AMERICAN JUSTICE

AMERICAN JUSTICE

Volume II
Feminism – Public order offenses

A Magill Book
from the **Editors of Salem Press**

Consulting Editor

Joseph M. Bessette
Claremont McKenna College

Salem Press, Inc.
Pasadena, California   Englewood Cliffs, New Jersey

Editor in Chief: Dawn P. Dawson
Consulting Editor: Joseph M. Bessette   *Project Editors:* McCrea Adams and R. Kent Rasmussen
Research Supervisor: Jeff Jensen   *Photograph Editor:* Valerie Krein
Proofreading Supervisor: Yasmine A. Cordoba   *Production Editor:* Janet Long
Layout: James Hutson   *Maps:* Moritz Design

Library of Congress Cataloging-in-Publication Data
American Justice / from the editors of Salem Press, consulting editor, Joseph M. Bessette
    p.   cm. — (Ready reference)
"A Magill Book"
Includes bibliographical references and index.
    ISBN 0-89356-761-2 (set : alk. paper). — ISBN 0-89356-763-9 (vol. 2 : alk. paper).
    1. Law—United States—Encyclopedias. 2. Justice, Administration of—United States—Encyclopedias.
I. Bessette, Joseph M.   II. Series.
KF154.A44   1996
349.73—dc20
[347.3]
                                                                                95-51529
                                                                                CIP

First Printing

CONTENTS

CONTENTS

ALPHABETICAL LIST OF ENTRIES

Volume I

Volume II

Volume III

AMERICAN JUSTICE

Feminism

Definition: The theory of the political, social, and economic equality of the sexes, or organized activity on behalf of women's rights and interests

Significance: Feminism, a topic of interest especially in the latter half of the twentieth century, has redefined the notion of equitable treatment based on sex in legal, social, political and economic spheres

Although the concept of feminism was introduced in the eighteenth century, it did not achieve wide popularity in the United States until the nineteenth century, when the Seneca Falls Convention of 1848, with its "Declaration of Sentiments," initiated the women's movement. Among the organizers of the convention were Lucretia Mott and Elizabeth Cady Stanton. In the nineteenth century, the women's movement was primarily concerned with suffrage and was not explicitly identified as feminist. Women at last gained the right to vote in 1920, with the ratification of the Nineteenth Amendment.

The Early Years. In the 1910's, a group of women, many of them identified with radical political movements, were the first to label themselves as feminists. These "modern feminists" addressed themselves to several issues of significance to women. Some began to work to make birth control available to women. Margaret Sanger, for example, was indicted for violation of the Comstock Law for using the mails to distribute a book discussing birth control. Others engaged in the suffrage movement, hoping to increase the voice women had in political and social circles. Many feminists dedicated themselves to reforming the workplace. They helped to organize labor unions in female-dominated occupations such as garment work, and they protested the low wages and dangerous conditions that many women faced.

The issue of labor reform divided the feminist movement in the 1920's. Mainstream feminists wanted to work for protective labor legislation. They believed that because women are physically different from men, they needed special protection in the workplace. Radicals in the movement argued that protective laws would differentiate women in the workplace and could be used to segregate jobs based on sex. They proposed working for an equal rights amendment (first introduced in 1923), which they believed would grant women the legal authority to be treated equally. Partly because of this difference of opinion, the movement remained stagnant from the 1930's until the 1960's.

Feminism in the 1960's and 1970's. During the Civil Rights movement of the 1960's, some feminists argued that the movement should be expanded to address various issues of significance to women. Some male civil rights organizers were hostile to offering equal rights to women and refused to include feminist demands as targets of social activism. Feminists, concluding that their needs would not be met within the Civil Rights movement, reunited to form an organized movement which has since attempted to address the injustices that they perceive. The largest single organization in the feminist movement, the National Organization for Women (NOW), was founded in 1966 by Betty Friedan and others. Friedan had published the influential work *The Feminine Mystique* in 1963. NOW adopted a Women's Bill of Rights in 1967.

The early 1970's is when the feminist movement truly came into its own; other than Friedan, leaders included Germaine Greer and Gloria Steinem. *Ms.* magazine began publication in 1972, under the leadership of Steinem and Patricia Carbine. Two watershed events in the 1970's were the Supreme Court's *Roe v. Wade* decision in 1973, upholding a woman's right to abortion, and the attempt ultimately unsuccessful to obtain ratification of the Equal Rights Amendment. It was also in the late 1960's and early 1970's that women's studies classes and curricula were established at many colleges and universities.

Since the 1970's, the feminist movement has focused on several issues. Feminists believe that women still occupy a subordinate role in American society because of social prejudices and because of long-standing practices of differential treatment in the workplace, in health care, in social standing, in education, in economic concerns, and in politics. In general, feminists argue that policy and practice are dominated by men and male prejudices.

Feminism in the Workplace. In the workplace, feminists point to long-standing inequalities in women's promotions and wages. In some cases, employers engage in discriminatory hiring practices because they believe that women are not capable of physical labor or that married women do not need jobs as badly as married males do. Even when women hold the same jobs as men, feminists often point to unequal pay scales and urge employers to address wage discrimination against women. In the 1990's feminists also focused on the workplace environment of women workers. A special concern is sexual harassment. Feminists argue that women continue to suffer from degrading comments about their appearance or their bodies and suggest that unscrupulous employers use sexual favors as a way to ensure women's dependence on male authority.

Sex and Sexual Expression. Some feminists have focused primarily on the issue of sexual freedom. They believe that unlimited access to birth control is needed so that women can have the freedom to plan their families and to limit the number of children that they might have. Beginning in the 1960's, the call for legal and medically approved abortions led to significant debate, both among feminists and the public at large. Finally, a small number of feminists have rejected heterosexual relations, believing that lesbianism is the only effective way to avoid what they believe is pervasive exploitation of women by men.

Health Care. Feminists are critical of the lack of health care for women. Often, health care available to women does not include basic protection for problems or concerns specific to women, such as recommended checkups for breast cancer, maternity and neonatal care, or gynecological services. Other medical services have become increasingly difficult to obtain, such as prescribed contraceptives for unmarried dependent women and abortions. The problems of physical and sexual abuse of women have led feminists to publicize the issues and to create shelters for battered women. In the home, the care of children is still often regarded as being the primary responsibility of women. Feminists are thus concerned that a general lack of child care facilities limits women's abilities to compete freely for work outside the home.

The feminist movement has had a significant impact on debates concerning equality and social justice in the United States as well as on the drafting of legislation dealing with these issues. In academic circles, gender issues are widely addressed in classroom curricula. Finally, legal support for women is increasingly being granted in the form of antiharassment statutes and the establishment of more effective procedures for hearing complaints of discrimination.   —*Sarah E. Heath*

See also Affirmative action; Battered child and battered wife syndromes; Birth control, right to; Comparable worth; Equal Rights Amendment (ERA); Family law; Gay rights; *Griswold v. Connecticut*; National Organization for Women (NOW); Rape and sex offenses; *Roe v. Wade*; Seneca Falls Convention; Sex discrimination; Sexual harassment; Woman suffrage.

BIBLIOGRAPHY

Sara M. Evans, *Born for Liberty: A History of Women in America* (New York: Free Press, 1989), is a useful general history of women in America. For some books that address feminist issues in whole or in part, consult Alice Echols, *Daring to Be Bad: Radical Feminism in America, 1967-1975* (Minneapolis: University of Minnesota Press, 1989); Sara M. Evans, *Personal Politics: The Roots of Women's Liberation in the Civil Rights Movement and the New Left* (New York: Vintage Books, 1980); Susan Faludi, *Backlash: The Undeclared War Against American Women* (New York: Crown, 1991); and Catharine A. MacKinnon, *Sexual Harassment of Working Women: A Case of Sex Discrimination* (New Haven, Conn.: Yale University Press, 1979).

Fiduciary trust

DEFINITION: An instrument by which one person holds property for the benefit of another

SIGNIFICANCE: A trust permits a person to provide for the welfare of a beneficiary through a trustee

Trusts were first used at the time of the Crusades. During travels abroad, crusaders would leave their lands in the care of another for the sake of convenience. A trust is an agreement created by two people, the trustor or donor, who donates the property, and the trustee, who holds the property for another, the beneficiary.

A trustee holding property for the benefit of another has legal title to the property but has no right to receive any benefits from it. The benefit, or equitable title, rests only with the beneficiary of the trust. A trustee acts under the laws of the state in which the trust is established. Even after a person is named as trustee, the relationship is not established until the trustee accepts.

There are several types of trusts. A direct or voluntary trust is a free act, deliberately created to bring about a certain outcome, which is attested by a written document. A declaration of trust permits the trustor to act as trustee during the trustor's lifetime and to receive the benefits of the trust. The benefits of the trust

pass to the beneficiary, whether individual or institution, after the trustor's death. Testamentary trusts are created by a will and come into existence only upon the death of the trustor. A Totten trust is created by an individual who places money in a bank account for another. There is no written trust instrument, but the person depositing the money must be described on the account as trustee for the other person.

A trust may be established for charitable, religious, scientific, or educational purposes. In these instances, the institution must meet certain Internal Revenue Service requirements.

Trusts have certain benefits for those who wish their financial affairs to remain private. In many states, trusts, unlike wills, need not be filed with the court upon the death of the trustor. They are not public documents and are not subject to public scrutiny.

See also Case law; Civil law; Wills, trusts, and estate planning.

Field, Stephen J. (Nov. 4, 1816, Haddam, Conn.—Apr. 9, 1899, Washington, D.C.)

IDENTIFICATION: U.S. Supreme Court justice, 1863-1897

SIGNIFICANCE: Field led the Court into a laissez-faire orientation toward the Constitution that would dominate Supreme Court rulings for more than half a century

Stephen J. Field was born into a family headed by a Congregational clergyman of Puritan stock whose uncompromising theology Field would later reflect in the righteous independence he exhibited on the bench. Early restlessness led Field to Marysville, California, where he served as *Alcalde*, the chief civil magistrate under the Old Mexican regime. After serving as a legislator, then a jurist in early California, he was tapped by President Abraham Lincoln when Congress created a tenth seat on the Supreme Court in 1863. On the Court, Field was at first a civil libertarian, but over time he came to champion the protection of private property. Field would become the most uncompromising proponent of constitutional laissez-faire the Court has ever seen, shaping the due process clause of the Fourteenth Amendment into a doctrine known as substantive due process, more a protection of the substantive right to hold private property than a protective procedural mechanism. He was also one of the longest-serving Supreme Court justices, and one of only two to be targeted by an assassination attempt (later the subject of a Supreme Court case, *In re Neagle*, 1890).

See also Due process of law; *Neagle, In re*; Supreme Court of the United States.

Fifteenth Amendment. *See* Civil War Amendments

Fingerprint identification

DEFINITION: The identification of individuals by the unique, complex pattern of ridges and valleys of skin on the tips of the fingers

SIGNIFICANCE: Since the beginning of the twentieth century, fingerprint evidence has been used to link suspects to specific crime scenes

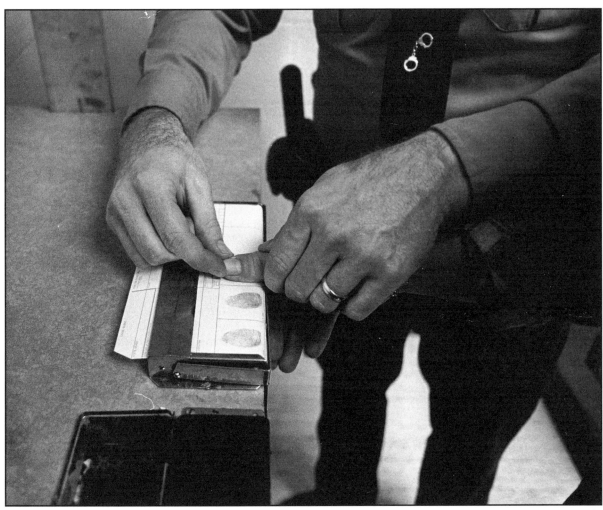

Twelve identification "points" are commonly used to compare fingerprints and determine whether they match. (James L. Shaffer)

Identifying suspects and placing them at the scene of a crime has always been a crucial part of determining guilt in criminal justice proceedings. Prior to 1900, the Alphonse Bertillon method of identification was used. This method relied on a system of human body measurements to compare a suspect with the recollections of witnesses. While some aspects of this approach are still in use to reduce the pool of potential suspects (most convenience stores, for example, have rulers that measure height at the exits), too often an innocent person was convicted of a crime because of a resemblance to the actual perpetrator.

In the late 1800's it was noted that when fingertips come in contact with a solid surface, the natural oils leave a latent mark. Argentinean Juan Vucetich developed a classification for these marks in 1888, and by 1893, the British home secretary had accepted the central tenet of fingerprint identification: No two individuals have the same fingerprints. The Galton-Henry system of classification was published in June, 1900,

and adopted by Scotland Yard a year later. Fingerprint evidence was first used in an English court in 1902.

Each fingerprint is unique, with features known as loops, whorls, dots, and splits combining to give an individual pattern. The British standard is sixteen identification "points"; in the United States it is common to use twelve. The points on a fingerprint left at a crime scene are compared with the prints of suspects. A number smaller than twelve can be used, when combined with other evidence.

Fingerprint identification has two primary requirements. Effective techniques for taking prints from the fingers—and, more important, techniques for lifting prints from the crime scene—had to be developed. It is routine for police departments to fingerprint every suspect; sometimes they find that the prints of a suspect in one crime match prints found at a different crime scene. Many military organizations also fingerprint inductees to develop a database for the identification of combat casualties. To collect fingerprints, the fingers are first cleaned to ensure that the ridges will be distinct. Next they are rolled onto a prepared card, transferring the ink to the paper's surface. In the past, storage and study of these collections was time consuming and tedious, but a system was devised to store the characteristics in a computer, so today searches can be conducted almost instantaneously.

Collecting prints from a crime scene is a more complex process. The oils left behind on a hard, smooth surface can be dusted and then lifted off for analysis. A rough surface can give the investigators a series of partial prints, which sometimes can be pieced together to provide a complete print. Porous material such as cloth or paper was long considered "unprintable," but with the use of silver nitrate or ninhydrin, these prints too can be developed. Ninhydrin can reveal prints even several years after the crime.

See also Detectives, police; DNA testing; Evidence, rules of; Forensic science and medicine.

Fletcher v. Peck

Court: U.S. Supreme Court
Date: Decided March 16, 1810
Significance: Upholding the contract clause of the Constitution, Chief Justice John Marshall not only strengthened the authority of the federal judiciary but for the first time also invalidated the act of a state legislature that contravened the Constitution

In 1795, the Georgia legislature sold land titles encompassing more than 35 million acres to the Georgia Company, the Georgia Mississippi Company, the Tennessee Company, and the Upper Mississippi Company, all speculative land companies. Including present-day Alabama and Mississippi, these so-called Yazoo lands reputedly were among the best cotton lands in the world and were made the more valuable by the recent invention of the cotton gin. While Native Americans occupied much of these areas, their rights were in the process of being extinguished. At the time of sale, it was confirmed public knowledge that the Georgia legislature was riddled with corruption, that most of its members had been bribed to effect the sale, and that the entire transaction was patently fraudulent.

Conscious of these facts, the succeeding legislature, nearly all of whose members were pledged to undoing the fraud, rescinded the land grants, which reverted to the state of Georgia. Meantime, however, the original speculators had sold millions of acres to innocent purchasers, mostly responsible residents of New England and the middle states. Eleven million acres, for example, were purchased for a penny an acre by leading citizens of Boston. Invalidation of the original land grants by Georgia's reformist legislature threatened to wipe out the investments of these honest purchasers. For years they importuned Georgia for relief, but the recently passed Eleventh Amendment (1798) was designed to prevent them from suing the state. Under constant pressure itself, Congress also failed to aid them.

John Peck and other Boston investors then entered into a "friendly" suit with Robert Fletcher of New Hampshire to secure a judgment from the federal courts in 1806. By 1809, on a writ of error, the case was argued before Chief Justice John Marshall and the U.S. Supreme Court. Marshall delivered the Court's unanimous opinion on March 16, 1810.

Although the Georgia legislature's original grants had been tainted by bribery and fraud and had provoked fifteen years of popular revolts, as well as bitter political controversy involving many of the most prominent figures of the day, Marshall delivered an opinion that cogent observers reported made him the most hated man in America.

In a brief decision, Marshall found that the rescinding act of the honest Georgia legislature violated the contract clause of the Constitution. It was irrelevant, he reasoned, whether the Georgia legislature that made the original grants was corrupt, for it was not the province of the Supreme Court to inquire into the motives of legislatures. The rescinding act of the succeeding legislature, therefore, impaired the obligation of contracts. The Court's decision was the first to invalidate a state law as unconstitutional, and it greatly strengthened the contract clause.

See also Contract, freedom of; Contract law; *Dartmouth College v. Woodward*; Marshall, John.

Food and Drug Administration (FDA)

Date: Originated as U.S. Department of Agriculture's Food, Drug, and Insecticide Administration in 1928; renamed Food and Drug Administration in 1931
Significance: Empowerment of the FDA made food, drugs, cosmetics, and other covered items safer and changed the basis of consumer protection from proving products are faulty to keeping unsafe products off the market

The Food and Drug Administration is a Health and Human Services Department agency that seeks to prevent harm from dangerous, unsanitary, or falsely labeled foods, drugs, cosmetics, and therapeutic devices. Article I, section 8 of the U.S. Constitution provides the basis for the Food and Drug Administration by stating that "Congress shall . . . promote the progress of Science and useful Arts . . . by securing . . . to the Authors and Inventors . . . the exclusive rights to their Writings and Discoveries." This provision led first to the creation of the U.S. Patent Office, where there were, from the start, a tremendous number of patent applications from the giant agricultural establishment. Thus, the need to regulate agriculture arose and led to the Department of Agriculture (1861), headed by a federally appointed commissioner. The first was Isaac Newton, who had spearheaded efforts to form the department. Along with Newton, President Abraham Lincoln appointed Charles Wetherill as the department chemist.

Consumer Danger Engenders the FDA. In the nineteenth century, many food manufacturers sold spoiled food as well as adulterated and underweight products. Furthermore, many patent medicines were worthless or even harmful. In the early twentieth century Harvey Wiley, chief chemist of the Department of Agriculture, loomed large in the developing struggle against such problems. His efforts, and Upton Sinclair's indictment (in the novel *The Jungle*, 1906) of meat procurement

Each regional FDA headquarters has a testing laboratory and its own team of investigators and scientists. (James L. Shaffer)

and packing, led Congress to enact the 1906 Pure Food and Drug Act. This law prohibited the transportation of adulterated foods and drugs in interstate commerce and required more honest product labeling. Its enforcement was carried out by the Bureau of Chemistry in the Department of Agriculture.

Despite these efforts, problems with inappropriate foods and drugs continued. In 1928 Congress authorized a separate Food, Drug, and Insecticide Administration to execute the provisions of the 1906 act more effectively. In 1931 the FDIA became the FDA. Disastrous problems—such as a killer "elixir of sulfonamide"—focused the attention of the public, president Franklin Roosevelt, and Congress on the deficiencies of the act. This led to the Food, Drug, and Cosmetic Act (1938), expanding FDA control and stiffening penalties for violations. Its main emphasis was on prevention rather than punishment. That is, the act aimed at preventing health problems by giving the federal government the mandate to require FDA approval for all covered items before they could be marketed.

To decrease external pressures on the FDA it was moved first to the Federal Security Agency (1940), then to the Department of Health Education and Welfare (1953), and finally to the Department of Health and Human Services (1980). Landmarks in FDA empowerment include requiring the testing of food additives (1957), the Delaney clause of the Food, Drug, and Cosmetic Act (1958) prohibiting the use in food of substances that cause cancer in animals, the FDA ruling (1962) that new drugs must be proven both effective and safe, the Orphan Drug Act (1983) inducing drug companies to develop therapies for diseases that affect only small segments of the U.S. population, and the 1992 requirement for more definitive food labeling.

FDA Operation. The FDA has its national headquarters in Washington, D.C. It is headed by a commissioner appointed by the secretary of Health and Human Services and approved by the U.S. president. A deputy commissioner and eight associate commissioners assist the commissioner. FDA divisions include Offices of Management and Operations, Health Affairs, Science, Legislative Affairs, Planning, Public Affairs, Consumer Affairs, and Regulatory Affairs. In the early 1990's the FDA employed approximately seven thousand administrative, technical, and service employees who were members of the civil service. For enforcement purposes the United States is divided into FDA regions. Each has its own headquarters, including complete testing laboratories manned by FDA field inspectors, scientists, and other staff. Mobile labs are also available.

FDA inspectors visit many manufacturing facilities suspected of illegal actions; however, routine examination of all 150,000 businesses the agency is empowered to police is infrequent because of its relatively small staff. Many enforcement visits reportedly deal with companies that performed poorly in the past or that make particularly suspect items. Usually, legal requirements for FDA approval before the dissemination of products to the consumer, publicity, and the honesty of most manufacturers suffice to prevent such problems. When problems do occur, the agency can move quickly to obtain cease-and-desist orders through the courts.

Varying Opinions of the FDA. Public opinion of the FDA has varied greatly. Initially, it was stated—and a strong case was made for this—that a strong FDA would stifle innovation in the food, drug, and cosmetic industries. Much evidence indicates that the reverse situation has occurred, as exemplified by the large variety and generally high quality of U.S. food industry offerings. Most Americans do not realize that labels on FDA-covered items as to contents and use directions (including various types of warnings) probably would not exist without the agency. Much attention has been given to "failures" of the FDA related to such things as the inappropriate actions of some employees, the agency's unwillingness to expedite the use of certain types of new drugs (such as acquired immune deficiency syndrome drugs), marketing of various therapeutic drugs and devices found to possess serious drawbacks, as well as incomplete policing of companies under the FDA's umbrella. —*Sanford S. Singer*

See also Acquired immune deficiency syndrome (AIDS); Animal rights movement; Consumer fraud; Consumer rights movement; Medical and health law; Pure Food and Drug Act; Sinclair, Upton.

Bibliography

For background on the FDA see William Patrick, *The Food and Drug Administration* (New York: Chelsea House, 1988). Books and articles identifying pros and cons of the FDA include James Harvey Young, *Pure Food* (Princeton, N.J.: Princeton University Press, 1989), and Herbert Burkholz, *The FDA Follies* (New York: Basic Books, 1994). The following articles shed light on FDA history: William Grigg's three-part "The Making of a Milestone in Consumer Protection, 1938-1988," *FDA Consumer* 22 (October, November, and December, 1988), and James S. Benson's "FDA Enforcement Activities Protect Public," *FDA Consumer* 25 (January, 1991).

Food stamps

Definition: A federally funded program to alleviate hunger adopted as part of the War on Poverty
Significance: The food stamp program, which became the largest of all federal food assistance programs, marked a shift in policy from aiding farmers in reducing surplus goods to a concern for social justice through improved nutrition for the poor

The Food Stamp Act of 1964 was intended to end malnutrition and hunger among the poor in the United States. Previous food programs had distributed surplus commodities, so that family diets had often been dependent upon excess production of certain items.

Republicans opposed food stamps as too expensive and as welfare financed by farmers. Northern Democrats supported the act, however, because fresh produce could be purchased throughout the month and because using food stamps would be less humiliating for poor families than the surplus commodities program had been. Southern Democrats supported the Food Stamp Act in exchange for northern Democratic support of a farm bill. The American Federation of Labor-Congress of Industrial Organizations (AFL-CIO), National Grange, National Farmers Union, and Americans for Democratic Action lobbied for the act, while the American Farm Bureau Federation opposed it.

Evidence suggests that the food stamp program has reduced malnutrition. Yet critics argue that the program is too costly, that fraud—estimated at $2.8 billion annually—is too high, that the nonparticipation rate is too high, and that amounts allowed for food are too low for a good diet.

See also Aid to Families with Dependent Children (AFDC); Great Society; Homelessness; Liberalism, modern American; Social Security system; War on Poverty; Welfare state.

Ford, Gerald R. (b. July 14, 1913, Omaha, Nebr.)

Identification: President of the United States, 1974-1977
Significance: Ford pardoned former president Richard M. Nixon and led the country during a difficult period of transition

Long-time conservative Republican congressman Gerald R. Ford became president through two unplanned events. First, Richard M. Nixon's elected vice president, Spiro Agnew, resigned because of a bribery scandal in 1973, and Nixon appointed Ford to replace him. Second, Nixon himself was forced to resign in 1974 to avoid impeachment. The eighth vice president to assume the presidency, Ford was the first to do so without having first been elected vice president. Upon taking office, Ford attempted to put the Watergate scandal in the past, declaring, "Our long national nightmare is over." Then, a month after becoming president, he announced that he was pardoning Nixon for any and all crimes he may have committed in the Watergate affair. The pardon was extremely controversial. Ford believed that it was a better option than subjecting the government and the country at large to the protracted spectacle of prosecuting a former president, but many disagreed.

Ford served as president at a time when the country was trying to regain its equilibrium after years of division caused by the Vietnam War and then the Watergate hearings, and he restored a measure of confidence and calm. In September, 1974, he offered a clemency, or limited amnesty, program, for Vietnam War draft evaders and deserters. Ford appointed one justice to the U.S. Supreme Court, John Paul Stevens. Democratic candidate Jimmy Carter narrowly defeated Ford in 1976, probably because Ford was connected with the party

Gerald R. Ford succeeded Richard Nixon to the presidency; a month later, he granted Nixon a full pardon before he could be prosecuted on Watergate charges. (Library of Congress)

responsible for Watergate and Carter campaigned as an outsider who would never lie to the American people.

See also Carter, Jimmy; Nixon, Richard M.; Pardoning power; President of the United States; Vietnam War; Watergate scandal.

Ford v. Wainwright

COURT: U.S. Supreme Court
DATE: Ruling issued June 26, 1986
SIGNIFICANCE: This case forced the criminal justice system to examine controversies surrounding mental illness and the death penalty, in particular what types of mental conditions should spare condemned prisoners from execution

On July 19, 1974, Alvin Bernard Ford was convicted of first-degree murder after shooting a Fort Lauderdale police officer in a robbery attempt. Ford was sentenced to death by electric chair in the Florida court system. During his trial and sentencing, Ford appeared to be mentally competent. After his first year of prison, Ford received only one disciplinary report for his behavior. In 1982, his mental condition gradually began to decline, and he started having delusions. For example, Ford thought that his family was being held hostage at the prison and that the Ku Klux Klan had made him a target of conspiracy. Ford's communication skills deteriorated; his writing and speaking became incoherent.

Florida law stipulated that if the governor is informed that a death row inmate may be insane, a commission of psychiatrists must be appointed to examine the person. The examiners must determine whether the person understands the consequences of the death penalty and why it is being imposed. After a thirty-minute interview, two of the three psychiatrists diagnosed Ford as psychotic, yet all three determined that Ford was competent enough to be executed. Relevant testimony of two psychiatrists who had worked with Ford over time, however, was not included in the fact-finding process. They concluded that Ford was severely psychotic and not competent to be executed. No opportunity was given to other knowledgeable experts to dispute the findings of the state-appointed commission. Based on the commission's results, the governor found Ford to be competent and issued a death warrant for his execution.

Florida's Eleventh Circuit Court of Appeals stayed the execution to hear the issues. The court decided against Ford. The U.S. Supreme Court agreed to hear Ford's appeal. In a 5-4 decision, the Supreme Court overturned the decision of the Florida court and ordered that the case be remanded to federal district court for a full hearing. Justice Thurgood Marshall wrote the majority opinion of the Supreme Court. He concluded that the Eighth Amendment prohibits the states from imposing the death penalty on prisoners who are insane. The court found that Florida's process of evaluating condemned prisoners did not provide adequately for deciding whether Ford was competent to be executed.

Before the federal district court could determine Ford's competency, Alvin Ford died in prison. His death left issues unresolved, such as how competency is defined, what should be done in cases where the inmate wavers between stages of competency and incompetence, whether medication should be used to restore an inmate's mental health before execution, and whether mentally retarded inmates are competent for execution.

See also Capital punishment; *Furman v. Georgia*; Insanity defense.

Forensic science and medicine

DEFINITION: The use of scientific and medical knowledge in the detection of crime and to answer questions of law
SIGNIFICANCE: Scientific evidence in the courtroom has given both victims and suspects powerful, convincing ways of proving their cases; increasingly sophisticated identification techniques, in particular, have made the incarceration of dangerous criminals easier and the risk of convicting the innocent much smaller

The area of forensic science and medicine, also known as medical jurisprudence, legal medicine, or criminalistics, encompasses a vast array of scientific techniques that are applicable in criminal and civil court cases. The testimony of a scientist or physician as an expert witness carries the weight of substantial knowledge and enormous societal respect. Many facts can be established from the examination of physical evidence at the scene of a crime, and the abilities of a well-equipped crime laboratory to deduce information from minute clues have

A forensics specialist "dusts" an automobile door for fingerprints. (James L. Shaffer)

grown dramatically in recent years. The lack of understanding of these techniques by the public, however, as well as the lack of standard methods in certain advanced areas, has also opened a number of loopholes in the criminal justice system.

Expert Witnesses. When an individual, whether a layperson, scientist, or physician, is asked to relate observations or general knowledge in court, the same rules apply that apply to an ordinary witness. When that person is asked to interpret these observations on the basis of professional knowledge, he or she becomes an expert witness. In theory, an expert witness is called upon to interpret the given facts without bias to either the prosecution or the defense. Normally an expert witness is asked to interpret facts that have been presented specifically for interpretation, or which he or she has been asked to gather for the case. If the facts have been learned through the course of a physician's personal practice, the physician is more likely to be called as an ordinary witness, since a bias in favor of the patient may be presumed. The lack of bias is the salient feature of the expert witness.

In practice, however, expert witnesses are called, and usually paid, by the lawyers on one side of a case. Other expert witnesses with opposing viewpoints are hired by the other side. While physical evidence does not lie, it is subject to interpretation, and occurrences, especially medical events, are less predictable than the courts might wish. Also, many crime laboratories work for the law enforcement systems of their state or county and so may feel obligated to support the prosecution's case. Many expert witnesses, too, have financial ties to one side of a case or the other. One must question the impartiality of the testimony of a witness for whom the advancement of acceptance of a particular technique would result in financial gain.

Physical Evidence. The most familiar uses of forensic science are in the area of physical evidence. Physical evidence can be used to gain information about the time at which, or method by which, a crime took place—or sometimes to determine whether a crime was committed at all. It may be used to identify victims and suspects or to prove an accused person innocent. It can be used to connect a person to a particular place or to show that a certain weapon was used. In some cases, it can provide evidence of personality traits that make it more or less likely that a given suspect is guilty. It is often the physical evidence in a case of violent crime that provides the court with the material needed to establish guilt or innocence beyond a reasonable doubt.

Evaluation of Mode and Time of Death. It is the physician who bears the responsibility for determining whether a death occurred from natural or suspicious causes. It is at the physician's instigation that many criminal investigations commence. The difference between suicide and murder, or between death from natural and artificial means, is often difficult to distinguish. For many crimes, an eyewitness is available to testify to the circumstances and actions. In a murder, however, there is rarely anyone who can testify directly as to the actual event. Therefore, for murder cases, more than any other, it is the physical evidence left behind that must bear witness on the victim's behalf.

The fast and correct determination of means of death can make a crucial difference in whether a murderer is caught. Much physical evidence fades quickly. For example, while time of death is usually an educated guess, the longer it is before this estimate is made, the more room for error. The time of death can be estimated reasonably well based on body temperature within the first eighteen hours after death, but a body cools to the temperature of its environment within twenty-four hours. Lividity, or the discoloration of areas of the body in which blood has settled after death because of gravity, develops in three to five hours and can give evidence (by its absence) of recent death or can indicate that the body has been moved. Rigor mortis (muscle rigidity) develops in different parts of the body at different times, and so provides good evidence of time of death, but it passes after about thirty-six hours. After this, the scientist must rely on such things as level of decomposition and insect infestation.

The cause of death is often a strong clue as to whether the death was an accident, suicide, or murder. The angle of a wound, access to poison, marks of self-defense, or evidence of self-induced strangulation can all lead the examining physician to consider or rule out any of the possibilities.

Identification. The positive identification or elimination of a victim or suspect can be the key evidence on which an entire case rests. Identifying bodies or remains grows more difficult as the body decays. Fingerprinting is the most familiar method of identification, but if the prints are not on file somewhere, it does no good to take them after death. DNA typing has been successful in some cases, but it is only useful to verify a suspected identification. Forensic odontology, or the examination of dental idiosyncrasies, is also useful only if there are dental records to which those of an unknown victim can be matched. More commonly, fingerprinting, deoxyribonucleic acid (DNA) typing, blood typing, body fluid, and hair matching are used to place a suspect at the scene of a crime or to eliminate a suspect.

Fingerprinting. Every individual has a unique set of fingerprints. Fingerprint evidence, when available, is the most compelling identification method there is. The fingers, however, are also easy to conceal through the use of gloves, and even if a person is not wearing gloves, many surfaces do not take prints well. Moreover, no one leaves prints all the time, and those prints that are left at the scene of a crime are often smudged and unreadable.

Fingerprints are caused by the ridges of skin on the fingers, which are lined with pores which exude perspiration. It is this perspiration which causes a print. The patterns of these ridges form before birth and do not change throughout a person's life. Whether a print is left on a surface depends on the condition of the skin, the way an object is handled, and whether the surface absorbs (and therefore dissipates) the perspiration. Glass, metal, and plastic surfaces all retain good fingerprints.

Fingerprints are classified by the patterns of the ridges and their locations on each finger. In this way they can be encoded and stored in computer files and can be transmitted or retrieved around the world. Each pattern consists of whorls, arches, and loops in different configurations and sizes. To match prints, an examiner looks for distinctive features, or points, on a print, and compares them to those on file. Most courts need at least eight, and usually twelve, points that match. Fewer matching points (as when only a partial print is available) may be used as evidence but do not constitute legal proof. Only one point that definitely does not match is needed to eliminate a suspect.

Blood Typing. There are three primary blood typing systems commonly in use today, although more than a hundred ways to type blood are known. Taken together, these three divide the human race into twenty-four blood groups. They are the ABO system, the MN system, and the Rh system. In each of these systems, different people produce different antigens and antibodies which make it impossible to mix noncompatible blood types (for example, through transfusion). There are four possible blood types in the ABO system, three in the MN, and two in the Rh. While a matching blood type provides evidence (but not proof) of identification, a nonmatching type provides definite elimination of a match. Since all three systems are independent of each other, investigators can use any or all to determine a match or elimination. The Rh factor is detectable only in relatively fresh blood, and so is not used as commonly as the other two.

Body Fluids. Other body fluids besides blood are often found at crime scenes. In about three-fourths of the population, the ABO antigens can be found in other body fluids, including perspiration, saliva, semen, and vaginal secretions, as well as hair and bone. These people are called secretors. Secretors also have H antigens in their body fluids. The body fluids of nonsecretors do not have any of these antigens.

Next to blood, semen is the most common body fluid at crime scenes. Usually it is found at the scenes of sex-related crimes. Its presence is useful to corroborate a victim's story as well as to test for antigens. With the advent of DNA typing, semen can sometimes be used as evidence of identification far more exact than that which can be provided by the blood typing systems.

DNA Typing. DNA typing is a way of identifying evidence as positively having come from a certain person. Each person's DNA is unique (barring identical twins) and is found in every cell of the body. DNA typing is a technique which analyzes the highly variable areas in the DNA sequence and then assesses the probability that the sample came from a certain person. Controversies have centered not on the technique itself, which is well accepted, but on the match probabilities (which have in some cases been given as low as one in seven billion) and the controls on the standards of the laboratories performing the tests.

Other Physical Evidence. At any crime scene, the perpetrator is likely to leave some physical evidence behind. Fibers, glass, hair, soil, and paint are all remains which can be linked to specific people and places. Tracks of tires or shoes, traces of poison, and explosion and fire patterns have all been used as evidence in court. Firearms can be particularly convincing as evidence, since every gun leaves its own unique pattern on the bullets it shoots. If a gun can be retrieved, experts can often determine whether it was the gun that shot a certain bullet.

Other Types of Evidence. Science has made great strides in psychological and behavioral areas as well as in the physical sciences. The use of polygraph (lie-detector) tests, voiceprints, and handwriting analysis is now common in the courtroom.

The testimony of court-appointed psychiatrists and psychologists is relied upon to assess both competency to stand trial (in the case of possible insanity) and likelihood that a person did or could commit a certain crime.   *—Margaret Hawthorne*

See also Autopsy; Coroner; DNA testing; Evidence, rules of; Fingerprint identification; Medical examiner; Simpson, O. J., trial.

BIBLIOGRAPHY

A slightly dated but very readable textbook on criminalistics is Frederick Cunliffe and Peter B. Piazza, *Criminalistics and Scientific Investigation* (Englewood Cliffs, N.J.: Prentice-Hall, 1980). Another excellent general overview, with gruesome pictures, is Keith Simpson and Bernard Knight's *Forensic Medicine* (9th ed. London: Edward Arnold, 1985). For varying viewpoints on the role of science in the courtroom, see *Forensic Science: Scientific Investigation in Criminal Justice* (New York: AMS Press, 1975) and Peter W. Huber's *Galileo's Revenge: Junk Science in the Courtroom* (New York: Basic Books, 1991). For more specialized textbooks aimed at those in the medical profession, see R. Keith Green and Arlene B. Schaefer's *Forensic Psychology* (Springfield, Ill.: Charles C

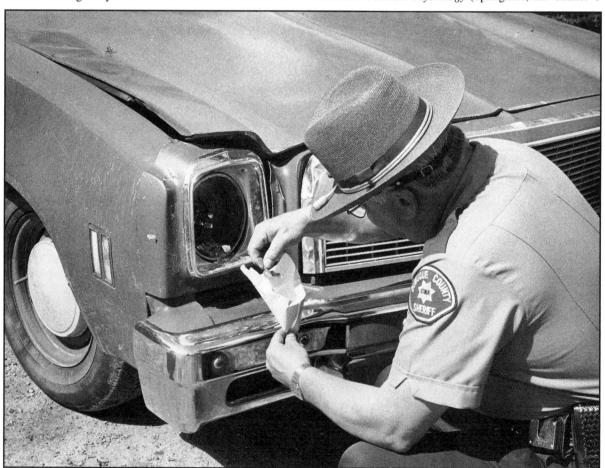

Remnants of glass and paint, as on this car involved in a hit-and-run accident, can be used as evidence in court. (James L. Shaffer)

Thomas, 1984) and D. J. Gee, *Lecture Notes on Forensic Medicine* (4th ed. London: Blackwell Scientific Publication, 1984). Finally, for an excellent overview of DNA typing techniques in lay terms, see William C. Thompson and Simon Ford's article "DNA Typing: Acceptance and Weight of the New Genetic Identification Tests," in *The Virginia Law Review* 75 (1989).

Forfeiture, civil and criminal

DEFINITION: Appropriation of goods by the criminal justice system that are owned by criminals and have been obtained illegally

SIGNIFICANCE: Forfeiture of items obtained through illegal means is used frequently as a method of punishing drug dealers

Forfeiture occurs when the criminal justice system seizes property and goods that have been stolen, used in the commission of a crime, or purchased using money obtained illegally. Forfeiture can be enacted through either civil or criminal law. If done through the criminal law, forfeiture takes the form of sanction (or punishment) by the court. This type of punishment can be used as an alternative to prison or in conjunction with a prison sentence. Forfeiture is a common element in the sentencing of drug dealers and distributors, whose possessions are almost entirely obtained through illegal drug sales. In some jurisdictions, property obtained through forfeiture is auctioned to the public or used by the police department itself. Typical items seized by police include vehicles, homes, and other personal property such as stereo equipment and televisions. When items are seized under civil law, a finding of guilt in the criminal court is not necessary.

See also Comprehensive Crime Control Act of 1984; Drug Enforcement Administration (DEA); Drug use and sale, illegal; Racketeer Influenced and Corrupt Organizations Act (RICO).

Forgery. *See* Counterfeiting and forgery

Fourteenth Amendment. *See* Civil War Amendments

Frankfurter, Felix (Nov. 15, 1882, Vienna, Austria— Feb. 22, 1965, Washington, D.C.)

IDENTIFICATION: U.S. Supreme Court justice, 1939-1962

SIGNIFICANCE: In his early political career a liberal reformer, and during his years on the Supreme Court a leader of the Court's conservative faction, Frankfurter was the most controversial justice of his day

Felix Frankfurter divided his early public career between teaching at Harvard Law School and public service in Washington, D.C. He turned down several official appointments, preferring instead to act informally as adviser to President Franklin D. Roosevelt, the National Association for the Advancement of Colored People (NAACP), and the National Consumers' League. He also found time to help found the American Civil Liberties Union (ACLU) and *The New Repub-*

lic magazine as well as to participate in the International Zionist Organization. Frankfurter was one of the formulators of the New Deal, so it was expected that once Roosevelt appointed him to the Court he would continue down a progressive track. Instead, although the Court became increasingly liberal during the years he was a member, Frankfurter became its leading conservative, opposing the commitment to abstract principles and political outcomes that dominated the Courts led by Chief Justices Fred M. Vinson and Earl Warren. He did, however, continue to exhibit the qualities that made him a great teacher, employing his intellectual rigor to tutor the lower courts with his closely argued opinions.

See also American Civil Liberties Union (ACLU); National Association for the Advancement of Colored People (NAACP); New Deal; Supreme Court of the United States.

Fraud

DEFINITION: The misrepresentation, distortion, or modification of facts, truths, terms in a business transaction, or one's identity in order to obtain property, funds, or performance of a contract to which one is not entitled

SIGNIFICANCE: The potential for fraud exists in every type of business, industry, or transaction, and businesses, financial institutions, consumers, and individuals lose millions of dollars every year from fraud-related activities

The concept of fraud was originally adopted from the English common law. The types of fraud are many and numerous.

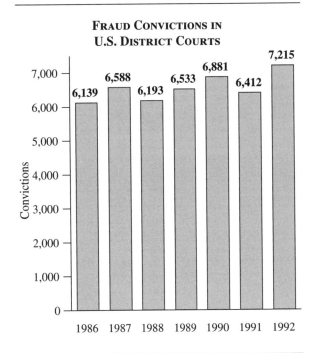

FRAUD CONVICTIONS IN U.S. DISTRICT COURTS

Source: U.S. Department of Justice, Bureau of Justice Statistics, *Sourcebook of Criminal Justice Statistics—1993.* Washington, D.C.: U.S. Government Printing Office, 1994.

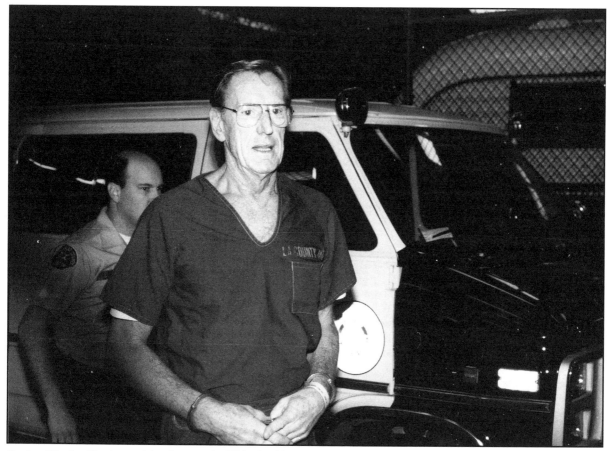

Banker Charles Keating arriving in court in 1990 after being charged with forty-two counts of fraud in the Lincoln Savings and Loan collapse. (AP/Wide World Photos)

Some of the more common types include representation of oneself as another, falsification of information, lying on a contract, misuse of credit cards, forgery, counterfeiting, and check fraud. Other areas where fraud is often perpetrated are sales, sales of securities, fraudulent conveyances (transfers), obtaining consent for marriage, wills, trademarks, and copyrights, and in areas related to product liability. All the above cases are viewed as legal offenses and can make perpetrators liable for both criminal and civil damages associated with losses that result from the fraudulent activity. Contracts that contain fraud are voidable, and in some cases employers can be held liable for the fraudulent activities of their employees and/or agents. According to the common law, in order to recover damages the plaintiff must prove the following: the fraud was deliberate and intentional, the defendant intended to benefit from the misrepresentation, the fraud was directly related to the harm done, and the plaintiff actually believed the misrepresentation. In the case of settlements, plaintiffs can receive up to treble (three times) damages. Criminal penalties can include fines and/or imprisonment.

Fraud has the potential to affect any type of business transaction. Certain other crimes, such as those listed above, derive their legal basis from the concept of fraud. The advancement of computer and information technologies creates new and ever more complicated opportunities for fraud. Computer and communications fraud happen on a global basis. As technology expands, so will the types of fraud and the number of fraudulent activities. New mechanisms must constantly be developed to limit criminals' abilities to commit fraud, because new schemes are always being developed.

See also Arson; Banking law; Computer crime; Consumer fraud; Consumer rights movement; Counterfeiting and forgery; Insider trading; Insurance law; Mail fraud; Tax evasion; Truth in Lending Act; White-collar crime.

Free Soil Party

DATE: 1847-1856

SIGNIFICANCE: As the Whig Party disintegrated, the Free Soil Party was one of the factions that filled the political vacuum; in time it resulted in the Republican Party

The slavery question was one of the most important of the time. In 1846 Representative David Wilmot introduced a measure to prohibit slavery in territories obtained as a result of the Mexican War, and almost immediately the political parties divided on the matter. Uniting with the Liberty Party and antislavery Whigs, the antislavery "barnburners" formed the Free Soil Party, which nominated Martin Van Buren for the presidency in 1848. He did not obtain a single electoral vote, but he won 291,000 popular votes in the North and Midwest. The election was won by Zachary Taylor, a hero of the Mexican War, who refused to state his political positions.

The Free Soilers next formed the "Free Democracy of the United States," which held a convention in 1852 during which it nominated John Hale for the presidency on the platform of "Free Soil, Free Speech, Free Labor, and Free Men." The Democratic nominee, Franklin Pierce, who favored the Compromise of 1850, won the election.

The nation seemed to want compromise and avoidance of war. This time the Free Soil candidate received only 156,000 presidential votes, and the party seemed to have lost influence.

Even so, the antislavery forces recovered, as antagonisms between the sections intensified. War actually erupted in Kansas, as the two groups contested for control of the territory. In July, 1854, antislavery elements came together to form the Republican Party. During the next two years Free Soilers filtered into the Republican ranks and were very much in evidence at the party's 1856 convention, which nominated John C. Fremont for the presidency. With this, the Free Soil Party dissolved.

See also Abolitionist movement; Democracy; Slavery; Whig Party.

Freedom of Information Act

DATE: Effective July 4, 1967
DEFINITION: The principal federal law on openness in government
SIGNIFICANCE: The Freedom of Information Act reversed long-standing government policies and practices regarding public access to information; it established the right of access to government information and agency records as essential to a free and open society

The Freedom of Information Act (FOIA) was the product of years of reform effort. Original passage was the result of a ten-year campaign in Congress, in which representatives of the media played a leading role. The legislation was drafted as a revision of the public information section of the Administrative Procedures Act (1946), which contained such expansive exceptions that most agencies were able to avoid public disclosures. Until 1967, public access to federal government records and documents was governed by a "need to know" policy. The burden was on the person requesting the information to demonstrate why such information should be made available. The FOIA represents a fundamental shift in policy and an official acknowledgment that secrecy is antithetical to democratic government.

Passage of the bill was largely attributable to the efforts of Democratic representative John E. Moss of California, who chaired the House subcommittee that examined myriad reports, testimony, and analyses of the practice of withholding

information by agencies of the federal bureaucracy. President Lyndon Johnson signed the bill into law on July 4, 1966.

The FOIA requires agencies to publish certain information regardless of whether it is requested and to disclose any other records that might be requested if such information is not covered by one of the nine exemptions contained in the act. The exemptions include classified documents related to national security, internal personnel rules, information exempt under other laws, confidential business information, internal government communications, information that would violate the privacy rights of an individual, information related to law enforcement activities, information regarding financial institutions, and geological information. The FOIA established several key principles: that disclosure be the general rule, not the exception; that all individuals have equal rights of access; that the burden is on government to justify the withholding of a document, not on the person requesting it; and that individuals improperly denied access to a document have a right to seek injunctive relief in the courts.

The original act fell short of expectations, largely because of the absence of deadlines for compliance and penalties for violation.

Bureaucratic agencies subverted the intent of the law with delays, excessive copying and search fees, and other tactics. Amendments to the FOIA resulted from concerns raised by public interest groups as well as the widespread concern over excessive government secrecy during the Watergate era. The FOIA has been amended three times—in 1974, 1976, and 1978—in response to expansive judicial interpretations of the exemptions and agency exploitation of procedural loopholes.

The Freedom of Information Act has been the subject of considerable debate since its original passage. Some see the act as a burden on government agencies, with the costs passed on to taxpayers. Others are critical of the complex procedures involved in identifying documents and processing requests used by some agencies, and of continued judicial deference to agencies in interpreting the exemptions to the act. The primary users of the FOIA are not the media, public-interest groups, or academic researchers, but rather business persons and attorneys.

See also Administrative law; Democracy; Rosenberg trial and executions.

Fries Rebellion

DATE: 1799
PLACE: Bucks County, Pennsylvania
SIGNIFICANCE: The Fries Rebellion was an early challenge to the ability of the United States government to collect federal taxes

Early in United States national history the power and authority of the federal government was challenged by a group of Pennsylvania farmers led by John Fries. The farmers objected to the concept of a federal real estate tax on their farms. In particular, they did not want to pay for an army and navy to protect American commerce during the wars of the French Revolution in Europe and in the West Indies.

Wearing a French tricolor cockade, John Fries and fifty farmers armed themselves and chased federal tax collectors out of Bucks County, Pennsylvania. President John Adams immediately ordered army regulars into Pennsylvania. Fries was arrested, tried for treason in Philadelphia, and sentenced to death. President Adams, however, pardoned him, and the incident ended quietly with the authority of the United States government vindicated.

See also Alien and Sedition Acts; American Revolution; Frontier, the; Jeffersonian democracy; Taxation and justice.

Frontier, the

DEFINITION: An area where formal societal institutions have not yet been established; most typically, the territory west of the Mississippi River in the nineteenth century

SIGNIFICANCE: The frontier and its justice institutions represent the development and application of some of the earliest forms of criminal apprehension, prosecution, and punishment in American history

As Americans moved westward in the nineteenth century, they took with them various elements of their culture—or rather, of their many cultures, as some were recent European immigrants to the United States. The Americans also took with them a cultural sense of justice. They carried a knowledge of what was right and wrong—that is, of what was deemed to be a crime and of how that crime should be prosecuted and punished.

Yet the western frontier produced a culture all its own. The unsettled lands and rough environment of the West mixed with the more stable culture of the East and produced a new type of American, one who was shaped by the unsettled environment of the frontier. There were no cities, villages, or communities of any kind when pioneers arrived at their new homes. There were no stores or merchants, no schools or teachers, no churches or clergy, and no courts, jails, or even constables to keep the peace. Life on the frontier was seemingly a life with no rules. Those who ventured into this wilderness, then, not only had to carve out a place to settle and make a living but also had to find ways to live in peace and security. This was a monumental task.

As the pioneers moved into this new frontier, the first order of business was often choosing a leader and setting the rules of conduct for the journey. Early wagon train guides often acted as sheriffs and judges for the traveling temporary communities. On many occasions representatives were selected from the male population of the wagon train to act as a quasi city council and jury if the need arose. Once settlements began, among the first priorities of the residents was establishing a system of law and order. Because there were no established laws and few lawmen on the frontier, dealing with crime and justice was of primary concern to everyone who desired to live in a stable community.

Creating Territories and States. Establishing a territory involved the surveying and laying out of fixed political and geographical boundaries. Once this was finished, the settlers would proceed to develop a territorial government. This government would provide the basis for a future state government.

A governor was appointed by the federal government, a legislature was elected by the territorial population, and U.S. marshals were appointed by federal authority to help enforce the law. Once these activities were completed, all that was necessary for the territory to petition for statehood was the assimilation of a large enough population, usually around thirty thousand people.

One of the first official positions created in the frontier areas was that of sheriff. Although the sheriff had responsibilities similar to those of his counterpart in seventeenth century England, the American officer was chosen by popular election and had broad powers to enforce the law. Sheriffs depended on the men of the community for assistance, and the *posse comitatus* ("power of the county"), or posse, a concept borrowed from fifteenth century Europe, came into being. This institution required local men (all able-bodied men ages sixteen to sixty-five) to respond to the sheriff's call for assistance.

Federal Marshals. Systems of marshalcy have been in effect for hundreds of years. First used in Europe in the sixteenth century, the concept was adapted by the Americans in the early eighteenth century as a means of policing the territory of the Old Northwest north of the Ohio River.

In September of 1789, Congress passed the Judiciary Act, which provided for the federal court system made up of district, circuit, and supreme courts. The act also provided for supporting personnel for the courts. In addition to judges, clerks, and district attorneys, a marshal was attached to each United States district court. When the circuit or supreme court convened in a particular district, the marshal also supported that session. Each marshal was responsible for maintaining law and order throughout the district (there were fifteen districts in 1789). The Judiciary Act authorized the marshal to execute decisions made by the federal judges. He was empowered to employ deputies and, when necessary, to form a *posse comitatus*. He was subsequently given other responsibilities, such as escorting prisoners to trial and carrying out orders for executing prisoners.

Federal marshals were appointed to a four-year term of office by the president of the United States with the consent of the U.S. Senate. The marshals fell under the immediate control of judges and U.S. district attorneys. The federal judges not only determined the process to be served by the marshals but also influenced the appointment of the lawmen. In time, federal judges were empowered to appoint interim marshals. As the country stretched westward in the nineteenth century, the system of federal marshals was expanded to keep up with the growth. From fifteen districts, the United States had increased to twenty-one states and four vast territories in 1850. Despite the fact that the marshals were allowed up to two deputies, the districts in the West were so large that the marshals had to rely on local sheriffs and other lesser officers for many services.

Nevertheless, among the agencies of the territories and states in the West, the marshals occupied a central place. Under the jurisdiction of the federal courts, they were expected to detect and apprehend violators of the law. The federal marshal was the first line of defense during times of domestic disturbance.

Notable Western Lawmen. The best known of the western lawmen have personal histories that are shrouded in legend and folklore. Numerous of the deputy U.S. marshals were really nothing more than hired gunmen, paid to use their guns to keep peace on a frontier that seemed far from civilization. Such men as Wyatt Earp, William (Bat) Masterson, Pat Garrett, and James "Wild Bill" Hickok were ready, willing, and often eager, to kill the lawbreakers of the frontier.

These men were not always hailed as heroes in the territories and towns in which they served. Wyatt Earp gained fame when he and his brothers outdueled the Ike Clanton gang in the shootout at the O.K. Corral. Some scholars believe that this gunfight was part of a larger struggle between cattlemen and sheep ranchers and that the Earps were only protecting the interests of the cattle ranchers when they fought the Clantons. Indeed, about half the population of the Arizona Territory wanted the Earps arrested and charged with murder after the fight.

Pat Garrett, too, is known more for his shooting exploits than his skills as a peacekeeper. Despite the fact that his commission as a deputy marshal was within days of expiring, Garrett and his posse closed in on, and eventually shot, outlaw William Bonney (Billy the Kid). Garrett was known as a remorseless gunman, and faced with the prospect of either bringing Billy the Kid in for trial or shooting him outright, he chose the latter. Yet considering the vast reaches of the territories and acknowledging that "good" lawmen must have been hard to find on an untamed frontier, it is not too surprising that gunmen were hired as law enforcement officials.

There were, however, some notable federal marshals who were not as suspect in their behavior or intentions. Crawley P. Dake, who was marshal of Arizona from 1878 to 1882, hired Wyatt Earp as a deputy marshal. It was Dake who brought order to the Arizona Territory by vigorously pursuing and capturing many bank and train robbers, thus securing the territory for expansion of the railroads.

John Pratt served as United States Marshal in the New Mexico Territory from 1866 to 1876. In his ten-year term, the territory witnessed important developments in federal law enforcement. Pratt regained public confidence in law enforcement in the territory and improved administration of the marshalcy by using local county sheriffs as deputies. He also increased the range of duties for the local authorities, allowing them to deal directly with crime in their own areas rather than waiting for him to arrive. This built up the confidence of the local citizenry and boosted the morale of the county sheriffs.

John E. Sherman, Jr., a nephew of General William T. Sherman, was marshal of the New Mexico Territory from 1876 to 1882. He introduced a measure of independence and professionalism into the marshalcy of the West. Unlike many, Sherman stayed above politics, investigating and prosecuting criminals no matter who their associates were. Though sometimes unpopular, he proved very effective. Others, among them Creighton M. Foraker, Secundino Romero, Francis H. Goodwin, and William M. Griffith, also endeavored to bring professionalism and administrative order to their terms as mar-

shals on the frontier. By the end of the nineteenth century, these lawmen had played a major role in establishing law and order in an area where none had existed fifty years before.

Vigilantism. Because the federal districts in the West were so vast and the numbers of federal marshals so few, responsibility for law enforcement often fell to the men of the territory. Members of "vigilance committees," otherwise known as vigilantes, were empowered to pursue and arrest lawbreakers. Unfortunately, these vigilance committees often took the law into their own hands and not only pursued and captured lawbreakers but executed them as well. Vigilante justice was quick and sure and frequently had little regard for such niceties as a trial. Vigilantes often avenged crimes never committed or mistakenly hanged the wrong man. To the vigilantes, such errors were an acceptable price to pay in the name of justice.

The men who were members of the vigilance committees usually thought of themselves as good, solid citizens exercising their rights and duties in preserving the peace. To some vigilantes, formal justice simply seemed too slow. In other cases, vigilantes operated in areas where formal systems did not yet exist; they were formulating and applying a makeshift criminal law until the real thing reached their part of the frontier. In the absence of a formal legal system, vigilantism was perhaps a prudent response to the criminal element of the West, necessary to avoid an otherwise ever-present risk of dying at the hands of the lawless. —*Kevin F. Sims*

See also Marshals Service, U.S.; *Posse comitatus*; Sheriff; Vigilantism.

BIBLIOGRAPHY

Perhaps the most informative book on the history of the federal marshals on the frontier is Larry D. Ball's *The United States Marshals of New Mexico and Arizona Territories, 1846-1912* (Albuquerque: University of New Mexico Press, 1978), which gives a detailed account of the development of the federal marshal program as well as brief biographies of notable lawmen. Two books present excellent historical surveys of the southwestern frontier: Howard Roberts Lamar's *The Far Southwest, 1846-1912: A Territorial History* (New Haven, Conn.: Yale University Press, 1966) and W. Eugene Hollon's *The Southwest Old and New* (New York: Alfred A. Knopf, 1961). These two texts give excellent details on the cultural and political development of the Southwest with an emphasis on justice issues. Walter Prescott Webb, one of the foremost writers of western history, chronicles the development of frontier justice in *The Texas Rangers: A Century of Frontier Defense* (Austin: University of Texas Press, 1965). Nathaniel P. Langford offers an informative look at the history of the vigilante movement on the frontier in *Vigilante Days and Ways: The Pioneers of the Rockies, the Makers and Making of Montana and Idaho* (New York: Grosset & Dunlap, 1912). One of the best studies on the development of American law and justice is Lawrence M. Friedman's *A History of American Law* (New York: Simon & Schuster, 1973). Friedman discusses the growth of American law from its earliest colonial roots and pays particular attention to the development of law and order on the frontier, including an interesting perspective on the vigilante movement.

Frontiero v. Richardson

COURT: U.S. Supreme Court

DATE: Decided May 14, 1973

SIGNIFICANCE: In this case, the Supreme Court held that a female member of the armed services who was not entitled to the same dependent benefits as a male had been unconstitutionally discriminated against

Under federal law, a male member of the armed services could automatically claim his spouse as a dependent and thus receive greater housing and medical benefits. A female member of the armed services, however, could only obtain such benefits if she demonstrated that her spouse was in fact dependent on her for more than half his support. After a servicewoman was denied benefits for failure to make the requisite showing concerning her spouse, she instituted a suit in federal court claiming that the law violated the equal protection component of the Fifth Amendment's due process clause. Although a majority of the Supreme Court could not agree on the precise standard by which to judge this claim, eight members of the Court agreed that the federal law at issue violated the Constitution.

Justice William J. Brennan wrote for four members of the Court and argued that legislative classifications based on gender are inherently suspect and should be accorded the same stringent review given laws that discriminate on the basis of race. Like race, Justice Brennan suggested, gender is an immutable characteristic. To disqualify an individual from some benefit purely on the basis of gender was, he claimed, inconsistent with the principles of justice that normally require legal burdens to bear some relation to individual responsibility. He concluded that the federal government could not justify its discrimination in this case and that the law therefore violated the equal protection requirements.

In a separate opinion representing the views of three justices, Justice Lewis Powell thought the case could be resolved without deciding upon a particular standard of review for all sex-discrimination cases. He thought it best to declare the law unconstitutional without attempting to elaborate a general constitutional doctrine concerning gender discrimination. Since the proposed Equal Rights Amendment was still being debated by the states, he believed that it would be premature for the Court to venture far in this area until the people of the United States had themselves deliberated the matter of sex discrimination. A single member of the court, Justice William Rehnquist, dissented without writing an opinion.

In the years following this case, the Court ultimately agreed that gender discriminations should be accorded some special review, though not so stringent a scrutiny as the Court had applied to instances of racial discrimination. *Frontiero* was important because, along with the Court's decision in *Reed v. Reed* (1971) two years earlier, it demonstrated that gender discriminations based on outmoded stereotypes would no longer be viewed with benevolence by the Court.

See also Due process of law; Equal protection of the law; *Reed v. Reed*; Sex discrimination.

Fugitive Slave Laws

DATES: 1793, 1850

DEFINITION: Provided for the seizure of, and return from one state to another of, runaway slaves

SIGNIFICANCE: The Fugitive Slave Laws further polarized the North and South in the decades prior to the Civil War

While the Constitution provided for the return of fugitive slaves across state borders, it did not specify the mechanism by which this would be accomplished. Congress therefore enacted the Fugitive Slave Law of 1793, by which slaves could be seized by masters or agents crossing state lines. State officials were made responsible for the enforcement of the federal law. For the slaves, the law embodied no protection of habeas corpus, trial by jury, or right to testify in their own behalf. In response, many Northern states passed laws granting slaves personal liberties.

The Fugitive Slave Law of 1850 made the federal government responsible for returning slaves to their owners. Interference with the law became a felony. Again, the alleged fugitive was denied personal rights. Furthermore, since commissioners received a higher fee for delivering a slave than for rejecting a claim, the law resulted in the confiscation of free people. The law's constitutionality was upheld in 1759 in *Ableman v. Booth*. Northern furor over the law and increasing abolitionist sentiment helped bring the country closer to the brink of war.

See also Abolitionist movement; Bill of Rights, U.S.; *Scott v. Sandford*; Slavery.

Fuller, Melville Weston (Feb. 11, 1833, Augusta, Maine—July 4, 1910, Sorrento, Maine)

IDENTIFICATION: Chief justice of the United States, 1888-1910

SIGNIFICANCE: Fuller reached the Supreme Court primarily because he was in the right place at the right time, but once there, he proved himself an able administrator

Fuller, who had never held federal office or served on the bench, was decried by some as the most obscure man ever to be appointed chief justice. To be sure, his appointment was largely a matter of luck. The U.S. seventh circuit, which included Illinois—second only to New York as a source of Supreme Court litigation—had been unrepresented on the Court for eleven years when Chief Justice Morrison R. Waite died. President Grover Cleveland heeded advice to look to Illinois for a replacement, and after his first choice declined, Cleveland turned to successful Illinois practitioner Fuller.

Fuller's confirmation was difficult, troubled by allegations of Copperhead sympathies during the Civil War and unethical business dealings. Once on the Court, surrounded by intellectual giants and devoid of all but a few original jurisprudential ideas, Fuller refined the role of chief justice as moderator. Favoring the status quo in his legal opinions, he funneled his energies into diplomacy, both on and off the Court. During his last ten years as chief justice, he also served as an arbitrator for

Chief Justice Melville W. Fuller led the Supreme Court for twenty-two years, refining the role of chief justice. (Painting attributed to Albert Rosenthal, collection of the Supreme Court of the United States)

the Venezuela-British Guiana Border Commission and the Permanent Court of Arbitration in the Hague.

See also Supreme Court of the United States; Waite, Morrison Remick.

Fullilove v. Klutznick

COURT: U.S. Supreme Court
DATE: Ruling issued July 2, 1980
SIGNIFICANCE: The Supreme Court held that setting aside a percentage of federal contracts for minority businesses was constitutional as long as it was intended to remedy demonstrated discrimination

After Congress passed the Local Public Works Capital Development and Investment Act in 1976, there was an outcry when minority business enterprises (MBEs) received only 1 percent of the contracts. Although minorities accounted for at least 15 percent of the U.S. population, only 3 percent of businesses were MBEs, and they earned only 0.65 percent of gross receipts.

Accordingly, in passing the Public Works Employment Act of 1977, Congress required 10 percent of local public works contracts to be "set aside" for MBEs—businesses with at least 50 percent ownership or 51 percent stockholding by African Americans, Spanish-speaking people, Asian Americans, American Indians, Eskimos, or Aleuts. Nonminority prime contractors were required, in subcontracting to MBEs, to provide guidance and technical assistance in making bids, to lower or waive bonding requirements, and to assist MBEs in obtaining working capital from financial institutions and government agencies.

Shortly after Juanita Krebs, U.S. secretary of commerce, issued administrative guidelines for bidding under the new law, several potential project grantees (H. Earl Fullilove and trustees of the New York Building and Construction Industry Board of Urban Affairs Fund, two general contractor associations, and a firm engaged in heating, ventilation, and air conditioning work) filed suit against Krebs, the city and state of New York, the New York Board of Higher Education, and the Health and Hospitals Corporation for a temporary restraining order to block implementation of the law. After they lost the case in the district court (in December, 1977) and on appeal (in 1978), they took the case to the Supreme Court. When the case was decided, Philip Klutznick was U.S. secretary of commerce. Chief Justice Warren Burger wrote the majority opinion; three justices provided concurring majority opinions, and two wrote dissents.

The Court answered the argument that government should act in a color-blind manner by noting that Congress had the power to spend money for the general welfare and thus to design a remedy for MBEs. The argument that nonminority businesses were deprived of equal access to contracts was rejected: a 10 percent set-aside rate was considered light in view of the larger percentage of minorities. The Court responded to the argument that the definition of "minority" was underinclusive and should have added other groups by noting that such a definition was entirely up to Congress. The argument that the "minority" definition was overinclusive and might favor MBEs unqualified to do the technical work was refuted by a reference to the statutory provisions that only bona fide minorities were covered by the law and that a waiver from the set-aside could be issued if no MBE was able to do the work.

The Supreme Court thus held that a numerical goal could be designed as a remedy for a statistically demonstrated inequality for minorities, with provisions tailored to removing specific, documented barriers to the success of minorities. Plans failing these tests have been consistently rejected by the Court, as in *Richmond v. J. A. Croson Co.* (1989).

See also *Adarand Constructors v. Peña*; Affirmative action; Civil Rights Act of 1964; Racial and ethnic discrimination; *Richmond v. J. A. Croson Co.*

Furman v. Georgia

COURT: U.S. Supreme Court
DATE: Decided June 29, 1972
SIGNIFICANCE: Ruling that existing laws for imposing capital punishment were unconstitutional because of their random and unpredictable application, the Court appeared to imply that any capital punishment laws might be found unconstitutional

William Furman, Lucious Jackson, and Elmer Branch were convicted and sentenced to death in the states of Georgia and Texas. After the three defendants were unsuccessful in their appeals to the supreme courts of the two states, their attorneys appealed to the U.S. Supreme Court, which granted review and consolidated the cases into one decision.

The majority of the Court voted 5 to 4 to strike down Georgia's and Texas' laws for imposing the death penalty, and the effect was to nullify all death penalty statutes in the United States. With the justices sharply divided, the majority announced the ruling in a short, unsigned *per curiam* opinion, followed by 231 pages of individual opinions by the nine justices. The majority agreed that existing laws allowed judges and juries so much discretion on whether to impose the death sentence that the result was arbitrary, irrational, and contrary to due process of law. Two members of the majority argued in concurring opinions that capital punishment was always unconstitutional, one concurring opinion emphasized the equal protection clause of the Fourteenth Amendment, and two other concurring opinions addressed only the arbitrary, unpredictable application of the penalty.

Justice William Brennan's concurrence presented a vigorous argument for the idea that capital punishment always was "cruel and unusual punishment." Like others of the majority, he quoted statements (called *dicta*) in *Trop v. Dulles* (1958) that the Eighth Amendment draws its meaning "from the evolving standards of decency that mark the progress of a maturing society" and that the amendment prohibited "inhuman treatment." From this perspective Brennan severely criticized capital punishment for four reasons: that it violated human dignity, that it was applied arbitrarily, that its declining use showed that it was increasingly unacceptable to contemporary society, and that it was excessive since it was not more effective than a less severe punishment.

In contrast, Justice William Rehnquist and the other dissenters emphasized that capital punishment was envisioned by the framers of the Constitution. They argued that it was undemocratic for judicial authority to strike down legislative enactments without being able to point to explicit statements in the Constitution.

Since *Furman* ruled that all existing laws providing for capital punishment were unconstitutional, the decision escalated controversy about capital punishment. Although the decision left the constitutionality of capital punishment unclear, thirty-five states soon enacted new legislation that took the concerns of *Furman* into account. Portions of these laws would later be declared unconstitutional, but in *Gregg v. Georgia* (1976) the majority of the Court would decide that capital punishment is constitutional so long as there are proper procedures and regulations.

See also Capital punishment; *Coker v. Georgia*; Cruel and unusual punishment; *Gregg v. Georgia*; *McCleskey v. Kemp*; *Robinson v. California*; *Rummel v. Estelle*.

Gambling law

DEFINITION: Legal efforts to regulate the placing of bets and playing of games of chance

SIGNIFICANCE: If all the money gambled legally in a year were totaled, gambling would be the nineteenth largest business in the United States, worth more than $329 billion; illegal gambling would add another $50 billion to the total

Since 1964, forty-eight states and the District of Columbia have legalized some kind of gambling. Utah and Hawaii have remained the only holdouts. Forty-seven states have legalized bingo, forty-two allow betting on horse racing, thirty-seven have lotteries, nineteen have dog racing, fourteen permit casino-type games such as poker, blackjack, and roulette, and four have betting on jai alai games. The federal government permits gambling on Indian reservations.

Gambling has a long history. Pharaohs played dice; Greeks and Romans loved games of chance, as did knights in the Middle Ages. The Chinese invented playing cards in the first century A.D., and sailors brought cards to Italy in the 1300's. The city of Florence sponsored a lottery in 1530; in 1566, Queen Elizabeth I of England did the same. In 1612, the Virginia Company raised money in London for its Jamestown Colony by selling lottery tickets. During the American Revolution, Congress approved a lottery to help raise money for George Washington's army.

Legal Gambling. The United States had legal gambling from 1790 to 1860. Twenty-four out of thirty-three states allowed games of chance, including lotteries and horse racing. States used money raised by lotteries to get funds for road and canal building and to support schools. Scandals led to a gradual decline in support for government-sponsored gambling, and by 1861, only three states still allowed it. By 1878, only the Louisiana lottery remained, and people across the country bought tickets by mail. In 1890, however, Congress outlawed lotteries, and the Louisiana game shut down. Only after the outbreak of the Great Depression in 1929 did states desperate for new sources of revenue return to legalized gambling. Twenty-one states made horse racing legitimate, though only Nevada authorized casinos.

The next expansion in legal gambling came in the 1960's, when state governments sought new sources of revenue. The turning point came in 1963, when New Hampshire created a lottery; soon after, New York and New Jersey started their own. Defenders called state lotteries a "painless tax," and the success of the three states encouraged twenty-eight others to follow. By 1990, lotteries sold more than $21 billion in tickets, with about half those funds going to the states and the rest divided between prizes and administrative costs. Lotteries are easy to play and require no skills, but they are bad bets because

of their long odds. Many states nevertheless prefer lotteries to tax increases.

Bingo games raised $3.9 billion for forty-five states in 1990. Money raised by states from other legal gambling totaled about $9 billion, less than 3 percent of total state revenues. States have found that regulating gambling and collecting their share of revenue is expensive. New Jersey spends more than one-third of each dollar collected from gambling to pay for the costs of policing its casinos. Other states spend more than 20 percent of the money raised from lottery sales on advertising and administration.

Illegal Gambling. Americans spend $50 billion a year on illegal gambling. Even in states with lotteries, the "numbers racket" continues to thrive. Players typically need to pick only three correct numbers to win such games, and they can place bets and collect winnings in their homes. Players can wager as little as a dime, and the payoff can be huge. Police seldom interfere with illegal gambling because they tend to see it as less important than other crimes. Corruption, too, plays a role in this lack of enforcement. One study of New York City found that some officers in antigambling units had collected an aver-

GAMBLING CONVICTIONS IN U.S. DISTRICT COURTS

Source: U.S. Department of Justice, Bureau of Justice Statistics, *Sourcebook of Criminal Justice Statistics—1993.* Washington, D.C.: U.S. Government Printing Office, 1994.

age of $1,000 a month in bribes. Illegal gambling on horse races amounts to more than $8 billion a year. Illegal bookies can remain in business because they pay off at higher rates than do the race tracks, and because winners can avoid paying taxes.

The relationship between organized crime and gambling dates to the 1920's. Mob figures helped to establish Las Vegas casinos in the 1950's, but beginning with the passage of the Organized Crime Control Act (1970), mob control diminished. The law prohibited interstate transportation of gambling devices and allowed wiretaps in connection with gambling investigations. Most laws concerning gambling come under state jurisdiction. Forty-eight states make gambling on sports events illegal. Nevertheless, in 1989 more than $27 billion was wagered on U.S. sporting events.

The Gamblers. A 1975 survey concluded that 61 percent of Americans had gambled during the previous year and that 80 percent approved of legalized gambling. Other surveys showed that people with lower incomes spent more on lotteries, numbers, and horse races than did middle- and upper-income Americans. More than 65 percent of lottery tickets are bought by only 10 percent of the population who tend to have low levels of education and income.

The American Psychiatric Association lists "compulsive gambling" as a disease. About 5 percent of gamblers fall into this category because of their "overwhelming, uncontrollable impulse to gamble." These addicts need counseling and assistance, and they frequently commit crimes such as fraud and embezzlement to support their habit. Most states stipulate that some of the funds from gambling be used to help these players, but only a few such programs actually exist.

—*Leslie V. Tischauser*

See also Commercialized vice; Organized crime; Organized Crime Control Act; Victimless crimes.

BIBLIOGRAPHY

Overviews of gambling and gambling law can be found in Jerome Skolnick's *House of Cards: Legalization and Control of Casino Gambling* (Boston: Little, Brown, 1978), David Weinstein's *The Impact of Legalized Gambling: The Socioeconomic Consequences of Lotteries and Off-track Betting* (New York: Praeger, 1974), and William N. Thompson's *Legalized Gambling* (Santa Barbara, Calif.: ABC-Clio, 1994).

Gandhi, Mahatma (Oct. 2, 1869, Porbandar, India— Jan. 30, 1948, Delhi, India)

IDENTIFICATION: Statesman and social reformer

SIGNIFICANCE: Gandhi developed and implemented a system of nonviolent resistance (*satyagraha*) to oppose the British rule in India during the first half of the twentieth century

Mahatma Gandhi's contribution to the Civil Rights movement in the United States is the idea that persistent nonviolent agitation can bring about peaceful social change. Gandhi was a successful attorney in South Africa from 1893 to 1901. In 1920, the British rulers in India made salt a government monopoly and imposed a salt tax. Gandhi led a peaceful march to Dandi and broke the Salt Law by making salt on April 5, 1920.

This aroused the Indian nation to fight for freedom. He attended a round-table conference in London in 1931 to discuss self-rule in India. He undertook many fasts to preserve Hindu-Muslim unity. In August, 1947, freedom from British rule was granted to the Indian subcontinent; two nations were born, India and Pakistan. Martin Luther King, Jr., discovered a method for social reform in Gandhi's emphasis on nonviolence and love. Nonviolent resistance was a practical weapon that King used in the American Civil Rights movement.

See also Civil disobedience; Civil Rights movement; King, Martin Luther, Jr.; Nonviolent resistance.

Gangs, youth

DEFINITION: Groups of juveniles, usually teenagers, whose behavior is characterized by both minor and serious crimes

SIGNIFICANCE: The increase of juvenile gangs in the late twentieth century has been blamed for large increases in property and violent crimes in urban areas

Gangs are groups of adolescents who engage in various forms of juvenile delinquency together. Gangs are typically made up of teenage juveniles, are male-dominated, and are usually racially homogeneous. Gang behavior in the United States has increased significantly since the early studies carried out by Frederic Thrasher in the early 1920's. Thrasher was one of the first researchers to study juvenile gang behavior, and many consider his work to be the standard. Gangs pose a problem for law enforcement, in that police officers have a difficult time apprehending gang members.

Gang Membership. Youth gangs in the United States are overwhelmingly male and adolescent, and they nearly always consist of members of the same racial group. Gang behavior seems to culminate in adolescence, and gangs consisting of children or adults are either extremely rare or nonexistent.

There has been much speculation about the reasons juveniles join gangs. Some believe that poor parental supervision is to blame for juveniles' becoming involved in gang activity. Poor parental supervision is usually attributed, in turn, to the increase of single-parent households in the United States. When parents are not home to monitor their children's activities, the children are more likely to be drawn into delinquency through gangs. Others have claimed that gang behavior stems from abusive treatment at the hands of parents. Prior abuse, whether sexual, physical, or emotional, sometimes is a reason that children try to escape their homes and find a new family in a youth gang. Most people who study gangs believe that the main reason juveniles join gangs is to gain a sense of belonging. On the other hand, some claim that there is active recruitment of new members—current gang members attempt to talk younger juveniles into becoming members of the gang. Many juveniles are pressured into joining gangs and do so for protection from other juveniles or from other gang members.

While there is much speculation about the reasons for joining a gang, few researchers have been able to identify those factors with any certainty. In general, however, most youth tend to join gangs for one of two reasons. Gang members are either search-

Members of warring Los Angeles gangs the Crips and the Bloods meet the press after three days of talks in 1988; they called for job availability to provide an alternative to gang life. (AP/Wide World Photos)

ing for a group of people to act as surrogate family or are interested in making a profit from illegal activities.

Criminal Behavior. Since the majority of youth gangs in the United States become involved in delinquent behavior, most definitions of a gang include mention of such behavior. The seriousness of criminal behavior varies across gangs, with some groups being much more serious offenders than others. On the less serious side is a practice known as "tagging." Some gangs tag territory by writing their gang names on walls, bridges, trains, and other public places. This form of vandalism can escalate into violence quickly when a rival gang crosses out another gang's or gang member's name. This is considered a sign of disrespect, and a fight usually ensues—sometimes ending in murder.

Youth gangs are largely blamed for the increases in violent crime in the United States since the early 1980's. When challenged by a rival gang, many gang members believe that they must show superiority by acting more violent or "wilder" than the rival gang. Gang violence began with territorial battles that usually consisted of physical fights. These fistfights led to much more serious crimes, including homicide. Modern gang members are frequently blamed for the killing of innocent

citizens who become trapped in the cross fire of drive-by shootings. In many such shootings, one gang is attempting to murder a member of a rival gang quickly, without being recognized or identified by witnesses. Not much evidence is available to police who attempt to investigate such crimes. While not all gangs or all gang members participate in homicide, the public perception of youth gangs is that they are responsible for a large number of homicides in urban America.

While most gangs are stereotyped as using or selling illicit drugs, not all youth gangs are engaged in this type of behavior. In fact, some research has shown that when gang members are arrested for drug offenses, the charge is usually low-level trafficking. This contradicts the stereotype of gang members acting as high-level distributors of drugs. While there are groups of people whose main focus is drug distribution, most of them are not youth gangs.

Types of Gangs. Carl Taylor has identified four types of gangs: territorial, scavenger, commercial, and corporate. Territorial gangs are the "traditional" type of gang; they recruit members to claim a certain territory or area as their own. Such gangs focus on petty crime (usually property crimes) and defending their territory from members of rival gangs. These types of gangs have been romanticized in such films as *West Side Story* (1961).

Scavenger gangs are groups of individuals whose main concern is survival. These people are usually from the lower classes, and the behavior they engage in is usually not criminal. They live together as vagrants, attempting to survive as a group. Anything recovered by one member (such as food or money) is shared with other members of the gang. Unlike most other gangs, scavenger gangs are not necessarily made up of one gender, nor are they racially exclusive.

Commercial gangs are scavenger gangs that have become more tightly structured and are interested in profit. They stay together to earn a profit, usually through drug sales, prostitution, and other illicit behavior. Corporate gangs differ from commercial gangs in that they are mostly interested in monopolizing a certain business. Instead of merely selling drugs, for example, they aim to monopolize the drug trade for a certain area. In many cases, they are tied to organized crime in some way, and their members are significantly older than the typical member of a youth gang.

Female Gangs. The majority of youth gangs are composed of males. It is much less common for a group of girls to come together to form a youth gang. This fact is usually attributed to the greater control that parents tend to exert over their daughters than over their sons. Girls are more closely guarded and are subject to higher levels of parental supervision. Yet because girls have significantly increased their participation in gang-related activities, some researchers believe that parental constraints on daughters are loosening.

When females become involved in gang behavior, they are usually girlfriends of male gang members. Sometimes, however, girls form their own gangs, which may or may not be tied to male juvenile gangs. When girls form gangs that are associated with male gangs, they are considered "auxiliary" gangs; their behavior and activities frequently focus on the activities of the male gang. Some have estimated that about half of all male gangs have female auxiliary gangs attached to them. In many cases, the girls provide sexual relationships for members of the male gang with whom they associate. Female gangs usually adopt names that are feminized versions of male gang names. For example, a female gang in Chicago in the 1960's called themselves the "Vice Queens"; they were an auxiliary gang tied to a male gang called the "Vice Kings."

Some female gangs have separated themselves from male gangs. Sometimes called "true gangs," these groups of girls are not tied at all to male gangs. Instead, they enjoy a fair amount of independence, are involved in their own activities, and tend to reject traditional ideas of femininity and female roles.

Gangs and Law Enforcement. Youth gangs pose a particular problem for law-enforcement officials. It is difficult for police officers to obtain information about crimes committed by gang members or about the gang members themselves. First, gang members are distrustful and reluctant to talk with police officers. They fear incriminating themselves—or fellow gang members—in crimes they have committed in the past.

When a member of a gang is killed by a rival gang, the survivors believe that it is their responsibility—not the job of the police or the justice system—to avenge the death of their member. Revenge is considered successful when a member of the rival gang, preferably the person responsible for the initial murder, is killed.

Members of the community are also reluctant to discuss details of gang-related crimes with police, usually out of fear of the gangs' retaliation. For many witnesses of gang-related crime, the threat of retaliation is an everyday fear. Many witnesses are coerced into silence by gang members who threaten to kill them or their family members if they testify against them in a trial or provide information to the police.

—*Christina Polsenberg*

See also Drive-by shootings; Drug use and sale, illegal; Juvenile delinquency; Juvenile justice system; Vandalism.

BIBLIOGRAPHY

One of the first researchers to report on gangs was Frederic M. Thrasher, in *The Gang* (Chicago: University of Chicago Press, 1927). Thrasher's work has been considered the standard for other researchers who followed. An anthology of various articles on gang behavior can be found in Scott Cummings and Daniel J. Monti, eds., *Gangs: The Origins and Impact of Contemporary Youth Gangs in the United States* (Albany: State University of New York Press, 1993). An extensive ethnographic study of gang behavior has been done by Carl Taylor, published in *Dangerous Society* (East Lansing: Michigan State University Press, 1990). More detailed information about girls in gangs can be found in Anne Campbell, *The Girls in the Gang: A Report from New York City* (New York: Basil Blackwell, 1984), and Carl Taylor, *Girls, Gangs, Women, and Drugs* (East Lansing: Michigan State University Press, 1993).

Garrison, William Lloyd (Dec. 10, 1805, Newburyport, Mass.—May 24, 1879, New York, N.Y.)

IDENTIFICATION: Abolitionist

SIGNIFICANCE: Garrison, an advocate of the immediate end of slavery and the equality of blacks, was the most influential American abolitionist

William Lloyd Garrison was one of the first Americans to support abolition. In 1831, he founded an abolitionist newspaper, the *Liberator*, which he edited until 1865. In 1833, he played a leading role in the formation of the American Antislavery Society (AAS).

In the 1830's and 1840's, Garrison's views became increasingly radical. He supported women's rights and nonresistance, a doctrine which claimed that governmental power, like slavery, was immoral because it suppressed human freedom. Garrison's views divided the AAS in 1839-1840, and anti-Garrisonian dissenters left the organization. In the 1840's, Garrison denounced the U.S. Constitution as a "covenant with death" because it protected slavery, and he urged the North to secede from the Union.

Yet for all his utopian idealism, Garrison realized that slavery could be ended only by practical politicians. His role as agitator was to proclaim truth and, in so doing, help governments increasingly make moral choices. During the Civil War, Garrison dropped his criticism of governmental power and supported the Union government's emancipation policy.

See also Abolitionist movement; Civil War; Douglass, Frederick; Slavery.

Garvey, Marcus (Aug. 17, 1887, St. Ann's Bay, Jamaica— June 10, 1940, London, England)

IDENTIFICATION: UNIA founder and black internationalist

SIGNIFICANCE: Garvey, an effective journalist and charismatic orator, advocated that American blacks return to Africa and organized the first black mass-protest movement in the United States

Marcus Garvey founded the Universal Negro Improvement Association (UNIA) in Jamaica. Achieving only limited success in uniting Jamaican blacks, he moved to the United States in 1916. In 1918 he founded the newspaper *Negro World*, which disseminated information about the UNIA. By the early 1920's, Garvey had somewhere between half a million and five million followers. He stressed black pride and argued that white racism had created self-hatred among blacks. He urged blacks to establish a nation of their own, encouraged black emigration to Africa, and worked to organize the UNIA on a worldwide basis.

At least partly because of his immense popularity among urban blacks, Garvey made numerous enemies among whites and blacks alike. In 1924, W. E. B. Du Bois described him as

Founder of the Universal Negro Improvement Association, Marcus Garvey advocated black business ownership as well as emigration to Africa. (Library of Congress)

"the most dangerous enemy of the Negro race and world." Garvey, who had little use for the black intellectuals of his day, filed numerous lawsuits for libel. Garvey criticized blacks for begging whites for jobs when they could create jobs for themselves. "Garveyism" influenced many black nationalists, including Elijah Muhammad and Malcolm X's father. His writings appeared in *African Times and Orient Review*, *Negro World*, and elsewhere.

The Black Star Line, Garvey's steamship and shipping company, was his favorite project, but it ultimately led to his downfall when he was convicted of mail fraud relating to the sale of its stock. He spent five years in prison. Upon his release he was deported and eventually settled in England, where he attempted to continue his work but died disheartened and alone. Garvey was, and remains, a controversial figure; he was both condemned as a charlatan and hailed as a black messiah.

See also Du Bois, W. E. B.; Mail fraud; National Association for the Advancement of Colored People (NAACP).

Gault, In re

COURT: U.S. Supreme Court
DATE: Decided May 15, 1967
SIGNIFICANCE: This decision established that juvenile court procedures must include the most basic procedural rights and evidentiary rules

In re Gault was the result of the 1964 arrest of Gerald Gault in Gila County, Arizona, for making a lewd telephone call to a neighbor. Gault, who was then fifteen years old, was on probation for an earlier minor offense. Although the state produced no evidence at Gault's hearing, the juvenile judge found him to be delinquent. The basis of the finding was evidently police rumors about him and statements elicited from him in the absence of his parents or his lawyer. He was committed to a state industrial school until his eighteenth birthday. Had an adult committed the same crime, the maximum penalty that could have been assessed under Arizona law would have been a fifty-dollar fine and two months' imprisonment. Gault's appeal to the Arizona Supreme Court was unsuccessful, and he brought the case to the U.S. Supreme Court. He argued that the Arizona juvenile code was unconstitutional on its face because it gives the judge almost unlimited discretion to take juveniles from their parents and commit them to an institution without notice of the charges, the right to counsel, the right to confront and cross-examine witnesses, the right to a transcript of the proceedings, or the right to an appeal. Arizona argued that because the main purpose of juvenile proceedings is to protect juvenile defendants from the full rigor and consequences of the criminal law, informal procedures are required. In Arizona's view, Gault's commitment to a state institution was protective rather than punitive.

The Supreme Court decided for Gault by a vote of 8 to 1. In an opinion by Justice Abe Fortas, the Court held that the due process clause of the Fourteenth Amendment requires that juvenile defendants are at least entitled to notice of the charges, right to counsel, right to confrontation and cross-examination

of witnesses, the privilege against self-incrimination, a transcript of the proceedings, and appellate review. Justice Fortas insisted that these are the minimal guarantees necessary to assure fairness. He argued that the guarantees would not unduly interfere with any of the benefits of less formal procedures for juveniles. Justice John M. Harlan wrote a separate concurrence agreeing with the result but suggesting that the crucial minimum guarantees should be limited to notice of the charges, the right to counsel, including assigned counsel for indigent families, a transcript, and the right to appeal. In dissent, Justice Potter Stewart argued that because juvenile proceedings are not adversary criminal actions the court is unwise to fasten procedural guarantees upon them.

In re Gault forces states to provide juvenile defendants with the central procedural guarantees of the Fifth Amendment. The possibility that young defendants will be unfairly judged to have committed crimes or been delinquent was substantially reduced.

See also Age discrimination; Criminal procedure; Due process of law; Evidence, rules of; Juvenile justice system.

Gay rights

DEFINITION: A broad range of civil rights and civil liberties guaranteed to gay, lesbian, and bisexual persons
SIGNIFICANCE: Discrimination against gay men, lesbians, and bisexuals is slowly being addressed through extensions of the legal protections provided to persons based on race, gender, ethnic origin, age, religion, and political affiliation

Gays, lesbians, and bisexuals historically have suffered severe discrimination in employment, housing, and other aspects of their lives. Perceptions that a person is gay, whether correct or not, can lead to discrimination in the workplace; they can also have a negative effect on an individual's ability to rent or buy a home, participate freely in social and political activities, and exercise the same rights of privacy that others have. Gay people have not enjoyed the same legal protections given to other groups in American society and often feel that they are singled out and harassed by law enforcement officers as well as by private citizens.

Discrimination. In large measure, discrimination has been quite similar to that suffered by racial and ethnic minorities and by women in American society. Unlike those groups, however, gays, lesbians, and bisexuals have not enjoyed the legal protection of the civil rights acts and other equal employment opportunity and equal housing acts. For that reason, the gay rights movement has supported legislation to provide gays, lesbians, and bisexuals with equal protection of the laws.

Studies indicate clear patterns of discrimination in the workplace that can affect a gay, lesbian, or bisexual individual's chances of being hired, promoted, and retained. A "lavender ceiling" exists, similar to the "glass ceiling" that limits women's prospects for advancement in the workplace. To help gay individuals cope with, and eventually overcome, such obstacles, networking and mentoring programs are being created for gay, lesbian, and bisexual employees in some organi-

Demonstrators at a gay rights rally in Madison, Wisconsin. (James L. Shaffer)

zations to provide support and encouragement. Employee benefits programs most often do not recognize gay, lesbian, or bisexual relationships or provide for "domestic partner" benefits, although that is changing as family law adjusts to new family groupings. For example, the legal definition of "dependent" is expanding beyond spouse and children to accommodate the growing number of employees supporting parents and other extended family members. Changes in law that permit marriages between partners of the same sex are also beginning to expand employee benefit programs and to clarify a variety of other legal issues relating to joint property.

Obstacles to Gay Rights. Several major factors have blocked the attainment of gay legal rights. Many religious groups have opposed granting equal rights protections based on sexual orientation because of their belief that gay lifestyles violate Christian doctrine. Acceptance of gay rights, particularly in the workplace, has also been opposed on economic grounds. Opponents of "domestic partner" benefits frequently argue that the costs of medical and other benefits to public organizations and private businesses will increase if they are extended to nontraditional family groupings. The fact that there are fewer and fewer "traditional" family groupings, however, is slowly nudging public organizations and businesses to broaden their benefits coverage.

Another complicating factor is the difficulty of identifying gays, lesbians, and bisexuals. Unlike gender and race, sexual orientation is not immediately evident, and to identify oneself openly as gay, lesbian, or bisexual is to leave oneself vulnerable to discrimination, harassment, and even hate crimes. Therefore, many individuals are unwilling to identify themselves as such. In some states, too, legal prohibitions against sexual relations between individuals of the same sex can discourage complaints of discrimination and may encourage harassment by police and civilians. The Supreme Court, in *Bowers v. Hardwick* (1986), held that such laws are constitutional and refused to extend the fundamental right to privacy to cover consensual acts of sodomy.

Activism and Change. Since the 1950's, small associations of gays and lesbians had sought to reduce antigay prejudice and pursue equal rights. By 1967, larger gay protests were becoming increasingly common. An event that occurred in 1969, however, is widely considered crucial in galvanizing the movement for equal rights for people of any sexual orientation. In June of 1969, the Stonewall Inn, a gay bar in New York City, was raided by police two nights in a row. Patrons resisted and protested, and a week of protests and riots—the Stonewall riots—ensued. The gay liberation movement was formed from this event. By the mid-1970's, hundreds of gay and lesbian organizations, including groups dedicated to pursuing legal rights, had formed. The National Organization for Women included a large lesbian faction and also began to work for lesbian rights.

In the 1970's, the first openly gay politicians were elected to office (most notably in San Francisco), the American Psychiatric Association removed homosexuality from its list of mental disorders, and a gay rights bill was introduced in Congress. The National Gay and Lesbian Task Force and the Lambda Defense and Education Fund were founded in 1973; the Civil Service Commission dropped its ban on employing gay people in 1975. The first national gay rights march on Washington occurred in 1977.

The 1990's. In the early 1990's, the issue of gay rights focused on the question of whether gays should be allowed to serve in the military openly. One of Bill Clinton's campaign promises in 1992 was to end the ban on gays in the armed forces. The proposal encountered such widespread and fierce opposition, however, that the administration abandoned the idea and accepted a compromise plan, the "Don't ask, don't tell" policy. In essence, it was accepted that there are—and always have been—gays serving in the military. The military was enjoined not to ask personnel about sexual orientation, and gay service members were assured that their service could continue as long as they did not identify themselves openly. The policy has been challenged in the courts as violating gay, lesbian, and bisexual service members' rights to free speech and privacy: Under "Don't ask, don't tell," self-identification amounts to self-incrimination.

Increasingly, a failure to protect gay, lesbian, and bisexual rights in the workplace can expose an organization to lawsuits and political protest. Antidiscrimination clauses are being added to personnel regulations and municipal laws to protect employees of all sexual orientations, but enforcement is uneven. Social acceptance of gays, lesbians, and bisexuals is still much greater in some communities than in others. The size of the community's gay community (and its degree of political influence) is still the best predictor of acceptance.

—*William L. Waugh, Jr.*

See also Acquired immune deficiency syndrome (AIDS); American Civil Liberties Union (ACLU); *Bowers v. Hardwick*; Civil liberties; Civil rights; Equal Rights Amendment (ERA); Family law; Feminism; Hate crimes; Privacy, right of; Victimless crimes.

BIBLIOGRAPHY

A broad overview of gay rights issues can be found in Mark Blasius, *Gay and Lesbian Politics: Sexuality and the Emergence of a New Ethic* (Philadelphia: Temple University Press, 1994). The major legal issues involved in gay rights are discussed in detail in Nan Hunter, Sherryl E. Michaelson, and Thomas B. Stoddard, *The Rights of Lesbians and Gay Men* (3d ed. Carbondale: Southern Illinois University Press, 1992), which is the gay rights handbook of the American Civil Liberties Union. New and continuing legal issues are addressed in the proceedings of the National Lesbian and Gay Law Association's biennial conferences; for example, see *Lavender Law IV* (Portland, Oreg.: Conference of the National Lesbian and Gay Law Association, 1994). Employment issues are discussed from the organizational and individual perspectives in Wallace Swan, ed., *Breaking the Silence: Gay, Lesbian, and Bisexual Issues in Public Administration* (Washington, D.C.: American Society for Public Administration, 1995).

Gerrymandering. *See* **Representation: gerrymandering, malapportionment and reapportionment**

GI Bill of Rights

DATE: Signed into law June 22, 1944

DEFINITION: Legislation that provided assistance to returning World War II veterans in securing employment, education, and homes, farms, and businesses

SIGNIFICANCE: The GI Bill, also known as the Servicemen's Readjustment Act of 1944 and as Public Law 346, provided the American people with a way of expressing their gratitude to veterans in a tangible manner; the law enabled some veterans to resume education and careers that had been interrupted and encouraged others to pursue opportunities that formerly would have been denied them

The GI Bill is considered to be among the most important and far-reaching pieces of social legislation in American history. The law, contained in six titles, helped returning World War II veterans secure employment and unemployment benefits as well as education and training. It also provided financial assistance to those wishing to purchase homes, farms, and businesses.

Prior to the passage of the GI Bill in 1944, the nation had a long tradition of caring for its disabled war veterans. In the years following World War I, the federal government and certain states, most notably Wisconsin, also began to make inroads into helping veterans without disabilities resettle into productive lives after their years of wartime service. Sponsors of the post-World War II veterans' legislation drew their central theme of resettlement and many of the law's rehabilitative features from practices developed between 1918 and 1943.

Resettlement to peacetime held a prominent place in the thoughts of all Americans at the end of World War II. Many feared the social consequences of demobilizing millions of displaced and unemployed veterans into an economy made fragile with the cessation of wartime spending. Supporters of veterans' legislation saw in the GI Bill an opportunity to stimulate the economy through direct financial assistance to veterans while achieving certain social benefits such as improved and expanded education and housing.

Legislative History. In the summer of 1940, President Franklin D. Roosevelt signed the Selective Service Act. One of the many features of this law was the guaranteed reemployment of all conscripted veterans. Subsequent legislation, passed in 1943 and 1944, that provided vocational rehabilitation and mustering-out pay also adumbrated later comprehensive efforts at resettlement for GIs.

Until the summer of 1942, President Roosevelt had eschewed efforts to plan for the postwar demobilization, preferring to keep the nation focused on winning the war. At the urging of his uncle, Frederick A. Delano, however, he acceded. Delano established the Post War Manpower Conference (PMC). The twelve-member committee issued a report in June, 1943, that dealt with the relationship of education and training to employment. Their program, to be administered by the U.S. Office of Education, provided for twelve months of schooling for all veterans and three additional years for the exceptionally talented. It would be administered competitively and sought to encourage education and training for growth occupations and professions. The armed forces also studied postwar demobilization. Their Osborn Committee issued its report in July, 1943, which concurred in all material respects with the work of the Post War Manpower Conference. A third evaluation, initiated by the American Council on Education, endorsed the findings of both the PMC and the armed forces committee.

Confident that consensus had been achieved and eager to gain political advantage, Roosevelt advanced the Osborn Report for legislative action in October, 1943. A month later he also called upon Congress to enact measures providing mustering-out pay, unemployment insurance, and credit in the Social Security program for years spent in service. The president's program was perceived by many to be a piecemeal approach to an enormous social issue.

Congressional deliberation lasted from late 1943 to June, 1944, and stayed within the broad outline drafted by the Osborn Committee. Senator Elbert D. Thomas, a New Deal Democrat

The GI Bill was enacted after World War II to assist returning soldiers—such as these fliers being addressed by General Dwight D. Eisenhower before the D-Day invasion. (Library of Congress)

from Utah, introduced a bill incorporating the Osborn-Roosevelt recommendation on November 3, 1943. The Subcommittee on Education and Labor reported the bill to the Senate on February 7, 1944. The American Legion, in the meantime, began a major campaign for a more comprehensive bill. The Legion wanted medical care, unemployment compensation, education and vocational training, home, business, and farm loans, and furlough pay for the soldiers' return to civilian life.

The Legion's proposal was advanced in a House bill introduced on January 10. The next day, Senator Joel Bennett Clark sponsored a similar bill in the Senate. After deliberations, he introduced another version of the bill on March 13. This bill, written in large part by the Legion, incorporated much that Senator Thomas had proposed several months earlier. Both House and Senate bills were approved in March, and a joint Senate-House committee approved the final version on June 13. The bill was signed into law on June 22, 1944.

Impact of the Law. The GI Bill had a profound effect on the social, cultural, economic, and political life of postwar America. By the fall of 1955, approximately 7.8 million veterans— slightly more than half of all World War II veterans in civilian life—had embarked on education or training under the GI Bill. Large numbers, 5.3 million and 3.8 million respectively, received readjustment allowances and home-loan guarantee benefits. Although the cost of the GI Bill has been placed at $14.5 billion, it produced a generation of well-educated professionals and business leaders; stimulated business, farm, and home ownership; and greatly strengthened the American middle class, repaying its cost many times over.   —*S. A. Marino*

See also Conscription; New Deal; Roosevelt, Franklin D.; Truman, Harry S; Veterans' rights; Welfare state.

BIBLIOGRAPHY

Good overviews include Keith W. Olson, *The G.I. Bill, the Veterans, and the Colleges* (Lexington: University Press of Kentucky, 1974); Davis R. B. Ross, *Preparing for Ulysses: Politics and Veterans During World War II* (New York: Columbia University Press, 1969); and Richard Severo and Lewis Milford, *The Wages of War* (New York: Simon & Schuster, 1989). A highly informative and enjoyable article that profiled several veterans who benefited from the GI Bill is Edwin Kiester, Jr., "Uncle Sam Wants You . . . to Go to College," *Smithsonian* 25 (November 1, 1994).

Gideon v. Wainwright

COURT: U.S. Supreme Court
DATE: Decided March 18, 1963
SIGNIFICANCE: The Supreme Court ruled that states must provide legal counsel to poor defendants in criminal trials because the right to counsel guaranteed by the Sixth Amendment applies without reservation to the states

Prior to this case, considerable confusion existed as to whether the Sixth Amendment's "right to counsel" provision applied to the states as well as to the federal government. In 1932, in the famous "Scottsboro" case of *Powell v. Alabama*, the Supreme Court had stressed the vulnerability of the accused and con-

Clarence Gideon, whose appeal to the Supreme Court led to the rule that poor defendants accused of serious crimes have a right to be represented by a lawyer. (AP/Wide World Photos)

cluded that their conviction transgressed the fair trial provisions of the Sixth Amendment because they had not benefited from legal representation. That case, however, teemed with qualifying circumstances. The accused were a half dozen young, transient black defendants with little education and, in some instances, with diminished intelligence, who were tried without effective counsel and sentenced to death for raping two white women. Nevertheless, it was believed that the Supreme Court had, in *Powell*, made the right to counsel provision of the Sixth Amendment applicable to the states.

This conclusion prevailed for a decade before the Supreme Court explicitly corrected that misunderstanding in *Betts v. Brady* (1942). Stressing the exceptional circumstances involved in the Scottsboro case, a majority concluded in *Betts* that the right to a fair trial does not require that the criminally accused be represented by an attorney under ordinary circumstances in state proceedings, even in capital cases. Following the *Betts* decision, it was generally supposed that the accused could adequately represent themselves, especially if they had previously witnessed the judicial system at work. Remarkable circumstances such as those of the *Powell* case were an exception to the rule.

Gideon v. Wainwright challenged this assumption. Clarence Gideon fit the *Betts* test. He had been on the wrong side of the bar more than once, and he had actively represented himself in his trial. In accepting the case on appeal, the Supreme Court committed itself to determining whether the concept of a fair trial requires counsel as a general proposition. No other basis existed for deciding the case.

From the outset it appeared that *Gideon* would be a landmark case. Abe Fortas, one of Washington's most celebrated lawyers and later a Supreme Court justice, represented Gideon on a *pro bono* basis. In Fortas' view, Gideon had repeatedly made errors in defending himself which most first-year law students would have avoided. The Supreme Court agreed, overturning *Betts* on the basis of the complex and often confusing nature of judicial proceedings to the ordinary citizen. "The right of one charged with crime to counsel may not be deemed fundamental and essential to fair trials in some countries," Justice Hugo L. Black summarized for the majority, "but it is in ours." Shortly thereafter, the right to counsel was extended to pretrial accusatory proceedings and custodial arrests (*Escobedo v. Illinois*, 1964; *Miranda v. Arizona*, 1966). Meanwhile, in his retrial, with a qualified attorney representing him, Gideon was acquitted of the crime for which he had been previously convicted.

See also *Argersinger v. Hamlin*; Assigned counsel system; Counsel, right to; Due process of law; *Escobedo v. Illinois*; Incorporation doctrine; *Miranda v. Arizona*; *Powell v. Alabama*; Public defender.

Gitlow v. New York

Court: U.S. Supreme Court
Date: Decided June 8, 1925
Significance: This decision weakened protection for free speech by establishing a "bad tendency" test for judging whether a person can be sent to prison for words advocating the overthrow of the government by force or violence

World War I and the Russian Revolution brought about a "red scare" in the United States. This was a period of feverish antiradicalism characterized by mass deportations of aliens and the adoption by many states of criminal syndicalism or criminal anarchy statutes. Benjamin Gitlow was the general secretary of the left-wing section of the Socialist Party, whose headquarters were in New York. He supervised the publication of sixteen thousand copies of a paper called *The Revolutionary Age*, which contained a "Left-Wing Manifesto." The manifesto attacked the moderate Socialists and advocated militant and revolutionary socialism based on the class struggle. It called for mass industrial revolts and strikes for the purpose of conquering and destroying the parliamentary state.

Gitlow was indicted and convicted for violating New York State's criminal anarchy statute. This act defined criminal anarchy as a doctrine that organized government should be overthrown by force or violence. Advocacy of criminal anarchy was made a felony. At trial Gitlow argued that his publication was protected by the First Amendment. There had been no evidence that the "Left-Wing Manifesto" had any effect. Gitlow insisted that his conviction could not stand unless the state showed that a "clear and present danger" resulted from the

publication. After losing in the New York courts, Gitlow appealed to the Supreme Court of the United States.

The Supreme Court held against Gitlow by a vote of 7-2. The majority's opinion, written by Justice Edward T. Sanford, limited the application of the "clear and present danger" test to cases not involving a direct legislative prohibition of particular kinds of speech. Under the test, utterances whose "natural tendency and probable effect" is to bring about revolutionary or violent activity are punishable by law. When the legislature does act to proscribe particular speech, a person may be punished for utterances which tend to bring about the evil whether or not there is any real danger. The Court's decision elicited a powerful dissenting opinion by Justice Oliver Wendell Holmes, Jr., with which Justice Louis D. Brandeis concurred.

The dissenting opinion attacks the majority for failing to distinguish between discussion and advocacy; only advocacy may be punished and even then only when it presents a clear and present danger of bringing about evil consequences which the legislature has the right to prevent. Justices Holmes and Brandeis often found themselves joining in dissent in free speech cases; their opinions collectively, and Holmes's dissent in this case, are the most powerful and compelling arguments for freedom of speech in the American legal canon.

Although this case was decided against Gitlow, the Court's assumption that freedom of speech is protected against invasion by state governments was a significant milestone in the development of free speech rights. In effect the Court held that freedom of speech is among the liberties protected against infringement by state government by the due process clause of the Fourteenth Amendment.

See also *Abrams v. United States*; *Brandenburg v. Ohio*; Clear and present danger test; *Dennis v. United States*; Due process of law; Holmes, Oliver Wendell, Jr.; *Schenck v. United States*; Socialist Party, American; Speech and press, freedom of.

Gompers, Samuel (Jan. 27, 1850, London, England— Dec. 13, 1924, San Antonio, Tex.)

Identification: Labor leader
Significance: Gompers' long leadership of the American Federation of Labor significantly shaped the ideas and practices of the labor movement in the United States

Born of Dutch immigrants of Jewish faith, Samuel Gompers came to the United States as a young teen. He became a cigarmaker. His career as a labor leader began in 1875 when he became president of the cigarmakers' local 144 in New York City. In 1886 he became president of the reorganized American Federation of Labor (AFL). As president of the AFL (1886-1924, except 1895), he pushed his conservative philosophy of labor, which became the standard mode of belief and practice for American labor.

He distrusted intellectual reformers and all radicals, fearing diversion from the economic gains sought by labor. He pushed for written, binding contracts, favored national labor organization dominance over both locals and international affiliates, and always kept the immediate concerns of skilled workers—

Samuel Gompers was influential in the labor union movement as president of the American Federation of Labor for more than thirty-five years. (Library of Congress)

better wages, working conditions, and work hours—in the forefront. His methods of accomplishing these goals were primarily collective bargaining, strikes, and boycotts.

See also American Federation of Labor-Congress of Industrial Organizations (AFL-CIO); Capitalism; Labor law; Labor unions.

Good time

DEFINITION: Time subtracted from a prison sentence for good behavior while in prison

SIGNIFICANCE: All felony prison sentences in the United States provide for release prior to service of the full sentence by reason of some form of good time if there is no parole

Good time (or "time off for good behavior") is defined as a number of days subtracted from a prison sentence. It is based on the notion that inmates should have some motivation for good behavior while serving their sentences. The control of good time can have a considerable impact on institutional discipline. Based on existing regulations and case law, an inmate's good time can be forfeited for misconduct or criminal behavior while in prison. Court decisions, however, have mandated that good time cannot be taken from an inmate without due process (*Wolff, Warden, et. al. v. McDonnell*, 1974).

Three factors should be noted with regard to good time. First, as a general rule, good time is based on the length of the sentence. The longer the sentence, the more good time

awarded per month of the sentence. Second, the amount of good time awarded per month varies considerably from government to government. Third, the way good time is calculated varies considerably from government to government. Some governments subtract good time from the total sentence, whereas others subtract it from other points in the sentence such as the minimum parole eligibility date.

See also Discretion; Mandatory sentencing laws; Parole; Prison and jail systems; Punishment; Sentencing; Sentencing guidelines, U.S.

Graham v. Richardson

COURT: U.S. Supreme Court

DATE: Decided June 14, 1971

SIGNIFICANCE: In this case, the Supreme Court declared alienage, like race, a "suspect classification" under the Fourteenth Amendment, thus subjecting state classifications based on alienage to strict scrutiny, under which states must promote a compelling government interest

Carmen Richardson, a Mexican citizen, was lawfully admitted to the United States in 1956. From that time, she resided continuously in Arizona, where she became permanently disabled. When she applied to the state for welfare benefits, she was denied them because she had not met Arizona's requirement that welfare beneficiaries who are not United States citizens must have resided in the state for fifteen years.

Richardson brought a class action on behalf of other similarly situated individuals against the Arizona commissioner of public welfare, claiming that the residency requirement violated their right to equal protection under the Fourteenth Amendment. She won her case in federal court, and the state appealed to the Supreme Court, claiming that limited public resources justified states favoring their own residents over aliens.

The Supreme Court unanimously upheld the lower court's decision. The Court agreed with the finding that residency requirements such as that at issue in *Graham v. Richardson* violate the Fourteenth Amendment's equal protection clause and that government classifications based on alienage, like those based on race, can only be upheld if they are closely related to a compelling state interest. Arizona's interest in husbanding its financial resources was clearly not compelling enough. In addition, the Court provided an alternate ground for striking down the Arizona statute: Because the Constitution empowers the federal government to control the conditions under which aliens reside in the United States, state laws addressing the same concerns were preempted because of the supremacy clause (Article VI of the Constitution).

The Court subsequently created a series of exceptions to *Graham*. In *Sugarman v. Dougall* (1973), for example, the Court indicated that states could bar aliens from certain posts in government. In *Foley v. Connelie* (1978), it employed only ordinary scrutiny (requiring the state to meet a much lower burden of proof) in upholding a New York statute barring aliens from becoming state troopers. Subsequent Supreme Court cases followed the political job function argument of *Foley* to uphold state laws barring aliens from employment as public school teachers (*Ambach v. Norwick*, 1979) and as deputy probation officers (*Cabell v. Chavez-Salido*, 1982). In the seminal case *Plyler v. Doe* (1982), although the Court voted 5 to 4 to invalidate a Texas law withholding public education from children of aliens who had migrated to the U.S. outside legal channels, it lowered the burden of proof to that of intermediate scrutiny. Thus a different standard of proof was made to apply in cases involving so-called illegal aliens than to those concerning lawful resident aliens. Unlike discriminatory racial classifications, which are inherently suspect, alienage has proven to be a more protean concept.

See also Burden of proof; Equal protection of the law; Illegal aliens; Immigration, legal and illegal; Supremacy clause.

Grand jury

DEFINITION: A body of citizens who investigate allegations of criminality and determine whether a particular suspect should be charged with and eventually tried for a crime

SIGNIFICANCE: The grand jury is a check against governmental authority because it, not the government, serves as the institution that determines whether a citizen should be charged with a crime

Originating in England in the eleventh century and serving as an integral part of English common law, the grand jury was created by judges to check the abuses of government and to prevent the prosecution of innocent persons. In the United States, the Fifth Amendment to the Constitution guarantees that no citizen may be charged with a crime "unless on a presentment or indictment of a grand jury." In *Hurtado v. California* (1884), however, the U.S. Supreme Court determined that the Fifth Amendment requires grand jury presentations only when a citizen faces charges brought by the federal government. Some states voluntarily authorize grand jury presentations.

Historically, the grand jury has served to protect individual liberties. For example, during American colonial and revolutionary times, grand juries refused to charge colonists with "political crimes," such as speeches denouncing the king. Today, grand juries, composed of up to twenty-three citizens, investigate cases and obtain evidence by issuing subpoenas, legal orders that compel witnesses to testify. If witnesses ignore the subpoena and fail to testify, they may be imprisoned for contempt of court. If witnesses lie in their testimony, they may be charged with perjury.

The grand jury may hear all types of evidence, including evidence that the police may have obtained illegally. In one important case, *United States v. Calandra* (1974), the Supreme Court permitted such evidence because the grand jury is designed to be a neutral investigative body. Therefore, the grand jury should consider as much relevant evidence as possible. Suspects may challenge improper evidence at their trials, which occur later and are by nature contentious and adversarial. Unlike virtually all other legal proceedings in the United States, the proceedings of the grand jury are secret. Secrecy encourages witnesses to provide complete and truthful testimony, while preventing suspects from learning about an investigation and fleeing before they are charged. If a grand jury determines that a suspect should be charged with a crime, it will issue an indictment, which is the legal document that details the charges the grand jury has authorized.

In colonial times, the grand jury was essential because there were few formal institutions or procedures that preserved the rights of citizens. Criminal suspects now have greater constitutional protections. The police and prosecutors also have legal and ethical obligations to pursue a suspect only when they believe that the suspect has committed a crime. Thus, the grand jury will often evaluate a case only after the case has been thoroughly investigated. Nevertheless, the grand jury, as the "conscience of the community," brings to the justice system a broad and realistic perspective of life, which in itself may lead to greater justice. The term "grand jury" simply refers to its size—it is composed of more members than a trial jury (a "petit jury").

See also Arraignment; Bill of Rights, U.S.; Criminal procedure; *Hurtado v. California*; Indictment; Information; Jury system; Prosecutor, public.

Great Society

DEFINITION: President Lyndon Baines Johnson's program for ending poverty and providing equality of opportunity to American citizens

SIGNIFICANCE: The Great Society program produced the largest growth in the United States welfare state in more than thirty years in enacting programs whose controversial nature was still being debated three decades later

In his inaugural address in 1965, President Lyndon B. Johnson declared an "unconditional war on poverty" and his intent to build a "Great Society" in which each individual would be able to realize his or her potential. To enable individuals to do so, access to education, training, and the necessary public services was to be significantly enlarged.

Johnson's inspiration was Franklin D. Roosevelt's New Deal program of the Depression years of the 1930's, the decade when Congressman Johnson first went to Washington. Thirty years later, President Johnson's opportunity to build a Great Society flowed from his Roosevelt-like control of Congress. His 1964 election was of landslide proportions, and his Democratic Party controlled majorities in both houses of Congress. Additionally, as the former majority leader of the Senate, Johnson possessed enormous legislative skills. By 1976, he predicted, poverty in the United States would end.

His was an ambitious program composed of many parts. Its centerpiece was the Economic Opportunity Act of 1964, a program designed to assist unemployed poor people in acquiring the skills necessary to escape poverty. Under the coordination of the Office of Economic Opportunity (OEO) were organized such innovative programs as the Neighborhood Youth Corps (to provide the young with part-time jobs and incentives

Lyndon B. Johnson's Great Society programs were in conflict with his desire to continue and increase funding for the Vietnam War. (Library of Congress)

to remain in school), Upward Bound (to help underachieving but intelligent youth from blighted backgrounds get into college), Project Head Start (to enroll preschool children from poor backgrounds in schools to improve their basic learning skills), and the Community Action Program, or CAP (to involve the poor in their own antipoverty programs in local communities). To these were added such non-OEO programs as food stamps to combat malnutrition and the Medicaid and Medicare health-care programs (targeting, respectively, the poor and the elderly, many of whom were statistically among the poor).

Almost uniformly attacked by conservatives as a manifestation of big, centralized government, the Great Society program actually moved large amounts of grants-in-aid money to the states and localities for disbursement. Moreover, a number of Great Society programs survived the wave of cost-cutting presidents who followed Johnson, from Richard Nixon to George Bush; Head Start was even targeted for increased support during the early Bill Clinton presidency.

On the other hand, of those programs that survived, most did so in very diminished form and with greatly reduced prestige. President Johnson's service approach to combating poverty is generally judged to have failed. Explanations for its failure include its underfunded nature as a result of the Vietnam War; the loss of opportunities in the frequent, debilitating power struggles between the CAPs and local governments; the inability of many of the enrollees in its retraining programs to profit from the system because of their serious learning disabilities; and the hugely bureaucratic, red tape-mired nature of the operation.

See also Aid to Families with Dependent Children (AFDC); Equality of opportunity; Food stamps; Johnson, Lyndon B.; Liberalism, modern American; Vietnam War; War on Poverty; Welfare state.

Greeley, Horace (Feb. 3, 1811, Amherst, N.H.—Nov. 29, 1872, New York, N.Y.)

IDENTIFICATION: Newspaper editor and reformer
SIGNIFICANCE: Greeley's was a strong voice for reform throughout the mid-nineteenth century because of his influential position as editor of the *New York Tribune*

Although he served as a congressman for three months (1848-1849), Greeley exerted the greatest influence on American society and politics through his work as an editor. He founded the first penny newspaper, *The New Yorker*, in 1834, and on April 10, 1841, began publishing the *New York Tribune*. He remained as editor until 1872, when, outraged by the Republican policy of revenge on the South that followed the Civil War, he ran for the presidency, supported by a coalition of liberal Republicans and Democrats. He was soundly defeated by the incumbent, Ulysses S. Grant, and died shortly thereafter.

Greeley is perhaps best remembered for coining the phrase "Go West, young man, go West." Yet as an editor he also called for numerous reforms, among them a protective tariff, temperance, and women's rights (he employed the feminist writer

Margaret Fuller on the *Tribune*). He favored the agrarian movement, which called for open land and a liberal policy for settlers, while opposing land grants to railroads. He also opposed monopolies and supported the organization of labor. An advocate of emancipation, he was one of the first members of the new Republican Party and was influential in the nomination of Abraham Lincoln, although he later embarrassed the administration with his antiwar sentiments. After the war he favored both black suffrage and amnesty for all southerners, signing the bail bond to release Jefferson Davis from prison.

See also Abolitionist movement; Civil War; News media.

Green v. County School Board of New Kent County

COURT: U.S. Supreme Court
DATE: Decided May 27, 1968
SIGNIFICANCE: In this case, the Supreme Court determined for the first time that school boards have an affirmative duty to desegregate their schools and disallowed "freedom-of-choice" desegregation plans that do not result in substantial pupil mixing

In the wake of the Supreme Court's 1954 decision in *Brown v. Board of Education* that outlawed school segregation, few southern school boards took action to integrate their schools. Finally, in the mid-1960's, under the threat of federal fund cutoffs and adverse court decisions, most southern school boards made some effort to integrate their schools. Many such school boards did so by adopting an assignment system whereby students were permitted to choose which school they wished to attend. Most such "freedom of choice" plans resulted in little racial integration. Black students typically chose to attend traditionally black schools, whereas white students chose to attend traditionally white schools. As a result, schools remained racially segregated in many southern school districts following the introduction of free-choice plans.

One school district that adopted a free-choice plan during the 1960's was the school district in New Kent County, Virginia. New Kent County is a rural county; its student population was about half black and half white, with blacks and whites scattered throughout the county. Prior to 1965, the schools in New Kent County had been completely segregated, with all the black students attending the county's one black school and all the white students attending the county's one white school. In 1965, the school board adopted a free-choice plan whereby every student was permitted to choose between the two schools. As a result of the free choice, all the white students chose to remain in the white school and 85 percent of the black students chose to remain in the black school.

A group of black parents, with the assistance of the National Association for the Advancement of Colored People (NAACP) Legal Defense and Educational Fund, filed a lawsuit challenging this free-choice plan. These parents contended that the plan was deficient because it did not effectively dismantle the old dual school system. The Supreme Court, faced with thirteen years of southern school board recalcitrance on school

desegregation, agreed that the school board's free-choice plan did not satisfy constitutional standards and announced that the school board had an affirmative duty to devise a desegregation plan that actually resulted in substantial pupil mixing. This decision, the Supreme Court's most important school desegregation decision since the 1954 *Brown* decision, helped transform school desegregation law by forcing school boards to devise assignment plans that resulted in greater integration. In the wake of the *Green* decision, lower courts throughout the South required school boards to take additional action to integrate their schools.

See also *Brown v. Board of Education*; Civil Rights movement; National Association for the Advancement of Colored People (NAACP); National Association for the Advancement of Colored People Legal Defense and Educational Fund; Segregation, *de facto* and *de jure*.

Gregg v. Georgia

COURT: U.S. Supreme Court
DATE: Decided July 2, 1976
SIGNIFICANCE: The Court ruled that the death penalty per se was not a cruel and unusual punishment but that procedural safeguards were required to prevent its use in an arbitrary and unpredictable manner

At the trial stage of bifurcated proceedings, a jury found Troy Gregg guilty of the murder of two men while engaged in armed robbery. In the penalty stage of proceedings, the judge instructed the jury to consider both mitigating and aggravating circumstances and not to impose the death penalty unless it found aggravating circumstances to exist beyond a reasonable doubt. Based on these instructions, the jury returned a verdict of death. The Georgia Supreme Court, which was required by law to review the record, upheld the sentence as not excessive or disproportionate to penalties in similar cases. Gregg and his lawyer then petitioned the U.S. Supreme Court for review.

A few years earlier, in *Furman v. Georgia* (1972), the Supreme Court had ruled that all existing laws allowing capital punishment were in violation of the Eighth Amendment because they failed to prevent arbitrary and unpredictable application. Many observers thought that it would be impossible to devise new laws that would satisfy the concerns expressed in the *Furman* decision, but between 1972 and 1976, thirty-five states, including Georgia, had passed new statutes authorizing the death penalty. With this background, observers were keenly interested in whether the Court would strike down Georgia's new legislation.

In *Gregg*, the Court voted 7 to 2 to uphold the statutory system under which Troy Gregg had been sentenced. The major idea in Justice Potter Stewart's majority opinion was that capital punishment is not unconstitutional per se. Stewart referred to the historical acceptance of capital punishment in American history and to the fact that the majority of state legislatures had recently indicated that they did not consider the punishment to be cruel and unusual. The death penalty, moreover, appeared to be a "significant deterrent" for some people, and the notion of retribution, while not the dominant goal in criminal law, was not forbidden or inconsistent with the recognition of human dignity. Stewart found that Georgia's laws prevented death from being imposed in an arbitrary or capricious manner, and he specifically endorsed three elements: first, the bifurcated proceedings; second, the judge's instructions to consider the defendant's character and the nature of the circumstances; and third, mandatory review by Georgia's high court to determine whether the death sentence was disproportionate.

Two liberal dissenters on the Court, Justices William Brennan and Thurgood Marshall, argued that capital punishment was always excessive, was not a significant deterrent, and was inconsistent with the concept of human dignity.

The *Gregg* decision indicated that in the foreseeable future the Supreme Court would allow capital punishment, but that its application would be slow, expensive, and rare because of the Court's insistence on procedural safeguards to prevent arbitrary or disproportionate sentencing. *Gregg* appeared to reflect the complex views of a public that was increasingly concerned about the growth of violent crime. By 1991 some twenty-five hundred persons were under sentence of death in the United States, but in that year there were only fourteen executions.

See also Capital punishment; *Coker v. Georgia*; Cruel and unusual punishment; *Furman v. Georgia*; *Robinson v. California*; *Rummel v. Estelle*.

Griffin v. Breckenridge

COURT: U.S. Supreme Court
DATE: Decided June 7, 1971
SIGNIFICANCE: This decision extended federal civil rights guarantees of equal protection of the law to the protection of personal rights not only from state action but from personal conspiracies as well

On July 2, 1966, a group of African Americans who were suspected of being civil rights workers were halted on a Mississippi highway near the Alabama border by Lavon and Calvin Breckenridge, whose car purposely blocked the road. The Breckenridge group forced the African Americans from their vehicle and then subjected them to intimidation by firearms. They were clubbed about their heads, beaten with pipes and other weapons, and repeatedly threatened with death. Although terrorized and seriously injured, the African Americans (who included Griffin) survived. They subsequently filed a suit for damages, charging that Breckenridge and others had conspired to assault them for the purpose of preventing them and "other Negro-Americans" from enjoying the equal rights, privileges, and immunities of citizens of the state of Mississippi and of the United States, including the rights to free speech, assembly, association, and movement and the right not to be enslaved.

A federal district court dismissed the complaint by relying on a previous U.S. Supreme Court decision, *Collins v. Hardyman* (1951), which in order to avoid difficult constitutional

issues had held that federal law extended only to "conspiracies" condoned or perpetrated by states. That is, the Court tried to avoid opening questions involving congressional power or the content of state as distinct from national citizenship, or interfering in local matters such as assault and battery cases or similar illegalities that clearly fell under local jurisdiction.

The *Collins* case, however, had been decided a decade before the nationwide Civil Rights movement of the 1960's, a period marked by the enactment of a new series of federal civil rights laws as well as by attentive regard by the U.S. Supreme Court of Chief Justice Warren Burger to cases involving civil rights violations. The Burger court heard the *Griffin* case on appeal.

The Supreme Court's unanimous decision in *Griffin* was delivered by Justice Potter Stewart on June 7, 1971. The Court broadly interpreted the federal statute under which Griffin brought damages, Title 42 of the U.S. Code, section 1985. Section 1985 stipulated that if two or more persons conspired or went in disguise on public highways with the intent to deprive any person or any class of persons of equal protection of the laws or of equal privileges and immunities under the laws, a conspiracy existed and damages could be brought. The Court waived consideration of whether the *Collins* case had been correctly decided. Instead, reviewing previous civil rights legislation, starting in 1866, the justices determined that the language of the federal statute clearly indicated that state action was not required to invoke federal protection of constitutionally guaranteed personal rights from impairment by personal conspiracies. *Griffin* effectively extended federal safeguards of civil rights to reach private conspiracies under the Thirteenth Amendment as well as under congressional powers to protect the right of interstate travel.

See also Civil Rights movement; Civil War Amendments; Conspiracy; Equal protection of the law.

Griggs v. Duke Power Co.

COURT: U.S. Supreme Court
DATE: Ruling issued March 8, 1971
SIGNIFICANCE: This case established the "adverse impact" test for discrimination so that an unequal statistical pattern could be used as *prima facie* evidence

The Civil Rights Act of 1964, Title VII, prohibited workplace segregation. Shortly after the law took effect in mid-1965, Duke Power Company in North Carolina rescinded its policy of restricting blacks to its Labor Department, so in principle they could transfer to other departments. Yet from 1955 on, all employees but those in Duke's Labor Department had to have a high school diploma. Beginning in 1965, all those applying for a transfer from the Labor Department needed a diploma. For those lacking a high school diploma (blacks were far less likely to have completed twelve grades than whites in that part of North Carolina), an alternative was to score at the national median on two standardized aptitude tests.

Willie Griggs and coworkers in the Labor Department at the company's Dan River steam-generating plant filed a class-action charge with the Equal Employment Opportunity Commission (EEOC), which ruled in favor of Griggs. When the company refused to conciliate the case, suit was filed in district court, which argued that a claim of prior inequities was beyond the scope of Title VII. The court of appeals rejected the suit because Griggs could not show that the requirements for a high school diploma or a passing score on standardized tests were intentionally discriminatory.

Chief Justice Warren Burger delivered a unanimous Supreme Court opinion (8 to 0), setting forth the adverse impact test. According to this principle, if statistics show that a job requirement screens out one race, the employer must prove that the requirement is relevant to the performance of the job. Since the percentage of black high school graduates and percentages of blacks who passed the two tests were substantially below percentages for whites, Duke Power had to prove that the jobs sought by Griggs and his coworkers required completing high school or having a level of intelligence at the national median. Since the company advanced no such evidence, the Court ruled that Title VII discrimination had occurred and decreed that "any tests used must measure the person for the job and not the person in the abstract."

The decision had an extremely broad impact: It called into question all lists of qualifications for every job in the United States. Employers were called upon to review job qualifications and to recalibrate job duties to job qualifications or risk successful discrimination suits.

In the 1980's the Supreme Court began to chip away at the *Griggs* ruling. In *Wards Cove Packing Co. v. Atonio* (1989), the Court shifted the burden of proof so that those filing suit must prove that specific job requirements alone cause statistical disparities. Congress responded by passing the Civil Rights Act of 1991, codifying the original *Griggs* ruling into law.

See also Civil Rights Act of 1964; Civil Rights Act of 1991; Equality of opportunity; Racial and ethnic discrimination; *Wards Cove Packing Co. v. Atonio.*

Griswold v. Connecticut

COURT: U.S. Supreme Court
DATE: Decided June 7, 1965
SIGNIFICANCE: This was the first case in which the Supreme Court recognized a constitutional right to privacy

Estelle Griswold, the executive director of Planned Parenthood of Connecticut, opened a birth control clinic in 1961 with the intention of testing the constitutionality of Connecticut's law prohibiting the use of contraceptives by married couples. Within three days she was arrested for violating the law.

The Supreme Court declared the state law unconstitutional. Writing for the majority, Justice William O. Douglas declared that certain provisions of the Bill of Rights applied against the states through the due process clause of the Fourteenth Amendment. Among these rights were some that were not listed in the Bill of Rights but that were necessary for the unfettered exercise of the explicitly enumerated rights. "Without those peripheral rights, the specific rights would be less secure. . . . [S]pecific guarantees of the Bill of Rights have penumbras, formed by

emanations from those guarantees that help give them life and substance." Among the rights emanating from the First Amendment, for example, were the right to free and private association, the right to educate a child in the school of the parents' choice, and the right to study any subject or any foreign language. Although the Bill of Rights never mentioned "privacy," its authors placed great importance on protecting citizens against government interference with their private lives, and that concern manifested itself in the explicit protection of various kinds of privacy in the First, Third, Fourth, Fifth, and Ninth Amendments. These amendments created broad "zones of privacy," and the marriage relationship falls within these zones. Since the Connecticut law forbade the use of contraceptives, and not merely their manufacture or sale, it allowed the police to "search the sacred precincts of the marital bedroom for telltale signs of the use of contraceptives . . . [an] idea repulsive to the notions of privacy surrounding the marriage relationship." The Court concluded that the Connecticut law invaded the privacy of the marriage relationship.

In *Griswold v. Connecticut* the opinions of the justices reflected differing judicial philosophies concerning the rights protected by the Constitution. Justice Douglas' majority opinion found such rights in the "emanations" of the Bill of Rights. Justice Arthur Goldberg found them in the rights reserved to the people by the Ninth Amendment (and incorporated in the Fourteenth). Justice John Harlan said that the meaning of the "liberty" protected by the Fourteenth Amendment could be found in the traditions of the American people. Justice Hugo Black dissented because he refused to acknowledge a right not protected by the literal language of the Bill of Rights.

The Court has expanded the right of privacy in a number of areas. The right to use contraceptives was extended to unmarried couples in *Eisenstadt v. Baird* (1972). The right of a woman to choose whether to have an abortion was announced in *Roe v. Wade* (1973). The Court, however, found that there was no zone of privacy covering homosexual sodomy in *Bowers v. Hardwick* (1986).

See also Abortion; Birth control, right to; *Bowers v. Hardwick*; *Eisenstadt v. Baird*; Privacy, right of; *Roe v. Wade.*

Grovey v. Townsend

COURT: U.S. Supreme Court
DATE: Ruling issued April 1, 1935
SIGNIFICANCE: The Supreme Court upheld "whites only" primaries when approved by state party conventions without any involvement or encouragement from the state legislature

One of the most successful devices in eliminating black voters in the South was the white primary. Since the Democratic Party dominated the solid South, whoever won the Democratic primary went on to win the general election. If blacks could not participate in the primaries, they were denied any real choice in selecting public officials.

In *Newberry v. United States* (1921), the U.S. Supreme Court held that primary elections were not constitutionally protected. Although the *Newberry* case took place in Michigan and involved the issue of vote fraud rather than racial discrimination, the South immediately took advantage of the ruling. In 1924 the Texas legislature passed a law that barred blacks from participation in that state's primary elections. Three years later, a unanimous Supreme Court struck down the Texas law in *Nixon v. Herndon* (1927), finding the actions of the Texas legislature a clear violation of the equal protection clause of the Fourteenth Amendment.

The Texas legislature then passed a law authorizing the executive committees of the political parties to determine eligibility for voting in primary elections. As expected, the executive committee of the Texas Democratic party excluded blacks from the primary. In *Nixon v. Condon* (1932), in a 5-4 decision, the U.S. Supreme Court ruled that the executive committee had acted as the agent of the state. As such, the attempt to bar black participation in the primary still violated the equal protection clause.

Texas succeeded on its third attempt to ban black voting. Immediately after the *Condon* decision, the Texas Democratic Party convention, without any authorization from the legislature, adopted a resolution restricting party membership to whites. R. R. Grovey, a black resident of Houston, brought suit against the county clerk who refused to give him a primary ballot. On April 1, 1935, a unanimous U.S. Supreme Court upheld the actions of the state party convention. According to the Court, there was no violation of the equal protection clause because there was no state action involved. The Democratic Party was a voluntary association of individuals who acted in their private capacity to exclude blacks from primary elections.

In 1941 the U.S. Supreme Court reversed *Newberry* in *United States v. Classic* (1941). The *Classic* decision brought primary elections under constitutional protection for the first time. *Classic* also paved the way for *Smith v. Allwright* (1944), the Supreme Court case banning white primaries.

See also *Classic, United States v.*; Equal protection of the law; National Association for the Advancement of Colored People (NAACP); *Newberry v. United States*; *Nixon v. Herndon*; *Smith v. Allwright*.

Guinn v. United States
COURT: U.S. Supreme Court
DATE: Decided June 21, 1915
SIGNIFICANCE: The decision in this case overturned Oklahoma's grandfather clause and marked a first step in the National Association for the Advancement of Colored People's campaign to use the courts to combat racial discrimination

Though the Fifteenth Amendment supposedly prohibited racial discrimination in voting, during the late nineteenth and early twentieth centuries Southern and border states found ways to prevent African Americans from voting in significant numbers. One method was the literacy test. One potential drawback to this practice, however, was that such a test would also prevent poorly educated whites from voting. A number of states solved this problem by adopting "grandfather" clauses, provisions that allowed anyone registered before a certain date or anyone descended from such a person to vote regardless of literacy. Since the date selected was usually set at a point when there would have been few black voters (1866 was popular), very few blacks would qualify. Thus a measure that was nonracial on the surface was decidedly discriminatory in its effects.

Many grandfather laws had only temporary application, and most Southern states moved away from them in the early twentieth century. In 1910, however, Oklahoma enacted a literacy test requirement with a permanent grandfather clause. The measure threatened not only black voting rights but also the position of the state's Republican Party. Fearing the loss of several thousand black votes, the U.S. attorney brought suit under the Reconstruction-era Enforcement Acts and won a conviction against state officials who were trying to enforce the literacy test.

The state appealed the case to the U.S. Supreme Court, attracting the attention of the National Association for the Advancement of Colored People (NAACP), which was just beginning to use litigation as a strategy for combating racial discrimination. Moorfield Story of the NAACP filed a brief in support of the government. In a unanimous decision, the Court upheld the convictions and ruled that the grandfather clause was a clear attempt to thwart the Fifteenth Amendment's ban on racial discrimination in voting.

The decision had relatively little immediate impact: Only one other state still had a grandfather clause at the time, and the Court carefully avoided declaring literacy tests themselves discriminatory. Nevertheless, the decision was not without its significance. Not only did it mark a modest revival of the Fifteenth Amendment, but it also encouraged the NAACP to continue its strategy of using litigation to put the Constitution on the side of racial equality.

See also Civil rights; Civil War Amendments; Enforcement Acts; Jim Crow laws; National Association for the Advancement of Colored People (NAACP); Vote, right to.

Gun control. *See* **Arms, right to keep and bear**

Habeas corpus

DEFINITION: A court order to bring a person being detained before the court or judge to determine whether his or her imprisonment is lawful

SIGNIFICANCE: *Habeas corpus* has long been part of the common law to protect people from unlawful imprisonment; the judicial branch of government has authority over the executive police power in this regard

Article I of the United States Constitution recognizes a long-standing tradition of the English common law that citizens have the "privilege of the Writ of Habeas Corpus." The executive authority detaining a prisoner has the burden of proof to show that there is sufficient lawful reason and legal evidence to take away temporarily a person's basic right to liberty. If the judge thinks that the evidence is not sufficient to hold the person, the judge will order the prisoner released.

This right was specified in the Constitution itself and not added as part of the Bill of Rights. Nevertheless, it is not an absolutely inviolable right, as most other civil rights are. The clause states, "The privilege of the Writ of Habeas Corpus shall not be suspended, unless when in cases of rebellion or invasion the public safety may require it." If the "privilege" is suspended and a judge issues a writ of *habeas corpus*, the jailer to whom the writ is directed does not have to obey the judge's orders.

President Abraham Lincoln, in fact, did suspend *habeas corpus* at the beginning of the Civil War, claiming war and Southern rebellion as the justification. A declaration of martial law automatically suspends *habeas corpus* rights because the military authorities are not subject to a civil judge. President Lincoln's actions, however, produced an outcry of protest, particularly since the clause quoted above is in Article I of the Constitution, dealing with the legislative powers entrusted to the Congress, and not in Article II, which enumerates executive powers, especially the powers of the president. It seems obvious, therefore, that the framers of the Constitution had Congress in mind and not the president when they provided for the suspension of *habeas corpus*.

Chief Justice Roger Brooke Taney issued a writ of *habeas corpus* in 1861 in an attempt to challenge Lincoln's suspension, and he tried to have the commanding general arrested for refusing to obey his order. Needless to say, he was unsuccessful. The Congress in 1863 did pass the Habeas Corpus Act, but Congress carefully limited the conditions under which suspension would be acceptable. President Lincoln even went so far as to order civilians tried in military courts. After the Civil War, in *Ex parte Milligan* (1866), the Supreme Court ruled unanimously that the president had no power to order civilians tried in military courts. Civil courts, the common law, and

habeas corpus remain crucial parts of the traditional liberties of Americans.

See also Civil War; Common law; Lincoln, Abraham; Magna Carta; Martial law; *Merryman, Ex parte*; *Milligan, Ex parte*; Police brutality; Speedy trial, right to; Taney, Roger Brooke.

Hammer v. Dagenhart

COURT: U.S. Supreme Court
DATE: Decided June 3, 1918
SIGNIFICANCE: In this case the Supreme Court strictly limited the federal government's power to bring about industrial and economic reform under its power to regulate interstate commerce. Over the powerful and now classic dissent of Justice Oliver Wendell Holmes, the Court held the first federal child labor law unconstitutional because its purpose was to regulate manufacturing practices, even though on its face the statute only reached interstate transportation

In September, 1916, Congress passed the Child Labor Act. This law prohibited the shipment in interstate commerce of goods made by a factory or mill in which children under certain specified ages had been employed within the previous thirty days. The law was challenged by Roland Dagenhart, whose two sons were employed in a cotton mill in North Carolina. Dagenhart argued that the purpose of the law was actually to regulate manufacturing and production. At that time, such regulation was beyond the direct power of Congress. A federal district court held for Dagenhart, and the United States appealed to the Supreme Court.

The Supreme Court ruled 5 to 4 in Dagenhart's favor in 1918. Justice William R. Day held that the real purpose of the act was not to regulate the shipment of goods in interstate commerce but to standardize the ages at which children could be employed. In other cases in which transportation in interstate commerce had been prohibited by the federal government, it was because the goods had been harmful or because the transportation was necessary to bring about the evil. According to the majority, that element was wanting in this case.

Day's opinion was countered by a brilliant dissent by Justice Oliver Wendell Holmes, Jr. In attacking the general premise of the majority opinion, that the government's commerce power must be read narrowly, Holmes argued that the majority was attempting to write laissez-faire economics into the Constitution. He insisted that the Court had been inconsistent in dealing with commerce limitation cases because every limit on interstate transportation affects business in some way. To Holmes it did not matter whether an evil preceded or followed the transportation. Congress could regulate the transportation regardless: "It is not for this court to pronounce when prohibition is necessary to regulation if it ever may be necessary—to say that it is permissible, as against strong drink, but not as against the product of ruined lives."

The rule established by the Court in *Hammer v. Dagenhart* was to last for about twenty years. It significantly limited industrial and economic reform measures from World War I to the early New Deal years. Holmes's dissent ultimately prevailed. In 1941 *Hammer v. Dagenhart* was explicitly overruled by *United States v. Darby Lumber Co.*, and Holmes's view, which had caught the imagination of the public, the press, and most of the bar, was vindicated.

See also Commerce clause; *Darby Lumber Co., United States v.*; Holmes, Oliver Wendell, Jr.; Property rights; *Wickard v. Filburn.*

Hand, Learned (Jan. 27, 1872, Albany, N.Y.—Aug. 18, 1961, New York, N.Y.)

IDENTIFICATION: U.S. federal judge

SIGNIFICANCE: Hand's opinions as a federal judge were influential because of their innovation, breadth of subject matter, and splendid writing style

Billings Learned Hand was born in 1872 into a family of judges: Both his father and grandfather were lawyers and judges. It was natural that he would go to Harvard University and eventually pursue a law career. Beginning his studies in 1889, he majored in philosophy under a faculty which included William James, Josiah Royce, and George Santayana. This philosophical bent would show in his thinking as a judge. He was a Phi Beta Kappa at Harvard and was graduated summa cum laude. Hand received a master of arts from Harvard in 1894; he then entered Harvard Law School and was graduated with honors in 1896. From 1897 to 1909, he practiced law. In 1909, President William Howard Taft appointed him to the Federal District Court for Southern New York. At thirty-six years of age, Hand was one of the youngest men ever appointed as a judge in a federal district up to that time. He served on that court for fifteen years.

In 1924, President Calvin Coolidge appointed Hand to the Federal Court of Appeals (the Second Circuit Court) for New York, Connecticut, and Vermont. Hand became the chief judge of the Second Circuit Court of Appeals in 1939. During his career, he wrote nearly three thousand opinions on nearly every conceivable subject. He retired in 1951 but stayed on call for assignments. At the time of his death in 1961, he had served on the federal bench longer than any other person.

Because the Second Circuit Court of Appeals is located in New York City, it decides much of the business law of the country. While Learned Hand was its chief judge, the Second Circuit Court became the most esteemed court in the country. During Hand's leadership, the Second Circuit had the largest docket of cases of any circuit court. The Second Circuit Court was required to specialize in many branches of the law. The range was as broad as American federal jurisprudence, and Hand was said to be a master of all fields. Hand's masterful writing style also helps explain the considerable acclaim given him. It is unusual for a lower court judge's views to influence the thinking of other judges, but the opinions of Learned Hand are the exception. Hand has been quoted by name in Supreme Court opinions and in academic publications more often than any other lower court judge. His decisions have thus had a strong impact on American law. During his later years, the press sometimes referred to him as the "tenth Supreme Court justice." Indeed, the great mystery surrounding Hand's career, about which much has been written, was why he was never appointed to the Supreme Court.

See also Appellate process; Jurisprudence; Law.

Harmelin v. Michigan

COURT: U.S. Supreme Court

DATE: Decided June 27, 1991

SIGNIFICANCE: Upholding a Michigan drug possession law that carried a mandatory term of life imprisonment, the Supreme Court rejected the plaintiff's argument that the sentence was "cruel and unusual punishment" and therefore in violation of the Eighth Amendment

Under Michigan law, the petitioner, Ronald Allen Harmelin, was convicted of possessing 672 grams of cocaine and sentenced to mandatory life imprisonment because the amount was in excess of the 650-gram threshold specified in the law for imposing the mandatory sentence. The Michigan State Court of Appeals upheld the sentence, rejecting Harmelin's claim that the sentence violated the protection against "cruel and unusual punishment" guaranteed by the Constitution. Harmelin argued that the sentence violated that restriction because it was "disproportionate" to his crime and, further, that because it was mandatory it provided for no "mitigating circumstances" that would allow a judge any latitude in sentencing.

Harmelin's appeal to the U.S. Supreme Court was denied and his sentence upheld. Justice Antonin Scalia delivered the Court's principal opinion. It concluded that because there is no proportionality provision in the Eighth Amendment, a sentence cannot be deemed cruel or unusual on the basis that it is disproportionate to the crime involved. Furthermore, it argued that Harmelin's claim that his mandatory sentence deprived him of his right to a consideration of mitigating circumstances had no precedent in constitutional law. It observed that mandatory penalties, though they could be harsh or extreme, were common enough in the history of the United States and had never been construed as cruel and unusual in the constitutional sense of that phrase. While granting that Harmelin's argument had support in the so-termed individualized capital-sentencing doctrine of the Court's death-penalty legal theory, the majority dismissed Harmelin's claim because of the qualitative difference between execution and all other forms of punishment.

Justice Anthony Kennedy, joined by Justices Sandra Day O'Connor and David Souter, although concurring with the judgment against Harmelin, claimed that the Eighth Amendment's cruel and unusual punishment provision does encompass "a narrow proportionality principle that applies to noncapital sentences." Citing various precedents, these justices argued that the Court, though not clearly or consistently, had previously determined the constitutionality of noncapital punishments based on that principle, although said precedents had taken under review only the length of a punishment's term, not its type.

Having again broached the issue of proportionality, the Supreme Court was likely to face more challenges to mandatory sentencing. From state to state, in statutes imposing mandatory sentences, there is no uniform-sentencing code governing types of punishment or their length. Although in *Harmelin* the Court argued that state legislatures must retain the prerogative of establishing their own penal codes, where there is a wide discrepancy between mandatory penalties imposed for the same crime by one state and another, plaintiffs may seek relief from enforcement of the more severe penalty.

See also Cruel and unusual punishment; Drug use and sale, illegal; *Hutto v. Davis*; Mandatory sentencing laws; Punishment; *Rummel v. Estelle*; *Solem v. Helm*.

Harmless error

DEFINITION: An error which is trivial and does not prejudice the substantial rights of the party declaring the error and does not affect the outcome of a legal action
SIGNIFICANCE: A party cannot obtain a new trial or set aside a verdict or otherwise disturb a judgment based on harmless error

The issue of harmless error arises when a party to a lawsuit has taken his or her case to trial and is not satisfied with the outcome. The party may declare that an error or errors took place at some stage of the lawsuit, thereby necessitating a new trial or reversal of the verdict on appeal. In order for the party to obtain a new trial or reversal of the verdict, the party must show that the error prejudiced his or her substantial rights and that the error affected the outcome of the case. If the error did not affect the substantial rights of the party or change the outcome of the case, the error is said to be harmless, and a new trial or reversal of the verdict will not be warranted.

One of the most common grounds for alleging error is in the admission or exclusion of evidence. In these cases courts generally look to the whole case to determine whether the erroneous admission or exclusion of the evidence prejudiced the party and would have changed the outcome of the case.

See also Civil procedure; Criminal procedure; Evidence, rules of; Mistrial; Reversible error.

Harper v. Virginia Board of Elections

COURT: U.S. Supreme Court
DATE: Ruling issued March 24, 1966
SIGNIFICANCE: The Court's decision in this case eliminated the use of poll taxes in state and local elections

Poll taxes, or the payment of a fee in order to vote, were widely used in southern states as a means to restrict the electorate, and in particular black voters. Because poll taxes led to corruption—as candidates and political organizations would pay the taxes of their supporters—and because there were more effective ways of eliminating black voters, many southern states started to repeal their poll taxes. Opposition to the poll tax was led by the National Committee to Abolish the Poll Tax and the National Association for the Advancement of Colored People (NAACP). On five occasions the House of Representatives passed legislation to ban the tax, but southern senators filibustered, blocking its passage in the Senate. In 1964, the Twenty-fourth Amendment to the Constitution was ratified, eliminating the use of poll taxes in federal elections. Five states—Alabama, Arkansas, Mississippi, Texas, and Virginia—continued to use poll taxes in state and local elections. Arkansas dropped its poll tax in 1964 after the passage of the Twenty-fourth Amendment.

In 1965 the U.S. House of Representatives passed a poll tax ban in state elections as part of the 1965 voting rights bill. The Senate failed to support the ban, however, and the final version of the Voting Rights Act of 1965 merely stated that the poll tax "denied or abridged" the constitutional right to vote.

Blacks in Virginia brought suit against that state's $1.50 annual poll tax as a requirement for voting in state and local elections. The U.S. district court, citing the 1937 case *Breedlove v. Suttles*, dismissed the claim. In *Breedlove*, the U.S. Supreme Court had held that, except where constrained by the Constitution, the states may impose whatever conditions on suffrage that they deem appropriate. On appeal, a 6-3 majority in the Supreme Court overruled *Breedlove* and held that the payment of a fee in order to vote violated the Constitution.

Interestingly, although the plaintiffs were black, the ruling was based on economic discrimination rather than racial discrimination. "To introduce wealth or payment of a fee as a measure of a voter's qualifications," wrote Justice William Douglas in the majority opinion, "is to introduce a capricious or irrelevant factor." In the view of the court's majority, voter qualifications had no relationship to wealth. The three dissenters believed that a "fairly applied" poll tax could be a reasonable basis for the right to vote. The *Harper* decision actually had little direct impact. Since only four states used poll taxes as a condition for voting at the time of the *Harper* decision, the ban on poll taxes barely generated a ripple on the surface of American politics.

See also Poll tax; Vote, right to; Voting Rights Act of 1965.

Harris v. McRae

COURT: U.S. Supreme Court
DATE: Decided June 30, 1980
SIGNIFICANCE: The Supreme Court determined that it was constitutionally permissible to deny funding under the Medicaid program for abortions deemed medically necessary

Under Title XIX of the Social Security Act, Congress established the so-called Medicaid program, providing federal financial assistance to states which fund medical treatment for the needy. After the U.S. Supreme Court invalidated restrictive abortion laws in *Roe v. Wade* in 1973, the Department of Health, Education, and Welfare (HEW) began reimbursing states for funding abortion services for poor women. In 1976, Congressman Henry Hyde offered an amendment to the HEW appropriations act prohibiting the use of federal funds to reimburse states for abortions under Medicaid. After Congress approved the Hyde Amendment, several plaintiffs (including

Nora McRae, a New York woman receiving Medicaid assistance who wanted an abortion that was deemed "medically necessary") filed suit in the District Court for the Eastern District of New York challenging the constitutionality of the amendment. Thus began the case that became *Harris v. McRae*. Federal district court judge Frank Dooling ruled that the Hyde Amendment was unconstitutional. Reversal of the ruling was sought by appellant Patricia Harris, the secretary of health and human services in the Carter Administration.

By a 5-4 margin, the U.S. Supreme Court decided that the Hyde Amendment was not unconstitutional, relying on a position it had taken in the earlier case of *Maher v. Roe* (1977), which had to do with Medicaid payments for abortions not medically necessary. The Court maintained that the constitutionally protected freedom recognized in *Roe v. Wade* barred the government from placing obstacles such as criminal sanctions in the way of a woman choosing an abortion, but it did not create an affirmative duty for the government to fund abortions. Justice Potter Stewart, writing for the majority, mentioned other cases such as *Griswold v. Connecticut* (1965), in which the Court had denied government the authority to prevent the use of contraceptives, observing that a case such as this did not entail the government having a duty to pay for contraceptives for persons wanting them. Furthermore, Justice Stewart noted that the Hyde Amendment did not violate the constitutional guarantee of equal protection. It was aimed at a legitimate state objective, protecting prenatal life, and was rationally related to achieving that objective by subsidizing childbirth but not abortion.

Three major lines of criticism were found in the dissenting opinions. Justice William Brennan urged that the Hyde Amendment burdened the constitutionally protected freedom of indigent pregnant women, in effect coercing them to bear children. Justices Thurgood Marshall and Harry Blackmun criticized the majority's reluctance to consider the social realities in the "other world" in which the poor live. Finally, Justice John Paul Stevens argued that the Hyde Amendment violated the equal protection clause in this type of case, where the issue is one of medically necessary abortions. Medicaid funds necessary medical treatment, he said, and exempting abortions is discriminatory in a constitutionally impermissible way.

The decision in *Harris v. McRae* placed the issue of abortion funding in the hands of Congress and the individual states. The Hyde Amendment, while undergoing some modifications, continued to stand. States could fund abortions without receiving federal reimbursements, and a small number of states chose to do so.

See also Abortion; *Maher v. Roe*; *Roe v. Wade*; Welfare state.

Harris v. United States

COURT: U.S. Supreme Court
DATE: Decided March 5, 1968
SIGNIFICANCE: This case established the principle that if evidence of a crime is in "plain view" of a law enforcement officer while the officer is fulfilling authorized duties, its use

in criminal proceedings does not violate a defendant's constitutional protection against unlawful search and seizure

James H. Harris, the petitioner, prior to his appeal to the U.S. Supreme Court, was tried for robbery in the U.S. District Court for the District of Columbia. Evidence used against him included his victim's automobile registration card, which the police found on the metal strip under the door of Harris' car after it had been impounded for its protection while Harris was being held as the robbery suspect. During his trial, Harris moved to have that evidence suppressed on the grounds that it was obtained through unlawful search. The district court denied the request, and Harris was convicted and sentenced to prison. Thereafter, a panel of the Court of Appeals for the District of Columbia reversed the conviction, concluding that the registration card had been obtained by unlawful search; however, it also granted the government's petition for a rehearing before the full court of appeals, which subsequently overturned the panel's determination, ruling that the conviction did not violate the petitioner's rights.

On *certiorari*, the U.S. Supreme Court upheld the decision, affirming the admissibility of the questionable evidence. Seven justices concurred in the majority opinion, arguing that nothing in the Fourth Amendment protects a suspect from the use of incriminating evidence found as a result of normal safeguards taken while a suspect's property is in police custody. According to the opinion, objects in the "plain view" of police officers authorized to be in a position to view the objects cannot be construed as the products of a search, are therefore subject to seizure, and may be introduced as evidence.

Various Supreme Court cases, including *Ker v. California* (1963), had established the right of law enforcement agents to seize objects in plain view to be used as criminal evidence, but none addressed the issue of whether evidence secured from a defendant's property while it was in police custody constituted an illegal search. Jurists concerned with the protection of an accused individual's rights argue that the *Harris* decision erodes the Fourth Amendment guarantees against illegal search and seizure. Because the circumstances were somewhat unusual, however, the application of *Harris* to other attempts to suppress evidence is likely to be fairly limited. Nevertheless, the ruling does reflect the Supreme Court's increasing unwillingness to broaden its interpretation of constitutional guarantees in favor of the accused to the disadvantage of criminal investigators and prosecutors.

See also Criminal procedure; Due process of law; Evidence, rules of; Search and seizure.

Harrison Narcotic Drug Act

DATE: Enacted December 17, 1914
DEFINITION: Legislation designed to control the production and dispensation of narcotics
SIGNIFICANCE: The most comprehensive federal drug legislation at the time, the Harrison Narcotic Drug Act involved issues of federal versus state authority and the protected physician-patient relationship

Prompted by international treaty obligations under the 1912 Hague Convention and concerns over drug abuse, Representative Francis Burton Harrison, a Democrat, introduced HR 6282 on June 10, 1913. The bill passed Congress on December 14, 1914, and President Woodrow Wilson signed it on December 17, 1914. The Harrison Act required the registration of all producers and dispensers of narcotics with the district internal revenue collector and the payment of an annual fee of one dollar. Violations carried a penalty of up to two thousand dollars and five years' imprisonment.

Section 8 of the Harrison Act declared as unlawful the possession of specified drugs by unregistered persons unless the drugs were prescribed by a physician, and it placed the burden of proof on the defendant. Federal district courts ruled, however, that addicts could not be arrested for possession as long as they had obtained the drug by prescription. In June, 1916, the Supreme Court ruled in *Jin Fuey Moy v. United States* (1916) that the Hague Convention (which had banned narcotics trafficking) did not require the police powers specified in section 8, which overturned central portions of the act.

See also Comprehensive Drug Abuse Prevention and Control Act of 1970; Drug legalization debate; Drug use and sale, illegal; Marijuana Tax Act; Opium Exclusion Act.

Hatch Act

DATE: Became law August 2, 1939
DEFINITION: An act restricting the political activities of federal employees
SIGNIFICANCE: The Hatch Act prohibited employees of the federal government from using their official authority to affect an election or to engage in political management or campaigns

The Hatch Act was enacted in response to a special Senate investigation showing that government officials had coerced federal workers to contribute to the reelection campaign of a U.S. senator in 1938. A second, and possibly more important reason for its passage was a fear that President Franklin D. Roosevelt would use the growing number of federal workers as a formidable political machine. In March of 1939, Senator Carl Hatch of New Mexico introduced legislation incorporating the recommendations of the special Senate committee prohibiting the involvement of federal employees in any political organization. They retained the right to vote and could privately express their political opinions. Political appointees and policy-making employees were not included in the act. By restricting the political activity of federal workers, the act addressed three objectives: It precluded the use of the federal workforce for political purposes; it prevented the bureaucracy from becoming a powerful political actor; and it reduced the influence of partisan politics in the hiring, promotion, and firing of federal employees. The Hatch Act was amended in 1993 to allow federal employees, acting as private citizens, to engage in any legal political activity while not on the job.

See also Civil service system; Machine politics; Political campaign law; Political corruption; Spoils system and patronage.

Hate crimes

DEFINITION: Criminal acts motivated by hatred of and directed against members of a particular group
SIGNIFICANCE: Hate crimes injure the victim and society in ways that other crimes do not; it has been argued that, because of their nature, they generate more injury, distress, and suffering than do other crimes

In 1984, Alan Berg, a Jewish talk show host on a Denver radio station, was fatally shot on his way home by several members of a neo-Nazi hate group. In 1986, three white teenagers attacked three black men in Howard Beach, New York, for no other reason than the fact that they were black. Both these actions were hate crimes—crimes motivated by the hatred of a certain group, such as a certain race, ethnic group, religion, gender, or sexual orientation. Since the mid-1980's, hate crimes have been on the rise.

Hate crimes are typically excessively brutal, and quite often they are carried out in a random fashion against strangers, as with the incidents involving the Howard Beach black men. Authors Jack Levin and Jack McDevitt have given several explanations as to why these crimes occur: the perpetrator's negative and stereotypic view of other people, the possibility that bigotry is becoming more widely tolerated, the resentment that one group feels toward another because it has been left out of the mainstream of society, a perpetrator's desire for the thrill of the action, a perpetrator's reaction to a perceived or imagined injury such as the loss of a job promotion or a benefit, and finally, a perpetrator's wish to rid the world of evil.

Federal Laws Against Hate Crimes. There are a number of different types of laws which victims of hate crimes can use against perpetrators. In recent years, most states have enacted laws to deal specifically with these types of crimes. Several statutes also address these crimes on a federal level. There are federal laws prohibiting conspiracies against the rights of citizens, prohibiting a deprivation of rights under color of law, and prohibiting damage to religious property and obstruction of persons in the free exercise of their religious beliefs. In addition, there are federal statutes that prohibit forcible interference with civil rights and willful interference with civil rights under the fair housing laws. These federal statutes have rarely been applied to hate crimes for several reasons. First, if a president does not emphasize civil rights, the attorney general in that administration will not be likely to prosecute these crimes. Second, since most of these statutes require that the victim be engaged in an activity involving a federally protected right, such as buying a house or eating in a restaurant, they do not apply to many victims. Third, the remedies under the federal statutes are limited. Fourth, only certain groups, such as racial and religious groups, are protected under these statutes. Sexual orientation is not. Thus, the most active prosecution of hate crimes has been at the state level.

State Laws Prohibiting Expressive Conduct. On June 21, 1990, two young white men burned a cross on the property of a black family in St. Paul, Minnesota. One of the men, designated by his initials, R.A.V., because he was only seventeen at the time, was charged in accordance with a new city "bias-motivated" disorderly conduct ordinance which read, "Whoever places on public or private property, a symbol, appellation, characterization, or graffiti, including, but not limited to, a burning cross or Nazi swastika, which one knows or has reasonable grounds to know arouses anger, alarm or resentment in others on the basis of race, color, creed, religion, or gender commits disorderly conduct and shall be guilty of a misdemeanor." R.A.V. could have been charged with simple trespass, disorderly conduct, breach of the peace, or even a more severe crime such as terroristic threats. Instead, in what was to become a test case of the statute and others similar to it, the prosecutor decided to invoke this law, which punished the expression of a viewpoint.

R.A.V.'s attorney, Edward J. Cleary, decided to challenge the constitutionality of the law under the First Amendment to the Constitution. A Minnesota district court agreed that the

ordinance was unconstitutional. The prosecutor decided to appeal the decision to the Minnesota Supreme Court. This court overturned the lower court ruling. R.A.V. appealed to the Supreme Court of the United States for a review of the case. On June 22, 1992, the Court issued a unanimous opinion in *R.A.V. v. City of St. Paul* declaring that the ordinance was unconstitutional. Five of the justices held that the ordinance was unconstitutional because it prohibited the expression of subject matter protected by the First Amendment. Four of the justices said that the ordinance was overbroad in that it included in its proscriptions expression which was protected by the First Amendment. The entire Court thought that the city had other means by which to prosecute R.A.V. Thus, the Court concluded that, offensive as the action in which R.A.V. had engaged was, the action was protected under the Constitution to the extent that it was expressive conduct.

State Hate Laws Prohibiting Conduct. In 1991, a nineteen-year-old black man, Todd Mitchell, and his friends came out of

Police investigating a cross-burning incident. In R.A.V. v. City of St. Paul *(1992), the Supreme Court held a "bias-motivated" crime statute to be unconstitutional.* (James L. Shaffer)

BIAS MOTIVATIONS IN HATE CRIMES KNOWN TO POLICE				
	1991		*1992*	
	Number	Percent	Number	Percent
Total	**4,755**	**100**	**8,075**	**100**
Race	2,963	62.3	5,052	62.5
Anti-white	888	18.7	1,664	20.6
Anti-black	1,689	35.5	2,884	35.7
Anti-American Indian/Alaskan Native	11	0.2	31	0.4
Anti-Asian/Pacific Islander	287	6.0	275	3.4
Anti-multiracial group	88	1.9	198	2.5
Ethnicity	450	9.5	841	10.4
Anti-Hispanic	242	5.1	498	6.2
Anti-other ethnicity/national origin	208	4.4	343	4.2
Religion	917	19.3	1,240	15.4
Anti-Jewish	792	16.7	1,084	13.4
Anti-Catholic	23	0.5	18	0.2
Anti-Protestant	26	0.5	29	0.4
Anti-Islamic (Muslim)	10	0.2	17	0.2
Anti-other religion	51	1.1	77	1.0
Anti-multireligious group	11	0.2	14	0.2
Anti-atheism/agnosticism/etc.	4	0.1	1	*
Sexual Orientation	425	8.9	944	11.7
Anti-homosexual	421	8.9	928	11.5
Anti-heterosexual	3	0.1	13	0.2
Anti-bisexual	1	0.0	3	*

Source: U.S. Department of Justice, Bureau of Justice Statistics, *Sourcebook of Criminal Justice Statistics—1993*. Washington, D.C.: U.S. Government Printing Office, 1994.

Note: Data are from an FBI statistical program on hate crimes. Asterisk (*) indicates less than 0.05 percent. Because of rounding, percentages may not add to 100.

a theater showing the film *Mississippi Burning* so enraged that, upon seeing a fourteen-year-old white youth (Gregory Riddick) on the street, they assaulted him. Coming out of the film, Mitchell said to others in his group, "Do you all feel hyped up to move on some white people?" Then, when Mitchell saw Riddick walking by, he added, "There goes a white boy—go get him." The group kicked and beat the boy for five minutes. Riddick remained in a coma for four days before he returned to consciousness with probably permanent brain damage. Mitchell was convicted of aggravated battery, normally punishable by a maximum sentence of two years. Because the jury found that the crime was motivated by racial animus, however, the sentence was increased to seven years in accordance with a state statute which read, "If a person commits the crime of aggravated battery and intentionally selects the victim 'in whole or in part because of the actor's belief or perception regarding the race, religion, color, disability, sexual orientation or ancestry of that person,' the maximum sentence may be increased by not more than five years."

Within hours after the Supreme Court announced its opinion in *R.A.V.*, the Wisconsin Supreme Court struck down this law as unconstitutional. The state appealed the decision to the Supreme Court of the United States, and on June 11, 1993, in a unanimous opinion less than half the length of *R.A.V.*, the Supreme Court reversed the decision and held that "enhancement" laws such as this which punish hate-motivated conduct are constitutional. The Court, in *Wisconsin v. Mitchell*, distinguished this case from *R.A.V.* by stating that *R.A.V.* dealt with expression and this case with conduct. The Court went on to state that with criminal acts, the more purposeful the conduct, the more severe is the punishment. Thus, when a defendant's beliefs add to a crime and motivate the defendant into action, the motive behind the conduct is relevant to the sentencing and punishment. Second, the Court stated that these enhancement laws are similar in aim to civil antidiscrimination laws and that they are justified because the conduct involved inflicts greater individual and societal harm than do other crimes. Some commentators, such as Edward J. Cleary, who argued *R.A.V.* before the Supreme Court, view *Mitchell* with alarm and sense that these enhancement statutes come dangerously close to punishing a person's thoughts and thereby infringing upon First Amendment rights. He would question why those who attack a person of another race should, because they hate that race and express it, be subject to stricter laws than those who attack in silence. By upholding the enhancement laws, Cleary suggests, the Supreme Court blurred the lines between speech and action.

Others believe that, because of the Court's emphasis on the analogy between these enhancement-type laws and antidiscrimination laws, these laws are constitutional. In sum, if a statute infringes upon expression, as in *R.A.V.*, it will be held unconstitutional; if a statute prohibits conduct, it will be upheld.

By 1991, thirty-five states had adopted some form of law to deter hate crimes. These laws, if they pass constitutional scrutiny, are not without practical problems. First, in many instances (as was the case in *R.A.V.*), prosecutors may wait to find the perfect case to fit the statute. The usefulness of the statute is thereby limited. Second, if there is a successful prosecution under the statute, there may be problems in carrying out a severe punishment. Most hate crime offenders are under twenty-one and do not have prior criminal records. Jails are overcrowded, and it seldom makes sense to jail the entire group involved in the crime. If only leaders are jailed, there is ample evidence that prison will make them worse.

—*Jennifer Eastman*

See also Anti-Defamation League (ADL); Civil rights; Ku Klux Klan (KKK); *R.A.V. v. City of St. Paul*; Vandalism; Vigilantism; *Wisconsin v. Mitchell*.

BIBLIOGRAPHY

Two overviews on the subject are Robert J. Kelly, ed., *Bias Crime: American Law Enforcement and Legal Responses* (Chicago: University of Illinois Press, 1991), and Jack Levin's and Jack McDevitt's *Hate Crimes: The Rising Tide of Bigotry and Bloodshed* (New York: Plenum Press, 1993), an anecdotal account. Two books which address the First Amendment problems raised by the hate crime statutes are *Beyond the Burning Cross: The First Amendment and the Landmark R.A.V. Case* by Edward J. Cleary (New York: Random House, 1994) and *"Speech Acts" and the First Amendment* by Franklyn S. Haiman (Carbondale: Southern Illinois University Press, 1993). Two law review articles which address and distinguish between the *R.A.V.* and the *Mitchell* cases are Brenda P. McCulloch's "*Wisconsin v. Mitchell*: Supreme Court Upholds Hate Crime Penalty Enhancer," *Journal of Contemporary Law* 1 (Spring, 1994) and Brian Resler's "Hate Crimes: New Limits on the Scope of First Amendment Protection? *Wisconsin v. Mitchell*, 113 S. Ct. 2194 (1993)," *Marquette Law Review* 77 (no. 2, Winter, 1994).

Hearsay rule

DEFINITION: The rule that oral testimony or written evidence regarding a statement made out of court generally cannot be accepted in court

SIGNIFICANCE: Hearsay evidence will not be admitted into evidence over the objection of the opposing party unless an exception is recognized by statute or case law

The hearsay rule is an exclusionary rule which often keeps what would otherwise be relevant evidence from a jury. The rule against hearsay was a somewhat late development in the common law of England and was not consistently applied until the eighteenth century. By that time the jury system was firmly established as the method for determining guilt or innocence in criminal cases and liability in civil cases through the presentation of witnesses who had knowledge of the events at issue. Judges considered hearsay evidence for a jury unreliable because the person who had made the statement was not under oath, not present at the trial, and not subject to cross-examination.

In its most common form, hearsay is elicited when a witness testifies about the statement of another person that was made out of court. The person making the out-of-court statement is the one who has first-hand knowledge of what was observed, but this declarant cannot be cross-examined to determine the opportunity and ability to observe or the tendency to lie.

This exclusionary rule precludes not only oral statements made out of court but also written evidence, including printed material such as newspaper articles. Hearsay may be admitted as evidence, however, unless the opposing party objects to it. Moreover, the hearsay rule is not applied as strictly in court trials in which a judge rather than a jury makes the final decision, or in hearings before administrative agencies. Greater latitude is permitted in these situations because judges and administrative hearing officers are typically well trained in the law and, presumably, can better evaluate evidence. Rules defining hearsay and describing circumstances in which its exclusion is required by the courts are set forth in federal rules, which govern proceedings in the United States courts, as well as in the statutes of the various states.

The exclusion of hearsay is not an absolute rule. Many exceptions are recognized in both federal and state law. The most important reason for allowing an exception to the hearsay rule is the likelihood that the hearsay testimony will be trustworthy. For example, an admission of guilt by a criminal defendant would be allowed in evidence if offered against him at his trial, assuming the admission was obtained without violating some other statutory or constitutional provision. Spontaneous statements are also admitted as exceptions to the hearsay rule when the statement describes or explains an event witnessed by a declarant who made the statement under the stress of some startling event. In these examples, as in the many other recognized hearsay exceptions, the circumstances surrounding the making of the statement by the person out of court confirm the reliability of the statement. The lost opportunity for the opposing party to cross-examine the declarant is outweighed by the benefit to the jury of hearing relevant evidence which is as trustworthy as that taken under oath in court.

See also Civil procedure; Criminal procedure; Evidence, rules of; Jury system; Reversible error; Self-incrimination, privilege against.

Heart of Atlanta Motel v. United States

COURT: U.S. Supreme Court

DATE: Ruling issued December 14, 1964

SIGNIFICANCE: This Supreme Court decision upheld the constitutionality of the public accommodations section (Title II) of the Civil Rights Act of 1964

After the Civil War, Congress passed the Thirteenth, Fourteenth, and Fifteenth Amendments in order to establish legal and political rights for the newly freed slaves. The Fourteenth Amendment, in part, was designed to protect black citizens from discrimination by state and local governments in the South. It did not address the issue of private discrimination against blacks in hotels, restaurants, and theaters. Was discrimination by private individuals therefore legal? The U.S. Congress addressed this question when it passed the Civil Rights Act of 1875. This law made it illegal to discriminate against individuals in public accommodations. In 1883 the U.S. Supreme Court declared the Civil Rights Act of 1875 to be unconstitutional. According to the Court, the Fourteenth Amendment only protected against state discrimination and not discrimination by private individuals in their private businesses.

Almost a century later, the U.S. Congress addressed this issue again. Congressional hearings were held concerning the difficulty African Americans faced in using public accommodations. According to the hearings, blacks traveling from Washington, D.C., to New Orleans, Louisiana, in 1963 would find that the average distance between hotel and motel accommodations available to them was 174 miles. As a result of the hearings, Congress incorporated a public accommodations section as part of the Civil Rights Act of 1964. The public accommodations section prevented discrimination in hotels, motels, restaurants, theaters, sports arenas, and other public facilities. Congress based its authority to regulate public accommodations on the basis of the "commerce clause" of the Constitution, which grants Congress the authority to "regulate Commerce with foreign Nations, and among the several States."

The *Heart of Atlanta* case involves the immediate challenge to the constitutionality of the public accommodations section of the Civil Rights Act of 1964. The Heart of Atlanta Motel, a local operation, refused to serve African Americans. As a local motel, it argued that its not serving blacks had no impact on interstate commerce. Attorneys for the U.S. government argued that interstate commerce was affected by the motel's policy because three-quarters of its clientele came from outside the state. In upholding the public accommodations section of the Civil Rights Act of 1964, a unanimous Supreme Court argued that it made no difference that the motel was a local operation. If interstate commerce is affected at all, "it does not matter how local the operation which applies the squeeze." A companion case, *Katzenbach v. McClung* (1964), involving a small, local restaurant in Birmingham, Alabama, which refused sit-down service to blacks, reached a similar conclusion. Although the Court was unanimous in upholding the public accommodations section of the Civil Rights Act of 1964, the justices did not all concur on the reasoning. A majority of the justices upheld the law on the basis of the commerce clause, but Justice William Douglas wanted to base the decision on the equal protection clause of the Fourteenth Amendment.

See also Civil Rights Act of 1964; Civil War Amendments; Commerce clause; Constitution, U.S.; Racial and ethnic discrimination; Segregation, *de facto* and *de jure*.

Herndon v. Lowry

COURT: U.S. Supreme Court

DATE: Decided April 26, 1937

SIGNIFICANCE: One of the first United States Supreme Court cases to reverse a state conviction on First Amendment grounds, *Herndon v. Lowry* limited the states' ability to prosecute political dissidents

Angelo Herndon, a black organizer for the Communist Party in the South, was convicted of an "attempt to incite insurrection" under a Georgia statute which defined insurrection as "any combined resistance to the lawful authority of the state . . . when the same is manifested by acts of violence." Herndon's conviction rested on a booklet found in his possession that listed the aims of the Communist Party. The Georgia court found that none of these was criminal on its face but that one of them—"equal rights for the Negroes and self-determination of the Black Belt"—showed criminality because the aim could not be accomplished without violence. Georgia argued that this "extrinsic fact" proved criminality.

The Supreme Court reversed Herndon's conviction in a 5 to 4 vote. The reversal rested partly on the First Amendment and partly on grounds of vagueness. Justice Owen Roberts' majority opinion emphasized that there was no evidence that Herndon had ever advocated forcible subversion. Unless it could be shown that Herndon had advocated violence, the dangerous tendency of his words could not be made the basis of a criminal conviction. If it were otherwise, anyone who solicited members for a political party that the state believed might later turn to violence could be convicted and—since the Georgia statute was capital—put to death.

The Court also attacked the statute on vagueness grounds. The law defined no specific acts that could be said to be criminal. As construed by the Georgia courts, a conviction under the law could rest on a jury's determination that any political speech might have a "dangerous tendency." Thus every speaker or party organizer must calculate whether some chain of causation might lead to violence. Justice Roberts said that "the law as construed and applied, amounts merely to a dragnet which may enmesh anyone who agitates for a change of government if a jury can be persuaded that he ought to have foreseen his words would have some effect on the future conduct of others." The Court insisted that this is so vague that it violates the guarantees of liberty contained within the Fourteenth Amendment.

Herndon v. Lowry is significant because it narrows state governments' powers to punish their political opponents. It is one of the first cases in which the Supreme Court overturned a state statute on First Amendment grounds. This case (and other cases of the 1930's in which speech convictions were overturned) left many free speech questions unsettled, however, and provided little guidance to the courts or to Congress when free speech issues were confronted again after World War II.

See also *Brandenburg v. Ohio*; Communist Party, American; *Dennis v. United States*; *Gitlow v. New York*; *Schenck v. United States*; Smith Act; Speech and press, freedom of.

Hirabayashi v. United States

COURT: U.S. Supreme Court

DATE: Ruling issued June 21, 1943

SIGNIFICANCE: In this case, which began during World War II, the Supreme Court ruled in favor of the military's use of a curfew in a wartime situation

In 1942, Gordon Kiyoshi Hirabayashi, an American citizen of Japanese ancestry, was arrested for violating the curfew set by General John L. DeWitt on the West Coast and subsequently failing to report to a designated Civil Control Station for assignment to a "relocation center" (internment camp). The military acted under the authority of Executive Order 9066, issued on February 19, 1942, by President Franklin D. Roosevelt. This order authorized the secretary of war and appropriate military commanders to establish military areas from which any or all persons might be excluded. The president issued this order solely on his authority as commander in chief of the army and navy. After Hirabayashi was found guilty of violating the curfew and failing to report to the Civil Control Station, he appealed to the U.S. Supreme Court.

In 1943, the U.S. Supreme Court ruled 9 to 0 in favor of the United States and upheld the military's right to authorize a curfew. The majority opinion was written by Chief Justice Harlan Stone, who emphasized the grave character of the national emergency that had confronted the nation in 1942 and the possible disloyalty of portions of the Japanese American minority. He further noted that "in time of war residents having ethnic affiliations with an invading enemy may be a greater source of danger than those of a different ancestry." The Court, he thought, ought not to challenge the conclusion of the military authorities that the federal power be interpreted as broadly as possible. While there was some question of the constitutionality of the military order under the Fifth Amendment, Justice Stone denied that the curfew was unconstitutional because the amendment contained no equal protection clause.

Interestingly, though the Court was unanimous in its holding, there were three separate concurring opinions, by Justices Frank Murphy, William O. Douglas, and Wiley Rutledge. Justice Murphy made it clear that he found restrictions upon minority rights on the basis of race odious even in wartime: "Distinctions based on color and ancestry are utterly inconsistent with our traditions and our ideals." He believed that the curfew order bore "a melancholy resemblance to the treatment accorded to members of the Jewish race in Germany and other parts of Europe." He nevertheless justified the order, constitutionally, because of the "critical military situation" on the West Coast.

While the Court upheld the act of Congress of March 21, 1942, authorizing the curfew, it seems clear that at least some of the justices were quite uncomfortable with the relocation program. Therein is the legacy of this case: Why did the justices not offer a decision on the Japanese Relocation Program? It seems evident that a majority of the justices were extremely reluctant to interfere with the program, primarily because they were unwilling to dispute the judgment of the president and military commanders as to what was necessary to win the war. Therefore, it was easier for them to determine only that the curfew order was constitutional and lay within the combined congressional and presidential powers.

See also Japanese American internment; *Korematsu v. United States*; Martial law; *Milligan, Ex parte*.

Hobbs Act

DATE: Enacted July 3, 1946

DEFINITION: Legislation that made it unlawful to interfere with interstate commerce by robbery or extortion

SIGNIFICANCE: In addition to protecting interstate commerce from criminal activities, the Hobbs Act limited labor unions' possibilities of enforcing the interests of their constituencies within the boundaries of the law

The bill that became the Hobbs Act (or Anti-Racketeering Act of 1946) was introduced by Congressman Carl Hobbs from Alabama on January 3, 1945, in response to a 1942 Supreme Court decision in favor of Local 807 of the Teamsters Union of New York. The Court decision had essentially nullified the Anti-Racketeering Act of 1934, and the purpose of the Hobbs Act was to put new antiracketeering legislation on the books by amending the 1934 act. Title I, section 2 of the Hobbs Act stated that it was a felony to obstruct, delay, or affect interstate commerce "in any way or degree" through robbery or extortion. To make the act effective, it redefined the key terms "commerce," "robbery," and "extortion."

Debate over the bill centered on its effect on workers and organized labor. Supporters of the bill argued that it protected farmers from harassment by the Teamsters Union and pointed out that Title II of the bill upheld previous laws guaranteeing labor's rights. Foes of the bill nevertheless questioned whether the bill was merely an antiracketeering measure or was also intended to be antilabor. They pointed out that the Hobbs Act would make it difficult for a union to picket a company effectively during a strike.

See also American Federation of Labor-Congress of Industrial Organizations (AFL-CIO); Anti-Racketeering Act; Labor law; National Labor Relations Act (NLRA); Organized crime; Racketeer Influenced and Corrupt Organizations Act (RICO).

Holmes, Oliver Wendell, Jr. (Mar. 8, 1841, Boston, Mass.—Mar. 6, 1935, Washington, D.C.)

IDENTIFICATION: U.S. Supreme Court justice, 1902-1932

SIGNIFICANCE: Universally acknowledged as one of the greatest justices ever to sit on the Supreme Court, Holmes was known both for his grasp of jurisprudence and his craftsmanship

Oliver Wendell Holmes, Jr., inherited his father's name and his mother's sensibilities. Although he shared with his father, a Boston physician and man of letters, an aptitude for writing and a marked loquaciousness, Holmes gained from his mother a powerful sense of duty—one mark of which was his attendance at every Supreme Court session for twenty-five years.

Throughout his life, Holmes also devoted considerable time to teaching and writing. His most distinguished literary effort was a series of lectures collected and published in 1881 as *The*

Common Law, a volume heralded ever since as one of the greatest works of American legal scholarship. In it Holmes developed the theory that legal decisions are based not so much on precedent as on "felt necessities" reflecting current attitudes. His identification of a new principle of American jurisprudence—that liability should be based on foreseeable injuries rather than on the transgressions producing them—greatly influenced tort and contract law.

Shortly after the publication of *The Common Law*, Holmes was appointed to the staff of the Harvard Law School, but he taught there for only one year before joining the Massachusetts Supreme Court, where he served for twenty years, the last three as chief justice. The Progressive opinions he authored there recommended him to President Theodore Roosevelt, who named him to the United States Supreme Court in 1902. Although, like many justices, Holmes sometimes disappointed the expectations of the president who appointed him, in most respects he remained a Progressive.

In one of his most renowned opinions, he objected to the majority's endorsement of an extreme form of freedom of contract in *Lochner v. New York* (1905), becoming one of the Court's great dissenters and exhibiting an eloquent pithiness that would become his trademark. "The Fourteenth Amendment does not enact Mr. Herbert Spencer's *Social Statistics*," he wrote, indicating that economic principles, such as those enunciated in that nineteenth century treatise, are not legal ones. A number of his dissents, particularly those concerning due process and free speech, have since been written into law. Writing for the majority in *Schenck v. United States* (1919), it was Holmes who developed the standard that speech presenting a "clear and present danger" was not protected by the First Amendment, a standard he modified later in *Abrams v. United States* (1919) to exempt political speech.

In his ninety-first year, after his health had begun to fail, Holmes was persuaded by his fellow justices to retire. When he died three years later, he left his estate to the nation. It has been used to produce a history of the Supreme Court.

See also *Abrams v. United States*; Clear and present danger test; Jurisprudence; *Lochner v. New York*; Progressivism; *Schenck v. United States*; Supreme Court of the United States.

Home Building & Loan Association v. Blaisdell

Court: U.S. Supreme Court

Date: Decided June 8, 1934

Significance: This interpretation of the U.S. Constitution's contract clause recognized an emergency power in government that would be able to deal with the crisis of the Great Depression

During the Great Depression, many states enacted debtor relief statutes that postponed the obligations of borrowers to repay their home mortgage loans. The Minnesota Mortgage Moratorium Act of 1933 authorized state courts to exempt property from foreclosure by the lender for two years, so long as the borrower paid the reasonable rental value of the property and taxes into the court. The statute prevented the lender from immediately taking back the property and reselling it upon the borrower's default.

The contract clause of the Constitution (Article I, section 10) provides: "No State shall pass any law impairing the obligation of contracts." This clause, along with the other clauses in this section, expresses a general mistrust of retroactive legislation, which is a statute passed after people's expectations are agreed on and settled. Between the Declaration of Independence of 1776 and the Constitution of 1787, debtor relief legislation was common in the states. This legislation caused immediate problems for creditors, who lost their investments. The framers of the Constitution were more worried about the long-term creditworthiness of the new nation, however, which needed capital from foreign investors, so the contract clause amounted to a federal guarantee of debts. Chief Justice John Marshall used the contract clause during his tenure to assert federal authority to protect vested interests in property.

The historical background, as well as earlier Supreme Court precedents, seemed to require that the Mortgage Moratorium Act be struck down. Instead, Chief Justice Charles Evans Hughes wrote for a five-member majority upholding the law. He explained that the prohibition of the contract clause is not an absolute and should not be read so literally that it interferes with the state's police power to legislate for the public good. While an emergency such as the Great Depression did not create additional legislative power, Hughes said, such a serious emergency was the occasion for the legislative exercise of a reserved power equal to dealing with the economic crisis.

The four dissenters argued that the original historical understanding of the contract clause and the Supreme Court's consistent interpretations of the prohibition could not be ignored because of political exigency. To this argument Hughes remarked, "If by the statement that what the Constitution meant at the time of its adoption it means to-day, it is intended to say that the great clauses of the Constitution must be confined to the interpretation which the framers, with the conditions and outlook of their time, would have placed upon them, the statement carries its own refutation."

This holding rendered the contract clause a rather inconsequential limitation on the legislative prerogative. The majority opinion also is an early example of judicial interpretation to "keep the Constitution in tune with the times."

See also *Charles River Bridge v. Warren Bridge Co.*; Constitutional interpretation; Contract, freedom of; Contract law; *Dartmouth College v. Woodward*; *Ex post facto* law; Property rights.

Homelessness

Definition: A broad category of conditions, including poverty, mental illness, and substance abuse, that result in a lack of permanent, secure, and adequate housing

Significance: The increasing number of homeless people in the United States has raised questions about the availability of low-income housing, mental health services, and other social programs as well as questions about crime and sanitation in inner cities

During the 1980's and 1990's, there was a noticeable increase in the number of people living on U.S. streets, in abandoned buildings, under highway overpasses, in vehicles, and in other inappropriate locations, as well as in overcrowded conditions and with family and friends. Begging or panhandling by indigent and homeless people has become a familiar part of city life. The public perception is that the number of homeless people has increased, but the scope of the problem is difficult to assess. In 1984, the U.S. Department of Housing and Urban Development estimated that there were roughly 250,000 to 350,000 homeless on any given night in December and January. In 1987, the Urban Institute expanded the definition of homelessness and estimated that there were about 600,000 homeless people in the United States. Later estimates have been much higher, particularly during the winter months when emergency shelters are operating.

It is very difficult to get an accurate count because many of the homeless hide from police and other representatives of government, many make their makeshift "homes" far from public view, and many will not admit being homeless. During the early 1980's, the "homeless problem" became a major public issue, principally because the numbers seemed to be increasing so rapidly. Levels of unemployment surpassed only during the Great Depression of the 1930's encouraged attention to the plight of the poor.

As the 1980's progressed, the "homeless problem" was recognized as being many problems rather than only one.

There are many reasons people find themselves without permanent shelter. Some are substance abusers, and their alcohol or drug habits leave them with too little money to afford housing. Some are mentally ill and have been released from mental health facilities because they have been judged not to be dangerous to themselves or others, although they may not be capable of taking care of themselves financially or socially. Some are simply indigents who have been left to fend for themselves because critical social programs have been eliminated. Some have lost their jobs or been overwhelmed by medical bills and cannot afford adequate shelter. Many are women with children. Many are veterans with mental health problems related to military service. Some are dangerous, although most are not.

The very breadth of the causes of homelessness has made it difficult to design and implement programs to address the problem, although some causes of homelessness are more easily addressed than others. For example, persons who lose their apartments or homes when they lose their jobs often simply need temporary homes in which to keep their belongings, day-care programs for their children while they look for work, and an address to give to prospective employers. Job hunting is difficult without clean clothing and a telephone number where one can be contacted by prospective employers.

The definition of homelessness is also a problem. Those living with relatives or friends because they cannot afford their own housing, those living in overcrowded conditions because

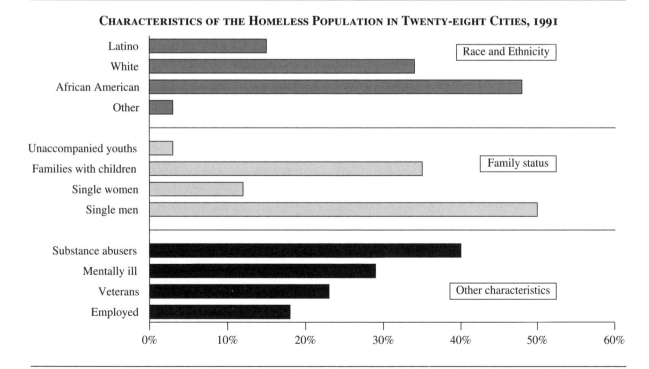

CHARACTERISTICS OF THE HOMELESS POPULATION IN TWENTY-EIGHT CITIES, 1991

Source: Data are from Carol Foster, ed., *Women's Changing Role*. Wylie, Tex.: Information Plus, 1992.

Note: Bars total more than 100% because most people fit into several categories.

that is all they can afford, and those camping out in rural areas because they cannot afford permanent housing may be missed in the count.

Beyond the personal causes of homelessness, American society itself has made it difficult for many to find permanent jobs and homes. Economic change has meant the loss of jobs in unsuccessful firms and declining industries. The decline of manufacturing and the rise of service industries have meant the loss of relatively high-paying jobs and the growth of relatively low-paying service sector jobs. As a consequence, hundreds of thousands of people have found themselves on the margins of American society. Along with growing unemployment, a shift in national policy brought severe cuts in the social "safety net" that formerly provided support to unemployed, mentally ill, and other indigent Americans. That, coupled with the deinstitutionalization of many mentally ill persons beginning in the 1960's, has put people on the streets. Programs that provided housing for low-income Americans have been cut. Urban development projects often tore down affordable housing and replaced it with expensive housing for middle- and upper-income citizens.

Furthermore, the demography of the United States began to change, with many more single-parent households, most often female-headed, with less economic stability than traditional two-parent households. The "baby-boom" bulge in population

An unidentified homeless person in Washington D.C., the day before Thanksgiving, 1989. (AP/Wide World Photos)

has strained resources of all kinds. The aging of the population, too, has meant fewer wage-earners and more elderly Americans. Sexual and racial discrimination has contributed to many people's struggle for adequate housing and jobs.

Homelessness is viewed as a major problem in many larger cities. Panhandling, loitering, threats of violence, petty theft, and public health problems are annoyances for many. At the same time, many people are concerned for the plight of the homeless. In some cities, strict enforcement of city regulations by police has been used to "sanitize" city parks and other areas, forcing the homeless into designated areas largely away from public view. Such actions are often viewed as violations of civil rights and liberties. Some cities have required developers to provide more single-room occupancy hotels for low-income people who are able to pay for housing only one day or one week at a time, as a condition for building more housing for moderate- and upper-income residents.

At the national level, Congress passed the McKinney Act in 1987 (amended in 1988), authorizing twenty programs to assist the homeless, with the Department of Housing and Urban Development as the designated lead agency. The act is designed to provide emergency food and shelter, including transitional and permanent housing; health care, including mental health care; drug and alcohol abuse programs; education; and job training. Funds are provided to local governments and nonprofit organizations to offer special programs for the poor. Yet despite some success, the level of funding has been inadequate.

—*William L. Waugh, Jr.*

See also American Civil Liberties Union (ACLU); Breach of the peace; Conservatism, modern American; Drug use and sale, illegal; Liberalism, modern American; Nuisance; Vagrancy laws; Welfare state.

BIBLIOGRAPHY

There are many books on the problem of homelessness; see, for example, Jennifer Wolch and Michael Dear, *Malign Neglect: Homelessness in an American City* (San Francisco: Jossey-Bass, 1993); Christopher Jencks, *The Homeless* (Cambridge, Mass.: Harvard University Press, 1994); Gregg Barak, *Gimme Shelter: A Social History of Homelessness in Contemporary America* (New York: Praeger, 1991); and Joel Blau, *The Visible Poor: Homelessness in the United States* (New York: Oxford University Press, 1992). For a description of federal programs, see U.S. General Accounting Office, *Homelessness: McKinney Act Programs Provide Assistance but Are Not Designed to Be the Solution* (Washington, D.C.: GAO, Author, May, 1994); and U.S. General Accounting Office, *Homelessness: McKinney Act Programs and Funding Through Fiscal Year 1993* (Washington, D.C.: Author, June, 1994).

Homicide. *See* Murder and homicide

Hoover, J. Edgar (Jan. 1, 1895, Washington, D.C.—May 2, 1972, Washington, D.C.)

IDENTIFICATION: Director of the Federal Bureau of Investigation, 1924-1972

J. Edgar Hoover with President John F. Kennedy and Attorney General Robert Kennedy in 1961. There was considerable animosity between Hoover and the Kennedys (Robert in particular), but Hoover was too powerful to remove. (AP/Wide World Photos)

SIGNIFICANCE: Hoover built the FBI into the world's foremost scientific law enforcement agency, but his abuse of his unregulated power precipitated a decline in his personal reputation

A lawyer at age twenty-two, Hoover entered the Justice Department in 1917, investigating aliens and communists during and after World War I. In 1924 he became director of the Bureau of Investigation, then under the cloud of Harding Administration scandals. Hoover upgraded recruiting and training standards and in 1935 renamed it the Federal Bureau of Investigation (FBI). With its extensive fingerprint file, crime-detection laboratory, training academy, and Crime Information Center (1967) to assist state and local police, the FBI gained a worldwide reputation for scientific law enforcement.

These achievements were enhanced by skillful public relations. During the Depression, Hoover and his agents became national heroes—glamorized through films and radio as well as Hoover's own books and articles—for hunting down criminals such as John Dillinger.

During World War II, the FBI guarded against enemy agents and saboteurs. After the war the target became American communism. Much publicized was the FBI's association with the House Committee on Un-American Activities, which convicted Alger Hiss and Julius and Ethel Rosenberg of espionage for the Soviet Union. Later, FBI files assisted Senator Joseph R. McCarthy's communist "witch-hunt."

Hoover's writings—*Persons in Hiding* (1938), *Masters of Deceit* (1958), and *A Study of Communism* (1962)—consis-

tently gave the impression that he alone was America's bulwark against every evil, from internal radicals to foreign agents. Beyond such self-aggrandizement, however, Hoover's personal life was well hidden. His own voyeuristic obsession with spying on others and amassing damaging information on their private lives undoubtedly made him acutely conscious of protecting his own privacy. A 1991 biography by Curt Gentry, *J. Edgar Hoover: The Man and the Secrets*, includes descriptions of Hoover as a secret transvestite.

From the 1950's to the 1970's Hoover's Counter-Intelligence Program (COINTELPRO) investigated individuals and organizations considered dangerous: Martin Luther King, Jr., the American Communist Party, the Ku Klux Klan, the Black Panthers, labor unions, student Vietnam War protesters, and civil rights organizations. Many legitimately feared the FBI's power and its stated mandate to investigate any radical opposition to conventional political beliefs. FBI agents were to act on the side of national security, needing only the "smoking gun" rule to burglarize organizations' offices. FBI wiretaps were coded and indexed in a top-secret "electronic surveillance card file."

Hoover consistently denied the existence of organized crime, despite its exposé by the Kefauver Senate committee, perhaps because his gambling in Mafia clubs made him vulnerable to the mob. The stormy relationship between Hoover and Attorney General Robert F. Kennedy stemmed from Kennedy's investigation of Mafia activities and from the FBI's laxity in enforcing federal civil rights laws.

By the 1970's demands for Hoover's resignation had become widespread. After his death, his reputation was tarnished by information published through the Freedom of Information Act and contained in a 1976 Senate study of intelligence activities. Hoover was found to have abused his power and, beginning in 1925, to have accumulated damaging files on twenty-five million people, including presidents and members of Congress. Even before Hoover's death, legislation limited FBI "information fishing expeditions" that placed Hoover beyond the control of the attorney general and the president. So great was his prestige and power that no president dared remove him from his position.

To some, Hoover was a symbol of law enforcement, patriotism, and anticommunism; to others he symbolized government repression and persecution of dissenters and reformers. All agree that he was one of the most controversial figures in American history.

See also Black Panther Party; COINTELPRO; Federal Bureau of Investigation (FBI); Freedom of Information Act; Kefauver investigation; Kennedy, Robert F.; King, Martin Luther, Jr.; Organized crime; Racketeer Influenced and Corrupt Organizations Act (RICO); Ten most wanted criminals.

House arrest

DEFINITION: A punishment which requires that convicted offenders remain in their homes at all times except to attend school or work

SIGNIFICANCE: This type of punishment is an alternative sanction that diverts offenders from secure incarceration and helps to reduce jail and prison populations

House arrest requires convicted offenders to remain in their homes. Most offenders are allowed to leave their homes to attend school or to go to their places of employment, but they must return to their homes immediately following school or work. The most lenient type of house arrest simply requires that the offender adhere to a specified curfew. More serious offenders may be monitored using an electronic device which straps around the ankle and allows free movement by offenders within their homes. Probation officers can then check on their probationers with a simple telephone call, which notifies them if the offender has left the home. House arrest is known as an alternative sanction, or an alternative to incarceration. When offenders are diverted from secure incarceration into an alternative such as house arrest, jail overcrowding problems are diminished. Some critics, however, have accused house arrest of being an attempt at "net widening" which increases control of the criminal justice system over offenders.

See also Diversion; Parole; Prison and jail systems; Probation; Punishment.

House Committee on Un-American Activities (HUAC)

DATE: Established 1938 as a special House investigatory committee; achieved standing committee status 1945; abolished 1975

SIGNIFICANCE: Established with a vague mandate to investigate un-American and subversive propaganda activities contrary to the form of government defined in the United States Constitution, the House Committee on Un-American Activities' operations raised serious freedom of speech and civil liberties issues

In 1938, the U.S. House of Representatives voted to establish a special committee to investigate the extent and nature of un-American and subversive propaganda activities in the United States that could also recommend corrective legislation to Congress. Although it was inspired by liberal Democratic representative Samuel Dickstein of New York, who sought a congressional investigation of the "un-American" German American Nazi Party's right-wing radicalism, the House Committee on Un-American Activities—also known as the House Un-American Activities Committee (HUAC)—adopted a conservative agenda and focused its investigations on left-wing radicalism under the leadership of its first chairman, Democratic representative Martin Dies, Jr., of Texas.

Approach and Authority of HUAC. HUAC's heyday lasted from the mid-1940's to the mid-1950's, coinciding with the height of the McCarthy-era "red scare." Reflecting the popular mood in a fiercely anticommunist period in U.S. history, HUAC most often aimed to expose in public hearings former and current members of the American Communist Party who held leadership positions or worked in occupations where they exercised a potential influence over the general American public, such as employees of government agencies, educational institutions, organized labor, or the entertainment industry. As an investigating committee, HUAC was empowered by Congress to subpoena witnesses and compel them to testify, under threat of contempt of Congress charges, to uncover "subversive and un-American activities." Relying on the Smith Act (1940), which made it a crime "to teach and advocate the overthrow of the United States Government by force and violence," HUAC sought to prove the "guilt" or "innocence" of subpoenaed witnesses.

HUAC questioned subpoenaed witnesses regarding their Communist Party membership, because membership in the Communist Party or a party-affiliated organization violated the Smith Act. HUAC deemed witnesses with Communist Party connections guilty with trial-like procedures but without allowing witnesses their constitutional rights as defendants to cross-examine their accusers. In theory, the courts could limit HUAC's authority to accuse witnesses and to compel testimony. When HUAC cited a witness with contempt, the U.S. attorney prepared a bill of indictment, which was followed by a grand jury indictment and a trial in a federal court. In practice, the courts upheld HUAC's authority and contempt citations.

Defense Strategies. Many subpoenaed witnesses chose one of two legal defense strategies to challenge HUAC's investigations of their Communist Party affiliations. Some witnesses claimed their First Amendment right to freedom of speech and challenged HUAC's right to inquire about their party membership, past or present. More often, witnesses claimed their Fifth

Amendment right and refused to give answers that could incriminate themselves. In 1947, when Republican representative J. Parnell Thomas of New Jersey chaired HUAC and led an investigation of "Communist infiltration of the motion-picture industry," prominent film stars, directors, and writers formed the Committee for the First Amendment to publicize their objections to HUAC proceedings. Ten witnesses whom HUAC subpoenaed during the investigation, who became known as the "Hollywood Ten," argued that the First Amendment right to free speech included the right to remain silent when asked about their political beliefs. A U.S. court of appeals, however, upheld their convictions for contempt in 1949 and stated that the question of Communist Party membership asked by HUAC was proper and that a witness' failure to disclose party membership was a punishable offense. This ruling seriously weakened the subpoenaed witnesses' use of the First Amendment defense.

More often, after 1947, subpoenaed witnesses took the Fifth Amendment and refused to answer HUAC's questions regarding Communist Party membership on the grounds that they would incriminate themselves. HUAC allowed witnesses to claim their Fifth Amendment rights without challenge because "taking the Fifth" implied guilt on the part of the claimant. If a witness had no crime or party association to hide, HUAC assumed, the witness would testify willingly in HUAC investigations. Unfriendly witnesses who claimed the Fifth Amendment and refused to answer HUAC questions about themselves or about the political beliefs of their associates escaped contempt of Congress convictions but became victims of other extra-governmental pressures such as public humiliation or inclusion on "blacklists" that prevented them from being employed in their chosen professions.

Support Declines. Public support for HUAC investigations waned in the 1960's as McCarthy-era anticommunism waned. The American Civil Liberties Union and the Emergency Civil Liberties Committee opposed HUAC proceedings. In 1960, the National Committee to Abolish HUAC, a single-purpose political action committee, was formed. In 1969, this growing opposition persuaded Congress to change HUAC's name to the House Committee on Internal Security (HISC) and to redefine its mandate to "monitor the activities of organizations bent on overthrowing the U.S. government" rather than to investigate "un-American activities," a concept that was open to much interpretation. In January, 1975, Congress abolished HISC. In 1976, Congress delivered the HUAC-HISC files to the National Archives of the United States, where they were sealed for fifty years. —*Karen Garner*

See also American Civil Liberties Union (ACLU); Assigned counsel system; Civil liberties; Communist Party, American; Palmer raids and the "red scare"; Self-incrimination, privilege against; Smith Act; Speech and press, freedom of; Truman, Harry S.

BIBLIOGRAPHY

A variety of perspectives on HUAC can be found in Carl Beck, *Contempt of Congress: A Study of the Prosecutions Initiated by the Committee on Un-American Activities, 1945-1957* (New Orleans, La.: Hauser Press, 1959); William F. Buckley, Jr., ed., *The Committee and Its Critics: A Calm Review of the House Committee on Un-American Activities* (New York: G. P. Putnam's Sons, 1962; Robert K. Carr, *The House Committee on Un-American Activities: 1945-1950* (Ithaca, N.Y.: Cornell University Press, 1952); Walter Goodman, *The Committee: The Extraordinary Career of the House Committee on Un-American Activities* (New York: Farrar, Straus and Giroux, 1968); and Jerold Simmons, *Operation Abolition: The Campaign to Abolish the House Un-American Activities Committee, 1938-1975* (New York: Garland, 1986).

Hughes, Charles Evans (Apr. 11, 1862, Glens Falls, N.Y.—Aug. 27, 1948, Osterville, Mass.)

IDENTIFICATION: U.S. Supreme Court justice, 1910-1916; chief justice of the United States, 1930-1941

SIGNIFICANCE: Between 1930 and 1941 Hughes presided over what amounted to two Courts, the first badly divided over New Deal legislation, the second fully supporting it

After a brilliant educational performance, Charles Evans Hughes entered private practice in New York City. He prospered, but illness and overwork caused him to accept a teaching post at Cornell University Law School. Two years later, following what would become a familiar pattern in his life, he bowed to financial pressures and returned to private practice.

In 1905, Hughes was named special counsel to a New York state committee investigating electric rates. He succeeded in unearthing a pattern of corruption. When the state legislature conducted a similar probe of the insurance industry, Hughes was again named special counsel and again produced impressive results. This record led to Hughes becoming the New York Republican nominee in the 1906 governor's race, which he won.

Hughes's record as governor was a good one, and when President William Howard Taft named him to the U.S. Supreme Court, the appointment proved popular. Taft had all but promised Hughes that he would succeed Chief Justice Melville W. Fuller, whose death was expected at any time, and this expectancy induced Hughes to disavow all further political ambitions. When Fuller died, however, Taft turned to Associate Justice Edward D. White, and in 1916, Hughes resigned to take up the Republican presidential nomination. His campaign was generally lackluster, but he lost to Woodrow Wilson by a slim margin.

In 1921 Hughes was named secretary of state by President Warren G. Harding. In 1925, however, suffering from overwork and a need to "recoup his fortune," he resumed his legal practice. Hughes kept a high profile, but his nomination as chief justice in 1930 was not met with the acclaim that had greeted his earlier appointment to the Court.

Hughes was eventually confirmed, and when he assumed the bench, he was at sixty-eight the oldest man ever to have been chosen chief justice. Nevertheless, Hughes's habits of hard work and commitment drove him to take on a large part

Charles Evans Hughes was chief justice when the Supreme Court grappled with the constitutionality of President Franklin Roosevelt's New Deal programs. (Harris and Ewing, collection of the Supreme Court of the United States)

of the heavy caseload generated by the effects of the Great Depression. His opinions during the early years of his tenure, like the Court itself, seemed to fall into two categories: On matters of civil liberties, he was an unqualified activist, but toward economic matters he exhibited an ambiguous attitude.

Like most of his brethren, he had been schooled in laissez-faire constitutionalism, a philosophical stance that led him to vote against some major New Deal legislation. Yet even before President Franklin D. Roosevelt announced his court-packing plan to engineer support for the New Deal, Hughes, joined by the other swing vote on the Court, Owen J. Roberts, began to foment a constitutional revolution, one in which the Supreme Court would defer to the will of the people as expressed by the legislative branch. The Court that Hughes led after 1937 was altogether different in jurisprudence and in personnel. In presiding over both and helping the nation through a time of crisis, Hughes exhibited the managerial skills and intellectual flexibility that make a chief justice great.

See also Court-packing plan of Franklin D. Roosevelt; New Deal; Roosevelt, Franklin D.; Solicitor general of the United States; Supreme Court of the United States; Taft, William Howard.

Hurtado v. California

Court: U.S. Supreme Court
Date: Decided March 3, 1884

SIGNIFICANCE: For the first time the Supreme Court indicated that the due process clause of the Fourteenth Amendment might apply some provisions of the Bill of Rights to the states

After Joseph Hurtado learned that his wife was having an affair, he shot and killed his rival. California authorities charged him with murder by filing an information—a formal accusation by a public prosecutor—in a state court. He was tried, convicted, and sentenced to death.

Hurtado appealed to the U.S. Supreme Court. He noted that on Fifth Amendment would have prevented the federal government from putting him on trial unless he had been indicted by a grand jury. He claimed that the Fourteenth Amendment's prohibition against a state's depriving "any person of life, liberty, or property without due process of law" meant that the state of California was bound to observe the same procedural limitations imposed on the federal government by the Fifth Amendment. The Supreme Court rejected his claim.

The Fifth Amendment contains a list of specific prohibitions on the federal government. It may not subject anyone to double jeopardy, self-incrimination, or trial without prior indictment by a grand jury. In addition it prohibits the federal government from depriving anyone of "life, liberty, or property without due process of law." Noting that the Constitution contained no superfluous language, the Court reasoned that had the framers of the Fifth Amendment meant "due process of law" to include the right to be indicted before trial, they would not have listed indictment as a separate, additional requirement.

The Fourteenth Amendment protects against state deprivation of due process of law. The Court ruled that the phrase has the same limitations it had in the Fifth Amendment. Consequently the Fourteenth Amendment due process clause does not prohibit the state's use of an information instead of an indictment.

Due process of law means that states cannot impose "arbitrary power" on their subjects. "Law," said the Court, "is something more than mere will exerted as an act of power." It excludes "acts of attainder, bills of pains and penalties, acts of confiscation . . . and other similar special, partial, and arbitrary exertions of power."

Justice John Harlan disagreed with the majority's interpretation of the due process clauses. He said that the framers of the Fifth Amendment listed certain prohibitions not because they were something other than due process of law but because they were essential to it.

Hurtado v. California is important for two reasons. Though the Court ruled that the due process clause of the Fourteenth Amendment did not incorporate the indictment requirement of the Fifth Amendment, it opened the door to incorporation by stating that certain standards of justice—some of which might be found in the Bill of Rights—did apply against the states. In addition the majority opinion is a classic statement distinguishing the rule of law from the arbitrary exercise of power.

See also Bill of Rights, U.S.; Due process of law; Grand jury; Incorporation doctrine; Indictment; Information.

Hutto v. Davis

COURT: U.S. Supreme Court
DATE: Decided January 11, 1982
SIGNIFICANCE: Narrowly interpreting the Eighth Amendment, the Court upheld a prison sentence of forty years for the possession and distribution of small amounts of illegal drugs

In 1973, Virginia police officers with a valid search warrant raided the home of Roger Davis, where they seized nine ounces of marijuana with a street value of two hundred dollars. The police already possessed a tape recording of Davis selling marijuana and other illicit drugs to a police informant. Davis was tried and found guilty in state court for the sale and distribution of illicit drugs, and his penalty was forty years' imprisonment and a fine of twenty thousand dollars. The federal district court, however, overturned the penalty, declaring that it was so "grossly out of proportion to the severity of the crime as to constitute cruel and unusual punishment in violation of the Eighth Amendment." The court of appeals agreed that the penalty was unconstitutional.

About the same time, the Supreme Court was taking a more conservative view of the Eighth Amendment; the majority in *Rummel v. Estelle* (1980) upheld a sentence of life imprisonment, with possibility of parole, for three offenses of fraud involving about $230. *Rummel* established the principle that federal courts should be most reluctant to use the proportionality doctrine to overturn legislatively mandated prison terms. In spite of *Rummel*, however, the court of appeals in 1981 reaffirmed that Davis' sentence was a cruel and unusual punishment. Virginia appealed the ruling to the Supreme Court.

The Court voted 6 to 3 to reverse the judgments of the lower federal courts. Following the logic of the *Rummel* precedent, the majority insisted in a *per curiam* opinion that the length of prison terms was a matter for legislative discretion and that any use of the doctrine of proportionality to overturn such sentences should be "exceedingly rare."

In a strong dissent, Justice William J. Brennan argued that Davis' sentence was cruel and unusual compared with other punishments for similar offenses. He observed that in Virginia at the time the average sentence involving marijuana was about three years and that even the district attorney who prosecuted Davis considered the penalty of forty years to be "grossly unjust."

The *Hutto* decision seemed to indicate that in the foreseeable future the Supreme Court would not allow the application of the proportionality doctrine to overturn penalties except in cases of the death penalty. Less than two years later, however, the majority of the Court in *Solem v. Helm* (1983) would make use of the doctrine to overturn a sentence of life imprisonment without possibility of parole. *Solem* did not appear to mark a long-term change in the Court's view of the Eighth Amendment, for in *Harmelin v. Michigan* (1991) the majority approved a lifetime sentence, without the possibility of parole, for possession of slightly over 650 grams of cocaine.

See also *Coker v. Georgia*; Cruel and unusual punishment; Drug use and sale, illegal; *Harmelin v. Michigan*; *Rummel v. Estelle*; *Solem v. Helm*.

Illegal aliens

DEFINITION: Foreigners who enter or reside in a country unlawfully or without proper documentation

SIGNIFICANCE: More than a million illegal or undocumented aliens are apprehended annually by the Immigration and Naturalization Service (INS) and other U.S. agencies; the seriousness of the problem of illegal immigration is a matter of considerable debate

The U.S. Immigration and Naturalization Service defines an alien as "any person not a citizen of the United States." An alien entering the United States or residing in the country in violation of immigration law is, therefore, typically referred to as an "illegal alien." The *INS Fact Book* glossary does not contain the term "illegal alien," however, as the Immigration and Nationality Act of 1952 states that an alien's unauthorized presence in the country is not, strictly speaking, a crime. Many people find the term "undocumented alien" to be preferable, as it does not imply that the individual has committed a criminal act. Moreover, some critics of the term "illegal alien" ask, how can a person be "illegal"?

Aliens residing in the United States occupy a unique place in the U.S. legal system. Aliens living in the country legally enjoy most of the rights guaranteed to "the people" by the Constitution, with the most notable exception being the right to vote. Unlike citizens, however, aliens can be deported for violations of the law (deportation can be appealed to the Board of Immigration in the Department of Justice or to the courts). There have also been periods in history during which aliens have been deported for their political views, as during the Palmer raids of 1919-1920. Until the early 1970's, states could discriminate against aliens in such ways as prohibiting them from certain employment and from receiving public assistance benefits.

Aliens living in the United States illegally or without adequate documentation are in a more precarious position. Considerable debate, particularly since the 1980's, has centered on issues such as the costs versus the benefits of the illegal alien population to American society and what the rights of illegal aliens should be. For example, conflicting statistics have been presented regarding whether illegal aliens are a drain on federal, state, and local governments because they use public services (such as health services) or whether the fact that many of them actually pay income taxes offsets such expenses. There are restrictions on the benefits that illegal aliens can receive from the government. Legal aliens are eligible for such things as food stamps and unemployment compensation; illegal aliens are not. The courts have held, however, that illegal aliens cannot be denied primary education and health care because of their status.

Legislative Background. No one is sure how many illegal aliens enter or reside in the United States each year. Throughout most of early U.S. history, all immigrants, with limited exceptions, were welcomed. It was not until 1875 that direct federal regulation of immigration was established. Prostitutes and convicts were the first categories of individuals specifically forbidden entry. The Chinese Exclusion Act of 1882 established further limits on entry by prohibiting Chinese laborers, along with persons guilty of political offenses, the mentally ill, "idiots," and persons likely to become public charges. The Bureau of Immigration, under the authority of the Treasury Department, was established in 1891 to administer all federal activities related to immigration. As the country entered the twentieth century, a series of immigration and naturalization laws were enacted, and the exclusion list was expanded to include polygamists, political radicals, persons with physical or mental defects, persons with tuberculosis, unaccompanied children, illiterates, alcoholics, vagrants, and others deemed undesirable. The first quotas were established to restrict Japanese immigration as well as the immigration of certain other ethnic groups. Such restrictions and quotas were fueled by the racial hostility that typified the period.

Twentieth Century Policies. The Great Depression heightened anti-alien attitudes, as millions of Americans were out of work and viewed aliens as competition for jobs. Aliens therefore became the target of violence in many cities. In 1931, Immigration Bureau "sweeps" to round up Mexican aliens began as the Depression deepened and public pressure for government action mounted. The U.S. Border Patrol, created in 1924, also stepped up efforts to enforce immigration restrictions and remove illegal aliens. Thousands of aliens were deported during this period, but few records are available. In fact, prior to 1927, no records were kept of illegal aliens apprehended or deported.

World War II brought great change in immigration policy. Workers were needed to replace those Americans called to military service. While many aliens entered the country legally in search of employment, primarily as agricultural workers, many more came illegally. There was little public interest in restricting the tide of cheap laborers. The INS has estimated that 5.6 million Mexicans illegally crossed the 1,945-mile border between the United States and Mexico between 1942 and 1967.

The economic recession of the late 1970's again brought the issue of illegal aliens to the forefront. The low wages paid to illegal aliens and the argument that they displaced citizens from jobs again became political issues. President Jimmy Carter reacted by calling for more INS inspectors and Border Patrol officers as well as for penalties for employers of illegal aliens. Carter's efforts failed for a number of reasons. Already in the

ALIENS EXPELLED AND IMMIGRATION VIOLATIONS, 1985 TO 1991							
Item	1985	1986	1987	1988	1989	1990	1991
Aliens expelled	**1,062,000**	**1,608,000**	**1,113,000**	**934,000**	**860,000**	**1,045,000**	**1,091,000**
Deported	21,000	22,000	22,000	23,000	30,000	26,000	28,000
Required to depart	1,041,000	1,586,000	1,091,000	911,000	830,000	1,019,000	1,063,000
Prosecutions disposed of	**17,688**	**23,405**	**18,894**	**18,360**	**18,580**	**20,079**	**18,882**
Immigration violations	16,976	22,751	18,200	17,590	17,992	19,351	18,297
Nationality violations	712	654	694	770	588	728	585
Convictions	**9,833**	**15,259**	**11,996**	**12,208**	**12,561**	**12,719**	**11,509**
Immigration violations	9,635	15,104	11,786	11,929	12,379	12,515	11,392
Nationality violations	198	155	210	279	182	204	117

Source: U.S. Department of Commerce, Bureau of the Census, *Statistical Abstract of the United States, 1992.* Washington, D.C.: U.S. Government Printing Office, 1992.

midst of a recession, many Americans were reluctant to spend millions of government dollars attempting to stop the flow of illegal immigrants. Besides, many argued, illegal aliens frequently took jobs that citizens were unwilling to perform.

A 1982 Supreme Court case, *Plyler v. Doe*, established that states cannot refuse to finance the education of illegal alien children or exclude them from public schools. The Court used the equal protection clause of the Fourteenth Amendment to support its decision. In 1986, the Immigration Reform and Control Act (IRCA) addressed the issue of illegal immigration. It outlawed the hiring of illegal aliens and strengthened controls to prevent illegal entry into the country. The law mandated that employers require their employees to provide documentation that they are legally residents of the United States. IRCA also established a program through which immigrants who had been residing in the country since 1982 could apply for amnesty. The law apparently did little to slow illegal immigration, as aliens could easily purchase forged documents. Using falsified Social Security cards and birth certificates, many received welfare, unemployment benefits, and public education. California voters, in a measure of their dissatisfaction with the size of the state's illegal Hispanic population, approved Proposition 187 in 1994. It prohibited illegal aliens from obtaining state welfare, health, and education benefits. The constitutionality of Proposition 187 was challenged shortly after it was passed.

Statistics on Illegal Aliens. In the mid-1990's, the U.S. Border Patrol estimated that only about a third of aliens entering the country without proper authorization are apprehended. In most years since 1977, more than a million illegal aliens have been apprehended annually, implying that perhaps three million or more people are able to enter the country illegally each year. The majority of these individuals are Hispanic, primarily of Mexican descent, and move back and forth across the border with regularity. Border Patrol statistics indicate that about one-third of those deported have been previously detained by the INS. Most deported illegal aliens are detained by the INS within seventy-two hours of entering the country. INS statistics indicate much about who these individuals are, where they

attempt to reside in the United States, what their occupations have been in the United States, and why they were required to leave the country. According to the INS, most are citizens of Mexico, reside in the southern and western United States, and are unable to find employment. Those who do find jobs are predominantly agricultural workers. The overwhelming majority of those required to leave were deported as a result of entry without inspection. Such INS data are probably somewhat misleading on some counts; for example, illegal immigration from Central American countries (via Mexico) increased markedly in the 1980's and 1990's, but many of these immigrants were unwilling to identify their actual place of origin to authorities. Also, many illegal immigrants find work in the United States' "underground economy," which similarly goes unreported.

Another aspect of the lives of illegal or undocumented aliens that is difficult to assess quantitatively is their unique vulnerability to various types of exploitation and crime, primarily because of their fear that going to authorities for protection will instead result in their deportation. A dramatic example of such exploitation surfaced in August, 1995, when it was discovered that a group of Thai immigrants had been held as virtual prisoners in an apartment complex that doubled as a sewing factory in El Monte, California. The immigrants were forced to work extremely long hours by the owners of the operation and were not allowed to leave the complex, which was locked and surrounded with barbed wire. —*Donald C. Simmons, Jr.*

See also Citizenship; Immigration, legal and illegal; Immigration and Naturalization Service (INS); Immigration laws; Immigration Reform and Control Act; International law; *Plyler v. Doe.*

BIBLIOGRAPHY

Perhaps the most easily accessible book related to illegal immigration is the Immigration and Naturalization Service's annual *INS Fact Book* (Washington, D.C.: INS Statistics Division), which provides up-to-date data on the entry, apprehension, and expulsion of illegal aliens as well as budgetary information regarding INS agencies. The INS also publishes the annual *Statistical Yearbook of the Immigration and Natu-*

ralization Service (Washington, D.C.: U.S. Government Printing Office). As its title suggests, *The Problem of Immigration* (New York: H. W. Wilson, 1985), edited by Steven Anzovin, deals with a variety of issues related to the problems of legal and illegal immigration. Robert Shafer and Donald Mabry's *Neighbors—Mexico and the United States: Wetbacks and Oil* (Chicago: Nelson-Hall, 1981) is perhaps one of the best works on the Mexico/U.S. border and illegal immigration. Also relevant is Abraham Hoffman, *Unwanted Mexican Americans in the Great Depression: Repatriation Pressures, 1929-1939* (Tucson: University of Arizona Press, 1974).

Illinois v. Krull

COURT: U.S. Supreme Court

DATE: Decided March 9, 1987

SIGNIFICANCE: In this case the Supreme Court held that the "good-faith exception," sometimes allowing the courtroom use of evidence seized illegally, could apply to certain warrantless searches

Illinois businesses that buy and sell used automobile parts or that process automobile scrap metal were required by a 1981 statute to obtain a business license, maintain detailed records of their transactions, and make these records and the business premises available to the state for inspection at any reasonable time to determine the accuracy of the records. On July 5, 1981, the Chicago police entered the premises of Action Iron & Metal, Inc., an automobile wrecking yard, to inspect its records and examine the vehicle identification numbers of cars in the yard. The clerk at the wrecking yard was unable to produce any records other than a paper pad on which approximately five vehicle purchases were listed. The inspection of the wrecking yard disclosed that three of the cars were stolen and a fourth car had no vehicle identification number. Two men (Krull, who held the license for Action Iron & Metal, Inc., and the clerk) were charged with various criminal violations of the Illinois motor vehicle statutes.

On July 6, 1981, a federal court held that the Illinois statute was an unconstitutional administrative search law. Based on this decision, the Illinois trial court held that the search was illegal. The Illinois trial court also held that the *United States v. Leon* (1984) good-faith exception to the exclusionary rule did not apply because it was limited to circumstances in which a warrant was issued by a neutral magistrate. The Illinois Supreme Court affirmed the trial court's decision. The U.S. Supreme Court, however, in a 5-4 vote, reversed the decision. It stated that the *Leon* good-faith exception to the exclusionary rule could apply when a police officer's reliance on the constitutionality of a statute authorizing the search was objectively reasonable, even though the statute is subsequently declared unconstitutional.

In Justice Harry Blackmun's majority opinion, the Court noted that *Leon* had reaffirmed that the purpose of the exclusionary rule is to deter future unlawful police conduct, not to provide a cure for past unlawful police conduct. Because the exclusion of evidence undermines the truth-finding process of

a criminal trial, the exclusionary rule remedy should be imposed only when the likelihood of deterring future unlawful police conduct outweighs the cost to the criminal justice system's primary purpose: determining the guilt or innocence of a defendant.

The statutory authorization for the warrantless search functions like the warrant for three reasons, the Court said. First, there is no evidence that legislators ignored the requirements of the Fourth Amendment in passing such legislation. Second, members of the legislature, like neutral magistrates, have no direct stake in the day-to-day conduct of law enforcement, so there is little incentive for them to overstep the limits of the Fourth Amendment. Third, no proof was offered that the application of the exclusionary rule would deter legislators from enacting statutes which may be declared unconstitutional or that exclusion of evidence in these cases will significantly deter future unlawful police conduct. Therefore, any marginal deterrent benefit in applying the exclusionary rule to cases such as this is outweighed by the cost of excluding reliable and relevant evidence from the process of determining guilt.

In this case the police acted in a reasonable manner in relying on the statute as authorizing a lawful search, because the Supreme Court had approved warrantless administrative searches in similar cases. In closing, the Court limited its decision by noting that if there was proof that the legislature wholly abandoned its responsibility to enact constitutional laws under the Fourth Amendment, or if a reasonable officer should have known the statute was unconstitutional, then the exclusionary rule should apply. Despite the caveat at the close of the opinion, the *Krull* case significantly expanded the scope of the decision in *Leon* by leaving open the possibility that it could be applied to other warrantless search circumstances.

See also Evidence, rules of; *Leon, United States v.*; Search and seizure.

Immigration, legal and illegal

DEFINITION: The permanent settling of persons in the United States from foreign countries, either pursuant to U.S. law or in violation of it

SIGNIFICANCE: Immigration constitutes a major source of population growth in the United States; it affects national and regional economic health, ethnic and cultural diversity, utilization of governmental services, and other domestic conditions

For much of the twentieth century, the United States has absorbed more legal immigrants than the other countries of the world combined. In addition to legal immigration, each year several hundred thousand persons enter the country to reside illegally. In the 1990's, about one in four foreigners settling in the United States did so in violation of immigration laws. Immigration affects American society in fundamental ways, but the costs, benefits, and moral obligations surrounding immigration are matters of dispute. The debate over immigration is fraught with conflicting statistics and conflicting values and centers on three primary topics: humanitarianism, economics, and nationhood.

Humanitarianism. A large part of the rationale for accepting immigrants into the United States stems from humanitarian concerns. In theory, U.S. policies seek to assist people of other nations who experience political oppression, discrimination, famine, civil war, or any number of other tribulations. In this context, allowing individuals to try to escape the worst of their problems by immigrating to the United States can be seen as a form of international aid.

The United States, like most other Western democratic countries, offers asylum to refugees of political repression. The United States distinguishes between political refugees fleeing persecution and economic refugees seeking a better standard of living. The system, however, is subject to inefficiency and abuse. Ascertaining whether a person is a political or economic refugee is a difficult and time-consuming task. Typically, there is a large backlog of asylum cases awaiting official action, and while the government is processing a case, the applicant may become "lost" within the general population. Such cases constitute one source of illegal immigration. Government efforts to locate and repatriate these illegal refugees are often ineffective. Moreover, many such enforcement actions raise justice issues of their own. Some groups in the United States have dedicated themselves to shielding illegal immigrants from immigration authorities and laws. Such efforts reached a peak in the 1980's, when a number of churches and even cities declared themselves "sanctuaries" for aliens who did not have official refugee status.

American public sentiment for political refugees has fluctuated widely over time. The anticommunist and anti-Soviet feelings prevalent during the Cold War made dissidents and defectors from Eastern Europe and the Soviet Union especially welcome. Unusually brutal governmental crackdowns, such as those by the Chinese government at Tiananmen Square in 1989, raise public sympathy for political refugees, particularly for activists fighting for democracy. Poignant examples of human tragedy, such as ethnic cleansing in Bosnia and the warehousing of orphans in postcommunist Romania, can spur Americans to adopt foreign children and to sponsor the immigration of adults and families. Some international crises, such as the fall of South Vietnam in the mid-1970's, dramatically increase the number of political refugees coming to the United States. These large waves of refugees can fatigue American public support for immigration. Further, incidents of international terrorism inflicted upon Americans can reduce public

An 1887 engraving of European immigrants arriving in New York Harbor. (Library of Congress)

acceptance of foreign immigrants (particularly when they belong to groups associated with terrorism, rightly or wrongly, in the public consciousness).

Economics. Persons without any claim of experiencing political repression can also apply to immigrate to the United States. Many are motivated by economic and societal opportunities. Traditionally, immigration of this sort has contributed significantly to the growth of the U.S. population and economy. A rapid influx of immigrants, however, may overwhelm the country's ability to assimilate them, burdening social services and housing stocks, absorbing employment opportunities, and heightening racial and ethnic tensions. The net economic effects of the presence of immigrants is a matter of debate. Proponents claim that immigrants tend to pay more in taxes than they receive in social services, that they perform jobs American citizens prefer not to take, and that they tend to have a strong work ethic. Yet to the extent that immigrants have lower levels of education and lower wage demands—both are particularly true of illegal immigrants—their presence may skew the economy toward more service-oriented, labor-intensive jobs. The presence of a surplus of cheap labor may reduce incentives to invest in greater mechanization. Some critics charge that large numbers of immigrants make finding employment more difficult for poor Americans, particularly for poor members of minority groups.

To regulate those effects, the federal government controls immigration through eligibility requirements and numerical limits. Deciding who will and will not be permitted to immigrate raises obvious justice issues. Until the mid-1960's, government established immigration quotas on the basis of nationality, at times excluding some national and racial groups entirely. Since the mid-1960's, permission to immigrate to the United States has been awarded largely by lottery.

Persons who are unable to secure legal resident status may resort to illegal means for entering the country. In response, the U.S. government has taken steps to block illegal border crossings. In 1924, the U.S. Border Patrol was established to police the country's borders. The Mexican border is more heavily policed than the Canadian and has been fortified with surveillance devices and metal fencing. These measures have led some critics to identify the U.S.-Mexico border with the infamous Berlin Wall, although others argue that the imprisonment of people within a country and the exclusion of people from a country concern different questions of morality.

U.S. efforts to limit immigration involve economic and market forces in a number of ways. The perceived promise of

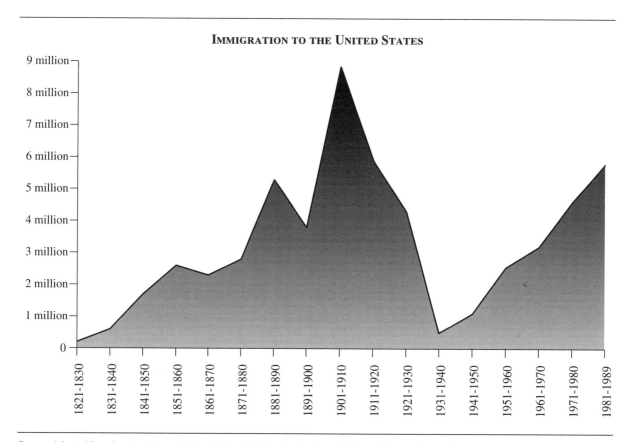

IMMIGRATION TO THE UNITED STATES

Source: Adapted from Immigration and Naturalization Service, *An Immigrant Nation: U.S. Regulation of Immigration, 1798-1991*. Washington, D.C.: U.S. Department of Justice, 1991.

economic opportunity in the United States, coupled with immigration restrictions, has given rise to human smuggling operations, particularly in Mexico. In the early 1990's, about half the aliens illegally entering the United States were assisted in some way by smugglers. In addition to taking police measures, the U.S. government has tried to stem illegal immigration by reducing the incentives for it. The 1994 North American Free Trade Agreement (NAFTA) was touted in part for its projected role in improving economic opportunities in Mexico, thus reducing the incentive to emigrate. At the same time, governmental benefits to illegal aliens were restricted, partly in the hope that such limitations will make the prospect of living illegally in the United States less attractive. Federal welfare payments, food stamps, unemployment compensation, and other federal benefits are available to legal, but not to illegal, immigrants; however, primary education and medical services cannot be withheld from illegal aliens. In ruling on such issues, the U.S. Supreme Court has held that the equal protection clause of the Fourteenth Amendment does not depend on citizenship status.

Border states have been especially sensitive to the economic and social costs of illegal immigration. These states often bear the brunt of service provision, infrastructure maintenance, law enforcement, and other social costs of illegal immigration. In 1994, California voters passed Proposition 187, a referendum that sought to deny state benefits, including health care, welfare, and education, to illegal aliens. (The referendum was immediately challenged as unconstitutional.) Some states have sued the federal government for the costs of supporting illegal aliens, asserting that the federal government was negligent in not stopping such aliens at the country's borders. Border states have also challenged federal census figures, arguing that the allocation of federal benefits (including apportionment of congressional seats) should account for illegal aliens.

Race, Ethnicity, and Nationhood. Although the humanitarian motives that ostensibly underlie many U.S. immigration laws seldom are defined in terms of race and ethnicity, the federal government frequently has controlled immigration on the basis of national origin. Beginning in the 1920's, the United States established immigration quotas defined by national origin. Immigrants from European countries historically have been favored.

Immigration patterns have shifted dramatically over time, however, and not always as a result of changes to U.S. immigration policy. In the 1950's, most immigrants came from Europe and Canada. By the 1970's, partly as a result of international events, the majority of immigrants were coming from Asia, Central America, and the Caribbean. The effects of different immigration patterns are compounded by higher birthrates among some immigrant groups; such effects are further accentuated by the disproportionate number of young adults among persons immigrating to the United States.

Consideration of immigration in terms of race and nationality raises the question of how the American people should be defined as a nation. The United States' sense of nationhood stems more from shared morals, values, and norms than from ethnic, racial, or even cultural characteristics. Yet the traditional conception of the United States as a "melting pot" of various ethnic and racial groups was challenged in the 1980's and 1990's by critics who claimed that such a concept unfairly pressures immigrants and racial minorities to conform to a largely white, middle-class culture. In its place, such critics offered a "salad bowl" metaphor of the United States, envisioning the various cultures of America's citizens as retained in a diverse mosaic. In this view, assimilation, including perhaps even the mastery of English language, is unnecessary and perhaps undesirable. Nevertheless, immigrant groups themselves overwhelmingly desire to adopt American mores and culture, believe that people who come to the United States should learn to speak English, and sense that the country suffers from excessive immigration.

Immigration policies thus cut to the heart of the United States' sense of nationhood. By defining who can live in the country, who can receive services, and what is required to become a citizen, the government defines what it means to be an American. These policies also describe the nation's sense of its moral obligations to foreign persons in need, and the enforcement of these policies helps to direct the future makeup of the American population.

Policies. American immigration policy has shifted widely over time. Although much of the country's early growth was fed by immigration, the United States has periodically restricted immigration in general or the entry of certain groups in particular. An example of the latter is the Chinese Exclusion Act of 1882, which was repealed in 1943. The first broad immigration control laws were established in the 1920's with the National Origins Act, which attempted to limit the inflow of immigrants and to fix the ethnic proportions of the U.S. population via national quotas.

World War II, the Holocaust, and the political dislocations that followed the war prompted the United States to revise its immigration laws. After a series of ad hoc alterations, in 1952 the Immigration and Nationality Act codified the disparate immigration laws and ended immigration and naturalization prohibitions by race. The Hart-Celler Act of 1965 expanded the 1952 law, ending national origin quotas entirely. In addition, this act established the reuniting of families as a goal of U.S. immigration policy. In a further move away from group- and nationality-based admissions policies, the Refugee Act of 1980 required that decisions to admit refugees be made on a case-by-case basis.

By the 1980's, the growing number of illegal immigrants had once again pushed immigration reform into the public spotlight. The Immigration Reform and Control Act (IRCA) of 1986, an attempt to balance the interests of anti-immigrant and immigrant-rights groups, took two approaches to the problem. To reduce illegal immigration, the act imposed sanctions on employers hiring illegal aliens and strengthened the country's border enforcement. At the same time, the IRCA granted amnesty to illegal aliens who had resided in the country since at least 1982. Further modifications to immigration and refugee laws and policies continued throughout the 1980's and early 1990's, prompted partly by the end of the Cold War and the increase in civil wars around the world. In 1990, for example, the Immigration Act raised immigration quotas by 40 percent, their highest level since 1914. —*Steve D. Boilard*

See also Chinese Exclusion Act; Illegal aliens; Immigration and Naturalization Service (INS); Immigration laws; Immigration Reform and Control Act; Mexican American Legal Defense and Education Fund (MALDEF).

BIBLIOGRAPHY

Numerous books on immigration, focusing on the various aspects discussed above, are readily available. A representative sample includes George J. Borjas, *Friends or Strangers: The Impact of Immigrants on the U.S. Economy* (New York: Basic Books, 1990); James D. Cockcroft, *Outlaws in the Promised Land: Mexican Immigrant Workers and America's Future* (New York: Grove Press, 1986); Brent Nelson, *America Balkanized: Immigration's Challenge to Government* (Monterey, Va.: American Immigration Control Foundation, 1994); Julian Simon, *The Economic Consequences of Immigration* (Cambridge, England: Basil Blackwell, 1989); and Virginia Yans-McLaughlin, ed., *Immigration Reconsidered: History, Sociology, and Politics* (New York: Oxford University Press, 1990).

Immigration and Naturalization Service (INS)

DATE: Established March 3, 1891

SIGNIFICANCE: The INS, an agency within the Department of Justice, is the most important agency in the enforcement of immigration law

The United States attorney general is charged with administering and enforcing all laws relating to aliens' immigration and naturalization. The attorney general delegates most such duties to the Immigration and Naturalization Service. The INS has jurisdiction over aliens in the United States, handling visa petitions, adjusting peoples' status (as from nonimmigrant to immigrant), granting citizenship, and dealing with deportations and exclusions.

The commissioner of the INS is appointed by the president, normally on the recommendation of the attorney general, with

European refugees in 1938 saluting the flag as they prepare to take citizenship exams. (AP/Wide World Photos)

ILLEGAL IMMIGRANTS APPREHENDED, 1925-1989

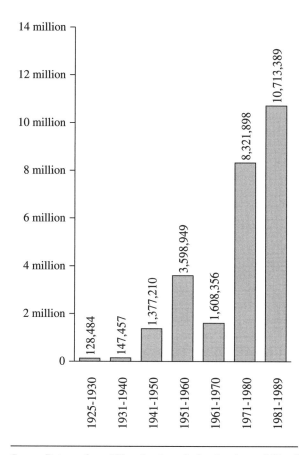

Source: Data are from Allison Landes, ed., *Immigration and Illegal Aliens.* Wylie, Tex.: Information Plus, 1991.

the consent of the Senate. INS headquarters is located in Washington, D.C. The headquarters handles administrative matters and general policy making almost exclusively. Directly under the headquarters are four INS regional offices. The basic function of the regional offices is fiscal management to assist INS field offices in their areas. Under the four regional offices are thirty-six district offices worldwide and twenty border patrol sectors throughout the United States. The district office is the basic operating unit of the INS. Each district director has authority and responsibility to grant or deny various applications or petitions submitted to the service, to initiate investigations and deportations, and to issue orders to show cause or warrants of arrest in deportation proceedings.

See also Citizenship; Illegal aliens; Immigration, legal and illegal; Immigration laws; Immigration Reform and Control Act.

Immigration laws

DEFINITION: Immigration laws govern the admission and exclusion of aliens and the process of attaining citizenship;

they also delineate various rights and restrictions regarding immigrants' activities in the United States

SIGNIFICANCE: Immigration laws have changed dramatically through time; they have affected millions of people directly and millions more indirectly throughout American history in such areas as civil rights, the distribution of wealth, employment, labor policy, foreign relations, and freedom of association

Generally, immigrants were officially welcomed to the United States for about a hundred years after American independence. Among the first laws that could be considered immigration statutes were the Alien and Sedition Acts (1798), which authorized the president to deport anyone who was dangerous to the peace and safety of the country. After the official ending of the slave trade in the 1850's, immigrants were often imported for specific jobs in response to the expanding economy. For example, the Irish were brought to the East Coast for manufacturing industries, and the Chinese to the West Coast for constructing railroads. These labor immigrants experienced considerable discrimination and were exposed to violent attacks. Under the influences of anti-immigrant hysteria, the federal government began to pass restrictive regulations controlling the entry of foreign workers and limiting their right to settle in the United States. The Chinese Exclusion Act (1882) was one of the most sweeping. It initially excluded all unskilled Chinese people from immigrating; amendments made it increasingly restrictive. The act was not repealed until 1943.

From the early twentieth century to 1952, Congress enacted several laws to restrict immigrants from southern and eastern Europe and to bar most Asians from coming to the United States. Laws favored immigration from northern and western European countries in order to preserve the northern and western European "character" of the United States population. In 1952, Congress enacted the Immigration and Nationality Act of 1952, the first comprehensive immigration law that consolidated previous immigration laws into one coordinated statute. It is still the basic immigration and nationality statute, although the 1952 act has been repeatedly amended. The racial exclusion and the national origins quota system were abolished in 1965, when Congress established a preference system for immigrants in order to facilitate the entry of relatives of United States citizens and those persons possessing certain professional qualifications or special skills.

In 1986, Congress adopted the Immigration Reform and Control Act (IRCA). The act focused on discouraging illegal immigration by penalizing employers for illegally hiring aliens who have no employment authorization. In 1990, Congress passed a series of amendments to the Immigration and Nationality Act, collectively referred to as the Immigration Act of 1990. The most visible change of the 1990 act was an overall increase in worldwide immigration quotas.

Scope of Immigration Laws. U.S. immigration law is primarily concerned with four broad areas: citizenship, admission, deportation and exclusion, and refugees and asylum. Most U.S.

An exhibit at New York's Ellis Island, once the point of entry for millions of European immigrants. (Mary Pat Shaffer)

citizens acquire their citizenship by being born on United States soil or by being born abroad of U.S. citizen parents. Some aliens may acquire citizenship through the naturalization process if they have resided continuously in the United States for five years as a lawfully admitted permanent resident, are English literate, and are of "good moral character."

All aliens admitted to the United States must obtain either immigrant visas (for persons who wish to become permanent residents of the United States) or nonimmigrant visas (for persons who want to come to the country temporarily and meet the requirement of a specific nonimmigrant class). There are two categories of immigrant visa. One is not subject to numerical limitations; these visas are given to immediate relatives of U.S. citizens. The second one is subject to the per-country quota limitation system. These immigrant visas are issued based on family-sponsored and employment-related preferences. Nonimmigrant visas have the following eighteen categories: diplomats, temporary visitors for business and pleasure, aliens in transit, crew members, treaty traders and investors, students, international organization representatives, temporary workers, foreign media representatives, exchange program visitors, children of and persons engaged to U.S. citizens, intracompany transferees, students in nonacademic institutions, parents and children of special immigrants, aliens

with extraordinary abilities, entertainers, cultural exchange program participants, and religious workers.

An alien may be deported or excluded based on a number of grounds. Gaining entry without inspection, violating nonimmigrant status, terminating conditional permanent residence status, or failing to maintain employment constitute grounds for deportation. Aliens who are convicted, postentry, of certain crimes or who are drug abusers or addicts may be deported or excluded, as may those who fail to register, falsify entry documents, or act in a way that threatens national security. Finally, aliens who become a public charge within five years of entry or who engage in immigration document fraud may be deported. An alien can be deported only through specific deportation processes and can be represented (at no expense to the government) by legal counsel to seek possible relief from deportation.

An alien may be considered for refugee or asylum immigration status if the alien has been persecuted or has a well-founded fear of persecution in his or her home country because of race, religion, nationality, or membership in a particular social or political group. Qualified refugee aliens can seek refugee status if they are outside the United States or apply for asylum status if they are already present in the United States or at its borders.

Agencies. The Immigration and Naturalization Service (INS) of the Department of Justice and the Bureau of Consular Affairs (including the Visa Office) of the Department of State are primarily responsible for the administration of immigration laws. Appointed by the United States attorney general but independent of the commissioner of the INS are the special inquiry officers (known as immigration judges, or IJs) who conduct exclusion and deportation hearings. The Board of Immigration Appeals (BIA) reviews exclusion and deportation orders of the IJs. The Executive Office of Immigration Review administers the BIA and IJs. The Public Health Service and the Department of Labor also share some immigration responsibilities. The Public Health Service is responsible for physical and mental examinations of arriving aliens, whereas the Department of Labor issues "labor certificates" for employment-based immigration. —*Wei Luo*

See also Alien and Sedition Acts; Chinese Exclusion Act; Coast Guard, U.S.; Illegal aliens; Immigration, legal and illegal; Immigration and Naturalization Service (INS); Immigration Reform and Control Act; Racial and ethnic discrimination.

BIBLIOGRAPHY

Good overviews of immigration law include David S. Weissbrodt, *Immigration Law and Procedure in a Nutshell* (3d ed. St. Paul, Minn.: West, 1992); Ira J. Kurzban, *Kurzban's Immigration Law Sourcebook: A Comprehensive Outline and Reference Tool* (4th ed. Washington, D.C.: American Immigration Law Foundation, 1994); and Stephen H. Legomsky, *Immigration Law and Policy* (Westbury, N.Y.: Foundation Press, 1992).

Immigration Reform and Control Act

DATE: Became law on November 6, 1986

DEFINITION: The first federal law to impose sanctions on employers who hire illegal aliens, it also provided amnesty for a class of aliens

SIGNIFICANCE: In order to compel employers to cooperate in controlling illegal immigration, the Immigration Reform and Control Act established an examining procedure for employers to verify that all potential employees are U.S. citizens or aliens with working authorization; the act also established penalties to be imposed on employers who violate the law

The Immigration Reform and Control Act (IRCA) originated from a bill introduced by Senator Alan Simpson and Representative Roman Mazzoli in March, 1982. The bill primarily tried to impose sanctions against employers who knowingly hired illegal aliens, to legalize the status of aliens who had continuously resided in the United States since January 1, 1978, to limit eligibility for adjustment of status, to expand the temporary worker program, and to reduce adjudication and asylum procedures and judicial review availability for undocumented aliens. The bill passed the Senate but died on the House floor. It failed mainly because of opposition by labor unions, farm groups, business groups, civil libertarians, and especially the congressional Hispanic caucus.

On May 23, 1985, Senator Simpson reintroduced the measure as the Immigration Reform and Control Bill of 1985.

Although the new bill contained the same major components as its predecessor, several important changes were incorporated, particularly in the areas of legalization of illegal aliens. After the Senate passed the bill on September 19, 1985, the bill was sent to the House, which considered it, amended it, and passed its version on October 9, 1986. The House version of the IRCA contained stronger provisions to prevent employment discrimination against United States citizens and lawful aliens, as well as broader farm labor provisions. The House-Senate conferees eventually adopted the House's version, with a few modifications. The compromise version mainly watered down the antidiscrimination protection, changed the cut-off date for legalization of illegal aliens to January 1, 1982, and included a compromise between the agricultural interest in labor and concern about exploitation of illegal alien workers. On November 6, 1986, President Ronald Reagan signed the bill into law.

Several years after the passage of the IRCA, the majority of respondents to a survey about implementing employer sanctions stated that they would comply with the act's employment verification system. Of this group saying they intended to comply, however, a majority had not actually done so. Concerning the antidiscrimination provisions, the majority of survey respondents believed that the act had already resulted in discrimination against workers with a foreign appearance. Some reports indicated that discrimination against Latinos and Asians had been particularly severe. In terms of providing amnesty to a certain class of illegal aliens, the Immigration and Naturalization Service originally estimated that between two and four million aliens would apply for amnesty. By May 4, 1988, however (the deadline for this amnesty), only 1.4 million applications had been filed.

See also Civil Rights Act of 1964; Illegal aliens; Immigration, legal and illegal; Immigration and Naturalization Service (INS); Immigration laws.

Immunity from prosecution

DEFINITION: Exemption from duty or penalty

SIGNIFICANCE: Immunity from prosecution encourages testimony that might not otherwise be given

The Fifth Amendment to the United States Constitution grants persons the right to refuse to incriminate themselves by testimony in a court of law. By the due process clause, the Fourteenth Amendment to the Constitution extends this same protection to individuals who are witnesses or defendants in state courts.

When it is difficult to find witnesses to a crime, and when the best witness is a person who participated in the crime, immunity from prosecution, or "use immunity," may be offered to induce that person to testify against others involved in the crime. The witness may then truthfully testify about the crime and escape prosecution for that crime or, in some cases, for other activities connected to the particular crime.

Once an offer of immunity is accepted, a witness may no longer claim self-incrimination during testimony. If a witness still refuses to testify after accepting immunity, the witness may be charged with contempt of court. A person may voluntarily waive the right against self-incrimination. In such a case, no immunity is offered, and the testimony given by the witness may be used in that proceeding, or in later proceedings, against that witness.

See also Contempt of court; Criminal procedure; Defamation; Due process of law; Immunity of public officials; Self-incrimination, privilege against.

Immunity of public officials

Definition: Exemption from duty or penalty, given under certain circumstances to public officials

Significance: Public officials may conduct proceedings without fear of reprisal for their official actions

Members of Congress are granted immunity as a protection from defamation suits, but only when they are acting in an official capacity. A slanderous statement made by a legislator outside official duties is as prosecutable as the same statement by a private individual.

Judges are protected from personal liability when acting in a judicial capacity but are not exempt from prosecution when acting as private individuals. Immunity also extends to judicial administrative officials when those officials are performing discretionary acts in honesty and good faith. Immunity for public officials never extends to matters of treason, felony, or breach of the peace.

The federal government and state governments are granted sovereign immunity, an exemption from suits brought by private individuals unless the government, through statute, consents to be sued. Under the Federal Tort Claims Act (1948), the federal government can be sued for torts committed by its employees or agents. This act nullifies sovereign immunity, except for the discretionary acts of public officials and certain other acts.

See also Immunity from prosecution; Self-incrimination, privilege against.

Impeachment

Definition: A constitutional provision for removing civil officers for abusing their power or violating their oath of office

Significance: Impeachment is an important check on governmental abuse of power; President Andrew Johnson was impeached, though not convicted, and President Richard Nixon resigned to avoid impeachment

Federal civil officers—including the U.S. president—can be impeached for abusing their power or violating their oath of office. Impeachment, like indictment, is a formal accusation of

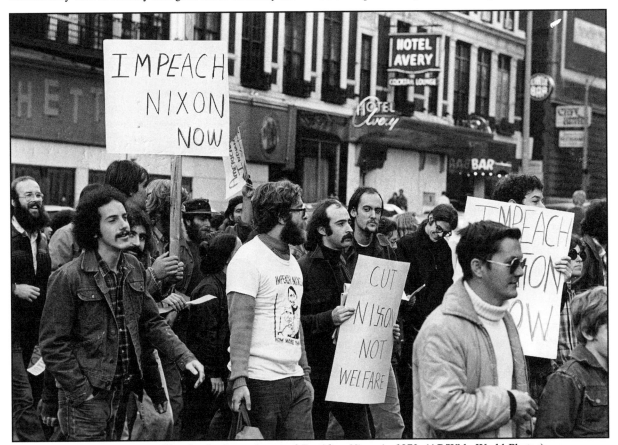

Demonstrators calling for the impeachment of President Nixon in 1973. (AP/Wide World Photos)

wrongdoing preliminary to trial and conviction. While no president has ever been impeached, convicted, and thereby removed from office, President Richard M. Nixon resigned when it became clear that impeachment and conviction were imminent. U.S. presidents, cabinet officers, and federal court judges may be impeached by majority vote in the House of Representatives for "treason, bribery, or other high crimes and misdemeanors." The Senate conducts the trial itself. To convict someone of impeachable offenses, two-thirds of the Senate must vote for conviction. The only U.S. president to be impeached was Andrew Johnson, and the Senate failed to convict him by a single vote.

Impeachment is used only for officials in the judicial and executive branches, since either house of Congress can simply expel any member for abuse of power by a simple majority vote. Military officers are not civil officers and so cannot be impeached, and cabinet officers have not been impeached because they may be fired by the president. If cabinet officers or lower administrators do something impeachable and are not fired, presumably their superiors (ultimately the president) could then be impeached. While the only constitutional penalty for impeachment and conviction is removal from office and debarment from holding further federal offices, any official so removed then becomes liable for indictment, trial, conviction, and punishment for the offenses that led to impeachment.

See also Nixon, Richard M.; Watergate scandal.

In forma pauperis petition
DEFINITION: A petition filed "in the character or manner of a pauper"
SIGNIFICANCE: The *in forma pauperis* petition extends the protection of the law to all persons
The Fourteenth Amendment to the U.S. Constitution guarantees all citizens equal protection under the law, regardless of nationality, age, sex, or financial circumstances.

A petition is filed to initiate an action. An *in forma pauperis* petition is a petition for which no filing fee is required because of the petitioner's poor financial circumstances. It permits those of truly limited financial means, or the indigent, to seek redress, without cost, for a wrong suffered. In some instances, not only are court fees and costs waived, but also the court appoints a lawyer to aid in the prosecution of the matter.

The *in forma pauperis* petition is not available to those who have the necessary financial means but consider court fees and costs burdensome or higher than they had expected.

See also Counsel, right to; Equal protection of the law; Litigation; Suit.

In loco parentis
DEFINITION: "In the place of a parent"; a temporary assumption of parental rights and responsibilities, such as care and control of a juvenile
SIGNIFICANCE: To the extent that families fail to perform the socializing role that traditionally has been expected of them, other institutions and individuals are allowed to fill that void

In loco parentis concerns both narrow legal questions about who possesses "parental" powers over individual minors and broader social questions about the extent to which children and juveniles should be controlled, socialized, and cared for by persons other than their parents. As regards the first question, *in loco parentis* has been taken to mean that an individual may assume temporary guardianship of a juvenile in the absence of supervision by the juvenile's natural or adopted parents. Boarding schools, for example, have assumed such status. Establishing a legal claim to a relationship of *loco parentis* at times can be a contentious, disputed matter resolvable only by courts. Broader questions about which persons and institutions should perform "parental" functions, particularly when families fail to do so, often are the hinge of public policy issues.

See also Family law; Gangs, youth; Juvenile delinquency; Juvenile Justice and Delinquency Prevention Act; Juvenile justice system; Majority, age of; School law; United Farm Workers (UFW).

In re cases. *See name of party*

Incapacitation
DEFINITION: An aim or rationale of punishment that seeks to control crime by rendering the criminal unable or less able to commit crime, such as by incarceration of the offender
SIGNIFICANCE: Incapacitation provides a justification for certain forms of punishment as well as a strategy for crime control
Incapacitation refers to the idea that certain forms of punishment are an effective means of reducing crime if they restrict the abilities and opportunities of criminals to commit crimes. For example, confining offenders in prison removes them from society and renders them unable to commit further crimes against the general public. Execution has the ultimate incapacitating effect. Even parole may help to incapacitate criminals by limiting their movement and thus restricting their opportunities for committing crimes.

The nineteenth century British utilitarian philosopher Jeremy Bentham discussed incapacitation in a treatment of the ends of punishment. Bentham regarded the principal end of punishment as control of conduct, and he used the term "disablement" to refer to the effect of punishment on the offender's "physical power." This was contrasted with reformation, which refers to the use of punishment to control conduct by influencing the offender's will, and with deterrence, whereby punishment sets an example and thus controls the conduct of people besides the offender. Contemporary discussions of the aims and effects of punishment follow Bentham, at least roughly, in distinguishing among reform or rehabilitation, incapacitation, and general deterrence by example or threat of punishment.

Incapacitation is an expected, or at least hoped for, effect of punishment. An incapacitative effect, however, does not occur in two types of situations. The first is the case in which the offender would not have committed any additional crimes even if he or she had not been punished. The second is the situation in which another individual takes the place of the incarcerated criminal, taking advantage of the opportunity that has opened. This often occurs in the case of criminal activity related to gangs, when the arrest and imprisonment of one member may not result in a decrease in crime. Other gang members or new recruits often fill the position vacated by the arrest of a gang member.

Studies have not established that a strict incapacitation approach to crime control is likely to lead to a significant reduction in the rate of crime. Skeptics point to periods during which crime rates have risen despite increased use of imprisonment. Studies have yielded mixed estimates of any incapacitative effect, with some research projecting a slight increase in crime (4 or 5 percent) with a reduction in prison use. Other research has projected a substantial decrease in crime if the prison population were increased. There is some evidence that the effect of incapacitation varies with types of criminal behavior. Some criminologists have recommended a policy of selective incapacitation—for example, of "career criminals" or violent criminals. Some states have enacted laws imposing life sentences on persons convicted three times of violent or serious crimes; these are sometimes colloquially called "three-time loser" laws or "three strikes and you're out" policies.

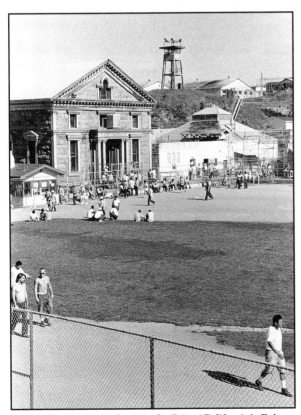

One of the purposes of prison facilities (California's Folsom Prison is pictured) is simply to incapacitate offenders—to keep them "off the street." (Ben Klaffke)

See also Bentham, Jeremy; Deterrence; Just deserts; Mandatory sentencing laws; Punishment; Rehabilitation.

Incest

DEFINITION: Sexual relations between individuals who are prohibited from marrying, either by custom or law

SIGNIFICANCE: The incest prohibition keeps the close male-female relationships formed inside families from being subjected to the disruptive effects of sexual pressures

In almost every society there are prohibitions against sexual relations between closely related individuals—the closer the biological relation, the stronger the taboo. Sexual intercourse between brother and sister, son and mother, and daughter and father are almost universally condemned. In most societies, relations between first cousins, nieces and uncles, and nephews and aunts are also generally prohibited. Why these restrictions have arisen can be broken into three distinct theories: biological, social, and traditional.

Biologically, incest involves a risk of reinforcing harmful recessive genes. Socially, it can have disastrous effects on family relations and family stability. The state has been able to show a "compelling interest" in prohibiting incest, so the right to privacy has not protected perpetrators of incest. Finally, traditional religions have a variety of restrictions that mirror the taboo against incest. The Old Testament book of Deuteronomy states, "A man is not to marry his father's wife," and "Cursed is the man who sleeps with his sister." Many such restrictions have been codified into law.

In the mid-1500's, England passed laws that protected boys from forced sodomy and girls under ten from rape. Most modern laws protecting children, however, stemmed from child labor laws such as the New York Child Labor Act of 1903. This act sought to prevent the neglect and abuse of children and was expanded nationally in 1974 with the Child Abuse Prevention and Treatment Act. This federal act called for the reporting of incidents of abuse. From its inception until the early 1980's, reported abuse rose by 150 percent. Of the reported abuse, only 15 percent was reported as sexual abuse, with much of this being incest. Historically it is clear that incest affects a small segment of any population, with physical abuse and neglect being more prevalent. Generally the laws that prohibit incest define the prohibited relationship in terms of what type of relationship would be legal in marriage.

Although these laws helped to codify sexual abuse and incest, the young age of many of the victims caused the right of the defendants to face their accusers to be modified. Two decisions that were important in defining the limits of adult perpetrator-child victim confrontations were the Supreme Court cases *Coy v. Iowa* (1988) and *Maryland v. Craig* (1990). The first found unconstitutional the practice of separating the perpetrator and victim by a screen; the second allowed for confrontation to occur with closed-circuit television. Twenty-six states allow this method to protect the young witness.

See also Child abuse; Child molestation; Family law; Rape and sex offenses.

Incorporation doctrine

DEFINITION: The extension of the Bill of Rights to protecting individuals against the states as well as against the federal government; incorporation has taken place gradually through individual court decisions

SIGNIFICANCE: Incorporation provides federal protection against state violations of most of the rights and guarantees of the Bill of Rights; it changed the federal-state relationship by increasing the power of the federal government

During debate over adoption of the U.S. Constitution, a major complaint was the lack of a bill of rights similar to existing state bills of rights. Continued agitation led supporters of the Constitution to agree that Congress should add a bill of rights during its first session. The First Congress proposed twelve amendments. Ten of the twelve were approved by the states and are known as the Bill of Rights.

The Bill of Rights limited the powers of the federal government, but the federal limitations did not apply to the state governments. The framers of the federal Bill of Rights thought it was unnecessary to provide protection against state governments, whose constitutions already provided the guarantees stated in the federal Bill of Rights. It was the Fourteenth Amendment (1868), one of the Civil War Amendments, that eventually became the basis for the incorporation of the states into the Bill of Rights.

The rights that were incorporated are in the first eight amendments, which protect the rights and privileges associated with the traditional liberties and freedoms of the people. These rights include freedom of speech, press, petition, and religion as well as the procedural rights guaranteed by the Fifth through Eighth Amendments, including indictment by a grand jury in criminal cases, protection against double jeopardy and self-incrimination, and prohibitions against depriving persons of life, liberty, or property without "due process of law."

Not until the decade of the 1830's were cases involving the Bill of Rights appealed to the Supreme Court. Before then, it was feared that Federalist judges would rule unfavorably. In 1833 the Court handed down a decision involving the Bill of Rights in *Barron v. Baltimore*. The *Barron v. Baltimore* case arose from economic injuries suffered by wharf owners John Barron and John Craig from street improvements that caused silting around the wharf. In 1822 Barron sued the city of Baltimore, claiming that the city had taken private property for public use without just compensation. Baltimore countered that under state law the city was not liable for incidental damage resulting from needed public improvements and that the compensation clause of the Fifth Amendment of the U.S. Constitution did not apply to the states.

When the case was appealed to the U.S. Supreme Court, it was dismissed for lack of jurisdiction. The Court unanimously stated that the compensation clause of the Fifth Amendment did not apply to the states. Later courts extended the *Barron* ruling to the rest of the Bill of Rights and prevented the federal government from interfering with state violations of civil rights. The *Barron* opinion was accepted without question until the Civil War Amendments (the Thirteenth, Fourteenth, and Fifteenth Amendments) were added to the Constitution between 1865 and 1870.

Civil War Amendments. The Thirteenth and Fifteenth Amendments are concerned with emancipation of the slaves and voting rights, respectively. The Fourteenth Amendment states:

> All persons born or naturalized in the United States, and subject to the jurisdiction thereof, are citizens of the United States and of the State wherein they reside. No State shall make or enforce any law which shall abridge the privileges or immunities of citizens of the United States; nor shall any State deprive any person of life, liberty, or property, without due process of law; nor deny to any person within its jurisdiction the equal protection of the laws.

The privileges and immunities clause, the due process clause, and the equal protection clause form the basis of incorporation.

The Supreme Court first gave attention to defining the privileges and immunities clause of the Fourteenth Amendment in the *Slaughterhouse Cases* in 1873. The cases developed during Reconstruction. The Louisiana legislature passed a law giving the Crescent City Landing and Slaughter House Company a monopoly of the slaughter and sale of livestock in New Orleans and the three surrounding parishes. The legislature based the measure on police powers that permitted states to restrict individual liberties and property rights in order to promote public health, safety, and welfare.

A group of about four hundred small, independent, local butchers obtained an injunction blocking the monopoly. The company in return got injunctions barring the local butchers from harassing the company and barring livestock dealers from building new stockyards. When the Louisiana Supreme Court upheld the law and the injunctions against the butchers and stockyard owners, the butchers appealed to the federal courts, claiming that the company monopoly violated the Thirteenth and Fourteenth Amendments to the U.S. Constitution. The federal circuit court in New Orleans ruled in this first judicial interpretation of the Fourteenth Amendment that the monopoly did violate the rights guaranteed in the Fourteenth Amendment.

On appeal, a sharply divided U.S. Supreme Court in a 5-4 decision upheld the Louisiana law and limited the privileges and immunities of the Fourteenth Amendment. The decision stated that the amendment was intended to protect the rights of the new freedmen and that the rights protected by the amendment were only those deriving from United States, not state, citizenship. Those rights included travel to and from the capital and on the high seas, access to navigable rivers and ports of the United States, *habeas corpus*, assembly, and the right to petition the government for redress of grievances, and the protection of the government abroad and on the high seas. The decision rejected the interpretation that all rights necessary to freedom were protected by the privileges and immunities clause of the Fourteenth Amendment.

Incorporation. In the post-Civil War period, the Supreme Court gave primary importance to the protection of property rights. In *Burlington & Quincy Railroad Co. v. Chicago* (1897), the Court incorporated the property rights of the Fifth Amendment, stating that the due process clause of the Fourteenth Amendment protected Fifth Amendment property rights against state actions.

The first steps in incorporating the traditional liberties included in the federal Bill of Rights occurred in the 1920's; the process increased during the 1930's. In 1925 the Court held in *Gitlow v. New York* that "[f]or present purposes we may and do assume that freedom of speech and of the press—which are protected by the First Amendment from abridgement by Congress—are among the fundamental personal rights and 'liberties' protected by the due process clause of the Fourteenth Amendment from impairment by the States." The Court used the due process clause (rather than the privileges and immunities clause) of the Fourteenth Amendment for incorporation. The Court continued to use the due process clause in the cases that followed.

During the 1930's the Court began the "modernization" of the Bill of Rights by incorporating most of the guarantees included in the Bill of Rights. Two cases in 1931, *Near v. Minnesota* and *Stromberg v. California*, applied the First Amendment rights of freedom of speech and press to the states. In succeeding cases, additional Bill of Rights guarantees were incorporated. The Sixth Amendment right to council in capital cases was added to incorporated rights by *Powell v. Alabama* in 1932, and freedom of assembly received federal protection in *DeJonge v. Oregon* in 1937.

Not until *Palko v. Connecticut* in 1937 did the Court address the relationship between the due process clause and the privileges and immunities clause of the Fourteenth Amendment. In its decision the Court extended the prohibition of double jeopardy (found in the Fifth Amendment) to the states, but it stated that not all the guarantees in the Bill of Rights apply to the states. The procedural rights in the Bill of Rights limit the federal government but not the states. Fundamental rights, however—freedom of speech and press, the free exercise of religion, peaceable assembly, and benefit of council—are protected from state encroachment by the due process clause of the Fourteenth Amendment. In this case the Court held that the rights in the Bill of Rights are privileges and immunities but that only some of them are so important that they cannot be violated by either the federal government or the states. The importance of each right would be decided on a case-by-case basis.

New attitudes and more liberal judges resulted in greater incorporation during the administration of Franklin D. Roosevelt. A few of the new justices, particularly Hugo Black, argued that the Fourteenth Amendment privileges and immunities clause limited both the federal and state governments. Although this opinion was not accepted by the majority, the Court did incorporate more of the Bill of Rights guarantees using the due process clause.

In the 1950's federalism was given less consideration and incorporation progressed rapidly. The rights of individuals, especially minorities, received increasing protection. By the end of the 1960's most of the Bill of Rights applied to the states as well as to the federal government. The federal-state relationship was changed significantly by the doctrine of incorporation. The federal government had attained the power to prevent state violation of the rights and guarantees of the Bill of Rights. One right not incorporated was the Second Amendment right to keep and bear arms. The Court held that the phrase "[a] well regulated Militia, being necessary to the security of a free state" qualifies the right and that regulation under state police powers is constitutional. Other rights not incorporated are the Third Amendment right that prohibits the quartering of troops in private homes, the Fifth Amendment right to a grand jury indictment, the Sixth Amendment right of twelve jurors in a criminal trial, and the Seventh Amendment right of a civil jury. The Court has held that state procedures are adequate to protect the values inherent in those Bill of Rights guarantees. —*Robert D. Talbott*

See also *Barron v. Baltimore*; Bill of Rights, U.S.; Black, Hugo L.; Civil War Amendments; Constitutional interpretation; *Gitlow v. New York*; Judicial review; *Palko v. Connecticut*; *Slaughterhouse Cases*; Supreme Court of the United States.

BIBLIOGRAPHY

Ellen Alderman and Caroline Kennedy, *In Our Defense: The Bill of Rights in Action* (New York: Avon Books, 1991), is a readable and popular explanation of the extension of the Bill of Rights. Lucius J. Barker and Twiley W. Barker, Jr., *Civil Liberties and the Constitution: Cases and Commentaries* (4th ed. Englewood Cliffs, N.J.: Prentice-Hall, 1982), discusses issues in civil liberties as determined by court cases and is written for the general reader. Raoul Berger, *Government by Judiciary: The Transformation of the Fourteenth Amendment* (Cambridge, Mass.: Harvard University Press, 1977), presents the extension of the Fourteenth Amendment by the Supreme Court and discusses Hugo Black's minority opinion in *Adamson v. California*, the most famous and cogent argument for total incorporation of the Bill of Rights. Milton R. Konvitz, ed., *Bill of Rights Reader: Leading Constitutional Cases* (5th rev. ed. Ithaca, N.Y.: Cornell University Press, 1973), is a revision of a pioneering work on civil rights as determined by court cases; heavy emphasis is on the 1960's and early 1970's, the period of rapid incorporation.

Indecent exposure

DEFINITION: Deliberate display of one's genitals in public or in other inappropriate circumstances

SIGNIFICANCE: Indecent exposure is one of the primary nonviolent sex crimes

The Model Penal Code suggests three elements necessary to a charge of indecent exposure: the knowing exposure of a suspect's genitals, the intention of sexual arousal or gratification of a person other than the suspect's spouse, and the performance of the act under circumstances that are likely to cause affront or alarm. Most states adopt antiexposure laws based on this or a similar definition.

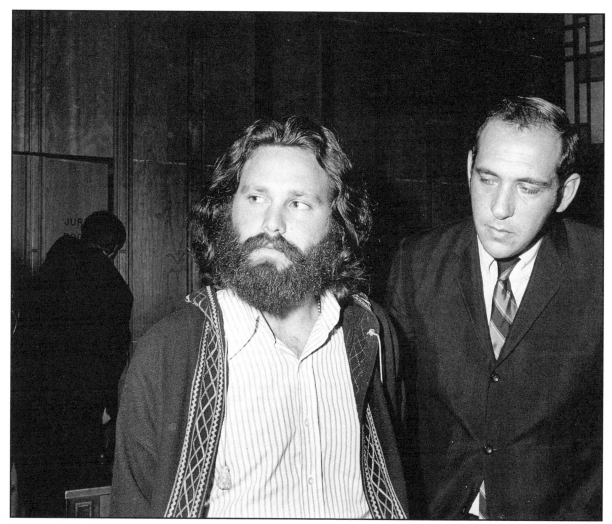

Rock singer Jim Morrison of the Doors was convicted of indecent exposure in 1970 because of an incident at a concert in Miami; charges were dropped on appeal. (AP/Wide World Photos)

In most states, a first offense of indecent exposure is ordinarily classified as a misdemeanor unless it occurs in the presence of a child, in which case the crime is usually classified as a felony. Subsequent offenses are also usually classified as felonies. Whereas laws against private sex crimes between consenting adults—such as fornication, adultery, and sodomy—are often not enforced, the public nature of indecent exposure usually results in enforcement.

See also Disorderly conduct; Felony; Misdemeanor; Model Penal Code; Moral turpitude; Public order offenses; Rape and sex offenses.

Indictment

DEFINITION: A formal written accusation made by a grand jury charging someone with a crime

SIGNIFICANCE: The indictment process is the first step in most criminal prosecutions

A bill of indictment is usually drafted by a prosecuting attorney and submitted to a grand jury along with witnesses and other supporting evidence. The people who serve on the grand jury convene to evaluate the prosecutor's evidence; if a majority finds that evidence warrants a trial, the jury then releases a bill of particulars informing the accused of the offense charged.

Grand juries can also conduct their own investigations and make accusations or "presentments" without a bill of indictment. Similarly, prosecutors in some states can make accusations without grand jury review. These non-grand jury charges, which are called "informations," were challenged in the case of *Hurtado v. California* (1884). Because the Fifth Amendment requires grand jury indictment for federal crimes, Hurtado argued, the Fourteenth Amendment's due process clause required states to do the same. The Supreme Court, however, upheld the process of information, finding that states may use various methods of initiating criminal prosecutions, provided that such methods are fair. The result is that the right to grand jury indictment applies only to federal crimes.

See also Arraignment; Arrest; Bill of particulars; Bill of Rights, U.S.; Criminal procedure; Due process of law; Grand jury; *Hurtado v. California*; Information; Prosecutor, public.

Information

DEFINITION: A prosecutor's written accusation of a crime in order to initiate a trial

SIGNIFICANCE: Serving the same purpose as an indictment by a grand jury, an information informs a defendant of criminal charges so that the defendant may prepare a defense

The Fifth Amendment guarantee of a grand jury indictment before a criminal trial is one of the few provisions of the Bill of Rights which has never been made applicable to the states. In *Hurtado v. California* (1884), the Supreme Court allowed the information alternative, with the rationale that it did not violate the principles of fairness required by the due process clause of the Fourteenth Amendment. The federal government, of course, must follow the common-law practice of initiating all criminal trials by indictment.

Although usually less cumbersome than the grand jury process, an information requires a preliminary hearing in which the defendant may appear with counsel, cross-examine witnesses, and see the prosecution's evidence. In 1993, some twenty states began all criminal trials by means of information, while the majority of the others used the procedure except in major felony cases.

See also Criminal procedure; Due process of law; Grand jury; *Hurtado v. California*; Incorporation doctrine; Indictment; *Palko v. Connecticut*.

Injunction

DEFINITION: A court order requiring a party to an action (or others acting for the party) to do something or to refrain from doing something

SIGNIFICANCE: Injunctions are used to provide equitable relief in cases where there is otherwise "no adequate relief at law"; they have played a major role in a number of important civil suits involving civil rights and business law litigation

A well-known and important distinction is between "preliminary injunctions," which are interim orders that apply while the litigation is in progress, and "permanent injunctions," which are final remedies in the case. In theory, preliminary injunctions should be available only when a party to an action is in imminent danger of being "irreparably injured" prior to the completion of the trial. All such injunctions are dissolved or replaced by a permanent injunction at the end of trial. A permanent injunction is available only when there is "inadequate remedy" at law: that is, when monetary award alone would be insufficient relief for the plaintiff.

Another common but somewhat less useful distinction is that between "affirmative" (or "positive") and "negative" injunctions. It is said that courts find it easier to issue negative injunctions (such as an order to a musician not to play for an orchestra in violation of a contract with another orchestra) than to issue an affirmative injunction, such as that the musician must play for an orchestra in performance of a contract with the orchestra.

The above seemingly simple description belies the very important role that the injunction plays in the American judicial system. Although an injunction is nominally directed only to a "party," the prominence of civil lawsuits to which governments are parties and the pervasive use of the class action device have resulted in some of the most controversial decisions in recent years involving injunctive relief. Examples include school desegregation, busing, and affirmative action cases, as well as lesser known but equally important business and economic litigation in such areas as antitrust, patent infringement, and international trade.

Finally, because of the historical origins of the injunction in the English "courts of equity," the Seventh Amendment to the U.S. Constitution's guarantee of a jury trial in certain types of civil cases does not apply to an action seeking injunctive relief. This exception, however, increasingly is being narrowly construed by the U.S. Supreme Court.

See also Affirmative action; Antitrust law; Busing; Civil procedure; Civil Rights movement; Class action; Contempt of court; Litigation.

Insanity defense

DEFINITION: Laws that allow the perpetrator of a crime to argue that because of some form of mental incapacitation, he or she is not "guilty" in the moral or legal sense

SIGNIFICANCE: The insanity plea is an outgrowth of the U.S. legal system's commitment to avoiding punishment of the innocent

In the United States there are several legal defenses that can be used by individuals who have committed a crime but who might still be considered blameless. The "insanity defense" is one of these. When it is used, the judge or jury must determine not whether the person committed the act but what the person's mental state or motive was at the time the act was committed. There are several versions of the insanity defense. The most common version, known as the M'Naghten rule, requires that the defendant must not have been able to distinguish between right and wrong at the time of the act. Because it relies solely on a basic cognitive capacity and ignores emotion or motivation, it is the strictest test.

The broadest version is the Durham rule, which specifies that the criminal act must have been committed as a result of a mental defect or disorder. This version allows any psychological disorder to be used in defense; thus, a defendant who is diagnosed, say, as a pyromaniac (someone who compulsively sets fires) may be considered "not guilty" because the crime was a symptom of the disorder. Because this rule is so broad and frequently elicits contradictory statements from expert witnesses, this version of the insanity defense has on occasion been abused. For this reason it is very uncommon.

The third major version of the insanity defense is the Brawner rule or the American Law Institute (ALI) rule. This rule falls between the M'Naghten rule and the Durham rule in terms of strictness. It allows an insanity defense for all cases that would fit under the M'Naghten rule, but also for individuals who could make the distinction between right and wrong but who were unable to control their behavior as a result of a mental disorder or defect. This rule could be used, for example, by a schizophrenic who heard voices telling him that he needed to commit a crime, even if he had the cognitive capacity to understand that the crime was illegal. The Brawner/ALI rule specifically states that the defense cannot be used by individuals who have a mental disorder that is defined solely or primarily by antisocial behavior; thus it excludes psychopaths, sociopaths, and people with compulsions (such as pedophiles and kleptomaniacs).

Despite popular belief, the insanity defense is very infrequently used, and when it is, the case is much less likely to result in acquittal than other cases—especially if the decision is being made by a jury.

See also Competency to stand trial; Criminal intent; Criminal procedure; Insanity Defense Reform Act; Malice; *Mens rea*; Psychopath and sociopath.

Insanity Defense Reform Act

DATE: Enacted 1984
SIGNIFICANCE: This act was the first federal law to establish a uniform definition of criminal insanity and require mandatory incarceration of the criminally insane; it significantly narrowed the opportunities for mounting a successful insanity defense

After the 1982 acquittal of John Hinckley, an allegedly insane defendant who had tried to assassinate President Ronald Reagan, public outcry spurred the Congress to place new restric-

The acquittal of John Hinckley, who had attempted to assassinate President Reagan in 1981, prompted the Insanity Defense Reform Act. (AP/Wide World Photos)

tions on the use of the insanity defense. Previously, insanity as a defense generally was defined in federal courts as lacking the capacity to understand the criminality of one's conduct (the "cognitive" test), or lacking the ability to conform one's behavior to the requirements of law (the "volitional" test). The Insanity Defense Reform Act limits the definition of insanity to the cognitive test. It also requires that the defendant prove insanity with "clear and convincing evidence."

Prior to the act, no uniform requirements had been established for the disposition of defendants found to be criminally insane. The act requires that all such defendants be committed to a mental hospital and makes them ineligible for release until after they can demonstrate that they pose no substantial risk to others.

See also Burden of proof; Competency to stand trial; Insanity defense; Psychopath and sociopath.

Insider trading

DEFINITION: The purchase or sale of a security by persons who have access to information which is not available to those with whom they deal or to traders generally
SIGNIFICANCE: Under the Securities Exchange Act, corporate "insiders" are discouraged from taking advantage of their access to information by engaging in short-term trading in the corporation's securities

Section 10 of the 1934 Securities Exchange Act makes it unlawful for any person to employ any device, scheme, or artifice to defraud or to engage in any act, practice, or course of business which operates as a fraud or deceit upon any person. This law was a response to a variety of fraudulent activities in the 1920's that manipulated stock prices and misled naïve investors. For example, an investment pool would "bid up" the price of a selected stock, often by trading the stock back and forth among members of the pool, and then sell to investors lured by the stock's upward movement. The spreading of false rumors was another popular tactic.

Early applications of the rules focused on persons who owned, either directly or indirectly, more than 10 percent of a registered stock. The law requires these owners to file a report with the Securities and Exchange Commission (SEC) at the time they acquire that status and at the end of any month in which they acquire or dispose of any equity securities of that company. To prevent unfair use of inside information, the law permits the company, or a security holder suing on its behalf, to recover any profit realized by the "insider" from any purchase or sale of any security of the company within a period of less than six months.

Inside Information. Inside information is not even mentioned in the 1934 act, let alone defined by the law, but over the years, through a series of cases it has been defined as material information not yet made public. Illegal insider trading occurs if the information was obtained wrongfully (as by theft or bribery) or if a person has a fiduciary responsibility to keep the information confidential. Further, investors are not allowed to trade on the basis of information that they know or

Michael Milken (right), "junk-bond" multimillionaire, was charged with insider trading in 1988 but managed to avoid conviction. He served twenty-two months in prison on related charges. (AP/Wide World Photos)

have reason to know was obtained wrongfully. The Securities and Exchange Commission is unlikely to press charges if it is convinced that a leak of confidential information was inadvertent—for example, a conversation overhead on an airplane. Many stock purchases and sales are made on the basis of tips and rumors from unknown sources and of questionable accuracy. The boundaries of insider trading represent a gray area that the courts are still shaping.

Three Cases. The courts have consistently ruled that the officers and directors of a company cannot profit from buying or selling stock in their own firm prior to the public announcement of important corporate news. In a series of administrative decisions and proceedings, beginning in 1961, the Securities and Exchange Commission has broadened the application of rule 10(b)-5 (the relevant part of Section 10 of the Securities Exchange Act) as a general prohibition against trading in "inside information" in anonymous stock exchange transactions as well as in face-to-face dealings. The three most significant decisions were *Cady, Roberts & Co.* (1961), *S.E.C. v. Texas Gulf Sulphur* (1968), and *Investor's Management Co.* (1971).

In *Cady, Roberts & Co.*, a partner in a brokerage firm received a message from a director of Curtiss-Wright that the board of directors had just voted to cut the dividend. He immediately placed orders to sell the stock of some of his customers, and the sales were made before the news of the dividend cut was generally disseminated. In *Texas Gulf Sulphur*, officers and employees of the company made substantial purchases of the company's stock after learning that exploratory drilling on one of the company's properties showed promise of an extraordinary ore discovery. In *Investor's Management Co.*, an aircraft manufacturer disclosed to its principal underwriter that its earnings for the current year would be substantially less than previously forecast. The information was passed on to the underwriter's sales force, which allowed major institutional clients to have access to it.

In all the above cases, the persons who effected the transactions were held in violation of rule 10(b)-5. *Cady, Roberts* held that the law extends beyond officers, directors, and major stockholders to anyone who receives information from a corporate source. *Texas Gulf Sulphur* established that a person who passes on inside information to another person who effects a transaction is as culpable as the person who utilizes it for his or her own account, and *Investor's Management* established the liability of the indirect "tipper," no matter how many links there are in the chain of information.

Changes in the 1980's. In the past, many cases were settled by the accused agreeing to give back the disputed profits rather than admitting guilt. Since August, 1984, the Securities and Exchange Commission has been empowered to seek not only a return of profits but also a penalty equal to three times the profit. The Securities and Exchange Commission has also become more aggressive in seeking prison terms, not only for securities violations but also for such related crimes as mail or wire fraud, obstructing justice, and income tax evasion.

One of the most publicized insider trading scandals erupted in the 1980's when the Securities and Exchange Commission charged Dennis Levine and Ivan Boesky with a wide variety of insider trades. The common denominator in most of their trades involved privileged information about potential corporate mergers. Levine and Boesky obtained tips from individuals who worked for the investment banking firms which were putting the mergers together. The indictment and conviction of these two insider traders have made most market participants very sensitive to illegal insider trading. The Securities and Exchange Commission tries to maintain a level playing field on which all traders have access to the same information. The commission worries that insider trading could undermine the integrity of financial markets and drive away honest players. —*Patricia C. Matthews*

See also Banking law; Computer crime; Fraud; Securities and Exchange Commission (SEC); White-collar crime.

BIBLIOGRAPHY

Overviews of insider trading include Harold F. Lusk, C. Hewitt, J. Donnel, and A. Barnes, *Business Law and the Regulatory Environment* (5th ed. Homewood, Ill.: Richard D. Irwin, 1982); Gary Smith, *Investments* (Glenview, Ill.: Scott Foresman, Little, Brown, 1989); and Glen G. Munn, F. L. Garcia, and Charles J. Woelfel, *Encyclopedia of Banking and Finance* (9th ed. Rolling Meadows, Ill.: Banker's Publishers, 1991).

Insurance law

DEFINITION: Legislation designed to regulate various aspects of the insurance industry, including applications of contract law

SIGNIFICANCE: The actions of insurance companies are governed by a vast array of regulations, mostly state regulations

The insurance industry is one of the most regulated businesses in the United States. Historically, government regulation of insurance started in Europe more than a century ago. The reason for regulation was that insurance policies are contracts, and their wording is complicated and often must be interpreted by the courts. The main concern of a government is to protect its people, so ambiguous language in contracts is generally interpreted against the maker of the contract (insurance companies) and in favor of the policyholder (the public).

The legality of an insurance policy is based on four contract validity requirements in contract law. There must be an offer and acceptance; the one who purchases the policy makes the offer. The payment made is another requirement, called consideration. When the insurance company approves the application and issues the policy, this is known as acceptance. Other elements of a contract are that it must have a legal purpose and be signed by competent parties. The policy will not cover intentional losses or unlawful activities. Incompetent people in the eyes of the law may be minors and mentally incapacitated adults.

The U.S. Supreme Court decided in *Paul v. Virginia* (1869) that insurance was not subject to interstate commerce laws. Insurance was regulated by the states until 1944 when, in *South-Eastern Underwriters Association v. United States*, the Supreme Court decided that the insurance business was commerce and was therefore subject to federal control. This caused such an uproar in the insurance industry that the following year Congress passed the McCarran-Ferguson Act, which again gave the states the right to regulate and tax the insurance industry.

Insurance Regulators. State regulations have three main sources, legislative, judicial, and administrative. State legislatures pass laws pertaining to insurance such as insurance tax laws and licensing requirements for companies and agents. Judicial regulations involve court decisions when lawsuits against insurance companies are involved. Often policy wording has to be interpreted by the courts for claims to be settled. The administrative branch is usually the state insurance department, which is headed by the state insurance commissioner, often a political appointment by the governor. This department has broad powers including licensing of agents and companies, keeping financial records of the companies to guard against insolvency, and approving policy provisions and premium rates.

One other source of insurance regulation is the insurance companies themselves. Many agents' associations set standards of conduct for the agents and recommend measures for companies to improve their standing in the community. Such self-regulation is quite effective in attaining and maintaining a professional level of competence among personnel in the insurance industry.

Unique Contract. Insurance law has a special nature in contract law because of certain notable features. For example, most contracts are bilateral, meaning that each party exchanges promises for performance in the future. Insurance policies are unilateral agreements, meaning that an act is exchanged for a promise: The insurance buyer exchanges the act of purchasing the policy for the insurance company's promise to perform (pay claims) in the future.

Also, the policy is an "aleatory" contract, meaning that it depends on an uncertain event. A claim for loss may or may not occur. The value given by each party is not equal. If there is never a loss, the only value received is the peace of mind of having the insurance (and, in some cases, the satisfaction of a legal requirement to have insurance). On the other hand, a large loss will result in a claim payment of many times the value given (premium paid) by the policyholder. Another feature unique to insurance law is that the contract is one of "adhesion," meaning that one party (the insurance company) writes the entire contract (the policy), and the other party (policyholder) simply adheres to it. Since the policy is written by one party, if there is a claim involving an ambiguity, the courts usually rule in favor of the policyholder, since that party did not write the contract.

One other feature that makes insurance an unusual type of contract is that most liability and property insurance policies are written to cover an indemnity payment. This means that the amount paid on a claim is sufficient to reimburse the policyholder for an actual loss but does not exceed the loss. There should be no profit as such; the policyholder should only be made "whole" again in a monetary sense.

Various categories of insurance, such as fire, auto, marine, and life, have their own special aspects. One predominant rule is that of insurable interest. For example, if one insures one's auto or home and then sells it to another party, the insurance does not transfer to the new owner without the insurance company's consent. A beneficiary of a person's life insurance policy must have an insurable interest in the person's life, as a dependent spouse or a bank where the person has a loan would have.

Claims. Those elements of contract law that are distinctive to insurance law play important roles in court cases. Property and casualty insurance companies routinely plan on allocating about 60 percent of their premium dollars to paying claims.

One of the large expenses associated with claim payments is attorney fees to defend lawsuits. Many of the larger insurance companies have their own staff of salaried attorneys because of the large percentage of legal resources devoted to litigation. Legal costs have a strong impact on insurance costs. Premiums are increased periodically to meet these and other loss-related expenses such as the increasing cost of hospital and medical care for injured claimants and the increasing costs of automobile parts and building supplies.

Insurance companies are routinely sued for large amounts because they are perceived by the public as having "deep pockets," or unlimited assets to pay claims. Many juries allow high awards for this reason. A number of lawyers actively solicit lawsuits against insurance companies from injured parties. There are also small but significant numbers of people who file fraudulent claims, and there are unscrupulous lawyers quite willing to promote such claims.   —*William M. Apple*

See also Contract law; Fraud; Litigation; Medical and health law; Workers' compensation.

BIBLIOGRAPHY

Irving Pfeffer and David R. Klock, *Perspectives on Insurance* (Englewood Cliffs, N.J.: Prentice-Hall, 1974), is a valuable source. Two multivolume encyclopedia sources are John Appleman (revised by Jean Appleman), *Insurance Law and Practice, with Forms* (St. Paul, Minn.: West, 1941-), and Ronald A. Anderson, *Cyclopedia of Insurance Law* (2d ed. Rochester, N.Y.: Lawyers Co-operative, 1984). Two one-volume references are recommended: Robert E. Keeton, *Insurance Law* (St. Paul, Minn.: West, 1971), particularly chapter 8, which discusses insurance institutions and the reach of insurance regulation; and Edwin W. Patterson, *Essentials of Insurance Law* (New York: McGraw-Hill, 1957), which also gives excellent coverage of governmental control of the insurance business. William R. Vance, *Handbook of the Law of Insurance* (2d ed. St. Paul, Minn.: West, 1930), is a law school classic.

Intellectual property. *See* Copyrights, patents, and trademarks

Internal Revenue Service (IRS)

DATE: Established July 1, 1862
SIGNIFICANCE: The Internal Revenue Service, the division of the U.S. Department of the Treasury responsible for collect-

ing federal taxes, is probably the best-known and most frequently maligned federal agency

The Internal Revenue Service (IRS) is a component of the United States Department of the Treasury. The IRS is headed by the commissioner of internal revenue, who is appointed by the president with the approval of the U.S. Senate. The commissioner's office, which is in the IRS national office, is located in Washington, D.C. Other major officers in the organization include a deputy commissioner, chief counsel, and eight assistant commissioners. Each of the eight assistant commissioners oversees one of the following functional areas: taxpayer service and return processing, compliance, inspection, administration, planning and research, technical, economic stabilization, and employee plans and exempt organizations. Most IRS employees (other than the top officers) are civil service workers.

For many years the nation was subdivided into seven IRS regions, each headed by a regional commissioner. That number was decreased to four regions on October 1, 1995. Each region has at least one service center that performs the data processing function for tax returns submitted from the region. The regions are further subdivided into districts, each headed by a district director. The district offices are typically the initial point of contact between the organization and taxpayers. For many years there were sixty-three districts, but as a cost-saving measure the IRS announced the reduction of the number of districts to thirty-three by October, 1996.

History of the Agency. Prior to the Civil War, the United States financed governmental operations primarily by means of tariffs. The 1861 outbreak of the Civil War brought national economic strains and pressure for Congress to implement other means of obtaining revenues—in particular an internal source of tax revenues. The income tax was the primary form in which these internal sources of revenue were to be obtained. The IRS, then called the Internal Revenue Bureau, came into being on July 1, 1862. The office of the commissioner of internal revenue was established in the Treasury Department by this law, and the president was authorized to divide the country into "convenient collection districts." The first commissioner, George S. Boutwell of Massachusetts, was appointed by President Abraham Lincoln on July 17, 1862. In addition to taxing income, the 1862 law imposed stamp taxes which had to be paid to negotiate certain types of documents such as checks, notes, bonds, and stock certificates.

Although sometimes controversial, the 1862 tax law was declared constitutional in the case of *Springer v. United States* (1881). The decision emphasized that Congress never intended the tax to be a direct tax of the type prohibited by the Constitution. The Supreme Court decision was essentially a moot point at the time, however, because the income tax had expired in 1871. The stamp tax lasted until 1883. The abolishing of these laws left the agency time to deal with other types of federal revenues. Among the most dangerous of the duties faced by revenue agents was the collecting of taxes on illicit distilleries, many of which were located in rural southern

locales. Many agents ("revenuers") were killed by owners of illegal stills, who were commonly known as "moonshiners." Because of duplicity by local law enforcement agents, an 1877 law was passed to protect revenue agents from arrest by local authorities for acts taken in the discharge of their responsibility to collect taxes. The Supreme Court upheld this legislation in the 1879 case of *Tennessee v. Davis*. In that case, Deputy Collector of Internal Revenue James Davis was indicted for murder after killing a moonshiner who had shot at Davis.

The need for reputable legal practitioners was recognized as early as 1884. In that year, Congress authorized the secretary of the treasury to prescribe rules for recognition of tax attorneys and agents and to disbar or suspend incompetent or disreputable practitioners.

Another income tax law was passed in 1894, leading to a temporary increase in the number of bureau personnel. That legislation was declared unconstitutional in the case of *Pollock v. Farmers' Loan & Trust Co.* (1895). Fourteen years later, a 1909 act levied an income tax on corporate income, and at about the same time Congress sent a constitutional amendment to the states that would legitimize an income tax. On February 25, 1913, the necessary number of states (three-fourths) had adopted what became the Sixteenth Amendment to the U.S. Constitution. The law taxing the income of individuals took effect March 1, 1913. The first tax returns were due a year later. Initially, in 1914, only about 350,000 tax returns were filed. By 1945, however, that number had increased to more than fifty million returns as the financial strains of World War II brought the income tax to the general population.

In its first year, the Internal Revenue Bureau collected just over $41 million. The total annual collections did not exceed $1 billion until the needs of World War I led to increased taxes and collections of $3.7 billion in 1918. Collections in 1945 amounted to more than $43 billion, a number not to be exceeded until 1951. The $100 billion level was not reached until 1963. The trillion dollar level was reached in 1989.

The Internal Revenue Bureau had 4,461 employees in 1866. That number had declined to 3,405 by 1881. The number remained relatively stable until 1918, when personnel increased to 9,597. A year later, the agency had 14,055 employees. World War II brought a greater need for revenue personnel, and the number of employees jumped to 59,693 in 1946—nearly four times the number of workers a decade earlier. By 1991, the IRS had more than 117,000 employees. As of 1995, the IRS staff averaged between 110,000 and 120,000 people throughout the year, making it one of the largest federal agencies.

The increase in the number of personnel in 1919 was only partially attributable to income tax needs. In addition, the agency was made responsible for the enforcement of the Volstead Act—the national experiment known as Prohibition. Most of the increase in personnel was in the national office. The most famed of Prohibition-era agents, Elliot Ness, joined the bureau in 1926. In 1927, Ness and the other agents of the Prohibition Unit were transferred out of the Bureau of Internal

Revenue and into the Treasury Department's new Prohibition Bureau. This was not, however, the end of the agency's involvement with Prohibition. In May, 1927, the Supreme Court reversed a lower court's decision and ruled that profits from crime were taxable. It was this concept which led the agency to its greatest coup—the imprisonment of gangster Al Capone. What Elliot Ness and his Prohibition agents could not accomplish was achieved by revenue agents who arrested Capone for income tax evasion in 1931. Conviction followed later in the year. Interestingly, Capone could have escaped indictment by agreeing to pay about $4,000, but he steadfastly refused to give in to the bureau's demands. Thus, the most noted criminal of the twentieth century was able to avoid all legal authorities except the Bureau of Internal Revenue.

In 1952, the Bureau of Internal Revenue was reorganized. Many functions were decentralized to new district offices, which replaced the former system of collectors' offices. At the same time, the name was changed to the Internal Revenue Service. By the early 1960's, the demands of processing millions of tax returns led to the implementation of a series of centralized processing facilities.

Functions and Role of the IRS. The primary function of the IRS is to enforce the nation's tax laws, including those laws dealing with corporate and individual income taxes, estate and gift taxes, Federal Insurance Contributions Act (Social Security) taxes, federal unemployment taxes, and excise taxes. Until 1972, the IRS also administered alcohol and tobacco tax laws, but that responsibility was transferred to the Bureau of Alcohol, Tobacco, and Firearms (ATF), another division of the Treasury Department.

In general, it can be said that the IRS is responsible for enforcing the requirements of the *Internal Revenue Code* (officially known as Title 26 of the Code of Federal Regulations). The IRS is given broad authority to issue various pronouncements to assist in administering the code. Through its pronouncements, the agency creates and implements laws as well as enforces them. These pronouncements include IRS Regulations, Revenue Rulings, Letter Rulings, and Revenue Procedures. Judicial precedents are also enforced by the IRS. The official IRS Regulations are the most comprehensive and authoritative interpretation of the code. Revenue Rulings are also official pronouncements, but they normally deal with only a specific set of facts and are not nearly as comprehensive as regulations. Courts typically do not accord Revenue Rulings the same legal standing as regulations. Technically, the IRS is not bound by Revenue Rulings and can even revoke rulings on a retroactive basis. The IRS usually relies on its rulings, however, and revocations are rare. A Private Ruling, sometimes known as a Letter Ruling, is issued at the request of a single taxpayer and binds the IRS for a specific transaction. The IRS is selective in agreeing to provide such private rulings. Determination letters are a form of tax ruling provided by an IRS district director. Determination letters are issued for completed transactions and provide an indication of how a district director applies the law with respect to a specific completed trans-

action. Revenue Procedures typically deal with administrative details of the tax laws.

Much of the IRS enforcement work involves the providing of tax return forms and instructional materials to taxpayers and tax preparers. The United States income tax system involves self-assessment by the taxpayer (voluntary compliance); thus, taxpayers must have the knowledge and the forms to provide such assessments. Another function performed by the IRS is to approve the status of certain types of entities—primarily tax-exempt agencies such as charitable organizations.

The function for which the IRS is most often criticized is the audit process. It is through the audit and enforcement process that IRS personnel are most visible to the general public. A small percentage of taxpayers, often representing less than 1 percent of all returns filed, are selected each year to be audited. The taxpayer must then prove that the data reported on the self-prepared tax return submitted during the preceding year are accurate. If the internal revenue agent auditing the return discovers an underpayment of taxes, the taxpayer is assessed the amount of the underpayment plus interest. If the agent thinks that the taxpayer intentionally tried to underreport income, a negligence or fraud penalty can be added. In the case of large frauds, the taxpayer can be convicted of felony tax evasion.

If a taxpayer does not agree to the finding of a deficiency that is the result of an audit, the taxpayer may file a protest and request a conference with the Regional Office of Appeals. If the taxpayer and appeals officer cannot reach a settlement, a so-called ninety-day letter is sent, advising the taxpayer that the tax deficiency will be assessed and collected unless a petition is filed in Tax Court within ninety days. The taxpayer receiving such a letter can either file the petition or pay the tax and file claim for refund. If the IRS rejects the claim or fails to act within six months, the taxpayer may file a suit for refund in the federal district court or a claims court. This means that a taxpayer who does not pay can only file in Tax Court. Thus, a taxpayer lacking the cash to pay an assessment is limited in the choice of courts. A jury trial is available only in federal district court.

The IRS is widely viewed as an agency that knows, or can know, everything about a person's life. Because of the increased computerization of the agency, this view is valid: The IRS does have access to considerable information about an individual's lifestyle and sources of income. In many respects, the success of the selfassessment system is attributable to the respect (or perhaps trepidation) with which the agency is viewed. Taxpayers have come to expect that the IRS will learn of most sources of income; thus it is a risky undertaking to underreport one's revenues. The impact of the IRS on the American justice system has been positive in that the agency is able to collect revenue at a very low cost to taxpayers. Yet the agency's mandate to collect taxes and its extremely broad powers carry with them the potential for abuse, and the agency sometimes oversteps its bounds. In a number of cases, the courts have been involved in debate over where the limits of the IRS's power should be and what the rights of individuals are in relation to the agency. Two Supreme Court cases involving the IRS are *Beckwith v. United States* (1976), in which the Court held that the right to counsel does not extend to talks between taxpayers and the IRS before formal charges of tax evasion have been made, and *Bob Jones University v. United States* (1983), in which it held that the IRS may withhold tax-exempt status from private schools that practice racial discrimination. —*Dale L. Flesher*

See also Alcohol, Tobacco, and Firearms (ATF), Bureau of; Capone, Alphonse (Al); Due process of law; Prohibition; Tax evasion; Tax revolt movement; Taxation and justice; Treasury, U.S. Department of the.

BIBLIOGRAPHY

Many books have been written about federal income taxes, and most include an introductory chapter on the role of the IRS in the tax-collecting process. Many such books are written for the general public, while others are written for accountants and lawyers. Among the good sources are Peter W. Bernstein, ed., *The Ernst & Young Tax Guide* (New York: John Wiley & Sons, published annually); William H. Hoffman, James E. Smith, and Eugene Willis, *West's Federal Taxation* (St. Paul, Minn.: West, published annually); and Kevin E. Murphy, *Concepts in Federal Taxation* (St. Paul, Minn.: West, 1995). One of the best books on the history of the IRS is Shelley L. Davis, *IRS Historical Fact Book: A Chronology, 1646-1992* (Washington, D.C.: Internal Revenue Service, 1993).

International Association of Chiefs of Police

DATE: Founded 1893

SIGNIFICANCE: The International Association of Chiefs of Police (IACP) provides a variety of consultation and research services and fosters professionalism in law enforcement

The primary goal of the International Association of Chiefs of Police is to foster police professionalism. It is overseen by a board of fifty-two police officers and has thirty standing committees comprising the chief executive officers of law enforcement agencies around the world. The organization has about fourteen thousand members in more than eighty countries; its headquarters is in Alexandria, Virginia. The IACP began in 1893 as a national organization but expanded to include Canadian members in 1902 and then expanded again to include chiefs of police (including assistant and deputy chiefs), commissioners, superintendents, and directors of national, state, provincial, and municipal departments from around the world. In the 1990's the organization's primary concerns included international narcotics trafficking, drunk driving, police use of force, civil disorder, and criminal aliens; it also expanded its training programs to make them more accessible to smaller jurisdictions. The IACP puts out a number of regular publications, including the quarterly *Journal of Police Science and Administration*, and maintains a speakers' bureau.

See also Chief of police; Police; Police corruption and misconduct.

International Brotherhood of Police Officers

DATE: Established 1970

SIGNIFICANCE: The International Brotherhood of Police Officers was the first nationwide union of police officers

This police union, affiliated with the American Federation of Labor-Congress of Industrial Organizations (AFL-CIO), includes law enforcement officers throughout the United States. Dedicated to protecting the welfare and security of municipal, state, and national law enforcement personnel, the organization maintains a legal department and insurance program and conducts seminars. It also publishes newsletters and the quarterly *Police Chronicle*. Police officers had begun organizing local unions early in the twentieth century, but the International Brotherhood of Police Officers was the first national organization. The union's headquarters is in Quincy, Massachusetts.

See also American Federation of Labor-Congress of Industrial Organizations (AFL-CIO); Labor law; Labor unions; Police.

International law

DEFINITION: That body of treaties and customary norms which sovereign national governments recognize as binding their behavior toward other nation-states

SIGNIFICANCE: In a world of complex interdependence, proliferating nation-states, and potential conflict, international law provides a coordinating mechanism whereby governments can accommodate and adjust their interrelations, enhance cooperation, and resolve disputes

As one of the world's great powers, the United States has an important responsibility to seek stability in international relations. One of the means through which the U.S. government seeks to do this is by promoting the development, application, and enforcement of international law. Great powers throughout history have had such an interest, and the United States is no exception in contemporary international relations.

Ancient Roots. The United States is a relative newcomer to international affairs, and international law actually traces its roots to the classical age of Greece and Rome. Even earlier, leaders had seen a need to send and receive diplomats, enter into treaties of commerce and alliance, and establish norms for treatment of aliens. It was during the Roman Empire, however, that important legal ideas emerged from which modern international law eventually issued. Holding sway over many different peoples, Roman jurisprudence distinguished between the *jus civile*, the laws which each people under Roman rule developed for themselves, and the *jus gentium*, composed of the customs and legal traditions common to all nations. Roman legal theorists also articulated the concept of the *jus naturalae*, or natural law. In this important concept they saw a link to the *jus gentium*: Why did so many diverse peoples have so many common legal customs and traditions? The Romans looked upon these principles of law they detected in all legal systems as transcendent legal norms, that is, as rules that could be reasonably deduced to apply to all human communities. Implanted in humanity was the capacity to comprehend exact and universal principles of law and justice through the use of right reason. The idea of natural law that could be discovered through reason deeply affected legal developments down through the Middle Ages to our own time. It also paved the way for the development of a *Jus inter gentes*, or a law among nations—international law. The Romans also developed codified systems of law which later had significant influence on the evolution of both national and international legal systems.

The Rise of Positivism. The unifying force of Christianity across national or feudal lines provided rules for international relations during the Middle Ages. Many rules regarding the use of force, the acquisition of territory, and the treatment of prisoners and hostages developed along customary lines. The Protestant revolt which was coupled with the rise of the nation-state in the sixteenth and seventeenth centuries, however, destroyed the unity of Christendom and ushered in the modern international system of sovereign states acknowledging no higher legal authority than themselves. In this context states began to view international law not simply as an expression of an abstract natural law but as the by-product of state-made customs and treaties. Law, in this positivist tradition, is not discovered by reason but made through acts of willful determination of sovereign states. The positivist view gradually gained ascendancy, although to this day the natural law tradition remains strong, as reflected in the human rights movement that arose during the twentieth century.

Sovereignty. With the Peace of Westphalia in 1648, which brought to a close the religious wars of the seventeenth century, the princes of Europe firmly established the principle of national sovereignty as the basis for international relations. The state, personified in the prince or monarch, was the highest legal authority. States were to be treated as independent and equal agents with full control over establishing their domestic legal system and their foreign affairs. No state could intervene legally into the internal affairs of other states. How a state dealt with religion or with its own citizens and subjects was its own business; internal order was to be maintained by states at their own discretion. External order in their foreign relations, however, would require a degree of cooperation and coordination among the various sovereigns, who might otherwise constantly be warring with one another.

Reciprocity and Obligation. One of the means employed by states to promote orderly relations was the time-honored principle of reciprocity. It was in the mutual self-interest of nations, if they wished to prosper and maintain peaceful relations, to limit their aggressive instincts. If, for example, a country desired to promote a thriving trade with other nations, it needed to permit merchants from other countries to enter its territory. It also needed to protect these merchants and their property and to provide them with avenues for legal redress. It could expect, in return, that the other state would extend similar privileges and rights to its merchants who traveled abroad. To promote commerce, the extension of diplomatic privileges and immunities to the emissaries of foreign governments was

necessary. In sending and receiving diplomats, countries reciprocally agreed to recognize their legal status, their immunity from local prosecution, and their personal inviolability. Governments even extended extraterritorial rights to embassy grounds, giving jurisdiction over acts committed on diplomatic property to the government occupying the embassy. By extending such legal rights, governments pursued their mutual self-interest even as they limited their own behavior.

In short, although states were sovereign and could not be bound by any law without their consent, nothing prevented them from limiting their own sovereignty, from entering into voluntary obligations, or from developing international law to which they would agree to be bound. International law, then, became a means through which states could order and regulate their interrelations through the establishment of mutual obligations. The primary means through which states made international law were customs and treaties, but in time other subsidiary sources of law, such as judicial decisions and the writings of important jurists and publicists, were acknowledged by states as useful interpretive sources of law, which, although not making law, helped governments to discern its existence or to shape it better to their purposes.

Rooted in the principle of obligation was the notion that once governments agreed to be bound by a custom or a treaty, that they would be expected by other governments to abide by such obligations in the future. Treaties were to be observed, not summarily ignored. Customs were to be followed, not casually discarded. Governments who failed to honor legal obligations could be legally punished by other states through various forms of retaliation. Outmoded treaties or customs obviously presented a potential problem, but through various mechanisms of treaty revision and amendment, or even through the development of new customary norms, peaceful change in the law could be effected without resort to force or conflict. Indeed, whole bodies of customary and treaty law gradually emerged. These dealt not only with the traditional law of diplomacy but also, especially with the onset of colonialism, with rules for the acquisition of territory, the waging of war, the treatment of aliens, the interpretation of treaties, and the mutual adjustment of disputes.

International Versus Municipal Law. To understand better how international law functions, it is useful to draw an analogy to the municipal (or domestic) law of nations. Normally, when one thinks about law, one assumes that there are supreme legislative, executive, and judicial institutions which have the capacity to make, enforce, and interpret the law, thereby ensuring that violators of the law are punished and that the rights of law-abiding citizens are protected. International law lacks supreme, centralized executive, legislative, and judicial functions such as are generally found in the municipal legal systems of sovereign states. For this reason some experts argue that international law is not really law. This view, however, fails to take account of the fact that, though often decentralized, international law is routinely observed rather than flouted by states and that coordinating mechanisms for making, enforcing, and interpreting the law do exist, if only through the cooperation of the sovereign governments.

The executive function in international law, for example, is routinely undertaken by the foreign ministries of governments. Sometimes in contemporary international relations, it is undertaken through the United Nations Security Council, which may legally punish countries that violate provisions of the U.N. Charter, as Iraqi leader Saddam Hussein discovered after his illegal invasion of Kuwait in 1990. The Security Council can only act when there is consensus among its member states to coordinate their responses to aggression. Thus, though sanctions may be collectively imposed by the Security Council, when a consensus to do so is lacking, states may also at their own individual discretion impose sanctions to punish an aggressor, as did the United States and many European powers when the Iranian government participated in the seizure of American diplomats as hostages in 1979.

Legislative functions in international law are also largely decentralized. The U.N. General Assembly may pass resolutions, but these are not normally binding on member states. Through international conferences and negotiations, however, governments frequently promulgate new treaties regarding various aspects of international law. Governments are free to participate or not participate in these negotiations and to sign and ratify agreements emerging from them as they please. Thus, there are *ad hoc*, decentralized means by which new international law can be made. Governments enter into hundreds of bilateral and multilateral agreements and treaties with other states every year in order to facilitate trade, technological and economic development, and political cooperation.

Similarly, the judicial function in international law is largely decentralized. It is true that there is an International Court of Justice (ICJ), but it does not have compulsory jurisdiction, as do the high courts of various states. (The ICJ, also known as

the World Court, is the judicial branch of the United Nations.) Governments may choose to give the ICJ compulsory jurisdiction over cases brought against them by other members, but they are not required to do so. By ratifying the optional clause to the Statute of the ICJ (which is part of the United Nations Charter), governments can submit to the compulsory jurisdiction of the court. The United States ratified the optional clause when it became a member of the United Nations but reserved the right to exclude cases from the ICJ's jurisdiction which fell under U.S. domestic jurisdiction. In the 1980's, the United States, in the wake of the Nicaragua Mining Case, announced that it would withdraw its recognition of the optional clause. Thus, even when states agree to the court's jurisdiction, they may withdraw.

Moreover, the ICJ has no power to establish a binding precedent on future international court decisions. Only states make international law; international courts do not. Thus the ICJ has only limited judicial powers. How then do states legally resolve disputes over interpretation of the law? The national courts of the various states routinely consider and rule on questions of international law that fall within their jurisdiction. National courts hear cases involving such things as international maritime law, disputes arising out of injuries to aliens, enforcement of laws relating to piracy and hijacking, extradition, and punishment of war criminals.

International law, then, is made, enforced, and adjudicated through a variety of centralized, though not always reliable, international mechanisms and, more important, through the decentralized municipal institutions of the various governments. There are occasions when states flagrantly violate the law and get away with it, but these are rare events compared with the routine observance of most international law.

Incorporation. One mechanism used by states to enforce international law is the doctrine of incorporation. Incorpora-

THE GENEVA AND HAGUE CONVENTIONS ON CONVENTIONS OF WAR

Year	Conference	Sample Declarations
1864	First Geneva Convention	Declared immunity from capture or destruction of facilities for the treatment of sick and wounded soldiers and personnel, protection of civilians aiding the wounded, and recognition of Red Cross symbol.
1899	First Hague Conference	Prohibited use of asphyxiating gases, expanding ("dumdum") bullets, projectiles from balloons; created Permanent Court of Arbitration.
1906	Second Geneva Convention	Amended and extended provisions of the First Geneva Convention.
1907	Second Hague Conference	Adopted conventions regarding force in the recovery of debts, rights and duties of neutral powers and persons, the laying of marine mines, and bombardment of naval forces.
1929	Third Geneva Convention	Amended and extended provisions of the first two Geneva conventions. Introduced provisions regarding humane treatment of prisoners of war.
1949	Fourth Geneva Convention	Following World War II, the most complete of the treaties. Provisions regarded care of the wounded and sick, fair treatment of prisoners of war, and protection of citizens of occupied territories (condemning torture, discrimination, hostage taking, and wanton destruction of property).
1977	Fifth Geneva Convention	Extended protection of international law to wars of liberation and civil wars.

tion occurs when a government decides to make international treaty or customary law a part of its domestic statutes. In the United States, for example, treaties are considered the law of the land, and they supersede prior conflicting domestic statutes. The U.S. Supreme Court upheld this principle in its *Missouri v. Holland* case (1920), in which Missouri attempted to prevent enforcement of the implementing legislation pursuant to Congress's ratification of the 1916 Migratory Bird Treaty and passage of the 1918 Migratory Bird Treaty Act as an infringement of its reserved powers under the U.S. Constitution. The Court held that only the federal government has constitutional authority to promulgate treaties, that such treaties are the supreme law of the land, and that any statute promulgated to implement a valid treaty is itself valid. The treaty had been, in effect, incorporated into U.S. domestic law. Many treaties are enforced in precisely this way. First an international agreement is made, and subsequently a national legislative body, such as the U.S. Congress, passes legislation to enforce it through domestic law.

International customary law is often also incorporated in this way. Thus Belgium was able to prosecute war crimes against German occupation officials. Even though it had no specific legislative statutes against certain war crimes, Belgium had incorporated the customary norms concerning war crimes that in turn had grown out of the 1899 and 1907 Hague Conferences and the 1907 Hague Convention. Modern efforts at promotion of human rights are also enforced in this way. Governments are very reluctant to place their own behavior before the scrutiny of international courts of human rights. Many of them do, however, incorporate various civil and political rights into their domestic constitutions or statutes, thus providing their citizens with domestic avenues of legal recourse should their rights be violated. The Universal Declaration of Human Rights passed by the U.N. General Assembly in 1948 was not a legally binding instrument. Eventually, however, many states, including states that subsequently obtained their independence, incorporated all or parts of the Universal Declaration into their own constitutions or statutes, thus giving its provisions a legally binding character within those countries' domestic legal systems.

American Involvement in International Law. The United States has always recognized the fundamental tenets of international law. With its rise to prominence in international relations in the twentieth century, the United States has asserted a leadership role in the promulgation and enforcement of international law. American presidents have been the principal architects of modern international organizations, such as the League of Nations after World War I, and the United Nations after World War II. The United States placed its military power at the service of the collective security principles built into the United Nations Charter. It fought a war in Korea under the banner of the United Nations. The United States took the lead in creating, financially supporting, and strengthening global specialized agencies such as the World Bank, the International Monetary Fund, the Food and Agricultural Organization, the General Agreement on Tariffs and Trade, and a variety of humanitarian agencies that deal with disasters, refugees, and displaced persons. It participated in global negotiations to codify rules of diplomatic and consular practice, international treaty law, and the law of the sea, although it did not always promptly ratify such treaties. Similarly, the United States participated in the drafting of human rights instruments, especially those related to civil and political rights.

During the Cold War, much of the U.S. effort at leadership in the global arena focused on preventing the spread of communism. Often, in that context, the global institutions it had helped to create could no longer be used effectively to achieve its interests. The collective security provisions of the U.N. Charter, for example, which called upon the Security Council to promote peaceful resolution of disputes and punish aggression, could not be implemented in the face of a veto by the Soviet Union. Thus the United States, along with its allies, fell back on traditional self-help principles to preserve their security. Other customary mechanisms, such as U.N. peacekeeping, were devised to promote peaceful settlements of disputes, short of collective sanctions or military interventions by the Security Council. With the end of the Cold War, however, the global institutions have been and can be more effectively used to enforce international law. —*Robert F. Gorman*

See also Admiralty law; Citizenship; Extradition; Illegal aliens; Immigration laws; Natural law and natural rights; Nuclear weapons; Skyjacking; Tariff; War crimes; World Court.

BIBLIOGRAPHY

One of the most comprehensive and readable works on international law is Gerhard von Glahn's *Law Among Nations: An Introduction to Public International Law* (6th rev. ed. New York: Macmillan, 1992). Another classic treatment on international law which deals with its traditional foundations and historical development is James L. Brierly's *The Law of Nations* (5th ed. Oxford: Clarendon Press, 1955). For a treatment of the political influences operating in international law see Morton A. Kaplan and Nicholas Katzenbach, *The Political Foundations of International Law* (New York: John Wiley & Sons, 1961). On U.S. policy toward Nicaragua, intervention in Grenada, and refugee policy, see David P. Forsythe, *The Politics of International Law: U.S. Foreign Policy Reconsidered* (Boulder, Colo.: Lynne Rienner, 1990). For a counterpoint to Forsythe's discussion, especially concerning the legality of intervention, see Louis Henkin et al., *Right v. Might: International Law and the Use of Force* (New York: Council on Foreign Relations Press, 1989). For a useful and broad collection of readings on contemporary issues in international law, see Richard Falk, Friedrich Kratochwil, and Saul Mendlovitz, eds., *International Law: A Contemporary Perspective* (Boulder, Colo.: Westview Press, 1985). For a systemic treatment of the political and legal aspects of U.S. policy concerning refugees, see Robert F. Gorman, *Mitigating Misery: An Inquiry into the Political and Humanitarian Aspects of U.S. and Global Refugee Policy* (Lanham, Maryland: University Press of America, 1993).

Interpol

DATE: Founded September, 1923

SIGNIFICANCE: Interpol was the first organization in modern history to promote multinational police cooperation in order to fight international crime

The purpose of Interpol, the popular name for the International Criminal Police Organization, is to ensure the widest possible mutual assistance between the world's police authorities and to establish institutions likely to contribute to the suppression of ordinary crime. It deals with criminals and crime that transcend national borders, such as terrorism, counterfeiting, drug trafficking, money laundering, illegal arms sales, electronic fraud, and the theft of artistic treasures. By charter, it may not investigate activities of military, political, religious, or racial character.

Interpol was founded in Vienna, Austria, in 1923 by a group of police officers from several countries, and Johann Schober, head of the Vienna police, was elected its first president. Although the organization grew quickly in membership and status, it in effect ceased to function after Nazi Germany occupied Austria in 1938. It was revived in 1946. Since that time, its headquarters has been located in or near Paris, until it moved to its new building in Lyon, France, in 1989. By then, some 150 nations were members of the organization. Within Interpol headquarters, a supervisory board is mandated to ensure that data on suspected criminals is accurate and used only for legitimate purposes.

Interpol does not have its own international police force; rather, it works through the National Central Bureaus (NCBs) of each member state. The NCB serves as the point of contact for police agencies of other countries and helps to transcend the problems of language and differing legal codes. Each national NCB functions within the laws and traditions of its country, and cooperation is entirely voluntary. The NCBs serve as valuable conduits of information in assisting the police of other countries in their criminal investigations, and they help by detaining suspects, identifying bodies, and providing descriptions of stolen property. Extradition of criminals, however, necessitates using diplomatic channels.

The United States has had an uneven record of cooperation within Interpol. It joined rather late, in 1938, and in the early decades J. Edgar Hoover, head of the Federal Bureau of Investigation, tightly controlled U.S. involvement in its work. The United States did not create an NCB until 1969. By the mid-1980's, however, the United States had begun to perceive Interpol as an effective instrument in combating international terrorism and quickly became a leader in encouraging the organization to improve efficiency and utilize the latest computerized technologies.

Care has been taken to prevent abuses in regard to civil liberties and personal privacy. The US-NCB is under the control of the attorney general of the United States. It is jointly supervised by the Departments of Justice and the Treasury, and more than one congressional committee oversees its activities. In addition, there are watchdog and advisory groups that establish guidelines for determining when and how much information can be released to other countries.

See also Extradition; Hoover, J. Edgar; Money laundering; Terrorism.

Interstate Commerce Commission (ICC)

DATE: Established February 4, 1887

SIGNIFICANCE: The ICC, established to regulate transportation carriers, settles disagreements between carriers and users over services, rates, and tariffs, and it has the power to rule on the sale of carriers, mergers, and stock issues

The Interstate Commerce Commission is a comprehensive and powerful commission that regulates the private transportation industry. It is an independent agency in the sense that it was created by the Congress, but the president appoints the commissioners. Historically the ICC has been blessed with highly qualified commissioners. Over the years there have been as many as eleven commissioners or as few as five. Generally it is an odd number. They are appointed for a term of seven years by the president, but the Senate must approve the appointments. Commissioners generally enjoy stable tenure, and it is very difficult to remove them during their term. The ICC is bipartisan in its composition and reports to the Congress; it is not considered to be part of the executive wing of the government.

The ICC has been described as a quasi-judicial, quasi-legislative, and quasi-administrative body. When it makes rules, establishes rates, and grants operating authority to carriers, the ICC is performing a legislative function. The commission acts in an administrative capacity when it enforces the rules and laws passed by the Congress. It is performing a judicial function when it hears cases and determines what is just and reasonable and what is unduly preferential. By performing all three of these functions, the ICC attempts to promote the public welfare. The most successful commissioners in the long history of the ICC have probably been Thomas Cooley, Martin Knapp, Franklin Lane, and Joseph Eastman.

History of the ICC. In the mid-nineteenth century, merchants, farmers, and manufacturers all suffered from railroad discrimination. By 1886, there was a major outcry for federal regulation. In response, the House passed the Reagan bill, and the Senate passed the Cullom bill; the two were combined into the Interstate Commerce Act. President Grover Cleveland signed the act into law on February 4, 1887. It required that all interstate rates be "reasonable and just." It also banned many trade practices, such as rebates, drawbacks, special rates, and pools. A five-member commission called the Interstate Commerce Commission (ICC) was established in 1887 to enforce these prohibitions. The ICC was authorized to investigate any railroad company engaged in interstate commerce. It could require a uniform accounting system and mandate that railroads submit annual reports. The first chairman of the ICC was Thomas Cooley.

The impact of the ICC has depended on the support it received from the Supreme Court. At the end of ten years in operation, the ICC suffered serious defeats in the Supreme

The ICC has regulatory power over transportation industries, including the trucking and railroad industries. (Jim West)

Court. The Court ruled that the ICC could not fix rates or prescribe any tariffs. In the late 1890's the commission was not supported by Congress, and the railroads ignored it. In 1906, however, the Hepburn Act was passed. President Theodore Roosevelt also strongly supported the ICC. The Hepburn Act gave wide regulatory powers to the ICC, including rate-fixing powers. The ICC's orders were to be obeyed or challenged in court. The caseload increased, and the ICC had about 4,500 informal complaints annually from 1907 to 1909. The commission had problems during World War I, but in 1920, when the Transportation Act was passed, the ICC's power was greatly increased. The commission could set minimum and maximum rates, and it could supervise all stocks issued by railroads.

The stock market crash in 1929 signaled the beginning of the Great Depression, during which American railroads fared badly. The ICC disintegrated and was powerless during the Depression. There was anarchy in the transportation industry, and bitter competition was the order of the day in the early 1930's. Under the leadership of Joseph Eastman, however, the ICC became powerful once again. In 1935, the Eastman bill became the 1935 Motor Carrier Act, which gave wide powers to the ICC: The commission could issue certificates of public convenience and necessity, and it was given powers over rates,

finances, accounting, organization, and management of common carriers. During World War II, the carriers prospered. The postwar years have seen the commission lose considerable prestige and power.

Public Perceptions. The political nature of the commission appointments has raised concerns regarding the qualifications of the commissioners in some quarters. Even though Congress wanted commissioners to run the ICC, staff members ran the commission in the postwar years. Some people believe that the ICC has sometimes acted more in the interests of the carriers than the public, and the commission's relationship with industry has been described as "intimate." Rail mergers approved by the commission have created local monopolies. Barriers to entry have been created by many actions of the commission, and many inefficiencies are consequently allowed to exist. Many studies have pointed out that regulatory costs are burdensome and cause misallocation of resources. The ICC budget may be modest, but the social costs imposed by the regulations are enormous. It has been argued, for example, that overregulation caused many railroads in the northeastern states to go bankrupt in the 1970's. The deregulatory acts of Congress in the 1980's decreased the role of the ICC. Nevertheless, the ICC is a powerful regulatory agency. —*Srinivasan Ragothaman*

See also Antitrust law; Clayton Antitrust Act; Commerce clause; Federal Trade Commission (FTC); Sherman Antitrust Act; Tariff; Transportation law.

BIBLIOGRAPHY
Perhaps the most comprehensive and readable book on the Interstate Commerce Commission is the work by Ari Hoogenboom and Olive Hoogenboom, *A History of the ICC: From Panacea to Palliative* (New York: W. W. Norton, 1976). Other overviews include Marver H. Bernstein, *Regulating Business by Independent Commission* (Princeton, N.J.: Princeton University Press, 1955); Robert C. Fellmeth, *The Interstate Commerce Omission: The Public Interest and the ICC* (New York: Grossman, 1970); I. L. Sharfman, *The Interstate Commerce Commission: A Study in Administrative Law and Procedure* (5 vols. New York: Commonwealth Fund, 1931-1937); John F. Stover, *American Railroads* (Chicago: University of Chicago Press, 1970); and John Meyer, Merton Peck, John Stenason, and Charles Zwick, *The Economics of Competition in the Transportation Industries* (Cambridge, Mass.: Harvard University Press, 1959).

Iran-Contra scandal

DATE: 1986-1990

PLACE: Washington, D.C.; Iran; Nicaragua

SIGNIFICANCE: The Iran-Contra affair raised anew the question of congressional versus presidential control over foreign policy

In November, 1986, the American people learned that officials in the administration of Ronald Reagan had traded arms for hostages and had used the profits from the arms sale to finance a rebellion in Central America. These acts, pored over by a presidential commission, congressional select committees, and an independent counsel, originated in Reagan's efforts to deal with anti-American terrorism in the Middle East and communist expansion in the Western Hemisphere.

Origins of the Scandal. In 1984, Shī'ite Muslim terrorists in Lebanon began kidnapping Americans who worked there. These terrorists were loyal to the Ayatollah Ruhollah Khomeini, the Shī'ite religious leader who ruled Iran. Hence there was hatched a scheme to sell antiaircraft missiles to Iran and thereby win the Iranian leaders' pledge to persuade the terrorists to release the hostages.

At the instigation of Marine Lieutenant Colonel Oliver North, an aide to national security advisers Robert McFarlane (October, 1983, to November, 1985) and Admiral John Poindexter (December, 1985, to November, 1986), profits from the arms sales were used to aid anticommunist rebels (the so-called Contras) in Nicaragua. In the early 1980's, as Nicaragua's new Sandinista regime proved more and more sympathetic to the Soviet Union and Fidel Castro's Cuba, Reagan, urged on by Central Intelligence Agency (CIA) director William Casey, asked the U.S. Congress to aid the Sandinistas' foes. Torn between the hope of saving Nicaragua from communism and the fear of American involvement in a bloody stalemate like the Vietnam War, Congress vacillated. It voted

money for the Contras in 1982 and 1983; in October, 1984, however, an amendment sponsored by Massachusetts Representative Edward Boland, banning all aid to the Contras for an entire year, became law. Congress voted for humanitarian aid to the Contras in June, 1985; only in June, 1986, did it again vote for military aid to them.

Although Reagan did not veto the appropriations bill that included the Boland Amendment, he failed to prevent North from circumventing the amendment by soliciting funds from private individuals and foreign governments and by using profits from the Iranian arms sales. North entrusted to retired Air Force General Richard Secord, and to Secord's Iranian-American business partner Albert Hakim, the task of expediting the transfer of funds from the Iranians to the Contras, and of weapons to both.

The Scandal Exposed. On October 5, 1986, Nicaraguan soldiers downed an airplane and captured an American, Eugene Hasenfus. On November 3, a news magazine in Beirut, Lebanon, revealed the arms-for-hostages swaps. On November 25, Reagan's attorney general publicly conceded that such a trade had occurred and that the profits from it had been diverted to the Contras. North was fired; Poindexter resigned.

In December, 1986, President Reagan set up a three-man commission chaired by former Texas senator John Tower. The Tower Commission Report, issued on February 26, 1987, exonerated Reagan from direct responsibility for the affair, while faulting him for insufficiently controlling his subordinates.

Senate and House select committees, created in early 1987, held joint televised hearings from May through August. CIA director Casey died before the hearings began. Witnesses included McFarlane, Secord, Hakim, North, Poindexter, Assistant Secretary of State for Inter-American Affairs Elliott Abrams, Secretary of State George Schultz, and Defense Secretary Caspar Weinberger.

Unlike Richard Nixon, who was forced to resign the presidency, Reagan cooperated fully with congressional investigators. Reagan's assertion that he had not ordered the diversion of funds to the Contras was never refuted. Hence the select committees' final report, issued on November 19, 1987, blamed Reagan for the scandal but did not urge his impeachment.

The Constitution and Foreign Policy. North's circumvention of the Boland Amendment, liberals contended, disregarded the power of the purse granted to Congress by the Constitution. Yet North's argument in 1987—that the Boland Amendment itself unconstitutionally encroached on the president's right to conduct foreign policy—appealed to many conservatives. After 1945, U.S. presidents had waged undeclared wars in Korea and Vietnam and had, through the CIA, waged covert warfare in Iran, Guatemala, and Cuba. Not until the 1970's had Congress tried to curb presidential discretion in such matters. The lack of consensus on the criminality of funding the Contras undermined attempts to prosecute the paymasters.

Iran-Contra and the Courts. Lawrence Walsh, named independent counsel by a three-judge panel in December, 1986, had some successes. Secord and Hakim, whom Walsh prosecuted in 1988, were convicted and sentenced to two years' probation. McFarlane pleaded guilty to misdemeanors in 1988, and Abrams in 1991.

To shed light on the scandal as quickly as possible, the congressional select committees had granted immunity from prosecution to North and Poindexter, in return for their agreeing to testify. Although North was convicted of several felonies in 1989, a federal appeals court threw out the convictions in 1990. The jurors might have been influenced by North's immunized testimony of 1987; hence, letting the conviction stand would have violated North's Fifth Amendment right against self-incrimination. Poindexter's 1990 conviction was thrown out by an appeals court on similar grounds in 1991. In 1989, a judge dismissed Walsh's case against CIA agent Joseph Fernandez after the Justice Department refused to order the release of relevant government documents.

In June, 1992, Walsh accused Weinberger of having lied to Congress; in November, a trial was scheduled for January 5, 1993. On December 24, 1992, however, President George Bush pardoned Weinberger, Abrams, McFarlane, and three CIA officials. The unpardoned included Secord, Hakim, and CIA official Thomas Clines, the only Iran-Contra defendant to go to prison. By January, 1994, when Walsh issued his final report, the conservative press was portraying him as having waged a legal vendetta for purely partisan purposes.

Aftermath and Consequences of the Affair. In late 1989, the Soviet-American Cold War ended. Although military aid to the Contras had ended in February, 1988, Sandinista leader

Oliver North, a central figure in the Iran-Contra scandal, maintained that President Reagan knew of the weaponry being illegally funnelled to the Contras. (AP/Wide World Photos)

Daniel Ortega was peacefully voted out of office on February 25, 1990. In December, 1991, Lebanon's terrorists freed their six remaining American hostages.

The issue of control over foreign policy was not resolved. Although the CIA officials implicated in the scandal were fired, Congress and the president did not agree on a new law governing CIA covert operations until August, 1991. President Bush cooperated with Congress in crafting the March, 1989, bill appropriating humanitarian aid for the Contras. Panama was invaded in December, 1989, without prior congressional consent; Bush did, however, request congressional approval for war with Iraq in January, 1991.

Widespread accusations of complicity in the scandal did not keep Bush from being elected president in 1988 or Robert Gates from becoming CIA director in 1991. In 1992, discontent over the economy probably played a greater role in Bush's defeat at the polls than did indignation over the Iran-Contra scandal. —*Paul D. Mageli*

See also Bush, George; Lying to Congress; Pardoning power; Reagan, Ronald; Terrorism; Watergate scandal.

BIBLIOGRAPHY

An exhaustive study by veteran journalist Theodore Draper, *A Very Thin Line: The Iran-Contra Affairs* (New York: Hill and Wang, 1991), views the scandal as an example of unconstitutional usurpation of power. For an interpretation by a pro-Reagan journalist, consult "The Scandal-Olympics: Iran-Contra," in Suzanne Garment, *Scandal: The Culture of Mistrust in American Politics* (New York: Times Books, 1991). Cynthia J. Arnson's *Crossroads: Congress, the Reagan Administration, and Central America* (New York: Pantheon Books, 1989) examines the dilemmas of Nicaragua policy; Don Lawson's concise *America Held Hostage: The Iran Hostage Crisis and the Iran-Contra Affair* (New York: Franklin Watts, 1991) offers more on the Middle Eastern side. Haynes Johnson, *Sleepwalking Through History: America in the Reagan Years* (New York: W. W. Norton, 1991), illuminates the domestic American political context. In *The National Security Constitution: Sharing Power After the Iran-Contra Affair* (New Haven, Conn.: Yale University Press, 1990), legal scholar Harold Hongju Koh ably analyzes the constitutional issues. A work by two senators, William S. Cohen and George J. Mitchell, *Men of Zeal: A Candid Inside Story of the Iran-Contra Hearings* (New York: Viking, 1988), helps explain why Reagan was not impeached. Walsh's activity as independent counsel is evaluated in Jeffrey Toobin, *Opening Arguments: A Young Lawyer's First Case—"United States v. Oliver North"* (New York: Viking, 1991).

Jackson, Jesse (b. Oct. 8, 1941, Greenville, S.C.)
IDENTIFICATION: Civil rights leader
SIGNIFICANCE: Jesse Jackson is the founder of Operation
PUSH (People United to Serve Humanity) and an advocate
for civil and human rights

The Reverend Jesse Jackson's civil and human rights advocacy
began in the 1960's, when Jackson joined the Southern Christian Leadership Conference (SCLC) in the fight to end segregation and discrimination against African Americans in the United
States. A protégé of Civil Rights leader Martin Luther King, Jr.,
Jackson founded Operation Breadbasket, a joint project with
the SCLC committed to ending hunger, and served as its national director from 1967 to 1971. Ordained as a Baptist minister in 1968, Jackson's ministry focuses on the political organization and mobilization of disfranchised people. In 1971, he
founded the Chicago-based organization Operation PUSH,
which has lobbied and developed programs for the fair treatment of all people for more than two decades. Jackson also
serves as national president of the Rainbow Coalition, an organization focusing on human rights in the United States and
around the world. Jackson was an outspoken critic of South
African apartheid until its demise in 1993. Jackson was a two-
time candidate for the Democratic presidential nomination
(1983-1984 and 1987-1988) and the first African American
candidate to gain a national audience, his campaigns were
characterized by his pulpit-style oration and liberal platform.

See also Civil Rights movement; Democratic Party; King,
Martin Luther, Jr.; Poor People's March on Washington;
Southern Christian Leadership Conference (SCLC).

Jacksonian democracy
DEFINITION: A movement involving a variety of reforms that
included expanding the suffrage base and restructuring federal institutions
SIGNIFICANCE: Although marked by contradictions, including
injustices toward American Indians and continued support

*Jesse Jackson in the late 1960's; he and other Operation Breadbasket members are being arrested at an antidiscrimination
protest in New York.* (AP/Wide World Photos)

for slavery, the Jacksonian movement instituted reforms that changed the character of American government

The Democratic Party (also known in its early days as the Jacksonian Party, as it was identified with Andrew Jackson) appeared in the early 1820's. It represented the first mass party in American history, replete with an internal organization that consisted of precincts, wards, and district political organizers; its own newspapers; and a set of state-level reforms that dramatically expanded the voting base. Jacksonians identified themselves with the "common man" and targeted farmers, laborers, small businessmen, and, in the South, some planters.

Jacksonian reforms in the electoral process included a movement away from caucuses that nominated candidates and toward nominating conventions (in which party leaders carefully orchestrated the party's nominee). A second major reform was the elimination of property requirements to vote, which had been carried out in some states even before the Democrats appeared. Finally, the Jacksonians emphasized mass numbers in voting, as opposed to an educated elite. That led them to "get out the vote" on election day by energizing the grassroots organization they established. The "spoils system," which rewarded party loyalists with higher party jobs or with positions in government, provided the lubrication and inducements to encourage local chiefs to "get out the vote."

Jacksonians' rhetoric about justice emphasized small government and its relationship to the economy; as one Jacksonian said, "[T]he whole objective of government is negative. It is to remove and keep out of [the businessman's] way all obstacles to . . . natural freedom." To that end, the Democrats opposed the Second Bank of the United States, redrafted bankruptcy laws to be less punitive, eliminated imprisonment for debt, and enacted general incorporation laws, wherein companies no longer had to obtain charters from the legislatures.

The issue of slavery illustrated many of the contradictions of the Jacksonians. Emphasis on states' rights led Jacksonian jurists to support the expansion of slavery, while other Democrats supported positive government intervention to protect slavery in the territories. Democratic jurists rarely grappled with the philosophical or legal reasons that people could be made slaves, which stood in stark contradiction to their elimination of penalties for debt.

Recently the notion that the Jacksonians were supporters of a free market has come under attack. Democratic state legislatures routinely supported monopoly banks in their states and threw the "full faith and credit" of their states behind speculative bond issues. More important, Jackson himself had laid plans for a national bank scarcely different from the one he killed. Most significant, the presidency under Jackson expanded the scale and scope of its authority more than all other presidents combined. That authority protected slavery and kept the South from facing a legislative challenge to "the peculiar institution" as long as the Democrats (or a Whig disinclined to fight over slavery) controlled the presidency.

See also Democracy; Democratic Party; Jeffersonian democracy; Machine politics; Slavery; Whig Party.

Japanese American internment

DATE: 1942-1946

PLACE: Western United States

SIGNIFICANCE: During World War II, the U.S. government's war powers were used to deny due process of law for aliens and U.S. citizens of Japanese ancestry, to the disapproval of the postwar generation

Historically there were severe restrictions on Japanese immigration and naturalization, and in 1941 there were in the continental United States only about 40,000 foreign-born Japanese people (Issei) plus about 87,000 American-born citizens (Nisei). Many were tenant farmers under West Coast state and local restrictions on land ownership, housing, employment, and education; Japanese Americans were a semisegregated community.

Evacuation. Following the December, 1941, Japanese attack on Pearl Harbor, the Federal Bureau of Investigation arrested 2,192 Japanese security risks, followed by German and Italian counterparts. False reports of Japanese American espionage at Pearl Harbor, Japanese victories in the Pacific, and radio and press rumors combined to create unfounded fears that traitors and saboteurs might assist a Japanese invasion of the West Coast. On February 14, 1942, Lieutenant General John DeWitt, with War Department encouragement, and misrepresenting rumors as security threats, recommended removing persons of the Japanese "enemy race," including American citizens, from his West Coast command area. The Justice Department acquiesced, and on February 19, 1942, President Franklin D. Roosevelt signed Executive Order 9066, authorizing the army to create restricted zones excluding "any or all persons." On March 21, 1942, Congressional Law 503 provided criminal penalties for noncompliance.

Internment. DeWitt put more than 100,000 West Coast Japanese Americans under curfew, exclusion, removal, collection, and evacuation orders, which resulted in permanent job and property losses. Their ten relocation camps in the Western United States were isolated, barren, crowded, and crude, with barbed-wire fences and armed guards. Liberals and conservatives alike generally seemed to approve this mass imprisonment, conspicuously limited to the Japanese race. Internees who hoped that compliance would demonstrate their loyalty to the United States became demoralized by camp conditions and popular hostility.

In 1943, Japanese American soldiers changed the situation. Aside from their Pacific theater intelligence service, Nisei already in uniform plus volunteers from the internment camps formed the 100th Infantry Battalion and the 442d Regimental Combat Team. Their European combat and casualty records earned public respect for the Nisei soldiers and a more positive policy for the internees. By early 1944, 15,000 Nisei civilians were on restricted camp leave; finally, on December 17, 1944, the West Coast exclusion order was lifted.

Following Japan's surrender on September 2, 1945, detention and exclusion were phased out, the last camp closing March 20, 1946. The 1948 Evacuation Claims Act offered meager compensations—about $340 per case—for those renouncing all other claims against the government.

Court Cases. Four significant wartime appeals by Nisei reached the U.S. Supreme Court. On June 21, 1943, in *Hirabayashi v. United States* and *Yasui v. United States*, the Court upheld convictions for curfew violations, ruling the curfews constitutional and the emergency real, and found that Japanese Americans "may be a greater source of danger than those of a different ancestry." The Court held that winning the war must prevail over judicial review, implicitly reversing *Ex parte Milligan* (1866). On December 18, 1944, the Court granted *habeas corpus* in *Ex parte Endo*, ruling that Congress had not authorized long-term detention for a "concededly loyal" American citizen; the Court avoided broader questions of internment. On the same day, however, in *Korematsu v. United States*, the Court upheld Korematsu's conviction, on the *Hirabayashi* precedent. Although three dissenting justices argued that the exclusion order was part of a detention process, that Korematsu's offense of being in his own home was not normally a criminal act, and that only his race made it a crime under the exclusion orders, the Court majority upheld the government's wartime powers.

Redress. America's postwar generation developed different priorities. The Civil Rights movement and Vietnam War protests emphasized racial justice and deemphasized "national security." In 1980 Congress established the Commission on Wartime Relocation and Internment of Civilians to review facts and recommend remedies. Their 1982 report, *Personal Justice Denied*, exposed General DeWitt's misrepresentations, finding that "not a single documented act of espionage, sabotage or fifth column activity was committed by an American citizen of Japanese ancestry," that Executive Order 9066 resulted from "race prejudice, war hysteria and a failure of political leadership," and that "a grave injustice was done," deserving compensation. Of the Supreme Court, the report contended that "the decision in Korematsu lies overruled in the court of history."

The commission's work enabled Yasui, Hirabayashi, and Korematsu to file motions to vacate their convictions in the original courts on writ of *coram nobis*, alleging prosecutorial misrepresentation and impropriety. Yasui died while his case was in progress. On April 19, 1984, U.S. district court judge Marilyn Patel granted Korematsu's petition, acknowledging the 1944 Supreme Court decision as "the law of this case" but

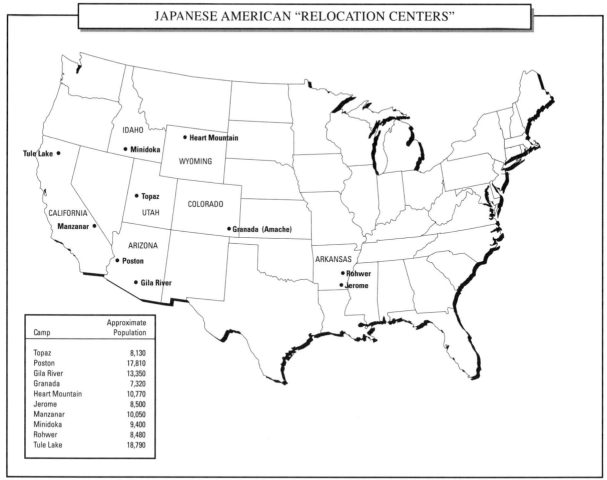

JAPANESE AMERICAN "RELOCATION CENTERS"

Camp	Approximate Population
Topaz	8,130
Poston	17,810
Gila River	13,350
Granada	7,320
Heart Mountain	10,770
Jerome	8,500
Manzanar	10,050
Minidoka	9,400
Rohwer	8,480
Tule Lake	18,790

JAY, JOHN / 411

The desolate internment camp at Tule Lake, California, in February, 1943. (National Archives)

terming it an anachronism, "now recognized as having very limited application." On this precedent, Hirabayashi's convictions were overturned in 1987.

In 1988, a congressional act signed by President Ronald Reagan accepted the findings of the 1980 commission, provided $1.2 billion in redress for 60,000 internees, and added, "for these fundamental violations of the basic civil liberties and constitutional rights of these citizens of Japanese ancestry, the Congress apologizes on behalf of the Nation." The history of Japanese American internment illustrates both the difficulty of limiting emergency powers during a popular war and the abuses caused by failing to do so.   —*K. Fred Gillum*

See also Citizen's arrest; Civil rights; *Habeas corpus*; *Hirabayashi v. United States*; *Korematsu v. United States*; Martial law; *Milligan, Ex parte*; Reparations; Warren, Earl.

BIBLIOGRAPHY

Jacobus Ten Broek, Edward Barnhart, and Floyd Matson, *Prejudice, War, and the Constitution* (Berkeley: University of California Press, 1968), relates the evacuation decision. Peter Irons in *Justice at War* (New York: Oxford University Press, 1983) and *Justice Delayed* (Middletown, Conn.: Wesleyan University Press, 1989) covers the court cases. See also the Commission on Wartime Relocation and Internment of Civilians,

Personal Justice Denied (Washington, D.C.: U.S. Government Printing Office, 1982), and Clinton Rossiter and Richard Longaker, *The Supreme Court and the Commander in Chief* (Ithaca, N.Y.: Cornell University Press, 1976).

Jay, John (Dec. 12, 1745, New York, N.Y.—May 17, 1829, Bedford, N.Y.)

IDENTIFICATION: First chief justice of the United States

SIGNIFICANCE: Jay determined the Supreme Court's original mode of operation

John Jay was graduated from King's College in 1764 and began practicing law in 1768. He was a member of the New York Committee of Correspondence. Elected to the New York Provincial Congress, he helped ratify the Declaration of Independence and, in 1777, was principal author of the first state constitution. He became the state's first chief justice in 1777. A delegate to the first two Continental Congresses and president of Congress in 1778, Jay was selected minister plenipotentiary to Spain in 1779, obtaining funds and munitions. In 1782, he joined the peace commission that concluded the revolution in 1783. Becoming foreign secretary in 1785, Jay encountered difficulties that made him propose replacing the Articles of Confederation. Later, in 1787, he contributed five

John Jay, the first chief justice of the United States, served from 1789 to 1795. (Painting by C. Gregory Stapko, collection of the Supreme Court of the United States)

papers on the Constitution and foreign affairs to the *Federalist Papers*.

Appointed chief justice in 1789, Jay organized the United States Supreme Court. His most important decision, *Chisholm v. Georgia* (1793), ruling that citizens of a state could sue another state, led directly to passage of the Eleventh Amendment to the Constitution. Jay's charge to the grand jury at Richmond (May 22, 1793) regarding the Neutrality Proclamation of 1793 established the principle that a presidential proclamation is implicitly declaratory of existing law. Remaining chief justice, Jay was sent to negotiate the treaty of 1794, resolving most postrevolutionary controversies with Great Britain.

Jay served six years as governor of New York beginning in 1795, signing a bill abolishing slavery. He retired from public life in 1801.

See also American Revolution; Constitution, U.S.; Declaration of Independence; Federalism; Supreme Court of the United States.

Jeffersonian democracy

DEFINITION: A conception of democracy emphasizing federalism and limited government

SIGNIFICANCE: Jefferson's conception of democracy was central to the founding of the United States, establishing a governmental framework and political philosophy that has endured for more than two centuries

The creation of the United States in the late eighteenth century established the world's first large-scale democracy. As one of the primary architects of the U.S. Declaration of Independence (and in various other capacities), Thomas Jefferson developed a democratic ideal which came to undergird the U.S. Constitution and traditional American political thought.

All forms of democracy rest on the ultimate sovereignty of the citizenry. Beyond this, however, there can be any number of variations. A primary distinction is made between direct democracy, wherein all members of the polity have direct input into the process of government, and representative democracy, in which the polity selects individuals to govern on their behalf. Virtually all modern democratic nation-states are of the latter variety.

Jefferson advocated a form of representative democracy with a number of features to help prevent the abuse of governmental power. Chief among these features is a federal structure, whereby power is divided between a central (national) government and several regional (state) governments. Jefferson also argued that individual rights and freedoms should be guaranteed, and thus he advocated specific constitutional limits on the powers of government. Finally, Jeffersonian democracy is characterized by checks and balances between the several branches of government in their exercise of power. All of these features were incorporated into the U.S. Constitution of 1789 and its Bill of Rights, ratified in 1791.

A critical assumption that underlies Jeffersonian democracy is the equality of individuals. This proposition, enshrined in the Declaration of Independence, informs Jeffersonian democ-

racy's commitment to universal suffrage and equal political rights. Although these principles today are commonly accepted (although not necessarily universally practiced) in the United States and many other countries, in Jefferson's time they were revolutionary. Their implications for the institution of slavery were particularly ominous. In a similar sense, it was Jefferson's belief in and commitment to the "common" people (especially farmers) which put him at odds with other political philosophers of the day. Unlike even the English philosopher John Locke, whose political writings influenced many of the founders of the United States, Jefferson assumed that all people have an innate moral sense and thus should be trusted to elect the best leaders.

The significant opposition to ratification of the new Constitution of 1789, and the unwillingness even of several members of the Constitutional Convention to sign it, illustrate that the new democratic framework conflicted with the beliefs of many Americans at the time. Although Jefferson was not present at the convention, the newly-ratified Constitution can rightly be seen as the first practical application of Jeffersonian democracy.

See also American Revolution; Bill of Rights, U.S.; Constitution, U.S.; Declaration of Independence; Democracy; Federalism; Jacksonian democracy.

Jeffersonian Republican Party

DATE: c. 1795-1828

SIGNIFICANCE: The rivalry between the Jeffersonian Republicans, an early liberal-populist coalition opposed to centralization, and the Federalists led to the landmark Supreme Court decision in *Marbury v. Madison* and an acceptance of the concept of judicial review

The U.S. Constitution did not say who should decide disputes over its meaning, and it left unclear the division of many powers between the states and the federal government. The Federalists, under Secretary of the Treasury Alexander Hamilton, supported a strong role for the federal courts and favored the principle of judicial review—the idea that the courts should have the final say in disputes arising over the meaning of the Constitution. The Jeffersonian Republicans (who later became the Democratic Party) were suspicious of a strong federal government. They instead favored leaving most powers with the states. The Jeffersonian Republicans won the election of 1800, but before they could take power, the Federalists appointed a slate of their own supporters as federal judges, including Chief Justice John Marshall.

President Thomas Jefferson tried to block these appointments, but an appeal of his decision led to one of the most important cases in U.S. constitutional history: *Marbury v. Madison* (1803). This judgment resulted in a proclamation by the Supreme Court of the principle of judicial review of acts of Congress and its assertion of a right to issue writs of *mandamus* even against the executive.

See also Democratic Party; Federalist Party; Jacksonian democracy; Judicial review; *Mandamus*, writ of; *Marbury v. Madison*; *Massachusetts Board of Retirement v. Murgia*.

Jim Crow laws

DATE: 1880's-1950's

DEFINITION: Laws passed by city governments and state legislatures in the southern United States to decree racial segregation in public and private affairs

SIGNIFICANCE: The so-called Jim Crow laws were part of an organized attempt throughout the American South to keep African Americans permanently in a socially subordinate status in all walks of life and to limit possibilities for any form of contact between people of different racial background

The precise origins of the term "Jim Crow" are unknown. It may have first appeared in 1832, in a minstrel play by Thomas D. "Big Daddy" Rice. The play contained a song about a slave; it was titled "Jim Crow." The expression was used commonly at least since the 1890's. In 1904, the Dictionary of American English listed the term "Jim Crow law" for the first time.

Jim Crow laws had predecessors in the so-called black codes, passed in many southern states after the Civil War to limit the freedom of the African Americans and assure a continuous labor supply for the southern plantation economy. Radical Reconstruction, which placed most parts of the South under military government, put an end to this. Even after the official end of Reconstruction in 1877, race relations in the South remained in a state of flux.

The Jim Crow Era. Jim Crow laws emerged during the 1880's and 1890's as conflict over political control in the South between different parties and between factions within parties intensified. Disfranchisement of African Americans and the segregation of whites and blacks were intended to assure the permanent subjugation of the latter and the prevention of future biracial political movements which could challenge white rule in the South. Domestic politics do not bear the sole responsibility, however: Jim Crow laws emerged at a time when the United States acquired colonies in the Pacific and the Caribbean and in the process subjugated the indigenous populations of those areas. Race theories used to justify American imperialism did not substantially differ from the white supremacy rhetoric of southern politicians.

The first Jim Crow law was passed by the state of Florida in 1887, followed by Mississippi in 1888, Texas in 1889, Louisiana in 1890, Alabama, Arkansas, Georgia, and Tennessee in 1891, and Kentucky in 1892. North Carolina passed a Jim Crow law in 1898, South Carolina in 1899, and Virginia in 1900. Statutes requiring racial segregation had been quite common in northern states before the Civil War, but only in the post-Reconstruction South did racial segregation develop into a pervasive system regulating the separation of white and black in all walks of life. Jim Crow laws segregated public carriers, restaurants, telephone booths, residential areas, workplaces, public parks, and other recreational spaces. Mobile, Alabama, passed a special curfew law for African Americans in 1909. In Florida, the law required separate textbooks, which had to be separately stored. The city of New Orleans segregated white and black prostitutes in separate districts. Many states outlawed interracial marriages. Jim Crow laws were not even limited to

life: Cemeteries, undertakers, and medical school cadavers were all subjects of segregation under the laws.

These laws, however, represented only symptoms of larger and even more pervasive patterns of discrimination and racial oppression. White vigilante groups, such as the Ku Klux Klan, often took it into their own hands to enforce their own brand of racial justice through violent means, frequently with the quiet consent and even cooperation of law enforcement officers. In addition, contract labor laws and corrupt law enforcement and prison officials created a system of peonage, which kept large numbers of African Americans in the turpentine and cotton belts in debt slavery.

U.S. Supreme Court. In the process of legally entrenching racial segregation through so-called Jim Crow laws, the U.S. Supreme Court served as a willing handmaiden. In the 1883 *Civil Rights Cases*, the Supreme Court ruled that segregation in privately owned railroads, theaters, hotels, restaurants, and similar places comprised private acts of discrimination and as such did not fall under the Fourteenth Amendment. In the 1896 case of *Plessy v. Ferguson*, concerning the constitutionality of a Louisiana Jim Crow law, the Supreme Court redefined segregation from a matter of private prejudice into a mandate of state law. In *Plessy v. Ferguson*, the Supreme Court approved of segregation as long as facilities were "separate but equal." In the 1930's and 1940's, the Supreme Court began to strike down segregation. Eventually, on May 17, 1954, the Supreme Court, in the landmark decision in *Brown v. Board of Education*, declared that separate facilities by their very nature were unequal, thereby reversing previous decisions.   —*Thomas Winter*

See also Black codes; *Brown v. Board of Education*; Civil rights; *Civil Rights Cases*; Civil War Amendments; Lynching; Marshall, Thurgood; National Association for the Advancement of Colored People (NAACP); *Plessy v. Ferguson*; Racial and ethnic discrimination; Restrictive covenant; Segregation, *de facto* and *de jure*; *Slaughterhouse Cases*; Slavery.

BIBLIOGRAPHY

An excellent starting point in understanding the Jim Crow era is C. Vann Woodward, *The Strange Career of Jim Crow* (3d rev. ed. New York: Oxford University Press, 1974). For a valuable survey of the relations between African Americans and the law, see Loren Miller, *The Petitioners: The Story of the Supreme Court of the United States and the Negro* (New York: Pantheon Books, 1966). See also Paul Finkelman, ed., *Race, Law, and American History, 1700-1900* (11 vols. New York: Garland, 1992). Of particular interest in this series is volume 4, *The Age of Jim Crow: Segregation from the End of Reconstruction to the Great Depression* (New York: Garland, 1992). On peonage, see Pete Daniel, *The Shadow of Slavery: Peonage in the South, 1901-1969* (Urbana: University of Illinois Press, 1972).

John Birch Society

DATE: Established December 9, 1958

SIGNIFICANCE: One of the best-known right-wing political movements in the United States in the 1960's, the John Birch Society held that communist infiltration was rampant

The John Birch Society was formed following a meeting hosted by Robert H. W. Welch, Jr., in Indianapolis, Indiana, in December, 1958. The purpose of the organization was to fight communism and counter the influence of liberal political groups. Welch named the group after Captain John Birch, an army intelligence officer who was killed by a Communist Chinese soldier ten days after the end of World War II. According to Welch, Captain John Birch represented the first casualty of the Cold War.

In 1959 and throughout the 1960's, the emphasis of the society was on a communist conspiracy. Welch claimed that President Dwight D. Eisenhower was a conscious agent of the communist conspiracy and denounced the Civil Rights movement as part of the conspiracy. The society also demanded the impeachment of the Chief Justice of the United States, Earl Warren. Later the society claimed that there was an internationalist conspiracy bent on destroying national sovereignty and creating a world government.

Operating out of Belmont, Massachusetts, the John Birch Society had a peak membership of approximately 100,000 in the 1960's. Welch stepped down as president in 1983; he died in 1985. The society's headquarters was moved to Appleton, Wisconsin, the hometown of Senator Joe McCarthy. It continued to oppose progressive movements and causes which it saw as promoting world unity. Its membership had declined to fewer than 25,000 by 1995.

See also Communist Party, American; House Committee on Un-American Activities (HUAC); McCarthyism; Warren, Earl.

Johnson, Lyndon B. (Aug. 27, 1908, near Stonewall, Gillespie County, Tex.—Jan. 22, 1973, en route to San Antonio, Tex.)

IDENTIFICATION: President of the United States, 1963-1969

SIGNIFICANCE: Johnson secured federal legislation outlawing almost all forms of racial discrimination

Lyndon Baines Johnson was graduated from Southwest Texas State Teachers College in 1930 and taught school thereafter until becoming Congressman Richard Kleberg's secretary. In 1935 he was appointed National Youth Administration administrator for Texas. He was elected United States Representative in 1937, serving until 1949, when he entered the Senate. His Civil Rights Act of 1957 established a bipartisan Civil Rights Commission and a Civil Rights Division within the Department of Justice and authorized the attorney general to litigate in protecting voting rights. He secured passage of the Civil Rights Act of 1960, authorizing judicially appointed referees to act upon complaints of a denial of voting rights.

In 1961 Johnson was elected vice president of the United States, becoming president November 22, 1963, after John F. Kennedy's assassination. In July, 1964, Johnson secured passage of the Civil Rights Act of 1964, prohibiting discrimination according to race, color, religion, or national origin. It provided a Civil Rights Division and authorized federal referees for voting rights complaints.

In 1965 more than eighty-six laws composing Johnson's "Great Society" program were passed. The Voting Rights Act of 1965 ended literacy tests for registration and instituted federal voter registration. In 1968 Johnson secured passage of the Civil Rights Act of 1968, mandating open housing and legal remedies for restriction of voting, running for office, jury service, attending public educational institutions, and access to public transportation and accommodations.

Johnson was frustrated when, in spite of such legislation, urban riots broke out in the late 1960's. His greatest frustration, however, was the Vietnam War, which he escalated repeatedly, leading to widespread and divisive protests. The war expenditures also placed the Great Society programs in jeopardy. Moreover, the controversy over the war brought Robert F. Kennedy into the 1968 presidential race, leading Johnson to withdraw from the race for the Democratic nomination. He published five books, including *Vantage Point: Perspectives of the Presidency, 1963-1969* (1973).

See also Civil Rights Act of 1957; Civil Rights Act of 1964; Civil Rights Act of 1968; Democratic Party; Great Society; Kennedy, John F.; Liberalism, modern American; Vietnam War; Voting Rights Act of 1965; War on Poverty; Warren Commission; Welfare state.

Lyndon B. Johnson being sworn in as president aboard Air Force 1; his wife Lady Bird is behind him, and Jacqueline Kennedy is at right. (Lyndon Baines Johnson Library)

Jones v. Alfred H. Mayer Co.

COURT: U.S. Supreme Court

DATE: Decided June 17, 1968

SIGNIFICANCE: Reversing many precedents, the Court held that the 1866 Civil Rights Act prohibited both private and state-backed discrimination and that the Thirteenth Amendment authorized Congress to prohibit private acts of discrimination as "the badges of slavery"

Joseph Lee Jones, alleging that a real estate company had refused to sell him a house because he was African American, sought relief in a federal district court. Since the case appeared before the passage of the Civil Rights Act of 1968, Jones and his lawyer relied primarily on a provision of the 1866 Civil Rights Act that gave all citizens the same rights as white citizens in property transactions. Both the district court and the court of appeals dismissed the complaint based on the established view that the 1866 law applied only to state action and did not address private acts of discrimination. The U.S. Supreme Court, however, accepted the case for review.

All the precedents of the Supreme Court supported the conclusions of the lower courts. In the *Civil Rights Cases* (1883) the Court had ruled that the Thirteenth Amendment allowed Congress to abolish "all badges and incidents of slavery," but the Court had narrowly interpreted these badges or incidents as not applying to private acts of discrimination. In *Hodges v. United States* (1906) the Court held that Congress might prohibit only private actions that marked "a state of entire subjection of one person to the will of another," and even in *Shelley v. Kraemer* (1948) the Court recognized the right of individuals to make racially restrictive covenants.

In *Jones*, however, the Court surprised observers by voting 7 to 2 to overturn its precedents. Writing for the majority, Justice Potter Stewart asserted that Congress under the Thirteenth Amendment possessed the power "to determine what are the badges and incidents of slavery, and the authority to translate that determination into effective legislation." In addition, the majority reinterpreted the 1866 law so that it proscribed both governmental and private discrimination in property transactions—an interpretation that is questioned by many authorities.

Justice John M. Harlan wrote a dissenting opinion which argued that the majority probably was wrong in its interpretation of the 1866 law. Harlan also wrote that the passage of the Fair Housing Act of 1968 eliminated the need to render this decision that relied on such questionable history.

Since the *Jones* decision was based on the Thirteenth rather than the Fourteenth Amendment, it was important in diluting the Court's traditional distinction between state and private action, and it appeared to grant Congress almost unlimited power to outlaw private racial discrimination. *Jones* became a precedent for new applications of the almost forgotten post-Civil War statutes in cases such as *Griffin v. Breckenridge* (1971) and *Runyon v. McCrary* (1976). In the quarter-century after *Jones*, however, the Congress did not pass any major legislation based upon the authority of the Thirteenth Amendment.

See also Civil rights; Civil Rights Act of 1968; Civil Rights Acts of 1866-1875; *Civil Rights Cases*; *Griffin v. Breckenridge*; *Moose Lodge No. 107 v. Irvis*; *Runyon v. McCrary*; Segregation, *de facto* and *de jure*; *Shelley v. Kraemer*.

Judicial review

DEFINITION: The power of the courts to review and declare unconstitutional the actions of the executive and legislative branches of government as well as the decisions of lower courts

SIGNIFICANCE: Judicial review is a preeminent means of enforcing the rule of the law in political systems operating under a written constitution; the process of judicial review has led to the federal judiciary assuming major policy-making authority in the United States

Although it has tangential roots in the lawmaking roles of the courts of medieval England, the process of judicial review—that is, of courts ruling on the constitutionality of statutory law, executive action, and the decisions of lower courts—may be regarded as one of the United States' contributions to the art of government. In the United States it has led to the federal judiciary assuming a major role in the evolving interpretation of the Constitution. Since World War II, the same device has spread widely to other democracies as a means of guaranteeing individual rights and the rule of law.

Development. One of the distinguishing characteristics of the Anglo-American legal system is that it is a common-law system composed not only of statutory law but also of bench (or judge-made) law. The system began with the emergence of the common-law and equity courts of medieval England. The former applied existing customs to the cases confronting its judges; the latter formed new rules to cover cases for which no relevant custom prevailed or where a rigid application of existing norms would create hardship or injury. In both instances the rulings of the courts became a part of the law of the realm, and it is in these courts that the power of the judiciary to make as well as apply the law has its origins.

It was not until the creation of the American political system at Philadelphia in 1787, however, that the process of entrusting the judiciary with the official task of reviewing the constitutionality of the actions of other branches of government, levels of government, and lower levels of the judiciary formally began. Two inventions at Philadelphia necessitated that development. First, in seeking a government based on a more permanent law than the statutory acts of momentary majorities as well as a system in which all would be subject to the same laws, the framers of the Constitution created the first political system founded on a single, written set of political rules declared "the supreme law of the land" (Article V of the Constitution). This higher law required an interpreter-enforcer, and in adopting Baron de Montesquieu's political model of three separate branches and powers of government (the law-making, law-enforcing, and law-adjudicating branches), the founders entrusted that task to the federal courts. Likewise, in adopting a system of dual (federal and state) levels of government, in which the powers of the federal government were enumerated and the states retained essentially what was left over, the constitutional system invited legal conflicts over jurisdictional issues. These had to be umpired, and the constitutional vehicle for umpiring them was also to be the judiciary.

Investing the Supreme Court with this authority provoked little controversy from the 1787-1789 period of constitution making through the first decade of the new Republic. In writing "Federalist Number 78" to urge the citizens of New York to ratify the pending Constitution, Alexander Hamilton linked the preservation of constitutionally limited government directly to the practice of judicial review by "the medium of courts of justice, whose duty it must be to declare all acts contrary to the manifest tenor of the Constitution void." The argument produced scarcely a ripple of contention, especially compared with the wrath which the Supreme Court incurred for not ruling unconstitutional the much-hated Alien and Sedition Acts enacted by Congress during the 1796-1801 presidency of John Adams.

Nor was there any serious criticism of the Supreme Court in 1796 when, in *Hylton v. United States*, it assumed that it had the power to declare an act of Congress unconstitutional in agreeing to review the constitutionality of the carriage tax enacted by the Congress. Even in *Marbury v. Madison* (1803), the heated reaction to the decision was far less because Chief Justice John Marshall declared an act of Congress unconstitutional than because he took the occasion to scold the Jeffersonians for wrongful actions even as he ruled that the Supreme Court lacked the ability to right that wrong (because the Judiciary Act was unconstitutional). Still, it was not until the decision in *Marbury* that the exercise of judicial review resulted in the invalidation of an act of Congress. Consequently, Marshall's decision in that case is properly revered as a precedent-setting moment in the development of both American constitutional law and the American political process.

Judicial Review and the American Political Process. In subsequent cases, the Supreme Court extended the power of federal courts to nullify as unconstitutional the decisions of state courts (*Martin v. Hunter's Lessee*, 1816), state laws (*McCulloch v. Maryland*, 1819), and presidential action (for example, President Harry Truman's 1951 attempt to seize steel mills during the Korean War, disallowed by the Supreme Court in *Youngstown Sheet & Tube Co. v. Sawyer*, 1952). Indeed, the willingness of federal courts to exercise judicial review vis a

The 1952 Supreme Court that declared that President Truman's attempt to put steel mills under direct government control was unconstitutional. Chief Justice Fred M. Vinson is in the center. (Harris and Ewing, collection of the Supreme Court of the United States)

vis state legislation and state court opinions was essential to the survival of federalism in the United States. Legal chaos would have resulted without the federal courts judiciously applying the supremacy clause to sustain the unfettered execution of the laws of Congress. Yet the willingness of the Supreme Court to assert the independence of the judiciary over the will of popularly elected majorities in Congress and popular presidents, also established by John Marshall in *Marbury v. Madison*, has been equally important to the development of the rule of law and separation of powers democracy in the United States.

Judicial review involves more than nullifying acts of government for contravening the Constitution. It embraces the power to interpret the Constitution to ascertain the validity of acts of government. In reviewing the authority of the federal government, the Supreme Court has historically taken a permissive approach. In so doing, the federal judiciary has been a major instrument for expanding the powers of the federal government and enabling government in the United States to function for more than two hundred years under a document written in the eighteenth century and intentionally made difficult to change by the formal amendment process. There are four broad categories of power which the federal government is today constitutionally recognized to possess: those expressly delegated to Congress and enumerated in Article I; those which may be reasonably implied from the delegated powers and represent appropriate means to their achievement; those inherent powers, such as the right to acquire land by conquest, which give the United States the same powers in foreign affairs as other countries; and the residual (or emergency) powers to do what is necessary to survive in the face of foreign or domestic crises. Of these, only the enumerated powers were explicitly conferred upon the federal government under the Constitution. The others have been "discovered" in the Constitution by the Supreme Court in such seminal cases as *McCulloch v. Maryland*. Moreover, the enumerated powers have been steadily given a much wider construction than was attached to them in 1789.

The expansion of the powers of the central government has not been at the expense of individual rights and liberties. The Supreme Court's interpretation of the provisions of the Bill of Rights and the Fourteenth Amendment has profoundly expanded the freedom of American citizens vis a vis all levels of government, profoundly influencing the nature of American politics and society in the process. The selective incorporation of most of the provisions found in the Bill of Rights into the due process clause of the Fourteenth Amendment, for example, resulted in an overhaul of the United States' system of justice during the 1949-1966 period framed by *Wolf v. Colorado* and *Miranda v. Arizona*. This period bestowed on Americans regardless of their state of residence the right to freedom from unreasonable searches and seizures, to confront their accusers, to a fair trial by jury in criminal cases, and to have an attorney not only in criminal trials but also in pretrial interrogation proceedings. Likewise, the emphasis given to the rights of citizens under the "equal protection of the law" clause

of the Fourteenth Amendment contributed greatly during the second half of the twentieth century to the emergence of a more integrated, empowered, and egalitarian society in the United States.

Restraints on Judicial Review. The ability of the federal courts to hear such controversial cases as those involving unwed women seeking the right to terminate unwanted pregnancies, and decisions such as that of *Roe v. Wade* (1973) recognizing a woman's constitutional right to do so, has led critics of the Supreme Court to attack it as acting above the law. This indictment is misconceived. Although it is true that once the Supreme Court rules on the meaning of the Constitution, its decision becomes the supreme law of the land and is only alterable by constitutional amendment or by the Supreme Court reversing itself in a later case, the federal judiciary does not lie outside the constitutional system of checks and balance. To the contrary, the president and Congress have three powerful tools at their disposal to influence the process of judicial review. First, the size of the Supreme Court is fixed by the Congress, not the Constitution. Although the sitting justices hold their positions for life (barring impeachment), additional justices could theoretically be added to turn a 6-3 majority on the Supreme Court into a 6-9 minority, as President Franklin Roosevelt contemplated doing in 1936 when the Supreme Court proved initially hostile to his New Deal legislation. Congress can also deny the judiciary the right to review certain types of cases, for the appellate jurisdiction of the federal judiciary is derived from acts of Congress, not the Constitution. If these steps are too direct and intrusive to find support in public opinion, critics of an active judiciary have long been able to delay the process of judicial review by slowing the process of filling vacancies on the lower federal courts and thus increasing the workload on the remaining judges.

These restraints, combined with the inherently controversial nature of many of the cases which the federal courts receive regarding safeguarding the rights of unpopular individuals, have prompted the federal courts to restrain themselves in their exercise of judicial review. Well aware that judicial review is a policy-making power and that nonelective bodies engage in it at their potential peril in a democratic political system, over the years the Supreme Court has developed an elaborate set of rules of judicial self-restraint for itself and the lower federal courts. Federal courts, for example, stay out of essentially political (and especially partisan) conflicts. Similarly, cases are heard only when there is an actual controversy (no advisory opinions are given), and the litigants must have a substantial interest in order to have legal standing. Above all, laws normally are presumed valid and are interpreted, as much as possible, in ways that uphold them. Issues of constitutional validity are considered only when there is no other basis upon which to decide a case. —*Joseph R. Rudolph, Jr.*

See also Constitution, U.S.; Constitutional interpretation; Constitutional law; Incorporation doctrine; Judicial system, U.S.; *Marbury v. Madison*; Marshall, John; Supremacy clause; Supreme Court of the United States.

BIBLIOGRAPHY

On the general need for judicial review, see Alexander Hamilton's essay "Number 78" in Hamilton, John Jay, and James Madison, *The Federalist: A Commentary on the Constitution of the United States* (New York: Random House Modern Library, 1941, reprint of 1787 *Essays Written in Support of the Constitution*). Among the many outstanding books on judicial review and constitutional law in the United States, see Edward S. Corwin's classic, *Court over Constitution: A Study of Judicial Review as an Instrument of Popular Government* (Princeton, N.J.: Princeton University Press, 1938); Henry J. Abraham, *The Judicial Process* (6th ed. New York: Oxford University Press, 1993); Michael J. Gerhardt and Thomas D. Rowe, Jr., *Constitutional Theory: Arguments and Perspectives* (Charlottesville, Va.: Michie, 1993); and Sylvia Snowiss, *Judicial Review and the Law of the Constitution* (New Haven, Conn.: Yale University Press, 1990).

Judicial system, U.S.

DEFINITION: The organization and interrelatedness of the courts of the federal government with the courts in the fifty states

SIGNIFICANCE: The United States has a dual judicial system composed of federal and state courts that are organized as separate and independent systems; these systems are integrated and coordinated in subtle and complex accommodations of judicial federalism

The basic duality of the U.S. judicial system, in which the federal judiciary coexists alongside the judiciaries of the fifty states, is a blueprint for conflicts. Although today this arrangement is taken for granted, the conceptual idea that two independent sovereigns could occupy the same territory and govern at the same time was a radical innovation of eighteenth century political philosophy. The framers of the Constitution of 1787 were uncertain that such a federal system would work; they were certain that there would be conflicts between the federal and state governments, particularly between the federal courts and the state courts. Judicial federalism is the term used to describe the ongoing accommodation of these conflicts.

Historical Origins. The study of the U.S. judicial system begins with two eighteenth century events: ratification of Article III of the U.S. Constitution and passage of the Judiciary Act of 1789. Article III settled the issue of whether Congress should be given the power to create independent federal courts. The debate over Article III at the Constitutional Convention of 1787 was protracted and intense. An early draft of the Constitution had provided for a federal judicial branch. The delegates had second thoughts, however, and voted to strike the provision and make no mention of national courts other than the Supreme Court. Their rationale was that the existing state courts were equal to the judicial tasks of the nation; all that was needed was to provide for appeals from state courts to some supreme national court to preserve the uniformity and the supremacy of the national law. The state courts would have been the chief expositors of federal law had

that position prevailed, and U.S. history would have developed far differently.

After further intense parliamentary wrangling, however, a compromise was reached, and the text of Article III was redrafted to read as it does today. It begins, "The judicial Power of the United States, shall be vested in one supreme Court, and in such inferior Courts as the Congress may from time to time ordain and establish." This language left the issue to Congress whether to create lower courts below the Supreme Court.

The delegates' compromise was the subject of controversy in the debates in the state ratifying conventions. The *Federalist Papers* (numbers 78 to 82, 1788) defended the wisdom of a separate and independent federal judiciary. Numerous amendments to Article III were proposed in the state ratifying conventions, and some of the provisions in the Bill of Rights, such as the Seventh Amendment right to a jury in a civil case, owe their origin to the controversy over Article III.

The anti-Federalists were mistrustful of the proposed Constitution. They campaigned against the document in most of its particulars and especially opposed the power to create a new federal judiciary. They feared that it would increase political power in the central government at the expense of the sovereign states. They wanted the state courts to remain supreme, and they nearly prevailed. The ratification outcome was in no measure certain, and the Federalists—who championed the Constitution—prevailed by the smallest of margins in several key states (the vote in Massachusetts was 187 to 168; Virginia, 89 to 79; and New York, 30 to 27). Thus, from the beginning, judicial federalism has been a theme in U.S. constitutional history.

Upon ratification, one of the transcendent achievements of the first Congress under the new Constitution was the passage of the Judiciary Act of 1789, also known as the First Judiciary Act. That statute established the tradition of a system of inferior federal courts. Today there are complex and detailed statutes in the U.S. Code and in the statutes of the fifty states describing the organization and jurisdictions of their judicial branches. The most controversial of these jurisdictions and procedures always have involved the interrelationship between the federal courts and the state courts.

Organization of Federal Courts. The structure of the federal judiciary is pyramidal. The Supreme Court, the courts of appeals, and the district courts form the three levels of federal courts.

At the apex is the Supreme Court of the United States, the only federal court created directly by the Constitution, which declares that there shall be "one supreme Court." The Supreme Court is the highest supervisory court within the federal judiciary. Therefore, it reviews the decisions of the lower federal courts, and it interprets the laws Congress enacts. The Supreme Court also has appellate authority over the state courts, but only for matters of federal law. It comprises nine justices, appointed by the president with the advice and consent of the Senate. Justices have lifetime tenure. Each justice is assigned to one of the courts of appeals for emergency matters, and the

STRUCTURE OF THE FEDERAL COURT SYSTEM

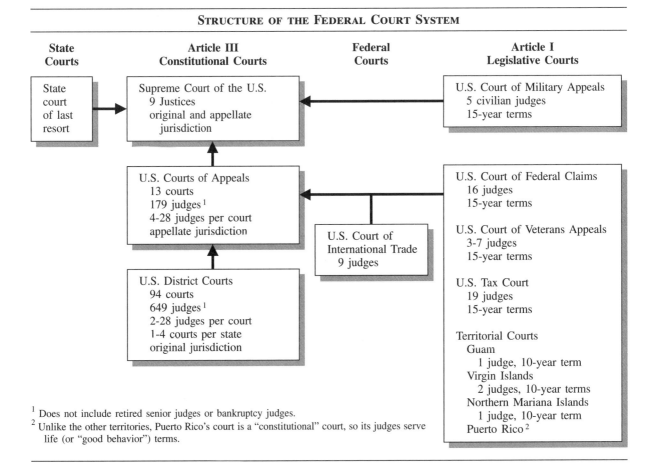

| State Courts | Article III Constitutional Courts | Federal Courts | Article I Legislative Courts |

State court of last resort

Supreme Court of the U.S.
9 Justices
original and appellate jurisdiction

U.S. Court of Military Appeals
5 civilian judges
15-year terms

U.S. Courts of Appeals
13 courts
179 judges [1]
4-28 judges per court
appellate jurisdiction

U.S. Court of International Trade
9 judges

U.S. Court of Federal Claims
16 judges
15-year terms

U.S. Court of Veterans Appeals
3-7 judges
15-year terms

U.S. District Courts
94 courts
649 judges [1]
2-28 judges per court
1-4 courts per state
original jurisdiction

U.S. Tax Court
19 judges
15-year terms

Territorial Courts
Guam
    1 judge, 10-year term
Virgin Islands
    2 judges, 10-year terms
Northern Mariana Islands
    1 judge, 10-year term
Puerto Rico [2]

[1] Does not include retired senior judges or bankruptcy judges.
[2] Unlike the other territories, Puerto Rico's court is a "constitutional" court, so its judges serve life (or "good behavior") terms.

chief justice of the United States has additional administrative duties. The Supreme Court sits only *en banc*, with all of its members participating. Its annual term begins on the first Monday of October and continues usually through the end of June. Its annual docket consists of more than seven thousand cases. Most of its jurisdiction is discretionary, and the Court exercises great care in selecting cases for full review. Most cases are disposed of, without a decision on the merits of the case, by a brief order denying the petition for review or dismissing the appeal for want of a substantial question. Of the thousands of cases presented each term, the Supreme Court selects about 120 of the most important for full briefing, oral argument, and decision by written opinion.

At the level of intermediate federal courts, there are thirteen United States courts of appeals and the Court of Appeals for the Armed Forces. Twelve of the courts of appeals have jurisdiction over federal cases in certain geographical areas, each covering a number of contiguous states. The thirteenth, the federal circuit, has a national jurisdiction over specific types of cases, mostly involving patents, trademarks, international trade, and claims against the United States. The number of judges appointed for each court of appeals varies from six to twenty-eight. These courts of appeals sit in panels of three

judges, subject to rare full court rehearings before all the circuit judges sitting *en banc*. Appeals to the courts of appeals, for the most part, are appeals as of right: The party who lost in the trial court files a notice of appeal, and the matter must be heard and decided. Most matters appealed from the trial courts are affirmed by the courts of appeals; the reversal rate hovers between 10 and 20 percent. The courts of appeals have evolved into what could be called "junior varsity" supreme courts that determine the federal law for their geographical region, unless and until the Supreme Court overrules them.

The court with primary original or trial jurisdiction in the federal judiciary is the United States district court. Federal statutes divide the country and territories into ninety-four geographical districts. Districts do not extend beyond state boundary lines; each state constitutes at least one district, and many states are divided into one, two, three, or four districts. Districts are sometimes internally arranged into divisions for administrative purposes. There are more than six hundred district judges, and each district has a chief judge, designated on the basis of seniority, who has additional administrative responsibilities. In a statistical year, the district courts decide more than two hundred thousand civil cases, including civil rights actions, personal injury or property damage actions, and prisoner petitions. There are nearly fifty thousand additional federal criminal cases, mostly felonies. Two additional federal judicial officers serve at the bottom of the federal court pyramid: U.S. magistrate judges and bankruptcy judges. Magistrate judges are appointed by the district judges and perform as their adjuncts, handling miscellaneous judicial tasks specified by statute and holding civil trials with the consent of the parties. Bankruptcy judges are appointed by the courts of appeals and preside over the various categories of exclusive federal jurisdiction for individual and business reorganizations.

Organization of State Courts. Because state court structures vary widely from state to state, only broad generalizations are possible. All the states have some version of the pyramid-shaped structure of the federal judiciary, although the specific names of courts and their particular jurisdictions are highly state-specific.

Most state judges are elected, in contrast to the appointed judges in the federal system who serve "during good behavior" (effectively for life), although state judicial elections frequently are solely retention elections and often are nonpartisan. Unlike the federal judiciary, most state court structures have a bifurcated trial level. In a bifurcated system, trial courts of limited jurisdiction hear disputes on specified matters, generally involving small monetary matters or minor criminal offenses. Trial courts of general jurisdiction have jurisdiction over more important civil matters and more serious criminal offenses. The courts of general jurisdiction usually are courts of record—transcripts of their proceedings are required. Their procedure is more formal, and they sometimes hear appeals from the courts of limited jurisdiction, commonly by a trial *de novo*, which means that an entirely new proceeding is held.

A growing majority of states has established intermediate appellate courts, often as a response to caseload pressure on the highest court in the state. These intermediate appellate courts hear appeals as of right from the trial courts of general jurisdiction and typically are arranged geographically within the state, usually hearing appeals from contiguous counties. It is not uncommon for state intermediate courts to have some reviewing authority of decisions issued by state administrative agencies.

Each state has a state supreme court, although jurisdictional provisions vary considerably. In some states, the appeal to the highest state court is discretionary, much like the U.S. Supreme Court, but in others such an appeal is a matter of statutory entitlement and the state supreme court is obliged to hear the appeal. The state supreme courts are the great common-law courts in the American judicial system. They have developed bodies of decisional law in torts and contracts, for example, that are comprehensive and highly sophisticated. The common law is developed by application of the principle of *stare decisis*, which basically obliges a court deciding an issue to follow the precedent established by an earlier court deciding the same issue unless there are compelling reasons to do otherwise.

When considered collectively, the fifty state judiciaries almost defy statistical measure. They dwarf the more elite federal courts. In 1992, there were nearly 28,000 state trial judges

presiding over approximately 16,500 state trial courts of general and limited jurisdictions in the fifty states. That year there were more than 250,000 appeals filed; more than 60 percent were mandatory appeals to intermediate appellate courts, and the rest were appeals to state courts of last resort. Many state trial and appellate courts have experienced great difficulty keeping up with accelerating increases in caseload. More generally, budget problems in the states have resulted in funding crises for state courts.

Comparisons with Other Countries. The jurisdictions of the state and federal courts in the United States overlap to a large extent. There are some jurisdictions that are exclusively assigned to the federal courts, such as bankruptcy and patent cases, but those are the exceptions. Most of the jurisdiction of the federal courts is concurrent with the state courts. This means that the same lawsuit can be filed in either the U.S. district court or in a state court of general jurisdiction. Sometimes the parties actually file two separate lawsuits. When this happens, the first proceeding to reach a final judgment is then deemed controlling in the other court, state or federal. Questions of federal law decided in state trial or appellate courts are subject to review by the U.S. Supreme Court. Besides these vertical conflicts between the federal and state courts, it frequently happens that horizontal conflicts arise—when, for example, the state courts in one state must decide a question by applying the law of another state.

Thus the United States has a comparatively complex judicial system. Other western democracies with federal systems use an entirely different model: The state/provincial courts perform the trial function, and the federal/national courts perform the appellate function. Australia and Canada, two federal systems that share the English common-law tradition with the United States, adhere to this alternative model, with some variations. In some federations, the federal authorities appoint all the judges, federal and state. In other federations, federal courts hear and decide only federal matters, and state courts hear and decide only state matters.

Conflicts Between State and Federal Courts. Issues of state court jurisdiction versus federal court jurisdiction are issues of constitutional power. Because federal courts are courts of limited jurisdiction, there is a presumption that the court lacks subject matter jurisdiction until it can be shown that the case falls within the appropriate constitutional and statutory authorizations. In contrast, a state court is not so limited. The presumption is that jurisdiction exists to hear and decide the matter and to afford appropriate relief. There are several points of regular conflict between state courts and federal courts.

The U.S. Supreme Court hears appeals from the highest courts of the states involving issues of federal law, interpretations of the U.S. Constitution, and federal statutes. State court judges are bound by their constitutional oath to follow the rulings of the U.S. Supreme Court, but the state court interpretations of state laws, including state constitutions, are binding on the U.S. Supreme Court so long as they are not inconsistent with federal law. Under the doctrine of the independent and adequate state ground, the Supreme Court will not hear a case if the decision of the state's highest court is supported by a state law rationale that is independent of federal law and adequate to sustain the result. The rationale is that it is better to decline to hear the case if a reversal of the state court's federal law ruling will not change the outcome of the case.

By federal statute, a person convicted for a state crime and serving a sentence in state custody may petition for a writ of *habeas corpus* in the U.S. district court. The petition must allege that the conviction and custody violate the U.S. Constitution. The U.S. district court can issue the writ and order the state authorities to release the prisoner unless a new trial is held. Appeals from the denial of the writ go to a U.S. court of appeals and then to the U.S. Supreme Court. This federal court jurisdiction is most controversial in cases in which the state prisoner has been sentenced to death and there are repeated federal appeals, often brought just before a scheduled execution.

Ever since the Judiciary Act of 1789, Congress has afforded federal courts jurisdiction in diversity cases, which are suits between citizens of different states or between a citizen of a state and an alien, when the amount in controversy exceeds a certain amount (set at $50,000 in 1988). When these requirements are satisfied, the plaintiff has a choice of filing in a U.S. district court or in a state court of general jurisdiction. Even if the plaintiff files in state court, the defendant may remove the case to the U.S. district court, under a federal statute. The policy behind this jurisdiction is a worry that a state court might be prejudiced against an out-of-state party. In theory, the federal judge hearing a diversity case must apply the law that a state judge would apply in state court. State judges, on the other hand, are not bound by the decisions of federal judges based on state law.

The principles of judicial federalism are not found in so many words in the U.S. Constitution, but nevertheless they are part of its deep structure. It would not simply be "bad form" for a federal court to entertain a case not within its jurisdiction; it would be an unconstitutional invasion of the powers reserved to the states. The intersovereign judicial interactions made possible by concurrent jurisdictions in such a complex court system cause problems that must be solved by complex statutes and sophisticated court doctrines. —*Thomas E. Baker*

See also Appellate process; Attorney; Civil procedure; Constitution, U.S.; Constitutional law; Criminal justice system; Federalism; Judicial review; Jury system; Juvenile justice system; Supremacy clause.

BIBLIOGRAPHY

The best single volume on the federal court system is Charles Alan Wright, *The Law of Federal Courts* (5th ed. St. Paul, Minn.: West, 1994). Two other sources focus on present and past issues: Richard A. Posner, *The Federal Courts: Crisis and Reform* (Cambridge, Mass.: Harvard University Press, 1985), and Erwin C. Surrency, *History of the Federal Courts* (New York: Oceana, 1987). Several other references emphasize the role of the state courts: Susan P. Fino, *The Role of State Supreme Courts in the New Judicial Federalism* (New York: Greenwood, 1987); Henry Robert Glick, *State Court Systems* (Englewood Cliffs, N.J.: Prentice-Hall, 1973); Daniel J. Meador, *American Courts* (St. Paul, Minn.: West, 1991); G. Alan Tarr, *State Supreme Courts in State and Nation* (New Haven, Conn.: Yale University Press, 1988). For comparative international treatments of different federal systems, see Henry J. Abraham, *The Judicial Process: An Introductory Analysis of the Courts of the United States, England, and France* (5th ed. New York: Oxford University Press, 1986), and Richard E. Johnston, *The Effect of Judicial Review on Federal-State Relations in Australia, Canada, and the United States* (Baton Rouge: Louisiana State University Press, 1969).

Judiciary Acts

DATE: September 24, 1789; February 13, 1801 (repealed March 31, 1802)

DEFINITION: The Judiciary Acts delineated the structure and powers of the federal judicial system

SIGNIFICANCE: Since the judicial branch had been left undefined in the Constitution, the Judiciary Acts established the initial federal judicial system

The Judiciary Act of 1789 provided for a Supreme Court with a chief justice and five associates as well as district and circuit courts. It also established the principle of appeals from the state courts to the federal judiciary created a fledgling federal justice system. Furthermore, the Supreme Court's right to determine the constitutionality of congressional laws was implied in the act.

With Federalist defeat in the 1800 election, the lame-duck Congress rushed passage of the 1801 Federal Judiciary Bill. During his last hours as president, John Adams appointed numerous Federalists to judicial posts, including Chief Justice John Marshall. Viewing it as a partisan measure, the Republicans immediately sought and gained repeal of the 1801 act. On March 31, 1802, the repeal became law, and the judicial system reverted to that established by the 1789 act. John Marshall remained chief justice until his death in 1835, however, and through his extraordinary leadership he extended and increased the powers of the federal judiciary. Marshall's decision in *Marbury v. Madison* (1803) firmly established the principle of judicial review.

See also Judicial review; Judicial system, U.S.; *Marbury v. Madison*; Marshall, John; Supreme Court of the United States.

Jurisprudence

DEFINITION: The philosophy of law, which seeks to discover the nature and justification of law

SIGNIFICANCE: Jurisprudence clarifies concepts used in law, exposes the law's presuppositions, and offers constructive criticism of legal doctrines

Jurisprudence seeks answers to fundamental questions about law and its function in society, questions that have been asked for thousands of years. Written discussions of law go back to the ancient Greeks, but the subject of jurisprudence has received increasing attention since the nineteenth century. Not merely the domain of scholars, jurisprudence is an integral part of the practice of law. Judges, particularly in appeals courts, typically consider the implications of their decisions beyond the case immediately at hand. Among the central aspects of jurisprudence are defining law and weighing the differing philosophies of what law should be based on and what it should accomplish.

Defining Law. By definition, law can be distinguished from related concepts such as morality. Some legal philosophers, it should be noted, such as H. L. A. Hart, reject attempts at definition and instead analyze law as a group of interrelated ideas. Actual definitions have varied widely according to time and place. The ancient Greek philosophers Plato and Aristotle viewed law as practical reasoning aimed at the common good of citizens in a city-state. The purpose of law was to enhance virtue and create a just social order. In the first century B.C.:, the Roman statesman Cicero extended Greek concepts into an explicit natural law theory: Law is reason in agreement with nature, and such law is unchanging. All positive law is derived from natural law. The scholastics of the middle ages, such as Thomas Aquinas, adapted natural law to Christianity and derived law from theological doctrines. One consequence of a belief in natural law is that any positive human law that is inconsistent with natural law is not really law and may be disobeyed. Natural law theories, after a period of disuse, regained acceptance in the twentieth century in the guise of fundamental freedoms that no law can override.

Opposed to natural law is positivism, which views law as a set of commands issued by a sovereign power and enforced by sanctions. Its representatives, such as John Austin and Hans Kelsen, denied that laws can be criticized or evaluated on nonlegal grounds such as morality.

Utilitarianism, identified with Jeremy Bentham and John Stuart Mill, equated a good law with rules that promote the happiness of the greatest number. Karl Marx, on the other hand, viewed law as an instrument of capitalism whose real purpose was to protect the ruling classes from the workers. Law, Marx theorized, would ultimately wither away along with capitalism. Legal realism in the twentieth century defined law in terms of what courts and officials do when deciding cases and not as a set of rules at all. Sociological jurisprudence, inspired by people such as Roscoe Pound, saw law as balancing the interests of various groups in society. It used a "social engineering" model to describe the function of law. Utilitarianism, legal realism, and sociological jurisprudence emphasized the operation of law in society. As a result, they spawned major law reform movements.

Law and Morality. Positivism saw no connection between law and morals. The tyrannies and atrocities of the twentieth century led to a revival of natural law, which sees a close connection. Minimalist versions of natural law, such as the version of Lon Fuller, based law on the needs of people who live in communities governed by rules. Legal realism and sociological jurisprudence granted the relevance of morality to law but grouped it with considerations such as social policy and economic efficiency. Even among philosophers who agree

that morality is relevant to law, there is intense disagreement over how the connection is to function and the ultimate effect of morality on particular laws.

Obligation to Obey the Law. Positivism identified the obligation to obey law with the threat of a sanction or punishment. Natural law and utilitarianism found threats inadequate and saw a moral basis for such an obligation. The moral basis of law is a sufficient reason to obey it. Thomas Hobbes and John Locke found the obligation in the social contract. People in a "state of nature" may have had an absolute right to do as they wished with no external restraint, but they gave up such rights when entering society, where the right to act was transferred to a sovereign or government. The social contract was a voluntary creation of an obligation to obey law.

Legal Rights and Duties. Law creates and enforces various rights and duties, such as the right of privacy and a duty to avoid inflicting unwarranted harm. The nature and sources of such rights and duties need some explanation. Legal rights and duties are sometimes reduced to nonlegal interests. Natural law theories easily identified legal rights and duties with moral rights and duties. Other concepts derived rights and duties from more basic wants and needs of individuals. For example, criminal laws against murder can be derived from the need for personal safety and security.

Besides identifying the sources of rights and duties, philosophers such as Wesley Hohfeld traced the relationships between fundamental legal conceptions. Rights and duties are correlative: For every right there is a duty. If an individual has a right of ownership in a piece of property, then others have a duty not to interfere with the property.

Justice in a Legal System. A fundamental purpose of law is the promotion of justice, if justice means equal treatment in similar cases. This notion was embodied in the equal protection clause of the Fourteenth Amendment to the U.S. Constitution. This general concept does not explain when people or situations are really alike, however, so jurisprudence seeks deeper meanings. Justice may be divided into the concepts of distributive and retributive justice. Distributive justice requires that benefits and burdens be divided equally, while retributive justice seeks to rectify denials of benefits by sanctions and punishments. The idea of justice as fairness, associated with John Rawls, argues for a minimal conception in terms of fair procedures used to allocate benefits and burdens. A distribution is just if the procedures used to accomplish it are viewed as fair, even if the final distribution is unequal. Such notions have obvious applications to a welfare state, where law allocates entitlements among a variety of recipients.

The standards to be used in passing a just law are also a matter for jurisprudence. Rawls insists on fair procedures. Utilitarians, on the other hand, base just laws on the happiness of the greatest number. Immanuel Kant advanced the principle that all persons are to be treated as ends in themselves and never merely as a means. Kant would reject slavery and discrimination as illegal because they treat victims as means, even if sometimes such treatment could result in overall happiness for most of society. The legal basis for U.S. laws forbidding race and sex discrimination can be seen as Kantian because they are based on a perception that people have inherent value.

Liberty Versus Paternalism. Most philosophers recognize fundamental rights such as freedom of expression, privacy, and the right to pursue an individual plan of life. When can law restrict the pursuit of such rights? John Stuart Mill argued that law is justified in restricting rights only when the action of an individual will harm someone else and that paternalism, which amounts to protecting people from the effects of their own acts, is never justified. Other philosophers do not use a harm-to-others criterion as the sole basis for law. They appeal to morality, the common good, and the social contract in limiting rights and liberties. Arguments concerning liberty and paternalism have direct consequences in law. For example, laws requiring motorcycle riders to wear helmets seem paternalistic because they are designed to protect people from the consequences of their own choices.

Punishment and Responsibility. Law imposes sanctions on persons found violating legal duties. Criminal penalties such as imprisonment are an example, as are money damages imposed in civil cases for tort and breach of contract. Not every action which causes an injury will result in a sanction, however; law normally requires a showing of fault on the part of the perpetrator and causation flowing from the perpetrator to the injury. Fault is usually defined in terms of intentional or negligent action. Liability without some element of fault is rare. When it occurs, jurisprudence must justify it. For example, modern tort law imposes strict liability without fault on manufacturers of dangerous products that injure consumers. Jurisprudence seeks to justify such a legal rule in terms of social policy or social insurance.

Criminal punishment, particularly capital punishment, raises profound questions because it involves the intentional infliction of pain. A utilitarian would punish only when the balance of pleasure over pain to be gained by punishment is greater than the balance of pleasure over pain for any alternative system (such as psychological treatment for the criminal or not punishing at all). Other philosophies view punishment as a matter of just deserts, the criminal having committed acts that allow the legal system to impose sanctions as a matter of principled justice. Punishment may also serve the purposes of reforming the offender and deterring others. Utilitarians reject punishment simply as a matter of just deserts because it obviously inflicts pain with no resulting pleasure; they evaluate criminal justice systems by how well they either reform or deter. A Kantian, however, would reject both reformation and deterrence because they involve treating the offender as a mere means to the ends of others. The subject of punishment remains highly controversial.

Legal Reasoning. Legal rules, even those found in very detailed statutes that begin with lists of legal definitions, are often indeterminate or open-textured. The application of legal rules to particular cases can be controversial, as in cases of negligence, in which a jury is required to decide if a defendant acted as a reasonable, prudent person. The test in such cases is to decide whether the defendant acted like the "ordinary person in the street." This is certainly not an obvious or well-defined concept but is the only test that can determine what is meant by negligence. Jurisprudence attempts to discover the limits of discretion in applying such indeterminate legal rules and to find ways to make particular applications consistent.

While legislatures and courts carefully seek to avoid inconsistency, the massive detail of law can result in glaring inconsistencies that must then be resolved. For example, in the famous 1889 New York case of *Riggs v. Palmer*, a grandson murdered his grandfather to inherit a farm. The grandfather had left the farm to the grandson in a will, and under New York law the grandson clearly inherited it. Yet this situation was inconsistent with such equitable maxims as "no one shall profit by his own wrong." The court resolved the issue by examining the apparent intent of the legislature in passing the statute on wills and then attempted to fit this intention with other legal rules such as the equitable maxim. As a result, the grandson did not inherit the property in spite of what the clear words of the statute said.

—David E. Paas

See also Blackstone, William; Common law; Crime; Criminal intent; Equal protection of the law; Holmes, Oliver Wendell, Jr.; Justice; Law; Legal realism; Moral relativism; Natural law and natural rights; Positive law.

BIBLIOGRAPHY

Anthologies containing standard readings on jurisprudence are John Arthur and William H. Shaw, eds., *Readings in Philosophy of Law* (Englewood Cliffs, N.J.: Prentice-Hall, 1984); Joel Feinberg and Hyman Gross, eds., *Philosophy of Law* (2d ed. Belmont, Calif.: Wadsworth Publishing, 1980); and R. M. Dworkin, ed., *The Philosophy of Law* (Oxford, England: Oxford University Press, 1977). Modern jurisprudence in English-speaking countries begins with H. L. A. Hart, *The Concept of Law* (Oxford, England: Oxford University Press, 1961). Detailed discussions of some topics are found in Ronald Dworkin, *Taking Rights Seriously* (Cambridge, Mass.: Harvard University Press, 1977), and John Rawls, *A Theory of Justice* (Cambridge, Mass.: Belknap Press of Harvard University Press, 1971).

Jury nullification

DEFINITION: The acquittal of a criminal defendant by a jury because the jury either thinks the law is unjust or believes the defendant or the crime to be commendable

SIGNIFICANCE: Jury nullification can be a significant restriction on the government's power to prosecute crimes successfully against the community's will

Under the American system of justice, three questions must be answered before a person can be convicted of a crime: What are the facts, what was the defendant's moral intent, and what is the law? The jury decides the first two under definitions of the law which are presented to it by the judge. "Jury nullification" takes place when the jury ignores (or nullifies) the law and acquits the defendant in spite of the judge's instructions. Under the constitutional provision forbidding "double jeopardy," the defendant cannot be tried again.

Historically, before juries could exercise this power, two great issues had to be settled. The first was whether judges have the power to punish jurors for bringing in the "wrong" verdict. A precedent was established in England in 1670, in what is generally referred to as Bushel's case. Bushel was one of twelve jurors who refused to convict William Penn (later to became governor of the American colony of Pennsylvania) of fomenting a riot. Penn had been preaching a Quaker sermon in public at a time when the Quakers were being persecuted. After the jurors refused to change their verdict, the judge fined them forty marks apiece. They refused to pay and were committed to Newgate Prison. Eventually they were released on bail, and when England's high court finally decided the case a year later, it was held that no jury can be punished for its verdict.

The second issue was whether juries could return "general verdicts" or only "special verdicts." A special verdict results when the jury is only allowed to answer specific questions of fact. A general verdict determines whether the accused is guilty or innocent. To render a general verdict, juries must judge the application of the facts to the law. In North America, the move from special to general verdicts was largely the result of unpopular prosecutions brought against printers by royal governors in the eighteenth century. At the trial of John Peter Zenger for seditious libel, Zenger's attorney argued that the jury had the power to decide whether Zenger was truly guilty of seditious libel. The prosecution argued that the jury could decide only whether Zenger had published the articles at issue in the case. Zenger was acquitted when the jury brought in the general verdict of "not guilty."

It is the general verdict that allows jury nullification. Juries may decide to disobey the judge's instructions if they believe either that the law is unjust or that the defendant's act was admirable or justified in some way. Prosecutors have no recourse, because acquittal is final in the American judicial system. During the nineteenth century, there was a substantial free jury movement in the United States, led by the radical American essayist Lysander Spooner. Although the movement subsided, many still argue that judges should inform jurors that they may "nullify" the law if they think it unjust. Regardless of whether juries are formally notified of this power, there are undoubtedly cases in which nullification takes place. For example, it is sometimes suggested that African American jurors are prone to acquit African American defendants, particularly on less serious charges, because they believe that there is considerable official harassment of blacks. It is difficult to tell with any certainty how common this practice may be.

See also Common law; Criminal procedure; Jury system; Mitigating circumstances; Seditious libel.

Jury system

DEFINITION: A system whereby groups of citizens representative of their communities hear testimony and assess evidence in court cases to determine the truth or falsehood of such testimony and evidence

SIGNIFICANCE: The jury system affords those accused of crimes to receive a hearing by a cross section of ordinary citizens in whose hands the determination of guilt or innocence rests

Four of every five jury trials in the world during the last half of the twentieth century occurred in the United States. Despite the inadequacies to which legal scholars, criminologists, and legislators have repeatedly pointed in such a method of judgment, the jury system is more securely entrenched in the American justice system than in the justice system of any other country. Despite modifications that various state governments have made in it, one can safely predict that the jury system will remain intact in the United States for many years to come.

The jury system is a fundamental part of the American justice system largely because the authors of the Declaration of Independence listed as one of their major complaints against the Crown that it was "depriving us, in many Cases, of the Benefits of Trial by Jury." Given this background, the nation's founders made provision for the jury system when they drew up the United States Constitution.

Constitutional Mandates. Article III of the Constitution promises those accused of any federal crimes (except for impeachment) the right to trial by jury. The Fifth Amendment specifies that no citizen shall be answerable for the commission of any capital or "otherwise infamous crime, unless on a presentment or indictment of a Grand Jury," thereby placing the judgment of testimony and evidence in the hands of a representative body of the citizenry.

The Sixth Amendment guarantees a speedy public trial "by an impartial jury of the State and district wherein the crime shall have been committed." The word "impartial" is particularly important in this amendment and has been the basis for empaneling disinterested jurors to hear both criminal and civil cases. The Seventh Amendment states that "in suits of common law, where the value in controversy shall exceed twenty dollars, the right of trial by jury shall be preserved, and no fact tried by a jury, shall be otherwise reexamined in any Court of the United States, than according to the rules of the common law." This amendment, which firmly establishes the right to trial by jury, also establishes the all-important guarantee against double jeopardy.

The Fourteenth Amendment guarantees the right of a jury trial to any defendant accused of a crime, federal or state, that carries a penalty of more than six months' imprisonment. The protection of this amendment, which has been tested in the courts, is not extended to those accused of minor offenses.

Given constitutional guarantees that resulted from zealous reactions to widespread dissatisfaction with Britain's governance of the colonies, the American judicial system would be hard pressed to move to any judicial system that did not involve juries. For all the faults jurists have found with the system, it is so fundamentally a part of the American justice system that it is inconceivable to envision the system without it.

The Grand Jury. Grand juries are bodies consisting usually of between sixteen and twenty-three jurors. They are subdivided into two types of juries, those that charge defendants and those that investigate.

The first of these examines the evidence brought forth against a suspect to determine whether it is sufficient to warrant a formal charge that will lead to a court trial by another, smaller jury. If the evidence suggests that there is probable cause for a trial, an indictment is issued that sets in motion the machinery for a jury trial. An investigatory grand jury, on the other hand, examines evidence against public officials suspected or accused of criminal misconduct in office. It also investigates alleged criminal activity in other segments of society, such as organized crime. It, too, can issue indictments if the testimony and evidence suggest probable cause.

Hearings held by grand juries are closed to the public. The rights of those suspected of violations are protected meticulously, and all suspects enjoy the presumption of innocence. Indictments are not declarations of guilt; they merely indicate the need for further investigation.

The Petit Jury. The jury with which most Americans are familiar is the petit or petty jury, so designated because of its size. In the United States it generally consists of twelve jurors and some alternates, although in some states juries may range from six to ten members.

In criminal cases, the petit jury decides whether defendants are guilty or innocent of the crimes of which they have been accused. In civil cases, juries establish liability and determine the damages awarded to successful complainants. The courtrooms in which cases are tried by petit juries are generally open to the public, although judges may limit the number of observers and are empowered, under certain circumstances, to clear the courtroom. All defendants in criminal cases that petit juries hear are deemed innocent until their guilt is proved to the jury beyond a reasonable doubt. Presumption of innocence is the keystone of the American justice system. If a reasonable doubt exists about any defendant's guilt, the verdict of acquittal must be returned.

Coroners' Juries. In most jurisdictions, coroners' juries are composed of six members. It is their purpose to hold investigations, termed inquests, into the cause of death where doubt exists. They are frequently called upon, for example, to determine whether a given death was murder or suicide. They work closely with forensic pathologists, who perform autopsies that provide them with the information they need to make reasonable judgments.

The Making of Juries. Stringent rules govern how juries are constituted. To begin with, pools of jurors must be representative of the general population. No United States citizen may be excluded from the pool of jurors on such arbitrary bases as race, gender, or class. Furthermore, jurors drawn from the jury pool to judge specific cases must also be representative of the community wherein the indictment has been issued.

The overall pool of jurors at one time was drawn only from those who owned property. This method of selection, however, was successfully challenged by those who contended that it imposed a class distinction upon jury selection. The pool then came to be drawn from the voting rolls. Before the enactment of the Nineteenth Amendment in 1920, however, women were excluded from the voting rolls in most states, and until the Voting Rights Act of 1965, the voting rolls in many southern states held the names of few black voters, making it impossible to impanel representative juries.

Toward the end of the twentieth century, other methods began to be employed to develop pools of jurors. The most common of these draws pools from lists of licensed drivers as well as registered voters. This method broadened substantially the composition of jury pools and constitutes a major advance toward making juries more representative of the general population than they had previously been.

In deciding who will serve on juries slated to hear specific cases, in a process known as *voir dire*, attorneys for both defense and prosecution question potential jurors drawn from the pool. The selection of an appropriate jury is essential to the successful defense or prosecution of any case. Effective attorneys select juries with great care and deliberation, sometimes employing consultants well trained in jury selection to guide them toward the best choices.

If their questioning uncovers obvious biases that might cloud a juror's objectivity or give reason to suspect that a potential juror has already reached a conclusion about the case to be tried, attorneys on either side may reject that person as a juror. Such dismissals are called objections for cause. Attorneys are permitted an unlimited number of such objections.

Attorneys are also allowed a limited number of peremptory challenges. These challenges do not require the attorney to offer any explanation or justification to the court, although such challenges clearly made solely on the basis of race or gender may lead to a mistrial. Peremptory challenges might legitimately be exercised, for example, to exclude a retiree dependent upon investment income from the trial of a stockbroker accused of fraudulent dealings with elderly clients or to exclude the local president of a temperance organization from serving on the jury in a drunk driving case.

The Jury's Decision. In most jurisdictions, the decision to find a defendant guilty in criminal cases must be unanimous. If even one juror votes against conviction and cannot be persuaded in subsequent balloting to change the not-guilty vote, a deadlock is declared and a "hung jury" is said to exist. There is no official limit on how many ballots a jury may take during its deliberations.

When jury deliberations result in a hung jury, defendants are still presumed innocent, although the accusations against them remain intact. Prosecutors can elect to reopen such cases and to hold retrials, although in many instances the press of other cases makes them reluctant to pursue such a course. They may also come under pressure to consider cost over the pursuit of justice. Some jurisdictions have sought to overcome the problem of hung juries by allowing specified majority votes of guilty—often ten out of twelve—to result in conviction. In Scotland, it has long taken only a simple majority to convict.

Defendants who are acquitted, under the constitutional prohibition of double jeopardy, cannot be tried again for the same crime even if additional evidence comes to light. Defendants

In most jurisdictions, a jury comprises twelve people, and the jury's decision must be unanimous. (James L. Shaffer)

who are found guilty, however, may appeal their convictions and, if compelling reasons are found for doing so, be retried.

The secrecy of the jury room has generally remained sacrosanct after a trial. Jurors, although they may be polled after their foreman has announced the verdict, are under no obligation to explain their votes.

The Beginnings of the Jury System. The jury system is a product of the past millennium. It grew out of the development of codified laws and statutes that came to be accepted by society to replace or at least supplement many of the controls that earlier resided in the family, whose eldest male member usually served a judicial function. The rules that governed such a system were often capricious, whereas law as society conceives it is meant to be uniform, and justice as society conceives it is ideally blind.

When William the Conqueror invaded England in 1066, right (which was often determined by combat) did not always triumph over might. A person who accused another of a crime besmirched the integrity of that person, who then felt honorbound to engage in combat with the accuser to avenge the insult. In such situations, might was right. The stronger combatant won regardless of whose case was more valid.

In many societies, trial by ordeal was a popular form of determining guilt or innocence until three or four centuries ago. Accused persons who could walk over glowing embers without blistering their feet or carry several pounds of hot coals in their hands without injury were considered innocent of all charges against them. Innocence, needless to say, was seldom the outcome in these primitive judicial procedures.

Before the year 1000, Ethelred I, king of England, recognizing that the English system of justice was deficient, appointed twelve of his most trusted followers to investigate illegal activities and to make formal accusations against suspects, much as grand juries do in modern society. After the evidence had been heard, a guilty vote by eight of the twelve would result in conviction. It is probably this early model of the jury that eventually caused most petit juries in the United States to have twelve members.

In the Anglo-Saxon era, with society centered in small villages or feudal keeps, people knew one another well. King Alfred, as early as 850, had divided every community in his empire into units of ten families that were mutually responsible for one another's behavior. Ten groups of such families, or "tythings," constituted a judicial unit called a "hundred."

County courts run by sheriffs met twice a year to hear cases brought by the "hundredors," as they were called. Cases were heard by twelve members of the hundredors who were selected because of their personal knowledge of each case being tried.

Among the early British, reputation carried great weight and honor was valued above all else. If people well respected in the community were accused of crimes by individuals, they either owned up to the accusation and made amends or, upon their honor, vowed innocence. Such vows were readily accepted from people who were known to be honest, although strangers who vowed innocence were often subjected to ordeals to prove their innocence.

When groups of people made accusations, the accused were expected to find eleven thanes who would swear to their hon-

JURY FEES IN STATE AND FEDERAL COURTS, 1994

Jurisdiction	Juror Fees per Day	Jurisdiction	Juror Fees per Day
Federal	$40.00	Missouri	$ 6.00
Alabama	10.00	Montana	12.00
Alaska	12.50	Nebraska	20.00
Arizona	12.00	Nevada	(d)
Arkansas	5.00	New Hampshire	10.00
California	5.00	New Jersey	5.00
Colorado	(a)	New Mexico	(e)
Connecticut	(b)	New York	(f)
Delaware	15.00	North Carolina	12.00
District of Columbia	30.00	North Dakota	25.00
Florida	(c)	Ohio	10.00
Georgia	5.00	Oklahoma	12.50
Hawaii	30.00	Oregon	10.00
Idaho	5.00	Pennsylvania	(g)
Illinois	4.00	Rhode Island	15.00
Indiana	7.50	South Carolina	10.00
Iowa	10.00	South Dakota	10.00
Kansas	10.00	Tennessee	10.00
Kentucky	12.50	Texas	6.00
Louisiana	12.00	Utah	17.00
Maine	10.00	Vermont	30.00
Maryland	10.00	Virginia	30.00
Massachusetts	(a)	Washington	10.00
Michigan	7.50	West Virginia	15.00
Minnesota	15.00	Wisconsin	8.00
Mississippi	15.00	Wyoming	30.00

Source: U.S. Department of Justice, Bureau of Justice Statistics, Sourcebook of Criminal Justice Statistics—1993. Washington, D.C.: U.S. Government Printing Office, 1994.

Note: Fees listed provide a point of general comparison, but there are various exceptions. A few variations are listed below, but there are others.

[a] No fee for first 3 days; $50.00 per day thereafter. Expenses for unemployed available. Employers must pay employees for first 3 days while serving.

[b] No fee for first 5 days; $50.00 per day thereafter. Expenses for unemployed available. Employers must pay employees for first 5 days while serving.

[c] If employer pays salary or wages of person on jury duty, then there is no fee paid for 3 days; then $30.00 per day thereafter. If individual is not employed or employer does not pay salary, then fee is $15.00 per day for first 3 days; then $30.00 per day thereafter.

[d] $15.00 per day while actually serving (sworn). $30.00 per day after 5 days of service. $9.00 per day if not sworn.

[e] $4.25 per hour.

[f] If employer has more than 10 employees, must pay at least $15 per day for the first 3 days. After 3 days, the court must pay $15 per day. If juror is not employed or if employer has fewer than 10 employees, then court must pay $15 per day from day 1.

[g] $9.00 for first 3 days; $25.00 per day thereafter.

esty and honor. If they could not persuade that many to testify, they were usually subjected to an ordeal and, predictably, adjudged guilty. These earliest juries of thanes selected by the accused were quite opposite to the impartial juries that are fundamental to modern jury systems. They were selected because they had made up their minds and were predisposed in favor of the defendant, whereas, under current judicial systems, if jurors are shown to have any bias for or against defendants, they are precluded from serving. A review of judicial decisions in England between 1550 and 1750 reveals that during those two centuries juries consistently voted to acquit people they knew and voted to convict people they did not know.

Objections to the Jury System. The jury system has been tried and abandoned in many countries. Generally it has been observed that where a nation attempts to impose such a system upon an established judicial system, the attempt soon fails. In such situations, modifications in the system are usually so great as to make it almost unrecognizable as a jury system.

In France, Germany, and Denmark, experiments with juries were eventually replaced with a trial system that involves judges and lay assessors who help to weigh evidence. The jury system seems most firmly entrenched in Britain, where it was established and refined quite early, Australia, New Zealand, the United States, and Canada, where it emerged as the original system.

A major objection to trial by jury is that many jurors lack the intelligence, backgrounds, or stamina to assess effectively evidence given within a legal context. This objection has been heard increasingly as law cases have involved an ever-growing need to understand highly technical evidence such as the results of polygraph tests, Deoxyribonucleic acid (DNA) testing, and other laboratory procedures that are now applied to gathering and evaluating evidence.

Complaints have substantiated that some jurors can be bribed, although this problem is eliminated in highly publicized cases that require the sequestration of the jury, sometimes for months at a time. In cases that involve organized crime, jurors have ample cause to fear for their physical welfare and safety during and after trials. Jurors assigned to spectacular cases are occasionally eager to serve because they have ulterior motives, such as post-trial plans to profit from their experience by writing a book about it or taking to the television talk-show circuit. Potentially competent jurors are sometimes excused because of the disruption that long sequestration might cause them. Sequestered jurors in some instances have, upon their release at the end of a long trial, found that their jobs have not been held for them and that their marriages or other personal relationships are foundering.

Civil suits that involve complicated fraud in the marketing or manipulation of securities, patent or copyright infringements, trusts or monopolies, or highly complicated labor-management relations are often beyond the ability of a typical jury drawn from a randomly selected jury pool to handle effectively or fairly. In some such cases, defendants may exercise the option to have their cases heard by one or more judges who will pass final judgment. Most defendants, however, prefer to take their chances with a jury, gambling that at least one of its members will not understand the proceedings well and will vote for acquittal as the only sure way to prevent sending an innocent person to prison.

Criticism has also been directed toward juries in civil cases that award unrealistically high settlements to complainants whose cases succeed. Appellate courts have often reduced or eliminated some of the most unrealistic settlements, but appealing a verdict is a cumbersome process that is costly to the complainants, the defendants, and the government.

—R. Baird Shuman

See also Burden of proof; Civil procedure; Civil rights; Common law; Criminal procedure; Grand jury; Juvenile justice system; Miscarriage of justice; Mistrial; Reasonable doubt; Simpson, O. J., trial; Standards of proof; *Voir dire*.

BIBLIOGRAPHY

Two exhaustive studies of the jury system are Maximus A. Lesser and William S. Hein's *The Historical Development of the Jury System* (Buffalo, N.Y.: W. S. Hein, 1992) and Jeffrey Abramson's *We, the Jury: Justice and the Democratic Ideal* (New York: Basic Books, 1994). Barbara Holland's lively and lucid article, "Do You Swear that You Will Well and Truly Try . . . ?," in *Smithsonian* 25 (March, 1995), presents accurate historical information with stylistic aplomb. W. R. Cornish's *The Jury* (London: Allen Lane, 1968) focuses on England's jury system and, although dated, presents valuable contrasts. John Guinther's *The Jury in America* (New York: Facts on File, 1988) views the American jury system with balance.

Just deserts

DEFINITION: The concept that the punishment for a crime should match the severity of the crime itself

SIGNIFICANCE: The concept of just deserts, related to the retributive philosophy of criminal justice, has gained in popularity as the crime problem in the United States has grown

In a 1976 report entitled *Doing Justice*, criminologist Andrew von Hirsch and other members of the Committee for the Study of Incarceration called for a turning away from the then-prevailing philosophy of rehabilitation of offenders and moving toward a sentencing model that emphasizes giving the criminal what he or she "deserves" for the particular crime committed. Under the rehabilitative model, indeterminate sentencing and wide discretion on the part of the sentencer are viewed as desirable. The so-called just deserts model (the term is from the French, hence the unusual spelling), by contrast, shifts the focus in sentencing to the seriousness of the offender's crime. Proponents of this approach generally favor reducing sentencing disparities and using guidelines that prescribe standardized sentences. The general aim is to give the same punishment to all individuals who commit the same crime.

The just deserts model draws some inspiration from the classical retributivist theory of punishment, such as that of the eighteenth century German philosopher Immanuel Kant. According to Kant, "[Judicial punishment] must in all cases be imposed on [the criminal] only on the ground that he has committed a crime." It is a matter of opinion and the subject of much debate what the appropriate punishment is for any given crime. Among the factors usually considered are the seriousness of the crime, the criminal's previous record, and the amount of harm done to the criminal's victim.

See also Criminal justice system; Discretion; Incapacitation; Mandatory sentencing laws; Punishment; Rehabilitation; Sentencing; Sentencing guidelines, U.S.; United States Sentencing Commission.

Justice

DEFINITION: The administration of rewards and punishments according to rules and principles that society considers fair and equitable

SIGNIFICANCE: Generally considered the most fundamental purpose of government and civil society, justice encompasses criminal law and the criminal justice system, civil law and civil courts, and social justice

In writing for the Federalist Papers in 1788, James Madison called justice "the end of government . . . the end of civil society. It ever has been and ever will be pursued until it be obtained, or until liberty be lost in the pursuit." For Madison and the other founders, justice meant a society in which people were secure in their persons and property, in which all enjoyed the rights to "life, liberty, and the pursuit of happiness," and in which citizens were governed only with their consent. In the American political tradition the Declaration of Independence is the single best articulation of the principles of justice that animated the nation's founding. While other nations embraced other notions of justice, such as the rule of the wealthy or the promotion of a specific religion, these were not to be the foundation of American government and civil society. American justice falls into three categories: criminal, civil, and social.

Criminal Justice. Encompassing the laws, procedures, and institutions that communities employ to apprehend, prosecute, and punish those who violate the property or persons of others, criminal justice is primarily a state and local concern in the United States. The federal government plays a minor role because the most typical crimes—such as theft, burglary, robbery, assault, and murder—violate state, not federal, law. The agencies charged with bringing offenders "to justice" are usually local police departments and municipal or county prosecutors. The courts, though established under state law, are commonly organized and run at the county level. Criminals punished by incarceration normally serve terms of less than a year in county jails or more than a year in state prisons.

The federal government actively investigates and prosecutes violations of federal law, such as counterfeiting, interstate drug trafficking, immigration violations, assaults on federal officials, violations of federal regulations governing such activities as environmental pollution and commercial transactions, terrorism, and espionage.

Key justice issues in prosecuting criminal defendants include how suspects or their homes are searched, how evidence is seized, the nature of interrogations, the admissibility of confessions, the provision of legal assistance to the indigent, and the number and types of appeals—particularly from state to federal courts.

There are many similarities among the criminal laws of the fifty states—in all of which murder, rape, robbery, burglary, and certain other negative behaviors are illegal. Nevertheless, disputes occasionally arise over whether governments even should prohibit certain behaviors. This is especially true of so-called victimless crimes, such as the personal use of illicit drugs, unauthorized gambling, and prostitution. Opponents of laws against such activities often argue that consenting adults should have the right to engage in any activities that do not directly harm others and that it is "unjust" for a state to limit personal choices in such ways. Defenders of such laws emphasize the function of the law and of government as a moral teacher. Upholders of the latter position maintain, for example, that a government's legalization of cocaine use would send a signal to the people that the community approves such behavior; the inevitable result would be an increase in harmful behavior and grave social costs.

Civil Justice. Generally less controversial than criminal justice, civil justice covers a wide range of legal matters governing the relations among individuals in civil society. These include contracts between private parties, marriage and divorce, parents' responsibility for their children's welfare, harms done without criminal intent, licensing of commercial or professional activities, and health and safety regulations. Civil courts provide forums for aggrieved parties to assert and vindicate their rights.

Perhaps the most controversial aspect of the civil justice system is the dramatic late twentieth century increase in awards to plaintiffs for harms done by government agencies or corporations. Proponents of "tort reform" have called for limits to "punitive damages" (those awarded to punish transgressors) and ceilings on attorney contingency fees.

Social Justice. In contrast to criminal and civil justice, social justice is a twentieth century concept. Embracing the idea that the government has an obligation to promote economic and social well-being, it is strongly associated with the administration of President Franklin D. Roosevelt, who broadly expanded the notion of rights contained in the Declaration of Independence. "Life, liberty, and the pursuit of happiness" were reinterpreted to encompass the "right" to be protected from hunger, unemployment, or the disabilities of sickness and old age. It thus became the task of government to correct inequities in the social and economic system, to redistribute income and wealth from those who had more to those who had less.

Another component of the movement for social justice was the Civil Rights movement, which peaked in the 1960's. Under such leaders as Martin Luther King, Jr., this movement sought to extend the promises of the Declaration of Independence and the Constitution to Americans of all races. It led to a national commitment in the landmark Civil Rights Acts of 1964 and 1965 to prohibit state and local discrimination in public facilities and employment and to enforce vigorously the right to vote. King summed up the aim of the movement in his famous "I Have a Dream" speech: "Now is the time to make justice a reality for all of God's children."   —*Joseph M. Bessette*

See also Civil law; Civil liberties; Civil rights; Criminal justice system; Declaration of Independence; Judicial system, U.S.; Jurisprudence; Law; Natural law and natural rights; Welfare state.

BIBLIOGRAPHY

Any study of American justice should begin with the documents on which the nation was founded, such as the Declaration of Independence and the Federalist Papers. The latter are essays that Alexander Hamilton, James Madison, and John Jay wrote defending the Constitution during its ratification struggle. An inexpensive standard edition is by Clinton Rossiter (New York: Mentor, 1961). Among many texts covering justice are Larry J. Siegel, ed., *American Justice: Research of the National Institute of Justice* (St. Paul, Minn.: West, 1990); James McClellan, *Liberty, Order, and Justice: An Introduction to the Constitutional Principles of American Government* (Cumberland, Va.: James River Press, 1989); and Howard Abadinsky, *Crime and Justice: An Introduction* (Chicago: Nelson-Hall, 1987).

Justice, U.S. Department of

DATE: Established 1870

SIGNIFICANCE: The Department of Justice serves as a link between the court system and the executive branch of the federal government; it brings suit against violators of federal law and defends the U.S. government against claims brought by persons, organizations, and local and state governments

American political thought traditionally divides the functions of a law-based society's government into three categories: the making of laws, the adjudication of laws, and the execution of laws. In the United States the three functions are carried out by separate branches of the federal government. Law execution is the primary responsibility of the executive branch, headed by the president. Because the functions and responsibilities overlap, the executive branch is limited in part by the judicial branch, which interprets the law and establishes guilt. The Department of Justice is the agency of the federal government which represents the executive branch in litigation connected with the enforcement of federal laws. This arrangement at once ensures both that the agencies charged with enforcing the law have a strong legal advocate and that a separation of powers is maintained between the judicial and executive branches. It is this balance of protecting the executive's power to enforce the law (through the Department of Justice) and protecting the public interest against possible abuses of power by the executive (through the courts and the Congress) which distinguishes American justice from that of most other governmental systems.

Organization. The U.S. Department of Justice was established in 1870. The attorney general, already an established position within the president's cabinet since 1789, was placed at the head of the new department. The attorney general is appointed by the president and confirmed by the Senate, as are the deputy attorney general, associate attorney general, solicitor general, inspector general, various assistant attorneys general, various bureau directors, and other political positions within the Department of Justice. In the mid-1990's, the department employed almost 100,000 persons. Attorneys, of which there are several thousand, are hired directly by the applicable division. Justice Department attorneys, Federal Bureau of Investigation (FBI) special agents, and other professional positions are not under the federal civil service.

As the chief law enforcement officer of the federal government, the attorney general advises the president and other executive officials on legal affairs and represents the United States in legal matters generally. As head of the Justice Department, the attorney general oversees what amounts to an enormous law office whose sole client is the United States government. The Justice Department is organized into six litigation divisions, which correspond to its six basic areas of responsibility: ensuring the enforcement of criminal law, antitrust statutes, civil rights, environmental law, and tax law, and defending the U.S. government against civil claims.

Criminal Law. The Criminal Division of the Justice Department is charged with the drafting and enforcement of virtually all federal criminal laws. Unlike the state and local authorities, the federal government is specifically charged by the U.S. Constitution with criminal jurisdiction over only counterfeiting and piracies and other felonies committed on the high seas. The criminal code of the United States nevertheless has expanded beyond that modest mandate to include a variety of laws justified under the constitutional authority to make laws deemed "necessary and proper for carrying into execution" the broad powers granted to it. By the mid-1990's the U.S. criminal code comprised an extensive and complex mosaic of about a thousand general criminal statutes (excluding statutes specifically within the jurisdiction of the other Justice Department divisions).

The Criminal Division was established with a general governmental reorganization under President Franklin D. Roosevelt in 1933. The scope of its authority is wide. Separate sections within the Criminal Division enforce laws on child exploitation and obscenity, money laundering, narcotics, internal security, and other areas. The largest component of the Criminal Division is the Fraud Section, which focuses in particular upon fraud which crosses district and national boundaries, which involves financial and insurance institutions, and which concerns government programs and procurement.

Although separate from the Criminal Division, an Office of Professional Responsibility ensures the continued ethical standards of employees within the Justice Department itself and investigates alleged criminal or ethical misconduct. The office reports directly to the attorney general. The existence of such an office highlights the strict ethical standards which the Justice Department must unequivocally maintain.

The headquarters of the U.S. Department of Justice in Washington D.C. (McCrea Adams)

Antitrust Division. Economic fairness is a fundamental aspect of American justice. The free enterprise principles that undergird the country's economic philosophy necessarily permit market forces to reward and punish the independent actions of consumers, producers, and investors. It is recognized, however, that some of those actors will try to take advantage of the system, engaging in unfair competition and otherwise intentionally distorting market forces for their benefit. The Antitrust Division of the Department of Justice, in cooperation with the Federal Trade Commission, seeks to identify and stop such practices.

In the late nineteenth century "trust-busting," as it was known, became a primary responsibility of the attorney general's office. Possible domination of the economy by monopolies was a major concern during the country's late industrial revolution. After Attorney General Richard Olney in the 1890's successfully sued the "sugar trust" under the Sherman Act, the way was paved for an increasing number of antitrust suits. With such a large workload of antitrust cases, a separate Antitrust Division of the Justice Department was established in 1933.

The Antitrust Division was charged with promoting and maintaining competitive domestic markets through the enforcement of federal antitrust laws. The most important antitrust acts historically have been the Sherman Act of 1890, the Clayton Act of 1914, and the Federal Trade Commission Act of 1914. Collectively, these and other laws prohibited the creation of unfair monopolies through mergers, price fixing, predatory practices, and other activities which threaten healthy competition. The antitrust laws pervaded all aspects of business, including distribution, marketing, and manufacturing, and they apply to virtually all industries.

As the twentieth century wore on, antitrust activities became less of a priority for the government and became overshadowed by competing demands on the department's resources. Much of the division's antitrust work increasingly has been in the area of international agreements. Yet the Justice Department still periodically brings high-profile domestic antitrust suits. One such suit against the American Telephone and Telegraph Company (AT&T) from the mid-1970's through the early 1980's, for example, had a tremendous impact on the telecommunications industry. The AT&T case suggested that the Justice Department was reconsidering some of the "natural monopoly" arguments that had exempted certain industries from antitrust suits. Other industries undergoing vast changes in terms of competition at the end of the twentieth century include health care and defense.

Civil Rights. In the mid-twentieth century, the enforcement of civil rights became a paramount justice issue. Particularly, although not exclusively, in the South, various local and state governments were not adequately protecting the most basic of civil rights. Indeed, in many cases it was these governments themselves which were violating civil rights, particularly those of blacks. Although the federal government would continue to pass various laws for the protection of civil rights, it would devolve on the Department of Justice to ensure their enforcement.

The Civil Rights Division of the Department of Justice was created in 1957. It is the governmental body charged with enforcing federal laws against discrimination based on race, sex, and other criteria. The Civil Rights Division grew rapidly after its inception and has come to occupy a high-profile place in the Justice Department. Many of its duties stem from the 1964 Civil Rights Act, the 1965 Voting Rights Act, the Fair Housing Act of 1968, and the Americans with Disabilities Act of 1990. The Civil Rights Division maintains separate sections which address these and other specific issues.

The Civil Rights Division encountered a dramatic challenge to its authority when the 1954 *Brown v. Board of Education* Supreme Court decision led to the court-ordered admission of black students to a Little Rock, Arkansas, high school in 1957. Governor Orval Faubus of Arkansas ordered state officers physically to prevent black students from entering the school. In response, U.S. marshals and federal troops were deployed to escort the black students to their classes. The Department of Justice further was able to secure an injunction against the governor's interference with the federal court's order. A similar victory was scored by the Justice Department against Governor George Wallace of Alabama. Although the Civil Rights Division, and the Department of Justice generally, have by no means always been successful in enforcing civil rights laws, the early civil rights victories provided the Civil Rights Division with a momentum that propelled it for a number of years.

Environment and Natural Resources. Increasingly, American justice issues have expanded from the various rights of individuals to the protection of the environment and natural resources. The Environment and Natural Resources Division of the Department of Justice enforces such laws as the protection of endangered species and the monitoring of hazardous waste disposal.

The work of the Environment and Natural Resources Division largely centers on three areas: environmental crimes, environmental defense, and environmental enforcement. The Environmental Crimes Section prosecutes persons and firms that violate the nation's environmental protection laws, such as the Clean Water Act, the Clean Air Act, and the Endangered Species Act. The Environmental Defense Section defends the U.S. government against legal challenges concerning federal enforcement of environmental laws (for example, challenges that federal enforcement is too strict or too lax). This section also defends the U.S. government against charges that it is itself in violation of environmental laws. The Environmental Enforcement Section litigates most of the civil suits brought by other federal agencies, including the Environmental Protection Agency, the U.S. Coast Guard, and the Departments of Interior, Commerce, and Agriculture.

Environmental law and policy are relatively new fields, and thus much of the Justice Department's work in the area is

precedent-setting. In *United States v. Robert Brittingham and John LoMonaco* (1993), for example, the Environment and Natural Resources Division obtained a $6 million criminal judgment against the chairman of the board and the president of Dal Tile Corporation. They were the highest-ranking corporate officials ever convicted of environmental offenses. The case establishes a strong precedent about personal liability for corporate violations of environmental statutes. If this and other legal trends continue, the potential influence of the Environmental and Natural Resources Division could be enormous.

Taxes. Another increasingly salient set of justice issues involves taxation. Although most of the issues are debated, decided, and administered by other agencies (such as the Congress and the Internal Revenue Service, or IRS), the preparation and conducting of the inevitable criminal and civil tax cases is done elsewhere. For many years these cases were conducted by the Treasury Department, but President Franklin Roosevelt's governmental reorganization shifted that responsibility. The Tax Division of the Department of Justice was created by executive order in 1933 to represent the United States in all criminal and civil suits connected with the internal revenue laws. The division's primary client is the IRS. Besides representing the government in tax suits, the division, in cooperation with U.S. attorneys' offices, also collects judgments.

Civil Claims. The department's Civil Division defends the various agencies, departments, and personnel of the United States government in noncriminal legal suits. The Civil Division is, in essence, the federal government's attorney. Its earlier name, the Claims Division, is perhaps more descriptive, highlighting the fact that the division defends the government against numerous claims stemming in one way or another from governmental operations: military tests, land sales, water diversion projects, and any number of other activities and mishaps. The sheer size of federal governmental operations virtually guarantees the likelihood of numerous civil suits. These suits turn on a wide array of justice issues.

Much of the work of the Civil Division is conducted by the Court of Claims Section. Congress established the Court of Claims in 1855 in response to a burgeoning number of claims against the U.S. government. Today the Civil Division's Court of Claims Section takes responsibility for all cases against the government with the exception of land, tax, admiralty, and American Indian claims.

Bureaus. In addition to the five divisions outlined above, the Department of Justice includes several more specialized bureaus. The Federal Bureau of Investigation (FBI) is the Justice Department's primary investigative arm. The Bureau of Prisons oversees the federal prison system. The U.S. Marshals Service provides security for the federal courts, executes court orders and arrest warrants, transports federal prisoners, and otherwise serves as a link between the executive and judicial branches of the federal government. The Immigration and Naturalization Service (INS) provides for the entry and resettlement of persons into the United States, prevents illegal entry, and administers employment and citizenship laws. The

Drug Enforcement Administration (DEA) enforces laws regulating narcotics and other controlled substances. The U.S. National Central Bureau represents the United States in the International Criminal Police Organization (Interpol), an association of police agencies from 169 countries.

In addition, the Office of Justice Programs (OJP) was established in 1984 to improve the overall efficiency and effectiveness of the country's justice system. The OJP primarily collects and disseminates data and analysis on various criminal justice issues and programs.

Context and Public Perceptions. The underlying principles and rationale of the Justice Department, whatever their value, seem to elude the general public's understanding of the agency. Indeed, the ethos of the department as a whole is limited by public (and in some cases intragovernmental) perceptions of the department's component parts. The public is generally cognizant of the FBI's investigative functions, the role of the Marshals Service in apprehending federal fugitives, and the DEA's seizure of assets derived from illicit drug trafficking, for example. The work of the litigation divisions, however, only infrequently commands public attention. In general, the litigation emphasis behind the Justice Department's slogans "the world's largest law firm" and "the nation's attorney" (which appear in department publications) is limited to only a small number of high-profile cases.

One example was the federal trial in 1993 of the four Los Angeles police officers who earlier had been acquitted by a state court on charges of assault against Rodney King. Much controversy surrounded the Justice Department's efforts to secure a conviction of the officers, whose previous acquittal had sparked racial riots in Los Angeles. Although the second trial (which resulted in the conviction of two of the officers) focused on civil rights violations rather than assault charges, some observers believed that it amounted to unconstitutional "double jeopardy." In any event, the case heightened public awareness of the Justice Department's litigation role, especially as distinguished from the state of California's role in the first trial.

In the mid-1990's, the Justice Department again began to garner considerable public attention, this time in the context of investigations of and litigation against high-level government officials. The Justice Department and independent counsels appointed by the attorney general investigated agency heads, White House officials, and even cabinet secretaries. In 1994 even the assistant attorney general himself was forced to resign as criminal allegations about previous activities headed toward an eventual guilty plea. The fact that the Justice Department was investigating various other parts of the executive branch lent some credibility to its role as the chief enforcer of laws, irrespective of the positions of those it investigates and prosecutes. To that can be added the "Saturday night massacre" of 1973, when the attorney general and deputy attorney general resigned rather than carry out President Richard Nixon's order to fire Watergate Special Prosecutor Archibald Cox.

The celebrity of these few events only emphasizes that the scope of the Justice Department's activities and the importance of its role are seldom recognized. The U.S. Department of Justice has become a large, diverse, and active agency with a tremendous impact upon American justice.　　*—Steve D. Boilard*

See also Alcohol, Tobacco, and Firearms (ATF), Bureau of; Attorney general of the United States; Drug Enforcement Administration (DEA); Federal Bureau of Investigation (FBI); Immigration and Naturalization Service (INS); Justice Statistics, Bureau of; Juvenile Justice and Delinquency Prevention, Office of; Marshals Service, U.S.; National Institute of Justice; Prisons, Bureau of; Solicitor general of the United States.

BIBLIOGRAPHY

The U.S. government makes available a number of publications explaining the operation of the Department of Justice and of its various divisions and bureaus. The *Annual Report of the Attorney General of the United States* is published by the Department of Justice (available through the U.S. Government Printing Office) and provides a current accounting of the department's operations and goals. The Department of Justice's *Legal Activities* describes the organization, activities, and recent cases handled by attorneys with the various divisions of the department. An annual publication, *Legal Activities* is aimed primarily at potential employees. The *U.S. Government Manual* covers the entire federal government, but its section on the Department of Justice provides a thorough accounting of the institutional structure, as well as addresses and phone numbers for more specific information. A history of the department, the full text of the act which established it, and a comprehensive analysis of its operation (as of the mid-1960's) is provided in Luther A. Huston, *The Department of Justice* (New York: Praeger, 1967). Finally, there are a number of books which focus on the Justice Department's policies under particular administrations. Two examples are Victor S. Navasky, *Kennedy Justice* (New York: Atheneum, 1971), which covers Justice Department activities under Attorney General Robert F. Kennedy, and Richard Harris, *Justice: The Crisis of Law, Order, and Freedom in America* (New York: E. P. Dutton, 1970), which provides a critical account of the Justice Department in the early Nixon years, under Attorney General John Mitchell.

Justice Statistics, Bureau of

DATE: Established 1979

SIGNIFICANCE: Crime data and publications put out by the Bureau of Justice Statistics are considered among the most authoritative and thus are used by law enforcement agencies, insurance firms, city planners, and a variety of other professionals

The Bureau of Justice Statistics collects, analyzes, and disseminates statistical information relating to crime and the operation of justice systems at all levels. This information is provided to the president, the Congress, various other governmental agencies, and the general public. Special Reports and Bulletins are published periodically to provide current data on various aspects of criminal justice.

Among the most important of the bureau's publications is the annual National Crime Victimization Survey, published under the title *Criminal Victimization in the United States*. The survey compiles household interviews to measure the incidence of violence and theft in the United States. Another major annual publication is the *Sourcebook of Criminal Justice Statistics*. Other statistical series concern various aspects of criminal justice, civil justice, law enforcement, and administration. The bureau also manages the Drugs and Crime Data Center and Clearinghouse, which compiles and analyzes existing data on drugs and the justice system, operates a clearinghouse/reference center, and prepares special reports of existing drug data.

See also Crime; Justice, U.S. Department of; National Crime Information Center.

Juvenile delinquency

DEFINITION: Illegal activities in which the offender is a juvenile (a person below the age of majority)

SIGNIFICANCE: Rates of delinquency have increased significantly since the 1970's; in addition, the increased seriousness of the crimes of youth gangs has helped to increase the attention on juvenile delinquency

Juvenile delinquency refers to crimes committed by individuals below the age of majority (usually someone under the age of eighteen). Crimes are defined as "delinquent" in order to

Urban gang activities have increased the level of violence involved in juvenile delinquency. Los Angeles gang members are pictured. (AP/Wide World Photos)

JUVENILE OFFENSES DISPOSED BY JUVENILE COURTS, 1991

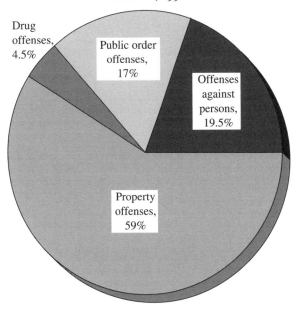

Drug offenses, 4.5%

Public order offenses, 17%

Offenses against persons, 19.5%

Property offenses, 59%

Source: U.S. Department of Justice, Bureau of Justice Statistics, *Sourcebook of Criminal Justice Statistics—1993*. Washington, D.C.: U.S. Government Printing Office, 1994.

Note: Total juvenile offenses disposed by juvenile courts, 1991, was 1,338,100.

separate juvenile offenders from adult offenders. Prior to the twentieth century, juvenile offenders in the United States were treated in much the same way as adult offenders. At the turn of the century, however, a group of reformers urged the creation of a special status for juvenile offenders. These reformers, known as the "child savers," argued that juveniles who commit crimes require special treatment. Juvenile delinquents were considered wayward youth who needed guidance and an appropriate environment to cure their delinquent behavior. Based on this idea, the juvenile justice system was created to deal with these offenders as a substitute parent. This philosophy is referred to as *parens patriae* and requires that the juvenile court act as a parent to the child, assuming that the child's parents have not lived up to their parental responsibilities. Many scholars have criticized the motives of the child savers, however, arguing that the intent of these reformers was to exert more control over juvenile delinquents by giving the government power to remove children from their homes.

Over time, the view of juvenile delinquents as wayward youth was transformed, and juvenile offenders were believed to be much more serious offenders. The focus on juvenile delinquency has increased in part because of the large number of juvenile gangs appearing around the United States. Some believe that these gangs become substitute families for youth who do not have strong relationships with their biological families. Juvenile gangs have been blamed for the dramatic increases in violent crime in urban America. Historically, most juvenile delinquents were arrested for crimes such as vandalism and petty theft. Today, delinquency includes violent crimes such as homicide, assault, and robbery, as well as drug-related crimes. Many juveniles in large cities are employed by drug dealers to run drugs, and they often become users themselves because of their increased exposure to the drug culture.

Increases in the seriousness of crime among delinquents has spawned debate over the best way to treat juvenile delinquents. The *parens patriae* view that characterized juvenile justice for nearly a century has been criticized as too lenient. Some critics advocate harsh and swift punishment for juveniles engaged in delinquency but worry that severe treatment will only increase future delinquency. Typical punishments for delinquents range from mild (probation, fines, community service) to more severe punishments that usually entail some type of incarceration (boot camps, juvenile detention facilities).

See also Boot camps; Contributing to the delinquency of a minor; Diversion; Gangs, youth; *Gault, In re*; *In loco parentis*; Juvenile Justice and Delinquency Prevention, Office of; Juvenile Justice and Delinquency Prevention Act; Juvenile justice system; Majority, age of; Status offense; Vandalism.

Juvenile Justice and Delinquency Prevention, Office of

DATE: Established 1974

SIGNIFICANCE: The Office of Juvenile Justice and Delinquency Prevention serves as a focus for policies and programs relating to juvenile delinquency and juvenile justice, coordinating its operations and funding with states and localities to curtail major national problems associated with juvenile crime

Amid growing national concerns over the nation's high incidence of street crime and its connections with juvenile delinquency, Congress created the Law Enforcement Assistance Administration (LEAA) in 1970, placing it within the U.S. Department of Justice. When Congress enacted the Juvenile Justice and Delinquency Prevention Act in 1974, the LEAA was given new life through the addition of the Office of Juvenile Justice and Delinquency Prevention (OJJDP) within the U.S. Justice Department. The primary mission of the OJJDP is to disseminate information on delinquency and juvenile justice programs in order to improve the nation's juvenile justice system and encourage state and local efforts to prevent delinquency. Juvenile delinquents are most often defined as individuals between the ages of fourteen and twenty-one who have, or are suspected of having, broken the law. The OJJDP also provides funds and technical assistance to government and private interests.

See also Juvenile delinquency; Juvenile Justice and Delinquency Prevention Act; Juvenile justice system; Law Enforcement Assistance Administration (LEAA); National Commission on the Causes and Prevention of Violence.

Juvenile Justice and Delinquency Prevention Act

DATE: Became law September 7, 1974

DEFINITION: An effort to reduce juvenile delinquency through prevention programs and reforms to the existing juvenile justice system

SIGNIFICANCE: This act emphasized education, counseling, and other programs over punishment of juvenile delinquency

Stating its finding that juveniles accounted for about half of the arrests for serious crimes, Congress enacted the Juvenile Justice and Delinquency Prevention Act as a broad attack on juvenile delinquency. The main provisions of the act provided federal block grants to states. The grants were intended for reforming juvenile justice procedures and for providing resources such as counseling and school programs to prevent delinquency. The act sought to decriminalize youth "status offenders," whose offenses would not be considered crimes if they were adults. Alternative sentences such as placement in a halfway house would be offered. The act also coordinated research on juvenile delinquency and established the Office of Juvenile Justice and Delinquency Prevention within the Department of Justice. This legislation was complemented by another measure from 1974, the Runaway and Homeless Youth Act. The act was amended and authorization extended in 1974, 1980, and 1984.

See also Juvenile delinquency; Juvenile Justice and Delinquency Prevention, Office of; Juvenile justice system; Status offense.

Juvenile justice system

DEFINITION: The various courts and agencies that administer the law as it is applied to, and on behalf of, persons under the age of eighteen in the United States

SIGNIFICANCE: This separate system of courts and agencies that the United States utilizes to administer justice to children reflects the important American value of protecting children by positive early intervention in their lives

The juvenile justice system is the description given to the courts, laws, personnel, and agencies that administer the laws to persons younger than the age of majority (the "legal age"). It is the statutory creation of state legislatures, there being no constitutional mandate for their existence or creation.

The juvenile justice system grew out of social reform movements of the nineteenth century and came into its own with the decision of *In re Gault* by the United States Supreme Court in 1967. Today, the juvenile justice system consists of myriad state and federal laws and even multilateral treaties.

Origins. The notion of a separate juvenile court developed from a convergence of historical trends. Historically, child criminal offenders were subject to the same procedures of arrest and detention as adults and were subject to most of the same punishments, without always enjoying the same rights.

One historical trend at work was society's changing beliefs about criminal behavior. A school of "positivistic criminology" propounded that criminal conduct was not completely

Juvenile courts evolved in the first half of the twentieth century in an effort to serve the best interest of the child. (James L. Shaffer)

the product of individual free will; it held that economic, political, psychological, and social forces contributed to such behavior. Its adherents believed that society should not simply react by making arrests subsequent to the occurrence of crimes, but should be proactive; in other words, society should engage in early or preventive intervention. Advocates of the positivist school of thought believed that society would best be protected by ameliorating the causes of crime and by reforming the criminal. Out of this philosophy grew the American public's increased concern regarding the fate of children in criminal court and the negative impact of the subculture of the urban poor on traditional middle-class values and the American way of life.

The second historical trend was the rise of the feminist movement. The "child saving" issue was one consensus-building, sympathetic cause around which this movement could organize. Commentators and historians disagree as to whether that occurred as a result of political ingenuity or coincidence. The convergence of these trends resulted in the creation of juvenile courts. State legislatures were persuaded to enact juvenile justice laws. Today the juvenile justice system encompasses the police, the courts, judges, lawyers, and social service personnel and agencies.

Illinois passed the first Juvenile Court Act in 1899. Over the next forty-six years, all the remaining states passed laws creating juvenile courts authorized to hear delinquency, neglect, and abuse cases. Separate procedures and nomenclatures developed, reflecting the focus of the juvenile court on the best

interest of the child; for example, there were "adjudicative hearings" as opposed to trials and "disposition hearings" as opposed to sentencings. The various states have disagreed on how to serve the "best interest of the child," or even what that may constitute.

In August of 1968, the National Conference of Commissioners on Uniform State Laws proposed a "Uniform Juvenile Court Act," with the motive of achieving some consistency in the juvenile justice system. The proposal was evidence of the national interest in "juvenile delinquency" issues and the increasing federalization of juvenile law. In 1974, Congress passed the Juvenile Justice and Delinquency Prevention Act, which for the first time provided a unified national program for dealing with the prevention and control of juvenile delinquency.

The juvenile justice system operates separately from, but as a junior partner to, the adult justice system. It was created almost as a hybrid of a social service agency and a court. Its function is to try to keep minors from becoming adult offenders by appropriate means of intervention. Intervention can run the gamut from incarceration in a youth detention center to a probationary period requiring periodic meetings with an assigned counselor.

Ordinarily, juvenile courts have exclusive jurisdiction over children through the age of fifteen. Between the ages of sixteen and eighteen, the juvenile courts have concurrent jurisdiction with the adult courts in most instances. Generally, after the age of eighteen, the juvenile court has no more jurisdiction. In short, individuals under the age of eighteen might find themselves in a juvenile court as the subject matter of its proceeding for one or more of three principal reasons. The child may be charged with a criminal offense in a juvenile delinquency proceeding, the child may be charged with a "status offense," or the child may be alleged to be a victim of abuse or neglect.

Whenever a juvenile enters the juvenile justice system for one of the foregoing reasons, a variety of procedures are set in motion. The law sets forth rules regarding the manner by which authorities can take a juvenile into custody. There are also regulations governing the place, length of time, and manner of detention as well as the preliminary aspects of getting the case before a judge.

Juvenile Delinquency Cases. In these cases the child enters the juvenile justice system because of criminal charges. Constitutional rights and procedural safeguards apply because of *In re Gault*, in which the Supreme Court held that juvenile defendants are entitled to such basic rights as notice of the charges, right to counsel, right to cross-examine witnesses, privilege against self-incrimination, a transcript of trial pro-

ceedings, and appellate review. (Other important Supreme Court decisions regarding juvenile justice include *Kent v. United States*, 1966, and *In re Winship*, 1970.) Typically there is some form of initial hearing at which an attorney will be appointed if the juvenile's family cannot afford to retain one privately, an arraignment will occur (where the youth enters a plea to the charges), the judge makes a determination whether the child will be detained or released pending trial, and a tentative trial date is set.

If the parties cannot work out a plea arrangement that is acceptable to all parties, then there is an adjudication hearing, similar to a trial in adult court. If the prosecutor does not prove the charges, then the youth is acquitted and goes free; if the youth is convicted, there is a subsequent dispositional hearing, similar to sentencing in an adult court.

It is this dispositional phase of a juvenile case that is most distinguishable from adult court. The express goal of juvenile dispositions is the rehabilitation of the offender. Thus the hearing focuses on the needs of the child rather than on the nature of the crime. It is this aspect, together with the jurisdictional cutoff at age eighteen, that frequently leads to society's frustration and dismay in cases where there are convictions for appalling and horrific crimes. Since the needs of the child are paramount, input from psychologists and social workers is crucial.

There is an extremely broad range of dispositional alternatives available to juvenile court judges. The court can dismiss the case, place the offender on probation (by far the most common disposition), or assign the offender to out-of-community incarceration. Each of these alternatives may include broad conditions, limited only by the imaginations of judges, lawyers, and counselors.

Status Offense Cases. These proceedings have a variety of names and acronyms, which vary from jurisdiction to jurisdiction. Frequently they are called PINS (person in need of assistance) or CHINA (children in need of assistance) cases. These are cases in which a juvenile is charged with an act which would not be criminal if committed by an adult. The rights available in delinquency proceedings are frequently not all available in status offense cases. There is often no standard of proof (proof beyond a reasonable doubt) requirement, no privilege against self-incrimination, and no right to counsel. The rationale articulated for this condition is that status offense cases lack a punitive purpose. Diversion, which means to divert the case out of the court system into some social program, is the most frequent outcome in these cases. Typically the juvenile is referred into a "diversion program," and upon successful completion, there are no further proceedings. Often the charge is removed from the individual's record.

The Juvenile Justice and Delinquency Prevention Act of 1974 included in its provisions a conditional mandate that any states wanting federal monies for the programs under this act had to agree not to incarcerate PINS/CHINA juveniles in secure facilities, to encourage community-based program alternatives, and to utilize a "least restrictive alternative" standard

JUVENILES TAKEN INTO CUSTODY IN U.S. CITIES, 1993

Referred to other police agency, 1%

Referred to welfare agency, 1%

Referred to criminal or adult court, 5%

Handled within department and released, 26%

Referred to juvenile court jurisdiction, 67%

Source: U.S. Department of Justice, Federal Bureau of Investigation, *Crime in the United States* (Uniform Crime Reports). Washington, D.C.: U.S. Government Printing Office, 1994.

Note: Total number of juveniles taken into custody in cities was 1,091,890.

in dispositions of these matters. In addition, if placement was required in a given case, it had to be in a location of reasonable proximity to the child's family and community.

Abuse and Neglect Proceedings. In these types of proceedings, children find themselves in the juvenile justice system, but not as respondents; the petition is filed against the parent or other adult caretaker. The state exercises its *parens patriae* and police powers (*parens patriae* is the state's right to usurp parental rights when in the best interests of the child) and charges the adult with abuse or neglect. Abuse may be an overt act, or pattern of acts, of physical and/or mental cruelty inflicted upon a child, or it may be inappropriate sexual or physical contact. Neglect is more vague, but it usually refers to an omission, or failure to act. Most often it involves a willful or deliberate failure to care for the basic needs of a child adequately or to protect a child from the infliction of abuse.

Before 1980, the various child protection laws were the province of the states. Since then, input from the federal government has had a dramatic impact on termination of parental rights and placement of children. In 1980, Congress enacted the Adoption Assistance and Child Welfare Act of 1980, and a plethora of federal case law ensued. Essentially this act strictly limited the circumstances in which courts can separate families, even temporarily, and further encouraged reunification when temporary placement of children outside the home is warranted.

In abuse and neglect proceedings, the adult defendant typically has an attorney; the affected juvenile often does not. Naturally, the defendant parents would not normally hire one for the child. Some jurisdictions appoint counsel for the child; others do not. A variety of jurisdictions will appoint a guardian *ad litem* (a guardian to represent the interests of the child) or other representative to assist the child. Frequently these representatives are not attorneys.

The juvenile justice system continues to expand in importance and influence as it expands in size and is more frequently involved in matters affecting children and families in American society. This increased demand on the system appears to be leading to a greater role for the juvenile courts and an increasingly imaginative involvement by state legislatures and the Congress in matters relating to the juvenile justice system.

—*David G. Hicks*

See also Battered child and battered wife syndromes; Child abuse; Contributing to the delinquency of a minor; Criminal justice system; *Gault, In re*; *In loco parentis*; Juvenile delinquency; Juvenile Justice and Delinquency Prevention, Office of; Juvenile Justice and Delinquency Prevention Act; Majority, age of; Status offense.

BIBLIOGRAPHY

Any serious study of the juvenile justice system in the United States should include a reading of the important cases, specifically *In re Gault*, 387 U.S. 1 (1967), and the various acts of Congress mentioned as particularly relevant. Among many texts and edited collections covering juvenile justice issues are Paul R. Kfoury, *Children Before the Court: Reflections on Legal Issues Affecting Minors* (2d ed. Salem, N.H.: Butterworth, 1991); Steven M. Cox and John J. Conrad, *Juvenile Justice: A Guide to Practice and Theory* (Dubuque, Iowa: Wm. C. Brown, 1978); Frederic L. Faust and Paul J. Brantingham, eds., *Juvenile Justice Philosophy* (St. Paul, Minn.: West, 1974); Malcolm W. Klein, ed., *The Juvenile Justice System* (Beverly Hills, Calif.: Sage Publications, 1976); Randy Hertz, Martin Guggenheim, and Anthony G. Amsterdam, *Trial Manual for Defense Attorneys in Juvenile Court* (Philadelphia, Pa.: ALI-ABA, 1991); Ira M. Schwartz, ed., *Juvenile Justice and Public Policy* (New York: Lexington Books, 1992); and S. Randall Humm et al., eds., *Child, Parent, and State: Law and Policy Reader* (Philadelphia, Pa.: Temple University Press, 1994).

JUVENILES HELD IN PUBLIC JUVENILE FACILITIES, 1991

Reason Held	Total	Male	Female
Total juveniles	**57,661**	**51,282**	**6,379**
Delinquent Offenses[a]	95%	97.3%	80.7%
Offenses against persons			
Violent[b]	19	20.5	10.3
Other[c]	12	12.1	9.4
Property offenses			
Serious[d]	24	24.4	17.1
Other[e]	12	12.5	12.9
Alcohol offenses	1	1.0	1.0
Drug-related offenses	10	10.4	5.3
Public-order offenses[f]	4	4.4	5.4
Probation/parole violations	8	7.2	12.9
Other	5	4.8	6.4
Nondelinquent Reasons			
Status offenses[g]	3	1.8	12.9
Nonoffenders[h]	1	0.7	4.2
Voluntary commitments	1	0.2	2.2

Source: U.S. Department of Justice, Bureau of Justice Statistics, *Sourcebook of Criminal Justice Statistics—1993.* Washington, D.C.: U.S. Government Printing Office, 1994.

[a] Offenses that would be criminal if committed by adults.
[b] Includes murder, nonnegligent manslaughter, forcible rape, robbery, and aggravated assault.
[c] Includes negligent manslaughter, simple assault, and sexual assault.
[d] Includes burglary, arson, larceny/theft, and motor vehicle theft.
[e] Includes vandalism, forgery, counterfeiting, fraud, stolen property, and unauthorized vehicle use.
[f] Includes weapons offenses, prostitution, commercialized vice, disorderly conduct, minor traffic offenses, curfew or loitering law offenses, and offenses against morals and decency and the like.
[g] Offenses that would not be considered crimes if committed by adults.
[h] Dependency, neglect, abuse, emotional disturbance, retardation, and other.

Kansas-Nebraska Act

DATE: Became law May 30, 1854

DEFINITION: Legislation that allowed for the expansion of slavery into territory in which it had been previously proscribed by the Missouri Compromise of 1820

SIGNIFICANCE: Viewed as a compromise between pro- and antislavery positions by its sponsor, Stephen Douglas, the bill gave encouragement to proslavery forces

Senator Stephen A. Douglas, chairman of the Committee on Territories, introduced legislation to organize the land west of Missouri and Iowa as the Nebraska Territory. New settlements in the region and the potential for a transcontinental rail route prompted Douglas' action. It soon became apparent to Douglas that obtaining support from the South required two major revisions. First, the region was split into the Kansas and Nebraska territories. Second, the bill called for repeal of that part of the Missouri Compromise of 1820 which prohibited slavery north of 36° 30′ latitude. Rather, settlers in each territory would vote to accept or prohibit slavery.

Douglas viewed slavery from economic rather than moral grounds, reasoning that its unprofitability in northern climates would be its demise. Douglas' concessions to slave states reflected both the desire to get on with nation building and the necessity of obtaining Southern support for his presidential ambitions. The act widened the growing rift between North and South and encouraged the formation of the Republican Party.

See also Abolitionist movement; Douglas, Stephen A.; Lincoln, Abraham; Lincoln-Douglas debates; Missouri Compromise of 1820; Slavery.

Katz v. United States

COURT: U.S. Supreme Court

DATE: Decided December 18, 1967

SIGNIFICANCE: The Supreme Court determined that electronic surveillance constitutes a search subject to the Fourth Amendment's warrant and probable cause provisions

Katz was convicted of transmitting wagering information over the telephone on the basis of information he gave over a public telephone which he habitually used. The Federal Bureau of Investigation gained access to this information by attaching an external listening device to the telephone booth. The lower court concluded that since the booth had not been physically invaded, this investigative method did not constitute a "search" within the meaning of the Fourth Amendment, which requires an antecedent showing of probable cause and the issuance of a warrant. The Supreme Court, however, finding that the government had violated Katz's "legitimate expectation" of privacy, declared that the government's methods did indeed constitute a search and reversed the ruling.

Katz v. United States substituted a "reasonable expectation of privacy" test for the physical intrusion test the Court had previously used to determine if a police search and seizure was constitutional. This new test was cogently phrased in Justice John M. Harlan's concurring opinion: "[T]here is a twofold requirement, first that a person have exhibited an actual (subjective) expectation of privacy and, second, that the expectation be one that society is prepared to recognize as 'reasonable.'" Harlan's opinion was used by lower courts to parse the meaning of *Katz*, but as he himself later recognized in *United States v. White* (1971), any evaluation of a questionable search must of necessity "transcend the search for subjective expectations." The government could, for example, defeat any expectation of privacy in telephone conversations by issuing a declaration that all such conversations are subject to third-party eavesdropping. The reasonableness requirement may mean that an expectation of privacy in a particular realm must be shared by a majority of Americans. Yet it might also mean that although there are areas in which reasonable individuals might legitimately expect to maintain their privacy, such expectations can be superseded by more important policy considerations, such as the need for railroad engineers to give blood and urine specimens for purposes of drug testing (see *Skinner v. Railway Labor Executives Association*, 1989).

In *White*, Harlan defined searches as "those more extensive intrusions that significantly jeopardize the sense of security which is the paramount concern of Fourth Amendment liberties," but the Supreme Court has applied the *Katz* doctrine narrowly. In *United States v. Miller* (1976), for example, the Court ruled that persons do not have a reasonable expectation of privacy as to bank records of their financial transactions. In *Smith v. Maryland* (1979), the Court found that while individuals might reasonably expect the content of their telephone conversations to remain private, they cannot entertain a similar expectation as to the telephone numbers they call. In both cases, the Court based its decision on the fact that the information plaintiffs claimed to be off limits to police was already accessed by others—bank employees and telephone companies, respectively.

See also Electronic surveillance; Evidence, rules of; Privacy, right of; Search and seizure.

Kefauver investigation

DATE: 1950-1951

PLACE: Washington, D.C.

SIGNIFICANCE: The Senate's Crime Investigation Committee, chaired by Estes Kefauver, in 1950-1951 investigated crime syndicates and their political connections

Tennessee senator Estes Kefauver gained national prominence in 1950 by leading an investigation of national crime syndi-

The Kefauver Committee explaining its report at a news conference in the Capitol, May 1, 1951. (AP/Wide World Photos)

cates. His committee's investigations brought to the American public one of its earliest exposures to televised senatorial hearings.

Kefauver, consciously seeking a national forum, proposed an investigation of national crime syndicates, although it was then unclear whether such syndicates actually existed. Kefauver urged the Eighty-first Congress to investigate the alleged syndicates and examine their political connections and influence. Senator Pat McCarran chaired the Judiciary Committee, which had to decide whether to bring Kefauver's proposal before the full Senate. As a senator from Nevada, McCarran was reluctant to broach the matter because his state's extensive gambling interests were connected to organized crime. Eventually, the press pressured McCarran into giving Kefauver his way. The Senate vote on Kefauver's proposal was 35 to 35, a tie broken by Vice President Alben Barkley in Kefauver's favor.

Kefauver chaired the resultant Special Committee to Investigate Crime in Interstate Commerce, popularly called the Crime Committee or the Kefauver Committee. Having the authority to create a task force that, for the first time in United

States history, could draw upon all the law enforcement agencies of the federal government, the committee verified links between crime syndicates and all levels of government. The Kefauver Committee, through attorneys of the Department of Justice, accumulated detailed information about some 150 of the most notorious crime figures in the United States, including such high-profile criminals as Jake and Meyer Lansky, Charles Fischetti, Frank Costello, Joe Adonis, and Mickey Cohen. They summoned many of these figures to give testimony before the committee.

The committee examined the bank accounts of public officials—sheriffs, mayors, state legislators—and made pointed inquiries about how, during their years of public service, their bank accounts grew out of proportion to their official incomes, which were matters of public record. Clearly, many of the public officials the committee investigated profited handsomely from providing protection for people connected with crime syndicates.

Some of those called to testify before the Kefauver Committee were mowed down gangster-style on the streets of

Chicago or other cities in which crime syndicates flourished before they could appear. Illinois voters, disgusted by what the Kefauver investigations unearthed, voted most of its national incumbents out of office in 1952.

William O'Dwyer, a former New York City mayor, was called before the committee to explain why he had not prosecuted known mobsters when he was Manhattan's district attorney. Governor Fuller Warren of Florida, exasperated that the committee exposed his having received campaign contributions from organized crime, sought to discredit Kefauver within the Democratic Party, as did former Speaker of the House Scott Lucas, who blamed Kefauver for his loss of the election in Illinois.

See also Crime; Organized crime; Organized Crime Control Act.

Kennedy, John F. (May 29, 1917, Brookline, Mass.— Nov. 22, 1963, Dallas, Tex.)

IDENTIFICATION: President of the United States, 1961-1963

SIGNIFICANCE: Kennedy is one of the best known and most celebrated of U.S. presidents; his primary interest lay in foreign affairs rather than domestic affairs, however, and his presidency accomplished little directly in the areas of civil rights and social justice

Between 1946 and 1952, John F. Kennedy was a Democratic representative from Massachusetts; from 1952 to 1960 he was a U.S. senator. In 1960, he won the presidency, defeating Republican candidate Richard Nixon. Kennedy established the Peace Corps, a volunteer organization to help developing countries, in 1961, as well as the Alliance for Progress, a pan-American alliance. Also in his first year in office, Kennedy gave approval to a Central Intelligence Agency plan to use Cuban refugees and exiles to invade Cuba and depose Fidel Castro. The plan was a dismal failure, but when Kennedy publicly accepted the blame for the debacle, his popularity rose.

Domestically, Kennedy's abbreviated term of office accomplished little. The Civil Rights movement was in full swing, but effective federal legislation on civil rights was not passed until Lyndon Johnson became president after Kennedy's assassination. Kennedy advocated civil rights and social legislation but lacked congressional support, and he generally did not lobby Congress for passage of his programs, so most of them were stalled or defeated. On the other hand, Johnson's success at pushing through the sweeping Civil Rights Act of 1964 owed much to Kennedy's submission of an omnibus civil rights bill to Congress in June, 1963, and to the national shock of Kennedy's assassination in November, when the bill was still pending in the House Rules Committee.

In the Cuban Missile Crisis of October, 1962, the United States and the Soviet Union came to the brink of nuclear war when Kennedy demanded the removal of nuclear missiles that the Soviet Union was placing in Cuba. When he instituted a blockade to force their removal, the Soviet Union relented and removed the missiles. The Cold War against the Soviet Union and the perceived worldwide communist menace cast a

The Civil Rights Act of 1964 was a strengthened version of legislation introduced by John F. Kennedy in 1963. (Library of Congress)

shadow over the politics of the 1950's and early 1960's, and it was in this context that Kennedy increased the numbers of American troops (called "advisers") in Vietnam from about three thousand to more than sixteen thousand.

Kennedy's term in office was cut short by his assassination in Dallas, Texas, by Lee Harvey Oswald on November 22, 1963. The Warren Commission, headed by Chief Justice Earl Warren, was charged with investigating the assassination. In a hasty and sloppy investigation, the commission concluded that Oswald had acted alone, thus setting the stage for decades of controversy and theories about a conspiracy to assassinate Kennedy.

See also Civil Rights Act of 1964; Democratic Party; Johnson, Lyndon B.; Kennedy, Robert F.; Nuclear weapons; Vietnam War; Warren, Earl; Warren Commission.

Kennedy, Robert F. (Nov. 20, 1925, Brookline, Mass.— June 6, 1968, Los Angeles, Calif.)

IDENTIFICATION: U.S. attorney general and presidential candidate

SIGNIFICANCE: Close adviser to his brother, President John F. Kennedy, and later a candidate for the nation's highest office himself, "Bobby" Kennedy was a champion of the disadvantaged

A graduate of Harvard University and the University of Virginia Law School, Kennedy served as attorney for the Criminal Division of the U.S Department of Justice (1951-1952), prosecuting income-tax cases; assistant counsel to Senator Joseph McCarthy's Permanent Investigations Subcommittee (1953-1956), until he resigned in protest of McCarthy's questionable methods; and chief counsel to the Senate "Rackets" Committee (1957-1959), where he gained fame by exposing organized crime and the illegal ties of Teamster's Union official James "Jimmy" Hoffa to organized crime. As attorney general (1961-1964), he continued his attacks on organized crime and furthered the cause of civil rights by prosecuting voting rights and school desegregation cases and banning segregation on interstate buses and in bus terminals.

Kennedy left President Lyndon B. Johnson's administration after being passed over for the vice presidency and became an outspoken critic of the Vietnam War. As U.S. senator from New York he built a strong base of support among the poor, African Americans, youth, and blue-collar workers by championing antipoverty programs, Medicare, education, and civil rights. In 1968 he entered the race for the Democratic presidential nomination. After winning five of the six primaries in which he ran, however, Kennedy was assassinated by Sirhan Bisharu Sirhan while leaving the Ambassador Hotel in Los Angeles after winning the California primary. Kennedy is the author of *To Seek a Newer World* (1967).

See also Attorney general of the United States; Johnson, Lyndon B.; Justice, U.S. Department of; Kennedy, John F.; Organized crime.

Kent, James (July 31, 1763, Fredericksburgh, N.Y.—Dec. 12, 1847, New York, N.Y.)

IDENTIFICATION: American jurist

SIGNIFICANCE: Kent's judicial decisions and writings helped shape the common law, equity, and other aspects of American legal culture during the formative years of the early nineteenth century

After practicing law in New York City, James Kent was appointed the first professor of law at Columbia University in 1793. His university lectures were later expanded into *Commentaries on American Law* (1826-1830), a treatise of enormous influence that had gone into fourteen editions by 1900. Also an influential judge, he was appointed to the New York Supreme Court in 1798 and was chancellor to the state's Court of Chancery from 1814 to 1823. Kent shaped the inchoate common law into a systematic organization and was one of the judges most instrumental in reviving equity jurisprudence. While he emphasized common-law

precedents, Kent also borrowed many concepts from Roman-derived civil law and international law. He helped establish many influential doctrines in American constitutional law, including judicial review, the nature of Indian sovereignty, and the use of truth as a defense in libel suits.

See also Common law; Defamation; Equity; Federalism; Judicial review.

Kent State student killings

DATE: May 4, 1970

PLACE: Kent State University, Kent, Ohio

SIGNIFICANCE: Because of litigation by representatives of college students killed by Ohio National Guardsmen, the U.S. Supreme Court held that the doctrine of sovereign immunity is not an absolute right

Protests against American involvement in the Vietnam War escalated immediately after President Richard Nixon announced on April 30, 1970, that American troops had moved into Cambodia. On May 4, four Kent State University students—Allison Krause, Jeffrey Miller, Sandra Scheuer, and William Shroeder—were fatally shot by Ohio National Guardsmen during an anti-Vietnam War protest. Nine other students were injured, two permanently. The incident shocked millions across the country. Several issues arose after the shootings, including a due process argument regarding the legality of using the Ohio National Guard to quell the civilian disturbance on the Kent campus. Regarding the civil action brought by representatives of the slain students, the U.S. Su-

Four Kent State University students were shot by National Guardsmen during anti-Vietnam War protests. (AP/Wide World Photos)

preme Court held in 1974 that the sovereign immunity of state officials against being sued for damages was not an absolute right. In other litigation, representatives of the slain students were unsuccessful in their attempt to prevent the building of a gymnasium on the site on which National Guardsmen had maneuvered moments before turning and firing the fatal shots.

See also Campus Unrest, President's Commission on; Civil disobedience; Immunity of public officials; National Guard; Vietnam War.

Keyes v. Denver School District No. 1

COURT: U.S. Supreme Court
DATE: Decided June 21, 1973
SIGNIFICANCE: This ruling extended *Brown v. Board of Education*; it outlawed *de facto* desegregation and expanded the prohibition on segregation to Hispanics

Brown v. Board of Education (1954) invalidated laws that required or permitted segregated black and white schools. Nevertheless, many school districts remained segregated, in part because of *de facto* segregation (segregation "in fact" rather than "by law"). Wilfred Keyes did not want his daughter, Christi Keyes, to attend any kind of segregated school in Denver. In 1970, when a newly elected school board rescinded a desegregation plan adopted by the previous board in 1969, he brought a class-action suit.

In 1970 the district court ordered Park Hill schools desegregated after hearing evidence that the school board deliberately segregated its schools through school site selection, excessive use of mobile classroom units, gerrymandered attendance zones, student transportation routes, a restrictive transfer policy, and segregated faculty assignment to schools. Keyes was also successful before the court in arguing that inner-city schools, with substantial black and Hispanic student populations, should also be desegregated, but Denver prevailed on appeal in 1971, arguing that the large percentages of black and Hispanic students in these schools resulted from a "neighborhood school" policy.

Justice William Brennan delivered the opinion of the U.S. Supreme Court. Six justices joined Brennan, one justice affirmed the decision in part and dissented in part, and the remaining justice dissented. The Supreme Court ruled that since intentional segregation was proved in one part of the city, there was a presumption of intentional discrimination in the other case. The burden of proof thus shifted to the school board to prove that the intentional segregation of one section of the district was isolated, separate, and unrelated to the pattern of pupil assignment to the "core city schools."

When the case was sent back to the district court in 1973, Denver was determined to have practiced unlawful segregation in both areas of the city, and the school board was required to desegregate. When the school board failed to design an adequate plan to desegregate by 1974, the court drew up a plan of its own.

The effect of *Keyes* was to open all northern school districts to the possibility of desegregation lawsuits. Eventually almost every city of at least moderate size then grappled with desegregation plans, voluntary or court ordered. The lone exception is the statewide school district of Hawaii, which has never been desegregated despite the existence of schools situated to serve certain geographic areas where only persons of Hawaiian ancestry by law can reside.

See also *Brown v. Board of Education*; Segregation, *de facto* and *de jure*; *Sweatt v. Painter*.

Kidnapping

DEFINITION: Seizing and holding by force or enticement a person who is unwilling to be held and/or is below a specific age
SIGNIFICANCE: Kidnapping is considered among the most serious crimes in the United States and carries with it a maximum federal penalty of life imprisonment

The term "kidnapping" is a combined form of the word "kid," meaning a young person or animal, and the word "nab" or "nap," meaning to steal. The term is somewhat misleading because people of any age can be kidnapped, as many adult political hostages over the years can attest. Records of kidnapping date to the ancient societies of Egypt, Palestine, and Babylon. Motivations vary; in the United States at present, most abductions occur when divorced or legally separated parents or other concerned persons, such as grandparents, are involved in bitter custody disputes.

The Categories of Kidnapping. Most records from ancient, pre-Christian societies indicate that kidnapping then was a capital crime. Under English common law this offense was subdivided into three types of offense. Taking people from their countries by force and transporting them to other countries was considered a misdemeanor, the punishment for which was slight. In situations where people from what are now called Third World countries were stolen and sold into slavery, punishment was seldom exacted. As late as the eighteenth century, when the United States was involved in a bustling slave trade with West Africa, most such kidnappings, which were carried out on a huge scale, went unpunished.

It was commonplace during this period for men to be taken forcibly aboard ships, where they were impressed into working involuntarily. The verb for this kind of kidnapping, "to shanghai," exists in the language today. Many women were kidnapped and sold either as domestics or as prostitutes. Until laws were enacted in the nineteenth and twentieth centuries to forbid such activities, kidnapping flourished in and was practiced by Western society.

A more serious kind of kidnapping under English common law involved the abduction of a person, usually a child, for ransom. This offense was punishable by death, as is still the case in many venues, particularly if bodily harm or death should befall the victim.

The third category, child stealing, involves snatching or forcibly confining a child below a specific age, usually between twelve and fourteen. Most of the kidnapping that comes before the courts in the United States falls into this category and involves custody battles. Such disputes are generally settled through compromise, although, on occasion, courts impose fines and/or prison sentences upon such child snatchers.

Tightening U.S. Kidnapping Laws. There were two major causes of the tightening of kidnapping laws in the United States during the twentieth century. Although the Mann Act of 1910 outlawed the interstate transportation of women for immoral purposes, this act touched only tangentially on kidnapping. It was not until 1932 that the nation took serious notice of the dangers that lurked for many families, especially the affluent, whose children might be taken and held for ransom.

In that year, the infant son of Charles and Anne Morrow Lindbergh was snatched from the second-floor nursery of his home in Hopewell, New Jersey, and held for ransom. Charles Lindbergh, the first person to fly solo across the Atlantic Ocean, was a national hero, so the abduction of this child focused enormous public attention on the kidnapping. In the end, the Lindbergh child was found murdered. In 1936, Bruno Hauptmann, after a trial based upon strong circumstantial evidence, was executed for murder.

The kidnapping and murder of the son of beloved hero Charles Lindbergh provoked a national outcry. (AP/Wide World Photos)

As a result of this kidnapping, Congress passed the Federal Kidnapping Act, commonly called the "Lindbergh law," which classifies kidnapping as a federal crime if the victim is taken across state lines. Under such circumstances, the Federal Bureau of Investigation is empowered to enter the case within twenty-four hours of the abduction. The severest penalty for conviction under this act is life imprisonment. A later law imposes severe penalties for any abduction that might occur during the robbery of a national bank.

A second reason for the tightening of laws related to kidnapping came during the 1970's, when a rash of airline hijackings and hostage situations in the Middle East, notably in Lebanon and Iran, added an international dimension to taking people by force and holding them for the purpose of achieving a given end—usually economic, religious, political, or a combination of these.

As a result of hijackings, airport security has become extremely stringent worldwide, and in the United States it is a federal offense to violate such security. Penalties extend even to people who make threats in jest to air security personnel at airport checkpoints. International law is involved in many cases of hijacking and in most political hostage situations. It has proved difficult to win extradition of foreign nationals who engage in such activities.   —*R. Baird Shuman*

See also Child abuse; Child molestation; Comprehensive Crime Control Act of 1984; Lindbergh law; Mann Act.

BIBLIOGRAPHY

The following sources provide varied insights into kidnapping: Ernest Alix, *Ransom Kidnapping in America, 1874-1974: The Creation of a Capital Crime* (Carbondale: Southern Illinois University Press, 1978); Martin Bloom, *Primary Prevention: The Possible Science* (Englewood Cliffs, N.J.: Prentice-Hall, 1981); Richard Clutterbuck, *Kidnap, Hijack, and Extortion: The Response* (New York: St. Martin's Press, 1987); Lela B. Costin, Cynthia J. Bell, and Susan W. Downs, *Child Welfare: Policies and Practice* (4th ed. New York: Longman, 1991); Anna Demeter, *Legal Kidnaping: What Happens to a Family When the Father Kidnaps Two Children* (Boston: Beacon Press, 1977); John E. Gill, *Stolen Children* (New York: Seaview Books, 1981); Geoffrey L. Greif and Rebecca L. Hegar, *When Parents Kidnap: The Families Behind the Headlines* (New York: Maxwell Macmillan International, 1993); and Robert H. Mnookin and D. Kelly Weisberg, *Child, Family, and State: Problems and Materials on Children and the Law* (2d ed. Boston: Little, Brown, 1989).

King, Martin Luther, Jr. (Jan. 15, 1929, Atlanta, Ga.—Apr. 4, 1968, Memphis, Tenn.)

IDENTIFICATION: Black American Baptist minister and civil rights leader

SIGNIFICANCE: King was the most famous twentieth century American moral crusader; he led the struggle for full citizenship and civil rights for the poor, disadvantaged, and racially oppressed

A leading Baptist clergyman, Martin Luther King, Jr., was the second of three children born to the Reverend Martin and Alberta Williams King. Educated at Morehouse College, Crozer Theological Seminary, and Boston University, he was pastor of the Dexter Avenue Baptist Church, Montgomery, Alabama, from 1954 to 1959. While at Boston University he met and married Coretta Scott in 1953. During his first year at Dexter Avenue, he was elected president of the Montgomery Improvement Association, which supervised the successful boycott of the local bus system from December, 1955, to December, 1956. After a year of struggle, the U.S. Supreme Court ruled that bus segregation was unconstitutional, and King became a national hero. In 1957, King and other African American leaders formed the Southern Christian Leadership Conference (SCLC) to coordinate civil rights activities. The neo-orthodox theology which he had adopted during his studies was tempered in his civil rights campaigns by the teachings of Mahatma Gandhi on nonviolent civil disobedience.

So that he could have more time to work with the movement, he left Montgomery in 1960 and became co-pastor, with

Martin Luther King, Jr., addressing demonstrators at the 1963 March on Washington in front of the Lincoln Memorial. (AP/Wide World Photos)

his father, of the Ebenezer Baptist Church in Atlanta. Thereafter he provided major leadership in the changes which led to an expansion of rights for minorities in the United States. Although he firmly committed the SCLC to voter registration campaigns throughout the South, his major efforts were in Albany, Georgia (1961-1962); Birmingham, Alabama (1963); and Danville, Virginia (1963). Arrested more than fifteen times, often receiving death threats, he came to personify the struggle of powerless people for justice. The high point of his life was the 1963 March on Washington, when 250,000 people demonstrated their support for civil rights. His "I Have a Dream" speech, delivered from the steps of the Lincoln Memorial, moved the nation. These events were major contributions to the passage of the 1964 Civil Rights Act and the 1965 Voting Rights Act. In January, 1964, *Time* magazine chose him as "Man of the Year," the first black American so honored. Later that same year, he became the youngest recipient of the Nobel Peace Prize.

In 1965, after leading a harrowing march from Selma to Montgomery, he expanded his work less successfully into the North. This shift in SCLC strategy was intended to "bring the Negro into the mainstream of American life as quickly as possible." Once he recognized the deeper relationship of poverty and economics to racism, King called for more fundamental changes in society. While supporting the War on Poverty, he condemned the war in Vietnam in 1967. His outspokenness on international issues of peace and imperialism earned him the enmity of many former supporters, while intensifying the opposition long waged against him by the Federal Bureau of Investigation.

In 1968, in the midst of planning a multiracial poor people's march on Washington to demand an end to all forms of discrimination and the funding of a twelve-billion-dollar "economic bill of rights," he flew to Memphis, Tennessee, to support a sanitation workers' strike. There, on April 4, he was assassinated. Although the immediate reaction to his death was violent rioting in the ghettos of many major United States cities, the more lasting effect of his life has been to provide the movement for social justice in the United States with an impressive hero and martyr. King authored five books: *Stride Toward Freedom* (1958), *Strength to Love* (1963), *Why We Can't Wait* (1964), *Where Do We Go from Here: Chaos or Community?* (1967), and *The Trumpet of Conscience* (1967). His birthday, observed on the third Monday in January, became a national holiday in 1986.

See also Civil disobedience; Civil Rights Act of 1964; Civil Rights movement; Gandhi, Mahatma; Hoover, J. Edgar; Jackson, Jesse; Nonviolent resistance; Poor People's March on Washington; Selma-to-Montgomery civil rights march; Southern Christian Leadership Conference (SCLC); Voting Rights Act of 1965.

King, Rodney, case and aftermath

DATE: March 3, 1991-June 1, 1994
SIGNIFICANCE: The trial of four white policemen in Los Angeles following the arrest and beating of Rodney King, a black man, sparked a major investigation of police brutality

in Los Angeles and violent race riots after a California court acquitted the police

Following a high-speed chase along a Los Angeles highway that ended just after midnight on March 3, 1991, California Highway Patrol officers Timothy and Melanie Singer stopped driver Rodney Glen King and his two passengers, Bryant Allen and Freddie Helms, for questioning. More than twenty Los Angeles Police Department (LAPD) officers soon arrived on the scene in Los Angeles' Lake View Terrace neighborhood. Police sergeant Stacey Koon, assisted by officers Theodore Briseno, Laurence Powell, and Timothy Wind, took over the investigation. The police quickly subdued and handcuffed Bryant Allen and Freddie Helms without incident. Their encounter with Rodney King, however, caused a controversy with far-reaching legal and social consequences.

King's Arrest. According to the four white police officers who arrested Rodney King, a black man, King refused at first to leave the car and then resisted arrest with such vigor that the officers had to apply two jolts from a Taser electric stun gun, fifty-six blows from aluminum batons, and six kicks (primarily from Briseno) to subdue King before they successfully handcuffed and cordcuffed King to restrain his arms and legs. The event probably would have gone unnoticed had not George Holliday, an amateur cameraman who witnessed the incident, videotaped the arrest and sold the tape to a local television station news program. The videotape became the crucial piece of evidence that the state of California used to charge the four LAPD arresting officers with criminal assault and that a federal grand jury subsequently used to charge the officers with civil rights violations.

Broadcast of Holliday's tape on national news programs elicited several responses from the LAPD. On March 6, 1991, the LAPD released King from custody and admitted that officers failed to prove that King had resisted arrest. On March 7, Los Angeles Police Chief Daryl Gates announced that he would investigate King's arrest and, if the investigation warranted it, would pursue criminal assault charges against the arresting officers. On March 14, a Los Angeles County grand jury indicted Sergeant Koon and officers Briseno, Powell, and Wind for criminal assault, and they subsequently pleaded not guilty.

Investigation of Police Brutality. Overwhelming public sympathy for King following the national broadcast of Holliday's videotape prompted Los Angeles Mayor Tom Bradley to investigate charges that instances of police brutality motivated by racism were commonplace during LAPD arrest operations. On April 1, 1991, Mayor Bradley appointed a nonpartisan commission, headed by Warren Christopher (who had formerly served as President Jimmy Carter's deputy secretary of state), to study the LAPD's past record of complaints regarding police misconduct. On April 2, Mayor Bradley called on Police Chief Gates, who had served on the LAPD since 1949 and had been police chief since 1978, to resign. In May, the LAPD suspended Sergeant Koon and officers Briseno and Powell without pay and dismissed officer Timothy Wind, a rookie without tenure, pending the outcome of their criminal trial. Rodney King then filed a civil rights lawsuit against the city of Los Angeles.

Several significant developments occurred as the officers awaited trial. On July 9, 1991, the Christopher Commission released the results of its investigation and its recommendations to the five-member Los Angeles Police Commission. The Police Commission employed the police chief and was responsible for the management of the LAPD. The Christopher Commission found that the LAPD, composed of 67.8 percent white officers in 1991, suffered from a "siege mentality" in a city where 63 percent of the population were people of color. The commission also found that a small but significant proportion of officers repeatedly used excessive force when making arrests and that the LAPD did not punish those officers when citizens filed complaints. Finally, the commission recommended measures to exert more control over the LAPD's operations, including limiting the police chief's tenure to a five-year term, renewable by the Police Commission for one additional term only. After the release of the Christopher Commission report, Police Chief Gates announced his retirement, effective April, 1992 (which he later amended to July, 1992). On July 23, 1991, a California court of appeal granted the police defendants' request for a change of venue for the upcoming criminal trial.

The State of California Court Trial. The trial of the four officers began on March 4, 1992, in the new venue—the primarily white community of Simi Valley in Ventura County.

The jury who heard the state of California's case against the four officers consisted of ten whites, one Latino, and one Asian. The officers' defense lawyers presented Holliday's videotape broken down into a series of individual still pictures. They asked the jury to judge whether excessive force—that is, force that was not warranted by King's "aggressive" actions—was employed at any single moment during the arrest. Referring often to the "thin blue line" that protected society from the "likes of Rodney King," the defense built a case that justified the police officers' actions. Rodney King's lawyer, Steven Lerman, a personal injury specialist, advised King not to testify at the trial out of concern that King's "confused and frightened" state of mind since the beating might impair his memory of events and discredit his testimony. The Simi Valley jury acquitted the four officers of all charges of criminal assault, with the exception of one count against officer Laurence Powell on which the jury was deadlocked.

The acquittal of the four police officers on April 29, 1992, ignited widespread and destructive riots led by poor and angry black Angelenos. The riots affected areas throughout Los Angeles but particularly devastated parts of impoverished South Central Los Angeles. Fifty-three people died during the riots, which raged until May 2, and more than one billion dollars' worth of property was damaged. There had long been friction between Los Angeles' neighboring Korean and black communities, and the Korean American community bore the brunt of the rioters' destructive attacks.

An amateur cameraman videotaped the beating of Rodney King, which quickly received national airplay. (AP/Wide World Photos)

The acquittal of the LAPD officers who arrested Rodney King provoked riots in which fifty-three people died. (AP/Wide World Photos)

The Federal Court Civil Rights Trial. On August 5, 1992, a federal grand jury indicted the four officers for violating King's civil rights. The grand jury charged Sergeant Koon with violating the Fourteenth Amendment, which obligated Koon, as the officer in charge of the arrest, to protect King while he was in police custody. Officers Briseno, Powell, and Wind were charged with violating the Fourth Amendment in using more force than necessary, and using that excessive force willfully, when they arrested King. King testified during the federal trial. On April 17, 1993, a jury of nine whites, two blacks, and one Latino found Koon and Powell guilty and Briseno and Wind not guilty. On August 4, 1993, Koon and Powell were sentenced to two-and-one-half-year prison terms. In May, 1994, a Los Angeles jury awarded Rodney King $3.8 million in compensatory damages in his civil rights lawsuit against the city, but on June 1, 1994, the jury denied King's request for additional punitive damages. —*Karen Garner*

See also Change of venue; Civil rights; Compensatory damages; Double jeopardy; Due process of law; Miami riots; Police brutality; Race riots, twentieth century.

BIBLIOGRAPHY

For accounts of the Rodney King incident that are sympathetic to King, see H. Khalif Khalifah, ed., *Rodney King and the L.A. Rebellion: Analysis & Commentary by Thirteen Best-Selling Black Writers* (Hampton, Va.: U.B. & U.S. Communications Systems, 1992), and Tom Owens with Rod Browning, *Lying Eyes: The Truth Behind the Corruption and Brutality of the LAPD and the Beating of Rodney King* (New York: Thunder's Mouth Press, 1994). For an account of the police officers' point of view, see Stacey Koon with Robert Deitz, *Presumed Guilty: The Tragedy of the Rodney King Affair* (Washington, D.C.: Regnery Gateway, 1992). For a collection of essays that places the Rodney King incident in the context of race relations in the late twentieth century United States, see Robert Gooding-Williams, ed., *Reading Rodney King/Reading Urban Uprising* (New York: Routledge, 1993).

Knapp Commission

DATE: 1970-1972

SIGNIFICANCE: The Knapp Commission investigated charges of bribery and corruption in the New York City Police Department

New York mayor John Lindsay appointed the Knapp Commission in 1970 in response to continuing rumors and charges of police misconduct. Police Commissioner Patrick V. Murphy opposed the investigations. During the proceedings, Sergeant

David Durk and Detective Frank Serpico testified to the existence of bribery and corruption in the department, and Officer William Phillips testified that bribes in the New York City Police Department amounted to several million dollars per year.

During the Knapp Commission investigations, more than fifty officers were indicted on charges of involvement in bribery, drugs, gambling, and prostitution. The mayor abolished the commission in 1972 amid considerable controversy. Nevertheless, the inquiries were important in stimulating public interest and concern about the problems of the police department. The Knapp Commission story later became a film, *Serpico* (1973), bearing the name of one of the state's star witnesses.

See also Bribery; Criminal justice system; Organized crime; Police corruption and misconduct.

Korematsu v. United States

COURT: U.S. Supreme Court

DATE: Ruling issued December 18, 1944

SIGNIFICANCE: In this case, the Supreme Court refused to rule in favor of the privacy rights of an American citizen of Japanese ancestry who was detained in a relocation camp during World War II

In 1942, American military authorities arrested Fred Toyosaburo Korematsu, an American citizen of Japanese ancestry, for remaining in San Leandro, California, a restricted region, in violation of a military order. The military acted under authority of President Franklin Roosevelt's Executive Order 9066, which authorized the secretary of war and appropriate military commanders to establish military areas from which persons might be excluded. The president issued this order on his authority as commander in chief of the army and navy. After being found guilty of violating the military order, Korematsu appealed his case to the U.S. Supreme Court.

In December, 1944, the U.S. Supreme Court ruled 6 to 3 in favor of the United States and in support of Korematsu's arrest. The majority opinion, written by Justice Hugo L. Black, sustained Korematsu's removal because "the properly constituted military authorities" feared an invasion of the West Coast and had decided that military urgency required the removal of persons of Japanese origin from the area. Black admitted that the exclusion order worked hardship on the Japanese American population, "but hardships are a part of war and war is an aggregation of hardships." Furthermore, the exclusion program did not constitute racial discrimination as such; Korematsu had not been excluded because of his race but because of the requirements of national security. As to the question of loyalty, Black stated that there was insufficient time to separate the loyal from the disloyal Japanese. The only recourse, then, was for the military leaders to take such action as they deemed necessary to protect the country and its citizens from possible aggression. The section of Black's opinion that has most often been cited, however, states that "all legal restrictions which curtail the civil rights of a single racial group are immediately suspect" and must be given "the most rigid scrutiny."

Three justices differed from the majority and registered vigorous dissents. Justice Owen J. Roberts objected on the grounds of both loyalty and race. This was a "case of convicting a citizen as punishment for not submitting to imprisonment in a concentration camp, solely because of his ancestry," without evidence concerning his loyalty to the United States. Justice Frank Murphy was equally adamant in his dissent. He denounced the removal of Japanese citizens as "one of the most sweeping and complete deprivations of constitutional rights in the history of this nation in the absence of martial law." He concluded that the exclusion program itself "goes over the 'very brink of constitutional power' and falls into the very ugly abyss of racism."

The importance of *Korematsu v. United States* lies in the difficulty that the Court had in determining the dividing line be-

Japanese Americans being relocated to camps. The Supreme Court upheld the relocation order in Korematsu v. United States. *(National Archives)*

tween the constitutional rights of the citizen and the nation's power to defend itself. In this case, the Court did not rule on the constitutionality of the internment of someone on the basis of race, only that the presidential executive order and the subsequent military orders were deemed necessary for the defense of the nation and its citizens. While it took the United States more than forty years officially to rectify and repudiate the internment of Japanese Americans (reparations payments were authorized by Congress in 1988), many commentators have long believed that the United States acted improperly and in violation of the civil rights of American citizens by its use of the internment camp program.

See also *Hirabayashi v. United States*; Jacksonian democracy; Martial law; *Milligan, Ex parte*; Racial and ethnic discrimination.

Ku Klux Klan (KKK)

DATE: 1866-1871; 1915-1944; 1946-present

SIGNIFICANCE: The terrorism of the Ku Klux Klan was instrumental in preventing blacks in the South from gaining their civil rights after the Civil War; in a later incarnation, the Klan terrorized and propagandized against blacks, Catholics, Jews, and Asian Americans

The original Ku Klux Klan was organized in the South after the Civil War in order to "keep the Negro in his place"—in the fields and subordinated to whites. It was founded in 1866 by former Confederate general Nathan Bedford Forrest, and it disbanded in 1871-1872. It has been estimated that the Klan murdered four hundred African Americans between 1866 and 1872; none of the people responsible was given more serious punishment than fines.

In 1915 William Joseph Simmons chartered the second version of the Klan, "The Invisible Empire, Knights of the Ku Klux Klan, Inc.," in Atlanta, Georgia. The new Klan was a tightly integrated secret fraternal organization dedicated to the "American" ideals of racial purity and traditional morality. Heavy initial recruitment coincided with the Atlanta filming of D. W. Griffith's *The Birth of a Nation* (1915), which glorified the Ku Klux Klan of post-Civil War Reconstruction.

After World War I, American blacks returned home proud of their distinguished service and filled with high expectations. Their hopes for full citizens' rights and status were similar to the dreams of the newly freed slaves which had called forth the original Klan. The Klan depicted blacks as seeking to "intermingle" the races.

The 1920's was the peak of the Klan's popularity. New immigrants (notably Italian, Irish, and Polish Catholics, Rus-

A Klan cross-burning rally in South Carolina in August, 1963—the same month that a massive civil rights march took place in Washington, D.C. (AP/Wide World Photos)

sian and Slavic Jews, and Asians) were altering the white Anglo-Saxon Protestant profile of the American population. The Klan's hate literature depicted Catholics and Jews as racial and religious threats to traditional American values. Asians were easy to stereotype and denigrate; like blacks, they simply looked different. Klan propaganda against these groups attracted millions of members. Membership was strong across the southern United States from Florida to Texas and in the Midwest, especially Indiana. Members came from all strata of white male society. In fact, the Klan's program reflected the feelings of many Americans in the 1920's. In 1924 the Klan helped elect eleven governors and sixteen congressmen, and in 1928 it helped defeat presidential candidate Al Smith.

Violence was perpetrated by only a minority of the group's members. In 1921 the exposure of Klan violence by *The New York World* and the ensuing congressional investigation of the Klan actually caused membership to burgeon. Under Hiram Wesley Evans, who replaced Simmons by a coup in 1922, the Klan renounced violence and worked more in the open arena of political lobbying and propaganda. In 1925, however, the murder conviction of David C. Stephenson, Grand Dragon of the Indiana Klan, and numerous other Klan outrages that made headlines diminished the Klan's popularity and effectiveness. Most Americans became disgusted with the Klan as an extremist group whose claims to protect American values proved false when it trampled on individual freedom and rights. In 1939 Evans sold the Klan to James A. Colescott, who dissolved the organization in 1944 rather than pay its back taxes.

The modern Ku Klux Klan began in the 1940's, its primary purpose being to oppose any civil rights gains by blacks. Although it was organized nationally in 1956, it has typically been very fragmented. The main result of its activities and headlines was to add impetus to the Civil Rights movement in the 1950's and 1960's, as people all over the country were outraged by the Klan's violent tactics. In 1991, Louisiana gubernatorial candidate David Duke was extremely controversial because he had formerly been a Grand Wizard in the Klan; he was defeated.

See also Hate crimes; Lynching; Reconstruction; Vigilantism.

Labor law

DEFINITION: Laws regulating relationships between employees, unions, and employers

SIGNIFICANCE: Labor law requires employers to bargain collectively with unions and protects the rights of employees to engage in union organizing activities

The National Labor Relations Act (NLRA), also known as the Wagner Act, established modern labor law in 1935. The law protects the rights of workers to organize and engage in concerted activities for the purpose of collective bargaining and other mutual aid or protection. Workers also have the right to refrain from such activity under the 1947 Labor-Management Relations Act, also known as the Taft-Hartley Act. Federal labor law further protects workers who join unions by giving union members a bill of rights under the 1959 Landrum-Griffin Act. Together, these three federal statutes regulate the field of labor law. There are many state labor laws, but because federal law usually preempts them, federal law effectively regulates this area.

Administrative Structure. The National Labor Relations Board, headquartered in Washington, D.C., is the administrative agency given broad powers to regulate labor relations. The NLRB is a five-member board whose members are appointed by the president and confirmed by the Senate for five-year terms. The board resolves disputes between labor and management. The NLRB also has a general counsel who serves as the chief administrative officer of the agency. The NLRB has thirty-three regional offices across the country. Each regional office is headed by a regional director who supervises a staff that investigates unfair labor practices, conducts union elections, and administers the law.

The U.S. secretary of labor has the power to regulate union internal affairs. The secretary is separate from the NLRB. The secretary receives copies of union constitutions and bylaws, as well as union and union officer reports, and investigates charges of union corruption.

Labor law is controversial in American society. Society is constantly balancing and weighing the rights and interests of labor with those of management. As a result, the law is constantly evolving as society attempts to reconcile these two divergent views of the law. The NLRB is criticized because it

These workers in Kennett Square, Pennsylvania, have just voted on whether to unionize; the votes will be counted by the state's Labor Relations Board. (Harvey Finkle, Impact Visuals)

changes its interpretation of the law depending on the political views of its members and the presidents who appoint them. It may go from a pro-labor view to a pro-management view in a relatively short time, as it did during the period from 1979 to 1985.

Concerted Activity. The heart of the Wagner Act is the right of employees under section 7 of the law to engage in "concerted activities." Concerted activities occur when employees band together for mutual aid and protection. Employees are protected from employer reprisal for engaging in union organizing activities such as discussing the benefits of a union, distributing union literature at work, conducting union election campaigns, and banding together to meet with the employer. Prior to the Wagner Act, employers could voluntarily bargain with a union but were not legally required to bargain. Employers had no incentive to bargain with unions and usually did not.

Unfair Labor Practices. Labor law prohibits certain employee and union actions that are deemed unfair labor practices. This prohibition protects worker rights to engage in concerted activities and permits the NLRB to use its expertise to determine what conduct is illegal. As a hypothetical case of employer unfair labor practices, one may imagine a union supporter who is fired for distributing union leaflets at work. The worker files a charge with the office of the regional NLRB director charging the employer with an unfair labor practice. The regional director assigns an investigator to investigate the charge. If the charge is found meritorious, the regional director will serve as a prosecutor at a hearing before an administrative law judge. The regional director and the employer will present evidence before the judge, who will make a decision on the charge. If the administrative law judge decides that the rights of the employee were violated, the judge may assess a remedy that includes reinstatement and back pay for the employee.

Union unfair labor practices may include illegal secondary strikes and boycotts. An employer who is the victim of an illegal secondary boycott may ask the NLRB for an injunction to stop the illegal boycott and may later seek money damages from the union.

Representation Elections. The NLRB conducts employee elections to determine whether a group of employees wish union representation. It also prohibits employer or union election campaign tactics that corrupt the "laboratory conditions" necessary for a free election. If the election is not free of undue interference, the NLRB may order a new election. If the employer unfair labor practices are so severe that they corrupt the chance for any fair election, the NLRB may order the parties to immediately begin collective bargaining.

Collective Bargaining. If the union wins the election, the employer must bargain in good faith with the union concerning wages, hours, and terms and conditions of employment. Bargaining in good faith requires the employer and union to meet and confer, with a goal of reaching agreement. The parties are free to negotiate their best contract based on their relative economic strength. The law does not require the parties to agree if they are unable to do so, only that they bargain in good faith and attempt to reach agreement. The NLRB will not force the parties to change the terms of a collectively bargained agreement even if a neutral person would view it as unreasonable or unfair toward one side.

Union Internal Affairs. Labor law also protects union members from union abuses and corruption. The 1959 Landrum-Griffin Act requires unions and union officials to file financial disclosure reports with the secretary of labor. The law also provides a bill of rights for union members. *—Scott A. White*

See also Affirmative action; Age discrimination; American Federation of Labor-Congress of Industrial Organizations (AFL-CIO); Equal Employment Opportunity Act; Equal Employment Opportunity Commission (EEOC); Equality of opportunity; Labor-Management Relations Act; Labor unions; Landrum-Griffin Act; National Labor Relations Act (NLRA).

BIBLIOGRAPHY

An overview of labor law is presented in Bruce Feldacker, *Labor Guide to Labor Law* (3d ed. Englewood Cliffs, N.J.: Prentice-Hall, 1990); Julius Getman and Bertrand Pogrebin, *Labor Relations* (Westbury, N.Y.:Foundation Press, 1988); William B. Gould, *A Primer on American Labor Law* (3d ed. Cambridge, Mass.: MIT Press, 1993); Douglas L. Leslie, *Labor Law in a Nutshell* (2d ed. St. Paul, Minn.: West, 1986).

Labor-Management Relations Act

DATE: Passed when the Senate overrode President Truman's veto on June 23, 1947; provisions became effective on August 22, 1947

DEFINITION: Popularly known as the Taft-Hartley Act, the Labor-Management Relations Act amended the National Labor Relations Act of 1935 by specifically limiting unions' powers

SIGNIFICANCE: This legislation addressed the public perception of excessive union power in the workplace

In the decade between passage of the National Labor Relations Act (NLRA, also called the Wagner Act) and the end of World War II, union membership tripled. By 1947, there were approximately fifteen million union members in the United States. In 1935, the NLRA had recognized the right of workers to organize and act collectively.

World War II was a period of labor-management harmony. The National War Labor Board, on which both labor and management were represented, controlled wage increases and minimized work stoppages and strikes in the national interest. With the end of the war in 1945, however, overtime pay ended and real income fell with rising inflation. As a result, union leaders came under pressure from the rank and file to secure wage increases which would help restore purchasing power.

In 1945-1946, hours lost to work stoppages and strikes hit a historic high. Employers and the public perceived a growing imbalance in labor-management relations, as unions seemed to be abusing their new-found powers. With the election of a Republican Congress in 1946, legislators were prompt in framing a bill that substantially amended the Wagner Act.

The intent of the Labor-Management Relations Act was to "rein in" the unions in the general public interest. The bill outlawed the "closed shop," which required union membership as a precondition of employment. It also enabled individual states to pass "right to work" legislation allowing a worker not to join a union, even though it represents him. The law itemized a list of "unfair labor practices" that included jurisdictional strikes between worker-competing unions, excessive union initiation fees, refusal to bargain in good faith with employers, and "featherbedding," or forcing employers to hire unessential workers. The act required unions to file financial reports with the Department of Labor and forbade coercion of workers regarding their rights to join or not join a union. It also declared that striking a third party to force that employer to cease doing business with the primary employer—a tactic known as a secondary boycott—is illegal.

The most important aspect of the Taft-Hartley Act was the eighty-day "cooling off" period, which the president, having declared a national emergency, can seek via court injunction. During this period, labor returns to work while union and management continue to seek an agreement.

Labor railed against the enactment of the Labor-Management Relations Act, calling it a suppression of the labor movement by a malevolent Congress. Membership in unions continued to grow to until 1954. The eighty-day cooling off clause was invoked seventeen times by Presidents Harry Truman and Dwight Eisenhower. The reality of a harsher environment for the labor movement was supplemental in the uniting of the American Federation of Labor (AFL) and the Congress of Industrial Organizations (CIO) in 1953.

See also American Federation of Labor-Congress of Industrial Organizations (AFL-CIO); Labor law; Labor unions; Landrum-Griffin Act; National Labor Relations Act (NLRA).

Labor unions

DEFINITION: Organizations of workers established to pursue collective interests related to employment

SIGNIFICANCE: Labor unions were organized to protect worker interests, balance the power of the employer, and promote justice in employment practices in the workplace

Labor unions emerged as a consequence of the growth and influence of powerful corporate actors in the U.S. economy. The employment relationship becomes increasingly complex as new forms of organization and modern technologies are introduced into the workplace. Workers in industrial societies organize because of the need to protect their common interests.

A History of Conflict. Beginning in local communities, skilled craftsmen began to organize into groups according to their individual trades. These small trade unions represented the first attempts by workers to improve their employment conditions through collective action. The small unions eventually began to affiliate with others in their trades. In 1886, national associations of trade unions organized as the American Federation of Labor. Manufacturers began to experience labor disputes as skilled craftsmen were replaced by workers on mass production lines and by massive teams of less-skilled workers. Working conditions in factories, mines, and railroads were often dangerous and unhealthy. Workers were required to work long hours, and wages were so low that entire families, including children, needed to work to pay for their own subsistence. Women and children were often assigned tedious and sometimes hazardous work.

Railroads, steel manufacturers, and other industrial companies significantly changed the employment relationship by moving toward mass production techniques and away from skilled craftsmen. As employees and managers adjusted to the change, major conflicts developed. Conflicts often centered on wages and hours, but many disputes were also the direct result of workers struggling to be recognized as a collective union. Owners and managers saw the conflict as a battle for control of their own firms, while workers sought a voice in their own working conditions and protested what they considered to be unfair wages or hours.

In spite of laws and public opinion which heavily favored employers during the nineteenth century, employees would withhold their labor to protest unlivable working conditions. These strikes often led to employees losing their jobs, but if the workers could stay unified, employers could be forced to make concessions to the workers. The earliest recorded strike in the United States, for example, occurred when the New York City Journey Printers struck in 1776. In 1828, nearly four hundred mill workers in Dover, Massachusetts, struck their textile employers to protest 13.5-hour workdays and low wages. As late as 1860, twenty thousand shoemakers from the New England states mounted a coordinated strike to protest their wage of three dollars per week.

After the Civil War, much of the American population went to the cities to find work, but they found more workers than jobs. Some large industrial corporations used the excess labor to reduce wages and require their workers to work in dangerous conditions. Miners lost a six-month strike in 1875 and were forced to accept a 20 percent wage cut. In the same year, the "Molly Maguires," composed of Irish immigrants in eastern Pennsylvania, used violence to emphasize their demands. Twenty-four were arrested on criminal charges, and ten were executed. The most violent strike occurred in 1877 against the railroads. Rail workers' wages had been cut for three years. Union leaders were fired if they caused trouble. When a 10 percent wage cut was announced in June, the workers revolted. Hundreds of workers were killed, and several hundred more were injured. Property damage was estimated at more than $10 million. In 1886, the Haymarket riot in Chicago claimed ten lives and thirty injuries, and it led to several laws restricting labor unions. The Homestead strike against Carnegie Steel in 1892 caused the death of more than twenty workers and Pinkerton guards hired by the steel company to break the strike. The Pullman strike of 1894 resulted in twelve deaths and extensive property damage. In each of these cases, workers were forced to end their job actions and return to work, often at lower wages.

Violence erupts during the 1869 New York streetcar strike. (James L. Shaffer)

By the early 1900's, conflict between workers and employers had spread to many industries and to government as well. In 1919 the Boston police strike resulted when more than twenty officers were suspended from their jobs after they decided to join a new union. After the city appealed to Governor Calvin Coolidge to intervene on their side, the governor sent a message that there was "no right to strike against the public safety by anybody, anywhere, anytime."

Despite the violence and obvious need for better working conditions, workers won few victories during this pro-business era. Although unions continued to use the strike as a tool to influence management, union leaders also began to consider other means of making their voices heard. The boycott, a unified effort of workers to stop buying products made by the offending company, was introduced in the 1880's. Other unions began to turn to politics to elect more pro-labor representatives to local, state, and national offices.

Legal Boundaries for Labor Unions. It has been noted by many observers that the success of labor unions in the United States has been dependent on the legal atmosphere of the times. In the corporate-dominated economy of the early twentieth century there was little sympathy for striking workers. The laws governing commerce and industry at the turn of the century were unfavorable to union activities. Congress passed the Interstate Commerce Act (1887) and Sherman Antitrust Act (1890) to ensure the free flow of trade in the United States. These laws were used routinely to condemn union actions as a restraint of trade and therefore as being against the national interest.

Management used two approaches in court to stop union actions. The first approach was to invoke the principle of criminal conspiracy. The usual argument claimed that there was undue control exercised by unions and injury caused to a company as a result of the collective action taken by its employees. The second approach was to seek an injunction, legally requiring striking employees to go back to work. Refusal of employees to return to work allowed the employer to bring in law enforcement officers to force workers to return to their jobs and to arrest and imprison union officials who would not cooperate.

The unions took a political approach to changing laws used against them. Their influence began to take effect in the early part of the twentieth century. The Clayton Antitrust Act of 1914 declared that human labor was not a commodity and therefore was not subject to antitrust laws originally meant to restrict business alliances. The act also limited court injunctions against strikes to cases where an injunction would prevent irreparable damage or injury. In 1916, two important acts were passed by Congress. The Adamson Act mandated an eight-hour day for railroad workers at no reduction in wages. The Child Labor Act prohibited employing children under the age of fourteen and restricted the number of work hours for a child between the ages of fourteen and sixteen. The Child Labor Act was declared unconstitutional in 1918, but it signified the willingness of Congress to deal with workplace issues. The Railway Labor Act of 1926 established a mediation board to help settle disputes in the railroad industry as a means of avoiding strikes.

A major change in public policy toward unions came about as a result of the Great Depression of the 1930's. In 1931, the Davis Bacon Act required all contractors working on government construction projects to pay the prevailing wage for labor. The next year Congress passed the Norris-LaGuardia Act, which prevented the use of court injunctions unless certain conditions were met, including giving the union adequate opportunity to respond to the court and argue against the request for the injunction. In 1933, under threat of a nationwide railway strike, Congress passed the Emergency Railroad Transportation Act, which recognized the railway unions as legitimate bargaining agents and gave railroad employees the right to organize and bargain collectively.

Early explanations of the causes of the Depression focused on production, but a number of influential economists and politicians saw the problem underlying the poor economy in the distribution of income. William Leiserson, of the Ohio Commission on Unemployment Insurance, noted that reduced consumer demand caused the loss of business and jobs and that reduced demand was caused by an unfair return of income to labor. Senator Robert F. Wagner of New York took up Leiserson's theme and introduced legislation to enhance the power of unions by recognizing unions and authorizing collective bargaining between management and labor. The National Labor Relations Act (NLRA), otherwise known as the Wagner Act, was passed by Congress in 1935. In only four years, union membership increased from 3.7 million to more than 6.5 million. The NLRA gave workers the right to organize, form unions, and bargain collectively. The act also specified

The opening of 1993 contract talks between the United Auto Workers and General Motors officials is representative of large-scale collective bargaining. (Jim West)

unfair labor practices which employers were prohibited from committing under penalty of legal action.

Other acts of Congress gave workers many of the rights and benefits they had been seeking for many decades. Strikes alone had failed to secure increases in wages and to improve working conditions, but politics combined with the threat of labor unrest provided many improvements in conditions. The Social Security Act of 1935 and its later amendments guaranteed workers old age retirement benefits and hospitalization insurance, unemployment insurance, workers' compensation, and disability insurance. Another important law was passed in 1938. The Fair Labor Standards Act was intended to eliminate "labor conditions detrimental to the maintenance of the minimum standards of living necessary for health, efficiency and well being of workers." The FLSA provided workers with a minimum wage and overtime pay for working beyond a maximum number of hours per week.

Many people believed that the laws passed during the administration of Franklin D. Roosevelt gave the unions too much power. The Labor-Management Relations Act (Taft-Hartley Act) was passed in 1947 to protect individual employees from unions. This act gave employees the right to sue unions and prevented unions from requiring union membership before being hired. Taft-Hartley provided for an eighty-day injunction at the discretion of the president of the United States in strikes that threatened public safety, and forbade union contributions to national elections. To balance against the provisions of the NLRA which listed unfair labor practices for employers, Taft-Hartley also listed unfair labor practices for unions. The Landrum-Griffin Act of 1959 extended further protection to individual workers from unions by requiring democratic union administration through election and public accounting, protecting freedom of assembly and speech for workers, placing union dues under member control, and requiring union leaders to file reports on finances to federal government officials.

Labor Relations in a Time of Change. The legal structure of labor relations developed with the purpose of stabilizing and bringing peace to the workplace. Lawmakers were as much interested in ensuring production in wartime or continued economic prosperity as they were concerned about the welfare of American workers. Peace in labor relations has widely been achieved, at least as long as the nation's economy is prosperous. Some unions are changing their approach to labor relations by forming partnerships with employers so both can adapt to significant changes in the national and world economies. In some ways, the relationship between management and labor is returning to the time before industrialization when small firms employed highly skilled workers. The industrial era was a time of massive corporations dealing with large numbers of workers for the collective interests of both sides. Now, many more people are employed by small companies than by large corporations. These small firms frequently hire specialized employees who are highly skilled and bargain with employers on the basis of their individual value to the firm.

The change from an economy dominated by agriculture and skilled artisans to the era of mass production and industrial giants promoted the growth of unionism. Today the economy is changing again. Manufacturing jobs are decreasing, and union membership is declining. Collective bargaining is changing from demands for higher wages and benefits to more concern for protections amid international competition. Union leaders are increasingly involved as partners with corporate management in making their organizations more productive.

—*W. David Patton*

See also American Federation of Labor-Congress of Industrial Organizations (AFL-CIO); Antitrust law; Boston police strike; GI Bill of Rights; International Brotherhood of Police Officers; Labor law; Labor-Management Relations Act; Landrum-Griffin Act; National Labor Relations Act (NLRA); Pullman strike.

BIBLIOGRAPHY

A good basic handbook of labor relations is John J. Kenny, *Primer of Labor Relations* (23d ed. Washington, D.C.: Bureau of National Affairs, 1986). Douglas L. Leslie's *Labor Law in a Nutshell* (2d ed. St. Paul, Minn.: West, 1986) gives the reader a good overview of the laws governing unions. James W. Hunt's *The Law of the Workplace: Rights of Employers and Employees* (2d ed. Washington, D.C.: Bureau of National Affairs, 1988) presents a good outline of the rights granted to management and labor by labor laws without much of the legal language. Christopher L. Tomlins' book *The State and the Unions: Labor Relations, Law, and the Organized Labor Movement in America, 1880-1960* (Cambridge, England: Cambridge University Press, 1985) offers a good review of the influence of the government on labor unions in the United States. Adrian A. Paradis and Grace D. Paradis' *The Labor Almanac* (Littleton, Colo.: Libraries Unlimited, 1983) provides an excellent chronology of labor history, organizations, leaders, laws, government agencies, and sources of labor information.

Landrum-Griffin Act

DATE: Signed September 14, 1959
DEFINITION: The Labor-Management Reporting and Disclosure Act of 1959, or Landrum-Griffin Act, served as a bill of rights for union members and a curb on union misconduct
SIGNIFICANCE: The act cracked down on criminal activity in unions and restored lost rights of union members

The Landrum-Griffin Act had its genesis in the hearings of the McClellan Committee from 1957 to 1959, which focused on crime within the labor movement. The Landrum-Griffin Act amended the Wagner Act (1935) and included a bill of rights for union members. It made explicit union members' right to assemble, speak out, vote, and attend meetings. The bill also required both national unions and local affiliates to file annual financial disclosure statements as a matter of public record.

The Landrum-Griffin Act limited the instances in which a national union could place a local under trusteeship. In some cases, the McClellan Committee had found, a trusteeship proviso had been misused by the national in order to obtain access to local funds or to silence dissent. The bill also required national and local unions to schedule regular elections. The Landrum-Griffin Act sought to close loopholes in the 1947 Labor-Management Relations Act (Taft-Hartley Act). It tightened restrictions on secondary boycotts, outlawed "hot cargo" agreements, and limited organizational and recognition picketing.

See also American Federation of Labor-Congress of Industrial Organizations (AFL-CIO); Labor law; Labor-Management Relations Act; Labor unions; National Labor Relations Act (NLRA).

Larceny. *See* **Theft**

Law

DEFINITION: A body of rules based on statutes, judicial decisions, and custom which are enacted by a politically organized society and backed by its sanctions

SIGNIFICANCE: Law is among the principal tools a civilized society uses to create order; in a modern constitutional democracy, law maintains a free society by restricting governmental power and forming boundaries within which citizens are free to act as they please

There is no single agreed-upon definition of law. It was once thought that law could be defined as "the commands of a sovereign backed by a force," but some people found this definition to be inadequate because some laws are permissions rather than commands. It is generally agreed, however, that laws are kinds of rules and that a legal system is a body of rules. Like other rules, law is intended to govern some aspect of human conduct. Rules in every arena of life are intended to mark out approved courses of conduct, from table manners and etiquette to the requirements of employers to the rules parents make for children. These rules do not have the force of law. Only those rules that are made in required ways by legitimate authority receive the sanction of society as a whole and are called laws. The rules that make up the legal system may be divided into four categories.

One is laws that regulate conduct. These laws make up the great bulk of what is ordinarily thought of as law. Some laws forbid some conduct, such as force or fraud; other laws command conduct, such as the performance of a public service—for example, military service or jury duty. These laws are generally enforced by courts and are backed by the state's coercive power.

Another category is fundamental (constitutional) law, which determines what valid law is. Some laws govern which institutions (such as Congress) are recognized by the legal system as authorized to make law. They are therefore more fundamental than other laws and are called "constitutional law." Constitutional law serves as a body of rules for determining what will count as valid law. Thus, while the people in a constitutional democracy are said to be sovereign, the rules of the constitution define the ways the people exercise their sovereignty.

A third category, rules for changing laws (usually called rules of legislation) specify how and by whom existing law may be changed or new law added. They are the rules that govern legislative procedure. Only laws that pass through a prescribed legislative process are recognized as valid by the legal system.

A final category is rules for interpreting law. Laws can seldom, if ever, be applied without being interpreted. Rules for interpreting law specify who is authorized to interpret law and what procedures must be used for interpretation. The process of authoritatively interpreting law is generally undertaken by courts. The last three of these categories of rules restrain authorities, setting limits to legitimate action in the eyes of the law—and in the eyes of knowledgeable citizens.

Purposes and Functions of Law. Law attempts to further central purposes of society and performs key functions. The overall purpose of law may be said to be a search for justice. Justice is usually taken, in general terms, to mean fairness. There is often disagreement, however, about what is and is not just or fair. Thus law is perennially subject to criticism regarding its fairness.

One of the functions of law is to serve as an instrument for reforming society and setting its future course. Thus a legislative program for a city or town, a state, or a nation as a whole can form the substance of social reform, whether it be a new departure for society or a return to the nation's original principles. Law protects people and property. Law restrains behavior, forbidding certain actions. The purpose of this restraint is the protection of people from harm arising from sources such as force, fraud, and negligence. A further function is resolving conflicts—keeping peace. Modern legal systems attempt to establish systems of courts whose procedures and decisions will be widely believed to be fair and just. If successful, legal systems remove demands for justice from the street to the courtroom. In criminal cases, legal systems attempt to substitute public justice for private vengeance. Similarly, in civil (noncriminal) disputes, the legal system moves grievances and disputes from the realm of private quarrel to public adjudication, in accordance with recognized principles of justice. The legal system is never entirely successful in fulfilling these purposes; to the extent that it is, however, society is civilized. Since the legal system cannot work without taxation, U.S. Supreme Court Justice Oliver Wendell Holmes, Jr., once remarked, "Taxes are the price we pay for civilization."

A further function is the creation of special legal facilities. Modern legal systems create facilities such as special courts and officials so that citizens may transfer property to their heirs through wills, establish trusts, register patents, and in other ways use or protect their property as they wish.

A most important purpose of modern legal systems can be summarized as "security of expectations." Law attempts to secure expectations by protecting citizens and their property from harm and abuse. Citizens can plan their lives with the expectation that if they act within the boundaries of the law, legal authorities will not interfere with them.

The idea of the "rule of law, not of men" has long been a fundamental principle of Western democracies, especially the United States. The rule of law can be understood in contrast to rule by the arbitrary whims of rulers and government officials—or, indeed, the whims of anyone in society. Criminals subject their victims to their arbitrary whims. Anyone exercising power in society, whether a public official, an employer, or anyone else, may act arbitrarily. Bullies are everywhere. Aspects of everyday life, such as driving automobiles, if left unregulated by law, would subject some to the whims of others, creating danger and arousing fear.

AMERICAN LAW: THE CONGRESSIONAL LEGISLATIVE PROCESS

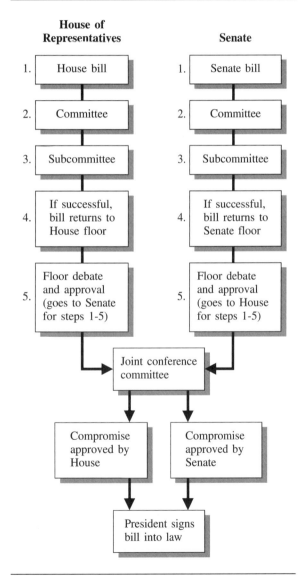

Source: Adapted from Jay M. Shafritz, *The Dorsey Dictionary of American Government and Politics.* Chicago: Dorsey Press, 1988. Primary source, Auraria Library, Government Documents Section, Denver, Colo.

In modern legal systems, the rule of law is intended to overcome all these problems, but it refers in particular to controlling public officials. Two ideas are central. First, the powers of officials to set and enforce rules are overseen by impartial tribunals that ensure that powers are exercised fairly, within legal limits. Second, everyone subject to legal authority must be liable to follow only preestablished laws and be given clear guidance about rights and duties under the law, and must not be subject to punishment without being able to follow the law.

"Freedom under law" has likewise been central in European and American thinking since the seventeenth century. In the 1680's the English philosopher John Locke wrote, "Where law ends, tyranny begins." According to this concept, in a fair legal system, law, while placing restrictions on citizens' behavior, also enlarges and enhances their freedom. This is so, it is argued, because an effective legal system removes significant obstacles to the exercise of freedom. Thus when people are terrified because they are threatened by violence, they can hardly be said to be free; when they are protected by an effective and fair legal system, their freedom is enlarged.

Types of Law. Law may be divided into several categories. Constitutional law sets up governmental offices and institutions and distributes power among them. In the American tradition, constitutional law also acts as a "higher law" that binds the people themselves as well as their elected representatives unless and until the Constitution is changed. Constitutional law thus provides government restricted to specified purposes and limited in the means to pursue them.

A second type of law is statutory law, which is enacted by legislative bodies. In the American constitutional tradition, however, statutory law must not conflict with constitutional law. If it does, the practice of judicial review empowers courts to declare such a law unconstitutional and therefore null and void.

A third type of law, common law (from the Latin *jus commune*), is created by judicial decisions, which act as the basis, or precedent, for future decisions. Courts in the Anglo-American tradition follow the idea of *stare decisis*, or "let the precedent stand." Decisions of courts accordingly become the basis for common law.

A fourth type of law, administrative law, governs the powers of administrative agencies to regulate areas such as food, drugs, the environment, industrial safety, and many others. The rules and regulations made by administrative agencies are also part of administrative law. Administrative law is overseen by the courts, which in the United States require administrative agencies to conform to administrative due process, such as the idea of fair hearing.

A fifth variety of law is international law. This law is the body of rule accepted as binding by independent countries or states. It is derived from both custom and explicit agreements and is created by the consent of sovereign states. International law addresses topics such as war and peace, human rights issues, the ratification of treaties, economic affairs, and environmental issues. Some deny that international law is law at all. There are many arguments regarding the extent to which

This quotation from William Pitt, echoing John Locke's words of a century before, is in Minnesota's state capitol building.
(James L. Shaffer)

international law is binding and the extent to which developments in international law erode national sovereignty.

Sources of American Law. Law in the United States is derived from several principal sources. One is statute law—that is, law passed by a legislative body such as Congress or a state legislature and approved by the executive, as constitutionally required. A variant of statute is the municipal ordinances passed by legislative bodies such as city councils. These laws are made under powers granted to cities by state government. A second source is the principles of the common law of England and the judicial decisions of American courts themselves. A third source is custom, although legal philosophers state that in the modern world custom is not an important source of law and is generally subordinate to other sources. Thus no American court would find that custom takes precedence over statute law in cases where they conflict.

The Place of Law in American Society. Since the beginning of the American republic, law has played an enormous role in U.S. society. One reason for this lies in the revolutionary origin of the new American state. Rather than evolving through many centuries, as occurred in much of modern Europe, certain basic rules of society had to be thought out and enacted "from scratch."

The United States was a new society in a "new world." One revolutionary said, "We have it in our power to start the world over again." Custom counted for less in America than in Europe, since it was less deeply ingrained. Indeed, customary ways of thinking, such as notions of the natural hierarchy of society and the deference resulting from it, were transformed by the new ideas of liberty and equality that swept the colonies prior to the outbreak of revolution.

Protecting the Innocent. One of the most significant aspects of law in modern constitutional states is its attempt to protect the innocent. A principal means of doing so is legal restraint of the actions of all members of society. Constitutional and statute law put special legal restraints on public officials. Of course, the innocent are protected only so long as public officials as well as ordinary citizens comply with the law. Thus, certain countries with written constitutions still fail to provide "constitutional" (limited) government, because in practice, constitutional and other law fails to restrain public officials. Similarly, laws that protect members of society from one another may not be enforced, either because government lacks the will or because social disorder makes enforcement impossible.

Assuming, however, that law is working as it should, how does it protect the individual? First, law prescribes the boundaries of behavior within which individuals are to act. By laying down rules specifying what may not be done or what must be done, law provides a framework for legitimate expectations. By enforcing law regarding property, for example, the legal system secures important individual expectations.

A principal way in which law and legal systems of modern constitutional democracies protect the freedom of law-abiding individuals is to ensure that public officials abide by legally prescribed procedures. Police cannot do as they please in dealing either with suspected criminals or with individuals caught *in flagrante delicto*, in the act of lawbreaking. In the United States, procedures enforced by courts ensure that police inform those arrested of their rights.

In Anglo-Saxon law, those arrested are accorded a "presumption of innocence" by courts and are protected by courtroom procedures, rules of evidence, provisions for legal representation, and other measures intended to ensure fair treatment at the hands of authority. Thus, in the United States, illegally obtained evidence may not be used to convict defendants. Police cannot go on unauthorized "fishing expeditions" for evidence of illegal activity in individuals' homes or stop them in public without probable cause that they have committed a crime. If judges convict defendants in violation of the rules of evidence and other procedural rules, or if in other ways they behave capriciously, their rulings are reversed on appeal to higher courts.

Americans generally favor the protection of the innocent, but there is a price to pay. Protections of the rights of innocents increase the chances that the guilty will go free. Diminishing these rights could increase the chances of convicting the guilty. It can be argued that such convictions would increase the security of the innocent, since more malefactors would be behind bars. In reply, it may be said that although the latter idea may be true, the argument that the innocent would be more secure is at best questionable.

American and Foreign Concepts of Law. The Anglo-Saxon system of law upon which the American legal system is based is often contrasted with the civil law system of continental Europe. The civil law system is so called because it is based on the Roman civil law, codified by the Byzantine emperor Justinian in the sixth century. While Anglo-Saxon law grew up in a haphazard way, civil law is set out in logical, orderly codes. The purpose of civil law codes such as the "Code Civil" is the creation of a purely rational body of law (as opposed to possibly contradictory or uneven law resulting from the judi-

cial decisions of a common law system), the equality of all citizens, separation of civil from ecclesiastical regulation, and the principles of the freedom of the person, freedom of contract, and the inviolability of private property.

Within these codes, there are national differences in civil law countries. The Netherlands, for example, uses Roman-Dutch law. The idea of law encompassed by civil law is not different from that of Anglo-Saxon, but the operation of civil law systems is different. First, judges are not bound by precedent, as they are in Anglo-Saxon systems. Second, while Anglo-Saxon systems are adversarial, civil law systems are "inquisitorial." That is, in criminal law cases, Anglo-Saxon systems pit prosecutors and defense attorneys in a contest. This is not so in civil law systems. Instead, there are three phases in criminal cases: an investigative phase, undertaken under the direction of a public prosecutor; an examining phase, which is not carried out in public and is primarily written; and then a trial. The trial phase differs from trials in adversarial systems, since the evidence has already been taken. The trial presents the case to a trial judge and jury, with cases made by prosecutor and defense counsel. The jury may not be required to reach a unanimous verdict.

An entirely different conception is found in various religious bodies of law. Islamic law, for example, does not apply to people by virtue of their citizenship or nationality but on account of religion. Islamic law is based upon a religious text, the Koran, and certain other Muslim religious texts. Further, this law is generally considered to have become unchangeable. Only God can make law; God is the only lawgiver.

This kind of law differs from Western law in general, and American law in particular, in several significant ways. American law is obligatory only upon those who are in territory governed by the United States; it is secular law, since it is known to be human-made and not created by legislators by virtue of their religion or religiosity. American law is not made to conform to a religious text and is not considered unchangeable; nor is God considered the only lawgiver.

—Charles Bahmueller

See also Administrative law; Case law; Civil law; Common law; Constitutional law; Contract law; Criminal law; International law; Judicial review; Jurisprudence; Justice.

BIBLIOGRAPHY

Among the classics of legal thought is H. L. A. Hart, *The Concept of Law* (Oxford: Clarendon Press, 1961), which argues a neopositivist view of law. Works by Ronald Dworkin, Hart's successor as professor of jurisprudence at the University of Oxford, such as his *Taking Rights Seriously* (Cambridge, Mass.: Harvard University Press, 1977), may also be consulted. Paul Edwards, ed., *The Encyclopedia of Philosophy*, 8 vols. (New York: Macmillan, 1967), has many pertinent articles on law and related topics. A convenient one-volume work is David M. Walker, *The Oxford Companion to Law* (Oxford: Clarendon Press, 1980); it covers a wide range of topics concerning the law, often from a British point of view. A general work on the place of law in society is Geoffrey Sawer, *Law in Society* (Oxford: Clarendon Press, 1965).

Law Enforcement Assistance Administration (LEAA)

DATE: Created 1968; eliminated 1982

SIGNIFICANCE: The Law Enforcement Assistance Administration was given responsibility for developing state and local law enforcement agencies' riot control capabilities following massive urban riots in the mid-1960's, but the infusions of federal dollars were principally used for police equipment rather than broader programs to reduce violence

The Law Enforcement Assistance Administration (LEAA) was created by Title I of the Omnibus Crime Control and Safe Streets Act of 1968. In response to a series of studies of urban violence in the 1960's and a growing fear of riots in more cities, the agency was established to provide federal funds and technical assistance to state and local law enforcement agencies. Its mandates were to encourage state and local officials to adopt comprehensive plans to deal with the specific kinds of urban violence they might encounter and to build local capacities to respond effectively to the violence. In support of that activity, LEAA provided block grants to state and local law enforcement agencies and undertook research on how to reduce the levels of violence and to improve the effectiveness of law enforcement efforts. The clear priority in the grant pro-

gram was to expand state and local capabilities in riot control, although relatively small amounts were also allocated to improve police-community relations and other programs to reduce racial conflict in some cities.

LEAA became a symbol of the "law and order" orientation of the federal government in the late 1960's and, later, of the ineffectiveness of that approach in reducing violence. Over the life of the agency, $5 billion was provided to state and local governments to respond to the threat of riots. The block-grant funding permitted local authorities to spend the money where they believed it was most needed, within the broad guidelines of the Omnibus Crime Control and Safe Streets Act. Most of the money was spent to improve policing capabilities rather than to address the causes of the violence or to reduce the level of tension between police and communities. In fact, so many local governments invested their LEAA grant money in police cars that the program was sometimes referred to as federal funding for "car buying." Money was also spent on communications equipment and weaponry for special weapons and tactics (SWAT) teams.

For the most part, the expenditures did little to reduce tension and violence. Subsequent studies of civil disorders even indicated that the police themselves tended to increase the levels

Many law enforcement agencies used LEAA grants to upgrade communications equipment and to purchase new vehicles. (James L. Shaffer)

of tension and often caused outbreaks of violence because of their poor training and insensitivity to community concerns. In the 1970's, studies by the Office of Management and Budget and other agencies severely criticized LEAA for not addressing the root causes of urban violence or improving relationships between police and other city officials and African American communities. The agency was eliminated in 1982.

See also National Commission on the Causes and Prevention of Violence; Nixon, Richard M.; Omnibus Crime Control and Safe Streets Act of 1968; Special weapons and tactics (SWAT) teams.

Law schools

DEFINITION: Institutions that prepare people to pass the bar examination and to practice law

SIGNIFICANCE: The first step to becoming a lawyer in the United States is to attend and be graduated from a law school

In the colonial and immediate postrevolutionary period, as was the case in most professions or trades, a person aspiring to be a lawyer apprenticed himself for an agreed-upon period of time to someone with knowledge of the field, who, in return for supervised work, would teach the nuances of the profession and would pay a subsistence wage, often including room and board. Although Litchfield Law School was founded in 1784, and several other institutions, including Harvard, shortly thereafter began to teach the subject of law, this was not the beginning of law schools as we know them today. The egalitarian impulses of the Jacksonian era were antithetical to all forms of professional training; as a consequence, all but Harvard's programs were shuttered. It was not until the 1850's, with the founding of schools at Columbia, New York University, and the University of Pennsylvania, that the institution of law schools truly began to flourish. By the time of the Civil War, there were at least twenty-one schools operating throughout the country.

Law Schools in the Nineteenth Century. The quality of education varied widely, but almost uniformly the standards for admission were low compared with other divisions of the same university. Furthermore, nonuniversity-based schools offering inferior training proliferated. For this reason, there grew a movement to extend the examination given to those who had completed their apprenticeship to all those seeking to practice. By 1890, successful passage of a bar examination was the normal prerequisite for practice, whether the candidate was a graduate from a law school or not. Shortly thereafter, one could not simply sit for the bar examination; in 1896, the American Bar Association (ABA), the professional association of all lawyers, promulgated more rigorous standards: a high school diploma and at least two years of law school or the practical equivalent thereof. In 1900, as part of the continuing effort to maintain and improve standards, the Association of American Law Schools (AALS) was founded.

Even with these improvements, the course and quality of study varied widely: Schools that were part of a university were often more theoretical, while proprietary schools were more practical, stressing specific facts and procedures appropriate to

their local area. In 1870, Dean Christopher Langdell of Harvard Law School introduced the "case method," in which the process and evolution of law is stressed. Very quickly most schools adopted this form of pedagogy, as it appeared to be effective and allowed for large classes, meaning that the schools could generate significant profit. As a result, admissions standards fell in many schools as administrators opted for a more Darwinian solution: Those who could surmount the rigors of the course could progress to the next hurdle, the bar examination. In 1926, 250 of Harvard's entering class of 700 failed. To inject some equity into the process, in 1928, Columbia included an aptitude test in the admissions process. From this would evolve the Law School Admission Test (LSAT).

Law Schools Today. Today's standards are rigorous. To qualify to sit for the bar examination, a student must have completed twelve hundred class hours in three years (if a part-time student, within four years) at an accredited law school and must have studied professional skills, torts, contracts, property, and procedure. These courses are usually taken in the first year of a three-year program. The range of additional courses is broad, covering interdisciplinary topics, social justice, and a wide variety of clinical exercises. Rarely do students specialize in narrowly defined areas of the law before entering the profession; rather, they are trained to "think like a lawyer." Essentially, this entails distilling arguments, identifying and ranking issues, and finding parallels with earlier cases. Accreditation standards therefore demand that the school have an adequate library, a student/faculty ratio that is low enough for easy interaction between student and faculty, and an admissions policy that is strict enough to ensure that those admitted will have a good chance of successfully completing the course of study. Only in the state of Wisconsin does graduation from an accredited law school guarantee admission to practice; elsewhere, all must pass a bar examination.

ABA and AALS efforts to raise and enforce standards put extraordinary pressures on the proprietary schools; to survive, many merged with universities or existing ABA-approved institutions. By 1958, there were only thirty unapproved institutions, most of which could be found in a smattering of states, notably California. By making its bar examination very rigorous, the state ensured the quality of those entering the practice without taking the potentially unpopular step of eliminating institutions which, for the most part, served those who could not gain admission to the more selective schools.

In 1995, with the approval of the School of Law at Roger Williams University in Rhode Island, there were 177 ABA-approved law schools throughout the nation plus several with provisional approval. Most required that for admission applicants take the LSAT, designed to predict how well the applicant will do in the first year of law school. Unlike the almost uniform requirements for admission to medical school, there is no specialized preparatory course of study prescribed for admission; any study that develops reasoning skills is seen as adequate training.

Both the ABA and the AALS have stressed the need for affirmative action in law school admissions, along with support systems to help ensure that those admitted will be able to complete the program. Since the early 1970's, the makeup of the typical law school class has changed dramatically. Whereas it used to be almost entirely composed of white males who were very recent college graduates, by the mid-1990's roughly 50 percent of law students were female, and often more than a quarter were members of minorities. —*Theodore P. Kovaleff*

See also American Bar Association (ABA); Attorney; Bar, the; Bar examinations and licensing of lawyers.

BIBLIOGRAPHY

Three works that provide interesting views on law schools are William C. Chase, *The American Law School and the Rise of Administrative Government* (Madison: University of Wisconsin Press, 1982); Randall R. Kelso and Charles D. Kelso, *Studying Law: An Introduction* (St. Paul, Minn.: West, 1984); and Robert Bocking Stevens, *Law School: Legal Education in America from the 1850's to the 1980's* (Chapel Hill: University of North Carolina Press, 1983). Each year the Law School Admission Services, with the Association of American Law Schools, publishes the *Prelaw Handbook: An Official Guide to ABA-Approved Law Schools*. They also publish materials designed to help students prepare for the Law School Admission Test, which are carried in many college book stores.

Legal ethics

DEFINITION: The standards of moral and professional behavior that members of the legal profession believe should govern their behavior regarding clients, courts, one another, and society at large

SIGNIFICANCE: American legal ethics evolved with the growth of the country, resulting finally in the American Bar Association's 1984 Model Rules of Professional Responsibility

Ethics are the set of moral beliefs and traditions by which societies and individuals govern themselves; they are a mixture of honesty, decency, manners, and etiquette. They are not rules or laws imposed by others; rather, they are personal, internal mechanisms arrived at through self-evaluation and self-knowledge. Legal ethics are also internal individual beliefs. In the narrowest sense, legal ethics concern professional conduct. More broadly, they encompass the moral lives of lawyers and their behavior toward clients, courts, and colleagues. Legal ethics are fraught with the potential for conflict, as members of the legal profession can find themselves with conflicting loyalties.

Lawyers are taught that loyalty to a client should be foremost; personal interests and the interests of others should be relegated to second place. Lawyers should counsel their clients on the best way to use the law to their advantage and, if necessary, how to escape or mitigate its effect. Conflict often arises between the public trust a lawyer owes as an officer of the court and the loyalty owed the client. A lawyer may have to make a decision whether to report a client's improper behavior to the court and put public trust first or to counsel the client to cease and put the client first. In some cases, conscientiously

and loyally representing a client may lead to civil disobedience or to the public impression that a lawyer is unethical and unprincipled.

Ethics and Common Law. In addition to being personal, legal ethics derive from discussion and meeting with other members of the legal profession and agreement as to what is expected and accepted behavior. This tradition is found in English common law. King Edward I of England decreed in 1292 that the Court of Common Pleas was to choose lawyers and students to take part in court business and that these individuals were to live together under the supervision of the court. Also in the thirteenth century, the Inns of Court were established. True inns, they became places for people studying and practicing the law to live and work together under the supervision of judges. From this community, through discussion, came a set of professional mores guiding those engaged in the law and setting certain ethical behaviors and standards. American law and ethics followed the English pattern for a time.

As the United States expanded westward, however, and as the nation's commercial enterprises diversified, new types of knowledge and expertise were needed. This knowledge had to come from experience rather than from books or from the court itself. At the same time, the tradition of spending evenings with colleagues at the end of a day in court—a time for discussing mutually accepted rules and self-government—was becoming a thing of the past. Because there was less internal pressure to be faithful to established legal principles, ethical problems began to arise more frequently, and there was a growing movement urging the state to begin regulating the practice of law. Yet the rapidly increasing complexity of American law made it obvious to many observers that those who knew the legal system best—the lawyers themselves—would have to be the ones to develop new ethical guidelines or rules of professional conduct. In 1836, one of the first extensive considerations of American legal ethics was published by University of Maryland professor David Hoffman. His *Fifty Resolutions in Regard to Professional Ethics* dealt with etiquette and ethics and attempted to discourage behavior that would reflect badly on the legal profession.

Written Rules. Pennsylvania judge George Sharswood's written lectures on professional deportment, *The Aims and Duties of the Profession of the Law* (1854), noted the differences between professional and personal ethics and served as the basis for the Code of Professional Ethics, enacted by the Alabama state bar in 1887. Alabama's was the first state bar to enact such a code. The American Bar Association's Canons of Professional Ethics, also drawing heavily on Sharswood, were promulgated in 1908. By 1920 the canons had been adopted by all but thirteen of the state bar associations, although not without modification.

The canons were detailed, dealing with the positive obligations of a lawyer, such as the duty to represent the poor and indigent. They were largely hortatory in nature, intended as professional rules rather than public laws. By 1969 the original thirty-two canons had grown to forty-seven, supported by more than fourteen hundred interpreting opinions, often lacking coherence and consistency.

The American Bar Association (ABA) recognized the shortcomings of the canons. It sought rules that would exhort lawyers to uphold the highest standards of justice upon which the country's legal system was based, that would weed out those whose standards could damage the reputation of all, and that would provide standards for new lawyers. The Code of Professional Responsibility was therefore adopted, amended as needed, by all state bar associations except California, which adopted its own similar rules. The code had three parts: canons, expressing standards of professional conduct; ethical considerations, setting aspirational objectives toward which all should strive; and disciplinary rules, setting the minimum standards of conduct to avoid disciplinary action. Supreme Court decisions in the 1970's that addressed legal advertising and fees as well as continuing problems with the ethical considerations necessitated a new document.

In 1984 the American Bar Association produced the final version of the Model Rules of Professional Responsibility. By the early 1990's most state bar associations had adopted the Model Rules, sometimes with substantial revision. The Model Rules focus more on mandatory guidelines for the legal profession than on moral considerations.

Bar association grievance committees have the ability to investigate complaints and, if necessary, refer the complaint to the court for further action. Disbarment may be recommended if a lawyer is found untrustworthy to advise and act for clients or if the lawyer's conduct reflects on the dignity and reputation of the court and the legal profession. Disciplinary codes cannot replace ethics and personal ethical behavior. They can only make it difficult for those guilty of unethical behavior to continue in the practice of law.   *—Elizabeth Algren Shaw*

See also American Bar Association (ABA); Attorney; Bar examinations and licensing of lawyers; Law schools; Privileged communications.

BIBLIOGRAPHY

Detailed explanations and examples of ethics in action include Geoffrey C. Hazard, Jr., *Ethics in the Practice of Law* (New Haven, Conn.: Yale University Press, 1978); Geoffrey C. Hazard, Jr., and Deborah L. Rhode, eds., *The Legal Profession: Responsibility and Regulation* (Mineola, N.Y.: Foundation Press, 1985); and Deborah L. Rhode and David Luban, *Legal Ethics* (Westbury, N.Y.: Foundation Press, 1992). A more general view of ethics in everyday practice is found in David E. Schrader, *Ethics and the Practice of Law* (Englewood Cliffs, N.J.: Prentice Hall, 1988), and a good general overview of the legal profession is Jethro K. Lieberman, *Crisis at the Bar* (New York: W. W. Norton, 1978).

Legal realism

DEFINITION: The legal realism movement, which reached its height in the 1920's and 1930's, sought to define law as what courts and public officials actually do rather than as a set of written rules to be followed

SIGNIFICANCE: Emphasizing the social, economic, and political elements in the law, the concept of legal realism contributed to law reform movements

Legal realism defines law as what actually happens in disputes and litigation. It rejects traditional definitions of law as a set of rules of conduct laid down by government. Oliver Wendell Holmes said, "The prophecies of what the courts will do in fact, and nothing more pretentious, are what I mean by the law."

Realism flourished in the first half of the twentieth century. This philosophy distrusted traditional legal rules and concepts because they did not describe what courts actually did. Legal rules as found in statutes and court decisions are important only if they help predict what officials will do in a particular situation.

Realists were impressed with the effects on nonlegal factors on law; changes in law, they observed, could not be explained in terms of the legal rules themselves. Even when clearly established legal rules are applied to a particular case, the courts have large discretion in interpreting and applying the rules. Such discretion cannot be explained by viewing law as a simple set of rules to be mechanically applied. Realism sought the unstated or unconscious factors underlying what courts said they did.

Legal realists were divided between "fact skeptics" and "rule skeptics." Traditional legal theory sees a trial as the application of fixed legal rules to a set of facts, yielding a final decision. Realists denied that the model of law was so simple. Fact skeptics doubted that juries or judges really "find" facts at all. Rather, the facts are opinions based on the opinions which witnesses have formed about their perceptions of events. All such opinions can be influenced by unconscious bias or prejudice, the social and economic standing of witness and juror, and other factors. Rule skeptics saw two flaws in traditional theory. First, different legal rules can be applied to a particular case to reach contrary results. Which rule is selected is often a matter of extralegal influences. Second, the creation of new legal rules often has little to do with legal issues. Instead, new rules are usually based on economic, political, and other factors. These must be identified and understood for law to be a rational enterprise.

Critics charged that realism emphasized a discretion which was obvious but noted that discretion could not be unlimited the way realists said. Some forms of discretion, such as bias and prejudice, are bad and must be rejected. The goal, they argued, is to develop law in such a way that it was not arbitrary.

Legal realism had the beneficial effect of emphasizing the policies, purposes, and social conditions behind the law. Law was changed when underlying bad policy became apparent. Realism thereby fueled law reform movements.

See also Common law; Holmes, Oliver Wendell, Jr.; Jurisprudence; Law; Moral relativism; Positive law.

BIBLIOGRAPHY

Classics of legal realism include Karl N. Llewellyn, *The Bramble Bush: On Our Law and Its Study* (Dobbs Ferry, N.Y.: Oceana, 1960); Jerome Frank, *Law and the Modern Mind* (Gloucester, Mass.: Peter Smith, 1970); and Oliver Wendell Holmes, Jr., "The Path of the Law," in *Harvard Law Review* 10 (March, 1897).

Legal Services Corporation

DATE: Established by Congress July 18, 1974

DEFINITION: An independent, nonprofit organization that uses public funding to support legal assistance for the poor in civil matters

SIGNIFICANCE: The Legal Services Corporation distributes grants to legal services programs operating at community offices throughout the nation

Congress created the Legal Services Corporation in order to continue the services that had been provided to the poor by the Office of Economic Opportunity. The corporation is governed by an eleven-member board of directors, appointed by the president and confirmed by the Senate. Lawyers and paralegals who work in local programs usually deal with problems such as housing, health law, workers' rights, and Social Security benefits, with an emphasis on hearings and grievance procedures. The corporation's funds may not be used on suits involving criminal charges, political activities, or school integration. Attorneys of the national support centers provide specialized assistance to the staff of local programs, and they sometimes directly represent clients in litigation. The corporation's Research Institute on Legal Assistance, created in 1976, investigates a broad range of issues related to poverty. Many conservatives, including former president Ronald Reagan, have criticized the Legal Services Corporation and its programs.

See also Civil law; Civil procedure; Counsel, right to; Public defender; Social Security system; Workers' compensation.

Lemon v. Kurtzman

COURT: U.S. Supreme Court

DATE: Decided June 28, 1971

SIGNIFICANCE: The Court established a three-part test to determine when governmental assistance to religious institutions violated the establishment clause of the First Amendment

After *Everson v. Board of Education* (1947) applied the establishment clause to the states while allowing states to reimburse students' costs for attending parochial schools, the U.S. Supreme Court found it difficult to arrive at standards for deciding which kinds of assistance were consistent with the "wall of separation" between church and state. In *Board of Education v. Allen* (1968), the Court upheld a New York law that provided secular textbooks to religious schools, ruling that the law had both "a secular legislative purpose and a primary effect that neither advances nor inhibits religion." In *Walz v. Tax Commission* (1970), the Court upheld property-tax exemptions for religious organizations but added that governments must not foster "excessive governmental entanglement with religion."

A Pennsylvania law of 1968, going beyond the New York program, directly reimbursed parochial schools for the costs of secular instruction, including teacher salaries, textbooks, and various instructional materials. Alton Lemon, a Pennsylvania taxpayer, challenged the law in a suit against David Kurtzman, state superintendent of education. A federal district court dismissed Lemon's complaint, but about the same time another district court ruled that a similar Rhode Island law violated the establishment clause. Granting review for both cases, the Supreme Court consolidated them into a single decision.

The Court unanimously decided that the Pennsylvania law was unconstitutional and voted 8 to 1 against the Rhode Island law. Writing the opinion, Chief Justice Warren Burger noted that the establishment clause was "at best opaque," but he interpreted it to forbid "a step that could lead to" the establishment of religion. Combining earlier precedents, he formulated a three-pronged test for evaluating the constitutionality of such laws. First, a law must have "a secular legislative purpose"; second, its primary effect must not be to advance or to inhibit religion; third, it must not lead to an "excessive entanglement" between church and state. Burger emphasized the danger that subsidies for teachers' salaries might be used in part for religious instruction. He argued that in order to certify that government funds were used only for secular purposes, the two laws required the kind of inspection and evaluation of religious content that fostered an impermissible degree of entanglement.

The *Lemon* decision was very important because of its three-pronged test, which provided a frame of reference for judging whether laws violated the establishment clause. In subsequent cases, the Court would disagree about whether the "Lemon test" was a strict standard or simply a loose guideline. The real question was whether the Court would allow governmental accommodation of religion or insist upon a strict separation between the two spheres, and the *Lemon* framework, while helpful, could be interpreted from either perspective.

See also *Abington School District v. Schempp*; *Engel v. Vitale*; Establishment of religion; *Everson v. Board of Education*; *Mueller v. Allen*; *Tilton v. Richardson*.

Leon, United States v.

COURT: U.S. Supreme Court

DATE: Decided July 5, 1984

SIGNIFICANCE: A "good-faith" exception to the exclusionary rule in search and seizure cases was created in this case

In August, 1981, an extensive drug investigation began in Burbank, California, based originally on tips received from an informant of unproven reliability. Search warrants were issued for the search of three homes in the area, including the house of Alberto Leon. The ensuing search resulted in the seizure of large quantities of cocaine and methaqualone. After the seizure, the defendants challenged the validity of the warrants. They argued that the state's affidavits had not presented the issuing magistrate—a California Superior Court judge—with appropriate evidence to establish probable cause. The reliability of the informant had not been properly established, and the information presented by the police was stale. A federal district court and the United States Court of Appeals for the Ninth Circuit both agreed with the defendants and ordered the evidence suppressed. The court of appeals rejected the government's suggestion that the Fourth Amendment exclusionary rule should not apply where evidence is seized in reasonable, good-faith reliance on a search warrant. The government asked the Supreme Court to reverse the decision of the court of appeals and establish such a good-faith exception.

Justice Byron White, writing for the majority of seven members of the Court, held that there is a good-faith exception. He argued that the exclusionary rule is not required by the text of the Fourth Amendment. It is a judge-made rule, whose purpose, as established in *Mapp v. Ohio* (1961), is to deter police misconduct. The rule discourages unlawful police searches by denying the investigating officers the "fruits" of their misconduct. In this case, however, there was no police misconduct. The officers relied on the warrant, believing it to be valid. To refuse to admit the evidence, Justice White argued, would have no deterrent effect on law enforcement personnel at all. Consequently the evidence should be admitted and Leon's conviction should stand.

Justices William Brennan and Thurgood Marshall dissented. Justice Brennan's opinion insisted that the exclusionary rule is required by the Fourth Amendment and that its purpose is to deter all official lawlessness, whether of police or courts. He charged that the majority had adopted a "crabbed" view of the amendment in order to limit its application and to do away with the exclusionary rule altogether. Once an unlawful search has taken place, the Fourth Amendment has been violated, whether or not evidence is found and whether or not evidence is admissible. Brennan concluded that the broader interpretation of the exclusionary rule should be adopted in order to prevent all invasions of people's privacy by government.

United States v. Leon is important because the good-faith exception to the exclusionary rule that it established remains valid and has become settled doctrine. The Court, however, has not been inclined to curtail the application or efficacy of the exclusionary rule beyond *Leon*. The decision may have been the high-water mark for that wing of the court which was anxious to restrict the scope of the exclusionary rule.

See also *Mapp v. Ohio*; Search and seizure; *Weeks v. United States*; *Wolf v. Colorado*.

Lewis, John L. (Feb. 12, 1880, Lucas, Iowa—June 11, 1969, Washington, D.C.)

IDENTIFICATION: American labor activist and union leader

SIGNIFICANCE: Lewis was a leader of the American labor movement as long-term president of the United Mine Workers of America and founder of the Congress of Industrial Organizations in 1936

John L. Lewis started work as a coal miner at age sixteen. In 1920, he was elected president of the United Mine Workers of America. He remained president until his retirement in 1960. In 1933, Lewis played a role in the enactment of section 7(a) of the National Industrial Recovery Act, which affirmed the right of workers to organize and bargain collectively. In 1936, Lewis founded the Congress of Industrial Organizations (CIO), which helped workers in mass-production industries to unionize.

Lewis became known for dealing with challenges to his leadership in an autocratic manner; on the other hand, he achieved crucial gains in the struggle of American workers for social and economic justice. In 1946 and 1948, for example, Lewis won agreements for mine workers that funded a welfare and retirement program. By 1956, the fund had helped to construct ten hospitals in the mining region of southern Appalachia.

See also American Federation of Labor-Congress of Industrial Organizations (AFL-CIO); Labor unions; National Labor Relations Act (NLRA); New Deal.

Libel. *See* Defamation

Liberalism, modern American

DEFINITION: An ideology that advocates egalitarianism and government intervention in people's economic affairs but minimum intervention in religious, moral, and intellectual matters

SIGNIFICANCE: Liberal ideas have dominated American political life since the beginning of the nation, and a form of liberalism emerged as the dominant ideology after the Great Depression; however, liberalism has been strongly challenged by neoclassical liberals and conservatives since the late 1960's

As an ideology and state of mind, liberalism began as a reaction to religious conformity, ascribed status, and political absolutism in medieval Europe. From the beginning, liberalism focused on individual liberty and freedom. In the nineteenth century, liberals defined freedom as the absence of restraint by human institutions, especially governmental institutions. These liberals wanted governments to interfere as little as possible in the lives of their citizens. In the twentieth century, however, liberals became divided on how best to define and promote individual freedom, especially in regard to the role of government, though they agree on the desired end—the creation of an open society in which every person enjoys liberty and has an equal opportunity to live as freely as possible.

Welfare Liberalism. Liberalism is deeply rooted in American thought. The American political tradition, which is antistatist and antimonarchical, is essentially liberal. Liberal and progressive ideas are enshrined in patriotic emblems such as the Declaration of Independence, the Pledge of Allegiance, and the Gettysburg Address. However, American liberalism changed in response to the Great Depression of the 1930's. Whereas liberals had earlier emphasized economic individualism and "negative freedom"—absence of restraint or government control—liberals in the wake of the Depression rethought their attitudes toward the state. Following T. H. Green's notion of "positive freedom" and John M. Keynes's economic theory, the majority of liberals began to subscribe to the philosophy of welfare liberalism, though a distinct minority continued to believe in the late-nineteenth century neoclassical view.

Welfare liberalism maintains that government is not merely a necessary evil. On the contrary, government can be a positive force when it provides equality of opportunity and assistance to certain individuals and groups by enabling them to have a substantive means of competing in a market economy. Welfare

The New Deal programs of President Franklin D. Roosevelt launched "welfare liberalism" in the United States. (Library of Congress)

liberals believe that government should be responsible for delivering welfare services such as health, housing, pensions, and education as well as for managing the economy. From Franklin D. Roosevelt's New Deal program through Harry S Truman's Fair Deal program, John F. Kennedy's New Frontier policies, and Lyndon B. Johnson's Great Society program, welfare liberalism dominated American political life and public policy for half a century. As a result, welfare liberalism came to be equated with liberalism in general.

Under President Johnson, the liberal commitment to equal opportunity was extended to "affirmative action," or positive discrimination for racial minorities, especially African Americans. The ideology of welfare liberalism remained dominant in the policy-making agenda of both Republican and, especially, Democratic presidents and congressional leaders into the 1970's. The biggest expansion of the social welfare program after Johnson's Great Society program took place under President Richard M. Nixon, a conservative Republican.

In the noneconomic areas, modern liberals continue to believe in the nineteenth century liberal view that government should intervene least in an individual's religious, moral, and intellectual life. Liberals therefore tend to favor separation between church and state—and hence to oppose prayer in school; to support a woman's right to abortion; and to oppose the suppression of pornographic material and the depiction of sex and violence in film or on television. The liberal views on cultural and social issues, espccially on race, family, "permissiveness," and crime, have thus been used by conservatives in the 1980's and 1990's in efforts to discredit liberalism.

The Reagan Revolution and the Decline of Welfare Liberalism. Welfare liberalism came under serious attack from neoclassical liberals and conservatives beginning in the late 1960's. The economic recession of the 1970's provided an environment in which critics questioned government spending on social welfare programs and the Keynesian doctrine that government should manage, or "fine tune," the economy. In doing so critics of "big government" and welfare liberalism revived the neoclassical liberal tradition, though under the rubric of conservatism, of viewing the government as the chief obstacle to individual liberty. These critics championed, among other things, the virtues of small government, commitment to free-market ideas, reduced regulation of business and the economy, and elimination of the welfare state.

To many observers, the election of President Ronald Reagan in 1980, followed by that of George Bush in 1988, marked the beginning of the end of welfare liberalism in American politics. In the 1992 presidential election, Bill Clinton's narrow victory over Bush hinged on his image as a "new Democrat" who was not wedded to welfare liberalism and had accepted conservative ideas on fiscal and economic policy, social welfare reform, and many other issues. While Reagan and Bush did not dismantle the welfare state, in the wake of the 1994 Republican landslide, Newt Gingrich, the new Speaker of the House, and other Republicans promised in their "Contract with America" to dismantle the welfare state brick by brick.

While liberal ideas—and democracy—generally triumphed around the world in the 1980's and 1990's, especially in most former communist countries and in the Third World, liberalism became "the L-word" in the United States after the 1988 presidential campaign. Nevertheless, the political discourse in America remained an essentially intramural debate between two wings of liberalism: welfare liberalism and neoclassical liberalism. —*Sunil K. Sahu*

See also Conservatism, modern American; Democratic Party; Great Society; Johnson, Lyndon B.; Kennedy, John F.; New Deal; War on Poverty; Welfare state.

BIBLIOGRAPHY
Influential works on American liberalism include Allen J. Matusow's *The Unraveling of America: A History of Liberalism in the 1960's* (New York: Harper and Row, 1984); Louis Hartz's *The Liberal Tradition in America: An Interpretation of American Political Thought Since the Revolution* (New York: Harcourt Brace Jovanovich, 1955); Alonzo L. Hamby's *Liberalism and Its Challengers: From F. D. R. to Bush* (2d ed. New York: Oxford University Press, 1992); Theodore J. Lowi's *The End of Liberalism: The Second Republic of the United States* (2d ed. New York: W. W. Norton, 1979); Randall Rothenberg's *The Neoliberals: Creating the New American Politics* (New York: Simon & Schuster, 1984); *The Liberal Tradition in American Thought* (New York: Capricorn Books, 1969), edited by Walter E. Volkmer; Francis Fukuyama's *The End of History* (New York: Free Press, 1992); Anthony Arblaster's *The Rise and Decline of Western Liberalism* (New York: Basil Blackwell, 1984); and David Greenstone's *The Lincoln Persuasion: Remaking American Liberalism* (Princeton, N.J.: Princeton University Press, 1993).

Lincoln, Abraham (Feb. 12, 1809, near Hodgenville, Ky.—Apr. 15, 1865, Washington, D.C.)

IDENTIFICATION: President of the United States, 1861-1865

SIGNIFICANCE: Lincoln led the nation during its most severe crisis, the Civil War, which resulted in the abolition of slavery

Abraham Lincoln was a lawyer, member of the Illinois General Assembly, member of Congress, and the president of the United States. Practicing law in Illinois in his forties, he was

angered by the 1854 Kansas-Nebraska Act, which repealed the Missouri Compromise. The Missouri Compromise had limited the spread of slavery in the western territories. Lincoln strongly opposed slavery, and he rapidly became a Republican Party leader in Illinois. He ran for the U.S. Senate against Stephen A. Douglas in 1858; at his nomination, he quoted the Bible in arguing against the feasibility of the nation continuing to contain both free states and slave states: " 'A house divided against itself cannot stand.' I believe this government cannot endure, permanently half *slave* and half *free*." This was strong language for the politics of the time: The suggestion that slavery eventually would have to end was generally considered a radical position. Lincoln gained national prominence debating the slavery issue with Douglas. He lost the Senate race to Douglas but only two years later was elected to the presidency.

Lincoln's election triggered the secession of the states in the South and the subsequent formation of the Confederacy. Lincoln viewed the preservation of the Union as his duty and highest goal, and the Civil War began within a month of his inauguration in March, 1861. Lincoln quickly took sweeping

Abraham Lincoln, president during the Civil War, used the powers of the presidency to the fullest in his struggle to preserve the union. (Library of Congress)

measures, pushing presidential power to its utmost. He proclaimed a blockade of the South, spent funds on the war without the authorization of Congress, and suspended the writ of *habeas corpus* in cases where the possibility of disloyal activity was involved. The *habeas corpus* issue was addressed by the U.S. circuit court in Baltimore in the case *Ex parte Merryman* (1861), in which the judge, Roger Brooke Taney (the U.S. chief justice), held that Lincoln's action was illegal.

The Supreme Court contained a number of southern justices at the time of Lincoln's election, and only one had resigned. Chief Justice Taney led the Court's southerners, and he tried—as in his circuit decision in *Merryman*—to block Lincoln's tactics in fighting the war. Taney had little success, however, in trying to convince other judges in the Union to follow his lead. The Supreme Court itself generally upheld Lincoln's actions, if by a narrow margin. Lincoln believed that the U.S. Constitution could cover any situation, including those arising during wartime. He made public the opinions of legal scholars that the war powers he was exercising were similar to those employed in previous national crises and were therefore constitutionally acceptable. During his presidency, Lincoln appointed three justices to the Supreme Court, including abolitionist Salmon P. Chase.

It had not been Lincoln's avowed goal to abolish slavery, even though he himself deplored the institution. As the war dragged on, however, proclaiming the freedom of all slaves in areas of the South still fighting against the Union came to be seen as an effective, even necessary, military move. It would weaken the South and add the manpower of escaping slaves to the North, and it would turn the war into a war of liberation. Lincoln therefore issued the Emancipation Proclamation on January 1, 1863. Later, realizing that the proclamation might not hold up after the war, Congress, with Lincoln's support, passed the Thirteenth Amendment, abolishing slavery. It was ratified on December 18, 1865.

Eleven months after issuing the proclamation (on November 19, 1863), Lincoln delivered what has become perhaps the most famous speech in American history, the Gettysburg Address, at the dedication of a cemetery at the Pennsylvania site of the Battle of Gettysburg (July, 1863). A few weeks later he issued an order that the states of the Confederacy would have to petition the Union for readmittance and meet certain requirements at war's end. After years of bloody, divisive fighting, the Civil War finally ended in May of 1865. On the evening of April 14, 1865, while watching a play at Ford's Theater, Lincoln was assassinated by John Wilkes Booth.

See also Abolitionist movement; Civil War; Emancipation Proclamation; *Habeas corpus*; Kansas-Nebraska Act; Lincoln-Douglas debates; *Merryman, Ex parte*; *Scott v. Sandford*; Slavery.

Lincoln-Douglas debates

DATE: August 21-October 15, 1858
PLACE: Illinois
SIGNIFICANCE: The most famous and consequential campaign debates in American history, the dialogue between Lincoln

and Douglas clarified how Democratic and Republican conceptions of justice differed and laid a foundation for a renewed national commitment to principles of freedom

In 1858 Abraham Lincoln, a leader of Illinois' recently formed Republican Party and a former one-term member of the House of Representatives, ran for the Senate against incumbent Stephen A. Douglas. A national leader of the Democratic Party, Douglas based his campaign, and his future presidential ambitions, on "the great fundamental principle" of "self-government," or "popular sovereignty." People of the federal territories, he argued, had the right to vote for or against allowing slavery, as they saw fit, and no outsiders had a right to interfere with their decisions. To Douglas, no principle was more fundamental to American democracy than this right of self-government, even if it meant countenancing slavery.

Lincoln viewed Douglas' position as a repudiation of the principles of freedom enshrined in the Declaration of Independence, which, if they meant anything, meant that slavery was wrong. Slavery had existed in the nation since before it began, but Lincoln echoed Thomas Jefferson in recognizing that the founders had been keenly aware of its incompatibility with principles of freedom and that they hoped for its eventual end. For Lincoln and other Republican Party leaders, the issue of extending slavery into the territories—the dominant political controversy of the 1850's—demanded that the nation make a choice. It must either recommit itself to the principles of freedom by refusing to extend this odious institution to new areas or adopt a position of moral neutrality toward slavery, thereby allowing it to spread into the territories and eventually into the free states. At stake was not only the fate of African Americans, but also the freedom of all Americans. If the American credo were to abandon the idea that "all men are created equal," tyranny of one form or other would surely follow.

These issues focused the seven debates that Lincoln and Douglas conducted throughout Illinois between August and October of 1858. In a format quite unlike modern political "debates," one man spoke for an hour, the other responded for an hour and a half, then the first finished with a half-hour rejoinder. They alternated speaking first.

Although Douglas was reelected to the Senate (the actual vote was by state legislators, who had pledged themselves to either Lincoln or Douglas in their own election campaigns), Lincoln's forceful defense of the antislavery position won him fame outside Illinois and greatly contributed to his election to the presidency in 1860. His elevation to the presidency, in turn, marked the political defeat of Douglas' position of moral indifference to slavery and led to a national reaffirmation that American justice would remain rooted in freedom and equality.

See also Abolitionist movement; Civil War; Democratic Party; Douglas, Stephen A.; Free Soil Party; Kansas-Nebraska Act; Missouri Compromise of 1820; Republican Party; *Scott v. Sandford*; Slavery.

Lindbergh kidnapping. *See* **Kidnapping; Lindbergh law**

Lindbergh law

DATE: Passed June 22, 1932

DEFINITION: The Lindbergh law made kidnapping for ransom a federal offense if the victim was transported across state lines or to a foreign country

SIGNIFICANCE: This law was one of many enacted during the 1930's which made crimes that transcend state borders federal offenses and thus placed them under FBI jurisdiction

In the late 1920's and early 1930's, kidnapping had become more prevalent as gangs often resorted to the crime for ransom. Congress had begun investigating measures to intensify penalties for the crime, and several citizens' groups from Chicago and St. Louis testified in front of the House Judiciary Committee seeking federal intervention. Despite these endeavors, the movement to pass a bill to make kidnapping a federal offense punishable by death was slow. It would be the kidnapping and murder of a small child that would move a nation to change the laws regarding kidnapping.

On March 1, 1932, Charles A. Lindbergh, Jr., the infant son of Charles and Anne Lindbergh, was kidnapped and subsequently found murdered. Charles Lindbergh, the first person to fly solo across the Atlantic Ocean, was a beloved national hero, and the public outcry resulted in a massive police investigation to find the perpetrator. While police forces in New Jersey and New York focused on the crime, Congress worked to pass a federal kidnapping law.

At the time, there were no federal statutes or a national agency charged with combating kidnapping. To compound the problem, interstate cooperation was minimal. Sentencing varied tremendously, with the death penalty used in seven states, life imprisonment in sixteen states, and prison terms ranging from one to ninety years in the remaining states. To further confuse the situation, only twenty-five states had laws specifically dealing with kidnapping for ransom.

Buoyed by public support, Congress passed a kidnapping bill, widely referred to as the "Lindbergh law," on June 22, 1932. The new law made kidnapping for ransom a federal offense when the victim was transported across state lines or to another country. Further, if the victim was not returned within twenty-four hours, there was a rebuttable presumption that the transportation had occurred. Initially, the maximum penalty for this crime was life imprisonment. Amended in 1933, the Lindbergh law made harming the kidnapping victim a capital offense punishable by death and allowed the Federal Bureau of Investigation (FBI) to enter and oversee the investigation within twenty-four hours. (In 1968, the U.S. Supreme Court ruled that the death penalty was unconstitutional in Lindbergh law cases.) Subsequent congressional measures during the mid-1930's enlarged the jurisdiction of the FBI and the definition of federal offenses to include other interstate crimes.

Ironically, Bruno Richard Hauptmann, who was arrested for the kidnapping and murder of Charles Lindbergh, Jr., could not be punished under the new law. Instead, the only charge available was statutory felony murder in the course of a burglary. Thus, the state of New Jersey convicted and executed Hauptmann on April 3, 1936, for committing a murder in the course of stealing the infant's pajamas.

See also Federal Bureau of Investigation (FBI); Kidnapping.

Litigation

DEFINITION: A lawsuit or the process of bringing a legal action, including all relevant proceedings

SIGNIFICANCE: Litigation is the primary means of seeking enforcement of rights and redress for grievances in a judicial setting

When two or more individuals or entities have a disagreement ostensibly based on a violation of law, often they find themselves embroiled in litigation. In a simple lawsuit, the plaintiff, the party who voices the initial complaint, files suit with a court against the defendant, the party who has allegedly wronged the plaintiff. The rules for filing and prosecuting a lawsuit are highly formalized and vary according to jurisdiction. As a case proceeds through a given court system, it can be rejected at a number of points, often for procedural violations. If a case actually goes to trial, it can be adjudicated by a judge or a panel of judges, or by a judge and jury. If the trial results in a judgment or verdict, that determination can often be appealed to a higher court by either party—again, often on procedural grounds. Appeals often result in further appeals, some of them taken all the way to the U.S. Supreme Court.

See also Appellate process; Civil law; Civil procedure; Class action; Contract law; Suit; Tort; Tort reform.

Little Rock school integration crisis

DATE: 1957

PLACE: Little Rock, Arkansas

SIGNIFICANCE: The first serious test of the 1954 Supreme Court decision requiring that all American schools be racially integrated

In the *Brown v. Board of Education* decision of 1954, the Supreme Court declared segregation unconstitutional, but its 1955 implementation order allowed the lower courts to develop plans to desegregate. It was the first time that the Court had not ordered immediate establishment of a constitutional right. In a state such as Arkansas, moderate and reluctantly willing to accept political and legal (though not social) equality, this approach seemed to suggest that a gradual process would be possible. Trouble seemed unlikely.

Little Rock school superintendent Virgil Blossom planned to start by enrolling a few black students at Central High School in 1957 and working down the grades year by year. The children, eventually pared down to nine, were chosen for strong scholarship and character; they were from middle-class families. When school opened on September 3, however, these children met serious resistance.

Governor Orval Faubus had decided that his best bet for future political success—most immediately a third term—lay in making himself the leader of the lower-class white segregationist element in the state. Despite the fact that he had not previously been particularly (or at least overtly) racist, Faubus

National Guard troops maintaining a pathway for nine African American schoolchildren during the Little Rock crisis. (Library of Congress)

announced that he could not keep the peace and called out the National Guard to keep order.

Daisy Bates, head of the local National Association for the Advancement of Colored People (NAACP) chapter, realized that families served by Central High School were predominantly lower class and were likely to be stirred to resistance by the governor's statements. She organized the students to arrive in a group. They were turned away at bayonet point. One student, Elizabeth Eckford, did not get the message and arrived alone to face a mob of angry whites. Blocked from the school by armed Guardsmen and cursed and reviled by the mob, she was rescued by a reporter from *The New York Times* and an older white woman. Such scenes as these were reported by the press and broadcast on television. The nation was forced for the first time to face the true ugliness of its prejudice.

President Dwight D. Eisenhower, not overly sympathetic to integration, was slow to act. He met with Faubus on September 14 and got what he thought was a promise to abide by the Supreme Court decision. When Faubus reneged, the president, on September 25, ordered elements of the 101st Airborne to Little Rock. The soldiers escorted the black children to school and protected them for several weeks. Then the state National Guard, placed under federal authority, took over. Despite con-

tinuing harassment by white students, all but one of the nine was graduated from Central High.

In Little Rock the *Brown* decision had been enforced, but resistance to school integration continued in many areas of the South. Faubus, who continued to fight, won a total of six terms as governor. The Little Rock crisis was a vital first step in desegregation, but it was no more than that.

See also *Brown v. Board of Education*; Civil rights; Civil Rights movement; Eisenhower, Dwight D.; National Association for the Advancement of Colored People (NAACP); National Guard; *Sweatt v. Painter*.

Livingston, Edward (May 28, 1764, Clermont, N.Y.— May 23, 1836, Rhinebeck, N.Y.)

IDENTIFICATION: American lawyer and statesman

SIGNIFICANCE: Livingston's criminal code for Louisiana, though never adopted, greatly influenced subsequent thought and practice in criminal justice

Edward Livingston was graduated from Princeton University (1764), read law in Albany and New York, and was admitted to the bar in 1785. He was a Republican representative in Congress for New York (1795-1801), later serving as U.S. district attorney for New York and as mayor of New York (1801-

1803). Moving to Louisiana, he prepared a provisional criminal code that was in force from 1805 to 1825. Elected to the legislature (1820-1823), he prepared a provisional criminal code to replace Louisiana's legal code. This code was not adopted, but it established Livingston as a preeminent legal scholar. He then served in the U.S. Congress (1823-1828) and U.S. Senate (1829-1831). Here, he again unsuccessfully introduced his criminal code. As secretary of state, he prepared Andrew Jackson's antinullification proclamation in 1832. He concluded public service as minister plenipotentiary to France from 1833 to 1835.

See also Criminal justice system; Jurisprudence; Law; Louisiana Civil Code.

Lochner v. New York

COURT: U.S. Supreme Court
DATE: Decided April 17, 1905
SIGNIFICANCE: Reflecting laissez-faire economics and emphasizing freedom of contract, this decision invoked the Fourteenth Amendment to negate a state labor law, thus by implication minimizing the effects of state and federal social legislation upon business

Between 1890 and 1937, the U.S. Supreme Court attempted to introduce the era's popular laissez-faire economic philosophy into constitutional law. Consequently, the Supreme Court's conservative justices delivered a series of decisions invalidating state legislation establishing minimum wages and maximum hours of employment, mandating workers' compensation, setting prices, and otherwise regulating business activities. The Court's authority for such decisions was drawn chiefly from the due process and equal protection clauses of the Fourteenth Amendment.

Ratified in 1868 during Reconstruction, the Fourteenth Amendment was drafted primarily to protect the extension of certain legal and civil rights to newly freed blacks. Its due process clause was then interpreted as guaranteeing individuals' procedural rights: the right to counsel, to *habeas corpus*, and to trial by jury in criminal and civil cases, among other procedural safeguards. The predominantly conservative Supreme Court of the late nineteenth century and early twentieth, however, began interpreting due process in a substantive manner, construing the due process clause as a device for protecting businesses and vested interests against "unreasonable" state and federal social legislation.

Substantive interpretation was brought to bear in *Lochner v. New York*. In 1897, New York State enacted a law limiting the hours of employment in bakeries and confectionery establishments to ten hours a day and sixty hours a week. New York justified this and similar laws as exercises of its police power: the obligation to protect public health, welfare, safety, and morals. Joseph Lochner, the proprietor of a Utica, New York, bakery, accordingly, was fined fifty dollars for violating this hours law—a conviction sustained by a New York appeals court. On a writ of error, Lochner's case then landed before the U.S. Supreme Court.

Justice Rufus W. Peckham, a lifelong opponent of social and economic legislation and a champion of laissez-faire policies, delivered the Court's opinion in 1905. The Court, he asserted, previously had been liberal in viewing the states' use of the police power. Since nearly any legislation, Peckham argued, could be justified as protective of the public's health, welfare, safety, and morals—thus leaving the states with "unbounded power"—the Fourteenth Amendment had to be invoked to set limits. The question at issue in *Lochner*, he reasoned, was whether New York's law represented a fair and appropriate employment of the police power, or whether it was an "arbitrary interference" with an individual's personal liberty and right to enter freely into contracts.

Peckham held for Lochner and invalidated New York's hours law, a victory for due process over the police power, by declaring that rights to personal liberty and freedom of contract should prevail when they clashed with the states' right to legislate. Justice Oliver Wendell Holmes, Jr., filed a brilliant dissent. By implication the *Lochner* decision was modified in *Muller v. Oregon* (1908) and was silently overturned in *Bunting v. Oregon* (1917).

See also Contract, freedom of; Due process of law; Labor law.

Long, Huey (Aug. 30, 1893, near Winnfield, La.—Sept. 10, 1935, Baton Rouge, La.)

IDENTIFICATION: American politician
SIGNIFICANCE: Long's Share Our Wealth plan for social justice was an alternative to President Franklin Roosevelt's New Deal during the Great Depression of the 1930's

Huey Long was chair of the Louisiana Public Service Commission, governor, and United States senator. He used the power of those offices to improve living standards throughout the state and to perpetuate himself and his allies in office. In 1932, Long supported New York governor Franklin Roosevelt for president, but he later broke with Roosevelt because he believed that Roosevelt's efforts to combat the Great Depression were inadequate. Long proposed the Share Our Wealth plan to redistribute resources more equitably. The plan included proposals to confiscate personal fortunes in excess of $3 million and give every American family $5,000 from the proceeds for shelter and transportation, provide $30 monthly pensions to all persons over sixty-five, grant cash bonuses to World War I veterans, guarantee $2,500 annual income to workers, and provide free college education to qualified students. His proposals attracted thousands of followers nationwide.

Long, who became known by the nickname "Kingfish," was also known for his ruthless consolidation of political power in Louisiana, and he was both loved and reviled. Long's political machine reached into every corner of the state, and at his peak he was powerful enough essentially to turn the state legislature into an extension of the Long machine. Long was assassinated in 1935 as he was planning a presidential campaign focused on social justice issues.

See also Machine politics; Political corruption; Roosevelt, Franklin D.; Socialism.

Lopez, United States v.

COURT: U.S. Supreme Court

DATE: Decided April 26, 1995

SIGNIFICANCE: For the first time since 1936, the Court ruled that a federal statute was unconstitutional because Congress had overstepped its authority to regulate interstate commerce

Responding to crime in the schools, Congress in 1990 passed the Gun-Free School Zone Act, making it a federal crime to possess a gun within one thousand feet of a school. More than forty states already had similar laws. After Alfonso Lopez, Jr., a high school student in San Antonio, Texas, was arrested for taking a .38-caliber handgun to school, he was tried under federal law because the penalties were greater than under state law. The federal court of appeals, however, ruled that the 1990 statute was unconstitutional, referring to it as a "singular incursion by the Federal Government into territory long occupied by the states." The federal government appealed the case to the Supreme Court.

The issue of the case was the nature of federalism. Not since 1936, in *Carter v. Carter Coal Co.*, had the Court overturned a statute because it exceeded federal prerogative to regulate commerce. In fact, in *Garcia v. San Antonio Metropolitan Transit Authority* (1985) the Court had ruled that the scope of the federal authority to regulate commerce was a question to be decided entirely by the political process rather than the courts. The *Garcia* precedent was usually applauded by liberals and denounced by conservatives, but few on either side expected it to be soon overturned.

In *United States v. Lopez*, however, the Court ruled 5 to 4 that the 1990 statute did exceed Congress' authority under the commerce clause. Writing the majority opinion, Chief Justice William H. Rehnquist noted that possession of guns near a school had nothing to do with interstate commerce and that such an issue is traditionally a concern of local police power. As a principle, Rehnquist argued that Congress could regulate only "those activities that have a substantial relationship to interstate commerce." The four dissenters argued that guns in schools interfere with education and thus affect interstate commerce by damaging the national economy. Even more, they expressed deep concern that the decision would create "uncertainty" about the validity of many federal laws on the books.

The *Lopez* decision had many possible implications for the future relationship between the federal government and the states. In concluding that Congress had gone further than the commerce clause allowed, the Court opened the door for additional restrictions on the powers of the national government. Since such an important decision was based on a 5-4 vote, the significance of *Lopez* as a precedent largely depended on the future membership of the Court; therefore, the decision appeared to increase the stakes of the presidential election of 1996.

See also *Carter v. Carter Coal Co.*; Commerce clause; Conservatism, modern American; *Darby Lumber Co., United States v.*; Federalism; *Hammer v. Dagenhart*; *Heart of Atlanta Motel v. United States*.

Los Angeles riots. *See* **King, Rodney, case and aftermath**

Louisiana Civil Code

DEFINITION: A compilation of short, logically interrelated articles designed to regulate civil society by means of general propositions

SIGNIFICANCE: The Louisiana Civil Code and civil law system are unique in the United States, as they are rooted in French, Spanish, and Roman traditions rather than English common law

Louisiana is the only state in the United States that has a civil law system and has enacted a civil code. While some common-law states have enacted codes addressing certain specific areas of law (such as commercial law), such codes typically attempt to reflect the law existing at the time of the codification without substantially altering or organizing it. In contrast, the Louisiana Civil Code provides logical organizations of general principles of law to be applied by deduction and extended to new circumstances by analogy. As law professor Ferdinand Stone has explained, this type of system requires attorneys to evaluate legal issues in different ways than their common-law counterparts do. The civil-law lawyer, Stone notes, has a written "blueprint plan of the universe" in his pocket; by consulting the plan, he can use "simple logic [to] deduce the appropriate answer." The common-law lawyer has no general rule but meets problems as they come, "bringing to bear upon them [his] experience and common sense."

Because the Louisiana Civil Code's vocabulary employs terminology and concepts of French, Spanish, and Roman law, attorneys from the other forty-nine states cannot readily understand it. For example, standard common-law concepts of property law such as "life estate" and "remainder" do not exist by that nomenclature. Their rough equivalents bear names derived from Latin and French, such as "usufruct" and "naked ownership."

The Structure of the Civil Code. The Louisiana Civil Code reflects a distinctively French perspective on law and society. The primary goal of early nineteenth century French civil codification was to render the law accessible by making it clear. To accomplish this goal, a civil code had to be complete in its field and had to lay down general rules in logical sequence.

In this spirit, the framers of the Louisiana Civil Code established three books that consist of a series of concisely written articles. Book 1, "Of Persons," encompasses legal personality, domicile, marriage, separation, divorce, legitimate and illegitimate children, adoption, parental authority, tutorship, and emancipation. This book regulates matters of personal status. Book 2, "Of Things and the Different Modifications of Ownership," covers the general law of movable and immovable property, personal and praedial servitudes, building restrictions, boundaries, and usufruct. Book 3, "Of the Different Modes of Acquiring the Ownership of Things," is the most comprehensive and lengthy of the three. It regulates the ways that citizens acquire and lose property, including successions, testaments, donations, delicts, community property, and many types of contracts—sale, lease, partnership, loan, deposit, mandate, surety, compromise, and pledge. In 1991, a fourth book, "Conflict of Laws," was added to the code.

Legal History of Louisiana. The legal history of Louisiana began in 1712, the year France granted Antoine Crozat a monopoly on commerce throughout the Louisiana Territory. The United States subsequently purchased Louisiana from France in 1803. The Louisiana Territory was then divided into territories, one of which, the Territory of Orleans, later became the state of Louisiana. At that time, United States officials, who were trained in the Anglo-American legal tradition, came to Louisiana and urged the adoption of a common-law system. In 1806, however, the first legislature of the Territory of Orleans passed a resolution to keep its civil law system intact insofar as it did not conflict with the U.S. Constitution. In 1808 the legislature enacted *A Digest of the Civil Laws Now in Force in the Territory of Orleans with Alterations and Amendments Adapted to Its Present Form of Government,* known as the Civil Code of 1808. The 1808 code was revised in 1825 and again in 1870; it remains the basis for the current civil code. —*David R. Sobel*

See also Civil law; Common law; Jurisprudence; Livingston, Edward; Natural law and natural rights.

BIBLIOGRAPHY

Among the good sources on Louisiana civil law are Shael Herman, *The Louisiana Civil Code: A European Legacy for the United States* (New Orleans: Louisiana Bar Foundation, 1993); Tulane Law School's *The Louisiana Civil Code: A Humanistic Appraisal* (New Orleans: Author, 1981); and A. N. Yiannopoulos, *Louisiana Civil Law System* (Baton Rouge, La.: Claitor's, 1971).

Lucas v. South Carolina Coastal Council

COURT: U.S. Supreme Court

DATE: Decided June 29, 1992

SIGNIFICANCE: In this case, the Court held for the first time that a state land-use regulation violated the Fifth Amendment's prohibition against taking private property without "just compensation" because, although it did not physically take property or transfer title, it reduced the land's value without compensation to the owner

In 1986, David Lucas, a South Carolina real estate developer, paid almost a million dollars for two oceanfront lots zoned for single-family residential construction. Two years later, before Lucas built, the state legislature changed its coastal regulations, moving the construction line inland. Lucas' lots, on each of which he had planned to build a house, were stranded seaward of that line.

Lucas sued, alleging that the Beachfront Management Act of 1988 (BMA), the legislation that revised the regulations, had effected a taking of the value of his property without just compensation. The trial court agreed that Lucas had suffered a total loss of the value of his property and concluded that a regulatory taking had occurred. On appeal, the South Carolina Supreme Court reversed the decision, on the grounds that the

BMA had been passed to prevent serious public harm. Lucas petitioned the U.S. Supreme Court to review the matter, and the Court sided with Lucas in a 6-2 opinion. Justices Harry Blackmun and John Paul Stevens dissented, and a separate statement was written by Justice David Souter.

Writing for the majority, Justice Antonin Scalia stated that it was impossible to ascertain whether the BMA had been designed to prevent harm or to obtain a free public benefit. Instead, he turned to the common-law principle that the right to use one's property is limited by the equal right of one's neighbor to an equivalent freedom of use. If a neighbor can bar a landowner's plan to put a nuclear plant on an earthquake fault, for example, the legislature may also act without compensation. Yet if a use is one permitted between private landholders—such as the construction of a private residence—the legislature cannot bar such a use without compensating the owner for its loss, at least when the loss is total. The use Lucas sought to make of his property fell into the category of such an "essential use" and hence could not be barred without compensation. The Court's opinion thus endorsed the proposition that the common law of private nuisance is the appropriate guide to the constitutionality of land-use regulation.

The Supreme Court's holding in *Lucas* applies only to total loss of value, an uncommon situation. The logic of the *Lucas* opinion, however, is not limited to the case of total loss. If the difference between a regulation that prevents harm and one that confers a benefit is indeterminate, it is so whether or not the loss caused by the regulation is total. Indeed, Justice Scalia, challenged by Justice Stevens to explain why a total loss would be compensated but a 95 percent loss would not, could give no principled reason for restricting the scope of the opinion. Such uncertainty suggests that a later court may further restrict the legislative power to enact incompensable land use and environmental regulation.

See also *Nollan v. California Coastal Commission*; Nuisance; Property rights; Takings clause; Zoning.

Lying to Congress

DEFINITION: Knowingly and willfully concealing material facts or making false statements in any matter within the jurisdiction of any federal department or agency

SIGNIFICANCE: The felony of lying to Congress provides a good illustration of problems associated with ambiguous legislation

The definition of lying to Congress is based on Article 1001 of the United States Code; this provision can be traced to 1934 amendments to Article 35 of the code. Both Oliver North and John Poindexter were indicted and prosecuted for lying to Congress in the Iran-Contra scandal under the provisions of Article 1001. Nevertheless, there has been considerable debate about whether this provision applies to Congress or only to the executive branch.

In an early effort to clarify the scope of Article 1001, the U.S. Supreme Court held that the word "department" applied to the legislative, judicial, and executive branches in *United*

Lieutenant Colonel Oliver North admitted lying to Congress about events in the mid-1980's that became known as the Iran-Contra scandal. (AP/Wide World Photos)

States v. Bramblett (1955). In *United States v. Hubbard* (1995), the Court reversed the Bramblett decision, holding that Article 1001 applies neither to the judiciary nor to the legislature but only to the executive branch.

See also Contempt of court; Iran-Contra scandal; Watergate scandal.

Lynch v. Donnelly

COURT: U.S. Supreme Court

DATE: Decided March 5, 1984

SIGNIFICANCE: The Court ruled that the inclusion of a Christian symbol in a city-sponsored display did not violate the Constitution's prohibition of religious establishment

For at least four decades, the city of Pawtucket, Rhode Island, had used public funds to erect and maintain a nativity scene, or crèche, as part of the Christmas exhibit in its shopping district. In addition to the crèche, which contained figures of Jesus, Mary, Joseph, shepherds, and angels, the display included figures and symbols of a secular nature, including a reindeer pulling Santa's sleigh, a clown, and a Christmas tree. A local resident, Daniel Donnelly, joined with the American Civil Liberties Union to bring suit against Pawtucket mayor Dennis Lynch in federal court. The challengers argued that the nativity scene created both the appearance and the reality of a governmental endorsement of a particular religion, contrary to the establishment clause of the First Amendment. Both the district court and the court of appeals ruled in favor of the challengers, and the city of Pawtucket appealed the case to the Supreme Court.

A sharply divided court voted 5 to 4 to reverse the lower court's ruling and to allow Pawtucket to continue its Christmas display. Writing for the majority, Chief Justice Warren Burger began with the argument that rather than requiring a complete separation of church and state, the First Amendment "affirmatively mandates accommodation, not merely tolerance, of all religions, and forbids hostility toward any." He observed that the first Congress of 1789 employed members of the clergy as official legislative chaplains and that historically the three branches of the federal government had not hesitated to acknowledge the role of religion in American life. Burger found that the display had the secular motive of encouraging community spirit, promoting downtown business, and depicting the historical origins of a national holiday, and that any benefit to religion was "indirect, remote, and incidental."

In a vigorous dissent, Justice William J. Brennan answered that the crèche retained a specifically Christian meaning and that Pawtucket's action was an unconstitutional endorsement of a particular faith. He quoted from the city leaders to show that their intent was to "keep Christ in Christmas."

In the *Lynch* decision, the Court allowed governments much discretion to accommodate the majority's religious culture by allowing governmental acts that appeared to encourage that culture. A few years later, however, the Court narrowed the importance of the decision in *Allegheny County v. American Civil Liberties Union, Greater Pittsburgh Chapter* (1989), a case involving a county-sponsored nativity scene that was not diluted with secular symbols and that proclaimed, "Glory to God in the Highest." In the *Allegheny County* case, the majority found the more pious crèche to be an unconstitutional endorsement of religion. The idea that a religious display is considered constitutional if it is accompanied by secular images is sometimes referred to as the "reindeer rule."

See also *Abington School District v. Schempp*; *Engel v. Vitale*; Establishment of religion; *Everson v. Board of Education*; *Lemon v. Kurtzman*.

Lynching

DEFINITION: An extralegal means of social control in which individuals take the law into their own hands to inflict corporal punishment and/or death upon persons who violate local customs and mores

SIGNIFICANCE: Lynching was a primary means of intimidation and control of blacks in the American South

Lynching, the deadliest form of vigilantism, has a long history in America. At the time of the American Revolution, lynchings were used to punish Tories or British sympathizers. Until the 1850's, lynchings were associated with nonlethal forms of punishment such as beatings and tarring and feathering. In the years immediately before the Civil War, lynching took on its fatal connotation as it was used to suppress slave insurrections. Although lynching is often associated with hanging someone, lynching includes all sorts of violent acts, including flogging, dismemberment, torture, burning, and shooting.

History of Lynching. After the Civil War, lynching became more widespread as former slaves came to be viewed as a threat by their former slavemasters. Accurate numbers on lynching are hard to come by, and it was not until 1872 that there was a systematic effort to obtain reliable data. Records kept by the Tuskegee Institute indicate that there were 4,743 lynchings in the United States between 1882 and 1968. Of those lynched, 3,446 (73 percent) were blacks and 1,297 (27 percent) were whites. Even these numbers underestimate what most scholars believe to be the actual number of lynchings. A more accurate estimate would be close to 6,000 lynchings.

Lynchings were most prevalent from the 1880's to the 1920's. During the last two decades of the nineteenth century, there was an average of 150 lynchings per year, with a high of 230 in 1892. Between 1901 and 1910 there was an average of 85 lynchings per year, and from 1911 to 1920 there was an average of 61 per year. Lynchings declined to an average of 28 per year during the 1920's, to 11 per year during the 1930's, and to only 3 per year during the 1940's. From 1951 to 1985 only 10 lynchings were reported in the United States. Although almost every state experienced lynchings, 82 percent occurred in the South. Mississippi ranks first with 581, followed by Georgia with 530 and Texas with 493.

Grounds for Lynching. Although lynching was often justified as a method of protecting white women from black rapists, only 25 percent of lynching victims were suspected of rape or attempted rape. In most cases, lynching victims were summarily executed before receiving any trial. Their guilt was never established at all, let alone beyond a reasonable doubt. The justification for lynching in the cases of rape was to protect the white woman from the agony of testifying in court.

Approximately 40 percent of lynchings involved murder or attempted murder allegations. Nine percent involved assault or robbery charges, certainly not capital offenses, and 2 percent involved blacks insulting whites, particularly white women. The most famous example of a black who was lynched for insulting a white woman was Emmett Till. Till, a fourteen-year-old Chicago native, was visiting relatives in Mississippi in 1955. Prodded by some friends, Till asked a white woman for a date. The woman immediately rejected Till and went to get a pistol. Till walked out of the store saying, "Bye, baby," and "wolf whistled" at her. Till's actions violated one of the major cultural taboos in the South, and he would pay with his life. That same day, the woman's husband and her half-brother abducted Till from the home he was visiting. Three days later, Till's decomposing body was found floating in the Tallahatchie River. Till had been beaten and shot before his weighted-down body was thrown into the river. The two white men who abducted Till were charged with his murder, but it took an all-white jury less than one hour to acquit them.

The Campaign Against Lynching. Few individuals who participated in lynchings were ever prosecuted. Coroners' juries repeatedly concluded that the death had come "at the hands of parties unknown." Seldom was anything further from the truth. Oftentimes lynchings took on a festive air, and local newspapers provided complete coverage, sometimes including photographs. In the event someone was arrested for the crime, such as the two white men accused of murdering Emmett Till, they would be found not guilty by all-white juries.

Leading the effort to abolish lynchings were the Commission on Interracial Cooperation, headed by Will Alexander, and Southern Women for the Prevention of Lynching, led by Jessie Daniel Ames. Ames, one of the leading social reformers in the South, had forty thousand members in her organization within nine years of its establishment in 1930. When alerted about a possible lynching, Ames contacted women in the area who were members of her organization or sympathetic to its objectives.

One of the earliest objectives of the National Association for the Advancement of Colored People (NAACP), a civil rights organization established in 1909, was to pressure the U.S. Congress to pass a federal antilynching bill. On several occasions, the House of Representatives passed such legislation, but it was always filibustered by southern senators when it reached the Senate. In the late 1940's President Harry Truman appointed a President's Committee on Civil Rights (PCCR). The PCCR urged Congress to pass a federal antilynching law, but without success.

The NAACP met with greater success in attempting to mobilize public opinion against lynching. The NAACP investigated lynchings and often sent special investigators into areas where a lynching had occurred. The NAACP prepared written narratives of the lynchings, including photographs if available, and distributed them to any media outlet that would publicize the

KNOWN LYNCHINGS BETWEEN 1882 AND 1968		
State	African Americans	Nonblacks
Alabama	299	48
Arizona	0	31
Arkansas	226	58
California	2	41
Colorado	3	65
Delaware	1	0
Florida	257	25
Georgia	492	39
Idaho	0	20
Illinois	19	15
Indiana	14	33
Iowa	2	17
Kansas	19	35
Kentucky	142	63
Louisiana	335	56
Maine	0	1
Maryland	27	2
Michigan	1	7
Minnesota	4	5
Mississippi	539	42
Missouri	69	53
Montana	2	82
Nebraska	5	52
Nevada	0	6
New Jersey	1	1
New Mexico	3	33
New York	1	1
North Carolina	86	15
North Dakota	3	13
Ohio	16	10
Oklahoma	40	82
Oregon	1	20
Pennsylvania	6	2
South Carolina	156	4
South Dakota	0	27
Tennessee	204	47
Texas	352	141
Utah	2	6
Vermont	0	1
Virginia	83	7
Washington	1	25
West Virginia	28	20
Wisconsin	0	6
Wyoming	5	30
Totals	3,446	1,287

Source: Data are from Low, W. Augustus, ed., *Encyclopedia of Black America.* New York: McGraw Hill, 1981.

Hundreds of spectators gathered to watch a lynching. (Library of Congress)

lynching. The effort was to try to shame the South into stopping this despicable practice.   —*Darryl Paulson*

See also Ku Klux Klan (KKK); National Association for the Advancement of Colored People (NAACP); Terrorism; Vigilantism.

BIBLIOGRAPHY

Among the best studies on lynching are Ray Stannard Baker, *Following the Color Line: An Account of Negro Citizenship in the American Democracy* (New York: Doubleday, Page, 1908); Richard M. Brown, *Strain of Violence: Historical Studies of American Violence and Vigilantism* (New York: Oxford University Press, 1977); James Chadbourn, *Lynching and the Law* (Chapel Hill, N.C.: University of North Carolina Press, 1933); Arthur Raper, *The Tragedy of Lynching* (Chapel Hill, N.C.: University of North Carolina Press, 1933); Walter White, *Rope and Faggot* (New York: Alfred A. Knopf, 1929); Stephen Whitfield, *A Death in the Delta: The Story of Emmett Till* (Baltimore: The Johns Hopkins University Press, 1988); Robert Zangrando, *The NAACP Crusade Against Lynching, 1909-1950* (Philadelphia: Temple University Press, 1980).

McCarthyism

DEFINITION: The practice of making wholesale accusations of disloyalty or treason, based on weak evidence, hearsay, and the presumption of guilt by association

SIGNIFICANCE: Between 1950 and 1954, unscrupulous and ill-founded accusations of treason and subversion made by Joseph McCarthy, a powerful senator, threatened to drown the presumption of innocence doctrine in presumption of guilt by association; McCarthyism destroyed the reputations and careers of thousands of innocent people

In its original sense, McCarthyism meant making charges of disloyalty, treason, or espionage against public figures or high officials—in particular accusing them of secret attachment to the cause of communism—based on doubtful and circumstantial evidence or prior association (however accidental or coincidental) with known communists, or even on the basis of no real evidence at all. Later, during the Cold War, it referred to any effort to restrict social dissent or political criticism, especially of foreign policy actions, by accusing the dissenter or critic of being unpatriotic or of harboring procommunist sympathies. Modern usage has broadened the term even further so that it refers to the tactic of unsupported charges of disloyalty or secret attachment to some repugnant political cause, which can be communism, fascism, or some other unfashionable or "un-American" ideology. McCarthyism in this sense no longer carries the exclusive connotation of extreme right-wing views but may be found on the left wing of the political spectrum as well.

The Rise of Joseph McCarthy. The term "McCarthyism" derives from the scurrilous practices of Republican Senator Joseph R. McCarthy (1909-1957) of Wisconsin. His agenda dominated debate in the U.S. Senate over a four-year period, from 1950 to 1954. A hint of what was to come in the 1950's was apparent as early as 1947, when the House Committee on Un-American Activities (HUAC) held hearings on the suspected communist infiltration of the major Hollywood studios. Still, the nation was shocked when, on February 6, 1950, McCarthy made a speech in which he claimed to have evidence that the State Department had at least 205 members of the Communist Party within its ranks and suggested that some of these individuals were spies working for the Soviet Union. He added that Secretary of State Dean Acheson (whom he sneeringly called "Red Dean") knew about these supposed communists but had refused to act against them. McCarthy never provided the list for scrutiny, and later he revised his claim to fifty-seven known "card-carrying members . . . [of] the Communist Party." The number was revised upward subsequently, but the list of names was never produced.

Acheson strenuously defended his department and, more problematically, accused spy and convicted perjurer Alger Hiss.

President Harry Truman, however, delayed a direct confrontation with the increasingly powerful senator. In March, 1950, the Senate established the Tydings Committee to look into McCarthy's charges. During its hearings, McCarthy was again unable to come up with a list of names or any other evidence. Instead of backing down, however, he cast an even wider net: In a series of new accusations he slandered several prominent academics, accusing them of being communist spies. In July, a majority on the Tydings Committee issued a report saying that McCarthy's charges were entirely without foundation. Yet not even this broadside from his Senate colleagues slowed down the crusading senator from Wisconsin or the wider "red-baiting" movement that was beginning to build steam.

The reasons for McCarthy's rising power and influence, even in the absence of any direct evidence for his charges, had much to do with the public's reaction to events outside the United States. By the late 1940's there was a growing fear among Americans that their country's historic security from external danger was evaporating, under the threat of overt hostility from Joseph Stalin's Soviet Union and, later, the People's Republic of China. This vague fear was deepened and made specific by Soviet detonation of an atomic bomb in 1949, several years ahead of expectations. The anxiety focused on espionage when a series of prominent spy discoveries and trials made it clear that the Soviets had achieved their breakthrough partly as a result of successful infiltration of the American and British nuclear weapons programs. Many conservatives, mainly Republicans but also some Democrats, blamed the Truman Administration for the "loss of China" to the communist camp in 1949, by way of Chairman Mao Tse-tung's victory over American ally Chiang Kai-shek in China's civil war. Added to that was criticism over the outbreak of war in Korea, where by the end of 1950 American and U.N. troops were fighting hundreds of thousands of communist Chinese "volunteers" as well as North Koreans.

Many Americans found it difficult to understand or accept such catastrophic events and apparent foreign policy failures, especially coming so soon after the enormous sacrifice and great victory in the war against Nazi Germany. The easiest response was to fix blame on domestic subversives and traitors, who were seen as in league with foreign villains. McCarthy and his followers thus were able to tap into a rich vein of anger, fear, and confusion as they set off their explosive charges that treason and conspiracy were behind all the ills of American foreign policy. Without this sense of physical insecurity in the face of nuclear weapons and the hostility of the communist states—a fear felt by Americans after 1949 for the first time in their history—it is doubtful that McCarthyism could have expanded beyond the unsubstantiated rantings of one extremist senator, to become a genuine threat to the nation's tradition of civil liberties and fair play.

A number of McCarthy's Republican colleagues in the Senate publicly disassociated themselves from his accusations. By 1951, however, McCarthy, hitherto a political nonentity, had assumed a position of public power and influence so great that even the most prominent Americans thought twice before confronting him directly. Carried away by ambition and worsening alcoholism, McCarthy viciously attacked nearly everyone associated with the Truman Administration and Truman's predecessor, Franklin D. Roosevelt. At one point he described the Roosevelt and Truman era as "twenty years of treason." McCarthy suggested that 1952 Democratic presidential nominee Adlai Stevenson was a communist dupe and sympathizer. He also accused World War II hero and former secretary of state George C. Marshall of secretly working for a Soviet victory over the United States. That alienated President Dwight D. Eisenhower, elected in 1952, who knew and had served under Marshall. Yet even "Ike," arguably the most popular man in America that year, hesitated to challenge McCarthy openly. Instead, Eisenhower waited, hoping that McCarthy would self-destruct.

The Fall of Joseph McCarthy. The Republicans recaptured Congress, for the first time in two decades, in the 1952 elections. The seniority system thus raised McCarthy to the chairmanship of a Senate subcommittee charged with investigating government operations. From this vantage point, McCarthy and several equally ruthless protégés expanded their assault on suspected communist agents and sympathizers. Government libraries were investigated and found to hold "subversive" and "communistic" books and other materials. Some civic librarians took up the cause, actually burning books they considered "un-American." This so outraged Eisenhower that he broke his silence and condemned all book burning, which many Americans had sharply criticized when Nazi Germany engaged in it in the 1930's. Still, McCarthy's subcommittee pressed on, next turning its attention to a purge of the Voice of America and other federal overseas operations.

The turning point came when McCarthy attacked an institution greatly admired by most Americans: the military. Starting in December, 1953, McCarthy held hearings into subversion and treason within the U.S. Army ranks. The nation watched, first in fascination and then in growing disgust, as McCarthy baited and badgered helpless witnesses, smeared people by associating them with known communists, accused them of belonging to "communist-front organizations," and demanded that they turn over the names of friends and colleagues for investigation by his subcommittee. In taking on the army

"Red-baiting" senator Joseph McCarthy finally found himself on the defensive during the "Army/McCarthy" hearings in 1954. (AP/Wide World Photos)

McCarthy had made a fatal mistake. In midyear, charges of corruption were brought against him by the secretary of the army, leading to an investigation of McCarthy by his own subcommittee.

Thus began thirty-six days of televised "Army/McCarthy Hearings," which proved the beginning of the end of McCarthy and McCarthyism. When subjected to intense grilling by army lawyer James N. Welch, McCarthy could only strike back with more unsubstantiated accusations designed to destroy junior colleagues in Welch's law firm. This naked display of personal indecency and gross abuse of Senate investigatory power shocked many people, even those who had thought the Wisconsin senator was serving the public interest by ferreting out traitors and foreign agents. After the hearings, the subcommittee voted to clear McCarthy of the charges, but he was spent as a political force. Eisenhower spoke publicly against the reckless use of power by elected officials. More charges were brought against McCarthy in the Senate, which voted to censure him on December 2, 1954. Cast into a political wilderness, he continued to level charges of disloyalty and conspiracy, but these now appeared to most people to be little more than the paranoid delusions of an alcoholic demagogue. He died of alcohol-related maladies in 1957, at the early age of forty-eight.

McCarthy never identified a single communist agent in the U.S. government. Yet his fall from media and political grace did not take place before a wave of red-baiting hysteria had unjustly destroyed many reputations and careers and seriously damaged the professional foreign service and the conduct of American foreign policy. Thousands of innocent people were hounded out of their jobs, or out of the country, by McCarthy and his supporters, and many never worked again. Reputations were unfairly destroyed and families, friendships, and individual lives broken apart. Social and political criticism, too, was temporarily stifled as a blanket of fear descended over public discourse.

Nevertheless, even at its worst McCarthyism did not begin to approach the horrors of political purges and show trials in nondemocratic countries. That false comparison is often made, but itself suffers from an almost McCarthy-like level of distortion and hyperbole.

McCarthy theorized a great conspiracy to subvert and spy on the United States. Had he insisted on the use of proper investigative techniques by the appropriate police and security authorities, with full respect for civil liberties and rules of evidence, there likely would have been little or no controversy. It was true that Soviet spies were in place within the U.S. government and in other Western governments, just as the United States had spies in place in Russia, as part of the age-old game of geopolitics. Thus what was truly pernicious about McCarthyism was not the charges of espionage or disloyalty as such but the gross abuse of investigatory powers by a small group of reckless fanatics and their demagogic insistence on deciding guilt by association or even mere innuendo. Perhaps most disturbing and damaging of all, however, was the shocking failure of elite opinion and political leadership in the United States to stand against such unprincipled, star-chamber proce-

dures. Only after the hysteria passed did the Senate introduce reforms to its procedures and the Supreme Court reaffirm civil rights and evidentiary rules in a series of cases that proceeded from the excesses of the McCarthy period.

In sum, the wild and groundless charges of subversion and treason made by McCarthy and his circle of advisers and supporters created a climate of near-hysteria, profoundly threatened the civil liberties of thousands of innocent Americans, severely damaged the internal morale and effectiveness of whole branches of the federal government, and, ironically, made it much more difficult in later years to marshal public support for policies aimed at countering the Soviet threat to the Western democracies. This paradox developed because the national experience with, and revulsion from, McCarthyism made it less acceptable among American intellectuals in later years to be avowedly anticommunist. In that respect, McCarthy himself was among the best friends the Soviet Union and the KGB ever had, as one prominent KGB defector later noted.

—*Cathal J. Nolan*

See also Communist Party, American; Eisenhower, Dwight D.; Espionage; House Committee on Un-American Activities (HUAC); Palmer raids and the "red scare"; Presumption of innocence.

BIBLIOGRAPHY

Numerous books have been written on McCarthyism. Yet readers need to be aware that despite the passage of years, the passions and even hatreds that characterized the period have not cooled for everyone. Most books vehemently denounce McCarthy. A rare few try unsuccessfully to defend his motive, even as they chide him for his methods. A good beginning, because it provides an overview but also allows the reader to see some of the evidence directly, is Ellen Schrecker, *The Age of McCarthyism: A Brief History with Documents* (Boston: St. Martin's Press, 1994). A more specialized work, by the same author, is *No Ivory Tower: McCarthyism and the Universities* (New York: Oxford University Press, 1986). Two general works are Mark Landis, *Joseph McCarthy: The Politics of Chaos* (Selinsgrove, Pa.: Susquehanna University Press, 1987), and William Ewald, *McCarthyism and Consensus* (Lanham, Md.: University Press of America, 1986). On McCarthyism and foreign policy issues, see Richard Freeland, *The Truman Doctrine and the Origins of McCarthyism* (New York: New York University Press, 1985).

McCleskey v. Kemp

COURT: U.S. Supreme Court
DATE: Decided April 22, 1987
SIGNIFICANCE: In this case, the Supreme Court rejected a death row inmate's claim that Georgia's system of sentencing people to death was unconstitutional because it discriminated on the basis of race

In 1978, Warren McCleskey, a black man, was convicted of killing a white police officer during an armed robbery of a store in Atlanta, Georgia. McCleskey's jury—which consisted of eleven whites and one black—sentenced him to die in

Georgia's electric chair. McCleskey sought a writ of *habeas corpus*, arguing, among other things, that the Georgia capital sentencing process was administered in a racially discriminatory manner and violated the United States Constitution. According to McCleskey, the jury's decision to execute him violated the Eighth Amendment because racial bias rendered the decision arbitrary and capricious. Also, the equal protection clause of the Fourteenth Amendment was violated because McCleskey, a black man, was treated differently than white defendants in the same position.

To support his claim of racial discrimination, McCleskey offered as evidence a sophisticated statistical study performed by Professor David B. Baldus and his colleagues at the University of Iowa (the Baldus study). The Baldus study showed that race played a dual role in deciding whether convicted murderers in Georgia would be sentenced to death. First, the race of the murder victim played a large role in whether a defendant would be sentenced to die. According to the study, defendants charged with killing whites received the death penalty in 11 percent of the cases. Defendants charged with killing blacks received the death penalty in only 1 percent of the cases. After taking account of thirty-nine variables that could have explained the disparities on nonracial grounds, the Baldus study concluded that, in Georgia, defendants charged with killing white victims were 4.3 times as likely to receive a death sentence as defendants charged with killing blacks.

Second, the race of the defendant played an important role during capital sentencing. According to the Baldus study, black defendants were 1.1 times as likely to receive a death sentence as other defendants. Thus, the study showed that black defendants such as McCleskey who had killed white victims had the greatest likelihood of receiving the death penalty.

By a 5-4 vote, the Supreme Court ruled against McCleskey. The Supreme Court accepted the validity of the Baldus study but held that McCleskey failed to prove "that decisionmakers in his case acted with discriminatory purpose." In other words, McCleskey failed to show that his constitutional rights were violated because he did not prove that anyone involved in his particular case intentionally discriminated against him based on his race. Justice Lewis Powell's opinion for the majority expressed special concern that if the Court accepted McCleskey's argument—that racial bias impermissibly tainted capital sentencing proceedings—all criminal sentences would be subject to attack based on allegations of racial discrimination. The *McCleskey* decision is a landmark ruling in the modern era of capital punishment.

Warren McCleskey died in Georgia's electric chair on September 25, 1991. That same year Justice Powell, whose 5-4 majority opinion sealed Warren McCleskey's fate, told a biographer that he would change his vote in that case (thus sparing McCleskey's life) if he could. Also, although executions had resumed in the United States in 1977, 1991 marked the first time in the modern era of American capital punishment that a white defendant (Donald "Pee Wee" Gaskins) was actually executed for killing a black person.

See also Capital punishment; *Furman v. Georgia*; Racial and ethnic discrimination.

Machine politics

DEFINITION: A non-ideological form of politics dominated by a small elite, usually corrupt, based on the exchange of material benefits for political support

SIGNIFICANCE: Machine politics was at its peak in the late nineteenth and early twentieth centuries, and it was a response to the needs of the growing urban population; its excesses generated numerous political reform measures that remain part of contemporary politics

Machine politics is characterized by a tightly organized political structure dominated by an individual "boss" or a small cadre of leaders who stay in power by brokering a variety of benefits such as jobs, contracts, protection, and other privileges in exchange for political support. This exchange frequently takes the form of benefits for money in the form of campaign contributions, kickbacks, and outright bribery.

Richard Daley, mayor of Chicago from 1955 to 1976, ran the city's powerful political machine. (AP/Wide World Photos)

The prototype of the political machine is as old as the American nation. The New York Society of Tammany was founded in 1785 as a social club named after a Delaware Indian chief. It rapidly evolved into a partisan organization that supported candidates for public office and remained a force in politics through the early twentieth century. Like other such organizations in the early nineteenth century, its strength increased with the expansion of voting during the Jacksonian era. The power of political machines further increased with the growth of immigration. By organizing the newly arrived voters through strict party discipline, Tammany Hall was able to control the political "spoils." It rapidly became a widely copied model of graft-ridden politics. When immigration increased after the Civil War, the political machine reached its zenith. In the case of Tammany, this period marked the rise of one of history's most famous bosses, William Marcy Tweed, or "Boss Tweed." Tweed became a Tammany leader or "sachem" in 1857. He was soon elected, with Tammany support, to the New York Board of Supervisors and from there expanded his base by controlling patronage and public contracts. By 1868, he was a state senator and a dominant force in politics. It has been estimated that his corrupt "ring" had stolen nearly two hundred million dollars from public funds and other sources. Tweed was eventually arrested and died in jail, but machine politics continued to prosper through the early twentieth century. Most cities had some degree of machine politics. Some of the most famous machine bosses include Frank Hague of Jersey City, James Curley of Boston, Ed Crump of Memphis, Tom Pendergast of Kansas City, Huey Long of Louisiana, and Richard J. Daley of Chicago. The growth of machines paralleled the rise of large cities. Though there were "courthouse gangs" or rural versions of the machine, the typical structure was a well-controlled urban population organized by a political party that cared primarily for staying in office for reasons of power and money rather than ideology.

Functions of the Machine. Though the corruption of machine politics cannot be minimized, scholars have found that the rise of machines can be explained by the unique set of social and economic conditions associated with immigration. As the United States became more urban, new tasks had to be performed to meet changing conditions. The political machine filled this vacuum. Most important, the machine performed a much-needed welfare function. It helped families and individuals find jobs through political patronage, obtain housing, and deal with personal crises such as fire or illness by providing financial and even emotional support. It also helped to socialize the newly arriving immigrants into both American culture and political life. It facilitated the assimilation of newcomers because it needed balanced tickets in which various ethnic voting blocks were included. This fact provided upward mobility and helped to lower the level of ethnic conflict. Machines also centralized power, which generated a measure of support from business and commercial interests. Centralization had become necessary, because a legacy of the Jacksonian era was the "long ballot" and the multiplying of elected of-

fices. By centralizing decision making, the machine increased the efficiency of a fragmented system and helped to personalize government.

Decline of Machines. Although machine politics persists in American politics, the classic machine organization had declined by the mid-twentieth century for a number of reasons. Primarily, a large-scale reform movement motivated by the corruption and waste of the machines was successful in passing a number of "good government" measures. Among these were civil service and merit system reforms which undermined the machine's patronage base, the short ballot, nonpartisan elections, city manager forms of government, direct primaries, and at-large elections. These structural reforms contributed greatly to the demise of the machine. Just as important, a growing middle class became far less tolerant of the scandals and corruption associated with the machine. Coupled with the rise of new management theories which aimed at removing politics from government in order to model it on a businesslike paradigm, the culture which supported the traditional machine disappeared. Finally, the growth of welfare programs initiated by the New Deal of Franklin Roosevelt in response to the Great Depression eliminated the functional basis of the machine. New agencies and programs took over the welfare activities of the machine.

Although the classical machine was undermined by reform efforts as well as changing social circumstances, machine politics continues in one form or another. Some would argue that machine politics, stripped of its corruption, represents a form of responsive politics in action. Nevertheless, the ultimate legacy of machine politics is the structural and social reforms that marked the end of the machine era. While some would argue that the reform legacy has weakened political parties too much and that the bureaucratic structures that accompanied reform have created their own set of problems, the positive functions of machines did not outweigh their corruption and the cynicism they caused, which served to undermine public faith in democratic institutions.   —*Melvin Kulbicki*

See also Civil service system; Jacksonian democracy; Long, Huey; Pendleton Act; Political corruption; Progressivism.

BIBLIOGRAPHY

Informative views of Tammany Hall include Seymour Mandelbaum, *Boss Tweed's New York* (New York: John Wiley & Sons, 1965), and William Riordon, *Plunkitt of Tammany Hall* (New York: Dutton, 1963). The Daley machine of Chicago is the subject of Milton L. Rakove, *Don't Make No Waves— Don't Back No Losers* (Bloomington: Indiana University Press, 1975). Broader perspectives are taken in Lincoln Steffens, *The Shame of the Cities* (New York: Sagamore Press, 1957); Alfred Steinberg, *The Bosses* (New York: Macmillan, 1972); Susan Welch and Timothy Bledsoe, *Urban Reform and Its Consequences* (Chicago: University of Chicago Press, 1988); and Edward C. Banfield and James Q. Wilson, *City Politics* (Cambridge, Mass.: Harvard University Press, 1963). A classic novel about machine politics is Edwin O'Connor, *The Last Hurrah* (Boston: Little, Brown, 1956).

Mack, Julian William (July 19, 1866, San Francisco, Calif.—Sept. 5, 1943, New York, N.Y.)

IDENTIFICATION: American jurist

SIGNIFICANCE: Mack, a leading Zionist and progressive reformer, was a pioneer in the development of the juvenile justice system and presided over several highly publicized trials in the 1920's

Julian Mack was one of the originators of the *Harvard Law Review* (1887), a professor of law at Northwestern University and the University of Chicago, a federal judge, and a leader in several social welfare and Zionist organizations.

After graduating from Harvard Law School, he studied comparative law in Leipzig and Berlin, then entered private practice in Chicago. He joined the faculty at Northwestern University in 1895 and moved to the University of Chicago when the latter opened its law school in 1902.

Mack became judge of the Circuit Court of Cook County (1903-1911) and presided over the newly formed Juvenile Court of Chicago (1904-1907), a project fostered by his friend Jane Addams and housed across the street from Hull House. He headed the Juvenile Protective League, forerunner of the Child Welfare League of America, and lobbied on behalf of protective legislation for minors and immigrant rights. In 1911 he was sworn in as a judge of the U.S. circuit court assigned to commerce court, becoming the highest-ranking Jewish person in the American judiciary at that time. He was a White House consultant on Jewish affairs in Russia during the William Howard Taft Administration, and he was appointed by President Woodrow Wilson to the Board of Inquiry on Conscientious Objectors during World War I.

His concerns over the anti-Semitism manifested in the prosecution of the cases of Alfred Dreyfus (in France) and Leo Frank (in the United States) led him increasingly to devote his political efforts to educational causes and to lobbying for the creation of a Jewish homeland in Palestine. He was active in the founding of the New School for Social Research, New York, and the Institute of Advanced Study at Princeton University. He served as president of the National Conference of Jewish Charities. President of the Zionist Organization of America (1918-1921), he attended the Paris Peace Conference of 1919. He raised funds for the defense committee in the Sacco and Vanzetti case and used his influence to try to convince Governor Alvan Fuller of Massachusetts to prevent the executions.

As judge of the U.S. Court of Appeals for the Second Circuit, New York, and the Southern District of New York, he presided over trials that received heavy publicity in the 1920's, including the mail fraud trial of Marcus Garvey, the breach of contract case of Lillian Gish, the perjury trial of theatrical producer Earl Carroll, the trials of former government officials Harry M. Daugherty and Thomas W. Miller, the bootlegging case of "Big Bill" Dwyer, and a series of extortion, blackmail, and racketeering cases. Citing the importance of the freedom of the press, he intervened in the attempted censorship of the *American Mercury* over the publication of an H. L. Mencken short story about prostitution. In the 1930's he ruled in several key antitrust, receivership, and bankruptcy cases, including that of the Interborough Rapid Transit, operators of the New York subway system. Mack presided over the World Jewish Congress in Geneva in 1936.

See also Anti-Defamation League (ADL); Censorship; Daugherty, Harry M.; Sacco and Vanzetti trial and executions; Taft, William Howard.

Magna Carta

DATE: June 15, 1215

PLACE: Runnymede, England

SIGNIFICANCE: This document established the principle that governmental authority is bound by law; it also contributed to the development of trial by jury, due process of law, and representative government

During the Middle Ages, King John of England, forced by his disastrous foreign wars to seek additional revenue, began imposing new taxes, confiscating property, violating his feudal obligations, and selling offices and justice to the highest bidders. His powerful nobility rebelled, and John was forced at Runnymede to grant his subjects a charter of liberties. The Magna Carta ("Great Charter") contains no stirring rhetoric. It simply comprises a preamble and sixty-three clauses, arranged in no particular order. Essentially a medieval document, most provisions dealt specifically with John's feudal obligations.

Certain clauses dealing with justice, however, became enshrined in English common law. The most famous was Clause 39, which stated that no free man should be taken, imprisoned, disposed, or outlawed, "except by the lawful judgment of his peers or by the law of the land." Eventually, over an extended period, "judgment of his peers" evolved into trial by jury, and "law of the land" into due process of law. Also significant was Clause 40, which stated, "to no one will we sell, to no one will we deny or delay right or justice." This too evolved into due process of law, that crucial principle of English common law which holds that not only must the law be just, but also the process of dispensing justice must be fair and reasonable.

The full impact of these and other clauses was not immediately felt, but by the fourteenth century, trial by jury had become an established legal concept. The Magna Carta was given an enormous boost in prestige when it was used in the seventeenth century struggle between Parliament and the Stuart kings, the latter hoping to reinstitute royal absolutism. By this time the Magna Carta was held to be part of the fundamental law of the land and a bulwark of liberty against capricious and unlimited government.

The Magna Carta played an important role in American legal history. Early American colonists were aware of its value in placing a check upon the excesses of English control. Some colonial charters contained language strikingly similar to that of the Magna Carta, and it was commonly cited in colonial assemblies and law courts. Copies and commentaries of the document could be found in the libraries of important colonial leaders. It played a particularly useful role during the revolutionary period, and influential pamphlets cited its provisions.

Some of the great figures of American history, including John Adams, James Otis, John Dickenson, and Samuel Adams, were familiar with it. Delegates to both the Stamp Act Congress and the First Continental Congress found comfort in its principles.

In the postrevolutionary period, it played no direct role in the Constitutional Convention, but the Magna Carta was mentioned frequently in the state ratifying conventions when debating whether to add a bill of rights to the new Constitution. Throughout the nineteenth and twentieth centuries, the supreme courts of the various states occasionally alluded to the Magna Carta in their decisions, particularly when dealing with legal concepts such as property rights or due process of law, which can be traced back to the English heritage. The Supreme Court of the United States exhibited similar behavior. Throughout the twentieth century, the Court's justices found wisdom and guidance in its principles. The American justice system has long seen in the Magna Carta a document that is not only noble and inspiring but useful and enduring as well.

See also Bill of Rights, U.S.; Common law; Due process of law; *Habeas corpus*; Jury system; Speedy trial, right to.

Maher v. Roe

COURT: U.S. Supreme Court

DATE: Ruling issued June 20, 1977

SIGNIFICANCE: The Court ruled that while a woman's right to abortion is constitutionally protected, states are not required to provide Medicaid funding for abortions that are not "medically necessary"

Connecticut adopted a law which refused Medicaid support for abortions for poor women which were not "medically necessary"—necessary to protect the life or health of the mother. To receive state funding, the hospital or clinic performing the abortion had to submit physician certification that the abortion was medically necessary. A case was filed on behalf of indigent women in U.S. district court against Edward Maher, the Connecticut commissioner of social services. The suit argued that the law violated Title XIX of the Social Security Act (Medicaid) and violated the constitutional rights of poor women, including the Fourteenth Amendment guarantees of due process and equal protection under the law. It further argued that by providing Medicaid support for childbirth but not abortion the state was favoring some procedures pertaining to pregnancy over others, thus limiting poor women's free choice. The district court found in favor of Roe, and the case was appealed to the Supreme Court.

In a 6-3 decision, the Court found in favor of Maher and the state of Connecticut. The majority argued that while *Roe v. Wade* (1973) guaranteed a woman's right to abortion, the Constitution does not require state funding of pregnancy-related medical procedures for indigent women. It ruled that states have the right to decide what will be covered under Title XIX. Additionally, it qualified *Roe v. Wade* by stating that it did not affirm an unconditional right to abortion but only required that states not impose undue burdens on women attempting to obtain an abortion. The majority argued that poverty may constitute a bur-

den, but it is not caused by the state and so the state is not required to alleviate the hardships pertaining to access to abortion that poverty causes. In response to the objection that Connecticut favored childbirth over abortion, the Court cited the trimester provision of *Roe v. Wade*, arguing that states do, indeed, have a vested interest in potential (fetal) life and may enact policies that encourage childbirth over abortion. Finally, the majority held that a statement from the attending physician attesting the medical necessity of a Medicaid-funded abortion was appropriate. The minority opinion objected that failure to fund elective abortions for the poor makes it almost "impossible" for many of them to obtain safe abortions and so violates their constitutional rights. The case is one of many which has qualified the right to abortion first affirmed in the *Roe v. Wade* decision.

See also Abortion; *Akron v. Akron Center for Reproductive Health*; *Doe v. Bolton*; *Harris v. McRae*; *Planned Parenthood of Central Missouri v. Danforth*; *Planned Parenthood v. Casey*; *Roe v. Wade*; *Thornburgh v. American College of Obstetricians and Gynecologists*.

Mail fraud

DEFINITION: Crime consisting of a scheme to defraud and the use of mails in furthering the fraudulent scheme

SIGNIFICANCE: Mail fraud legislation has developed into a powerful weapon that allows the federal government to assert its jurisdiction over fraudulent acts not otherwise covered by federal law

A wide variety of schemes to swindle and defraud the public appeared in the nineteenth century, largely because of society's increasing mobility and access to information. Fraud via the newspapers and the mails were among the most prevalent. Mail fraud legislation had its beginnings in 1865. The initial advocate for a federal statute in this area was the postmaster general, who believed that the U.S. mail system was too often used to distribute obscene materials. By the late 1860's it had become apparent that the U.S. mails were being used for fraudulent purposes such as deceitful lotteries and gift schemes. Yet it was not until 1872 that the first mail fraud statute was instituted. Generally known as the Mail Fraud Act, this legislation is still in effect.

The act made it a crime to mail any material intended to put into effect "any scheme or artifice to defraud," and the major debate following the enactment of the law centered on the meaning of this phrase. Some courts interpreted the statute narrowly, while others believed that it was intended to cover more comprehensive types of fraud than were specifically enumerated. In response to this debate, Congress amended the act to expand the crime of mail fraud to include cases in which there was an intent to defraud through the mails. The result was broad application of the statute by the federal government and the courts. Another reason for its broad application is that the Mail Fraud Act employs a less technical definition of "fraud" than is found in other fraud statutes. It has been interpreted to include pyramid schemes, welfare and insurance fraud, schemes involving bad checks, and debt-consolidation fraud.

MAIL FRAUD CASES HANDLED BY THE U.S. POSTAL INSPECTION SERVICE

Year	Arrests	Convictions
1984	1,272	1,042
1985	1,142	887
1986	1,435	1,131
1987	1,304	1,206
1988	1,488	1,015
1989	1,543	1,225
1990	1,699	1,486
1991	1,772	1,297
1992	1,904	1,582
1993	1,965	1,900

Source: U.S. Department of Justice, Bureau of Justice Statistics, Sourcebook of Criminal Justice Statistics—1993. Washington, D.C.: U.S. Government Printing Office, 1994.
Note: The U.S. Postal Inspection Service is the law enforcement arm of the U.S. Postal Service.

The Politics of Mail Fraud. The crime of mail fraud, like tax evasion, has provided a way for the federal government to prosecute criminals that it cannot reach any other way. A good example of how the statute has been used by the federal government is the case involving Marcus Garvey, the leading black nationalist of the 1920's. Through his work with the Universal Negro Improvement Association (UNIA) and his publishing of Negro World, Garvey became a nationally known figure. He also attracted the attention of the federal government and was constantly being investigated. After several race riots occurred in Washington, D.C., and Chicago, the Justice Department began to pursue Garvey, viewing him as a dangerous agitator. In particular, J. Edgar Hoover, head of the Federal Bureau of Investigation, was convinced that Garvey was a threat to the government. The government found a way to prosecute Garvey when his steamship company, the Black Star Line, distributed through the mails a picture of a ship represented as belonging to the company. The Black Star Line did not actually own the ship. Garvey was indicted and convicted of violating section 215 of the U.S. Code: using the mails for fraudulent purposes.

Court Challenges and Constitutionality. Many cases involving the Mail Fraud Act have come before the Supreme Court. The Court's decision in Ex parte Jackson (1877) upheld the right of Congress to regulate activities carried on through the mails. It also implied that sealed mail could not be opened without a warrant and that the enforcement of mail fraud law could not override freedom of the press. The Court's decision in Durland v. United States (1896) stated that the act should be interpreted broadly to cover "everything designed to defraud by representation as to the past or present, or suggestions and promises as to the future." Through the years the Court has refined its interpretation of the act, but not without inconsistencies. In the 1987 Supreme Court decision McNally v. United States, the Court ruled that application of the act is limited to protecting money and property rights and can no longer be used as a tool for prosecutors to tackle local corruption or political "agitators," as was done in the Garvey case. The debate over how narrowly or broadly the mail fraud statute should be applied has yet to be resolved, however; in Carpenter v. United States (1987), for example, the Supreme Court essentially contradicted its McNally decision. Here the Court affirmed that the defendants were rightly convicted on mail fraud charges based on their intent to deprive people of confidential business information.

Enforcement. There have been several problems in enforcing mail fraud legislation. First, the Supreme Court's reluctance to define the mail fraud statute clearly as either limited or broad has left federal prosecutors, investigators, agents, and lower court judges somewhat confused about what the criminal boundaries are. Second, sentencing guidelines for such white-collar offenses are not as stringent as they are with other crimes. In fact, mail fraud offenders enjoy a low rate and average length of imprisonment as well as a low average size of fine and compensation to their victims. Third, the characteristics of these white-collar offenders make their conviction more difficult for federal government agents and prosecutors.

The Bureau of Justice Statistics has shown that persons who commit mail fraud tend to be wealthy, older than most other criminals, well educated, and employed; they tend to have no prior convictions and no history of drug abuse. Thus, they are harder to detect and convict than typical federal criminal offenders. Finally, although statistics indicate that fraudulent activity in the United States has increased since the 1980's, many fraud cases are not reported to government agencies. This fact makes these criminals even more difficult to track down, arrest, and convict. —Maria A. Hernandez

See also Consumer fraud; Embezzlement; Fraud; Garvey, Marcus; Organized crime; White-collar crime.

BIBLIOGRAPHY

Overviews of mail fraud are included in David Nelken, ed., White Collar Crime (Brookfield, Vt.: Dartmouth, 1994), and Irwin Ross, Shady Business: Confronting Corporate Corruption (New York: Twentieth Century Fund Press, 1992). Current governmental legislation on mail fraud is included in Tony G. Poveda, Rethinking White-Collar Crime (Westport, Conn.: Praeger, 1994); Ellen S. Podgor, "Mail Fraud: Opening Letters," South Carolina Law Review 43 (no. 2, 1992); and Brian Behrens, "18 U.S.C. Sec. 1341 and Sec. 1346: Deciphering the Confusing Letters of the Mail Fraud Statute," Saint Louis University Public Law Review 13 (no. 1, 1993). For the Garvey case, see Judith Stein, The World of Marcus Garvey: Race and Class in Modern Society (Baton Rouge: Louisiana State University Press, 1986).

Majority, age of

DEFINITION: The age at which a person is recognized as an adult
SIGNIFICANCE: The age of majority (generally eighteen) sets the standard for when individuals are held responsible for their own affairs

Defining the age of majority, also known as "legal age," dates back to common law. Once individuals reach the age of majority, they are no longer considered minors and are entitled to full social and legal rights. Further, a person is legally bound and responsible for any contract or other legal partnership such as marriage in which they enter *sui juris* (of their own right). In some cases, minors have successfully petitioned the court to enter into contracts prior to reaching the age of majority.

Generally set at eighteen, the legal age can vary depending on the activity in question. For example, many states allow driving privileges at age sixteen, while the purchase and consumption of alcohol are generally forbidden until age twenty-one. Another element of obtaining legal age is acquiring voting rights. The voting age was originally set at twenty-one, but the Twenty-sixth Amendment, ratified in 1971, lowered the voting age to eighteen. Subsequently, many states lowered their legal age to coincide with federal voting regulations.

See also Contributing to the delinquency of a minor; *In loco parentis*; Juvenile delinquency; Status offense; Statutory rape.

Mala in se and mala prohibita

DEFINITION: A distinction between actions which are wrong in and of themselves and actions which are illegal because they are prohibited by law

SIGNIFICANCE: This legal principle recognizes the existence of an absolute moral law as distinguished from the relativism of pragmatic politics which fluctuates from time to time and from society to society

Mala in se is a Latin term referring to immoral acts that are wrong in and of themselves. Examples include murder, robbery, theft, burglary, and rape; these are actions which are universally condemned as evil. Historically they have been considered to be wrong in virtually every society, regardless of culture or historical period. As such they have a long history in the common law.

Mala prohibita (singular, *mala prohibitum*) refers to those things that are wrong because they have been prohibited by legislative law. Actions that are unlawful by statute are such actions as running a traffic light or failure to register one's car. These are wrong or illegal because they are prohibited by law, not because they are inherently and essentially evil.

Something that is inherently wrong can, of course, also be prohibited by law. For example, it is wrong to drive recklessly and endanger one's life and the lives of other people, but that is also legislatively illegal and a violation of motor vehicle codes. Similarly, contaminating a source of drinking water by dumping toxic materials is both immoral and illegal.

Most or all of the offenses punishable under the common law are considered *mala in se*. A basic presupposition of the common law, time-honored through the centuries, is that law and morality cannot be separated. The strongest argument for something being wrong in the eyes of the law is that it is morally wrong. Ordinary citizens are much more ready to accept the inherent wrongness of an act than they are its mere prohibition by a body of elected legislators. This fact is what gives the "oughtness" and moral strength to lawful obedience.

The laws of evidence are different in the two types of cases. *Mala in se* offenses require a consideration of motivation. One's mental state, attitude, and intention may be weighed in assessing the degree of guilt or innocence. In *mala prohibita* cases, only the factuality of whether the accused actually committed the offense is at issue. For example, where it is illegal to sell alcoholic beverages to minors, the question is whether a person did, in fact, sell those drinks to a minor. It makes no difference in the eyes of the law that the person selling them sincerely believed the person was of the proper age or even that the minor lied to the seller.

See also Common law; Criminal intent; Criminal law; Malice; Moral relativism; Natural law and natural rights; Positive law.

Malcolm X (May 19, 1925, Omaha, Neb.—Feb. 21, 1965, New York, N.Y.)

IDENTIFICATION: Black nationalist leader

SIGNIFICANCE: A Nation of Islam spokesperson and leading black militant voice in the 1950's and 1960's, Malcolm X's demands for an end to racial injustice "by any means necessary" made him a hero to many blacks and made him feared by many whites

When Malcolm X (born Malcolm Little) was six years old, his father, a Baptist minister and organizer for Marcus Garvey, was brutally murdered, presumably by a gang of racist whites. His mother eventually suffered a mental breakdown and was confined to a state mental hospital for twenty-six years. The state broke up the family; some of his brothers and sisters were raised in foster homes.

Malcolm moved from Lansing, Michigan, to Boston in 1940 to live with his sister, Ella. He earned a reputation as a street hustler. He later moved to New York City where he sold drugs to popular black musicians in 1944 and 1945 before his arrest and conviction for burglary in 1946.

He educated himself in prison and became a follower of Elijah Muhammad and the Nation of Islam (Black Muslims), a black nationalist group that encouraged black pride, self-reliance, and self-discipline. Rejecting his past, Malcolm changed his name to Malcolm X. Following his release in 1953, he moved to Detroit, where he held several menial jobs but quickly rose to the post of minister and then became the national spokesman for the Nation of Islam. The Nation of Islam encouraged blacks to separate from whites, who were considered a race of devils, and advocated the establishment of a separate black nation as the only way to remedy the plight of blacks in the United States.

After he had helped to build the Nation of Islam as a prominent force, internal jealousy led to his suspension. He eventually broke with Elijah Muhammad in 1963 after becoming disillusioned over allegations that Elijah had fathered children with his secretaries. Malcolm went on a religious pilgrimage to Mecca, Arabia, and traveled throughout Africa and the Middle East. Upon his return in 1964 he abandoned his belief that all whites were devils in order to work with all persons committed to racial justice. He also took a new name, El-Hajj Malik El-Shabazz.

Malcolm X denounced white racism and advocated black pride and self-reliance in terms strong enough to make many whites uneasy. (Library of Congress)

Malcolm X was assassinated in 1965 in New York City; although three former members of the Nation of Islam were convicted of the crime, controversy remains regarding who else may have been involved. Malcolm X's ideas greatly influenced the black power movement of the 1960's and 1970's. The 1990's witnessed a renewed interest in Malcolm X, encouraged by Spike Lee's *Malcolm X* film in 1992. Malcolm X's 1965 autobiography, *Autobiography of Malcolm X*, written with Alex Haley, appeared on *The New York Times* bestseller list in 1992.

See also Muhammad, Elijah; Nation of Islam.

Malfeasance, misfeasance, and nonfeasance

DEFINITION: Malfeasance is the performance of an unlawful act; misfeasance is the improper performance of a lawful act; nonfeasance is the failure to perform a lawful act

SIGNIFICANCE: The commission of these acts undermines public confidence in the justice system and its officials

Malfeasance, misfeasance, and nonfeasance are the wrongful actions of those in public office, whether the person is hired, elected, appointed, or an officer of the court. They are acts of misconduct.

Malfeasance is the performance of a totally unlawful act which has no authority of law. It is the wrongful deed of the person performing the action, even if that act was contracted for or instigated by a third party. The embezzlement of public monies is an example of malfeasance.

Often confused with malfeasance, misfeasance is the improper, wrongful commission of what is otherwise a lawful act. It is an action which may infringe upon the rights of a third party. Issuing a traffic ticket for a lesser offense than that committed is misfeasance.

Nonfeasance is dereliction of duty. It is the total failure to perform a lawful act (which may have been contracted or requested by a third party). It must be a substantial omission for which there is no adequate excuse. Failing to arrest someone in the act of committing a crime is nonfeasance.

Although closely related, malfeasance, misfeasance, and nonfeasance are separate and distinct actions, and each may be committed separately from the others. Because they are so closely allied, however, they may also be part of the same, single act, as in the following example. A lawyer is hired to represent the estate of a decedent. In such cases, the lawyer has contracted with the fiduciary of that estate to perform certain acts, including rendering an accurate account of the monies received by the estate and the expenditures made. That written account must be presented to the court. The lawyer for no apparent reason fails to do so. Upon investigation, the court finds that in addition to failing to file the proper account, the lawyer has taken monies from the estate for personal use.

The taking of monies from the estate to which the lawyer is not entitled is theft, an unlawful act. The court may allege that the lawyer has committed malfeasance. The failure of the lawyer to file the account, the filing of which is a lawful act, is a failure to perform. The court may allege that the lawyer has committed nonfeasance. The lawyer has not performed the duties that the fiduciary expected and for which the fiduciary has contracted. The court may allege that the lawyer has committed misfeasance.

Malfeasance, misfeasance, and nonfeasance are particularly grievous crimes because they undermine the public's expectation and right to an honest system of justice and ethical officials. The commission of these crimes by anyone in the public eye casts doubt upon all officials, the majority of whom are hardworking and honest.

See also Bribery; Color of law; Embezzlement; Frankfurter, Felix; Police corruption and misconduct; Political corruption; Teapot Dome scandal.

Malice

DEFINITION: The intentional causing of harm to another, without justification or excuse

SIGNIFICANCE: Malice is an indication of the mind of the criminal and may determine with which crime a person is charged

Malice is an indication of a person's mental state, a desire to cause specific or general harm with complete disregard of the possible consequences of the action and the possible resulting harm or hurt caused to others. Malice is deliberate, not accidental, and demonstrates a lack of social duty toward others.

There are several types of malice. Express malice is a deliberate, premeditated action intending harm; implied malice is inferred from the commission of an act. At its most serious, malice is malice aforethought, the specific intent to injure or kill another individual. Malice aforethought must be present prior to the commission of a murder and indicates an awareness of the outcome of the action. It is this intention prior to the action which separates murder from manslaughter. Under common law, when such a mental state exists, murder may be committed even if it was not originally intended. Universal malice, similar to malice aforethought, is marked by a desire to take the life of any person, not a specific individual.

Malice is not only associated with a physical act. It is the intention to do harm to another by slander or libel. A person who makes a statement that he or she knows is false, or at least doubts but makes no attempt to check its accuracy, and who had the intention of causing harm to another by that statement, is guilty of malice. For example, a person who refers to another as an alcoholic in front of that person's employer, knowing or suspecting the statement to be false, is guilty of malice.

See also Competency to stand trial; Crime; Criminal; Criminal intent; Insanity defense; *Mens rea.*

Malloy v. Hogan

COURT: U.S. Supreme Court
DATE: Decided June 15, 1964
SIGNIFICANCE: The Supreme Court reversed prior decisions by holding that the privilege against self-incrimination is safeguarded by the due process clause of the Fourteenth Amendment

William Malloy was arrested during a gambling raid in Connecticut in 1959. After pleading guilty to a gambling misdemeanor he received a light jail sentence, was fined $500, and was placed on probation. Sixteen months later he was summoned to testify before a state court referee—a procedure similar to a grand jury investigation—on his gambling activities. Several questions were asked regarding the events surrounding his arrest and conviction. He refused to answer any question on the ground that to answer "may tend to incriminate me." The Superior Court held him in contempt and sentenced him to prison until he was willing to answer the questions. Malloy appealed to Connecticut's Supreme Court of Errors, which held that the Fifth Amendment's privilege against self-incrimination did not apply to state proceedings and that the Fourteenth Amendment's due process clause did not confer such a privilege. Malloy petitioned the Supreme Court for a hearing on the issue.

The Supreme Court reversed the state court's decision. Justice William J. Brennan, Jr., wrote the opinion for the majority. In it he argued that the right not to incriminate oneself is fundamental to an adversary system of justice. Therefore it is one of the rights which operate against state governments through the due process clause of the Fourteenth Amendment. Brennan held that the Fifth Amendment self-incrimination clause in its entirety limits state governments. The question in the case then became whether Malloy had in fact been asked to incriminate himself. The questions he had been asked had to do with the identity of the person or persons who employed him at the time of his gambling convictions. Connecticut was trying to find out who was in charge of the gambling operation. The state argued that Malloy was in no danger of incriminating himself: He had already been convicted and could not be tried again for the same crime. Justice Brennan's opinion argued that Malloy's answers might furnish a link in a chain of evidence which might convict him of some new crime or more recent crime, particularly if he were still connected to the person who was running the gambling operation. Because "injurious disclosure" might result, Malloy was protected by the privilege against self-incrimination.

Four members of the Court dissented in two separate dissenting opinions. Justice John M. Harlan's dissent begins by pointing out that this issue was first encountered by the Supreme Court in 1908 in *Twining v. New Jersey. Twining*, and all the Court's subsequent cases regarding the privilege against self-incrimination, left it to the states to decide the extent of the self-incrimination privilege. Harlan argued that the Court should adhere to the precedents. First, it is not absolutely clear that the right is "fundamental." It is not necessarily unfair to ask a person to give an accounting of himself or even to compel an answer by legal means. Second, the decision fastens federal criminal procedure to the states, depriving them of the ability to experiment or to establish procedures that their own citizens wish to have. Finally, Harlan argued, Malloy's commitment for contempt would have been proper even under the federal standard espoused by the majority. Even if Malloy had answered the questions he would not have incriminated himself.

Malloy v. Hogan has had an immense impact on state legal procedures. As a result of this case, states have far less power to compel witnesses to testify in grand jury or other investigatory proceedings.

See also *Adamson v. California*; Due process of law; Self-incrimination, privilege against.

Malpractice. *See* Medical malpractice

Mandamus, writ of

DEFINITION: An order issued by a superior court to a lower court, official, corporation, or person directing the recipient to perform some official duty or to restore to some party rights or privileges of which the party has been improperly deprived
SIGNIFICANCE: The writ of *mandamus* is used most commonly by a superior court to correct an abuse of power by a lower court

The writ of *mandamus* is an extraordinary order, providing a drastic remedy for unusual circumstances. It is a writ of great antiquity, intended to provide a remedy when normal judicial proceedings did not provide one. In more recent times, the writ is provided for in most jurisdictions by either a constitution, statute, or rule and is issued where an applicant for the writ has a legal right to some action and the court or officer to whom the writ is directed has a legal duty whose performance is ordered. The writ of *mandamus* is used, for example, by a superior court to respond to unauthorized actions by a lower court whose effect, if not corrected, would be to deprive the superior court of jurisdiction in a particular case.

See also Appellate process; Civil procedure; Criminal procedure; Judicial system, U.S.

Mandatory sentencing laws

DEFINITION: Laws that impose certain specific sentences for certain crimes that judges are not allowed to change

SIGNIFICANCE: Mandatory sentencing laws are intended to reduce disparities in sentencing and dictate appropriate punishments, but they do not always have the desired effect

In the American colonial era, legislatures fixed the sentences for most criminal offenses, and courts enjoyed little flexibility in sentencing defendants. In the nineteenth century, however, legislatures relaxed their hold on sentencing, allowing trial courts to impose sentences based on the circumstances of the situation. Renewed interest in mandatory sentencing appeared in the early 1970's, when state legislatures began enacting a variety of mandatory sentencing programs for felony prosecutions. Federal mandatory sentencing guidelines were enacted in 1987, and by 1991 they were being applied to more than 75 percent of federal criminal defendants. Some states have also experimented with mandatory sentencing for misdemeanors.

Mandatory sentencing laws take a variety of forms, but all seek to narrow the scope of discretion exercised by the trial court in imposing sentence on the defendant. The principal goals of mandatory sentencing laws are to eliminate unwarranted disparity in the sentences imposed on similarly situated defendants, to impose appropriate punishments for particular crimes, and to ensure consistent punishment for similar crimes. Some states, such as California, prescribe a sentence for each offense, the imposition of which may be rebutted only by a showing of specified factors. Other states, like the federal mandatory sentencing rules, require judges to follow guidelines that enumerate a number of relevant characteristics of the defendant and the crime. In these systems, courts weigh the aggravating and mitigating circumstances of the offense. Both these types of mandatory sentencing systems may also involve "minimum" sentences as well as enhanced sentences for particular crimes, for crimes committed within a particular context (with a child victim, for example), or for a certain number of convictions of a particular type of crime. The best-known example of this third type are "three strikes" laws, in which the third conviction for a felony results in a mandatory and lengthy prison term.

Mandatory sentencing laws, though popular with citizens and legislatures, are controversial. They are criticized as excessively rigid and technical, time-consuming to apply, and overly harsh in effect. Perhaps the most serious criticism is that the guidelines fundamentally change the balance of power between prosecutors and defendants. It is universally recognized that the criminal justice system relies on the vast majority of cases never going to a full trial, but instead being resolved through plea bargaining. A prosecutor and defense attorney may avoid the imposition of a mandatory sentence by avoiding trial and negotiating a plea, and the specter of mandatory sentencing may increase the prosecutor's ability to influence a criminal defendant to accept a plea bargain.

A related criticism is that, in systems where a specified number of felonies results in a lengthy sentence, defendants facing that sentence have no incentive to plead guilty to a felony: It makes more sense to go to trial and take their chances on an acquittal. When the resulting heavy burden of cases taxes prosecutorial and judicial resources beyond their limits, a prosecutor may be more willing to charge a defendant with a lesser crime in the hope of generating a plea bargain. As a result, two different defendants could receive very different sentences for the same conduct, depending on whether the defendant accepted a plea bargain. Thus, the disparity in sentencing that mandatory sentencing laws are enacted to eliminate reappears in the process of plea bargaining.

See also Criminal justice system; Discretion; Plea bargaining; Sentencing; Sentencing guidelines, U.S.; United States Sentencing Commission.

Manhattan Bail Project

DATE: Established 1958

SIGNIFICANCE: The Manhattan Bail Project sought to gather data and establish effective guidelines for the granting of bail

Established in 1958, the Manhattan Bail Project operated under the auspices of the philanthropic Vera Foundation. Under the direction of Herbert Sturtz, New York City law students developed a system for the rapid collection of information regarding an arrested person's residential stability, employment history, family situation, prior criminal record, and other relevant topics. Using a point system to estimate the arrestee's reliability, the project leaders would then recommend whether or not the offender should be granted bail.

The project found that fewer than 1 percent of all defendants released on bail failed to appear for trial. Although the study proved to be statistically flawed, the Department of Justice incorporated the project's results into its recommendations on bail reform.

See also Bail system; Criminal justice system; Criminal procedure; Preventive detention.

Mann Act

DATE: Enacted June 25, 1910

DEFINITION: The Mann Act, officially designated the White Slave Traffic Act, prohibits the interstate transportation of women for immoral purposes

SIGNIFICANCE: The Mann Act was the first national legislation specifically to outlaw sexually oriented activities considered immoral and detrimental to the public welfare

Prostitution in the United States is as old as the country. Until the Mann Act, it was regulated by state statutes that generally prohibited the practice. Enforcement, however, was universally lax. The powerful men who controlled the syndicates that owned many of the brothels and controlled the women who worked in them had the political influence it took to protect their operations even though laws existed in virtually every state that specifically prohibited illicit sexual enterprises.

Vigorous enforcement of antiprostitution laws generally occurred only after vice commissions or outraged citizens' groups, often religiously oriented, raised a loud outcry against prostitution in their communities. Enforcement stepped up when such outcries arose, then died down quickly and continued to be sporadic. Many law enforcement officials across the nation grew wealthy from the bribes they accepted from those who controlled prostitution.

Beginning in the reform era of the 1890's and continuing into the early 1900's, however, sensational reports began to surface about the widespread existence of "white slavery," the name given to the transportation of women from depressed rural areas to large cities, where they were forced into prostitution.

Such reports alarmed a public that had already been shocked by Stephen Crane's *Maggie: A Girl of the Streets* (1896) and Theodore Dreiser's *Sister Carrie* (1900), two influential novels that drew widespread attention to prostitution and aroused strong public sentiment against it. Lincoln Steffens' *The Shame of the Cities* (1904), which focused attention on the corruption that pervaded most major American cities of that period, also aroused the public.

At this time, it must be remembered, the many women's suffrage groups actively crusading to gain the franchise for women were focusing considerable attention upon women's rights. Also active in the 1890's and early 1900's were temperance groups, most of them dominated by women, who were calling for a constitutional amendment that would prohibit the sale of alcoholic beverages in the United States. Members of these groups, most notably members of the Anti-Saloon League, founded in 1893, were active in calling for strict enforcement of antiprostitution statutes.

Responding to public sentiment and, assuredly, with an eye toward furthering his own political ambitions, James Robert Mann, U.S. Representative from Illinois, introduced legislation in 1910 that would ban the interstate transportation of women for immoral purposes. This legislation, which Congress passed on June 25, initially imposed a fine of up to five thousand dollars and a prison term of up to five years, or both, upon those who violated this law. These penalties were doubled if the victims were minors.

See also Adultery; Commercialized vice; Comstock Law; Temperance movement; Victimless crimes.

Manslaughter
DEFINITION: A crime of homicide, distinct from murder, involving no premeditation or malice aforethought but some degree of culpability

SIGNIFICANCE: Manslaughter, sometimes used as a lesser charge in plea bargaining, is a catch-all category for homicides ranging from those provoked by the victim to those resulting from negligence

Most current homicide laws preserve the traditional common-law distinction between voluntary and involuntary manslaughter, even if those explicit terms are not used. Voluntary manslaughter, the more serious offense, involves willful homicide. Involuntary manslaughter, the lesser offense, involves unintended but negligent homicide not wholly accidental or inadvertent.

Voluntary manslaughter is distinguished from murder in that it involves no premeditated intent to kill. There are usually mitigating circumstances that to some extent excuse the crime. There must be provocation by the victim—some act that could motivate an "ordinary, reasonable person" to react with violence before a "cooling-off period" could lead to rational self-control. Typically, homicides committed in fear, anger, or other circumstances of "diminished capacity" are interpreted as voluntary manslaughter. Examples might be the killing of a physically abusive person or a spouse caught in a flagrant act of adultery.

Involuntary manslaughter is an unintended homicide that involves a degree of culpable behavior. It is normally distinguished from an unintended homicide that occurs in the commission of a felony, such as burglary or armed robbery. It must, however, involve willful negligence, whether unlawful or not. It is committed under circumstances that put the victim at risk. An example is the unintended death of a victim of corporal punishment or hazing.

In some states there is a distinction between "criminal-negligence manslaughter" and "unlawful-act manslaughter," a more serious offense. Unlawful-act manslaughter occurs when death results during the commission of a misdemeanor. Criminal-negligence manslaughter occurs when there is "gross negligence" involved but no actual crime. There may be, however, a dereliction of duty or inordinate risks involved. A standard variety of criminally negligent manslaughter is vehicular homicide.

In voluntary manslaughter cases, distinguishing between reasonable and unreasonable provocation has proved a sticking point. As a rule, if a victim's threats are only verbal or are restricted to mild physical aggression, such as pushing and shoving, courts have found the provocation unreasonable. With increasing frequency, however, courts have occasionally ruled that threats alone are sufficient provocation in cases in which the victim has a history of violent behavior, as in repeated spousal abuse. Another problem involves an interpretation of what constitutes rational behavior and appropriate cooling-off periods. These concepts invite subjective interpretation and have led to complaints of arbitrary or inequitable applications of homicide statutes.

Under the provisions of the Model Penal Code, manslaughter is either a second-degree or third-degree felony, reflecting the residual distinction between voluntary and involuntary manslaughter. The penalty in most instances of voluntary manslaughter, the second-degree felony, is imprisonment. Manslaughter describes a broad category of homicides, however, and in involuntary manslaughter cases in which only minor negligence is involved, courts have reduced penalties to suspended sentences, community service, or even light fines.

See also Criminal intent; *Mens rea*; Murder and homicide; Negligence; Plea bargaining; Self-defense.

Mapp v. Ohio

COURT: U.S. Supreme Court

DATE: Decided June 19, 1961

SIGNIFICANCE: The Court required that illegally obtained evidence must be excluded from criminal trials in state courts, a rule that previously had been applied to federal trials in 1914

In 1957, Cleveland police officers went to the home of Dollree Mapp, acting on information that a suspect in a recent bombing and related paraphernalia were located in her home. After Mapp refused to admit them, the officers forcibly entered, conducted a widespread search of the house, and discovered some illegal pornography. Mapp was arrested and convicted of violating Ohio's antiobscenity statute. Unable to demonstrate that the officers had possessed a valid search warrant, the state of Ohio argued that even if the search had been illegal, precedents of the U.S. Supreme Court did not forbid the admission of the resulting evidence in a state trial.

For many years the Supreme Court had been debating the issue of the so-called exclusionary rule. Earlier in the century, in *Weeks v. United States* (1914), the Court had required that illegally obtained evidence be excluded from federal prosecutions. Thirty-five years later, in *Wolf v. Colorado* (1949), the Supreme Court applied the Fourth Amendment right of privacy to the states through the due process clause of the Fourteenth Amendment, but the Court decided against imposing the exclusionary rule as an essential element of that right. By 1961, nevertheless, about half the states had adopted the *Weeks* rule.

In *Mapp v. Ohio*, the Court ruled 5-3 to make the exclusionary rule binding on the states. In the majority opinion, Justice Tom Clark declared that the rule was "an essential part" of the constitutional rights of individuals, but he also pointed to the rule's deterrence as a justification for the decision. Experience demonstrated, he wrote, that other remedies were "worthless and futile" in preventing officials from disobeying the prohibition against unreasonable searches and seizures.

Three members of the Court were opposed to overruling the *Wolf* precedent. They objected that the briefs and oral arguments of the case had dealt more with the obscenity issue than with the exclusionary rule, but even more, they insisted that the principle of federalism should allow states to have flexibility in devising alternative remedies to deter unreasonable searches and seizures. Justice Potter Stewart wanted to decide the case on the basis of the First Amendment and refused to join with either the majority or the minority.

The *Mapp* decision, a landmark of the Warren Court years, has been one of the most controversial opinions ever rendered by the Supreme Court. Since most criminal prosecutions take place in state courts, the decision's impact was much greater than that of *Weeks*. Many state officials resented *Mapp* as an intrusion into the traditional prerogatives of the states, and members of the public had difficulty understanding why there were not other means to enforce the right to privacy implicit in the Fourth Amendment. In later cases such as *Massachusetts v. Sheppard* (1984), the majority of justices of the Court have accepted the deterrent rationale for the exclusionary rule, and this has resulted in flexibility in its application.

See also *Escobedo v. Illinois*; Evidence, rules of; *Illinois v. Krull*; *Leon, United States v.*; *Massachusetts v. Sheppard*; Search and seizure; *Terry v. Ohio*; *Weeks v. United States*; *Wolf v. Colorado*.

Marbury v. Madison

DATE: Decided February 24, 1803

SIGNIFICANCE: In this case, the Supreme Court for the first time exercised the power of judicial review to invalidate an act of Congress

This case evolved out of the political conflict between the Federalist Party, which had controlled the government since the Constitution had been ratified, and the new Democratic-Republican party headed by Thomas Jefferson. The Federalists favored a strong national government, including the power of the federal courts to interpret the Constitution, while Jefferson and his party supported the idea that state legislatures, not the courts, should have the final say in disputes centering on the meaning of the Constitution.

The Midnight Appointments. In the elections of 1800, Jefferson not only defeated President John Adams but also carried a Democratic-Republican majority into Congress on his electoral coattails. Adams and his fellow Federalists were horrified; they considered Jefferson and his political followers dangerous radicals. Adams was still president, however, and the Federalists still controlled Congress, so they decided to take advantage of the time prior to Jefferson's inauguration to place as many judges in the federal court system as possible.

Since Article III, section 1 of the Constitution says that federal judges "shall hold their Offices during good Behavior," they had every reason to believe that these would be lifelong appointments. When the new justices were in place, the Federalists hoped they could be relied upon to check the worst consequences of the Democratic-Republican takeover until the Federalists made a political comeback.

Adams immediately began to appoint dozens of new justices. On March 3, 1803, the day before Jefferson was to take the oath of office, he worked into the night signing the last of what became known as his "midnight appointments." He then handed them over to his secretary of state, John Marshall, for delivery. The more important of the commissions were delivered without mishap. Possibly because Marshall, whom on January 27 Adams had appointed chief justice of the United States, was preoccupied preparing for the events of the next day when he would administer the oath of office to the new president, or perhaps because of an oversight on the part of a clerk, seventeen minor commissions were left for the incoming secretary of state, James Madison, to deliver. Upon assuming office, however, Jefferson, angered by the last-minute attempt to "pack" the federal judiciary with Federalist justices, ordered Madison not to deliver the commissions.

New president Thomas Jefferson told his secretary of state, James Madison (above), not to deliver judicial commissions to William Marbury and sixteen others. (Library of Congress)

One of the midnight appointees who did not receive a commission was William Marbury. Adams had appointed Marbury justice of the peace for the District of Columbia. The forty-one-year-old Marbury, a little-known aide to the first secretary of the navy, was a staunch Federalist. In an attempt to acquire his commission and, at the same time, strike a blow at Jefferson and the Democratic-Republicans, he sought redress before the Supreme Court. Specifically, Marbury asked the Court to issue a writ of *mandamus* to force Madison to deliver his appointment. A writ of *mandamus* is a court order directing a government official to perform an act required by law, and it was Marbury's contention that Section 13 of the Judiciary Act of 1789 granted the Supreme Court the authority to issue such writs. The stage was set for one of the most momentous Supreme Court decisions of all time.

Marshall's Dilemma. Marshall, the man who had failed to deliver Marbury's appointment and was now chief justice, seemed to be faced with two equally unpalatable alternatives. The Supreme Court, at that time, had nowhere near the power and prestige that it would later acquire, and Marshall had every reason to believe that Jefferson would defy an order to deliver Marbury's commission. He also knew that with no military or police at its disposal, the Court would be helpless in the face of such noncompliance. On the other hand, if he failed to issue the writ, the damage to the Court's prestige could be irrevocable. It would appear as if he was caving in to the Democratic-Republicans and would add credence to their belief that the courts had no power to intrude on the executive branch.

Marshall's Opinion. To no one's astonishment, the Court's unanimous decision, written by Marshall, held that Congress had authorized the Supreme Court to issue writs of *mandamus* in Section 13 of the Judiciary Act of 1789. Therefore, Marshall declared, under this provision of the law Marbury was entitled to his commission. Then he shocked both his Federalist allies and their political opponents by declaring Section 13 unconstitutional.

When Congress passed Section 13, according to Marshall, it had overreached its constitutional authority by adding to the Court's original jurisdiction, which Article III, section 2 of the Constitution specifically restricts to cases involving ambassadors, foreign ministers, and states. In one bold stroke, he avoided weakening the Court by rendering a decision that Jefferson would in all likelihood ignore and, at the same time, chastised the Democratic-Republicans by establishing the power of the Court to declare a federal law invalid. Judicial review—the power of the Court to declare a congressional act unconstitutional—is not mentioned anywhere in the Constitution, but by declaring Section 13 unconstitutional Marshall set the precedent for judicial review and established the Supreme Court as a coequal branch of government.

—*Thomas J. Mortillaro*

See also Federalist Party; Jeffersonian Republican Party; Judicial review; Judiciary Acts; *Mandamus*, writ of; Marshall, John.

BIBLIOGRAPHY

An accessible overview of *Marbury* is John A. Garraty, "The Case of the Missing Commissions," in John A. Garraty, ed., *Quarrels That Have Shaped the Constitution* (rev. ed. New York: Harper & Row, 1987). Albert J. Beveridge, *The Life of John Marshall* (Boston: Houghton Mifflin, 1916), provides historical context. Concerning judicial review, Charles A. Beard, *The Supreme Court and the Constitution* (Englewood Cliffs, N.J.: Prentice-Hall, 1938), explains its origins; John Hart Ely, *Democracy and Distrust: A Theory of Judicial Review* (Cambridge, Mass.: Harvard University Press, 1980), discusses its modern applications; and Jesse H. Choper, *Judicial Review and the National Political Process* (Chicago: University of Chicago Press, 1980), examines its pros and cons.

Marijuana Tax Act

DATE: Enacted August 2, 1937

DEFINITION: An occupational excise tax imposed on everyone involved with producing, processing, trading, or using the various products of the hemp plant

SIGNIFICANCE: With the Marijuana Tax Act, the federal government set out to suppress illicit uses of the hemp plant while not disrupting its industrial or medicinal uses

Harry J. Anslinger, commissioner of narcotics of the Federal Bureau of Narcotics of the U.S. Treasury Department, drafted the proposal for the Marijuana Tax Act. On April 14, 1937, Representative Robert L. Doughton (North Carolina) introduced the bill, which was designed to control the trade in marijuana and suppress illicit use of the substance. Anybody involved with handling the plant or its products was to obtain a license and register with the Internal Revenue Service. Taxes on the handling of marijuana would range from one to twenty-four dollars. In response to criticism from hemp producers, their tax was reduced from five dollars in the original bill to one dollar in the final act. Hemp producers believed that the higher tax would have forced small growers out of business.

See also Comprehensive Drug Abuse Prevention and Control Act of 1970; Drug legalization debate; Drug use and sale, illegal; Harrison Narcotic Drug Act.

Marshall, John (Sept. 24, 1755, Germantown [now Midland], Va.—July 6, 1835, Philadelphia, Pa.)

IDENTIFICATION: Chief justice of the United States, 1801-1835

SIGNIFICANCE: Widely regarded as the greatest chief justice the Court has ever known, Marshall was responsible for consolidating the Court's power, making it into an instrument of American federalism

John Marshall's ardent federalism first became public knowledge at the 1788 Virginia convention to ratify the Constitution. President George Washington, a family friend, offered Marshall a series of government posts, all of which Marshall refused until 1797, when he accepted an offer to become a special envoy to France. In that role Marshall achieved acclaim for his public chastisement of French agents who had tried to bribe the American government in the "XYZ Affair."

As a member of the House of Representatives, he successfully defended the administration of President John Adams against Republican charges that it had surrendered Thomas Nash, a murderer masquerading as an American sailor, to the British for trial. In 1800, a grateful Adams named Marshall secretary of state and, the next year, chief justice of the United States.

Marshall briefly served in both roles simultaneously, but soon his judicial responsibilities became all-consuming. In 1801, the Republican Thomas Jefferson, Marshall's distant cousin and arch antagonist, assumed the presidency, and Marshall had to devote his energies to resisting Jefferson's attempts to diminish the power of the Supreme Court. He did so through such means as persuading his fellow justices to abandon the practice of delivering serial opinions in favor of speaking through one voice—usually his own. He also worked very hard: During his thirty-four years as chief justice, he wrote roughly half the 1,106 opinions issued by the Court.

One of the earliest and most lasting expressions of Marshall's judicial philosophy was *Marbury v. Madison* (1803), which was the Court's first clear expression of its power of judicial review: the authority to determine constitutional issues involving the states and other branches of the federal government. Later opinions authored by Marshall expanded this power, while others reinforced the strength of the entire national government through broad readings of such sections of the Constitution as the "necessary and proper" clause, endowing Congress with the capacity to create substantive laws enabling it to exercise powers already enumerated in the Constitution, and the commerce clause, granting federal government the power regulate commerce with foreign nations and between the states. In decisions such as *Dartmouth College v. Woodward* (1819), Marshall employed the law to protect private property and promote the growth of American business by providing corporations with a stable investment environment.

The theme running through most of Marshall's opinions is the separation between the states and the federal government, with Marshall favoring curtailment of the powers claimed by the states. In the last decade he presided over the Court, he was confronted with the increasing power of the states' rights movement and the election of its champion, Andrew Jackson, as president. By that time, however, he had irrevocably suc-

Chief justice from 1801 to 1835, John Marshall established the Supreme Court's power of judicial review. (Rembrandt Peale, collection of the Supreme Court of the United States)

ceeded in changing the status of the Court, fashioning it into the ultimate explicator of the Constitution.

See also Advisory opinion; *Barron v. Baltimore*; Constitutional law; *Dartmouth College v. Woodward*; Federalism; *Fletcher v. Peck*; Judicial review; *Marbury v. Madison*; *Ogden v. Saunders*; Supreme Court of the United States.

Marshall, Thurgood (July 2, 1908, Baltimore, Md.— Jan. 24, 1993, Bethesda, Md.)

IDENTIFICATION: Civil rights attorney and Supreme Court justice

SIGNIFICANCE: Thurgood Marshall was a prominent civil rights attorney for the National Association for the Advancement of Colored People (NAACP); he was also the first African American U.S. Supreme Court justice

Thurgood Marshall was the son of a schoolteacher and Pullman train porter. He attended an all-black college, Lincoln

Thurgood Marshall in 1958, when he was an NAACP attorney, arriving at the Supreme Court to file papers in the Little Rock school integration case. (AP/Wide World Photos)

University, in Chester, Pennsylvania, where he developed a reputation for excellence as a debater. After graduation in 1930, he was accepted to Howard University Law School in Washington, D.C., and was graduated first in his class in 1933.

Marshall has been nicknamed "Mr. Civil Rights" because of his dedication to and preeminence in the field. Marshall became a litigator for the NAACP following graduation from law school, working first with the Baltimore branch, then with the national legal staff. In 1938, he became chief legal officer for the NAACP. In 1940, the NAACP established the Legal Defense and Educational Fund (LDF), the legal arm of NAACP. Marshall was appointed as the fund's director and counsel.

In his twenty years with the NAACP, Marshall led efforts to topple racial segregation in all of its dimensions—in housing, public accommodations, voting, and education. The LDF's litigation strategy was to erode the doctrine steadily by bringing cases which challenged the underpinnings of the "separate but equal" doctrine established in the case of *Plessy v. Ferguson* (1896). In case after case, the LDF chiseled away at the edifice of segregation. Its ultimate goal was to overturn the doctrine of separate but equal.

Marshall was chief counsel in the landmark case *Brown v. Board of Education* (1954). In this case, the Supreme Court directly overruled the separate but equal doctrine in a case involving segregation in public elementary and secondary schools. The Court reasoned that even if educational facilities were equal in terms of their tangible qualities, the very fact of separation resulted in inequality by creating feelings of inferiority in those black students attending the separate schools. In the *Brown* case, social science evidence was provided to demonstrate the impact of segregation on black students. While the dismantling of segregated school systems took many years, the impact of *Brown* on the Civil Rights movement itself was monumental.

Marshall was appointed by President John F. Kennedy to the U.S. Court of Appeals in 1961. He was selected by President Lyndon Johnson to be U.S. solicitor general in 1965. Marshall was the first African American to be appointed to this prestigious position (the U.S. government's chief advocate before the Supreme Court). Marshall himself was a prolific litigator, arguing thirty-two cases before the Supreme Court as a private attorney and as solicitor general. He won twenty-nine of those cases.

On June 13, 1967, President Johnson nominated Marshall to the Supreme Court. He was confirmed August 30, 1967, and served twenty-three years on the Court, retiring June 17, 1991. On the Court, Marshall was known as an outspoken opponent of the death penalty and as a civil libertarian. Marshall believed in the power of the courts to be the great equalizers in the area of social justice. Throughout his career, he was known as someone with firm convictions who fought tenaciously for the less powerful persons in society. In the 1970's, under a more conservative court, Marshall became known as a frequent dissenter from the more conservative legal positions of many of his colleagues.

See also *Batson v. Kentucky*; *Brown v. Board of Education*; Civil Rights movement; Jim Crow laws; National Association for the Advancement of Colored People (NAACP); National

Association for the Advancement of Colored People Legal Defense and Educational Fund; *Payne v. Tennessee*; Solicitor general of the United States; Supreme Court of the United States; *Sweatt v. Painter*.

Marshals Service, U.S.
DATE: Established 1789

SIGNIFICANCE: U.S. marshals, appointed by the president, are responsible for protecting the federal court system and implementing the orders of the federal judiciary, thereby providing executive powers to the judicial branch of government

The U.S. Marshals Service is responsible for providing support and security for federal courts, judicial officers, and trial participants and for executing court orders. The agency was created by the Judiciary Act of 1789 and is the oldest federal law-enforcement agency. The institution of "marshals" as judicial officers was brought to the United States from England. English marshals represented and enforced the king's law in England after the Norman invasion, and early in U.S. history, American federal marshals similarly represented the national government in the new states and territories. Federal marshals have perhaps been best known for their role in the settlement of the West. "Wild Bill" Hickok and Wyatt Earp served as deputy U.S. marshals for a time, and many marshals were politically influential in the new states of the West. Marshals were called upon to perform a variety of duties, most relating to law enforcement. The reason for the variety of tasks was that the Marshals Service was responsible to several agencies, including the White House and the Department of the Treasury, as well as the Department of Justice, during the 1800's. The result of the multiple masters was conflict and confusion, and as a consequence, the agency was put into the new Department of Justice and made directly responsible to the attorney general in 1861.

The marshals and their staffs operate 427 offices nationwide and provide support to federal judicial officers and courts in ninety-four federal judicial districts. The Marshals Service is responsible for protecting more than seven hundred judicial facilities in the United States and its overseas territories, almost two thousand federal judges and magistrates, and thousands of lawyers and witnesses involved in federal trials. The service operates the Federal Witness Security Program to protect witnesses testifying in federal cases. The service is also responsible for apprehending fugitives sought by federal courts and transporting federal prisoners to and from correctional facilities, as well as for maintaining custody of federal prisoners.

The director of the Marshals Service, like the attorney general, is appointed by the president. The agency has a deputy director for operations who is responsible for the law enforcement, security, witness protection, prisoner transport, and property seizure and disposal functions and a deputy director for administration who is responsible for human resource management, facilities, communications, procurement, and the operation of the U.S. Marshals Service Training Academy.

U.S. marshals are individually appointed by the president, and the political nature of the appointment has sometimes been

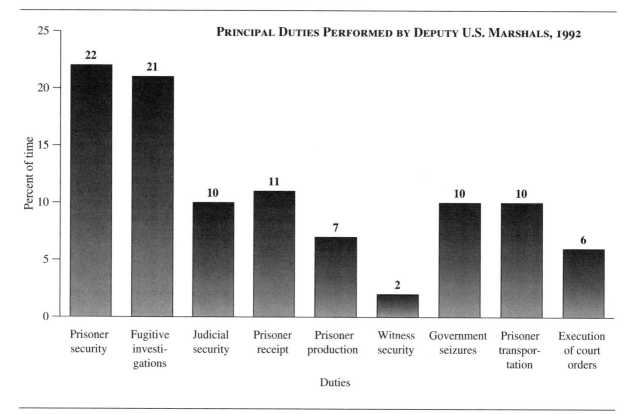

PRINCIPAL DUTIES PERFORMED BY DEPUTY U.S. MARSHALS, 1992

Source: U.S. Department of Justice, Bureau of Justice Statistics, *Sourcebook of Criminal Justice Statistics—1993.* Washington, D.C.: U.S. Government Printing Office, 1994.

very controversial. That was certainly the case early in U.S. history, when political corruption and cronyism characterized national and state politics. For many years, the U.S. Marshals Service was held in very low regard because of the perceived low quality of its personnel. That changed considerably in the late twentieth century with the increased professionalization of the agency. The reputation and effectiveness of the service have improved dramatically.

See also Federal Crimes Act; Frontier, the; Judiciary Acts; Justice, U.S. Department of; Martial law.

Martial law

DEFINITION: A temporary form of government operated by the armed forces of a country when civilian authorities cannot function in an area

SIGNIFICANCE: When martial law is declared, normal civil rights are generally suspended and the civilian population becomes subject to military law and military justice

The concept of martial law in democratic countries rests on the theory that under certain emergency conditions it may become necessary for government leaders to declare martial law and send troops into a specific area until such time as the civilian authorities can again perform the functions of government. Peacetime emergencies may include such disruptive occur-

rences as natural disasters, economic crises, insurrection (actual or threatened rebellion), and riots. During wartime, martial law may be declared in the event of invasion or in zones of military operations. Under martial law a military officer takes full command and substitutes military law and proceedings for civil laws and courts.

Authority to Declare Martial Law. In the United States, the concept of martial law has evolved. It is usually the constitutionally designated commanders in chief of either the U.S. armed forces or the individual state militias who declare martial law— that is, the president of the United States or the governor of an individual state. Exceptions, however, are to be found in history.

While virtually every state has a constitutional provision authorizing its governor to proclaim martial law, no such statement is found in the U.S. Constitution regarding presidential powers. Such authority, however, is attributed to the presidency through the implied constitutional powers granted to the chief executive, under Article II, section 2, "[t]o provide for calling forth the Militia to execute the Laws of the Union, suppress Insurrections and repel Invasions."

Historical Examples. Like many American legal practices, martial law has its basis in old English law, though it was hardly used in the colonial period because it was looked upon with disfavor by both the English Crown and the people. In fact, in America there was no real conception of martial law or its use until a military commander—General Andrew Jackson—called it into service during the Battle of New Orleans in the War of 1812. When it became evident that the United States faced extreme peril from the impending British capture of New Orleans and from the confused condition and questionable loyalty of some of the citizenry, Jackson proclaimed martial law in the zone of military operations. This early occurrence is of tremendous legal significance for several reasons: Jackson's censure over its use, his defense of the practice (which essentially defined its main characteristics as Americans would come to view it), the tremendous debate it sparked in Congress and the cabinet, and, ultimately, its tacit acknowledgment as a legitimate constitutional action.

As history demonstrates, declarations of martial law are intricately tied to the legal concept of *habeas corpus*. At the outbreak of the Civil War, President Abraham Lincoln suspended the writ of *habeas corpus* (as Andrew Jackson had done earlier) and, in essence, placed sections of the country under martial law. The question of whether the president's action was too broad came before the circuit court in *Ex parte Merryman* (1861), which decided that it was.

Since that time, there have been several declarations of martial law. It was proclaimed by Hawaii governor Joseph Poindexter on December 7, 1941, after the bombing of Pearl Harbor, and approved by President Franklin Roosevelt two days later. It has also been declared during labor disputes and violence associated with strikes. Martial law was invoked on five occasions to counter resistance to federal desegregation orders in southern states. Martial law has also been declared in response to urban rioting.

Restraints on Martial Law. In countries outside the United States, martial law is often synonymous with absolute power, but an opposite trend has developed in the United States. Even before the *Merryman* case, an important instance of martial law signaled that the judicial branch of American government leaned toward restraint and the protection of individual rights. In 1842, when agitation over reform of Rhode Island's outdated charter led to Dorr's Rebellion, the assembly and governor of that state proclaimed martial law. This action spawned an important court case, *Luther v. Borden* (1849), in which the Supreme Court officially sanctioned the use of martial law but also laid down some rules regarding the parameters of its employment.

From that time on, the Supreme Court produced a series of rulings which put restraints on the power of martial law regimes regarding their administration of justice. In 1866, *Ex parte Milligan*, the Court held that there could be no military trial of a civilian (and thus no suspension of writs of *habeas corpus*) in domestic territory when the civilian courts were open. In 1932 the Court decreed that the allowable limits of military discretion had been overstepped in a case involving the governor of Texas, who had declared that a state of insurrection existed and invoked martial law in order to enforce state restrictions on oil production and maintain existing prices. Finally, in 1946, the

Court ruled that a military court did not have jurisdiction over a civilian employee of the Honolulu Navy Yard even though martial law had been declared in Hawaii.

History teaches that martial law should be considered an emergency measure used to restore civil law and civil justice. It is constitutional but is subject to the disallowance of the civil courts, which have favored its use only with restraint. There are different forms of martial law, depending on whether the country is at war or at peace. Martial law in time of war may extend to both enemies and U.S. civilians. In time of peace martial law may be either preventive or punitive (used to respond to insurrection or rebellion). Martial law has never been intended to supplant the Constitution but rather to be used temporarily as a means to restore it to full operation.   —*Andrew C. Skinner*

See also Civil War; *Habeas corpus*; *Merryman, Ex parte*; Military justice; *Milligan, Ex parte*; Reconstruction.

BIBLIOGRAPHY

Succinct, updated, accessible resources on martial law are not abundant. The best one-volume work is probably Robert S. Rankin, *When Civil Law Fails: Martial Law and Its Legal Basis in the United States* (New York: AMS Press, 1965). See also volume 1 of Abraham D. Sofaer, *War, Foreign Affairs, and Constitutional Powers* (Cambridge, Mass.: Ballinger, 1976); Daniel Walker, ed., *Military Law* (New York: Prentice-Hall, 1954), especially chapter 13, "Martial Law and Military Government," which presents an excellent review of legal cases bearing on martial law in a democratic society; and William Whiting, *War Powers Under the Constitution of the United States* (10th ed. Glorieta, N. Mex.: Rio Grande Press, 1971). For a modern foreign (Filipino) perspective on martial law, see Jose M. Crisol, *The Armed Forces and Martial Law* (Manila: Agro Printing & Publishing House, 1980).

Marxism

DEFINITION: The political and economic theory named for Karl Marx that rejected capitalism in favor of communism

SIGNIFICANCE: Marxism challenges as unjust many ideals traditionally regarded as fundamental to American life, especially private ownership, free enterprise, and the central importance of personal freedom

Philosopher Karl Marx tried to uncover scientific laws governing societies throughout history in an effort to facilitate the creation of a more just world. According to Marx, matter is all there is (he called religion the "opiate of the masses"), and the most basic fact of human existence is physical need. To survive, people must produce food, clothing, and shelter. How this is done in any society is determined by who controls the "means of production": such things as raw materials, tools, and machinery. Societal structure determines the way classes relate to one another and how workers feel about their work.

According to Marx, humanity has passed through successive stages: a primeval commune stage, a slave era, feudalism, and capitalism; the final, ideal stage will be communism. All but the last stage include oppression and a resultant clash between classes. Marx thought that under capitalism the industrial working class is exploited by the owning class, the bourgeoisie, which makes considerable profit from goods while paying workers just enough to keep them alive and working. This abuse alienates workers from their work, themselves, their human nature, and other people. Marx predicted that the working class in industrial countries would sink into poverty, causing it to rise up and overthrow the owning class. It was inevitable, he believed, that revolutions would begin in industrial countries. He predicted an eventual classless communist utopia in which free producers would contribute all they could to society and in return would take only what they needed. The resulting abundance and lack of exploitation would eliminate the causes of crime and, internationally, the causes of war. Unneeded, the state would wither away, leaving a worldwide utopia. Marx did not foresee the twentieth century reforms of industrial capitalism that ameliorated some of its worst excesses. At least partly because of these reforms, Marxist revolutions did not sweep the industrialized world; where Marxist revolutions did occur, they were in less-developed countries.

Marxism views the capitalist United States as inherently unjust and as a force that creates global injustice and strife. As Marxism evolved under various idealists and tacticians, it challenged principles central to American society and American views of justice. It advocated dictatorship by an elite—in theory, a temporary measure—on the grounds that the masses could not soon be trusted to act in their own interests and that counterrevolutionaries threatened the realization of the communist utopia. The United States' commitment to due process and to freedom of speech, press, and religion are regarded by many Marxists as virtually worthless in the light of the more fundamental economic injustices of capitalism. Marxism considers individual rights expendable in the struggle to establish a more just (communist) society—creating the paradox of establishing a just society through otherwise unjust means. Since private ownership is seen as an expression of selfishness and a root of society's ills, the sanctity of personal property is condemned. Privacy and individuality are regarded as obstacles to the creation of a communist state. Marxists generally regard the American system as one that sanctions greed and exploitation rather than one that allows individuals to be free from pervasive government control of life and belief. Thus American protection of individual freedom is perceived as a failure of social vision.

See also Capitalism; Communist Party, American; Debs, Eugene V.; Smith Act; Socialism; Socialist Party, American.

Maryland v. Craig

COURT: U.S. Supreme Court
DATE: Decided June 27, 1990
SIGNIFICANCE: In this case, which upheld a Maryland statute permitting a child to testify via one-way, closed-circuit television, the Supreme Court determined that the witness-confrontation rights of defendants guaranteed by the Sixth Amendment are neither absolute nor an indispensable part of criminal hearings

In 1986, Sandra Ann Craig, an operator of a Maryland child-care center and kindergarten, was indicted for sexually abusing a six-year-old child in her care and was subsequently convicted. Under a state statute, the victim and other children were allowed to testify on a closed-circuit television without directly confronting the defendant. On the grounds that the law violated a defendant's right to face an accuser, guaranteed by the Sixth Amendment, Craig appealed the conviction. Although the Maryland Court of Special Appeals upheld the conviction, the next higher court, the Court of Appeals of Maryland, ordered a new trial, finding that the state prosecutors had not sufficiently justified their use of the closed-circuit television procedure. It also questioned the statute's constitutionality but did not determine it per se.

On *certiorari*, the U.S. Supreme Court vacated the lower court's order and remanded, holding that the confrontation clause of the Sixth Amendment did not invalidate the Maryland statute's procedure. Justice Sandra Day O'Connor, writing the 5-4 majority opinion, argued that under "narrow circumstances," when there are "competing interests," dispensing with witness-confrontation rights is warranted. Further, the Court stated that the term "confront" as used in the Sixth Amendment cannot be defined simply as "face-to-face." A state's concern for the psychological and physical well-being of a child abuse victim, as reflected in the Maryland statute, was deemed important enough to supersede a defendant's right to face an accuser. The majority also argued that in previous cases other Sixth Amendment rights had been interpreted "in the context of the necessities of trial and the adversary process."

A vigorous dissenting opinion, presented by Justice Antonin Scalia, argued that "confront" as used in the Sixth Amendment clearly means "face-to-face," whatever else it may also mean. The majority was also chided for distorting explicit constitutional text to suit "currently favored public policy." Although granting that the procedure authorized by the Maryland statute may be fair, the dissenters maintained that it violated the constitutional protection afforded defendants in the confrontation clause of the Sixth Amendment.

A controversial case, *Maryland v. Craig* left in its wake the likelihood of additional problems of interpretation precisely because it held a constitutional guarantee to be less than absolute and incontrovertible. Determining which "narrow circumstances" will validate a suspension of a defendant's right to a face-to-face confrontation with an accuser will be an ongoing issue in jurisprudence, because it must be decided virtually on a case-by-case basis.

See also Bill of Rights, U.S.; Child molestation; Due process of law.

Massachusetts Board of Retirement v. Murgia

COURT: U.S. Supreme Court
DATE: Decided June 25, 1976
SIGNIFICANCE: In this age discrimination case, the Court restrained extensions of previously expanded categories of discrimination and the applicability of the equal protection clause to them

Robert Murgia was a fifty-year-old uniformed officer with the Massachusetts State Police. Annual medical examinations required by the state had consistently shown him to be in excellent physical and mental health. Health notwithstanding, Murgia, like all uniformed officers, was subject to a state statute that mandated retirement on his fiftieth birthday. Murgia challenged the law, arguing that his compulsory retirement by Massachusetts discriminated against him on the basis of his age and therefore violated the equal protection clause of the U.S. Constitution's Fourteenth Amendment.

A three-judge federal district court upheld Murgia's challenge, concluding that the Massachusetts statute "lacked a rational basis in furthering any substantial state interest." The Massachusetts Board of Retirement, however, appealed to the U.S. Supreme Court, then headed by President Richard Nixon's appointee, Chief Justice Warren Burger, who had succeeded Chief Justice Earl Warren. Unlike Warren, Burger was a moderate conservative who advocated judicial restraint, in which he often was supported by Justices William Rehnquist, Lewis Powell, Byron White, and Harry Blackmun. By the mid-1970's, however, the Burger Court was in a difficult position. Through the 1960's, the Warren Court's antidiscrimination rulings had lent a literal interpretation to the equal protection clause, namely that no state should deny to any person within its jurisdiction equal protection of the laws. The clause was therefore applied to an increasing number of alleged civil rights discriminations.

This represented a significant shift for the Court. Previously the equal protection clause had been invoked almost exclusively in cases involving the civil rights of blacks. Thus the Warren Court launched so-called substantive due process and substantive equal protection. Under the Fourteenth Amendment, people's federally protected rights were also applied to violations of those rights by the states. Under Burger, the Court sought rational grounds to restrain this process by "strict judicial scrutiny." It was in this context that the Murgia appeal came before the Court.

In a 7-1 decision, the Court ruled against Murgia. It did not deny the adverse effects that premature retirement can have on individuals, nor did it suggest that the Massachusetts statute was well-drafted or wise. Rather, it decided that drawing lines that created distinctions—age, in this case—was a legislative task, that the statute was rational, and that the Massachusetts legislature had not denied Murgia equal protection of the laws. Determining the appropriate applications of substantive equal protection has continued to trouble the Supreme Court.

See also Age discrimination; Age Discrimination in Employment Act; Due process of law; Equal protection of the law.

Massachusetts v. Sheppard

COURT: U.S. Supreme Court
DATE: Decided July 5, 1984
SIGNIFICANCE: The Court ruled that, the Fourth Amendment notwithstanding, a search authorized by a defective warrant was proper because the police had acted in good faith in executing what they thought was a valid warrant

Osborne Sheppard was convicted in a Massachusetts state court of first-degree murder. Sheppard appealed his conviction to the Massachusetts Supreme Judicial Court on the basis that the police had knowingly searched his residence with a defective search warrant.

Boston police detective Peter O'Malley had drafted an affidavit to support an application for an arrest warrant and a search warrant authorizing the search of Sheppard's residence. The affidavit stated that the police wanted to search for such items as the victim's clothing and a blunt instrument that might have been used on the victim. The affidavit was reviewed and approved by the district attorney.

Unable to find a proper warrant application form, O'Malley found a previously used warrant form used in another district to search for controlled substances. After making some changes on the form, it and the affidavit were presented to a judge at his residence. The judge was made aware of the defective warrant form, and he made further changes before he signed it. He did not change the substantive portion, however, which continued to authorize a search for controlled substances, nor did the judge alter the form to incorporate the affidavit. The police believed that the warrant authorized the search, and they proceeded to act in good faith. The trial judge ruled that the exclusionary rule did not apply in this case because the conduct of the officers was objectively reasonable and largely error free. On appeal, Sheppard argued that the evidence obtained pursuant to the defective warrant should have been suppressed. The Supreme Judicial Court of Massachusetts agreed and reversed the lower court's conviction of Sheppard. The court held that it did not recognize a good-faith exception to the exclusionary rule.

Massachusetts filed a petition for writ of *certiorari*. Speaking for the U.S. Supreme Court, Justice Byron White stated that the police officers who conducted the search should not be punished. They acted in good faith in executing what they reasonably thought was a valid warrant—one that was subsequently determined invalid—issued by a detached and neutral magistrate (*United States v. Leon*, 1984). The exclusionary rule, White said, did not apply because it was adopted to deter unlawful searches by police, not to punish the errors of judges. He stated that an error of constitutional dimension may have been committed by the judge who did not make the necessary changes, but not the police. Judgment of the Supreme Judicial Court was therefore reversed and remanded for further proceedings consistent with the U.S. Supreme Court's opinion.

See also Evidence, rules of; *Leon, United States v.*; Search and seizure.

Medical and health law

DEFINITION: The field of law that addresses quality of health care and its costs, equitable access to health care, informed consent, confidentiality of medical information, and decision-making capacity
SIGNIFICANCE: Policies aimed at reforming the health care system, and tort law generally, have been proposed in order

to provide equitable access and a systematic approach to health care

Health law and medical malpractice are related yet different. Malpractice suits are filed when patients are injured allegedly because of a physician's negligence or deviation from the generally accepted standard of care. A bad result alone is not a sufficient basis for commencing a malpractice action. Rather, proof of negligence requires evidence that the physician's conduct failed to conform to that of a reasonable person acting in the same or similar circumstances.

The standard of care in the medical profession emerges from a synthesis of clinical policy, reports in the literature, scientific conferences, and peer discussions. The notion that there are variations in treatment approaches resulting from some physicians' inferior knowledge and practice limitations—the so-called locality rule—has been largely discredited, as technology and training have made medical practice national in scope. Therefore, a national standard of care is generally applied.

The general tort rule is that experts are held to the standard of their profession. That standard is normally established through testimony, both to establish the standard itself and to establish a defendant's failure to conform to the standard. In an effort to deter malpractice claims against themselves, many doctors conduct costly, unnecessary tests on their patients. This trend, commonly called "defensive medicine," significantly drives up the cost of health care.

Informed Consent. The doctrine of informed consent, recognizing that individuals have the right to be free from nonconsensual interference with their person and the right to determine what is to be done with their bodies, requires physicians to disclose all material risks, benefits, and alternatives to any proposed invasive procedure—any elements that might influence the patient's decision to undergo the procedure. Nondisclosure would be deemed the cause of the harm if a jury concluded that a reasonable person in the patient's position would have elected to forgo a procedure had certain information been disclosed. The absence of consent is grounds for an action for battery.

Patients facing major decisions, however, may well be irrational, anxiety-ridden, and biased, giving disproportionate weight to certain benefits and discrediting certain risks in the hope of gaining a certain result. Religious beliefs or social factors may also strongly influence treatment decisions. Some patients have poor memories or do not completely understand the information presented to them by physicians. Such factors complicate the process of obtaining true informed consent.

Other consent issues involve competence to consent and proxy consent. Competence necessitates that the patient understand, assimilate, and have an opportunity to question the information provided and weigh any options. Although it can be argued that generally the doctor-patient relationship is a partnership, the decision ultimately belongs to the patient.

Aimed at enhancing patient autonomy, self-determination, and well-being, the informed consent doctrine requires a decision maker with sufficient knowledge and capacity, mental and physical, to make a reasoned choice. The decision maker must be alert, recognize the importance of relevant information, and have the capacity to retrieve or remember factual material. Clearly, patients who are comatose, autistic, delusional, irrational, or mentally disabled or impaired cannot give informed consent.

Conflicting Values. Health care delivery involves a network of intersecting and overlapping issues: access, quality of care, costs, government regulation, and market competition. The equality principle holds that health care should be distributed regardless of race, gender, income, or social status. Need should dictate how care is to be allocated, and those with the greatest need should have the greatest claim on resources. That concept, however, must not be grossly distorted by providers seeking to maximize their incomes or by patients' desire to minimize their uninsured or unreimbursed costs. Distributing health care on the basis of need rather than as a commodity has been defended on the grounds that equal respect for all human beings requires an egalitarian approach to their needs, including health care. Market competition is a response to government's failure to regulate or provide health care in an equitable manner.

The notion of a "right" to essential medical care sometimes conflicts with the concept of individual liberty. The government has attempted to mediate this conflict in part through various legal mandates on hospitals, both public and private, to provide emergency care and necessary medical care for the indigent. Financing health care for one out of five Americans and representing three-quarters of all public spending for health care by the mid-1980's, Medicare and Medicaid assumed primary importance in the government's health care policy. Yet there has been ongoing controversy over their adequacy, impact, and cost. Burgeoning costs, along with the failure of President Bill Clinton and his administration to implement a national health care plan in 1994, led to a reassessment of government programs. The estimation that Medicare would deplete its resources by 2002 sparked much congressional debate and discussion about reform and the future course of health care funding.

Medical Technology. There is general agreement that the skyrocketing cost of medical care is attributable to rapidly expanding technology. There is no one method to determine when a new technology will be covered by private insurance, Medicare, or Medicaid. Cost-benefit analysis, in which the cost of a procedure is weighed against the benefit to be derived from it, is often a useful tool for determining how much should be spent on geriatric care. Cost-effectiveness analysis compares the efficiency of various means to achieve a particular goal. Its outcome, however, depends largely on the alternatives and practices considered in the comparison.

The mapping of cells in the human genome (the sequences of genes making up each human being), begun in 1990, could make traditional genetic screening obsolete. Theoretically, when the project is completed, it will be possible to identify genetic sequences for cancer, cystic fibrosis, heart disease, manic depression, and intelligence, and to manipulate genes governing such characteristics as race, eye color, and height. The most practical way to use the new technology is in genetic screening, but there is much disagreement over what to do with unfavorable prognoses. Advocates of genetic engineering tout its useful properties to cure disease, while its opponents fear that altering human genes is "playing God." —*Marcia J. Weiss*

See also Acquired immune deficiency syndrome (AIDS); *Cruzan v. Director, Missouri Department of Health*; Family Medical Leave Act; Food and Drug Administration (FDA); Forensic science and medicine; Insurance law; Medical malpractice; Negligence; Suicide and euthanasia.

BIBLIOGRAPHY

Malpractice issues are taken up in Frank M. McClellan, *Medical Malpractice: Law, Tactics, and Ethics* (Philadelphia: Temple University Press, 1994); Mark A. Hall and Ira Mark Ellman, *Health Care Law and Ethics in a Nutshell* (St. Paul, Minn.: West, 1990); and Joseph H. King, Jr., *The Law of Medical Malpractice in a Nutshell* (St. Paul, Minn.: West, 1977). Becky Cox White, *Competence to Consent* (Washington, D.C.: Georgetown University Press, 1994), examines questions of competence and informed consent. Edward P. Richards and Katharine C. Rathbun, *Law and the Physician: A Practical Guide* (Boston: Little, Brown, 1993), surveys a number of issues in the field.

Medical examiner

DEFINITION: A physician certified to conduct autopsies

SIGNIFICANCE: Through an autopsy, a medical examiner can determine the cause of death and provide evidence to help police in their investigation

A medical examiner is an employee of a municipality. Unlike a coroner, who is usually elected to the position, a medical examiner is appointed either by the chief official of a municipality or by a commission.

To be certified as a medical examiner, a person must be a graduate of an accredited four-year college, attend an accredited medical school, receive the degree of Doctor of Medicine, and spend five years as a resident in general pathology and forensic pathology. At the end of this residency, the doctor must pass a national examination and be recognized as a diplomate by the American Board of Pathology. The doctor also may be certified by the American Board of Pathology in general pathology. In addition, the medical examiner may be trained in the law, particularly as it affects forensic medicine; however, legal training is not a requirement.

The functions of medical examiner and coroner may overlap. In some municipalities, both offices are held by one person, although they may also be separate and distinct duties. When the duties are separate, the coroner has the power to

The medical examiner, a physician and certified pathologist, is qualified to examine evidence and perform autopsies in order to determine time and cause of death. (James L. Shaffer)

order an autopsy but not necessarily the qualifications to perform one. A medical examiner cannot order an autopsy but has the expertise to conduct one.

A medical examiner may be characterized as a detective who, using evidence gathered from internal and external examination of a body, plus evidence gathered where the body was found, tries to determine how and approximately when death occurred. The evidence gathered at the scene of the death can aid the medical examiner in determining whether death actually occurred where the body was found. This evidence is presented to the coroner and the coroner's jury, who render a formal verdict.

Information gathered by medical examiners over the course of many years has been collated to show how general facial and body characteristics correspond with age, sex, and nationality. A medical artist can use such information to draw a likeness of the person based upon these general characteristics and any specific facts provided by the medical examiner. These renderings have proved to be extremely accurate.

The first medical examiner may have been the physician Antisius, who determined that, of the twenty-three dagger wounds inflicted upon Julius Caesar, the fatal thrust was one that perforated his thorax.

See also Autopsy; Coroner; Forensic science and medicine; Murder and homicide.

Medical malpractice

DEFINITION: Certain acts by doctors, nurses, or other medical personnel that result in iatrogenic injury—injury that is a result of medical care—or to the death of a patient; such acts include dereliction of professional duties and failure to exercise an acceptable degree of professional skill or care

SIGNIFICANCE: The costs of medical malpractice insurance and litigation are often said to be significant factors in the increasing cost of medical care as well as a reason for some physicians choosing to leave the practice of medicine or the practice of high-risk specialties

The medical services market is very different from the market for other services or products. A situation of "asymmetrical information" exists, in which it is assumed that the health care professional knows what to do and the patient does not. The average patient (medical "consumer") does not have the background knowledge to question this assumption or the actions of a physician. The patient therefore finds it very difficult, if not impossible, to evaluate meaningfully a physician's skills or the quality of medical care received. The "product" produced in medical treatment is not a mass-produced, homogenous good; rather, medical treatment is a patient-specific service.

The Medical Malpractice System. The current system for addressing the problem of medical malpractice in the United States is a tort system. In order for the plaintiff to prevail in a medical malpractice suit, the patient must demonstrate that an iatrogenic injury (an injury that is the result of medical care) was the result of a physician's failure to take "due care." A physician has the legal duty to provide the patient with a "standard of care," which may be defined as the "customary practice of physicians in good standing with the profession, or a significant minority of such physicians."

There has been considerable debate regarding whether the current medical malpractice tort system is efficient and effective. Is the current system cost-effective, for example? If the current system is intended simply to compensate victims of injury, it is very inefficient. The compensation offered by the tort system is arbitrary, unpredictable, and often unfair. Some claims are overcompensated, while other valid claims receive little or no compensation. The course and results of legal proceedings are uncertain. One cannot help but conclude that there is an element of chance (some have compared it to a lottery) in the tort system. The overhead costs and litigation costs together consume 55 percent of all malpractice premium dollars, leaving only 45 percent to compensate victims of injury. (The comparable overhead cost of large health and disability plans is around 20 percent.)

Studies of the Malpractice System. Empirical studies of medical malpractice and malpractice suits are particularly difficult to conduct, because the data used in such studies were collected for other purposes and tend to be rather old. The very lengthy litigation process involved in medical malpractice means that studies often must use data that are a decade or more old to allow for a closure of the legal process.

Both the number of medical malpractice suits and the dollar value of awards have risen significantly. Between 1975 and 1985, malpractice claims increased at about 10 percent per year per hundred physicians. The dollar value of out-of-court settlements and jury awards increased twice as fast as the Consumer Price Index. During the five-year period from 1985 to 1989, the dollar value of claims stabilized, even though there had not been any fundamental changes in basic common-law rules governing medical malpractice suits.

While high monetary awards can increase the potential value of even marginal claims, changes in the legal or medical environment as such do not seem to explain the growth of malpractice litigation. Changes have been small, subtle, and numerous. Subtle changes in case law and the rules of evidence, for example, have reduced the cost of a medical malpractice suit. Moreover, it is probably easier now than it was in the past for a patient to establish a cause for action and to get a claim to a jury. The fact that the current system permits contingency fees—in which the lawyer gets a portion of the settlement or court award if he or she wins—is often said to be a major factor in the rapid growth of medical malpractice suits. Yet neither Canada nor the United Kingdom permits contingency fees, and claims for medical malpractice there have grown at approximately the same rate as in the United States.

In two extensive studies, legal medical experts who studied hospital records concluded that many valid claims for malpractice are never made. Two studies that were reported in the November 23-30, 1994, issue of the *Journal of the American Medical Association* attempted to determine what factors would trigger a malpractice claim. The studies examined the quality of medical care—in this case, obstetrical care—and physicians' interpersonal communication skills. Obstetrics is a high-risk specialty for malpractice claims. Medical charts were reviewed to assess the quality of medical care; no correlation could be found between the quality of medical care and the physician's claim history. The studies did indicate, however, that physician-patient communication was a critical factor. A patient who believed that her physician was concerned about her and took the time to discuss treatment options was much less likely to be sued. The patients of physicians who had frequent prior claims were significantly less satisfied than were the patients of physicians who had no claims. The patients of the physicians with frequent claim histories indicated that the physicians spent little time with them, that the physicians did not give them adequate explanations or advice, and that they felt as though they were being rushed or ignored. Both verbal and nonverbal communications—once called the physician's "bedside manner"—are apparently extremely important to patients.

Studies indicate that the high cost of medical malpractice insurance is passed on to patients in the form of higher fees rather quickly. Higher premiums for malpractice insurance seem to have little measurable effect on physicians' net incomes. Furthermore, contrary to some suggestions, doctors do not seem to choose to leave, or to avoid practice in, states where the malpractice environment has worsened relative to other states.

According to some studies most claims for medical malpractice result from performance rather than from purely judgmental issues. That is, most claims are the result of a procedure performed, often surgical, by a physician rather than the result of a diagnostic error. The evidence suggests that some injuries could be avoided if physicians simply took more time and were more careful. There is some evidence, although it is rather weak, that the current tort system may be causing physicians to spend more time per patient, a possible indication of a greater preventative effort.

Two studies have indicated that approximately 1 percent of all hospitalized patients suffer iatrogenic injuries. More than half of these injuries are the result of negligence. While most of these injuries are minor, 14 percent are fatal. Put another way, eight out of every ten thousand hospital admissions result in iatrogenic injuries that cause the death of the patient.

Conventional wisdom is that most medical malpractice involves the actions of a small number of poor-quality hospitals and a minority of incompetent physicians. A less widely recognized problem is the occasional mistake or inadvertent lapse of a normally very good physician that results in a claim. Empirical studies indicate that both these factors—incompetent care and rare lapses by competent personnel—play a role in medical malpractice claims. One interpretation of the evidence regarding lapses by otherwise highly regarded physicians is that some competent physicians may be sued because they treat cases that are medically very difficult. Another is that a relatively high frequency of claims may be the result of a large volume of patients.

Suggested Reforms. Some reformers have suggested that the current American malpractice system be replaced with a no-fault system similar to the workers' compensation system. Under workers' compensation, if a worker demonstrates that he or she was injured on the job, the worker will be compensated for actual economic loss. Workers cannot, however, be compensated for any pain and suffering.

Yet the situations that arise under workers' compensation are not always simple. While the concept of a job-related injury is well defined, the issue of occupational disease is much less clear. It can be difficult or impossible, for example, to distinguish the effects of lifestyle from the effects of occupational hazards. The problem with attempting to apply a no-fault system to medical malpractice is that it will often be very difficult to determine where the disease process ends and the iatrogenic injury begins. Virginia and Florida have instituted no-fault systems, but only for birth-related neurological injuries.

Premiums for medical malpractice insurance are somewhat puzzling when one compares them to those for other types of insurance. Malpractice insurance, for example, generally does not use an experience rating system: A physician's premiums are unrelated to his or her past experience, and the physician with a clean record pays the same insurance premium as a physician with a number of expensive liability claims. Rates are generally based on the medical specialty, the geographic location, and whether the physician performs certain high-risk procedures.

Many commercial insurance companies have withdrawn from the medical malpractice insurance market, forcing physicians to form mutual not-for-profit insurance companies to provide liability coverage. As of 1994, more than half of all malpractice insurance was being written by such mutual companies, and their loss experience has been better than that of the commercial insurance companies. Physician-owned mutual companies may have a greater ability to separate meritorious claims from spurious ones as well as the ability to recognize and avoid high-risk practitioners.

A physician's inability to obtain malpractice insurance, when such insurance is being written by physician-owned mutual companies, could represent a collective peer judgment that the physician should stop performing certain medical procedures. It may also indicate that physicians should seek additional medical training to increase their competence or should receive training in interpersonal skills to increase patients' trust in, and satisfaction with, their performance.   —*Daniel C. Falkowski*

See also Civil law; Compensatory damages; Medical and health law; Negligence; Suit; Tort; Tort reform.

BIBLIOGRAPHY

For a good treatment of "standard of care," see George J. Annas, *Standard of Care: The Law of American Bioethics* (New York: Oxford University Press, 1993), and Larry Palmer, *Law, Medicine, and Social Justice* (Louisville, Ky.: Westminster/John Knox Press, 1989). For a guide on how to handle the practical legal problems that occur in medicine, see George D. Pozgar, *Legal Aspects of Health Care Administration* (5th ed. Gaithersburg, Md.: Aspen, 1993). For a series of twenty-four professional conference papers by leading medical and legal educators, see A. Everette James, Jr., ed., *Legal Medicine with Special Reference to Diagnostic Imaging* (Baltimore, Md.: Urban and Schwarzenberg, 1980). Two studies of factors contributing to obstetrics malpractice claims are G. B. Hickson et al., "Obstetricians' Prior Malpractice Experience and Patients' Satisfaction with Care," and S. S. Entman et al., "The Relationship Between Malpractice Claims History and Subsequent Obstetric Care," both in the *Journal of the American Medical Association* 272 (November 23-30, 1994). Also see the study by Patricia M. Danzon, Mark V. Pauly, and Raynard S. Kington, *The Effects of Malpractice Litigation on Physicians' Fees and Incomes* (Chicago: University of Chicago, Center for the Study of the Economy and the State, 1990), and Patricia M. Danzon, "Liability for Medical Malpractice," *Journal of Economic Perspectives* 5 (Summer, 1991).

Mens rea

DEFINITION: A "guilty mind"

SIGNIFICANCE: *Mens rea* requires an awareness of the wrongness of an act

The idea of *mens rea* is based in the practice of English common law, when judges decided that a wrongful act in itself was not enough to establish guilt. A wrongful act must be composed of two parts: the physical, or *actus reus* (the "act itself"), and the mental, or *mens rea* (the "guilty mind").

Mens rea is usually applied to acts in which criminal rather than civil liability is at issue. To be criminally liable, a perpetrator not only must have committed the act but also must be found to have done so knowingly, intentionally, or recklessly, or to have been grossly negligent. The prosecution must prove, beyond a reasonable doubt, that at least one of these four states of mind existed, although all may have been present. Any of these states of mind also require that an act be committed with a particular outcome in mind.

An act that is *malum prohibitum* (wrong because it is prohibited), such as speeding, does not require specific intent, but only the knowledge that such an act is wrong. In contrast, civil liability laws do not require knowledge of an act's wrongness, but only that the act is voluntary.

Because the prosecution must prove beyond a reasonable doubt that *mens rea* existed, several defenses exist. These include insanity, intoxication, or simple mistake.

See also Criminal intent; Insanity defense; *Mala in se* and *mala prohibita*; Reasonable doubt; Standards of proof.

Merryman, Ex parte

COURT: U.S. Circuit Court, Baltimore

DATE: Issuance of Chief Justice Taney's writ, May 26, 1861; Taney's ruling, May 28, 1861

SIGNIFICANCE: President Abraham Lincoln's suspension of the writ of *habeas corpus* as an executive emergency act at the outbreak of the Civil War provoked a clash with the Chief Justice of the United States and became the first of several celebrated wartime civil liberties cases

For centuries, wherever Anglo-American law prevails, a citizen's right to a writ of *habeas corpus*—that is, the right not to be arrested and held by government authorities without being charged—has been regarded a basic civil liberty. As secession continued and fighting that signaled the opening of the Civil War erupted, President Lincoln authorized Union military commanders to suspend the privilege of *habeas corpus*. Article I, section 9 of the U.S. Constitution stipulates that this privilege "shall not be suspended" unless "in cases of rebellion or invasion the public safety may require it."

Of particular concern to Lincoln were the border states which teetered on the brink of secession. Maryland, adjoining Washington, D.C., was one of these states and, indeed, hostile actions against Union forces were already under way there. John Merryman was a wealthy and well-born Maryland landowner—in fact, a descendant of Francis Scott Key, who had written the national anthem. Merryman was also a lieutenant in a secessionist cavalry unit that had destroyed bridges and telegraph lines during April, 1861. Along with other suspected traitors, Merryman's arrest was ordered by a Union general, William H. Keim. Merryman's lawyer promptly petitioned a federal circuit court in Baltimore for a writ of *habeas corpus*. Merryman, meantime, was imprisoned at Fort McHenry.

In 1861, justices of the U.S. Supreme Court still were assigned individually to preside over one of nine federal circuit courts. In this instance, Chief Justice Roger Brooke Taney, a Marylander, was presiding over the federal court in Baltimore when Merryman's petition reached him. Taney denied the president's right to suspend the writ. The chief justice reasoned that the Constitution placed the right of suspension in the Congress and that Congress had not exercised that power. Further, Taney argued that the Constitution neither sanctioned the arrest of civilians by army officers without prior authorization by civil courts nor allowed citizens to be imprisoned indefinitely without trial. Lincoln refused to obey Taney's ruling, declaring before a special session of Congress on July 4, 1861, that suspension was necessary in order to quell the rebellion and preserve the nation.

Opinions concerning both Lincoln's action and Taney's ruling were divided. As had been true of earlier clashes between presidents and the Supreme Court, the president could enforce his view, and without his acquiescence the Court could not. Nevertheless, in a few weeks Merryman was released. Although he was indicted by a U.S. circuit court, he was never brought to trial. Passage of the Habeas Corpus Act of 1863 represented an effort to respect authority of the courts while not seriously restricting executive and military decisions.

See also Civil War; *Habeas corpus*; Lincoln, Abraham; Martial law; *Milligan, Ex parte*; Taney, Roger Brooke.

Mexican American Legal Defense and Education Fund (MALDEF)

DATE: Established 1968

SIGNIFICANCE: MALDEF protects the civil rights of Mexican Americans

Founded by San Antonio lawyer Pete Tijerina, MALDEF works through litigation and other legal avenues to battle discrimination and integrate Mexican Americans into the U.S. mainstream. Headquartered in Los Angeles, MALDEF maintains regional offices in Fresno, Sacramento, San Francisco, and Santa Ana, California; El Paso and San Antonio, Texas; Detroit, Michigan; Chicago, Illinois; and Washington, D.C. The organization has a professional staff of about sixty-five and relies on volunteers to perform the bulk of its work.

See also Immigration, legal and illegal; Race riots, twentieth century; Racial and ethnic discrimination.

Miami riots

DATE: May 17-19, 1980
PLACE: Miami, Florida
SIGNIFICANCE: Brutal race riots were triggered by indignation over the failure of the criminal justice system to convict police officers in the death of a black businessman

Many of Dade County, Florida's, poorest black residents live in Liberty City, a five-hundred-square-block unincorporated area created in the 1920's by a black realtor who wanted to establish a place for blacks to live in "liberty." Conflicts between the police and Liberty City residents were common. Between 1970 and 1979, there were thirteen violent racial confrontations. In the five years preceding the Miami riot,

more than 930 charges of police brutality were filed, an average of one every two days.

At 1:15 A.M. on December 17, 1979, Arthur McDuffie, an African American insurance agent, left his sister's house on his motorcycle. Almost immediately, police officers were in pursuit of McDuffie for traffic violations. After an eight-minute chase, McDuffie was stopped and beaten by at least six and perhaps as many as twelve officers. He lapsed into a coma and died four days later.

While McDuffie was being transported to the hospital, several officers demolished his motorcycle in an effort to make it appear that he had been in a traffic accident. The initial police report attributed McDuffie's death to injuries he had suffered in a motorcycle accident while fleeing police. Five police officers who were eventually charged with McDuffie's murder had been named in forty-seven citizen complaints, thirteen internal reviews, and fifty-five "use-of-force" incidents.

All five officers were tried at the same time, and the trial was shifted to Tampa, Florida. The defense used its challenges to remove all blacks from the jury pool, and the case was heard by an all-white six-person jury. After deliberating for less than three hours, the jury found all defendants not guilty.

At 6:00 P.M. on May 17, 1980, approximately three hours after the verdict was read, riots began in Liberty City. After three days of rioting, the death toll stood at seventeen, with

Fires spread in Miami in May, 1980, during rioting sparked by the acquittal of five white police officers who beat a black man to death. (AP/Wide World Photos)

eight whites killed on the first day and nine blacks killed on the second and third days. Some six hundred blacks were arrested, and property damage amounted to $200 million.

In the aftermath of the riots, Dade County spent $100,000, and the Chamber of Commerce another $40,000, for studies on economic revitalization. No action was taken. On the state level, the response was minimal. Liberty City was designated as an enterprise zone, providing state and local tax credits to businesses that moved into the area. On the federal level, the administration of President Jimmy Carter provided financial assistance to damaged businesses through the Small Business Administration. The officers who were acquitted in the state courts of killing McDuffie were later tried in federal courts and convicted of violating McDuffie's civil rights. More than one-half of the damaged businesses closed or relocated, and the economic climate deteriorated further in the years following the riots.

See also Deadly force, police use of; King, Rodney, case and aftermath; National Commission on the Causes and Prevention of Violence; Police brutality; Race riots, twentieth century; Reasonable force.

Military justice

DEFINITION: The system of apprehension, judgment, and punishment designed to maintain order, efficiency, security, and discipline in a military organization

SIGNIFICANCE: A military justice system isolates its members from civilian control of legal issues for which the civilian judicial system is deemed inadequate or inappropriate; it also provides for the handling of crimes which are exclusively military matters

A military justice system is usually administered by a particular arm or department of the military branch it serves. It is commanded by officers of rank comparable to those heading other departments to avoid situations in which judicial matters might be influenced—or appear to be influenced—by a higher authority in another branch.

As in any other system of justice, military systems have provisions for investigation, gathering of evidence, arrest and detainment of alleged wrongdoers, trial, review, sentencing, punishment, and record keeping. Legal counsel must be provided for the accused and for those bringing charges. Sites are reserved for detainment of the accused, processing and studying evidence, trial, review, sentencing, and punishment. The severity of the charges determines to what extent isolation from the civilian population is necessary. In cases where civilian political activism is likely because of the severity or notoriety of the alleged crime or cases in which legal action against an accused is unpopular among the civilian population, the entire proceedings may be removed from civilian surroundings and made off-limits to the public and the press.

For minor lapses of discipline the accused may elect to face his accuser before only his or her immediate unit commander. While this removes safeguards involved with a formal trial by disinterested strangers, it has the benefit to the accused of being swift and private. For more serious offenses, there is a system of courts-martial.

Despite extremely detailed instructions and regulations in official military documents, there are also provisions for crimes that are not predictable or are difficult to define. These are covered in what are usually called "general articles" and relate to offenses not familiar to civilians. The very lack of specificity of these articles has placed them under attack by civil liberties advocacy groups.

In the United States, constitutional safeguards such as the Bill of Rights extend to military personnel except when the freedoms guaranteed by these rights are limited by "military necessity." The personal property of a military person, for example, is open to examination by superiors. In the closeness of military living conditions and because of the hazard that contraband poses to discipline, inspections may be conducted without prior announcement or a warrant. These examinations include the sort known familiarly as "shakedowns," in which a detailed search of living quarters is conducted if a crime is suspected. This is a violation of U.S. constitutional provisions but is generally assumed to be necessary.

Another constitutional guarantee withheld from military personnel is freedom of speech. Criticism and calumny against the president, vice president, members of Congress, secretaries, governors, and state legislators is forbidden. Activism against war or any usages of the military is also considered sowing dissension and may be acted upon.

In the military, the accused is denied access to a random selection of court, to trial by peers, to access to counsel in the lowest level of court, and to a verbatim record of the trial—all of which are guaranteed to civilians. The functions of the court, normally divided in the civilian milieu into "prosecution" and "defense," are combined in a single group, usually a judge advocate's staff appointed by the unit commander. This is justified by the cardinal military precept of "singleness of command," intended to avoid the inefficiencies of multiple command paths.

These exceptions to civilian practice have varied widely according to public reaction to the activities of the armed forces at any given time. In time of war some exceptions to the rights of military personnel are made in the name of secrecy and security. Yet military assignments which are thought "inhumane" may be refused with impunity if public opinion brings enough political pressure on the military. Cases of nonperformance of duty on the grounds of the enemy's human rights, for example, produced considerable legal wrangling during the Vietnam War.

An individual may not be tried by both military and civilian courts for any federal offense, including military offenses. Individuals tried for offenses under the laws of the states or of foreign countries, however, may be tried by the military as well.

Structure of the System. For the following discussion of a military justice system, the terms used will be those of the U.S. Army. (Parallel titles, structures, and procedures apply generally to many other modern systems.) All military justice activ-

Three of the six U.S. Army officers who found Lieutenant William Calley guilty of premeditated murder in 1971; the charges stemmed from the My Lai massacre, which occurred in Vietnam in 1968. (AP/Wide World Photos)

ity except that of the informal procedure mentioned above is conducted by the organization directed by the judge advocate general. The document of law and procedure for military justice in the United States is the Uniform Code of Military Justice (UCMJ), which was adopted in 1951 to replace the antiquated Articles of War in use since revolutionary times. An auxiliary work, the Manual of Courts Martial (MCM) provides procedural rules for the conduct of courts-martial.

In addition to specific offenses, the UCMJ provides two nonspecific articles: one for officers, making it an offense to indulge in "conduct unbecoming an officer and a gentleman," the other for enlisted men, forbidding "disorders and neglects to the prejudice of good order and discipline in the armed forces, all conduct of a nature to bring discredit upon the armed forces." In the MCM these are divided into more specific, but still subjective, offenses such as "being grossly drunk and conspicuously disorderly in a public place." While these "general articles" have been criticized as vague and allowing selective persecution, they have parallels in civilian law. Additionally, although the UCMJ and MCM are specific to the American armed forces, they have parallels in other modern military entities, reflecting the legal and social cultures of the various nations.

In U.S. territory, the military justice system has no responsibility for crimes not involving military property or personnel, leaving these to the civilian judicial systems. For nonmilitary offenses in foreign countries, however, the military justice

system assumes responsibility. This protects the accused from possible draconian civilian jurisprudence, and it protects the civilian populace of the country from abusive behavior by military personnel.

Procedures and Provisions. Military justice differs from civilian justice in ways that reflect the danger to a nation's military mission posed by offenses which in civilian life present a much lesser danger. Except for a person committing multiple capital crimes, a criminal in civilian life seldom imperils those much removed from his own sphere of action, whereas in the military similar actions may have national consequences. In the United States armed forces, for example, quick and consistent response is expected to every order, however minor. Since the courts are formed of command personnel taken from their other duties (except for civilian counsel), there must be a system that provides for hearing minor accusations in a simplified way so that the entire command organization is not burdened.

At the least serious end of the range of offenses, an individual may be tried in an informal session, called an Article 15 in the military because it is defined by the article so numbered in the UCMJ. In this action the accused person's immediate unit commander convenes, hears, judges, and sentences the accused without outside assistance, although the accused may have recourse to counsel if requested. Often in these minor actions the punishment is assignment of short periods of onerous but necessary chores within the unit, such as food preparation, maintenance, refuse removal, or sentry duty. There are limits to the allowed punishment consistent with the minor nature of the offenses. If the accused wants, he or she may request trial by a court-martial.

In the U.S. military, there are several levels of courts, with each higher level giving the accused as well as the prosecutor greater freedom. The highest of these courts are usually convened only for serious crimes involving what would, in civilian life, be criminal cases. Typically, these offenses involve major bodily harm to others, large-scale theft, or insubordination of a nature that may threaten the outcome of a major military operation. While any planned rebellion against orders is mutinous in the sense of refusing to follow orders, the charge of mutiny is usually reserved for action against authority in the face of enemy activity.

Individuals have the right to claim redress for unfair or unusually harsh treatment by superiors. Like the courts-martial that hear accusations against individuals, a court may be requested to hear and adjudicate an individual's complaints. It is incumbent upon the person bringing the complaint, however, to perform whatever action he or she is assigned by competent orders. Only then, the mission satisfied, may the individual bring complaint. This policy is necessary to avoid having a mission jeopardized by an individual who wishes to take the time to protest an order.

Police. The military branches provide their own police forces. These are specially trained personnel who serve many of the same functions as civilian police. On each military base there is one organization under the command of a provost marshal and the provost marshal's staff. Not under the command of any other entity on that base, the provost marshal has responsibility for order, traffic control, and property security on the base. In off-base situations, military police have the additional responsibility of protecting civilians from risks such as intoxicated and belligerent personnel on leave.

Military police carry out surveillance, arrest of wrongdoers, accumulation of evidence, and presentation of evidence in court. They are supported by the same sort of scientific facilities and communications systems as, for example, the state police of a populous state. In addition, they have the responsibility for apprehending and transporting accused personnel. They have access to federal criminal records for issues of national security. Confinement of prisoners on military bases and escort of prisoners during trials is also provided by the military police organization. In addition, it is responsible for apprehending and returning illegally absent personnel to their base for trial.

Courts-Martial. In the U.S. Army there are three levels of court-martial. In the first, or "summary" court, the convening officer serves simultaneously as judge, jury, prosecutor, defense counsel, and court reporter. If requested, a military lawyer is provided for the accused. The safeguards of individual rights found in a civilian court are not required to be observed, but the summary court is restricted in the severity of its sentences—typically they involve a short (not exceeding forty-five days) confinement, reduction of pay, or demotion of one grade level.

The next higher, or "special" court-martial, provides competent, trained counsel and three experienced officers as judges. While the special court involves greater safeguards of the accused person's rights, it also carries with it the potential of severe sentences, including "bad conduct" discharges or prolonged imprisonment.

A general court-martial is heard by at least five officers of senior rank, when available, and is preceded by an investigation to determine whether assurance of guilt is sufficient to warrant pressing the charge. If convicted of a serious offense in the general court-martial, an individual may face a "dishonorable" discharge, prolonged imprisonment, or, in cases involving default in the face of enemy action, the death penalty. In the two higher courts, the accused may request the replacement of up to one-third of the officers hearing the case by enlisted (non-officer rank) personnel. This is intended to lower the cultural and social bar between the accused and his judges. Should the accused desire, the trial may be conducted by a single officer rather than a board.

The protections against self-incrimination and double jeopardy are identical to those guaranteed for civilians by the Bill of Rights and are specifically described in the UCMJ. Because of the intimidation implicitly present in a situation involving personnel interrogated by those of substantially superior rank (and therefore, power) the UCMJ requires that the accused be informed of their rights and the nature of the accusation. This is a parallel to the "Miranda" procedure in civilian police procedure, in which a person is warned that testimony, freely given, may be used against the person in court.

Review and Appeal. Upon conviction, the prisoner is allowed an "administrative review," an interview with the presiding (trying) officer at which the prisoner and counsel may make arguments for mitigation or suspension of the sentence. It is common for the commander bringing the charges to ask for the maximum sentence provided by the UCMJ so that he can mitigate it if indicated.

After the administrative review, judgments may be reviewed by a civilian court of military appeals (COMA). The COMA is a board appointed by the president, each member serving fifteen years. In major issues, such as cases involving top-grade officers or in offenses providing for the death penalty, review by the COMA is automatic.

For offenses such as those providing for the dismissal of an officer, for a bad-conduct discharge from service, or for more than one year's incarceration, the accused may request review by a court of military review (COMR). In addition to these avenues of review, cases which may have involved the alleged denial of the prisoner's constitutional rights may be heard by the U.S. Supreme Court.

If no relief is allowed by these reviews and an individual believes that he has been wrongly treated, he may request a formal legal procedure in which the judge advocate general's staff serves in the role of judge and arranges for counsel for the plaintiff if necessary. The accused may request counsel from others in the military, such as a doctor or chaplain.

Military justice procedures contain additional safeguards for the accused person awaiting trial. While in confinement the accused is exempt from any work not involved in the cleanliness of his own living quarters and person. He is not usually required to live in close proximity with convicted prisoners. He is protected from hazing or unusually severe discipline. Mail pertaining to his case is exempt from invasion. Any physical force applied to his person and the conditions of his confinement are limited in severity to those needed to ensure his presence at the trial. Unlike civilian practice, however, there is no provision for release on parole or bail.

Punishment. Convicted offenders may be reduced in rank, fined, or imprisoned. Incarceration of convicted military personnel for limited periods (less than a year) may be in a facility (stockade) on the military installation to which the accused is assigned unless the antisocial nature of his offense makes a change of station advisable. For longer terms of confinement, federal prisons are employed.

There are several offenses for which the death penalty may be invoked. Mutiny, deserting in the face of enemy action, and murder are the most likely. In most countries having a military force, the crime of desertion in war is a capital crime, but the death penalty for military crimes in the U.S. has generally become obsolete in the light of the extensive appeals available to condemned criminals.

There have been executions since World War II, including one of a deserting soldier in the period immediately following the Vietnam War, but these occurred during the period of conscription. Pressure from antiwar activists led to the cessation of the draft in 1972. With one of the few all-volunteer military establishments in the world, the U.S. is unlikely to suffer further desertions of any consequence. —*Loring D. Emery*

See also Bill of Rights, U.S.; Conscription; Constitution, U.S.; Criminal procedure; Martial law; *Milligan, Ex parte*; My Lai massacre.

BIBLIOGRAPHY

A historical perspective of the military is found in Samuel Huntington's *The Soldier and the State* (Cambridge, Mass.: Belknap Press of Harvard University Press, 1967), which treats the evolution of military leadership and documents the struggle between American political culture and the military. The social and political development of the military is treated by Peter Karsten in *The Military in America* (New York: Free Press, 1986), which discusses the development of civilian control of the military and the emergence of human rights movements in the military. In *The Military Establishment* (New York: Harper & Row, 1971) by Adam Yarmolinsky, one finds a carefully annotated attack on every phase of the United States military, from the military-industrial "conspiracy" to the arbitrary nature of military justice. The rights of personnel in the military justice system are described by Robert Rivkin in his *The Rights of Servicemen* (New York: Avon, 1972), a handbook prepared by the American Civil Liberties Union for dealing with military justice and securing individual rights in the system. *History of the United States Army* by Russell Weigley (Bloomington: Indiana University Press, 1984), is a comprehensive work on the history of the American military establishment from colonial times to 1983.

Miller v. California

COURT: U.S. Supreme Court
DATE: Decided June 21, 1973
SIGNIFICANCE: In this landmark obscenity case, a relatively unified Supreme Court, under Chief Justice Warren Burger, formulated specific guidelines for regulating "hard-core" sexually explicit material

In this case, the defendant, Marvin Miller, was convicted by a California jury of violating a state statute prohibiting the distribution of obscene materials. Miller had conducted an aggressive mass mailing campaign to advertise sale of "adult materials." A pamphlet, sent to California residents who had not necessarily requested the information, included explicit pictures and drawings of sexual acts with genitalia prominently displayed. Miller's conviction was upheld by the California Superior Court. In *Miller v. California*, the U.S. Supreme Court by a vote of 5 to 4, remanded, or sent back, the decision of the lower courts for further deliberations consistent with its revised obscenity standards.

The Court had struggled with the issue of obscenity for nearly two decades prior to the *Miller* ruling. In *Roth v. United States* (1957), the Court obtained majority agreement for the following obscenity standard: whether to the average person applying contemporary community standards, the dominant theme of the material, taken as a whole, appeals to prurient interests. *Roth* was also important because in it the Court explicitly stated that obscenity was not protected speech under the First Amendment. In *Roth* and subsequent decisions leading up to *Miller*, the Court's standards became increasingly more liberal. In *Jacobellis v. Ohio* (1964), a Supreme Court opinion by Justice William J. Brennan clarified that contemporary "community" standards are national standards, those of the "society at large." National standards are likely to be more permissive than those of local communities. Further definitional clarification by the Court in *Jacobellis* held that the material must be "utterly without redeeming social importance" to meet the criteria for obscenity. The standard made obscenity convictions difficult.

In the 1960's, the Supreme Court was internally divided on the obscenity issue. For example, in *Jacobellis*, Justice Brennan was assigned to write the majority opinion, but all eight of the other justices wrote either concurring or dissenting opinions, indicating their factiousness. The task of writing clear guidelines for determining what is obscene is daunting, as a result of the value-laden nature of "obscenity." Justice Potter Stewart suggested this when he declared in his opinion in *Jacobellis* that he found it difficult to articulate a definition of obscenity, but "I know it when I see it." A lack of consensus and firm principles on the part of the justices resulted in a case-by-case examination of materials in obscenity cases. Case-by-case determination left lower federal and state courts perplexed about what standards to use.

The *Miller* Court, led by Chief Justice Warren Burger, reformulated obscenity standards, building on the doctrine established in *Roth*. These standards were intended to provide clearer guidance to lower courts and to prevent the need for the U.S. Supreme Court to review allegedly obscene materials. The standards established were:

(a) whether the average person, applying contemporary community standards, would find that the work, taken as a whole, appeals to the prurient interest; (b) whether the work depicts or describes, in a patently offensive way, sexual conduct specifically defined by the applicable state law; and (c) whether the work, taken as a whole, lacks serious literary, artistic, political, or scientific value.

The *Miller* standards eliminated the "utterly without redeeming social value" test. In addition, the new standards placed emphasis on local community standards rather than national standards, recognizing the differences in values that exist in different parts of the country. Despite clearer standards in *Miller*, debate about the meaning of obscenity continues, with significant challenges from libertarians, who support broader free expression rights, from some conservatives, who support stronger regulation of obscenity, and from some feminists, who believe that the emphasis in *Miller* on offensiveness is misplaced and should be refocused on the harms of pornography to women.

See also *Barnes v. Glen Theatre, Inc.*; Bill of Rights, U.S.; Censorship; *New York v. Ferber*; *Osborne v. Ohio*; *Roth v. United States*.

Milligan, Ex parte

COURT: U.S. Supreme Court
DATE: Ruling issued April 3, 1866; opinions released December 17, 1866
SIGNIFICANCE: In this case, which began during the Civil War, the Supreme Court for the first time limited the authority of military courts acting under presidential authority to try civilians for acts subverting a war effort

In October, 1864, Union military authorities in Indiana arrested Lambdin P. Milligan, a civilian, and several other Confederate sympathizers for conspiring to attack federal arsenals and free Confederate prisoners. The military acted under authority of President Abraham Lincoln's order stipulating that military courts could try and punish persons "guilty of any disloyal practice affording aid and comfort to the rebels." After a military commission found Milligan and two others guilty and sentenced them to be hanged, Milligan disputed the commission's jurisdiction and sought a writ of *habeas corpus* asserting his constitutional right to a trial by jury.

In 1866 the U.S. Supreme Court ruled 9 to 0 in Milligan's favor and ordered that he be released. Though unanimous in its holding, the Court split, 5 to 4, in its reasoning. The majority opinion, written by Justice David Davis, held that "it is the birthright of every American citizen, when charged with crime, to be tried and punished according to law." Military authority could thus not lawfully supersede civilian authority "where the courts are open and their process unobstructed"—as was the case in Indiana. In what became a famous statement of a fundamental principle of American constitutionalism, Davis wrote: "The Constitution of the United States is a law for rulers and people, equally in war and peace, and covers with the shield of its protection all classes of men, at all times, and under all circumstances. No doctrine, involving more pernicious consequences, was ever intended by the wit of man than that any of its provisions can be suspended during any of the great exigencies of government."

While such sweeping language appears to deny martial law any trace of legitimacy, Davis argued in the same opinion that if "courts are actually closed" because of foreign invasion or civil war, then within a "theater of active military operations" the military may "govern by martial law until the laws can have their free course." Four justices differed from the majority in maintaining that the military's actions in the Milligan case would have been legal had Congress expressly authorized them; however, the majority held that even Congress lacks power to establish a system of military rule where civil courts are open and functioning.

The importance of *Ex parte Milligan* is twofold. While it establishes the legitimacy of martial law when invasion or rebellion makes normal law enforcement impossible, it also prohibits such martial law if the civil courts are functioning, even during wartime. *Milligan* has stood as a landmark for more than a century. Although the Court has never expressly repudiated it, some commentators believe that its principles were violated by the internment of Japanese Americans in World War II—an action that the Supreme Court upheld in *Korematsu v. United States* (1944).

See also Civil War; *Habeas corpus*; Japanese American internment; *Korematsu v. United States*; Martial law; *Merryman, Ex parte*; Military justice.

Milliken v. Bradley

COURT: U.S. Supreme Court
DATE: Decided July 25, 1974
SIGNIFICANCE: In this case, the U.S. Supreme Court decided that courts did not have the authority to order school desegregation plans that required moving schoolchildren across school district lines unless it could be shown that school district lines had been constructed in a manner designed to preserve segregation

By the early 1970's, many urban school districts continued to operate schools with a majority black population because of the dearth of white students in those school districts. In 1971, the U.S. Supreme Court in *Swann v. Charlotte-Mecklenburg Board of Education* had held that urban school boards could be required to engage in extensive school busing to integrate their schools. The *Swann* decision, however, did not address the issue of how to integrate urban school districts that had few white students.

In the early 1970's, a group of black parents, with the assistance of the National Association for the Advancement of

Colored People (NAACP) Legal Defense and Educational Fund, brought suit seeking to desegregate the Detroit school system. In 1972, federal district court judge Stephen Roth ruled that the Detroit schools were in fact illegally segregated and ordered a multidistrict desegregation plan involving the Detroit city school district along with fifty-three surrounding suburban school districts. One year later, the U.S. Court of Appeals for the Sixth Circuit affirmed, holding that the Detroit schools could not be adequately desegregated without such a multidistrict plan. Shortly thereafter, the U.S. Supreme Court agreed to hear the case.

In 1973, the Supreme Court had considered a similar multidistrict desegregation plan involving the Richmond, Virginia, schools. In that case, the Court had divided 4 to 4, with Justice Lewis Powell recusing himself because of his prior membership on the Richmond School Board. The Court took the Detroit case to decide the question whether multidistrict desegregation plans were required when inner-city school districts could not otherwise be desegregated. In the meantime, the specter of multidistrict desegregation prompted a firestorm of activity in Congress, as many members of Congress backed both legislation and amendments to the Constitution restricting the ability of federal courts to order extensive desegregation plans.

The Supreme Court held in the *Milliken v. Bradley* decision, with a 5-4 vote, that a district court should not order an interdistrict remedy unless it could be shown that the school district lines had been constructed in a manner to preserve segregation or unless state government officials had taken other action that contributed to the interdistrict segregation. This was a burden of proof that would prove difficult to meet. The *Milliken* decision marked the first time that the Supreme Court had declined to refine existing school desegregation jurisprudence to further integrationist goals.

In the wake of the *Milliken* decision a few metropolitan areas did adopt interdistrict desegregation remedies, but for the most part, the decision undermined desegregation efforts in America's cities. Unable to utilize an assignment plan that included children from surrounding suburban school districts, inner-city school boards were greatly restricted in their efforts to desegregate their schools.

See also *Brown v. Board of Education*; Busing; Racial and ethnic discrimination; Segregation, *de facto* and *de jure*; *Swann v. Charlotte-Mecklenburg Board of Education*.

Minnick v. Mississippi

COURT: U.S. Supreme Court

DATE: Decided December 3, 1990

SIGNIFICANCE: The Supreme Court found that a reinitiated interrogation of a murder suspect who had been advised of his Miranda rights and received counsel still violated the suspect's Fifth Amendment rights because it was conducted without counsel being present

Robert S. Minnick, the petitioner, sought reversal of his conviction for murder in the circuit court of Lowndes County, Mississippi, on the grounds that his constitutional rights against self-incrimination had been violated when his confession was taken during an interrogation conducted without counsel present. Minnick, a fugitive from prison, had been arrested and held in a California jail, where two federal agents, after reading the Miranda warnings to him, began an interrogation on a Friday. He requested that they return on the following Monday, when he would have counsel present. The agents complied, breaking off their questioning. An appointed attorney then advised Minnick to speak to no one about the charges against him. After an interview with the agents on Monday, Minnick was questioned by a deputy sheriff from Mississippi. The deputy advised Minnick of his Miranda rights, and the accused, who refused to sign a waiver of those rights, confessed to the murder for which he was subsequently tried and sentenced to death.

At Minnick's murder trial in Mississippi, he filed a motion to suppress the confession, but his request was denied. The conviction was then upheld by the Supreme Court of Mississippi, which ruled that Minnick's right to counsel, as set forth in the Fifth Amendment, had been granted in accordance with the guidelines established in *Edwards v. Arizona* (1981), which stipulates that a defendant who requests counsel during questioning cannot be subjected to further interrogation until the counsel is "made available" to the defendant. According to the Mississippi Supreme Court, that condition had been met when Minnick consulted with his appointed attorney.

The U.S. Supreme Court, on *certiorari*, reversed and remanded in a 6-2 decision. In the majority opinion, written by Justice Anthony Kennedy, the justices ruled that in a custodial interrogation, once counsel is provided, questioning cannot be resumed without counsel being present. It stipulated that the *Edwards v. Arizona* ruling regarding protection against self-incrimination is not met, nor is that protection terminated or suspended, by the mere provision of counsel outside the interrogation process. The majority found that Minnick's confession to the Mississippi deputy sheriff should have been inadmissible at his murder trial. In a dissenting opinion, Justice Antonin Scalia argued the contrary, holding that the *Edwards v. Arizona* rule excluding self-incrimination without counsel was not applicable after Minnick's first interview with his appointed attorney.

The Court's relatively narrow interpretation of what constitutes right to counsel leaves a legacy of stringent procedural requirements on law enforcement agencies, which must comply with a suspect's right to have counsel present during custodial interrogations that had been broken off and later resumed. From the point of view of such agencies, its practical effect is to inhibit an expeditious interrogation of suspects.

See also Counsel, right to; *Miranda v. Arizona*; Self-incrimination, privilege against.

Miranda v. Arizona

COURT: U.S. Supreme Court

DATE: Ruling issued June 13, 1966

SIGNIFICANCE: In this case, the Supreme Court established a broad interpretation of the Constitution's Fifth Amendment

The Miranda v. Arizona *decision required that the "Miranda rights" be read to all criminal suspects upon arrest.* (James L. Shaffer)

protection against forced confessions and established the "Miranda rights" which are read to suspects upon arrest, informing them of their full Fifth Amendment protection Ernesto Miranda was arrested by Phoenix police at his home on suspicion of kidnapping and rape. After two hours of interrogation, police produced a confession signed by Miranda. Also on the document was a statement that the confession had been made voluntarily and with Miranda's knowledge of his Fifth Amendment rights. All who were present agree that Miranda was not subjected to physical violence or threats to that effect.

Miranda was convicted on all counts against him. After his appeal to the Arizona Supreme Court was denied, his case was taken to the U.S. Supreme Court, which granted a writ of *certiorari*. The Court, by a 5-4 vote, overturned Miranda's conviction. The majority reasoned that Miranda had been effectively denied his Fifth Amendment protection against forced confessions. Because police could not clearly establish that Miranda had been informed of his right to remain silent, of his right to an attorney, and that his testimony could be used against him in a court of law, the majority held that a form of psychological coercion had been used to compel Miranda to testify against himself.

Based on its decision, the Court established guidelines for informing suspects of their Fifth Amendment rights. Under these guidelines, now known as the Miranda rights, suspects are informed immediately of their right to remain silent, that anything they say may be used against them in a court of law, and that they have a right to representation by an attorney (including a court-appointed attorney if they cannot afford to hire one).

Miranda v. Arizona was one of the landmark criminal justice cases during the Warren Court era. These cases dramatically expanded Fourth, Fifth, Sixth, and Eighth Amendment protection against abuse of the criminal process by police. As crime statistics swelled from the late 1960's until the early 1980's (after which they have lingered at high levels), popular support for protecting the constitutional rights of suspected and accused criminals greatly diminished. In addition, the subsequent Burger and Rehnquist Courts included many appointees of Republican presidents. These appointees resist both broad interpretations of the Bill of Rights and imposition of federal standards of due process on the states. As a result, subsequent cases have tended to dilute the full force of Miranda. (*New York v. Quarles*, 1984, for example, established a "public safety" exception to Miranda protection.) They have not, however, completely reversed *Miranda*. The Miranda rights are still read, and psychological coercion remains outside the parameters of legal police methods.

While Miranda himself won reversal of his conviction, he did not profit much from the victory. He accumulated a substantial criminal record and was ultimately stabbed to death by an assailant who, upon arrest, was dutifully read his Miranda rights.

See also *Arizona v. Fulminante*; Arrest; Assigned counsel system; Bill of Rights, U.S.; Counsel, right to; Criminal procedure; *Escobedo v. Illinois*; *Gideon v. Wainwright*; *Minnick v. Mississippi*; Self-incrimination, privilege against.

Miscarriage of justice

Definition: Damage to a party's rights sufficient to require reversal of a judgment

Significance: A claim of miscarriage allows a higher court to examine a proceeding to determine whether its outcome was just

A miscarriage of justice occurs when the outcome of a proceeding is inconsistent with justice. A finding of miscarriage is generally made by an appellate court, which examines the proceedings of the lower court upon application of one of the parties. The appellate court may order a new trial, but only if it is clearly convinced that the outcome might not have been the same if errors had not occurred. The decision to come to a finding of miscarriage of justice is based upon provisions of law that define right conduct, not the adjudication of rights.

Miscarriage is not concerned with the belief by one of the parties to the proceeding that they have been wronged by the outcome; it addresses only the conduct of the proceeding.

See also Appellate process; Due process of law; Evidence, rules of; Justice; Mistrial; Scottsboro cases.

Miscegenation laws

Definition: Laws that prohibited interracial marriages and/or attached criminal penalties to sexual relations and cohabitation between whites and nonwhites

Significance: State miscegenation laws were examples of explicit racial discrimination in U.S. statutory law; they criminalized and penalized the unions of persons of differing racial heritages and denied legal legitimacy to mixed-race children born to such interracial couples

Thirty-eight of the states at one time had miscegenation laws in force; seven of those thirty-eight repealed their laws before 1900. All southern states (not including the District of Columbia) had miscegenation statutes. Many western states (including Arizona, California, Montana, Nevada, Oregon, Utah, and Wyoming), in addition to forbidding intermarriage between blacks and whites, also specifically prohibited unions between whites and Native Americans or whites and Asian Americans. Penalties upon conviction varied from a maximum imprisonment of more than two years in most of the South and some other states (ten years in Florida, Indiana, Maryland, Mississippi, and North Carolina) to sentences ranging between a few months and two years in other states. Enforcement of the laws was random and irregular.

The key case in ending miscegenation laws was *Loving v. Virginia* (1967). At the time that the U.S. Supreme Court heard the *Loving* case, sixteen states still had miscegenation laws in force. Virginia's laws dealing with racial intermarriage were among the nation's oldest. They stemmed from statutes formulated in the colonial period (1691) and had been strengthened by more stringent miscegenation legislation passed in the mid-1920's in which whiteness was very narrowly defined. The codes that became law in 1924 were aimed primarily at discriminating against people of mixed African American and white heritage and/or of American Indian background.

In the *Loving* case, Richard Perry Loving, who was white, had married Mildred Delores Jester, who was African American, in Washington, D.C., in June, 1958. The Lovings made their home between Fredericksburg and Richmond in Caroline County, Virginia. They were issued warrants of arrest in July, 1958, and in January, 1959, they were convicted before the Caroline County court of violating Virginia's antimiscegenation statute. Their minimum sentences (of one year imprisonment each) were suspended on agreement that they would leave the state. They moved to Washington, D.C., until 1963, when they returned to their farm in Virginia and worked with attorneys Bernard Cohen and Philip Hirschkop of the American Civil Liberties Union (ACLU), who placed their case under appeal. The miscegenation law and the Lovings' convictions were upheld by the Virginia Supreme Court of Appeals in March, 1966, but in June, 1967, the U.S. Supreme Court overruled the appellate finding. The Supreme Court ruled that use of race as a basis for prohibiting marriage rights was unconstitutional under the Fourteenth Amendment's equal protection and due process provisions. The ruling nullified all remaining laws forbidding interracial marriage. Previous to the unanimous 1967 ruling, the U.S. Supreme Court had taken a conservative approach to this civil rights issue. It had repeatedly avoided reviewing lower court convictions based on state antimiscegenation laws (*Jackson v. Alabama*, 1954; *Naim v. Naim*, 1955; *McLaughlin v. Florida*, 1964).

See also American Civil Liberties Union (ACLU); Civil War Amendments; Due process of law; Equal protection of the law; Racial and ethnic discrimination.

Misdemeanor

DEFINITION: A criminal offense viewed as less serious than a felony; examples include prostitution, disorderly conduct, and many traffic offenses

SIGNIFICANCE: Federal and state definitions of felony and misdemeanor vary somewhat, but in all states the distinction is important

Felony and misdemeanor are large categories that indicate the seriousness of various types of crime. Misdemeanors are less serious offenses, such as disorderly conduct, many traffic offenses, and many "vice" offenses such as prostitution and some gambling activities. Felonies are more serious crimes, such as murder, rape, and armed robbery. Federal guidelines define a felony as any crime "punishable by death or by imprisonment for a term exceeding one year."

Most states maintain similar definitions, although some states classify crimes according to the place of incarceration for offenders. If incarceration is to be in a state prison, the offense is a felony; if it is punishable by a term in a local jail, it is considered a misdemeanor. In some jurisdictions an offense may be considered either a felony or a misdemeanor depending on a number of factors. Larceny (theft), for example, may be classified as a felony (grand larceny) if the value of the item or items stolen is sufficiently high or a misdemeanor (petty larceny) if their value is relatively small. Occasionally the first conviction for an offense

is a misdemeanor, with subsequent convictions being defined as felonies; an example is driving under the influence (DUI).

In most states there are separate court systems for felonies and misdemeanors. Felonies are tried in county courts, or courts of general jurisdiction. Misdemeanors are handled by local courts with limited jurisdiction. These local courts (also called minor or inferior courts) are not "courts of record"; that is, transcripts of the proceedings are not kept. By far, most criminal cases are handled by local courts, partly because so many charges are only misdemeanors and partly because felony charges are sometimes reduced to misdemeanor charges before a trial begins. Misdemeanor cases proceed through the courts very quickly (the process has been called "factory-like" and has been the subject of considerable criticism), and many of the safeguards of defendants' rights that apply in felony cases are not required. In contrast to felony cases, misdemeanor cases are usually decided at one time, with hearing, arraignment, and sentencing all combined in one short hearing. Many local courts must process a tremendous volume of misdemeanor cases every day. The handling of felony cases, on the other hand, is complex, and cases may take more than a year.

The term "misdemeanor" derives from a combination of the French words *mes* and *demener*, and therefore means "to conduct oneself ill." The felony and misdemeanor categories come from English common law; in England, misdemeanor originally meant a "trespass against the peace." Eventually the term broadened to incorporate any criminal act that was not considered a felony or treason. The misdemeanor/felony distinction was discontinued in England in 1967, but in the United States most jurisdictions maintain the classifications.

Another classification of lesser criminal acts is infractions, or violations. Many traffic offenses are infractions, as are such things as peddling without a license. Infractions are punishable only by fines, not by incarceration.

See also Arraignment; Arrest; Commercialized vice; Common law; Counsel, right to; Crime; Criminal law; Criminal procedure; Felony; Indictment.

Missouri Compromise of 1820

DATE: Passed by Congress March 3, 1820

DEFINITION: This measure allowed Missouri to enter the Union as a slave state and Maine to enter as a nonslave state

SIGNIFICANCE: This first major congressional controversy involving slavery was resolved by preserving the balance between slave and nonslave states

During the early nineteenth century, the issue of slavery was simmering beneath the surface of American life. Politically, by 1818, there was a balance of eleven slave and eleven nonslave states. It was understood that, east of the Mississippi River, the southern border of Pennsylvania and the Ohio River marked the dividing line between the two types of states. There was no such understanding for new states in the Louisiana Purchase west of the Mississippi River. In February of 1819, when Congress began considering Missouri's application for statehood, the territory had about ten thousand slaves, and it anticipated becoming a slave state; however, congressmen from nonslave states argued that to allow it to do so would upset the balance between the states.

The solution to the Missouri dilemma appeared when Maine applied for admission as a nonslave state. After a year of congressional maneuvering, led in the House of Representatives by Speaker Henry Clay of Kentucky, both states were allowed to join as planned. The compromise also prohibited slavery, except in Missouri, in the Louisiana Purchase north of 36° 30′, the southern boundary of Missouri.

In 1854, the 36° 30′ provision of the Missouri Compromise was repealed when the Kansas-Nebraska Act allowed for the possibility of slavery north of that line. In *Scott v. Sandford* (1857), Supreme Court Chief Justice Roger Taney declared that the 36° 30′ line actually had been unconstitutional because it deprived citizens of their property (slaves) without due process of law.

See also Civil War; Clay, Henry; Kansas-Nebraska Act; Lincoln-Douglas debates; *Scott v. Sandford*; Slavery.

Mistrial

DEFINITION: A trial that is aborted or ruled invalid because of either a fundamental error or a hung jury

SIGNIFICANCE: Since a mistrial is equivalent to no trial, a retrial is necessary if a defendant is to be convicted of a crime

The most common reason for a mistrial is the inability of the jury to agree on a verdict. A judge may also declare a mistrial when a violation of evidentiary or procedural rules is so prejudicial that a fair trial becomes impossible. A "harmless error" provides no basis for a mistrial, because it does not affect substantive rights.

In order to protect a defendant's Fifth Amendment right against double jeopardy, the Supreme Court in *Oregon v. Kennedy* (1982) divided mistrials into two categories. First, when a mistrial is declared over the defendant's objection, a retrial is not permitted except when the judge acts from "manifest necessity." Second, when the mistrial occurs with the consent of the defendant, a retrial is permitted unless the prosecution intentionally commits an error designed to obtain a second trial.

See also Double jeopardy; Due process of law; Evidence, rules of; Harmless error; Jury system; Miscarriage of justice; Reversible error.

Mitigating circumstances

DEFINITION: Circumstances that may be considered extenuating in nature but not to the extent of excusing an offense or crime

SIGNIFICANCE: Mitigating circumstances may affect the seriousness of criminal charges and, in civil cases, the levels of damages awarded

Mitigating circumstances, although they do not provide a justification or excuse for an offense, may lessen the seriousness of the crime or the culpability of an offender. For example, if an accused party had been provoked to commit a crime in the sudden heat of passion, it might be said that mitigating circumstances existed. The accused would not have an excuse for the crime, but the extenuating circumstances under which the accused acted might lessen the charge from a more serious offense to a lesser offense.

Mitigating circumstances may also affect damage claim awards, not by negating the claim for damages but by moving the amount of award either upward or downward. Mitigating circumstances may also come into play in cases of defamation (libel and slander). If the accused spoke or wrote the offending words in good faith, not malevolently, and with honest intentions, then these circumstances may warrant a lessening of culpability.

See also Compensatory damages; Criminal procedure; Defamation; Reparations.

Model Penal Code

DEFINITION: A suggested criminal code drafted by the American Law Institute in 1962

SIGNIFICANCE: The Model Penal Code has strongly influenced a number of states in the drafting of their criminal law statutes

Before the American Law Institute sponsored and published the Model Penal Code in 1962, the criminal codes of the fifty states were far from uniform. In criminal law matters, states were guided by the decisions of the common law, often replete with inconsistencies and contradictions. The Model Penal Code was drafted by judges, lawyers, and law teachers with the goal of eliminating the inconsistencies found in the common law and providing a uniform set of criminal codes. It was designed as a model for state legislatures to follow in drafting their own criminal codes, and as such it has influenced the drafting of criminal codes in approximately forty states.

See also Bentham, Jeremy; Common law; Criminal law; Criminal procedure; Federal Crimes Act; Sentencing guidelines, U.S.; United States Code.

Money laundering

DEFINITION: Crime involving the turnover or conversion of funds, normally funds obtained through illegal activities, in order to avoid payment of appropriate taxes and disclosure of an audit trail

SIGNIFICANCE: Individuals involved in crime need to have a mechanism to exchange, transfer, and/or eliminate traces of ownership of funds obtained through various criminal activities

Money laundering is a key component of the exchange of funds obtained through various criminal activities. The process is often affiliated with organized crime. Illegal businesses such as prostitution, gambling, and drug dealing all generate large amounts of untraceable cash. Money laundering acts as the mechanism to convert those funds into legitimate businesses or place it in the hands of organized crime leaders. Legitimate cash businesses such as bars, vending companies, grocery stores, and laundromats all can be effective fronts for money laundering. Financial institutions, a natural source of money transfers, are regulated by the Bank Secrecy Act, which strictly prohibits them from engaging in this process. Banks

MONEY LAUNDERING CENTERS IN THE WESTERN HEMISPHERE

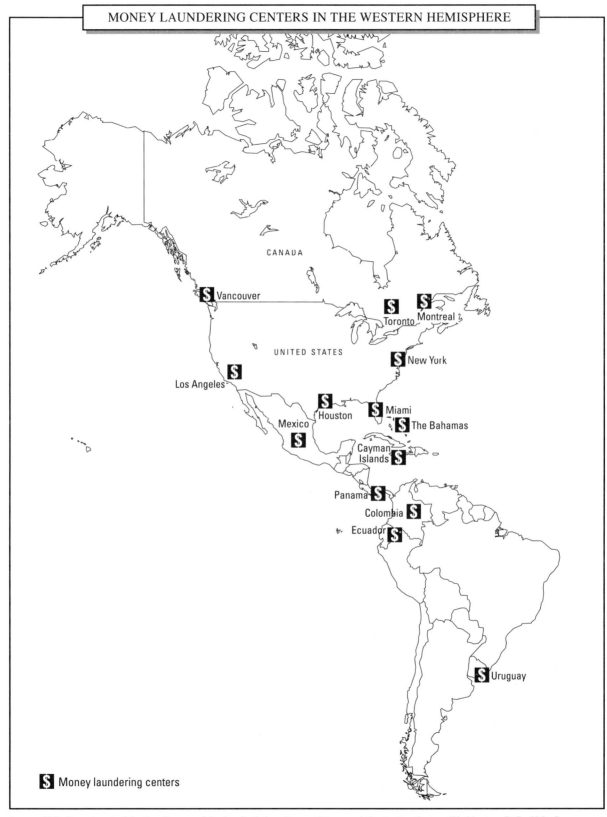

Source: U.S. Department of Justice, Bureau of Justice Statistics, *Drugs, Crime, and the Justice System.* Washington, D.C.: U.S. Government Printing Office, 1992.

are required to report any cash transaction exceeding ten thousand dollars, or multiple transactions by the same party adding up to ten thousand dollars, to the federal government.

See also Commercialized vice; Drug use and sale, illegal; Interpol; Organized crime; Racketeer Influenced and Corrupt Organizations Act (RICO); Tax evasion; Treasury, U.S. Department of the.

Montgomery bus boycott

DATE: December 1, 1955-December 21, 1956
PLACE: Montgomery, Alabama
SIGNIFICANCE: This action ultimately led to the demise of racial segregation on Montgomery buses and, more important, served as the catalyst for the rise of Martin Luther King, Jr., to national prominence as the leader of the Civil Rights movement

On December 1, 1955, Rosa Parks, a black seamstress, was ordered by a Montgomery city bus driver to surrender her seat to a white passenger as required by law. When she refused, Parks was arrested and fined for failure to obey the seating instructions of a bus driver.

In response to the arrest, black leaders in Montgomery distributed leaflets throughout black sections of the city calling for a one-day boycott of the city bus system. The move proved so successful that black leaders decided to continue it until their demands were met. The demands of the black community were that all passengers be seated on a first-come, first-serve basis. Martin Luther King, Jr., a young minister, was selected as president of the newly formed protest organization, which was named the Montgomery Improvement Association (MIA). As the boycott continued into January of 1956, it became apparent that no compromise was possible despite the loss of bus company and city revenues. The determination of the MIA was strengthened when King was arrested and jailed for speeding, followed by the bombing of his home four days later. The leadership of the boycott, at that point, decided to file suit in federal court to challenge the constitutionality of bus segregation. The MIA suit, *Browder v.*

Rosa Parks being fingerprinted by Montgomery police. Her arrest provided the impetus for a citywide bus boycott by African Americans. (AP/Wide World Photos)

Gayle, argued that racially segregated seating violated the Fourteenth Amendment's guarantee of equal treatment of all citizens as implied in the recent landmark Supreme Court decision *Brown v. Board of Education* (1954).

In May, 1956, a three-judge panel met at the federal courthouse in Montgomery to hear arguments regarding segregated seating on the city bus line. The federal judges were all natives of Alabama. Walter Knabe, attorney for Montgomery, argued before the justices that not only was segregation constitutional, but it was also necessary for the welfare of the citizens of Montgomery. To end segregation, according to the witnesses called by the city, would ultimately lead to violence between the races.

The decision of the justices was split, but it favored the plaintiffs. The majority decision held that Montgomery laws regarding the segregation of buses did violate the Fourteenth Amendment, as argued by the plaintiffs. Montgomery officials appealed the decision, but to no avail. In December, 1956, U.S. marshals served a Supreme Court order to desegregate the buses in Montgomery. The following morning, Parks, King, and other boycott leaders boarded a city bus and occupied seats formerly reserved for white passengers. The decision in *Browder v. Gayle* was a tremendous victory for the Civil Rights movement. The following year, King was elected president of the Southern Christian Leadership Conference (SCLC), an organization established to coordinate the Civil Rights movement in the United States.

See also *Brown v. Board of Education*; Civil Rights movement; King, Martin Luther, Jr.; Racial and ethnic discrimination; Segregation, *de facto* and *de jure*; Selma-to-Montgomery civil rights march.

Moose Lodge No. 107 v. Irvis

Court: U.S. Supreme Court
Date: Decided June 12, 1972
Significance: The Court ruled that a state did not deny the equal protection of the law when it granted a license to serve alcohol to a racially discriminatory private club

Moose Lodge No. 107 was a private club in Harrisburg, Pennsylvania, that served both food and alcohol, the latter under a license granted by the Pennsylvania Liquor Control Board. The club was often used by members of the state legislature for lunch breaks and after-hours relaxation. A white member of the lodge brought an African American fellow legislator, K. Leroy Irvis, into the club's dining room and bar, where the pair were refused service on the grounds of Irvis' race.

The Fourteenth Amendment to the Constitution forbids state action in furtherance of racial discrimination. Since the lodge's refusal to serve Irvis amounted to racial discrimination, the Supreme Court was asked to determine whether Pennsylvania's granting of a liquor license constituted state action in furtherance of that discrimination.

The Court ruled in a 6-3 vote that mere state licensing of a private club on private land did not make every action of the club an action of the state. The majority noted that the impetus for discrimination did not have to originate with the state in

order for there to be state action, so long as the state was involved in enforcing private discrimination in a significant way. If the lodge had been a tenant in a state-owned building and had opened its facilities to all members of the pubic except African Americans, the state would have been engaged in a joint venture with the club, and the club's discrimination would have been state action. Here, however, the building was privately owned, it rested on privately owned land, and its facilities were open not to the public in general, but to members only. The Court observed that the state provided many services, among them water, electricity, licensing, and police and fire protection. The mere provision of such services was not enough to convert every action of the beneficiary into state action.

The dissenters argued that there was state action, since the liquor regulatory scheme was pervasive, regulating "virtually every detail of the operation of the licensee's business." They also observed that since the quota for liquor licenses had been exceeded in Harrisburg, the state's renewal of the Moose Lodge's license prevented a different facility with nondiscriminatory policies from opening.

This important case limited the reach of the Fourteenth Amendment by defining state action narrowly. It remains possible for victims of discrimination to find recourse in federal and state antidiscrimination statutes. Leroy Irvis was able to do just that when he brought suit against Moose Lodge No. 107 under Pennsylvania's public accommodations law. He eventually gained admission to the club's facilities and was later elected speaker of the Pennsylvania House of Representatives.

See also Equal protection of the law; *Jones v. Alfred H. Mayer Co.*; Racial and ethnic discrimination; Restrictive covenant; Segregation, *de facto* and *de jure*; *Shelley v. Kraemer*.

Moral relativism

Definition: The ethical belief that what is morally right depends on one's culture or varies from person to person
Significance: The belief is commonly held to be conducive to tolerance and to show the wrongness of laws that seek to prohibit "immoral" behavior that does not directly harm others

A wide variety of moral codes exists among different cultures, and this fact suggests that ethical universalism—the belief that there are moral norms valid for all human beings—is false. Instead, it seems that what is right or wrong is relative to one's culture. This type of ethical relativism is known as cultural or social relativism. Cultural relativists commonly hold that if in a particular society bribery, for example, is a widely accepted business practice, then bribery is right in this society. Conversely, if in a different society bribery is generally morally condemned, then it would be wrong to bribe in this society.

The most extreme form of ethical relativism is individual relativism, defined as the belief that what is right or wrong is relative to each individual. The individual relativist maintains that suicide, for example, may be right for one person, while it may be wrong for someone else in a similar situation. The individual relativist typically views moral judgments as subjective and similar to judgments of taste. Just as people like different foods, so they have different moral values, and, just as it is wrong to criticize people for their culinary preferences, so it is wrong to criticize their values.

The law has traditionally prohibited many forms of conduct that do not lead to direct harm to others but are considered to be immoral, such as sodomy, suicide, gambling, and prostitution. The claim that such victimless immoral practices should be legally prohibited is sometimes met by the relativist's response, "Who is to judge?" The point of this individual relativist response is that, since what is right is relative to each individual, it would be wrong for the law to impose one particular moral viewpoint on the citizens. To most people, this response is inadequate. Citizens should be free to make their own moral choices in some areas, but the relativist's view implies that all legal prohibitions are ultimately arbitrary because all morality is relative. It is true that by emphasizing the idea that different moral codes of different cultures have equal validity, the cultural relativist may increase open-mindedness concerning moral practices opposed to one's own. Yet the relativist is also committed to the view that one should be intolerant if one lives in a society in which intolerance is the dominant norm. Only the ethical universalist can consistently claim that everyone should be tolerant.

Western moral philosophy has been predominantly universalist, and this is reflected in the American legal and political tradition. The Declaration of Independence and the Bill of Rights assume that all human beings have certain moral or natural rights. An appeal to universal moral principles is also not uncommon in judicial decision making. A rejection of ethical relativism is also embedded in U.S. foreign policy insofar as it aims to promote human rights.

See also Jurisprudence; Justice; Morality and foreign policy; Natural law and natural rights; Positive law.

Moral turpitude

DEFINITION: Term describing an act or behavior, whether illegal or not, that violates the accepted moral standards of a community

SIGNIFICANCE: Like disorderly conduct, vagrancy, loitering, trespassing, and contributing to the delinquency of a minor, moral turpitude has been used by the police as a vague charge against individuals who cannot be accused of more tangible offenses

Moral turpitude is most generally applied to several of the so-called victimless crimes, most often involving sexual conduct or substance use. Developments such as sexual liberation movements of various kinds have tended to change public opinion about certain forms of behavior often classified as moral turpitude.

There have been concomitant changes in public policy. Some states have overturned their antisodomy laws in court decisions or by statute. The U.S. Supreme Court's ruling in *Bowers v. Hardwick* (1986), however, upheld Georgia's challenged antisodomy laws as constitutional even when the act is consensual. U.S. immigration laws continue to bar an alien from citizenship on account of "moral turpitude," interpreted as involving, among other things, fornication, prostitution, and homosexuality.

See also Disorderly conduct; Indecent exposure; *Mala in se* and *mala prohibita*; Pandering; Pedophilia; Vagrancy laws; Victimless crimes.

Morality and foreign policy

DEFINITION: The role that ethical judgments and values should play in the conduct of a nation's foreign affairs

SIGNIFICANCE: The notion of a "moral" foreign policy is central to the idealist perspective of international politics, a perspective which seeks to enhance peace and justice by placing moral values above narrow conceptions of the national interest

The appropriate role for moral values in foreign policy has been a divisive issue for scholars and statesmen alike. The issue is particularly relevant to the long-standing debate between proponents of the idealist and realist perspectives of international politics.

Idealism. The philosophical perspective known as idealism emphasizes the potential for good in human nature and therefore in the behavior of nation-states as well. Idealists view war and other forms of conflict as aberrant and attributable to a combination of misunderstandings, negative stereotypes about others, and the failure of leaders and diplomats to elevate moral and ethical concerns above the selfish pursuit of national interests (what the seventeenth century French minister Cardinal de Richelieu called "reasons of state"). The central premise of the idealist perspective is that world peace is achievable, but only if governmental leaders are willing to sacrifice parochial interests on behalf of values such as justice, equality, and compromise. Supporters of the idealist approach, including American presidents Woodrow Wilson, Jimmy Carter, and Bill Clinton, have consequently been in the forefront of movements to strengthen international law, use negotiations to reduce armaments, and uphold universal standards of human rights. Important to their approach has been the belief that nation-states should be guided and judged by the same moral standards as individuals.

Human Rights. While the idealist perspective has long championed a variety of moral causes, perhaps the most important to contemporary idealists has been the protection of human rights abroad. In this view, leaders of democratic countries have a moral obligation to speak out on behalf of rights such as freedom of speech and press and against violations of those rights by foreign governments. As such, the policies pursued by the United States toward other nations should be strictly determined by the extent to which their governments adhere to certain moral standards in the treatment of their people—standards which are codified in documents such as the Universal Declaration of Human Rights (1948) and the International Covenant on Civil and Human Rights (1966). This idealist perspective explicitly rejects notions of cultural relativism or "different" standards of human rights for different countries, arguing instead that no government has the right to engage in acts such as torture and genocide. This emphasis

A 1982 march in Washington, D.C., protesting U.S. support of the El Salvador government, which perpetrated many human rights violations during a civil war. (Jim West)

upon human rights has also been responsible for the founding of various nongovernmental organizations dedicated to monitoring human rights violations, including Amnesty International, Freedom House, and Americas Watch.

Promotion of Democracy. Related to the idealist support for human rights is the belief that the spread of democratic institutions and practices enhances both adherence to human rights and prospects for peace and justice between nations. Idealists see democracy as the only legitimate form of government, because they believe that it is the only kind which has historically guaranteed basic human liberties. They also argue, in agreement with the views of scholars dating back to the eighteenth century German philosopher Immanuel Kant, that democratic governments are more peaceful in nature and therefore less likely to become involved in foreign conflicts. President Woodrow Wilson, for example, justified American intervention in World War I as an effort "to make the world safe for democracy" and explicitly blamed the war upon the autocratic governments of Europe. Thus, for Wilson, as for his idealist contemporaries, policies which promote the spread of democracy abroad are both morally desirable and help to expand a "zone of peace and justice" in the international system.

The Realist Critique. The realist approach to international politics has been sharply critical of what its supporters see as the excessive moralism inherent in idealism. For prominent realists such as scholar Hans Morgenthau and former American secretary of state Henry Kissinger, statesmen have an obligation to protect the vital interests of the nations they represent and should avoid elevating their own personal moral values above such interests. While realists, too, claim an interest in moral standards, they differ with idealists in arguing that such moral values can only be realized through prudent policies that also secure the national interest. In their view, the utopian moralism of the idealists is a recipe for hypocrisy, perpetual conflict, and eventual national disillusionment.

The idealist response to the realist critique has been to argue that their attention to moral concerns, far from sacrificing the national interest, represents a higher conception thereof. By avoiding the temptation to conduct an amoral foreign policy, and doing instead that which is morally correct, idealists claim that leaders can encourage others to do the same and thereby advance the causes of peace and justice. If the realists believe that no good can come of foreign policies conducted on a basis other than the national interest, idealists argue that true national interests are indistinguishable from moral values.

—Bradley R. Gitz

See also Carter, Jimmy; Democracy; International law; Wilson, Woodrow.

BIBLIOGRAPHY

For the idealist view see Stanley Hoffmann, *Duties Beyond Borders: On the Limits and Possibilities of Ethical International Politics* (Syracuse, N.Y.: Syracuse University Press, 1981), and Felix Oppenheim, *The Place of Morality in Foreign Policy* (Lexington, Mass.: Lexington Books, 1991). An analysis of the idealist-realist tension in American foreign policy is Robert E. Osgood, *Ideals and Self-Interest in America's Foreign Relations* (Chicago: University of Chicago Press, 1953). A representative idealist endorsement of the human rights cause by a former American secretary of state is Cyrus R. Vance, "The Human Rights Imperative," *Foreign Policy* 63 (Summer, 1986). The realist critique of a prominent role for morality in foreign policy can be found in Hans Morgenthau, *Politics Among Nations* (5th ed. New York: Alfred A. Knopf, 1973), and Henry Kissinger, *Diplomacy* (New York: Simon & Schuster, 1994).

Mothers Against Drunk Driving (MADD)

DATE: Established 1980

SIGNIFICANCE: MADD has been a vital force in passing antidrunk driving legislation on the federal and state levels and encouraging citizen participation in working toward the elimination of the drunk driving problem

Mothers Against Drunk Driving (formerly called Mothers Against Drunk Drivers) was formed in 1980 by Candy Lightner after her thirteen-year-old daughter was killed by a drunk hit-and-run driver in California. The driver, who had four prior driving under the influence (DUI) arrests, served less than two years jail time. His light sentence prompted Lightner to form the organization for the purpose of tightening drunk driving laws. By the time Lightner left MADD in 1985, there were more than 320 chapters nationwide, and all fifty states had tightened their drunk driving laws. MADD is a nonprofit volunteer organization with more than three million members and affiliates in Canada, New Zealand, Australia, and England.

National initiatives supported by congressional efforts resulted in the passage of a number of federal laws, including the National Minimum Drinking Age Law in 1984 and the Drunk Driving Prevention Act of 1988. This amendment to the Anti-Drug Abuse Act of 1988 grants monetary incentives for states that adopt administrative license revocation, self-sufficient DUI enforcement funding programs, open container laws, mandatory alcohol testing in fatal/serious injury crashes, license plate confiscation, and age twenty-one enforcement measures.

MADD was also instrumental in the reauthorization of the 1984 Victims of Crime Act, extending the category of crime victims to include victims of drunk driving crashes. Other federal legislation in which MADD was involved includes the 1988 federal law requiring that alcoholic beverage containers carry warning labels citing the risks of fetal alcohol syndrome and impairment of driving skills, the revision of section 410 of the Federal Intermodel Surface Transportation Efficiency Act of 1991, which grants incentives to states passing countermeasure laws, the 1994 crime bill's Child Protection Act, carrying penalties for DUI offenders apprehended driving with a child in the vehicle, and the revision of federal laws which previously allowed DUI offenders to discharge their obligations to victims by declaring bankruptcy. MADD also closely monitors state legislation related to drunk driving, publishing annual "report cards" on each state's efforts.

MADD credits its organization with helping to pass more than fourteen hundred pieces of victim rights and victim compensation legislation. Victim services include providing information for victims and their families on bereavement groups, the judicial system, and other assistance groups. The victim outreach program aids victims by taking them through the court process step by step.

In addition to legislative involvement and the provision of counseling services, MADD's methods include media exposure and contacts, offering educational workshops, constant updating of compendium resources, increasing public awareness, networking with other concerned citizens' and safety groups, running youth programs, and monitoring alcohol advertisements.

See also Driving under the influence; Victim assistance programs; Victims of Crime Act.

Candy Lightner, founder of MADD, holds a photograph of her daughter who was killed by a drunk driver. (AP/Wide World Photos)

Motor vehicle theft

DEFINITION: The unauthorized, illegal taking of an automobile or other motor vehicle

SIGNIFICANCE: Motor vehicle theft is one of the leading property crimes in the United States

According to the Insurance Information Institute, a motor vehicle was stolen every twenty seconds in the United States in 1994. Somewhat surprisingly, new, expensive, or luxury-model cars are not the most likely targets of car thieves. The most commonly stolen cars are about ten years old and of relatively low value; they are often stolen because thieves can resell their parts for use in other vehicles. Car thieves are rarely caught; on average, only about 14 percent of all U.S. car thefts reported end in an arrest.

Data on car thefts is collected by a number of sources. Local police departments report citizen complaints to the Federal Bureau of Investigation (FBI), which publishes the Uniform Crime Reports, a national survey of crimes in the United States. The National Insurance Crime Bureau also collects information on car theft using claims received by insurance companies. All sources report that automobile theft is by far the most reported crime in the United States, largely because of insurance requirements that prevent policy recovery if the theft is not reported. Most surveys, however, indicate a decline in motor vehicle theft. This decline can be attributed to a number of factors: tougher state and federal legislation, increased public awareness, and the proliferation of antitheft devices and alarm systems, among others.

State and Federal Law. Although every state has a criminal statute punishing automobile theft, several key federal statutes have also addressed the crime. The first federal motor-vehicle theft law was enacted in 1919, when the federal government intervened against car thieves with the passage of the Dyer Act. The Dyer Act made interstate transportation of stolen vehicles a federal crime. Since then, federal intervention has largely

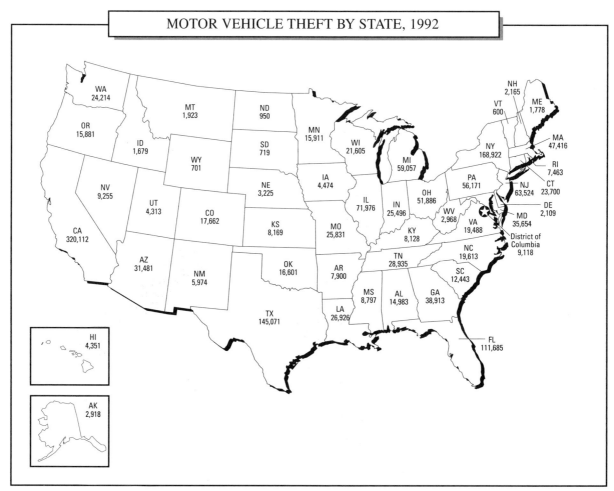

MOTOR VEHICLE THEFT BY STATE, 1992

WA 24,214
MT 1,923
ND 950
MN 15,911
NH 2,165
VT 600
ME 1,778
OR 15,881
ID 1,679
SD 719
WI 21,605
NY 168,922
MA 47,416
WY 701
MI 59,057
RI 7,463
NV 9,255
NE 3,225
IA 4,474
PA 56,171
NJ 63,524
CT 23,700
UT 4,313
CO 17,662
IL 71,976
IN 25,496
OH 51,886
WV 2,968
DE 2,109
CA 320,112
KS 8,169
MO 25,831
KY 8,128
VA 19,488
MD 35,654
District of Columbia 9,118
AZ 31,481
NM 5,974
OK 16,601
AR 7,900
TN 28,935
NC 19,613
SC 12,443
TX 145,071
LA 26,926
MS 8,797
AL 14,983
GA 38,913
FL 111,685
HI 4,351
AK 2,918

Source: Data are from U.S. Department of Justice, Federal Bureau of Investigation, *Crime in the United States, 1992* (Uniform Crime Reports). Washington, D.C.: U.S. Government Printing Office, 1993.

Note: The five states with the highest motor vehicle theft rates, as opposed to total numbers of motor vehicle thefts, were, in descending order, California, New York, Florida, Texas, and Arizona.

It has been estimated that only about 14 percent of motor vehicle thefts end in arrest. (McCrea Adams)

Motor Vehicle Theft, 1993: Percentages by Type			
Region	Autos	Trucks and Buses	Other Vehicles
Total U.S.	**79.2**	**15.4**	5.5
Northeastern states	92.3	4.6	3.2
Midwestern states	82.1	11.8	6.1
Southern states	75.2	18.0	6.8
Western states	72.5	22.0	5.5

Source: U.S. Department of Justice, Federal Bureau of Investigation, *Crime in the United States* (Uniform Crime Reports). Washington, D.C.: U.S. Government Printing Office, 1994.

Note: Because of rounding, percentages may not add to 100 percent.

occurred as regulation on automobile manufacturers or in response to an upward surge in thefts. In the late 1960's, federal laws were enacted that focused on preventing theft by requiring that automakers identify vehicles through a system of numbering. Vehicle identification numbers are now common for all cars. In the 1980's, when the number of reported car thefts reached an all-time high, federal measures were imposed to require automakers to begin including some antitheft measures in new cars with high-theft records. Cars with dealer-installed antitheft devices that disable the vehicle's electrical system and activate sirens and flashing lights to discourage car theft have been stolen less frequently than their nonequipped counterparts. The trend toward built-in antitheft devices has continued, in part because of federal legislation requiring automakers to place the vehicle identification numbers on frequently resold parts and on other components of vehicles with high incidences of theft, thus making such items easier to track. Additional requirements include warning alarms that sound if the keys are accidentally left in a vehicle after the car door is opened. These initiatives are only some of the requirements put into place by the Motor Vehicle Theft Law Enforcement Act of 1984.

In recognition of the international market for stolen cars and the parts from stolen cars, the Motor Vehicle Theft Law Enforcement Act of 1984 also included a provision aimed at curtailing the business of international sale. The 1984 act made illegal the sale of stolen vehicles and parts taken from stolen vehicles both in the United States and internationally, gave customs officers greater authority to inspect and arrest, and instituted stiffer fines, sentences, and penalties for those convicted of violating its provisions. The Anti-Car Theft Act, which became law in 1992, extends the provisions of the Motor Vehicle Theft Law Enforcement Act of 1984.

State laws have also been bolstered in the past decade. Model laws gained significant attention in the 1980's. The most significant model law is the Vehicle Chop Shop, Stolen and Altered Property Act. The Chop Shop Act was aimed at combating organized theft rings, which typically consist of a three-part operation to steal cars, strip them of their valuable components, and resell those components for profit. Seven states had adopted this law as of 1995. Numerous other states have strengthened existing motor vehicle theft statutes to include stiffer penalties for those convicted of motor vehicle theft and additional penalties for resale of stolen goods.

Organizations formed to increase citizen awareness and reporting of theft and illegal chop shop operations have also contributed to the decline in motor vehicle thefts, as have commercially available antitheft devices and alarms that are easily installed by consumers themselves.

Carjacking. Perhaps as a result of these measures, the FBI's Uniform Crime Reports showed car theft declining in the mid-1990's. Yet carjacking, a violent form of car theft that often involves danger to car owners, was on the rise in urban areas. Although law enforcement officials do not consider carjacking a new crime, it has only relatively recently been reported as separate from car theft. The Department of Justice reports that in every year between 1987 and 1992, approximately thirty-five thousand carjackings occurred, with about half that number resulting in the actual theft of a car. Although this amounts to only about 2 percent of all car thefts, the greater risk in a carjacking incident is of physical harm to the victim. FBI data suggest that one of every four carjacking attempts ends with the victim being injured by the carjacker. In addition to providing for increased car marking to prevent sale of parts, the Anti-Car Theft Act of 1992 makes carjacking a federal crime punishable by fifteen years in prison. The Violent Crime Control and Law Enforcement Act of 1994 adds the provision that the death penalty may be sought if a victim dies as a result of injuries sustained in a carjacking.   *— Karyn E. Langhorne*

See also Carjacking; Crime; Crime Index; Motor Vehicle Theft Act; Motor Vehicle Theft Law Enforcement Act.

BIBLIOGRAPHY

The House of Representatives report *Anti-Car Theft Act of 1992: Hearings Before the Subcommittee on Crime and Criminal Justice* (Washington, D.C.: Government Printing Office, 1992), Michael R. Rand's *Carjacking: National Crime Victimization Survey* (Washington, D.C.: Bureau of Justice Statistics, 1994), and Caroline Wolf Harlow's *Motor Vehicle Theft* (Bureau of Justice Statistics, 1988) provide good official overviews of automotive theft in the United States. Steven Cole Smith's "Have Screwdriver, Will Steal" (*Car and Driver*, July, 1994) contains interviews with car thieves. John L. Russell III's *Involuntary Repossession: Or, In the Steal of the Night* (Boulder, Colo.: Paladin Press, 1979) is a fascinating, though somewhat dated, how-to manual on the mechanics of car theft.

Motor Vehicle Theft Act

DATE: Became law October 29, 1919

DEFINITION: An act that established penalties for motor vehicle theft involving interstate commerce

SIGNIFICANCE: This act was one of a series of bills utilizing the Constitution's commerce clause to expand federal involvement in the enforcement of criminal law

In 1919, approximately 6.5 million motor vehicles were registered in the United States. Criminals and criminal rings, particularly in larger cities, were taking advantage of this rapidly expanding opportunity, so that automobile theft was a burgeoning problem and insurance rates were rising significantly. Although all states already had established laws against automobile theft, the Motor Vehicle Theft Act (the Dyer Act) made the theft of motor vehicles and the receipt of stolen vehicles a federal offense when state boundaries were crossed. It specified penalties of five thousand dollars and/or up to five years in prison.

The commerce clause of the Constitution thus was used to justify federal involvement in what had been the jurisdiction of state and local authorities. Some opposed the legislation out of concern for states' rights, and President Woodrow Wilson did not support the bill, which became law without his signature. In following years, federal regulation of business and labor would be expanded significantly on the basis of the commerce clause.

See also Carjacking; Motor vehicle theft; Motor Vehicle Theft Law Enforcement Act.

Motor Vehicle Theft Law Enforcement Act

DATE: Became law October 25, 1984
DEFINITION: Established criminal penalties for trafficking in stolen vehicles and their parts
SIGNIFICANCE: This law required automobile manufacturers to mark fourteen major car parts with a vehicle identification number (VIN)

Pressure for legislation to combat vehicle theft stemmed from a dramatic increase in the number of stolen automobiles. Organized crime controlled networks of "chop shops" that dismantled stolen cars and sold their parts, costing the nation five billion dollars annually. The law required manufacturers to place vehicle identification number (VIN) marks on major parts of automobile models that were subject to higher than average theft rates. In response to company complaints that the proposal added to car costs, the final act signed by President Ronald Reagan limited the number of marked parts to fourteen and required each manufacturer to mark no more than fourteen of its models. It established penalties for altering VIN marks (a fine of up to five thousand dollars and/or a maximum of five years in prison) and for trafficking in stolen vehicles and their parts (up to twenty-five thousand dollars and/or ten years in prison). The secretary of transportation selected the parts and models to be marked.

See also Carjacking; Motor vehicle theft; Motor Vehicle Theft Act.

MOVE, Philadelphia police bombing of

DATE: May 13, 1985
PLACE: Philadelphia, Pennsylvania
SIGNIFICANCE: A bungled attempt to evict illegal squatters resulted in eleven deaths and the destruction of sixty-one homes

MOVE, founded in 1972 by Vincent Leaphart, who adopted the name "John Africa," was a group of "back-to-nature" activists with an unusual and inconsistent philosophy. Although they advocated going back to nature, they were an urban movement. They shunned modern technology but used an elaborate loudspeaker system to bombard neighbors with their views. They decried pollution but littered property with their garbage and human waste.

The origin of the term "MOVE" is unclear. Not an acronym, it is generally believed to be merely a shortened form for the term "movement." MOVE first received media attention in 1978, when Philadelphia police clashed with members when police tried to evict them from an illegally occupied house. One police officer was killed, and eight officers and firefighters were wounded. Nine MOVE members were convicted of murder.

After failing to win the release of their imprisoned colleagues, MOVE members barricaded their new residence in a middle-class neighborhood, hooked up an elaborate sound system, and bombarded their neighbors for twelve hours per day with their profanity-laced speeches. This continued for more than two years, despite repeated appeals to the city by neighborhood residents. Philadelphia Mayor Wilson Goode, that city's first African American mayor, chose to ignore the appeals of local residents. At one point, Mayor Goode announced that he preferred "to have dirt and some smell than to have death." The denouement, however, included dirt, smell, and death.

After local residents held a press conference on May 1, 1985, criticizing the city's inaction, city officials decided to take aggressive action. On May 13, 1995, Police Commissioner Gregore Sambor told MOVE members to vacate their two-story row house. Tear gas was fired into the house, and a gun battle commenced. Twelve hours later, MOVE members still occupied the house. Police officials requested and received Mayor Goode's permission to drop a satchel filled with explosives onto the roof of MOVE's house. The goal was to dislodge a rooftop bunker; the result, however, was a fire that quickly got out of control. By the time the fires were controlled, eleven MOVE members, including four children, were dead. Only one thirty-year-old woman and one thirteen-year-old boy escaped alive. In addition to the deaths, two city blocks were destroyed, and sixty-one homes were reduced to embers.

Newspapers across the nation and throughout the world condemned the mayor's decision to drop the bomb, but a majority of local residents, both black and white, supported Goode and the police department. By the mid-1990's, the MOVE bombing had cost Philadelphia $30 million, and legal action was still pending. The city rebuilt the sixty-one destroyed homes, paid settlements to residents for lost belongings, and paid damages to the families of slain MOVE members. A 1986 citizens' commission concluded that Mayor Goode and the police and fire commissioners had "exhibited a reckless disregard for life and property." Goode was reelected to another four-year term in 1987.

See also Branch Davidians, federal raid on; King, Rodney, case and aftermath; National Commission on the Causes and Prevention of Violence.

Mueller v. Allen

COURT: U.S. Supreme Court

DATE: Decided June 29, 1983

SIGNIFICANCE: The Supreme Court upheld a state law that allowed taxpayers to deduct educational expenses that mostly benefited parents of children in private religious schools

A Minnesota statute authorized state taxpayers to deduct up to seven hundred dollars from their gross income for expenses incurred in school tuition, textbooks, and transportation for dependents who attended elementary or secondary schools in the state. Although the law extended the benefits to parents of children attending both public and private schools, more than 95 percent of the benefits went to those whose children were in religious schools. Several Minnesota taxpayers contested the law in federal court, arguing that it violated the separation of church and state required by the establishment clause of the First Amendment. After the trial and appellate courts ruled that the law was constitutional, the plaintiffs took their case to the U.S. Supreme Court.

The precedents of the Court appeared to suggest that the statute would be ruled unconstitutional. In *Committee for Public Education and Religious Liberty v. Nyquist* (1975), the Court had struck down a New York law that had provided tuition grants and tax credits for parents of children in church-related institutions. *Nyquist* and other precedents had established that a state may not aid parochial schools either by direct grants or by indirect tax credits to the parents.

In *Mueller*, however, the Court voted 5 to 4 to uphold the Minnesota law. Writing for the majority, Chief Justice William Rehnquist argued that the law was consistent with the three-pronged test of *Lemon v. Kurtzman* (1971). First, the law had the secular purpose of educating children and promoting diversity of educational institutions; second, it was religiously neutral, because it was designed to benefit parents of children in both public and private schools; third, it did not result in "excessive entanglement" between church and state, since there was no program for monitoring instructional materials.

The three dissenters argued that the Minnesota law was unconstitutional because it had the effect of providing financial assistance to sectarian schools. They emphasized that parents of public school children were unable to claim large deductions for tuition and textbooks, and that 95 percent of the law's financial benefits went to parents with children in religious schools. Also, they observed that the statute did not restrict private schools to books approved for the public schools, with the result that the state became entangled in religious questions when deciding which books might qualify for tax exemption.

The *Mueller* decision was important because the majority of the Court went further than in perhaps any other case toward allowing an indirect subsidy for religious education. In *Aguilar v. Felton* (1985), however, the Court appeared to return to the idea of strict separation. Few observers expected that future cases would consistently defend either the state's right to accommodate religion or the duty to maintain a high wall of separation.

See also Establishment of religion; *Everson v. Board of Education*; *Lemon v. Kurtzman*; *Lynch v. Donnelly*; School prayer; *Tilton v. Richardson*.

Muhammad, Elijah (Elijah Poole; Oct. 7, 1897, Sandersville, Ga.—Feb. 25, 1975, Chicago, Ill.)

IDENTIFICATION: Black nationalist leader of the Nation of Islam

SIGNIFICANCE: Elijah Muhammad was the leader of the Nation of Islam from the mid-1930's to the mid-1970's

Elijah Poole was the son of sharecroppers; his father was also a Baptist preacher. He attended school through the fourth grade and in his youth witnessed a white mob lynch an innocent black man.

He married Clara Evans in 1917 and moved to Detroit in 1923. After meeting Wallace D. Fard, the founder of the Nation of Islam, he joined the organization; his name was changed to Elijah Muhammad in 1931. Muhammad began to lead the Nation of Islam after Fard's disappearance in 1934. The Nation of Islam under Muhammad advocated black pride, self-reliance, and black separatism. Whites were considered a race of devils.

In 1942 Muhammad was imprisoned for refusing military service. By the 1950's the Chicago-based Nation of Islam was growing dramatically, partly because of another charismatic leader, Malcolm X. Although the group's membership probably never exceeded 500,000, its influence was widely felt. Muhammad authored the book *Message to the Black Man*, published in 1965. After his death in 1975, the largest faction of the Nation of Islam, led by his son Wallace, abandoned the Nation's black nationalist tradition to embrace Sunni Islam. A smaller faction, however, led by Louis Farrakhan, remains staunchly black nationalist and continues the teachings and traditions established by Elijah Muhammad.

See also Malcolm X; Nation of Islam.

Muller v. Oregon

COURT: U.S. Supreme Court

DATE: Decided February 24, 1908

SIGNIFICANCE: For the first time in an important case, the Supreme Court sanctioned the use of sociological jurisprudence and adopted the position that the meaning given to law should evolve in relation to social needs

In 1908 attorney Louis D. Brandeis defended before the Supreme Court an Oregon law prohibiting the employment of women in factories and laundries for more than ten hours a day. That statute had been challenged by employers who argued that it impaired women's freedom of contract and violated their rights under the due process clause of the Fourteenth Amendment. In his now famous 104-page brief, in which only two pages dealt with abstract logic and legal precedents, Brandeis argued that existing law acknowledged that the right to purchase or sell labor was part of the "liberty" protected by the Constitution and that such liberty was subject to such reasonable restraints as a state government might impose, in the exercise of its police power, to protect the health, safety, morals, or general welfare. The question at issue, argued Brandeis, was whether Oregon's maximum-hour law was a necessary restraint. The answer to that question, said Brandeis, could not be answered by legal logic, only by facts.

In his defense Brandeis argued that a woman's special role (her child bearing and maternal functions) and her lack of physical strength relative to men required restricting her hours of work to ten per day. Armed with data from reports of factory inspectors, physicians, experts in hygiene, and special industrial commissions that had been gathered for his use by the National Consumers' League, Brandeis submitted seventy-five thousand words of facts to prove that long hours of work are dangerous to the health and safety of women. In a unanimous decision, the Supreme Court agreed and affirmed Oregon's ten-hour law. "Woman's physical structure, and the [maternal] functions she performs in consequence thereof," said the Court, "justify special legislation restraining or qualifying the conditions under which she should be permitted to toil."

Muller v. Oregon is important for several reasons. Although the decision related solely to the number of hours worked by women and could not be taken as a reversal of the Court's earlier ruling in *Lochner v. New York* (1905) that restricting the hours that men worked in a bakery was not a legitimate use of a state's police power, it did suggest a change in the Court's thinking. As a result, the *Muller* decision revived the entire field of protective labor legislation. Over the next eight years, forty-one states enacted new or revised hour laws for working women. In a broader sense, however, and for the first time in an important case, the Supreme Court allowed a new means of legal argumentation and accepted the position that the meaning given to the law should evolve in relation to social needs. The decision, in effect, sanctioned what came to be known as "sociological jurisprudence"—presenting factual data to establish the need for social legislation.

See also Brandeis, Louis D.; Constitutional interpretation; Judicial review; Jurisprudence; Labor law; *Lochner v. New York*; Sex discrimination.

Murder and homicide

DEFINITION: Homicide is the killing of one human being by another; murder is an unlawful homicide committed with "malice aforethought"

SIGNIFICANCE: Depending on the circumstances, a homicide may be criminal or may be either justified or excused by the law; murder is the most serious felony offense and is punishable by death in some states

Distinguishing Murder from Homicide. The words "murder" and "homicide" are often used interchangeably by the public; however, the terms are not synonymous. Any killing of one human being by another is homicide, but some acts of homicide are not criminal. A soldier who slays an enemy during war, an executioner who carries out a lawful sentence of death, or a peace officer who kills a suspect during a legal arrest or when preventing an escape (if only reasonable and necessary

force is used) are considered to have committed justifiable homicide because, in each instance, the act was authorized or commanded by law.

A homicide may also be justified or excused if committed in self-defense, in defense of others, or in defense of the home. Such killings are justified or excused depending on the circumstances of the act and the intent and beliefs of the one who acted. One who kills another who has aimed a loaded weapon and threatened to shoot has committed a justifiable homicide. If the threat is specious and the weapon unloaded, however, the slaying will not be justified, but it may be excused if the person reasonably but erroneously believed that the deadly defensive action was required to repel an attacker intent on killing or inflicting serious bodily harm. The defense of others is analyzed in a similar manner, but the defender can resist the attack of a third person with only the same force as can the victim.

An example of an excusable homicide is death caused by an accident in which the person responsible acted lawfully and was not criminally negligent. A motorist traveling within the speed limit and exercising reasonable caution while looking out for pedestrians should not be charged and convicted of murder or manslaughter if the car strikes and kills a person who suddenly darts into the road. The act is excusable.

Another special case is the killing of a fetus, whether in the case of an abortion or the rare case of another party killing a fetus as a consequence of killing (or trying to kill) the mother. At common law, and in the statutes of some states, these acts are not considered homicide because the fetus is not considered a human being. Those jurisdictions, which exclude the killing of a fetus from the proscription against murder or manslaughter, typically rely on a separate statute proscribing feticide or fetal infanticide to protect the unborn. When a distinction is drawn between a fetus and a human being to assess liability under criminal statutes, a child must be born alive—that is, it must be capable of existence independent of its mother—before it can be the victim of a homicide. In California and some other states, however, the killing of a fetus is specifically included within the statute defining murder. Feticide statutes do not necessarily conflict with state abortion laws or with decisions of the U.S. Supreme Court such as *Roe v. Wade* (1973). Statutes that define the unlawful killing of a fetus as murder or that proscribe such killing as infanticide carefully exclude therapeutic abortions, which are sanctioned by statute and by the constitutional right of privacy.

Elements of Murder. A conviction for murder requires proof beyond a reasonable doubt not only that a homicide has been committed but also that the accused has acted unlawfully and with "malice aforethought." Although the common understanding of the word "malice" connotes an attitude of ill will, hatred, or hostility, the legal definition means simply an intent to do a wrongful act without justification, excuse, or mitigation. Thus a person could be guilty of murder even if the intentional act that caused death was preformed to end the suffering of one who is terminally ill. Malice—and, therefore, intent—can be express or implied. Malice is express if the

MURDERS BY STATE, 1992

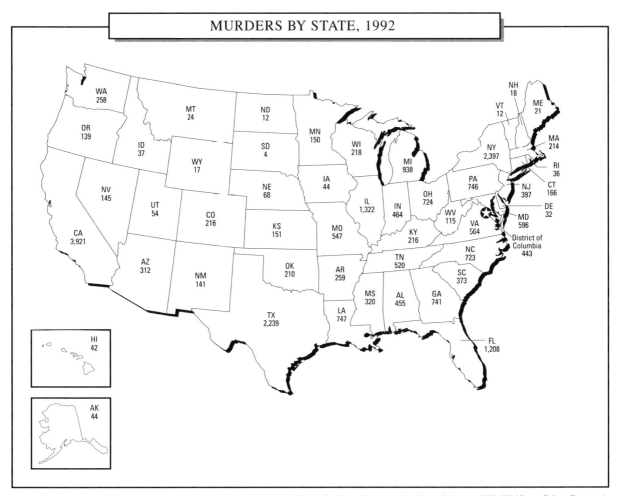

Source: Data are from U.S. Department of Justice, Federal Bureau of Investigation, *Crime in the United States, 1992* (Uniform Crime Reports). Washington, D.C.: U.S. Government Printing Office, 1993.

Note: The five states with the highest murder rates, as opposed to total numbers of murders, were, in descending order, Louisiana, New York, California, Texas, and Mississippi.

slayer intends to kill or to inflict serious bodily harm. The distinction between the two types of malice is significant only because of the nature of proof used to show guilt. Evidence that a defendant lay in wait for a victim or assembled and delivered a letter bomb, for example, demonstrates express malice. Malice is implied when the act manifests a wanton and willful disregard for human life or poses an unreasonable human risk. In some U.S. cities, drive-by-shootings have become endemic. If the shooter aims and fires intending to kill or cripple a rival, malice is express. If, however, the wrongdoer fires into a house in which people are obviously present even though the purpose is only to frighten the inhabitants, malice is implied because of the unreasonable risk and wanton disregard for the safety of the occupants.

Although many state statues still define murder by employing the term "aforethought," this usage is primarily of historical interest. Common law judges centuries ago in England

appear to have used the term to describe a well-thought-out plan to kill. In modern law, a showing of intent formed even at the same instant as the act causing the death is sufficient to support a conviction of murder.

One who perpetrates or attempts to perpetrate an inherently dangerous felony that results in a homicide is also guilty of murder. This rule, the felony murder rule, was well established under the common law of England and has been adopted in America by the various states. The rule does not require an intent to kill or even a finding of implied malice. In fact, the killing can be quite unintentional as long as there is some causal connection between the underlying crime or attempted crime and the homicide. An armed street robber whose gun accidentally discharges and kills a robbery victim who grabs at the weapon has committed murder. Moreover, if two felons join together to commit a dangerous felony and one is killed by a victim or by someone defending the victim, the surviving felon will be charged with murder under the felony murder rule. An arsonist who burns a structure believing no one to be inside and having no intent to kill may be responsible for the death not only of any building occupants whose presence was unknown but also of any firefighters who battle the blaze and die doing so. This rule made good sense in the early period of English common law, when all felonies were punishable by death and by the forfeiture of lands and possessions. The criminal risked his life by committing any serious wrongful acts such as arson, burglary, rape, or robbery, and the law considered it unimportant that the wrongdoer might be punished for murder even though the intent was to commit another felony. Under the common law, an attempted felony was only a misdemeanor; however, one who caused a homicide unintentionally during the attempted commission of a felony was punished as severely as if the attempted felony had been completed. The felony murder rule has been abolished in England and has been criticized in the United States, but it survives as a method of imposing liability for a criminal homicide without the necessity of proving intent.

Degrees of Murder. The early common law did not recognize degrees of murder, nor did it draw a distinction between murder and manslaughter. All murders were punishable by death. As the law developed in the years after the American Revolution, state legislatures recognized that applying capital punishment to all criminal homicides was unjust because of the widely differing circumstances involved in various homicides. Pennsylvania adopted the first American statute distinguishing between "degrees" of murder, providing the death penalty for first-degree murder and life imprisonment for second-degree murder. Other jurisdictions adopted similar laws, and states now typically divide criminal homicide into murder in two or three degrees and manslaughter. All such statutes recognize that some criminal homicides are more brutal and deserve greater punishment than others.

Most statutes define first-degree murder as murder that is willful, deliberate, and premeditated, that is perpetrated by poison, torture, or lying in wait, or that is caused by the perpetration or attempted perpetration of an inherently dangerous felony such as arson, rape, robbery, or burglary. Other statutes add a wider range of felonies such as child abuse, mayhem, or kidnapping, and some distinguish degrees by defining the characteristics of the murder—that is, whether multiple victims were killed or whether the victim was a peace officer engaged in discharging his duties. Under this type of statutory scheme, all murders that do not fit the definition of first-degree murder are considered second-degree murder.

For a murder to be of the first degree because it is willful, deliberate, and premeditated, it must be a well-considered action. "Willful" means intentional, and the intent must be express. "Premeditated" means that the action must be thought out before the crime, and "deliberate" means that the crime must have been considered, contemplated, or weighed in the mind in a calm and reflective state. Deliberation presupposes the absence of sudden passion caused by some provocation. Judges often speak

of deliberation as requiring a "cool state of blood." No specific length of time must be shown to establish that murder is deliberate and premeditated, but the length must be appreciable. Deliberation must occur before, not during, the act of killing.

An impulsive homicide committed with the intent necessary to constitute malice aforethought would be murder in the second degree rather than murder in the first degree. Also, one who acts with intent to cause serious bodily harm to another or acts in a manner posing a grave risk of death to others, but without the premeditated design to cause death, may be guilty of second-degree, rather than first-degree, murder. In those states that divide murder into three degrees, murder in the third degree includes those criminal homicides that are included in the definition of second-degree murder in other jurisdictions but that are the least atrocious of the crimes of murder.

Manslaughter is not a degree of murder but a separate offense. At common law, it was considered to be murder, but various statutory changes beginning in England have enumerated special rules defining the crime. Manslaughter is a criminal homicide committed without malice aforethought. It may be an intentional or unintentional act. The law regarding manslaughter evolved in a way so as to punish those killings that could not be justified or excused but that were not committed with malice aforethought. Voluntary manslaughter is often defined as an unlawful killing of another that is committed intentionally but in a sudden heat of passion as the result of adequate provocation. Involuntary manslaughter is the unintentional killing of another as the result of an unlawful act that is not a felony or as the result of a lawful but negligent act or failure to act when legal duty requires otherwise.

Murder in American Society. Murder is the most grave of those offenses committed by one person against another. Its consequences are tragic and permanent, and they profoundly affect the victim's family and friends. Consequently, modern American society reserves its harshest penalty, capital punishment, for convicted murderers, typically for those whose offense is first-degree murder. Some states refer to this crime, which is subject to capital punishment, as "capital murder" or "aggravated murder."

Murder rates rose dramatically in the last half of the twentieth century. Between 1960 and 1990, the chances of becoming a murder victim in the United States almost doubled. Such violence is particularly troublesome in large cities, where juvenile delinquency, gang violence, and drug-related crime radically altered inner-city areas. The nature of most criminal gangs was quite different before the 1970's. Gangs in earlier years, although frequently engaged in criminal activity, did not usually have access to the range of weapons that became readily available. Drug sales also appear to have had a significant effect on murder rates. Arrests and trials for drug possession and sales dominate the calendars of both state and federal courts. Those involved in illicit drug activity often have large amounts of cash to purchase assault weapons and other firearms, which then can be used to commit other crimes, including murder, to assist in the criminal enterprise.

According to the U.S. Department of Justice, firearms are by far the most common implement used to commit murder, constituting typically more than 60 percent of the weapons used to kill. Knives and other similar weapons used to cut or stab rank second and are used in approximately 20 percent of murders. The statistical predominance of firearms used in the rapidly escalating numbers of criminal homicides makes the issue of gun control a critical topic for Congress and the various state legislative bodies.

The victims of criminal homicides are typically male and relatively young. The Department of Justice reports that nearly 80 percent of U.S. murder victims are male. Nearly one-third of all victims are between the ages of twenty-five and thirty-four, with a slightly lower percentage of victims between the ages of fifteen and twenty-four. African Americans have a much greater statistical chance of dying as the victim of criminal homicide than do members of other races. Figures released by the Department of Justice show that at the beginning of the 1990's, a black male had one chance in thirty of being a victim of homicide, a black female one chance in 132, a white male one chance in 179, and a white female one chance in 495. The Department of Justice also reports that African American males and females are both overrepresented among convicted killers. Most killers murder within their own race.

HOMICIDES INVOLVING BLACK OR WHITE OFFENDERS AND VICTIMS, 1992

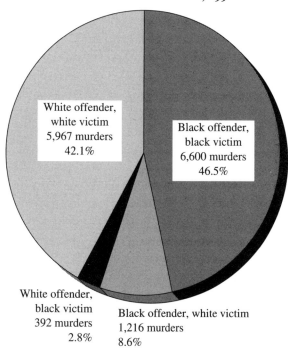

White offender, white victim
5,967 murders
42.1%

Black offender, black victim
6,600 murders
46.5%

White offender, black victim
392 murders
2.8%

Black offender, white victim
1,216 murders
8.6%

Source: Data are from *Newsweek,* August 15, 1994. Primary source: National Crime Analysis Program, Northeastern University.

For many people, especially residents of large metropolitan areas, one of the greatest fears is of being a victim of a violent confrontation with a stranger. Nevertheless, the majority of homicide victims are attacked by a relative or acquaintance. Bureau of Justice Statistics reports reveal that more than 75 percent of criminal homicide victims are killed by people they knew. Nearly 40 percent of all murders are the product of arguments, while about 18 percent occur during the commission of some other felony. Many murders occur between spouses or between other domestic partners. Most of the victims of domestic violence are women, although some well-publicized cases have focused attention on battered women who have slain an abusive partner after enduring long periods of emotional and physical trauma. Child abuse is also recognized as a widespread problem. Children are particularly vulnerable because of their inability to protect themselves and to seek help. Both physical abuse and neglect of children can end in murder unless police or social service agencies discover the abusive family and intervene.

Murder Prosecutions. The crime of murder is one over which the states usually have jurisdiction, and it is typically prosecuted by states unless the crime has occurred on federal territory or against a federal officer or agent. Federal prosecutions for murder typically derive from violation of specific congressional legislation protecting federal interests or involving matters of interstate concern. Each state adopts its own statutes proscribing criminal conduct and establishes its own rules of criminal procedure, subject only to the limitation that such law must conform to the Constitution. Thus the definitions of murder and manslaughter, the punishments imposed on those convicted, and the procedural steps from arrest to conviction, sentencing, and imprisonment differ somewhat among the various states.

The decision whether to prosecute a suspect for murder rests with the local prosecutor within the jurisdiction in which the crime occurred. The prosecutor has the discretion to reject cases when available evidence to prove guilt is weak, and the prosecutor may decline to file a case even when police have recommended that charges be brought. When this discretion is abused by local prosecutors, state authorities may intervene. However, when both the local and state prosecutors decline to go forward for improper reasons or when a jury fails to convict a defendant in a murder case under suspicious circumstances, federal prosecutors may seek to file charges under federal statutes such as those making it unlawful to deprive a person of civil rights guaranteed by the Constitution. This type of intervention has been employed when local authorities have declined to prosecute or juries have failed to convict Caucasians accused of murdering African Americans.

Murder prosecutions are conducted procedurally like other felony prosecutions, and the same constitutional safeguards apply. Nevertheless, the consequences to society and to the defendant—especially in murder cases in which capital punishment is a sentencing option—are so great that exceptional efforts are typically expended by both sides to contest all legal

A murder suspect being taken into custody. The crime of murder is generally prosecuted in state courts. (James L. Shaffer)

and factual issues. Usually, the most experienced prosecutors and defense attorneys try murder cases.

All criminal cases have a *corpus delicti*, which literally means the "body of a crime." In a murder prosecution, it is a reference to more than the deceased victim's corpse. It is evidence of the components of the crime: evidence that the victim is actually dead, that the death was caused by the criminal act of another, and, in some jurisdictions, that the defendant is that criminal. The importance of the *corpus delicti* rule, which is of practical significance primarily in murder cases, is that a conviction cannot rely upon the uncorroborated out-of-court statement or admission of the accused. The prosecution must offer additional evidence to establish the *corpus delicti* in order to obtain a conviction. Of course, a plea of guilt or other confession made in court is ordinarily sufficient to prove the *corpus delicti* and to support a conviction in a murder prosecution.

Murder is punished by imprisonment, sometimes for life without possibility of parole, and by death. Criminal sentencing is usually left up to the discretion of the judge, within guidelines set by statute, even in cases tried before a jury. Some states, however, require that the jury determine or participate in the determination of whether capital punishment should be imposed. Many state statutes declare that the death penalty is proper only when certain aggravating factors occur during the crime. Those who oppose capital punishment contend that it is imposed arbitrarily, has little deterrent effect, and constitutes cruel and unusual punishment in violation of the Eighth Amendment to the Constitution. Nevertheless, most polls indicate that the majority of Americans support the use of the death penalty, and the Supreme Court has upheld the validity of properly drafted death-penalty legislation against constitutional challenges. — *Scot Clifford*

See also Capital punishment; Child abuse; Civil Rights Acts of 1866-1875; Crime; Crime Index; Malice; Manslaughter; Murders, mass and serial; Self-defense.

BIBLIOGRAPHY

Murder in America (Thousand Oaks, Calif.: Sage Publications, 1994), by Robert M. Holmes and Stephen T. Holmes, studies various types of murder, mass murder, serial murder, terrorism, and sex-related homicide and contains useful statistical information. Colin Wilson's *A Criminal History of Mankind* (New York: G. P. Putnam's Sons, 1984) reviews the crime of murder and other serious criminal offenses from a historical perspective. Martin Daly's *Homicide* (Hawthorne, N.Y.: Aldine De Gruyter, 1988) reviews murder and other criminal homicide from a psychologist's perspective. Philip E. Devine's *The Ethics of Homicide* (Ithaca, N.Y.: Cornell University Press, 1978) is a fascinating study of the ethical aspects of homicide and of the homicides that society considers justified: abortion, capital punishment, and war. *The Human Side of Homicide* (New York: Columbia University Press, 1982), edited by Bruce L. Danto et al., is a collection of insightful essays on various topics pertinent to the issue of homicide in American society.

Murders, mass and serial

DEFINITION: Mass murderers characteristically slay several persons at one time and in one place, while serial murderers kill many persons over periods ranging from one month to many years

SIGNIFICANCE: Because of their distinctions from ordinary homicides, crimes of passion, and political terrorism, mass and serial killing have devastating impacts on the families and friends of victims and generate profound communal fears and dislocations

During the last half of the twentieth century, the incidence of mass murder in the United States had not decreased and the incidence of serial murders appeared to have increased significantly. Other than general suggestions by experts that Americans have created and live in a culture of violence, there are not yet definitive, overall explanations for the high incidences of either of these distinctive categories of crime. There is common agreement, however, that because of their savagery, superficial randomness, and sensational characters, mass and serial murders have devastating effects. Families and relatives of the slain are themselves tragically victimized, while widespread fear, panic, and a sense of vulnerability often blight the communities in which these crimes erupt. Such murders have been difficult and costly to predict, prevent, contain, or detect. Moreover, the public outrage they incite has swelled popular demand for capital punishment, which often seems thwarted by defense attorneys' pleas that their clients were not guilty by reason of mental incompetence, schizophrenia, or criminal "insanity."

Mass Murder. Typically mass murders occur in one place at one time when three, four, or more persons (experts disagree on the lowest number of victims constituting a "mass"), most of them strangers to the killer, are slain. The killer often turns his weapon upon himself or creates a suicidal situation in which police must kill him. Weaponry employed by mass murderers has included bombs, fires, poisons, handguns, rifles, and automatic assault guns. Mass murders are not novel, and the phenomenon has not been confined to the United States. Authorities are unclear about whether the incidence of these crimes has been rising or whether researchers' statistics have improved. Between 1949 and 1995, there were sixty-one mass murders in the United States (and among American citizens in Guyana), individually involving the deaths of from three to 912 victims.

The factors that produce a mass murderer largely seem to exclude genetic-biological disorders as well as socioeconomic factors such as poverty and dysfunctional family life. Rather, the mass murderer seems to have been subjected to a nightmarish combination of the worst social stresses (though only a few persons of the many who have experienced such combinations turn homicidal).

For purposes of study, prevention, apprehension, and prosecution, typologies of mass murders have been developed since the 1960's. These include murderers who are disciples of a "charismatic" leader such as Charles Manson or Jim Jones; family annihilators, who specialize in killing family members; pseudocommandos, or "gun fanatics," who want to teach the world a lesson; disgruntled employees who seek to avenge themselves on the persons or institutions that employed them; and set-and-run killers who, for material gain, murder by means of time-delayed bombs or by the contamination of food or medicinal products. Nearly all mass murderers have been males whose instabilities or potential for murder might possibly have been discernible by family, acquaintances, neighbors, institutional personnel, or teachers and social workers, because often they have not fit readily into normal social situations.

Serial Murder. Serial murder is an old and worldwide phenomenon. Except for evidence of higher intelligence among many of them, such killers have been hard to distinguish from the general population in behavioral terms, since they frequently blend into many social landscapes quite well. In the United States, the Department of Justice estimated in 1989 that as many as thirty-five serial killers were active in the nation. That figure may be far too low; criminologists and other researchers estimated in the early 1990's that the real figure might be three hundred active serial murderers, whose victims probably numbered about five thousand annually.

Not surprisingly, by the 1990's serial killers had become the subjects of intensive study. These have resulted, despite terminological differences among researchers, in serial killers being defined as a distinct species of murderers who can be classified, if not inclusively, under five major categories based on analyses of their motivations. Visionaries feel impelled to kill because they hear voices, have visions, or are driven to kill by internal demons or beasts. Mission-oriented killers concentrate on eliminating what they regard as "undesirable" types of humans, which can mean almost any group, from prostitutes to priests. Thrill killers derive aberrant sexual pleasure from necrophilia, dismemberment, cannibalism, coprophilia, or varieties of sadomasochism. Others kill to "play God," to exert complete control over helpless victims both before and after the victim's death. To this typology must be added team killers, so-called hit men for whom murder is a business for profit, women "comfort killers" who murder for financial gain, and human hunters whose joy comes from stalking and killing complete strangers.

Known serial killers, whose ranks include a growing number of women, appear to share three common traits. They are remorseless, feeling that those they murder are depersonalized objects. They become psychologically addicted to murdering. They are motivated by acquisitive, demonic, or sexual fantasies. Apprehending such killers requires careful profiling of crimes and victims and extremely close, if costly, collaboration among police authorities throughout the country. Creation of the computerized National Center for the Analysis of Violent Crime in the 1970's was a step in this direction.

— *Mary E. Virginia*

See also Capital punishment; Child abuse; Civil Rights Acts of 1866-1875; Crime; Crime Index; Malice; Manslaughter; Murder and homicide; Psychopath and sociopath; Self-defense.

BIBLIOGRAPHY
Publicity and communal shocks attending mass and serial murders have generated fine "true crime" works such as Tru-

Mass murderer Colin Ferguson after being sentenced to six consecutive life terms for a 1993 shooting spree on the Long Island Railroad in which six people died. (AP/Wide World Photos)

man Capote's *In Cold Blood* (New York: Random House, 1966), biographies of killers, and scholarly studies. Among the excellent crime portraits is Vincent Bugliosi's *Helter Skelter* (New York: W. W. Norton, 1974), a description of the infamous Manson family's murders. Stephen A. Egger's *Serial Murder* (New York: Praeger, 1985), using statistical and psychological profiling analyses, concentrates on the elusiveness of serial killers, while Ronald M. Holmes and James De Burger, *Serial Murder* (Newburn Park, Calif.: Sage Publications, 1988), along with Ronald M. Holmes and Stephen T. Holmes, *Murder in America* (Thousand Oaks, Calif.: Sage Publications, 1994), distinguish between mass and serial murders and suggest classifications for them. Jack Levin and James A. Fox, *Mass Murder* (New York: Plenum Press, 1985), discuss mass murder and its cultural context.

My Lai massacre

DEFINITION: The March, 1968, killing of more than five hundred Vietnamese civilians, including women, children, and elderly people, by United States military forces

SIGNIFICANCE: The attempts of some army officers and high-ranking officials to cover up the actions of American troops at My Lai illustrated the problem of military oversight of its own conduct in wartime

In 1968, the American military had become increasingly frustrated with the guerrilla war in Vietnam. Lacking a clearly defined strategy from Washington for achieving military victory, the military leadership defined victory as the destruction of villages that assisted communist forces. The most important measure of victory in the war against the elusive communist forces in 1968 was an estimate of enemy forces killed in combat, the so-called body count.

My Lai 4. In late February, 1968, American troops began to suffer an increasing number of casualties in Quang Ngai Province. With their morale diminished by random attacks by Viet Cong guerrillas, the Americans suspected the civilian population in the area of aiding and abetting communist forces. On March 16, 1968, elements of Charlie Company, a unit of the 11th Light Infantry Brigade, were ordered by Lieutenant Colonel Frank Barker to "search and destroy" villages suspected of sympathizing with the Viet Cong.

That morning, members of the company entered the village of Tu Chung, designated My Lai 4 by American troops. While the exact sequence of events has never been ascertained, what is clear is that unarmed civilians of Tu Chung were beaten, tortured, raped, and executed by American troops. A number of soldiers who took part in these events, later described as an "incident" by the army and a "massacre" by others, were commanded by Lieutenant William Calley, Jr. Charlie Company suffered only one casualty during the operation—a private who shot himself in the foot to avoid participating in the killing of civilians.

An army helicopter pilot, Hugh Thompson, Jr., witnessed the brutality from the air and threatened to turn the helicopter guns on the American troops if the carnage did not cease. Soon afterward, Charlie Company was ordered to cease fire, and many of the soldiers took a lunch break only yards from the piles of dead Vietnamese.

Exposure of the Massacre. Almost immediately after Charlie Company left My Lai 4, a number of army personnel began trying to clarify what exactly had happened on March 16. Officially there was a "body count" of 128 hostile forces killed in combat operations in and around My Lai 4. Lieutenant Colonel Barker told a briefing, "It was tragic that we killed women and children, but it was a combat operation." The operation was deemed a tactical success. A conspiracy among officers inside Charlie Company concealed the atrocities committed at My Lai 4 from top-level military officials in Vietnam. Helicopter pilot Thompson did inform his superiors about the carnage he had witnessed, but after a brief investigation the charges were dismissed.

Rumors about My Lai 4 continued to spread through the 11th Light Infantry Brigade. Shortly before a transfer out of Vietnam, Specialist Fourth Class Tom Glen wrote to General Creighton Abrams, commander of U.S. forces in Vietnam. Glen had not taken part in the My Lai operation but had heard

Lieutenant William Calley was convicted of murder for his role in the My Lai massacre, but he served little time in prison. (AP/Wide World Photos)

MY LAI MASSACRE / 539

firsthand accounts of the brutality. Concerned about what he perceived as widespread violence against civilians, Glen warned General Adams that this conduct was undermining U.S. efforts to defeat Viet Cong guerrilla tactics. Still, lacking specific accounts of brutality, high-level army officials failed to investigate Glen's charges. A memorandum prepared for General Adams by Colin Powell, later chairman of the Joint Chiefs of Staff, suggested that Glen's charges of widespread brutality were ill-founded: "In direct refutation of this portrayal is the fact that relations between American soldiers and Vietnamese people are excellent."

The events at My Lai 4 might never have been exposed had it not been for the efforts of two men, Ronald Lindenhour and Ronald Haeberle. Like Glen, Lindenhour had not participated in the My Lai operation but had heard a number of firsthand accounts. In March, 1969, Lindenhour wrote a letter to a number of congressional representatives outlining what he had learned about My Lai. Under pressure from Congress, the military began an investigation. It was not until August, 1969, when investigators interviewed retired army photographer Haeberle, that proof of the killings was obtained. Haeberle had used his own camera to record the dead at My Lai. The color photographs proved that killings indeed had taken place and that U.S. troops were responsible. Soon afterward, William Calley, Jr., was charged with multiple murder charges.

After free-lance journalist Seymour Hersh published an explosive account of his interview with Calley, the army moved forward with its charges against Calley and a number of other officers. Public opinion about the allegations of murder by American troops illustrated the divisive nature of the Vietnam War. When Haeberle's photographs were published in November of 1969, opponents of the war called for a full-scale investigation. Yet many supporters of the war saw My Lai as an aberration, and many also saw Calley as a scapegoat. Georgia governor Jimmy Carter even proclaimed an "American Fighting Men's Day" and asked Georgians to turn on their headlights to support Calley's service to the country.

Military Justice. The Nixon White House was extremely reluctant to push for a full investigation of My Lai. The Joint Chiefs of Staff, horrified at the allegations of misconduct, ignored White House advice and appointed Lieutenant General William Peers to lead an official military investigation. The report, completed in March, 1970, recommended that charges be brought against thirty soldiers who were found to have committed violations of the code of military conduct during the killings and the subsequent coverup. Army lawyers later charged fourteen, including two generals and three colonels. The army had chosen to charge only individuals who were still on active duty. Retired soldiers, many of whom had publicly detailed their involvement in the killing, were not charged.

Only four of the individuals charged were court-martialed; three were dismissed because of lack of evidence. Of the thirty officers cited in the Peers Report, only Calley was convicted by a military court. In 1971, he was found guilty of the premeditated murder of twenty-two villagers at My Lai 4. Originally given a life sentence, Calley was held for two months in a military prison and was later paroled by the secretary of the army. After years of legal motions, Calley's conviction was upheld in appeals court, but he remained free on parole.   — *Lawrence Clark III*

See also International law; Military justice; Vietnam War; War crimes.

The attempt to cover up the killings at My Lai by members of the American military was exposed in Seymour M. Hersh, *Cover Up: The Army's Secret Investigation of the Massacre at My Lai* (New York: Random House, 1972). For a comprehensive examination of the Peers Report and a historical examination of the legal aspects of war crimes, see Joseph Goldstein, Burke Marshall, and Jack Schwartz, *The My Lai Massacre and Its Cover-Up: Beyond the Reach of Law?* (New York: Free Press, 1976).

Nader, Ralph (b. Feb. 27, 1934, Winsted, Conn.)

IDENTIFICATION: Consumer advocate

SIGNIFICANCE: The leader of the modern consumer protection movement, Nader has focused national attention on unsafe and unethical practices by big business and government

From credit card and insurance scams to nuclear power plant safety, Ralph Nader has uncovered or publicized countless examples of fraudulent and unsafe practices on behalf of the American consumer. Nader's first major foray into consumer protection came while he was working in a Hartford law practice. Bothered by high automobile accident and death rates, he captured national attention with his case against de-

fective design in the auto industry. Nader's book *Unsafe at Any Speed* (1965) and his subsequent testimony before the U.S. Congress on auto safety in 1966 were instrumental in the passage of the National Traffic and Motor Vehicle Safety Act (1966) and federal regulation of automotive design.

Educated at Princeton University and Harvard Law School, Nader was the driving force behind "Nader's Raiders," college students and activists who investigated issues in the consumer interest. He founded the Center for Study of Responsive Law (1969) and the consumer lobbying group Public Citizen, Inc. (1971) and utilized published reports, lobbying, testimony before Congress, and appearances on television and the lecture

Ralph Nader became a prominent consumer rights activist in 1965 with the publication of his book Unsafe at Any Speed. (Library of Congress)

circuit to advance his points. Nader was instrumental in the passage of the Wholesome Meat Act (1967) and active on behalf of congressional term limits and automobile air bags.

See also Class action; Consumer fraud; Consumer rights movement.

Nation of Islam

DATE: Established 1930

SIGNIFICANCE: The Nation of Islam is the oldest and largest African American nationalist movement in the United States; it advocates self-sufficiency as the means for achieving justice for blacks

The Nation of Islam, or Black Muslims, was started by Wallace D. Fard, a silk peddler who appeared in Detroit in 1930. Fard claimed that he was from Mecca and that he was sent to bring freedom, justice, and equality to his black brethren in America. Fard mysteriously disappeared in 1933 or 1934, and Elijah Poole, the son of a rural African American preacher in Georgia, became the leader of the church. Poole, renamed Elijah Muhammad, began to preach that Fard had actually been Allah himself in human form. From the 1930's until his death in 1975, Elijah Muhammad headed the Nation of Islam and preached a dogma which combined elements of Islam, black separatism, black self-sufficiency, and the belief that whites were devils.

The sect's greatest period of growth occurred during the 1950's and early 1960's when Malcolm X headed the New York City temple of the Nation of Islam. Membership peaked at an estimated 100,000. Following a trip to Mecca in 1964, Malcolm X converted to traditional Islam, broke with the Nation of Islam, and formed his own group. In 1965, Malcolm X was assassinated.

Following the death of Elijah Muhammad in 1975, the Nation of Islam split. One faction, the American Muslim Mission, was led by Elijah's son Wallace D. Muhammad. It followed more orthodox Islamic teachings and ceased to preach separatism. The other faction, led by Louis Farrakhan, reaffirmed the doctrines of Elijah Muhammad and continued to preach that whites were devils and that African Americans were Allah's chosen people. Farrakhan modified his stance on separatism and became involved in Jesse Jackson's presidential campaign in 1984. The Nation of Islam was undeniably the most widely known and influential black separatist organization in the latter twentieth century, and it remains a controversial group in both the African American community and American society.

See also Jackson, Jesse; Malcolm X; Muhammad, Elijah.

National Advisory Commission on Civil Disorders

DATE: Established July 29, 1967; report issued March 1, 1968

SIGNIFICANCE: The commission, commonly known as the Kerner Commission, was created by President Lyndon B. Johnson to investigate the causes and possible future prevention of racial violence and unrest; it placed the primary blame on continuing discrimination by whites

The National Advisory Commission on Civil Disorders was created by executive order in 1967 with Governor Otto Kerner of Illinois as chairman and Mayor John V. Lindsay of New York City as vice chairman. The commission had eleven members, including four members of Congress as well as labor, civil rights, and law enforcement leaders. Other public officials and private citizens participated on advisory panels studying such things as private enterprise and insurance in riot-affected areas.

Racial violence had escalated with the riots in Watts in 1965 and, by the summer of 1967, was spreading to other American cities. After extensive study, the commission recommended new and expanded employment and educational opportunity programs, national standards for welfare programs, and increased access to housing. The commission's report stated that the United States was becoming "two societies, one black, one white—separate and unequal." It was the first major study to place the blame for creating black ghettos on white society.

The commission studied the major race riots, identified patterns in the violence, developed profiles of participants, and analyzed the conditions prior to and following the disorders. Despite concern among some officials that the violence was being encouraged by radical groups, the commission determined that the principal causes were widespread discrimination and segregation and the increasing concentration of the black population in inner-city ghettos offering little opportunity. These conditions, according to the report, lead to pervasive frustration, the acceptance of violence as a means of retaliation, and growing feelings of powerlessness. A spark was all that was necessary to ignite violence, and the police often provided it. The commission recommended new federal programs to address the problems of poverty, unemployment, education, and housing and the expansion of existing urban programs, such as the Model Cities Program, to provide economic opportunity to residents of the inner city. Guidance was also offered to state and local officials for identifying potentially violent conditions, reducing the likelihood of violence, providing training to police to lessen tensions in minority communities, and organizing emergency operations in response to escalating violence.

See also Civil rights; Great Society; Johnson, Lyndon B.; Race riots, twentieth century; Racial and ethnic discrimination; War on Poverty.

National Association for the Advancement of Colored People (NAACP)

DATE: Established 1910

SIGNIFICANCE: The NAACP, the first civil rights organization established in the twentieth century, has worked for social, political, and economic equality for African Americans

The Niagara movement, founded in 1905, was the forerunner to the National Association for the Advancement of Colored People (NAACP). A group of African American leaders headed by W. E. B. Du Bois and William Monroe Trotter met at Niagara Falls, Canada. Their chief purpose was to develop an aggres-

The executive committee of the NAACP meeting in 1963; those present include Thurgood Marshall and Roy Wilkins. (Library of Congress)

sive campaign for the full citizenship of African Americans. They were dissatisfied with the approach of Booker T. Washington, who advocated black achievement while submitting to the injustice of segregation. Race riots, in which a number of African Americans were shot, beaten, burned, or hanged by lynch mobs in the early twentieth century, served as the backdrop for the meeting. Among the primary goals of the Niagara movement were erasing all distinctions based on race, gaining respect for all working men, and attaining black suffrage. The Niagara movement was the first attempt to organize African Americans after the Reconstruction Era and its mob violence against them. Open-minded whites, moved to action by the race riots, called for a national conference on Lincoln's birthday in 1909 and invited Niagara movement members.

The NAACP was formally founded in May of 1910, and the Niagara movement was incorporated into it. Most charter members were white rather than people of color. They had a wide range of expertise and resources. One of its most notable African American members was W. E. B. Du Bois, the great African American leader and scholar. The new organization vowed to fight *de jure* segregation and to work for equal education for white and black children, complete suffrage for African Americans, and the enforcement of the Fourteenth and Fifteenth Amendments (dealing with citizenship and voting rights, respectively). During its first year, the NAACP established programs for blacks in economic development and job opportunities. It pushed for more police protection in the South and for antilynching and lawlessness initiatives in the nation. *The Crisis*, the official publication of the NAACP, served as the "cutting edge" of critical thought regarding the "race question," publicizing injustices against African Americans. Du Bois served as editor.

Development. Early tension within the NAACP centered on the question of whether the budding organization should focus primarily on civil rights or should tackle economic issues as well. Noneconomic liberalism became the guiding light for the organization, since a consensus could not be reached over the importance of economic issues. The liberal white who served as president starting in 1930, Joel E. Spingarn, believed that once the racial issue in the United States had been resolved, African Americans would be able to compete on an equal footing in the economic and educational arenas. Future leaders of the NAACP would include Walter White, Roy Wilkins, Benjamin Hooks, and Benjamin Chavis.

There was considerable debate over whether African Americans should pursue a social agenda of equality and civil rights as opposed to economic development and independence. In its most acute form, this involved public debate between W. E. B. Du Bois and Booker T. Washington. Washington was renowned as the founder and president of Tuskegee Institute (now University) in Alabama. He was often consulted by presidents and invited to the White House. Washington argued that African Americans should focus on vocational education and training. He viewed politics as secondary and social equality for blacks as less important—a philosophy that pleased white southerners and presidents. Civil rights, to his way of thinking, would gradually evolve as African Americans developed their own business enterprises. Until then, African Americans should not be too pushy, for fear of alienating whites. In short, blacks should remain subservient to whites and, particularly in the South, reconcile with the prevalent racism.

Du Bois, on the other hand, argued that Washington's approach was inadequate and asked African Americans to give up too much. Du Bois held that African Americans needed higher education. He held that a "talented tenth," meaning those with higher education, would be in the position to lead the masses and working class. Unlike Washington, Du Bois maintained that economic progress was irrelevant without political participation and political power. To his way of thinking, political power would nurture economic development, not vice versa.

The failure of noneconomic liberalism can be seen in the results of the Great Depression. While the NAACP focused on social status and targeted race and racism, African Americans were devastated by the Depression. Already on the bottom of the economic ladder, many African Americans began to migrate to northern industrial cities in search of job opportunities and an improved standard of living relative to the South. The timing of their migration, however, collided with the Great Depression. African Americans in the South still survived at a subsistence level, trying to make a living as sharecroppers in an agricultural economy. The arrival on the political stage of Marcus Garvey in the early 1920's stirred the black masses. Preaching black nationalism and economic independence, Garvey urged African Americans to return to the Mother Country (Africa), emphasizing self-determination and independence. Garvey developed a large following in a short period of time between 1919 and 1925. Du Bois realized that the Garvey phenomenon, combined with the effects of the Depression of the 1930's, revealed a critical flaw in the thinking and philosophy of the NAACP. In 1934 Du Bois challenged the NAACP to question its organizational philosophy of noneconomic liberalism and to stress economic development and issues. The organization, still with Spingarn and a board of directors dominated by whites, failed to heed the call. Their agenda remained centered on racial equality. It was at this point that Du Bois broke with the NAACP.

Role in Justice and Equality. A black and white team of lawyers of the NAACP, constituting its legal committee, won three significant legal cases during the first fifteen years of the NAACP's existence. In *Guinn v. United States* (1915) the Supreme Court invalidated the grandfather clause in Maryland and Oklahoma, ruling that it was unconstitutional under the Fifteenth Amendment. Two years later, in the case of *Buchanan v. Warley* (1917), the Court voided a Louisville ordinance requiring African Americans to live in certain sections of the city. In the case of *Moore v. Dempsey* (1923), the Court ordered a new trial in a case in which an African American had been convicted of murder in Arkansas. The poverty-stricken defendant had been tried before an all-white jury. As a result of these early victories, the NAACP soon realized that the court system could be a valuable ally in the fight against racial injustice and the struggle for equality.

In addition, the NAACP supported or provided the legal expertise in a number of cases that successfully challenged aspects of the "separate but equal" doctrine of racial segregation established in *Plessy v. Ferguson* (1896). This doctrine was premised on the notion that it was legal to have separate facilities for blacks and whites as long as those facilities were equal. Successful challenges included restrictive covenants in

the case of *Corrigan v. Buckley* (1926) and the legality of the white primary in *Nixon v. Condon* (1927, 1932). In the wake of *Smith v. Allwright* (1944), which finally sounded the death knell for the white primary, the NAACP began to organize local voter leagues in the South. Repression from local governments and the White Citizens Council, however, led to the decrease of the NAACP's influence in the South in the 1950's, to be replaced by younger organizations such as the Southern Christian Leadership Conference.

The 1954 U.S. Supreme Court case of *Brown v. Board of Education* gained the greatest notoriety for the NAACP and its sister organization, the NAACP Legal Defense and Educational Fund. Thurgood Marshall argued this landmark case. In its decision, the Court ruled that the pernicious "separate but equal" doctrine of racial segregation in the public schools was unconstitutional, stating that separate schools for whites and blacks were inherently unequal. The *Brown* case served as the defining moment for the NAACP and the Civil Rights movement in the 1950's.

The NAACP Legal Defense and Educational Fund (LDEF) was founded in 1939. It was designed to be the chief legal arm of the NAACP. It claimed to be a nonprofit entity, yet it had an interlocking membership with the NAACP. As a result of objections by the Internal Revenue Service in 1957, the legal and educational arm formally separated from the NAACP. Thus, the NAACP Legal Defense and Educational Fund developed its own staff, board of directors, budget, and policies. Thurgood Marshall became the first director-counsel until 1961, followed by Jack Greenberg, who served in this capacity until 1984, when Julius L. Chambers took over. The LDEF had represented thousands of cases in education, employment, prisoners' rights, housing, health care, voting rights, and other areas by the end of the 1980's.

The NAACP continued to push for civil rights and racial integration in the 1950's and 1960's as the Civil Rights movement intensified its efforts to overcome racial segregation in every phase of American society. Like other civil rights organizations of the time, the NAACP engaged in a number of nonviolent activities. The NAACP, along with a number of other organizations, was partly responsible for the Civil Rights Act of 1964. The NAACP, and the Civil Rights movement as a whole, reached its zenith in this decade, as the 1964 Civil Rights Act, the 1965 Voting Rights Act and the 1968 Civil Rights Act were passed. In the 1970's and 1980's, the organization became increasingly irrelevant, since constitutional civil rights guarantees were in place and had been upheld by the courts. At the same time, the social movement in African American communities switched increasingly toward community control, black nationalism, and separatism, which were diametrically opposed to the organizational goals of the NAACP. In the 1980's, as the federal government and the Reagan Administration became increasingly hostile toward civil rights and previous black gains, the NAACP Legal Defense and Educational Fund continued to play an important role in the legal arena. —*Mfanya D. Tryman*

See also *Brown v. Board of Education*; Civil rights; Civil Rights Act of 1964; Civil Rights movement; Congress of Racial Equality (CORE); Du Bois, W. E. B.; Equality of opportunity; Garvey, Marcus; National Association for the Advancement of Colored People Legal Defense and Educational Fund.

BIBLIOGRAPHY

Informative sources include Gerald David Jaynes and Robin M. Williams, Jr., eds., *A Common Destiny: Blacks and American Society* (Washington, D.C.: National Academy Press, 1989); Harold Cruse, *Plural but Equal* (New York: William Morrow, 1987); John Hope Franklin, *From Slavery to Freedom* (New York: Alfred A. Knopf, 1967); Jack Greenberg's article "NAACP Legal Defense and Educational Fund," in *Civil Rights and Equality*, edited by Leonard W. Levy, Kenneth L. Karst, and Dennis J. Mahoney (New York: Collier Macmillan, 1989); Talcott Parsons and Kenneth B. Clark, eds., *The Negro American* (Boston: Houghton Mifflin, 1966).

National Association for the Advancement of Colored People Legal Defense and Educational Fund

DATE: Founded 1939

SIGNIFICANCE: The NAACP Legal Defense and Educational Fund emerged as the legal arm of the Civil Rights movement in the 1950's and 1960's and since that time has organized litigation campaigns on a variety of key equity issues, bringing suits on behalf of individuals and of major civil rights groups seeking to end legal discrimination against African Americans and other people of color (sometimes abbreviated as LDF, sometimes as LDEF)

The NAACP Legal Defense and Educational Fund (sometimes abbreviated as LDF, sometimes as LDEF) was established in 1939-1940 as a tax-exempt corporation by the National Association for the Advancement of Colored People. Its charter was handwritten in March, 1940, by Thurgood Marshall, who stated the new organization's dual purpose: to provide legal aid to African Americans "suffering legal injustices by reason of race or color" and to create education opportunities for African Americans that had been denied them by reason of race or color.

The LDF was founded to carry on litigation in the spirit of the social change agenda already established by the actions of NAACP attorneys in the American courts. It provides or supports legal representation on behalf of African Americans and other people of color in defending their legal and constitutional rights against discrimination in education, employment, land use, recreation, transportation, housing, voting, health care, and other areas. It has successfully argued against grandfather clauses, restrictive housing covenants in city ordinances, white primaries, white juries, capital punishment, and segregation of public facilities. Since the 1950's the LDF has operated independently from its parent organization, which maintained its own legal department, and at times the relationship between the LDF and NAACP has involved some conflict. The LDF both represents individuals and brings suit on

behalf of civil rights groups. Its clients have included the Congress of Racial Equality (CORE), the Southern Christian Leadership Conference (SCLC), the Student Nonviolent Coordinating Committee (SNCC), and local branches of the NAACP. It has been based in New York City since its formation and also maintains a center in Washington, D.C.

Funding. Fund-raising for the Legal Defense and Educational Fund is conducted by the Committee of 100, a volunteer group. In the formative years of the 1940's, the fund-raising drives of the committee were spearheaded by Harold Oram and Anna Caples Frank; during the Civil Rights movement, they were led by Allan Knight Chambers and Paul Moore. The LDF is supported by thousands of individual donations and by sustaining grants from smaller foundations, notably the Field Foundation. The largest contributions to the LDF come from major foundations, including the Ford, Carnegie, and Rockefeller foundations, and from corporations.

Civil Rights Litigation. The LDF has litigated many hundreds of court cases on the state level and has argued many of the key civil rights cases heard before the U.S. Supreme Court since World War II. While always pursuing cases on a variety of fronts—including, in the 1940's, victories in white primary cases, which ended the exclusion of African Americans from the Democratic Party in the South (*Smith v. Allwright*, 1944), and the restrictive covenant cases, which held unconstitutional covenants prohibiting the sale of property to people of color—the initial focus of the LDF was the desegregation of American schools. Its landmark case was *Brown v. Board of Education* (1954), argued before the U.S. Supreme Court by the LDF team of Thurgood Marshall, Jack Greenberg, Louis Redding, George E. C. Hayes, Howard Jenkins, James M. Nabrit, Jr., and Spotswood W. Robinson III.

In *Brown* the Court, under Chief Justice Earl Warren, ruled in a unanimous decision that racial segregation of public schools was inherently unequal. At its inception the LDF had begun challenging the legal precedent of the "separate but equal" doctrine established in regard to transportation by the U.S. Supreme Court in *Plessy v. Ferguson* (1896) and extended through other cases to educational institutions. In a series of cases argued by Marshall and LDF staff, the LDF chipped away at the strength of the separate but equal doctrine. Beginning with higher education, the LDF initiated suits in several different states and won favorable rulings from the U.S. Supreme Court that opened professional and graduate schools to African American applicants. One of the key cases in this effort was *Sweatt v. Painter* (1950), in which the Court found against the University of Texas Law School, which had been refusing admission to blacks, on the grounds that a separate black law school did not meet the criteria for equal professional education. *Brown v. Board of Education* broadened the issue of equal access to education to the more comprehensive level of elementary and secondary schools. In their ruling, the Supreme Court justices found that the black children represented by the LDF had been denied equal protection under the laws as guaranteed by the Fourteenth Amendment, thus—at long last—reversing the separate but equal mandate of *Plessy v. Ferguson.*

In the years following *Brown*, the LDF initiated hundreds of civil rights demonstration cases in support of the public actions initiated by organizers and activists of the Civil Rights movement. These included the defense of Martin Luther King, Jr., Ralph Abernathy, and other SCLC activists in their criminal contempt case arising from their defiance of a court injunction prohibiting marches during the 1963 Birmingham demonstrations (*Walker v. City of Birmingham*, 1967). (In *Walker*, the U.S. Supreme Court ultimately upheld the ruling of the Alabama Supreme Court, diminishing the constitutional protection afforded protestors under the Bill of Rights.) The 1957 "Little Rock Nine" action in Arkansas was one of the LDF's key school desegregation cases. In the Little Rock case, members of the local NAACP aided nine black high school students who challenged the school district and the state to admit them into a previously all-white high school. Their admittance was eventually secured under federal military guard. Another major LDF desegregation case was that of James Meredith. In that suit the U.S. Court of Appeals for the Fifth Judicial Circuit in New Orleans ordered the University of Mississippi to admit its first African American student (*Meredith v. Fair*, 1962). The Meredith case was argued by Constance Baker Motley, who had been one of the central figures in the LDF staff since the 1940's. LDF lawyers also defended the organizers of sit-ins, participants in the Freedom Rides, and those who spearheaded other public protests. Their court victories, combined with the public activism of the Civil Rights movement, led to passage of the Civil Rights Act of 1964 and the Voting Rights Act of 1965. An LDF case, for example, created the doctrinal base for Title IV of the 1964 act, which made federal funding of institutions that discriminate against minorities illegal.

In addition to desegregation, voting, residential discrimination, and other civil rights causes, the LDF has devoted campaigns since the late 1960's and early 1970's to overturning the death penalty and initiating prison reform. In response to the women's movement, the LDF established a program in the 1970's to promote educational and employment opportunities for black women. Key victories came in 1972, when LDF attorneys succeeded in separate cases in getting the U.S. Supreme Court to rule that the death penalty was unconstitutional as then administered and that towns with primarily white residents could not withdraw from school systems in which the student population was predominantly African American.

In the post-Civil Rights movement era, the LDF expanded into poverty law and began taking the cases of Mexican Americans, Native Americans, gays and lesbians, women, and others bringing suits on discrimination grounds.

Educational Work. In addition to bringing litigation, the LDF lobbies for equal rights legislation and monitors federal programs for compliance with civil rights aims. LDF staff members give advice to lawyers involved in rights cases and supply information on current legal trends and decisions affecting the status of people of color. Funds are also allocated to provide counsel and to train attorneys to do activist work. Since the late 1970's, the Herbert Lehman Education Fund, an LDF scholarship program established in 1965, has awarded African American students some two hundred scholarships per year to offset the costs of state college tuition. In 1962 the LDF began providing internships to recent law school graduates to work in the LDF offices and then to go into the field and work in integrated firms in areas of the South where there were few African American attorneys. Marian Wright Edelman (founder of the Children's Defense Fund) and Julius Chambers (later a president of the LDF, and director-counsel of the organization beginning in 1984) were among the early interns. The internship process was formalized in 1971 with the creation of the Earl Warren Legal Training Program, funded with grants from the Carnegie and Rockefeller foundations. Over time, as increasing numbers of African Americans began working in legal practices in the South, the internship aspect of the program was abandoned, but the Earl Warren Legal Training Program continues to grant fellowships to black students attending formerly all-white law schools in the South and to give financial assistance to lawyer training.

Other Programs. The LDF supplies community assistance through its Division of Legal Information and Community Services. The LDF also sponsors several publications, including its *Annual Report*, the *Equal Justice* quarterly, and numerous legal materials, brochures, and pamphlets. It also issues press releases on current legal and political events and prepares watchdog reports. It hosts an annual institute to encourage public awareness of current problems faced by people of color.

Headquarters and Leadership. Thurgood Marshall headed the LDF for more than two decades, from its inception in 1939 until 1961. Jack Greenberg, who had been an LDF staff member since the 1940's, succeeded Marshall as LDF director-counsel when Marshall was appointed by President John F. Kennedy to the U.S. Court of Appeals. Like Marshall, Greenberg had a long tenure as head of the LDF. He resigned in 1984 to accept a position as a professor at the Columbia University School of Law. Greenberg, who is white, was the subject of a 1983 boycott by African American students at Harvard University who believed that the legal rights organization should be headed by a person of color. Julius Chambers succeeded Greenberg as head of the LDF. During the early 1980's, the LDF moved from its old location at 10 Columbus Circle to new offices at 99 Hudson Street in the Tribeca area of New York, joining with the Puerto Rican Legal Defense and Education Fund, the Asian American Legal Defense and Education Fund, the NOW Legal Defense and Education Fund, and the Council of New York Law Associates to constitute the Public Interest Law Center. Elaine Jones (the first black woman graduate of the University of Virginia Law School), who, as part of her long career with the LDF, had worked closely with LDF staff lawyer Lani Guinier on voting rights issues in the 1970's, became the director of the LDF office in Washington, D.C., in 1977. She became the director-counsel of the LDF in 1993.
— *Barbara Bair*

See also *Brown v. Board of Education*; Civil Rights Act of 1964; Civil Rights movement; Little Rock school integration crisis; Marshall, Thurgood; National Association for the Advancement of Colored People (NAACP); Voting Rights Act of 1965.

BIBLIOGRAPHY
The LDF is put in a larger context in Derrick A. Bell, Jr., *Race, Racism, and American Law* (2d ed. Boston: Little, Brown, 1980). Jack Greenberg wrote of his years with the LDF, his fellow staff members, and the cases they fought over four decades in *Crusaders in the Courts: How a Dedicated Band of Lawyers Fought for the Civil Rights Revolution* (New York: Basic Books, 1994). See also Richard Kluger's history of the LDF's most famous case, *Simple Justice: The History of Brown v. Board of Education and Black America's Struggle for Equality* (New York: Vintage Books, 1977); the LDF's own account of its history, National Association for the Advancement of Colored People Legal Defense and Educational Fund, *Thirty Years of Building American Justice* (New York: Author, 1970); and Mark V. Tushnet's history of NAACP legal efforts that preceded the founding of the LDF, *The NAACP's Legal Strategy Against Segregated Education, 1925-1950* (Chapel Hill: University of North Carolina Press, 1987). Tushnet also wrote a study of the legal career of Thurgood Marshall, *Making Civil Rights Law: Thurgood Marshall and the Supreme Court, 1936-1961* (New York: Oxford University Press, 1994). Finally, Stephen L. Wasby, Anthony A. D'Amato, and Rosemary Metrailer, *Desegregation from Brown to Alexander: An Exploration of Supreme Court Strategies* (Carbondale, Ill.: Southern Illinois University Press, 1977), deals with many LDF cases.

National Commission on the Causes and Prevention of Violence

DATE: 1968-1969
SIGNIFICANCE: The commission was appointed to investigate causes of violence in the United States and make recommendations for reducing its incidence

Established after the assassination of Senator Robert F. Kennedy, the commission was a response to the high levels of violence in American society—the highest of any stable democratic society. While it also studied social and political violence, its main focus was on street crime and family violence. The commission located the primary causes in the existence of a large number of poor, uneducated young males trapped in deteriorating neighborhoods with no opportunities for social success. Crime was a means of income and an expression of social resentment. Racial prejudice was identified as another contributing factor.

The commission recommended programs to upgrade neighborhoods, improve education, increase job training, provide access to jobs, and eliminate racial discrimination. It supported hand-gun control and focused on ways to make the criminal justice system more equitable and efficient. The United States has responded primarily to the issue of criminal justice reform, leaving social factors unchanged. Crime has continued to increase; the United States still has the highest crime rate among industrialized nations.

See also Crime; Crime Index; Kennedy, Robert F.; National Advisory Commission on Civil Disorders; President's Commission on Law Enforcement and Administration of Justice.

National Crime Information Center

DATE: Established 1971
SIGNIFICANCE: The National Crime Information Center (NCIC), a powerful computer database run by the U.S. Federal Bureau of Investigation (FBI), provides law enforcement agencies with access to recorded criminal justice information through its computerized database and library collection; NCIC allows agencies to gather cross-boundary criminal justice information efficiently

Since its creation in the 1970's, the National Crime Information Center has amassed a substantial collection of criminal justice databases. Topics include missing persons, wanted persons, stolen and recovered guns, stolen securities, stolen and recovered motor vehicles, stolen license plates, and other stolen articles. NCIC users are able to access these data when they need them. Users have expressed satisfaction with NCIC and have requested enhancements over time.

To enhance the NCIC, the FBI is establishing NCIC-2000, which will allow full on-line computer search and retrieval of crime incidents nationwide. Police officials will be able to check liens, images (such as photographs and fingerprints), license plates, and other routine items instantly. It is hoped that this increased functionality will help greatly in reducing false arrests.

The FBI has merged NCIC with the National Incident-Based Reporting System (NIBRS) and Automated Fingerprint Identification System (AFIS) to create the Criminal Justice Information Services Division (CJIS). CJIS serves as a single source for state, local, and private law enforcement officials seeking crime analysis data, incident information, and criminal imaging data. In addition, the division provides information services for the FBI and its direct enforcement divisions. Among the stated goals of the CJIS are to develop consistent crime information collection and recording standards and to develop and implement a strategy for assisting state and other users in creating linkages to the FBI's computer systems. CJIS will also offer training and support services for federal, state, and local CJIS users.

See also Crime; Federal Bureau of Investigation (FBI); Motor vehicle theft.

National Crime Victimization Survey

DEFINITION: An annual publication that reports the results of a survey of criminal victimization
SIGNIFICANCE: Along with the Uniform Crime Reports, the National Crime Victimization Survey (NCVS) is one of the major sources of national crime statistics

The National Crime Victimization Survey has been performed annually since 1975; it is published by the Justice Department's Bureau of Justice Statistics under the title *Criminal Victimization in the United States*. Formerly known as the

NCVS ESTIMATED RATES OF PERSONAL VICTIMIZATION, 1978-1992

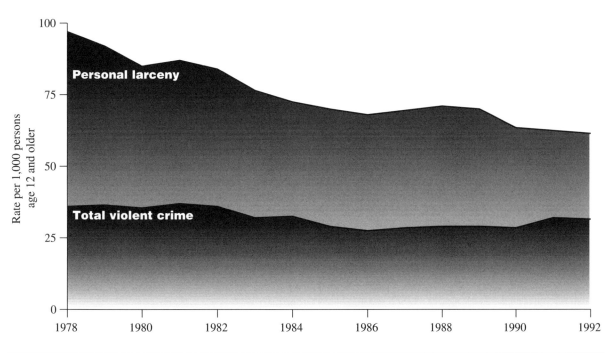

Source: U.S. Department of Justice, Bureau of Justice Statistics, *Sourcebook of Criminal Justice Statistics—1993.* Washington, D.C.: U.S. Government Printing Office, 1994.

National Crime Victim Survey, the National Crime Victimization Survey is one of two major sources of crime statistics. Unlike its counterpart, the Uniform Crime Reports (UCR), which is an annual report of crimes reported to police and other authorities across the nation, the National Crime Victimization Survey polls individual households. Interviewers ask participants if anyone in the household has been the victim of a crime within the past year. Because many crimes are never reported to police, the National Criminal Victimization Survey uncovers more crimes than the UCR. The amount of crime that goes unreported to police is sometimes called the "dark figure of crime." Analysts compare the two crime surveys to determine how frequently crimes are reported.

Interviewers ask people about murders, assaults, burglaries, thefts, rapes, robberies, and other crimes, excluding only certain kinds of manslaughter and arson. Recent comparisons of the survey to the UCR show that Americans are increasingly reporting crimes, particularly rapes, robberies, and thefts. In spite of increased reporting, however, only 39 percent of crimes were reported in 1992. The two surveys also show contrasting results on the spread of crime. UCR statistics showed crime rising almost 17 percent between 1973 and 1992. On the other hand, the National Crime Victimization Survey finds the number of households experiencing a crime dropping from 32 percent to 23 percent in the same period.

See also Crime; Justice Statistics, Bureau of; Uniform Crime Reports (UCR); Violent Crime Control and Law Enforcement Act of 1994.

National debt

DEFINITION: The debt owed by the public as a result of the accumulation of annual budget deficits

SIGNIFICANCE: During the last three decades of the twentieth century the national debt of the United States grew significantly; since debt is often passed from one generation to the next, questions of ethics and justice between generations emerge

Whenever government spending exceeds tax revenue, a budget deficit results. The budget deficit accumulates from year to year in the national debt, which is held in the form of government financial securities, Treasury bills, bonds, and notes. Private individuals, corporations, and foreign investors hold these securities as investments. The debt of the United States is owed by the people of the United States to the investors, who are also primarily the people of the United States.

The Treasury debt securities are issued for terms as small as three months and as long as thirty years. When Treasury securities mature, they can be paid when there is a surplus or be refinanced through the issuance of new securities. Each annual budget must contain sufficient funds to pay the interest due on

THE NATIONAL DEBT	
Accumulation of the National Debt	
From President George Washington Through President Jimmy Carter (1789-1981)	$1.1 trillion
Under Presidents Ronald Reagan and George Bush (1981-1993)	$3.1 trillion
Debt Accumulated from 1963 to 1993	
Lyndon Johnson Administration (1963-1969)	$0.05 trillion
Richard Nixon Administration (1969-1974)	$0.1 trillion
Gerald Ford Administration (1974-1977)	$0.2 trillion
Jimmy Carter Administration (1977-1981)	$0.3 trillion
Ronald Reagan Administration (1981-1989)	$1.8 trillion
George Bush Administration (1989-1993)	$1.3 trillion

Source: William Pemberton, *George Bush.* Vero Beach, Fla.: Rourke, 1993.

the securities. As the national debt grows, the portion of the annual budget required to make the interest payment increases.

An ethical concern is who bears the burden of paying the cost of the national debt: Is the burden felt by the generation that incurs the debt or by the next generation? The most critical cost of the national debt is the interest cost, since the principal can be indefinitely refinanced. Public money used to pay the interest is not available for other public goods. The burden of the debt is paid by the potential benefactors of the public goods that are forgone. These benefactors may be welfare recipients, defense contractors, or scientists doing medical research. The public suffers because the benefits which may have resulted from the forgone public goods are lost—possible benefits such as less poverty, better national defense, and cures for diseases.

Another cost of carrying a large national debt is the phenomenon known as "crowding out." Within an economy there is a limited availability of funds for investment purposes of all kinds. When the national debt is large, public funds absorb an ever-increasing portion of investment funds and crowd out private investment. The lack of funds for private investment reduces the capacity of the economy to expand.

The true effect of transfers of debt between generations is complex. If the deficits cause the economy to grow, as some economists predict, the burden of the debt may be lighter on the subsequent generation, who may benefit from the economic growth. If the debt causes the economy to stagnate, however, the burden on the future generation would be significant and could result in reduced living standards. The issue

becomes more complex if the demands of foreign investors and trading partners increase the negative implications of a large national debt.

See also Social Security system; Treasury, U.S. Department of the.

National District Attorneys Association

DATE: Founded 1950
SIGNIFICANCE: The National District Attorneys Association (NDAA) provides educational and technical services to prosecuting attorneys in the United States

The NDAA serves prosecuting attorneys and their staffs. Particularly, the group provides technical assistance as well as informational services in the areas of juvenile justice and the prosecution of child abuse. Membership is about sixty-five hundred, with about two thousand being prosecuting attorneys (active members), and the remainder (termed associate members) being assistants, deputies, investigators, and other staff members. Headquartered in Alexandria, Virginia, the NDAA puts out a number of regular publications, including *The Prosecutor* and a monthly digest of state and federal court decisions. It also prepares *amicus curiae* briefs. The organization conducts research through the American Prosecutors Research Institute and is affiliated with the National Center for the Prosecution of Child Abuse.

See also Attorney; District attorney; Prosecutor, public.

National Firearms Act and Federal Firearms Act

DATE: Enacted in 1934 and 1938
DEFINITION: The first federal statutes that restricted the keeping and bearing of arms
SIGNIFICANCE: The 1934 and 1938 firearms acts represented the first significant federal involvement in taxing and controlling firearm possession; they also established the struggle between the federal government and the National Rifle Association

The 1934 National Firearms Act required a license for the interstate transfer of machine guns, silencers, and short-barreled rifles and shotguns. The licensing procedure involved a $200 transfer tax and the use of a tax stamp. Although the law's initiator, Attorney General Homer Cummings, wanted the act to apply to all concealable firearms, records of congressional hearings show that it was concealable automatic weapons with which lawmakers were primarily concerned. As a compromise between the bill's advocates and opponents, handguns were removed from the law. Major opposition to the bill came from the National Rifle Association.

The 1938 Federal Firearms Act established a general licensing and record-keeping procedure for manufacturers and dealers shipping or receiving any firearms or ammunition across state lines. Restrictions included forbidding the interstate sale of guns by unlicensed dealers. The act prohibited the interstate sale of guns to fugitives and to people who had been convicted of violent crimes; also prohibited was transporting stolen firearms across state lines. These two acts were to be the only federal firearms legislation until the government again became interested in firearm legislation in the late 1960's.

See also Arms, right to keep and bear; Bill of Rights, U.S.; Constitution, U.S.; National Rifle Association (NRA); Search and seizure; Taxation and justice.

National Guard

DATE: Uniform Militia Law of 1792 authorized nationwide militia; National Guard Association established 1878

SIGNIFICANCE: The National Guard, in peacetime, consists of units in each state, the District of Columbia, and three territories; the National Guard may be called by the state governor in times of local emergencies, such as natural disasters or civil disturbances, or by the president in times of national emergency

The National Guard is the term for the reserve units of the U.S. Army and U.S. Air Force that are organized by state. These units are distinct from the regular armed services; they are composed of citizens who enlist to serve on a reserve basis for eight years. They undergo training for six months at the beginning of their service, and thereafter they generally serve for a weekend each month and for two weeks of field training per year. The federal government funds weapons and equipment; the states pay for armories and other storage facilities. The National Guard is separate from the nation's Organized Re-

serve, which is organized nationally rather than by state and is directly under the armed services.

The modern National Guard evolved gradually from the state militias of colonial times. The early American settlers adopted the concept of the "citizen soldier"—in which citizens moved into and out of military service as required—from European practices. The standing militia, or force composed of citizen soldiers, was the origin of the National Guard.

The National Guard is unique in that it may be called to duty by either the state or national government. In peacetime, the National Guard and Air National Guard are under the command of state (or territorial) governors. They may be called to active duty by the governor to help maintain or restore order during civil unrest, working with state and local branches of law enforcement. During a war or other national emergency, the National Guard and Air National Guard may be called to active duty by the president or Congress. The National Guard is the primary source of augmentation for the Army and the Air Force. The National Guard Bureau (NGB), a federal agency in Washington, D.C., formulates and administers National Guard programs to ensure the continued development and maintenance of Army and Air Guard units. The NGB is the primary channel of communication between the states and the Departments of the Army and Air Force.

Federal Activation of the Guard. Since 1916, the president of the United States has had two methods available to him

National Guard troops called up in 1968 to help quell rioting in Washington, D.C. (AP/Wide World Photos)

to bring members of the National Guard into federal active service. The first is the "call," authorized since 1792. Under the call, the troops are considered to be in the service of the United States. While on active duty in the service of the United States, the National Guard is subject to all of the regulations that govern the regular Army, except that the governor of the state retains the right to appoint and promote officers. The second method is the "order," provided for the first time by the National Defense Act of 1916. The entire National Guard was first drafted into the service of the United States in 1917, after Congress had declared war.

Relationship with Federal and State Governments. When ordered to active duty in the service of the United States, the state designation of the unit is dropped and the federal designation is used. In 1933, amendments to the National Defense Act created a new force, the National Guard of the United States. This designation was declared to be a reserve component of the Army. When the term "National Guard" is used alone, it refers to the units in their state status. The terms National Guard of the United States (NGUS) and Air National Guard of the United States (ANGUS) refer to the same units and personnel but in their federal status as reserve units, reserve officers, reserve warrant officers, and reserve enlisted members of the Army and/or Air Force.

The Armed Forces Reserve Act of 1952 reiterated that, except when so ordered, members of the NGUS and ANGUS shall not be on active duty in the service of the United States. The president must go to Congress for authority before ordering any part of the National Guard of the United States to active duty. No prior congressional approval is required, however, in order for the president to call the National Guard into active federal service in its militia or state status. In March, 1965, President Lyndon Johnson used this provision when he signed an executive order federalizing more than eighteen hundred members of the Alabama National Guard over the protests of Alabama governor George Wallace. The Guard was used to provide security during a potentially volatile fifty-mile civil rights march led by Martin Luther King, Jr., from Selma to Montgomery, Alabama.

The Guard and Civil Disturbance. The state mission of the National Guard is to provide organizations in each state that are sufficiently trained and equipped to function efficiently in the protection of life and property and the preservation of peace, order, and public safety. This mission has led state units of the National Guard to be involved in a number of difficult situations that have provoked controversy. In May, 1970, in the midst of national anti-Vietnam War student protests, the Ohio National Guard was called to restore order at Kent State University. On May 4, during a heated confrontation between students and guardsmen, several members of the National Guard fired live ammunition into a crowd, killing four students. The national shock over this tragedy was profound, heightening the debate over the Vietnam War and highlighting the polarization that the war was causing in American society. The event also spawned civil suits that continued for many years.

Another event in which the National Guard was prominently in the news occurred in April, 1992. After a jury acquitted four white police officers on trial for beating a black motorist, Rodney G. King, the city of Los Angeles erupted into chaos. In conditions of general social disorder, fifty-three people were killed, looting was widespread, and hundreds of fires burned out of control. Four thousand members of the California National Guard were called by the governor. The initial deployment, however, was slowed by a shortage of ammunition and by difficulties in organizing the command structure. These problems prompted concerns about communication between the National Guard and other agencies and about the National Guard's ability to respond quickly and effectively to severe law enforcement emergencies. Beyond such controversies, however, a large part of the National Guard's role is to help out during natural disasters. It has been an extremely valuable resource through the years in helping local organizations fight forest fires and cope with storms, floods, and their aftermaths.

National Guard Strength. As of the mid-1990's the Army National Guard comprised more than three thousand units located in twenty-six hundred communities throughout the fifty states, Puerto Rico, Guam, the Virgin Islands, and the District of Columbia. The Air National Guard maintained more than ninety flying units and five hundred mission support units which, upon mobilization, would be gained by one of the major commands of the United States Air Force.   —*John L. Farbo*

See also Kent State student killings; King, Rodney, case and aftermath; Little Rock school integration crisis; Martial law; Selma-to-Montgomery civil rights march.

BIBLIOGRAPHY

Jerry M. Cooper, *The Militia and the National Guard in America Since Colonial Times* (Westport, Conn.: Greenwood Press, 1993), and John K. Mahon, *History of the Militia and the National Guard* (New York: Macmillan, 1983), both present excellent accounts of the National Guard from colonial times. National Guard Association of the United States, *The Nation's National Guard* (Buffalo, N.Y.: Baker, Jones Hausauer, 1954), a document created by the National Guard Association that includes a condensed history, is dated but useful.

National Institute of Justice

DATE: Established 1968

SIGNIFICANCE: The National Institute of Justice has been a major national and international center for criminal justice research, for policy experimentation aimed at professionalizing law enforcement, and for more effective ways of controlling crime

Following recommendations from President Lyndon B. Johnson's 1967 Committee on Law Enforcement and Administration of Justice, Congress enacted the Omnibus Crime Control and Safe Streets Act of 1968. The law created, within the Department of Justice, the Law Enforcement Assistance Administration (LEAA), which in turn established the National Institute of Justice (NIJ). The NIJ has multiple research responsibilities aimed at revising extant criminal justice policies and practices, producing new crime control programs, encouraging the professionalization of law enforcement, sponsoring experimental training programs, and assessing law enforcement and criminal justice standards and performance. It also collects and disseminates relevant data and information. During its first quarter-century of operations, the NIJ provided important resources for the study of violent crime, career criminals, sentencing, rehabilitation, the use of police resources, community crime prevention, and pretrial processes.

See also Justice Statistics, Bureau of; Law Enforcement Assistance Administration (LEAA); Omnibus Crime Control and Safe Streets Act of 1968; President's Commission on Law Enforcement and Administration of Justice.

National Labor Relations Act (NLRA)

DATE: Became law July 5, 1935
DEFINITION: Known also as the Wagner Act, the NLRA was the first effective federal law pertaining to labor unions
SIGNIFICANCE: The NLRA established federal protection of workers' right to form unions and bargain collectively; it also defined and prohibited various unfair labor practices on the part of employers

The National Labor Relations Act climaxed decades of conflict between management and labor over the right of American workers to form unions and bargain collectively. Earlier federal court decisions had rendered federal legislation—such as the Clayton Antitrust Act (1914), Norris-LaGuardia Act (1932), and National Industrial Recovery Act (1933)—ineffective at securing workers' collective bargaining rights. To remedy this situation, Senator Robert F. Wagner of New York and Representative William Patrick Connery, Jr., of Massachusetts introduced legislation in early 1935 to provide a federal right to collective bargaining. President Franklin D. Roosevelt signed the bill into law on July 5, 1935.

Most important, the NLRA established under federal law the right of workers (except agricultural and domestic laborers) to form or join labor organizations and to bargain collectively with their employers through representatives of their choice. The act also defined and prohibited a variety of unfair labor practices, such as interfering with the formation of labor organizations, discouraging workers from joining such organizations, and discriminating against employees for filing charges under the act. Finally, the act created a new National Labor Relations Board (NLRB) that was authorized to determine bargaining-unit jurisdictions, hold elections, and certify those unions receiving the majority of votes as the legally binding representatives of the workers.

Although previous federal laws on collective bargaining had failed to pass constitutional scrutiny in federal courts, the U.S. Supreme Court upheld the constitutionality of the NLRA on April 12, 1937, in the case of *National Labor Relations Board v. Jones & Laughlin Steel Corp.* In this case the steel company—one of the largest in the nation—maintained its own unions and refused to allow employees to organize separate unions. After the company fired ten workers for engaging in union activities, the NLRB issued a cease and desist order and demanded that the company rehire its workers. A federal appeals court sided with the company, ruling that the NLRA was beyond the authority of Congress. The Supreme Court overruled this decision, however, adopting a broad interpretation of Congress' commerce power and deeming it a "fundamental right" for employees to bargain collectively "without restraint or coercion by their employer."

A direct result of the NLRA was the formation of strong, independent unions. Although Congress amended the act in 1946 by passing the business-supported Labor-Management Relations Act (Taft-Hartley Act) over President Harry S Truman's veto, the right of workers to bargain collectively with their employers remained enshrined in federal law.

See also American Federation of Labor-Congress of Industrial Organizations (AFL-CIO); Clayton Antitrust Act; Labor law; Labor-Management Relations Act; Labor unions; Landrum-Griffin Act; New Deal; Pullman strike.

National Narcotics Act

DATE: Became law October 12, 1984
DEFINITION: Chapter thirteen of the Comprehensive Crime Control Act of 1984
SIGNIFICANCE: The act created the National Drug Enforcement Policy Board (NDEPB) as a high-level interagency council to coordinate federal drug-enforcement activities

The National Narcotics Act was part of an omnibus crime package that had been eleven years in the making. Congress passed this package, the most extensive revision of the federal criminal code since 1968, after President Ronald Reagan made it a high-priority item. The narcotics act proclaimed that the flow of illegal narcotics into the United States fed drug use that had reached epidemic proportions. Drug trafficking was an eighty-billion-dollars-a-year industry, and government agencies were able to interdict only 5 to 15 percent of the illegal product crossing American borders. The law created the National Drug Enforcement Policy Board (NDEPB) as a high-level board to coordinate drug interdiction activities. The attorney general chaired the board, which included the secretaries of state, defense, treasury, and health and human services along with other officials. It authorized the board to develop and coordinate all U.S. efforts to halt national and international drug trafficking.

See also Comprehensive Crime Control Act of 1984; Drug Enforcement Administration (DEA); Drug use and sale, illegal; Reagan, Ronald.

National Organization for Victim Assistance (NOVA)

DATE: Founded 1975
SIGNIFICANCE: This organization offers help to crime and disaster victims, lobbies for legislation, and provides services to professionals who deal with victims of crime

Based in Washington, D.C., the National Organization for Victim Assistance both serves as a national advocacy group for

Marchers in suffragist clothing participating in NOW's 1987 March for Equality in Philadelphia. (AP/Wide World Photos)

victims of crime and provides direct services to victims themselves. It also provides assistance such as training services and conferences to prosecutors, police, and health and social workers, and maintains an extensive library and informational clearinghouse. In its advocacy capacity, NOVA has played a prominent role in federal and state enactments of "victims' bills of rights" and in the passage of legislation allowing or requiring the impact of a crime on the victim to be considered in the sentencing of the offender. Its activities have also enabled many victim assistance and service programs, including rape crisis centers and domestic violence shelters, to continue operations. When it was founded, NOVA did not intend to provide direct help to victims, but the demand for such help was too great for the organization to ignore. NOVA established a referral program to help crime victims find counseling and other services in their communities, but it also provides direct counseling to victims.

See also Assault; Battered child and battered wife syndromes; Domestic violence; Rape and sex offenses; Victim assistance programs; Victims of Crime Act.

National Organization for Women (NOW)

DATE: Established 1966

SIGNIFICANCE: The National Organization for Women, the largest feminist organization in the United States, works toward full equality for women

Founded in 1966 by Betty Friedan and other women opposed to the second-class status of American women, the National Organization for Women (NOW) has grown from a small organization devoted to working for women's equality to a large mass-membership organization of approximately 280,000 members. NOW has a national organization, fifty state groups, and approximately eight hundred local groups.

The National Organization for Women seeks full equality for women in all spheres of American society, including government, industry, education, the professions, churches, political parties, the judiciary, labor unions, science, medicine, law, and religion. It supported passage of the Equal Rights Amendment, enforcement and enhancement of abortion rights, and an end to discrimination based on gender or sexual orientation.

NOW's early years saw conflict both within the group, over issues including abortion and lesbianism, and with the larger society regarding the attitudinal, behavioral, and legal changes sought by the organization on behalf of women. Within a few years of its creation, however, NOW had firmly sided with the abortion rights camp and stood resolutely in support of the right of women to define and express their own sexuality and to choose their own lifestyle, be it heterosexual, bisexual, or lesbian.

While still the largest feminist activist organization in the United States, over the years NOW has become more of a mainstream interest group and less of a social movement organization. It is essentially a civil rights group seeking an end to legal inequities and seeking the creation of formal rights. NOW works to change formal policies by litigation, lobbying, and, increasingly, attention to electoral politics. In addition, it seeks to change attitudes and behavior by education and consciousness raising. It has its own political action committees and legal defense fund.

NOW has enjoyed a number of successes, as well as some dramatic failures, in its battles to win equal treatment for women. For example, NOW's first big success came with a sex-discrimination suit brought by female flight attendants against the airlines' policy of forcing them to retire at age thirty or thirty-five or when they married. NOW also fought and won a ruling that sex-segregated newspaper employment advertising constitutes discrimination. Other successes came with the support of abortion rights and the U.S. Supreme Court's *Roe v. Wade* ruling in 1973. The most notable failure, perhaps, was the inability of NOW and other feminist groups to secure ratification of the Equal Rights Amendment to the U.S. Constitution.

Through its many activities on behalf of women's rights, NOW has been a significant force in American politics since the mid-1960's.

It has secured rights and changed policies at the national, state, and local levels. Beyond that, the organization can be credited with helping to change entrenched attitudes toward women and their role in American society.

See also Abortion; Comparable worth; Equal Pay Act; Equal Rights Amendment (ERA); Equality of opportunity; Feminism; *Roe v. Wade*; Sex discrimination; Sexual harassment.

National Rifle Association (NRA)

DATE: Founded August, 1871

SIGNIFICANCE: Since its inception in 1871, the National Rifle Association has become the principal, and most controversial, defender of the Second Amendment in the face of an increasing violent crime rate that includes the use of guns

The formation of the National Rifle Association (NRA) came as the result of a debate. In August of 1871, after months of discussion about how prepared the American military was to use the more advanced breach-loading rifles that had been developed since the Civil War, William Conant Church, a Boston journalist, joined with a New York lawyer, George Wingate, to create the organization that became the National Rifle Association. Church claimed that the purpose of the new organization was to do what the government itself should have been doing: providing for military preparedness. By providing target-shooting competitions and training in the latest firearms, Church believed that "the National Guard would be turned into sharpshooters." While the group centered on military life and included mostly active military personnel, it was officially independent from the armed forces.

In its early years, the NRA sponsored target-shooting competitions to advance the group's work and provide the opportunity and incentive for riflemen to improve their skills. The emphasis on target shooting and the subsequent development of sharpshooters continued to dominate NRA concerns until after World War II. The end of the war brought a new wave of members into the organization and, more important, provided a significant change in the purpose of the association. The new members had little interest in the target-shooting competitions; their interest was in hunting. While the NRA did not drop its shooting-competition program, it did shift its emphasis to education in the use of weapons and in hunting safety. This proved to be a wise decision on at least two counts. First, it met a marketing need. Former soldiers wanted to learn more about hunting and being good hunters. Second, it was a blessing to many farmers, who had found everything on their farms from windmills to windows being shot by careless hunters.

This widely favorable impression of the NRA changed significantly in the 1980's. In response to a steady increase in the use of handguns in violent crimes throughout the previous decade, the American public began to reassess the value of allowing citizens to own firearms, particularly handguns and military-type "assault rifles," with little or no regulation. Some people began to view the NRA as an organization protecting the criminals who use these weapons in the course of their crimes. Reacting to this change in the public attitude, the NRA chose the tactic of defending assault-rifle ownership and denouncing government actions and agents who attempted to implement more strict policies on gun ownership. As a result, in the view of some Americans, the NRA in the 1990's had become an advocate of dangerous weapons rather than a legitimate defender of the Second Amendment or a promoter of firearm safety.

See also Arms, right to keep and bear; Bill of Rights, U.S.; Crime; Drive-by shootings; Murder and homicide; National Firearms Act and Federal Firearms Act; National Guard; Self-defense.

National Treasury Employees Union v. Von Raab

COURT: U.S. Supreme Court

DATE: Decided March 21, 1989

SIGNIFICANCE: In this case the Supreme Court expanded the scope and discretion of public employers to utilize mandatory drug testing in their efforts to promote a drug-free work environment

The rules of the drug-testing program of the U.S. Customs Service required a very closely monitored urine test for employees seeking transfers or promotions to specified job classifications. Positions covered included those involved with classified materials, drug interdiction, and the carrying of firearms. The National Treasury Employees Union (NTEU) challenged these rules in federal district court on the grounds that they called for an unlawful search, a violation of employees' Fourth Amendment rights.

The court agreed, arguing that the drug testing was an overly intrusive violation of the employees' privacy and an unlawful search, given the lack of any actual evidence of drug abuse. An injunction was issued to keep the Customs Service from implementing the rules.

This injunction was later vacated by the circuit court of appeals, which, while it agreed that the testing did represent a

"search," in the meaning of the Fourth Amendment, concluded that the Customs Service rules were "reasonable." This conclusion was based on the Customs Service's strong law enforcement function and its related need to maintain public confidence that key employees were drug free.

The U.S. Supreme Court, in a 5-4 decision, upheld the majority of the testing program, based largely on the rationale of *Skinner v. Railway Labor Executives' Association* (1989). The Court ruled that there must be a balance between an employee's legitimate expectation of privacy and the government's legitimate public policy interest, a balance that must be evaluated on a case-by-case basis. Thus, for example, the Court excluded the drug-testing procedures for Customs Service positions dealing with "classified materials," concluding that the term was too vaguely defined.

The ongoing need to strike a balance was further demonstrated by the dissenting opinion of Justice Antonin Scalia. Though he had voted with the majority in *Skinner*, Scalia argued that in this instance the Customs Service did not adequately demonstrate a potential for great harm in the absence of drug testing and thus the government's interest in this case should not supersede the employees' Fourth Amendment protection.

NTEU v. Von Raab, in conjunction with *Skinner*, established that the Fourth Amendment does not exclude all drug testing of employees. Rather, some searches are "reasonable" and are therefore lawful. On the other hand, the government employer does not have an unfettered right to impose drug testing. The government must, in each instance, demonstrate that there is a rational connection between drug testing and the broader public interest. Properly and reasonably crafted drug-testing procedures are legal, and thus *NTEU v. Von Raab* both expanded and defined the scope of public sector drug testing.

See also Drug use and sale, illegal; Privacy, right of; *Skinner v. Railway Labor Executives' Association*.

National Urban League

DATE: Founded 1910

SIGNIFICANCE: The National Urban League is a nonpartisan interracial community service organization and research institution that works as a development and advocacy group for disadvantaged African Americans and other people of color; in the 1960's it evolved into a major civil rights advocacy organization

The National Urban League is one of a group of associations, like the National Association for the Advancement of Colored People (NAACP), that was founded at the beginning of the twentieth century for the advancement of African Americans. It was founded in 1910 as the National League on Urban Conditions Among Negroes, an organization that helped black migrants coming from the rural South to find work and make transitions to living in northern cities. The league merged in 1911 with the Association for the Protection of Colored Women and the Committee for Improving the Industrial Conditions of Negroes in New York, both groups founded in 1906 to aid urban migrants, and adopted its shorter title. The emphasis of the organization has shifted over the years from serving black workers in the cities of the north to assistance to the rural and urban poor in all regions of the country, and from an educational, service, and investigational association to one involved in political action. A nonmembership organization, it has a centralized structure, with a main headquarters in New York and local units in major cities; the local units have their own boards and budgets and adapt national policies to local needs. The league maintains regional bureaus in Washington, D.C.; Akron, Ohio; St. Louis, Missouri; and Atlanta, Georgia. The national governing board is, according to organization by-laws, interracial, and 25 percent of its members are under the age of thirty.

From 1923 until 1948 the National Urban League published the influential magazine *Opportunity*, which, along with the NAACP's *Crisis*, also based in New York, was a voice for black intellectuals, writers, and social reformers. From 1910 through the Depression, the league focused on services to those seeking jobs and housing, and lobbied to end discrimination in federal policies and the labor movement. The league grew in size and influence during World War II, when many thousands of blacks moved to northern industrial cities to do war-related work. The organization was conservative in its approach until the 1960's, when the severity of the problems of segregated housing, ghetto conditions, and inferior education called for more activist policies. The league emerged as a major advocate for civil rights under the leadership of Whitney M. Young, Jr., who became its executive director in 1961. Under the influence of the Civil Rights and Black Power movements, Young and the National Urban League pursued active protest politics, including a sponsorship role in the 1963 March on Washington. Young's successors, Vernon E. Jordan, Jr., and John Jacob, have established several community-based improvement programs. These include street academies to aid high school dropouts in finishing school; job training and placement services in computer skills, law enforcement, and the construction industry; voter registration drives; a Business Development Program for black businesspersons; and a National Consumer Health Education Program to supply health workers to local neighborhoods.

See also Civil rights; Civil Rights movement; National Association for the Advancement of Colored People (NAACP).

Natural law and natural rights

DEFINITION: Those laws and rights that are believed to exist by nature as opposed to those laws and rights that exist by convention

SIGNIFICANCE: Natural rights and natural laws have often been viewed as the guiding principles behind the development of legitimate legal systems

The relationship between natural law and natural rights varies considerably between ancient and modern traditions. As a general rule, one can argue that a more thorough notion of natural law existed among the ancients and a more thorough notion of natural rights exists among moderns. The relation-

ship between the two is presented with some clarity in the Declaration of Independence which started the United States of America. The most important feature common to both is a firm rooting in, and dependence on, human reason.

Both natural law and natural rights depend on a rational understanding of right and wrong that is universal and timeless. In contrast, conventional laws are those which pertain to particular political regimes and particular times. A good example of this distinction can be found by examining the documents that shaped the United States. The Declaration of Independence is one of the best modern statements on both natural law and natural rights.

The Declaration refers to such things as "the laws of nature," "self-evident truths," and "unalienable rights." In contrast the Constitution of the United States makes no claim to establishing natural laws. Since the Constitution creates conventional laws, it includes a provision describing how it can be amended and changed. There is no provision for amending the "truths" set forth in the Declaration of Independence, because they are natural and permanent.

An examination of the historical development of natural law and natural rights will help clarify their importance and role within the Western and American systems of justice.

Natural Law. Greek and Roman philosophers were the true originators of the tradition of natural law. The Greek philosophers Plato and Aristotle were the first writers to pay strict attention to the rational foundation of law. They liberated laws from their previous masters: theology and conventions. Laws that were neither divinely inspired nor subject to the whim of kings and aristocrats were hard for many people to understand at that time.

Plato's understanding of the "ideas" or "forms" was a central feature of this teaching. According to his doctrine of the forms, everything can be fully understood by the abstract notion that precedes and guides its existence. Natural law is the ideal form of law that exists independent of human endeavors. To understand law fully, one must first come to an understanding of what law is by nature. The philosophical quest for knowledge about human nature was the point of origin for the natural law tradition.

Aristotle followed Plato in the development of natural law. In his writings, the natural law tradition takes a slightly different turn. Aristotle believed that everything was determined by its end. Accordingly, natural law could only be determined by understanding what ends laws were meant to achieve. As with Plato, the desire to understand natural law was driven by an understanding of nature; however, Aristotle's nature was not found in abstract forms but in the final or ultimate purpose of the object.

Aristotle believed that there was a best or natural political system to go with natural law, but he provided for varying interpretations of the law to accommodate varying political circumstances. Nevertheless, there was a natural standard which he believed should guide all deliberations about legal matters. Reason was a central component of his natural law teaching, because one must understand the best laws before one can attempt to approximate those laws. Consistent throughout the teachings of Plato and Aristotle is their commitment to laws that are just and noble. Roman laws present a break from this particular aspect of the Greek natural law tradition.

The two dominant Roman teachings about natural law can be traced to Cicero and Thomas Aquinas. The Romans attached their beliefs about natural law to the gods. Their understanding of natural law is closely associated with divine law. This linking of natural law to divine law made Roman law more rigid. The relationship between the gods and the law was necessary for human development. Reason still played a central role in their understanding of natural law; however, reason was aided by divine inspiration or revelation.

Natural Rights. The close relationship between natural law and natural rights continued with the development of modern philosophy; however, the nature of that relationship was significantly altered. Niccolò Machiavelli, a medieval Italian philosopher, described one aspect of the change adequately in *The Prince* (1513). Machiavelli argued that people could no longer use abstract notions about how one ought to live as their guide

to law and government. Instead, he advocated that philosophers examine how people actually live to establish their main point of reference. With this philosophical shift from the "ought" to the "is," a new nature became the guiding principle behind both natural law and natural rights.

This shift altered the relationship between natural law and natural rights by placing rights first. At the very time scientific philosophers were discovering that the earth was not the center of the physical universe, political philosophers were making humans the center of the legal universe. Appetites and aversions, rather than ideas and ends, became the guiding principles of natural rights and law.

The development of modern natural rights also witnessed the popularization of both natural rights and natural law. The American and French revolutions were the most obvious results of this popularization. Phrases such as the "rights of man" and "human rights" became part of the new natural rights doctrine. Another important notion that developed with modern philosophy was the idea of a social contract or compact.

Two seventeenth century English philosophers who were instrumental in shaping the modern natural rights and natural law tradition were Thomas Hobbes and John Locke. Both placed considerable emphasis on the social contract theory and, as a result, were important contributors to the emerging belief that governments possessed only those rights which were consistent with the principle of modern natural right. The social contract theory relied on the belief that governmental powers were derived from the consent of the governed. Any rights that are not delegated to government through this consent are maintained by the citizens.

Many modern thinkers believe that rights are not only natural but also prepolitical—another important departure from the traditional understanding of natural rights. Hobbes, Locke, and eighteenth century French philosopher Jean-Jacques Rousseau all trace natural rights back to a prepolitical "state of nature." There are significant differences among their descriptions of the state of nature, but they are common in that the rights humans possess can be traced back to that original state. In fact, for all three of these writers, natural rights can be explained only by reference to their original state of nature.

The natural rights that one possessed in the state of nature are the basis for the natural laws that govern the state of nature. These laws are the only ones that people can transfer to civil society and government. Modern teachings about natural rights and law limit the nature of legitimate governmental power in three distinct ways. First, governments can never possess more powers than the individual possessed in the state of nature. Second, the only powers a government can exercise are those the citizen transfers to the government through consent. Third, no matter what type of government is established, there are certain basic rights and liberties that citizens can never give up.

A basic assumption of modern natural rights is that governments are designed to ensure and strengthen those rights which exist by nature. For this reason, positive laws (those made by governments) can never exceed or conflict with natural laws.

HUMAN RIGHTS THAT EVOLVED FROM NATURAL RIGHTS CONCEPTS

Natural Rights Concept	Human Rights
Freedom	Self-determination: rights to food, shelter, education, medical care, and social security
Liberty: freedoms of expression and religion	Liberty: freedoms of assembly, expression, religion, thought, culture, nationality, and movement; right to asylum
Equality	Equality: equality before the law, equal education, equal employment
Property	Property: right to employment, equal pay
Self-government	Representative government: fair elections, participatory government, equal suffrage, equal access to public service
Freedom from arbitrary arrest	Due process: presumption of innocence, right to fair trial; freedoms from torture, detention, and exile
Personal privacy	Right to privacy: domestic privacy, privacy of correspondence; rights to family, marriage, honor, reputation, and leisure

Citizens have a clear right, if not an obligation, to overthrow any government that oversteps the boundaries of natural right.

Natural Rights and Law Within the United States. Few countries have a closer or more direct tie to the natural rights tradition than does the United States of America. The Declaration of Independence was the first governmental document to justify the development of a political regime on the principles of natural rights. The U.S. Constitution and the Bill of Rights further reveal the strong natural rights basis of the United States government.

The Declaration of Independence established American independence from Great Britain on the grounds that the British government had violated the natural rights of the colonists. The Declaration of Independence's appeal to the "laws of nature and of nature's God" would fit into the Greek and Roman natural rights tradition as well as the modern tradition. The "self-evident" truths and the "unalienable rights" are clearly references to modern natural rights beliefs. The most undeniably modern statement in the Declaration is the reference to governments "deriving their just powers from the consent of the governed."

The preamble to the Constitution continues the natural rights assumptions that are part of the American system. The phrase calling for a "more perfect union" as well as the reference to securing "the blessings of liberty to ourselves and our posterity" could easily have been taken from Rousseau's *The Social Contract* (1762).

The Bill of Rights expresses those rights which cannot be removed or infringed upon by government. The understanding when these were proposed and ratified was that such rights were beyond the reach of any government. They were necessary to ensure "life, liberty, and the pursuit of happiness."

— Donald V. Weatherman

See also Bill of Rights, U.S.; Civil disobedience; Civil liberties; Civil rights; Constitutional law; Declaration of Independence; Jurisprudence; Moral relativism.

BIBLIOGRAPHY

A fine collection of essays that provides a good perspective is M. P. Golding, ed., *The Nature of Law: Readings in Legal Philosophy* (New York: Random House, 1966); the best overviews are Carl J. Friedrich, *The Philosophy of Law in Historical Perspective* (Chicago: University of Chicago Press, 1973), and Leo Strauss, *Natural Right and History* (Chicago: University of Chicago Press, 1953). The most accessible classic work is Thomas Pangle, trans. and ed., *The Laws of Plato* (New York: Basic Books, 1980). Two of the most insightful works related to the American context are Harry V. Jaffa, *Original Intent and the Framers of the Constitution* (Washington, D.C.: Regnery Gateway, 1994), and Carl L. Becker, *The Declaration of Independence: A Study in the History of Political Ideas* (New York: Harcourt, Brace, 1922).

Neagle, In re

COURT: U.S. Supreme Court

DATE: Decided April 14, 1890

SIGNIFICANCE: This case, involving an attack on Supreme Court Justice Stephen J. Field, expanded federal power by making certain acts committed under color of federal law subject to the jurisdiction of federal law rather than state criminal law

While sitting as a circuit court judge in his native California in 1888, Justice Stephen J. Field delivered an opinion invalidating the purported marriage between William Sharon, a wealthy Nevada mine owner, and Sarah Althea Hill. During Sharon's federal action to nullify a state court award to Hill of a judgment of divorce and alimony, he died, and Hill married David S. Terry, one of Field's former colleagues on the California Supreme Court. Hill and Terry were outraged by Field's ruling, precipitating a courtroom brawl that resulted in Field citing them for contempt and sentencing them to jail.

Terry began a campaign of public vilification of Field, going so far as to threaten to kill him. Against all warnings, in 1889 Field returned to California for circuit duties. He traveled with David Neagle, a federal marshal who had been assigned to protect him. While eating breakfast on his way to Los Angeles, where he was to hold court, Field was attacked by Terry, who struck him twice. Neagle, who believed Terry to be reaching for a weapon, drew his own gun and shot Terry dead.

Neagle was arrested by state officials and charged with murder under California law. He appealed to federal circuit court for a writ of *habeas corpus*, which federal law author-

Justice Stephen J. Field is third from the right in this 1887 Supreme Court photograph; a complex chain of events, including an attack on Field by David S. Terry, precipitated In re Neagle. *(Harris and Ewing, collection of the Supreme Court of the United States)*

ized if a person was being held against federal law. California then appealed the grant of the writ, and the release of Neagle, to the U.S. Supreme Court.

Justice Field did not participate in the case, which by a 6-2 vote upheld the lower court's grant of the writ. While the majority interpreted the authority under which the writ was granted to mean that federal "law" included Neagle's performance of his assigned duties as a federal marshal, the minority objected that this was a strained interpretation formulated solely to justify the intrusion of the federal government into the jurisdiction of state criminal law.

To be sure, the Court wanted to save Neagle—who had possibly saved the life of one of their own in the course of doing his job—from the vagaries of California law. In effect, however, the Supreme Court decided that the federal circuit court had the authority, on the basis of a petition for a writ of *habeas corpus* and without benefit of the fact-finding process afforded by a trial, to make a determination that Terry's murder had been justifiable homicide. The majority of laws governing criminal behavior are promulgated by individual states, and when criminal matters come before federal courts, customarily it is state law that applies. *In re Neagle* thus expanded federal judicial and executive power into a realm normally reserved for the states.

See also Color of law; Federalism; Field, Stephen J.; *Habeas corpus*; Judicial system, U.S.

Near v. Minnesota

COURT: U.S. Supreme Court
DATE: Decided June 1, 1931
SIGNIFICANCE: In this case the Supreme Court held for the first time that injunctions on the press to prevent publication are presumptively unconstitutional "prior restraints" and that the parties seeking them have a heavy burden to overcome; however, it also suggested that prior restraints could be acceptable under certain circumstances

Based on a statute that allowed a court to enjoin (prohibit) the publication of a newspaper if it was detrimental to public morals and general welfare, a Minnesota district attorney requested an injunction against the *Saturday Press* because of its anti-Semitic and racist remarks. The trial court concluded that the publication was chiefly devoted to malicious, scandalous, and defamatory articles and enjoined the editors from publishing, editing, producing, and circulating their publication. The Supreme Court of Minnesota affirmed this decision, but the Supreme Court of the United States reversed it.

The Court held that the statute amounted to a prior restraint in violation of the First Amendment. Since the effect of the application of the statute was the suppression of information, the Court held that it operated as a system of censorship. The Court suggested that prior restraints are the most dangerous infringement on freedom of the press because their effect is to suppress speech totally and because of the inability of the press to challenge the constitutionality of the order by disobeying it. The Court suggested, however, that prior restraints

could be acceptable in limited circumstances, including cases of obscene material, cases of fighting words and incitement to violence or to overthrow the government, and cases of national security during war where the information to be published could endanger U.S. troops or the success of a mission. The Court offered no explanation for these exceptions.

Justice Pierce Butler wrote a dissenting opinion joined by three other justices. They argued that the original court order did not have the effect of a prior restraint but of punishment imposed after publication to preserve law and order. They also emphasized the fact that the statute did not authorize administrative, licensing, or censorship control by the government. Therefore, they suggested, the statute did not amount to censorship.

The decision of the Court stated clearly for the first time that by issuing an injunction against the media prior to publication the state would be abridging freedom of the press. In reaching this conclusion, the Court gave the concept of prior restraint a much broader meaning than it had been afforded before. Traditionally, the phrase "prior restraint" was used to describe an administrative licensing system which allowed the state to determine in advance what could be published. The Minnesota statute did not create a licensing system; the decision to enjoin a publication was made by a court after a hearing and not by an administrative licenser or censor prior to publication. Yet the Court declared that the primary purpose of the First Amendment is to protect against governmental actions that have the ultimate effect of a prior restraint, whatever their character might be. Since *Near v. Minnesota*, therefore, the doctrine against prior restraints on the media has been related to the effects on speech notwithstanding the method used by the government in regulating it.

See also Bill of Rights, U.S.; Censorship; *New York Times Co. v. United States*; News media; Speech and press, freedom of.

Negligence

DEFINITION: A theory of liability that allows an injured party (a plaintiff) to recover compensation for damages caused by a defendant's careless conduct; the term is also used to describe the particular conduct of the defendant
SIGNIFICANCE: American law presupposes that people have a duty to act with reasonable care; many civil suits involve charges of negligence, or acting carelessly or recklessly

When a person suffers an injury caused by someone else's conduct, the injured person may have the right to "recover," or collect an award to compensate for damages, for the injury. The injured party (the plaintiff) could bring a cause of action against the defendant under one of several theories of liability, depending on the facts of the case.

The law imposes on everyone a duty to act carefully. This means that people should not act in a way that creates unreasonable risks of harm to others. This duty is usually referred to as the duty of the "reasonable person under the circumstances." A person is negligent when his or her conduct is below this standard of care. The test for negligence is thus objective in that it does not matter whether the person intended or knew the consequences of the act. The conduct is compared with, and judged against, that of the hypothetical reasonably prudent person under the same circumstances. If the person's conduct is an act that the reasonable person would not have done under the circumstances, or if it is failure to act under circumstances where the reasonable person would have acted, he or she is considered "negligent" and may be found liable for the damages others suffer because of the risk created.

The word "negligence" is also used to describe that legal right, or cause of action, that the plaintiff has against the defendant to recover damages for the injury. In addition to showing the damages suffered, in order to have a cause of action the plaintiff will have to show that the defendant had a specific duty toward him or her, that the defendant breached that duty, and that the defendant's conduct that constituted the breach caused the injury.

There may be instances where the law has designed a different standard of conduct for particular circumstances. For example, the standard of conduct for children is that of similar children of the same age, experience, and intelligence under the circumstances. The standard for physicians is that of the medical profession's recognized practice in the particular field.

See also Malfeasance, misfeasance, and nonfeasance; Malice; Medical malpractice; Products liability; Strict liability; Tort.

Neighborhood watch programs
DEFINITION: Organized community efforts at self-policing
SIGNIFICANCE: Neighborhood watch programs are among the most successful civilian crime-reduction efforts

Officially organized neighborhood watch groups cooperate with local police departments, reporting suspicious activities. (McCrea Adams)

Neighborhood watch programs range from loose organizations of citizens simply looking out for unusual activity in their neighborhoods to well-organized patrols by civilian volunteers. Official neighborhood watch programs cooperate with local police departments; they are distinguished from self-organized patrols that act without police consent and resemble vigilante groups. Police often establish official watch programs, forming groups of volunteers who attend meetings and receive police training. Members of such groups are warned not to accost suspicious persons but to contact regular police if they suspect criminal activity; some patrols carry citizen's band radios. Neighborhood watch groups aid also in police public relations and information programs and can help to build community-police rapport.

See also Burglary; Community-oriented policing; Police and guards, private; Theft; Vigilantism.

New Deal
DATE: Began March 4, 1933
PLACE: Washington, D.C.
SIGNIFICANCE: The New Deal program of President Franklin D. Roosevelt vastly expanded the size and economic role of the federal government and gave rise to long-time political domination by the Democratic Party

Franklin D. Roosevelt was elected president in November, 1932, at a time when the United States was in the depths of its worst economic depression. He persuaded Congress to enact a vast array of legislation aimed at achieving "relief, recovery, and reform." Through the relief measures, the federal government for the first time provided direct handouts to needy individuals. These began with the Federal Emergency Relief Act of 1933, followed by the Works Progress Administration (WPA) in 1935 and certain provisions of the Social Security Act of that same year.

Recovery from the Depression was sought in 1933 through the National Industrial Recovery Act (NIRA) and the Agricultural Adjustment Act (AAA). Both reflected the view that the Depression was a problem of overproduction, to be remedied by measures which would raise product prices, even if production had to be curtailed. Both were held unconstitutional, but portions were reenacted. Agricultural price supports and production controls became a permanent part of the national farm policy. Public works projects were greatly expanded to provide jobs and incomes as well as construct useful facilities.

"Reform" meant a variety of measures to regulate business and redistribute incomes toward the poor. An epidemic of bank failures was brought to a halt in March, 1933, followed by stringent examination of surviving banks, creation of federal deposit insurance, separation of commercial banking from investment banking, and establishment of the Securities and Exchange Commission to regulate issue and trading of securities. Federally financed housing for low-income families was developed, particularly through the United States Housing Act of 1937.

The federal government became a strong promoter of labor unions, particularly through the National Labor Relations Act

The New Deal was a response to the devastating Great Depression, during which millions were thrown out of work. (Library of Congress)

(Wagner Act) of 1935. Union membership more than tripled between 1933 and 1940, and unions became a powerful support for the Democratic Party. The Fair Labor Standards Act of 1938 prohibited child labor and established minimum wages and maximum hours for wage earners. The Social Security Act of 1935 created an enormous program of federal transfer payments for retirement pensions, unemployment compensation, and assistance to specific categories of low-income families. The Tennessee Valley Authority (created in 1933) constructed dams for flood control, hydroelectric power, and recreational development. A variety of programs spurred a flow of credit into lending for home purchases, notably the Federal Housing Administration (FHA) program of mortgage guarantee.

By taking the dollar off the gold standard in 1933, Roosevelt opened the way for a large increase in the money supply, which helped promote economic recovery but also contributed to the inflation of the 1940's.

The greatest achievement of the New Deal was in restoring the public's confidence in a free-market economy (admittedly much regulated) and in a democratic political system. On the other hand, the New Deal programs did not quickly restore the economy to full employment. While federal expenditures nearly doubled from 1933 to 1940, much of the potential stimulus to aggregate spending was offset by the constant increases in tax rates, and the unemployment rate was still about 15 percent in 1940.

See also Court-packing plan of Franklin D. Roosevelt; Democratic Party; Labor law; National Labor Relations Act (NLRA); Roosevelt, Franklin D.; Securities and Exchange Commission (SEC); Social Security system; Welfare state.

New Jersey v. T.L.O.

COURT: U.S. Supreme Court

DATE: Decided January 15, 1985

SIGNIFICANCE: This decision established the standards by which the protections of the Fourth Amendment apply to searches of students by school officials

A teacher at Piscataway High School in New Jersey found two students smoking cigarettes in a school restroom in violation of the school's rules. After being sent to the school office, one of the students, "T.L.O.," a fourteen-year-old freshman, denied smoking. Based on the report he had received from the teacher, the assistant vice principal searched T.L.O.'s purse and discovered a pack of cigarettes. As he reached for the cigarette pack, he then noticed other items, including cigarette rolling papers, which he associated with marijuana use. He then searched the purse more thoroughly and discovered marijuana, a pipe, plastic bags, a large sum of money in single dollar bills, a list of students who owed T.L.O. money, and two letters which suggested T.L.O. was involved in marijuana sales. School officials notified T.L.O.'s mother and the police.

On the basis of this evidence and a later confession, the state brought delinquency charges against T.L.O. T.L.O. appealed the charges, arguing that because the search of her purse was improper under the Fourth Amendment, the evidence was inadmissible. The U.S. Supreme Court, however, ruled that the search was conducted within the constitutional standards of the Fourth Amendment. In its opinion, the Court established standards to be used by school officials in searches of students' pockets, purses, and other items associated with the student's person. The Court specifically did not address searches of school lockers.

Until this case, public school officials had typically relied on the doctrine of *in loco parentis*, whereby school officials had broad search powers akin to those of a student's parents. The U.S. Supreme Court rejected this argument and held that when public school officials conduct a search of a student, they may be held to the same Fourth Amendment standards as government officials. In its analysis, the Court recognized that public school students maintain an expectation of privacy in their personal effects even on a public school campus, but the Court did not go so far as to hold school officials to exactly the same standards as police officers in conducting searches. While police officers are usually required to show they had probable cause to believe the person has violated the law, the Court allowed that school officials may need to show only that they had a reasonable suspicion that a search would produce evidence that the student had violated a school code. The Court justified this relaxed standard for school officials by citing the major social problems evident in schools nationwide and a school's need to maintain an educational environment.

See also Evidence, rules of; *In loco parentis*; Probable cause; School law; Search and seizure; *Tinker v. Des Moines Independent Community School District*.

New Mexico State Penitentiary riot

DATE: February 2 and 3, 1980

PLACE: Approximately ten miles south of Santa Fe, New Mexico

SIGNIFICANCE: This riot was the bloodiest and one of the most costly prison riots in American history as inmates engaged in a reign of terror and destruction lasting thirty-six hours

Around 2:00 A.M. on February 2, sixty-two inmates, many drunk on an intoxicating "home brew" of fermented yeast, sugar, and raisins, overpowered the four guards responsible for securing their dormitory residence. Possessing keys and weapons, the prisoners surprised four more officers and, within twenty minutes, overran the prison's control center, giving them access to the entire institution.

The next thirty-six hours took on a nightmarish quality as roving inmate gangs engaged in sadistic and brutal acts of violence. Thirty-three prisoners were killed by other inmates. Twelve guards, taken as hostages, and another one hundred prisoners suffered torturous beatings and sexual assaults. Some estimates place the riot's final monetary costs as high as $100 million.

The riot's causes were multiple and overlapping. Corrections suffered from years of neglect and poor leadership. There was a lack of staff, training, and funding; equipment failed regularly, and standard procedures were not followed. On February 2, twenty-two officers were guarding 1,157 inmates in a facility designed to hold fewer than 1,000. The riot prompted the state to enter into a federal court decree concerning confinement conditions at the penitentiary. Almost two decades and millions of dollars later, the penitentiary was still operating under judicial supervision.

See also Attica prison riot; Prison and jail systems.

Prisoners not wanting any part of the rioting at the New Mexico State Penitentiary gathered outside in the prison's recreation area. (AP/Wide World Photos)

New York Times Co. v. Sullivan

COURT: U.S. Supreme Court

DATE: Decided March 9, 1964

SIGNIFICANCE: In this case, the Supreme Court ruled that the press and public have wide latitude against claims of libel when commenting on the official conduct of public officials

On March 29, 1960, *The New York Times* ran a full-page advertisement sponsored by the "Committee to Defend Martin Luther King and the Struggle for Freedom in the South." The advertisement appealed for financial support for the Civil Rights movement in the South. In the ad, various incidents of discriminatory action in southern cities, including Montgomery, Alabama, were described. The ad was ostensibly endorsed by sixty-four well-known persons in the fields of religion, trade unions, public affairs, and performing arts. (Later, many proclaimed that they had never been contacted before the ad was released.)

The description of events in the advertisement relating to Montgomery, Alabama, was contested by L. B. Sullivan, an elected Montgomery commissioner with supervisory responsibility for the police department. The ad made several references to wrongdoing by police, which, Sullivan maintained, implicated him and defamed his reputation. Sullivan himself was not mentioned by name.

Sullivan pointed to several erroneous factual statements in the description of events. For example, the ad described an incident in which students were expelled following a protest on the Montgomery capitol steps, at which they had recited "My Country 'Tis of Thee," and it stated that truckloads of police had surrounded the Alabama State College campus with shotguns and tear gas. In reality, Sullivan said, the police had not surrounded the campus, as claimed, but had been on campus several times in response to events; the protesting students had sung the National Anthem, not "My Country 'Tis of Thee"; and the students were expelled for a demonstration at which they had demanded service at a courthouse lunch counter, not for a capitol demonstration.

The Montgomery County Circuit Court found that Sullivan had been defamed and awarded him $500,000, an unprecedented amount in a libel trial. Sullivan effectively convinced the Court that *The New York Times* had been irresponsible in printing the ad with the factual errors, since its own files contained articles with conflicting information. The Supreme Court of Alabama affirmed the lower court judgment.

The U.S. Supreme Court reversed the judgment, holding that the Alabama courts had failed to place sufficient weight on First and Fourteenth Amendment claims. The Supreme Court determined that constitutional free press guarantees extend to an advertisement with political content, especially since members of the public without access to the press may need to buy space to publicize their ideas. The Court further pointed to a potential chilling effect on freedom of press by damage awards for criticism of public officials' conduct, even if factual errors are involved. In an opinion authored by Justice William J. Brennan, the majority held that "erroneous statement is inevitable in free debate" and that it "must be protected if the freedoms of expression are to have the breathing space they 'need to survive.' " Brennan argued that forcing critics of government action to guarantee the truth of their assertions could bring about self-censorship as a result of fear of potential libel suits.

The Court's opinion pointed out that the Constitution's framers believed in debate which is robust and uninhibited, even if it includes "vehement, caustic, and sometimes unpleasantly sharp attacks on government and public officials."

In *New York Times Co. v. Sullivan*, the Court fashioned a federal standard for libel cases involving public officials. The standard prohibits public officials from recovering damages for defamatory falsehoods relating to official conduct unless an official "proves that the statement was made with 'actual malice'—that is, with knowledge that it was false or with reckless disregard of whether it was false or not."

New York Times Co. v. Sullivan recognized the importance of allowing the public and press to criticize freely the official conduct of public officials without the crippling fear of libel suits in retaliation for that criticism. While the decision has been refined and clarified in subsequent cases, the principle of encouraging free debate of public officials' conduct and actions has been strongly preserved.

See also Defamation; News media; Speech and press, freedom of.

New York Times Co. v. United States

COURT: U.S. Supreme Court

DATE: Decided June 30, 1971

SIGNIFICANCE: This was the first Supreme Court decision involving a restraint directly on the media under the national security exception to the prior restraint doctrine

During 1971, Daniel Ellsberg, one of the original writers of a secret government study of the United States' involvement in Vietnam, leaked a copy to *The New York Times*. Two days after the newspaper published some sections of it, the government filed a petition for a restraining order, arguing that further publication would threaten national security. This petition was originally denied, but the denial was later reversed by a court of appeals. Meanwhile, the government also filed a petition for an injunction against *The Washington Post*, which had also begun to publish the report. Eventually, this petition was denied. Both cases were then appealed to the Supreme Court. The issue before the Court was whether the media could be enjoined from publishing truthful information of public interest because it would allegedly endanger the nation's security. The media argued that such injunction would constitute censorship in violation of the First Amendment.

A total of ten separate opinions were published by the Supreme Court. The opinion of the Court was very short and unsigned. It merely reiterated that any order prohibiting publication has a heavy presumption against constitutional validity, and that the petitioner has a heavy burden of showing that such a remedy is justified. It then held that the government had not met the burden that would justify the restraining order. Therefore, it was implied that the state could have enjoined the

A New York Times *editor looks over the paper's "Pentagon papers" story on July 1, 1971, the morning after the Supreme Court's decision to allow publication.* (AP/Wide World Photos)

media had it been able to produce better evidence of the danger to national security.

Each justice filed a separate opinion. Seven of them accepted the idea that there could be a national security exception to the prior restraint doctrine, as had been suggested in passing in the 1931 decision *Near v. Minnesota.* Suggesting that the Court had not provided clear standards for future decisions, Justice Harry Blackmun called for the creation of clear standards to be used in prior restraint cases. Only Justices William Brennan and Potter Stewart suggested such standards. Brennan suggested that only in cases where the petitioner could prove that the publication would "inevitably, directly and immediately cause the occurrence of an event kindred to imperiling the safety of a transport already at sea" can a prior restraint be issued. Stewart suggested the standard should be proof that the publication would "surely result in direct, immediate and irreparable damage to our Nation or its people."

Even though the Supreme Court was dealing for the first time with the national security exception mentioned in *Near*, it did not explain the meaning of the burden needed to justify the order. The Court did not create any standards to determine the constitutionality of restraining orders. It is also nearly impossible to get an accurate idea of what standards would have been acceptable to a majority of the justices. The Court did not provide any discussion on the restraining order itself and did not discuss the evidence used by the government to support its

claim. In essence, the Court failed to provide any guidelines for future litigants as to what would constitute sufficient evidence to overcome the presumption of invalidity of a petition for an order banning publication by the press.

See also Bill of Rights, U.S.; Censorship; *Near v. Minnesota*; News media; Speech and press, freedom of.

New York v. Ferber

COURT: U.S. Supreme Court
DATE: Decided July 2, 1982
SIGNIFICANCE: The Court ruled that pornography depicting sexual performances by children was a category of material not protected by the First Amendment

The state of New York, like nineteen other states, had a statute that criminalized the dissemination of material depicting sexual conduct of children under the age of sixteen, regardless of whether the material satisfied the legal definition of obscenity. The owner of a Manhattan adult bookstore, Paul Ferber, was tried and convicted under the statute for selling films that depicted young boys masturbating. The New York Court of Appeals, however, reversed the conviction, holding that the statute violated the First Amendment because it was inconsistent with the recognized legal standard of obscenity. The state then appealed the case to the U.S. Supreme Court.

The Court voted unanimously to uphold the conviction of Ferber under the New York statute. Justice Byron White, writing for the Court, proclaimed that child pornography was "a category of material outside the protection of the First Amendment." He emphasized five points. First, the state had a compelling interest in safeguarding minor children from sexual exploitation and abuse. Second, the distribution of materials depicting the sexual activity of juveniles was intrinsically related to their sexual abuse. Third, the advertising and selling of child pornography provided an economic motive for an activity that was everywhere illegal. Fourth, child pornography was of very modest literary, scientific, or educational value. Finally, the recognition of a category of material outside the protection of the First Amendment was compatible with earlier decisions of the Court. White concluded that the test for child pornography was much less demanding than the three-part test in *Miller v. California* (1973), but he also wrote that the prohibited conduct must be adequately defined in state law.

The most important aspect of the *Ferber* decision was that all the justices agreed that the state's interest in protecting children was sufficiently compelling to justify more discretion in criminalizing child pornography than when dealing with other forms of pornography. The majority of the Court was unwilling to consider the possibility of constitutional protection of any material depicting juveniles engaged in sexual conduct. A liberal minority cautioned, however, that such material would be protected by the First Amendment if its depictions were found to contain serious literary, artistic, scientific, or medical value.

See also *Barnes v. Glen Theatre, Inc.*; Censorship; Child molestation; *Miller v. California*; *Osborne v. Ohio*; Pedophilia; *Roth v. United States*; Speech and press, freedom of.

Newberry v. United States

COURT: U.S. Supreme Court
DATE: Decided May 2, 1921
SIGNIFICANCE: The Supreme Court concluded that the federal government lacked the constitutional authority to regulate party primaries, a ruling that had the unintended consequence of disfranchising black citizens in the single-party South

In 1918, Truman H. Newberry, Republican candidate for the U.S. Senate, was tried in Michigan, along with more than one hundred associates, for conspiring to violate the Federal Corrupt Practices Act of 1910. The statute violated had set a limit on campaign financing, and the indictment claimed that Newberry had exceeded this limit in primary and general election expenditures. Newberry and his associates were found guilty in the U.S. District Court for the Western District of Michigan.

The U.S. Supreme Court reversed the conviction and sent the case back to the lower court, finding that the statute on which Newberry's conviction rested had no constitutional authority. The Court argued that prior to the Seventeenth Amendment, the only part of the Constitution empowering Congress to regulate the election process was to be found in Article I, section 4, which pertained only to the time, place, and manner of holding general elections and failed to address such matters as party primaries and conventions, additions to

the election process unforeseen by the framers of the Constitution. Consequently, the Court ruled that in the relevant section of the Corrupt Practices Act, Congress had exceeded its authority. The Court also maintained that because the statute antedated the ratification of the Seventeenth Amendment, which extended congressional authority, it was invalid at the time of its enactment. The Court held that a power later acquired could not, *ex proprio*, validate a law that was unconstitutional at the time of its passing. The Court did not question a state's right to regulate primaries and campaign financing, claiming that "the state may suppress whatever evils may be incident to primary or convention."

The *Newberry* ruling imposed an important barrier to the enfranchisement of black Americans in the single-party South. Although the Court would strike down laws expressly prohibiting African Americans from voting in primaries, as late as 1935, in *Grovey v. Townsend*, it upheld legal measures taken in Texas to bar blacks from participating in the state Democratic convention, arguing that such "private" discrimination did not come under constitutional purview. *Grovey* and *Newberry* were finally successfully challenged in *United States v. Classic* (1941), which held that Congress had the authority to regulate both primary and general elections for federal offices.

Three years later a final legal blow to *de jure* disfranchisement of African Americans was dealt in *Smith v. Allwright* (1944), which held that laws governing all elections—local, state, and federal—could be invalidated if they violated Article I, section 4 of the Constitution. Sponsored by the National Association for the Advancement of Colored People, the plaintiff argued that Texas Democratic Party officials had denied him a primary ballot because of his race. The Supreme Court concurred, noting that state laws regulated both primary and general elections and were therefore responsible for barriers to the ballot box erected on racial grounds.

See also *Classic, United States v.*; *Grovey v. Townsend*; Jim Crow laws; Poll tax; *Smith v. Allwright*; Vote, right to; Voting Rights Act of 1965.

News media

DEFINITION: Entities that gather and disseminate news, either in print (newspapers and magazines), over the airwaves (radio and television), or via cable systems
SIGNIFICANCE: The news media hold a unique place in the American legal system and constitutional scheme; the Supreme Court consistently confirms freedom of the press as a fundamental right

The American constitutional system of government is based on interaction between three branches: the executive, the legislative, and the judicial. These branches react to one another and check one another to protect society from autocracy. Within this system, the news media are expected to exercise an additional check on the power of the three branches of government. To protect this function from being controlled or impeded by the government itself, the framers enacted the press clause as part of the First Amendment to the Constitution. The framers understood that a free, independent press was needed to assure a responsible government.

The First Amendment states, among other things, that Congress shall make no law abridging freedom of the press. In 1925, the Supreme Court held in *Gitlow v. New York* that the protection contained in the First Amendment applied to the states through the Fourteenth Amendment. Therefore, the press can claim the protection of the First Amendment in state actions. For these reasons, any definition of "the news media" must be closely tied to an understanding of the First Amendment.

The extent of the protection provided by the Constitution depends on the particular circumstances and the governmental interests that may be at stake. For example, it may depend on whether the press is claiming a right in relation to information that has been already published or whether it is making a claim of a right of access to information while gathering news. Also, the Constitution cannot provide a guarantee of responsibility or ethical behavior. It would be ideal if all the media were neutral, objective, truthful, and responsible; however, this is something the Constitution does not guarantee and that the government cannot impose. A press subject to governmental control over media ethics would not be a free press.

Although there are many aspects of news media law and practice that are not derived directly from constitutional protections, the First Amendment always plays an important role. For example, it limits the way the states can protect the reputations of its citizens, the way states regulate access to trials, and the way states protect the rights of criminal defendants to a fair trial.

Access to the Media. Given that the press is protected under the American constitutional scheme because it serves the role of eyes and ears of the public, it seems to follow that the government could intervene to make sure the press is accountable to those whom it is supposed to serve. In *Miami Herald v. Tornillo* (1974), however, the Supreme Court determined that such intervention would be unconstitutional. The Court held that the government cannot force a printer to print the different points of view on an issue. The Court reasoned that once the press is forced to be responsible, it ceases to be free and independent.

News-Gathering Function. The role of the media involves two distinct functions: news-gathering and publishing. Both functions raise important legal issues. The process of getting access to the information is the "news-gathering" function. If the press is going to serve as a check on government and be the eyes and ears of the public, it must have access to information.

The right of broadcast journalists to use television cameras in courtrooms is not absolute but is left to the presiding judge's discretion. Here a murder trial is being broadcast and videotaped. (James L. Shaffer)

Many issues regarding access to information are regulated by statutes such as the Freedom of Information Act and the open meeting laws, which guarantee that certain government documents and meetings will be open to the public and the press. Many other issues regarding access to information are not covered by statutes, and the media have claimed the right to access the information directly under the First Amendment. Recognition of this right and its limits depends on the legal context under which it is claimed.

For example, the relationship between the news media and the judicial system creates unique legal problems. On the one hand, courts have a duty to protect the criminal defendant's right to a fair trial under the Sixth Amendment to the Constitution. On the other, media coverage of criminal matters and of the judicial system is a valuable component of the democratic form of government. Indeed, the Supreme Court has repeatedly stated that public scrutiny of criminal trials is an effective restraint on possible abuse of judicial power and that such scrutiny enhances the quality and integrity of the process. In *Richmond Newspapers, Inc. v. Virginia* (1980) the Supreme Court balanced these interests and held that there is a limited First Amendment right of access to criminal trials. The Court held that this right could be curtailed, however, if there was a clear finding of an overriding state interest and the order limiting access was narrowly tailored to serve the interests. Through a series of decisions, the Court later extended this analysis to pretrial proceedings.

The use of injunctive orders to prohibit or delay publication of information regarding a criminal trial to make sure the jurors are not exposed to pretrial publicity creates a conflict between the Sixth Amendment right to a fair trial and the First Amendment right to freedom of the press. When an order banning publication is requested, the courts have to determine whether the order would constitute an unconstitutional prior restraint. In *Nebraska Press Association v. Stuart* (1976), the Supreme Court reiterated that such orders were presumptively unconstitutional prior restraints. The Court stated, however, that orders banning publication could be constitutionally valid under very limited circumstances.

Certain controls on the media's presence in the courtroom do not violate the First Amendment. The fact that there is a limited First Amendment right of access to trials does not mean that the media have a constitutional right to bring cameras into the courts. The First Amendment prevents the courts from closing access to the media but does not prevent the imposition of restrictions on the manner in which access is conducted. It has been argued that the use of cameras in the courtroom affects the decorum of the trial, intimidates witnesses, and distracts juries. Others argue it provides the best assurance of fairness in the court system. Although the federal courts decided not to continue an experiment which allowed cameras in some civil trials, most states allow the use of cameras in at least some categories of trials.

Journalist Privilege. Also important to the news-gathering efforts of the press is its claim of a privilege to refuse to provide the identity of its sources of information. The media insist that the law should recognize their right to keep their sources confidential because otherwise the sources might disappear and the press would not have access to necessary information. The existence of such privilege varies tremendously among the states. In many cases it is created by the courts, but in many others it is created and regulated by statutes. Most statutes are narrowly construed and provide only limited protection. The recognition of a limited privilege also depends on the context in which the claim is made. The decision can be influenced by such factors as whether the claim is made in a criminal trial, whether the media are a party to the case, or whether the claim is made in response to an ongoing criminal investigation. Every year there are nationally reported instances of journalists being sent to jail on contempt of court charges for refusing to reveal sources.

Publishing Function. The second important function of the press is the publishing function. In publishing, the media also have limited First Amendment protection. The First Amendment protects the press from governmental orders that have the effect of censorship prior to publication. The phrase "prior restraint" was used in the common law to describe an administrative licensing system which allowed the state to determine in advance what could be published. In 1931 the Supreme Court gave the concept of prior restraint a much broader meaning. In *Near v. Minnesota* (1931), the Court held for the first time that judicial injunctions on the press to prevent publication are presumptively unconstitutional prior restraints and that the parties seeking them have a heavy burden to overcome. Yet it also suggested that prior restraints could be acceptable under certain circumstances, such as the publication of obscene material, information that could endanger a mission during wartime, and information that could incite violence. The Court declared that the primary purpose of the First Amendment is to protect against governmental actions that have the ultimate effect of a prior restraint, whatever their character might be. Therefore, since this decision, the doctrine against prior restraints on the media is related to the effects on speech notwithstanding the method used by the government in regulating it.

Defamation. The law of defamation is very important to the news media. It allows people who believe their reputations have been damaged by a published false statement to be compensated for the injury. Because the fear of liability may have a chilling effect on the press, the Supreme Court has created standards to balance the interests. In *New York Times Co. v. Sullivan* (1964) and *Gertz v. Welch* (1974), the Supreme Court "constitutionalized" the law of defamation by altering the degree of fault a plaintiff needs to show to have a cause of action. If the plaintiff is a public figure, he or she must show that the publisher knew the published statement was false or that it published it with "reckless disregard" for the truth. Plaintiffs who are not public figures can satisfy the burden by showing whatever degree of fault their state requires, which is usually a showing of negligence. For this reason, the distinction between a public and a private person becomes very important. A public figure is someone who is a household name or who voluntarily participates in an issue of public interest in a visible role.

In addition to reporting the news, the media play the role of "commentator" by providing a forum for authors to express their opinions. This valuable role has led the Supreme Court to recognize some protection for the media in those cases where the plaintiffs want compensation for statements of opinion.

The news media have these protections from defamation actions because they are expected to be reasonably free to report and comment on the conduct and character of people involved in issues of public interest. In fact, the media have often played an important role in uncovering government corruption and misconduct, as in the case of the Watergate scandal that eventually led to the resignation of President Richard Nixon.

Privacy. Laws governing the individual's right to privacy are also very important for the news media. Many observers believe the media too often intrude in people's privacy. To a certain extent, this is part of the media's role, yet there is a government interest in protecting the privacy of the public. The Courts have limited the causes of action for which people can recover damages for invasion of privacy. (Some states do not recognize these causes of action at all.) For example, a person could recover damages if the media reveal an embarrassing, non-newsworthy private fact that the person did not want anyone to know or if the media make a statement that places the person in a false light in the eyes of others. Invasion of privacy also may occur if the media appropriate a person's name or likeness for commercial gain or if the media invade a person's protected personal space or sphere to gather news. This last type of claim against the media can have a substantial effect on the way the news-gathering process is conducted.

Broadcast Media. Television and cable television provide perhaps the two most popular sources of news in the United States. First Amendment protection has different meanings when applied to broadcast media and to print media. Whereas the government is essentially precluded from regulating the print media, the broadcast media are directly regulated by the Federal Communications Commission (FCC). The specific characteristics of the television medium, such as the scarcity of the airwaves and the pervasiveness of the system, led the Supreme Court to conclude that government regulation is not unconstitutional. Thus, for example, the FCC is allowed to regulate access to the broadcast media by political candidates and to limit the broadcasting of indecent language. Even though cable television is a different medium, the FCC has also been granted jurisdiction over it because it has a direct relationship with, and effect on, the broadcast media.

— *Alberto Bernabe-Riefkohl*

See also Defamation; *Near v. Minnesota*; *New York Times Co. v. Sullivan*; *New York Times Co. v. United States*; News sources, protection of; Privacy, right of; Speech and press, freedom of.

BIBLIOGRAPHY

A good discussion of many legal issues affecting the news media appears in Rodney Smolla, *Free Speech in an Open Society* (New York: Vintage Books, 1993). For a history of the development of libel law, see Norman Rosenberg, *Protecting the Best Men* (Chapel Hill: University of North Carolina Press, 1986). For a discussion of the issues regarding contemporary libel law, including issues of libel reform, see Rodney Smolla, *Suing the Press* (New York: Oxford University Press, 1986); Anthony Lewis, *Make No Law* (New York: Random House, 1991); Donald Gillmor, *Power, Publicity, and the Abuse of Libel Law* (New York: Oxford University Press, 1992); Everett Dennis and Eli Noam, eds., *The Cost of Libel* (New York: Columbia University Press, 1989); and Randall Bezanson, Gilbert Cranberg, and John Soloski, *Libel Law and the Press* (New York: Free Press, 1987). For a discussion of the political economy of the mass media, see Edward Herman and Noam Chomsky, *Manufacturing Consent* (New York: Pantheon Books, 1988), and Ben Bagdikian, *The Media Monopoly* (3d ed. Boston: Beacon Press, 1990). For a discussion of the relationship between the First Amendment right to freedom of the press and the Sixth Amendment right to a fair trial, see Peter Kane, *Murder, Courts, and the Press* (Carbondale: Southern Illinois University Press, 1992). For a discussion of the debate regarding the regulation of the broadcast media, see Lee Bollinger, *Images of a Free Press* (Chicago: University of Chicago Press, 1991), and Lucas Powe, Jr., *American Broadcasting and The First Amendment* (Berkeley: University of California Press, 1987).

News sources, protection of

DEFINITION: Journalists sometimes promise to keep confidential, or protect, the identity of sources so that the sources will provide information that they otherwise would not

SIGNIFICANCE: Reporters are sometimes ordered to reveal the identity of their sources in court proceedings; the press frequently responds that to do so would jeopardize its ability to gain information that the public has a right to know

A study by the Reporters Committee for Freedom of the Press in 1989 found that 1,042 news organizations had been asked to respond to 4,400 subpoenas asking for notes, tapes, photographs, or testimony concerning their sources of information. These sources often do not wish to be identified, either because they could be implicated in criminal activity, because they could be harmed or fired from their jobs, or simply because they do not wish to be hassled.

When wrongdoing has occurred, the justice system has a right to require testimony from anyone who may have knowledge of the crime. When journalists report wrongdoing, the courts believe that they should testify as to what they know of the events they have written about. Reporters are often asked to reveal the identity of their news sources to aid police in criminal investigations, to assist the defense in a criminal case, or to aid the establishment of negligence or malice in a defamation suit.

Journalists respond that the public's right to know would not be satisfied unless journalists were exempted from the obligation to testify about their sources in court proceedings. There would be a "chilling effect" such that potential sources would not be willing to provide information for fear that their identity would be revealed in open court. This requirement, it is argued, would violate the First Amendment.

The Supreme Court of the United States resolved this constitutional issue in *Branzburg v. Hayes* (1972). Branzburg was a reporter for the Louisville *Courier-Journal* who wrote a series exposing drug use in Jefferson County, Kentucky. Branzburg was called to testify before a grand jury about his knowledge. He refused to do so, arguing that he had a journalist's privilege not to provide testimony under the First Amendment. The Court found that there was no such constitutional privilege, but it also stated that there was no constitutional prevention of a legislature from passing laws, called shield laws, granting such a privilege.

Although Congress has never passed a federal shield law, slightly more than half the states have. Shield laws do not grant a privilege to protect news sources if the reporter has been a witness to a crime. They also require the reporter to have made an explicit promise of confidentiality to his or her source. Generally, the reporter will be asked to testify only if three conditions are met. The information must be relevant to the hearing, there must be a compelling need for disclosure of the information, and there must be no alternate sources for the information. If reporters still refuse to provide the information, they may be held in contempt of court and fined or jailed.

See also Contempt of court; News media; Privileged communications; Speech and press, freedom of.

Ninth Amendment

DEFINITION: States that the "enumeration in the Constitution, of certain rights, shall not be construed to deny or disparage others retained by the people"

SIGNIFICANCE: The Ninth Amendment has great potential significance as a source of unenumerated rights; since most justices have interpreted the amendment in a limited fashion, however, it has had less actual significance than it could

For much of American history, the Ninth Amendment lay "forgotten." In a 1965 concurring opinion in *Griswold v. Connecticut*, however, Justice Arthur Goldberg cited the Ninth Amendment as a source of an unenumerated right of privacy. Since then, the amendment has been cited in more than a thousand cases and has received considerable scholarly attention. Yet the Court has been reluctant to rely upon this amendment. Justice William O. Douglas' majority opinion in *Griswold* maintained that the right of privacy emanated from "penumbras" surrounding various provisions in the Bill of Rights which created zones of privacy. In other cases, justices have found additional unenumerated rights as part of the "liberty" protected by the due process clauses of the Fifth and Fourteenth Amendments.

The Ninth Amendment seems to embody the concept of natural rights enjoyed by the people and protected against governmental infringement. Responding to anti-Federalist calls for the inclusion of a bill of rights in the U.S. Constitution, Federalists such as Alexander Hamilton and James Wilson claimed that a written bill of rights was unnecessary and dangerous: unnecessary because the national government would possess only powers delegated to it and dangerous because the inadvertent omission of some natural right from a written list might imply that no such right existed. James Madison, author of the Bill of Rights, shared Hamilton's and Wilson's concerns. In a speech to the House of Representatives, he explained that the Ninth Amendment was designed to guard against the presumption that rights which were not enumerated "were intended to be assigned into the hands of the General Government, and were consequently insecure."

While the Ninth Amendment supports the idea that the American people enjoy constitutional rights beyond those enumerated in the written text of the Constitution, the amendment's open texture provides little guidance for judges attempting to define those rights. Testifying before Congress, Robert Bork argued that the Ninth Amendment should not be used if its meaning is not truly known. For example, if an amendment said that "Congress shall make no" and the rest of the sentence was covered by an inkblot, a court should not "make up what might be under the inkblot." Critics of the Supreme Court's decision in *Lochner v. New York* (1905) and subsequent related cases have argued that the Court used "due process" to create fundamental values favored by the justices but not directly traceable to the text, history, or structure of the Constitution. Some commentators on the Court's more recent right-of-privacy decisions suggest that the Court continues to "Lochnerize" by giving constitutional status to rights and interests not explicitly mentioned in the text of the Constitution.

See also Bill of Rights, U.S.; Civil liberties; Civil rights; *Griswold v. Connecticut*; *Lochner v. New York*; Natural law and natural rights; Privacy, right of.

Nixon, Richard M. (Jan. 9, 1913, Yorba Linda, Calif.— Apr. 22, 1994, New York, N.Y.)

IDENTIFICATION: President of the United States, 1969-1974

SIGNIFICANCE: Nixon had a number of significant achievements in both foreign and domestic policy, but he was also forced to resign from office in the face of near-certain impeachment for wrongdoing

Richard Nixon, a lawyer and Republican, began his political career as a member of the U.S. House of Representatives, where his work on the House Committee on Un-American Activities established his reputation as a staunch anticommunist. He was subsequently a senator, then vice president of the United States under President Dwight Eisenhower. He was narrowly defeated by John F. Kennedy in the 1960 presidential race, and from this defeat he learned never to take an election victory for granted—a lesson that twelve years later would lead to illegal activities intended to ensure victory but instead driving him from the presidency in disgrace.

Nixon was elected president in 1968; the times were grim. The Vietnam War was polarizing the country, as was the black militancy that followed the crumbling Civil Rights movement; there were extensive white fears of black violence and calls for "law and order."

President Richard Nixon's achievements will always be viewed alongside his wrongdoing in the Watergate cover-up. (Library of Congress)

Nixon had a number of achievements in his years in office. He institutionalized affirmative action as federal law, instituted wage and price controls to stop inflation, and formulated a plan for American withdrawal from Vietnam. Yet he also ordered the bombing of neutral Cambodia and the extension of the war into Laos. Internationally, Nixon is noted for signing nuclear agreements and achieving "detente" with the Soviet Union and for reopening U.S. relations with China. Nixon was reelected in 1972 by a huge margin.

Nixon's legitimate achievements, however, will forever be viewed alongside the events of the Watergate scandal—the burglary of Democratic campaign headquarters and the subsequent cover-up, which involved Nixon himself as well as his top advisers. Nixon is the only American president to have been forced to resign from office. The unfolding of the Watergate hearings, the revelations of White House wrongdoing, and Nixon's extravagant claims of "executive privilege," which, he essentially argued, should put him above the law, formed a political drama unlike any other in U.S. history. The Supreme Court twice handed down decisions directly involving Nixon, in *United States v. United States District Court* (1972) and *United States v. Nixon* (1974), in which it ordered Nixon to surrender the "White House tapes" to prosecutors. Nixon's primary legacy may well be the increased distrust of government, and of the power of the presidency in particular, caused by the Watergate events.

See also Campus Unrest, President's Commission on; Impeachment; International law; Pardoning power; Republican Party; Vietnam War; Watergate scandal.

Nixon v. Herndon

COURT: U.S. Supreme Court
DATE: Decided March 7, 1927
SIGNIFICANCE: The Supreme Court voided an attempt by the Texas legislature to restrict black participation in primary elections

In 1921, the U.S. Supreme Court ruled in *Newberry v. United States* that Congress lacked authority to regulate primary elections. Southern state legislatures immediately took advantage of this decision to prohibit black participation in state primary elections. "White primaries" were quickly adopted throughout the South. Texas, during the first half of the twentieth century, was part of the Democrat-dominated South. The only competition that mattered was within the Democratic Party, so if blacks were not allowed to participate in the Democratic primary they would effectively be denied any meaningful choice in the electoral process.

In 1924, the Texas legislature passed a law barring blacks from voting in the Democratic primary. L. A. Nixon, a black resident of El Paso, attempted to vote in the primary and was refused by Herndon, an election judge. Nixon and the National Association for the Advancement of Colored People (NAACP) claimed that the Texas law violated the Fourteenth and Fifteenth Amendments. The Supreme Court did not deal with the issue of the Fifteenth Amendment, but a unanimous Court found that the Texas white primary law violated the "equal protection clause" of the Fourteenth Amendment.

The NAACP won the battle but temporarily lost the war. Texas responded to the Court's decision by engaging in the strategy of "legislate and litigate." By passing a different white primary law after their defeat in *Nixon v. Herndon*, the Texas legislature forced the NAACP to institute another attack on the white primary. When the second law was declared unconstitutional in *Nixon v. Condon* in 1932, Texas came up with a third variation of the white primary. This time, in *Grovey v. Townsend* (1935), the U.S. Supreme Court upheld the Texas white primary, arguing that no state discrimination was present. According to the Court, the Texas Democratic Party, a private voluntary association, decided to exclude blacks from voting in the primary elections. It was not until *Smith v. Allwright* (1944) that a unanimous Supreme Court declared that the Fifteenth Amendment could be used as a shield to protect the right to vote in primary elections.

From the passage of the first white primary law in 1924 until the final abolition of white primaries in the *Smith* case in 1944, blacks were denied the right to vote in Democratic Party primaries, the only election of significance at that time. The white primary cases illustrate one of the dilemmas in using the federal courts—the fact that justice delayed is justice denied.

See also Civil War Amendments; *Classic, United States v.*; *Grovey v. Townsend*; National Association for the Advancement of Colored People (NAACP); *Newberry v. United States*; *Smith v. Allwright*.

Nollan v. California Coastal Commission

COURT: U.S. Supreme Court

DATE: Decided June 26, 1987

SIGNIFICANCE: In this case, the Supreme Court substantially expanded the protection of property rights by limiting the power of states to force land owners to consent to physical occupations of their property by third parties as a precondition to obtaining government permission to develop the property

James and Marilyn Nollan planned to demolish a dilapidated bungalow and replace it with a three-bedroom house on a beachfront lot in California located between two public beaches to the north and south. Pursuant to state law, the Nollans sought a development permit from the California Coastal Commission to enable them to proceed. The Coastal Commission conditioned the granting of the permit on the Nollans' agreeing to create an easement that would allow the public to cross their beachfront to gain better access to the adjacent public beaches. The Nollans challenged this condition in state court on the grounds that it violated the Fourteenth Amendment by "taking" their property without the payment of just compensation. When the state court of appeal ruled against them, the Nollans sought review from the U.S. Supreme Court.

In a 5-4 decision, the Supreme Court held that the Coastal Commission had violated the Constitution and reversed the ruling of the court of appeal. Justice Antonin Scalia, writing for the majority, argued that the commission could not directly require property owners to grant an easement to the public to cross their land unless the state paid the owners just compensation as the Constitution required. The issue before the Court in *Nollan* was whether the state could avoid the constitutional obligation of paying for this property interest by denying the owners the right to develop their property unless they agreed to grant the sought-after easement to the public without receiving compensation in return.

The Court conceded that a state agency might impose lawful conditions on the development of property even to the point of requiring owners to dedicate easements to the public. Such conditions would comply with the takings clause of the Fifth Amendment, made applicable to the states by incorporation into the Fourteenth Amendment, if the condition mitigated or offset some externality caused by the proposed development. Thus, if the anticipated use of private property resulted in a burden to the community in which the property was located, the state could refuse to allow the development of the property to protect the public from the anticipated externality, or it could condition the development on the owners taking appropriate steps to reduce or eliminate the problems their development would cause.

Without this "essential nexus" between the conditions placed on development permits and some legitimate state interest in avoiding harms caused by the development, however, the state's demand for concessions from the property owner amounted to a constitutionally impermissible use of the state's regulatory power to take property interests without paying for them.

The majority did not find the required "nexus" in the facts before it. There seemed to be no connection whatsoever between any burden to the public that might result from the construction of the house and the public easement the Coastal Commission was requiring. The Nollans' house would not interfere with the public's rightful access to any public beach. Therefore, the easement could not be upheld as a legitimate regulatory response. If the Coastal Commission still wanted a public easement on the Nollans' land, it would have to acquire it through the power of eminent domain and pay for it.

Nollan is an important land use decision because many states and cities throughout the United States regularly impose land dedication conditions on property owners as a way of offsetting the burden on municipal services and infrastructure created by new land development in a community. *Nollan* is the first case in which the Supreme Court indicated that this "dealmaking" form of land use regulation is limited by constitutional constraints. Subsequent cases, particularly *Dolan v. City of Tigard* (1994), expanded on this foundation and further limited the state's ability to regulate land use by placing conditions on development permits.

See also Eminent domain; Environmental law; *Lucas v. South Carolina Coastal Council*; Property rights; Takings clause; Zoning.

Nonviolent resistance

DEFINITION: The active use of nonviolent strategies to resist laws and policies regarded as unjust and to promote social and political change

SIGNIFICANCE: A central method for expressing political dissent and marshaling the power necessary to bring about political change in the United States

Although the term "nonviolent resistance" is a twentieth century concept based on analysis of the strategies and conditions necessary for successful nonviolent action, its practice is deeply rooted in United States history. Religious groups from Europe such as the Amish and the Society of Friends (Quakers), who practiced a literal understanding of Jesus' teachings forbidding the use of violence, fled to North America to escape persecution. Their continued witness to principles of pacifism has influenced a tradition and philosophy of nonviolent protest. Additionally, the early colonists engaged in nonviolent resistance against British rule. In 1766, Britain passed an import tax, the Stamp Act. American merchants organized a boycott of goods, causing the repeal of the act. This action marked the first organized resistance to British rule and led to the establishment of the First Continental Congress in 1774. The legal basis for nonviolent action was established in the First Amendment to the Constitution, which protects the rights of persons to "freedom of speech," peaceful assembly, and petitioning the government "for a redress of grievances." The United States has a long history of expression of such rights.

Nineteenth and Twentieth Centuries. In 1845, Henry David Thoreau was jailed for refusing to pay a poll tax in protest of the Mexican-American War. In his essay "Civil Disobedience," Thoreau proclaimed the moral necessity of resistance in the face of immoral government action. Nonviolent protest has accompanied every war in which the United States has engaged, and it was so widespread during the Vietnam War that it became a central reason for United States' withdrawal from Vietnam in 1974. Nonviolent protest has also been central to various movements seeking to ban and limit nuclear weapons and in war tax resistance movements, in which members refuse to pay taxes to support the military budget. Strategies of nonviolent resistance were also employed by the women's rights movement, which culminated in the right to vote (1920) and in greater social and economic equality for women. The labor movement has used nonviolent tactics in the form of strikes, labor slowdowns, and boycotts to force improvement of working conditions and income. Despite strong, often violent responses by corporate owners, the Wagner Act, passed by Congress in 1935, recognized the legal right of workers to organize and use such methods. César Chávez effectively used consumer boycotts in the 1970's and 1980's to win better conditions for farmworkers. Nonviolent strategies have been used by environmental groups to block construction of nuclear power plants, stop the cutting of forests, or alter policies considered to be ecologically hazardous. They have also been employed since the 1980's by antiabortion groups attempting to close abortion clinics.

The most prolonged, successful use of nonviolent resistance, however, came in the Civil Rights movement led by Martin Luther King, Jr., in the 1950's and 1960's. Drawing on the work of Mahatma (Mohandas) Gandhi, the movement used marches, sit-ins, and boycotts to force an end to legal racial segregation in the South and informal (*de facto*) segregation in the North. This campaign demonstrated the ambiguity of governmental response to such tactics. Often participants were arrested and convicted under local statutes, only to have such laws ruled invalid by higher courts; this occurred during the Montgomery

At a Jackson, Mississippi, lunch counter in 1963, sit-in demonstrators are covered with sugar, mustard, and ketchup by whites opposing integration. (AP/Wide World Photos)

bus boycott. On the other hand, King and his followers were under constant surveillance by the Federal Bureau of Investigation and were considered threats to political stability by many government officials. The debate has also focused on what constitutes "freedom of expression" and "peaceful assembly." The "plowshares eight," in 1980, protesting nuclear weapons, entered a General Electric plant in Pennsylvania and dented the nose cone of a warhead. They were sentenced to prison on grounds of trespass and destruction of private property.

Theory and Strategy. Nonviolent resistance has two distinct traditions. The religious tradition centers on the moral claim that it is always wrong to harm another and that only love of the "enemy" can transform persons and societies. Violence and hatred cannot solve social problems or end social conflict, for each act of violence generates new resentments. This spiral of violence can be ended only if some group absorbs the violence and returns only nonviolence and love. Central to this vision is a commitment to justice that requires adherents to engage injustice actively wherever they find it. The political tradition focuses on strategies for organizing political and social power to force another, usually a political authority, to change policies. As Gene Sharp, a leading analyst, notes, government requires the consent of its citizens. In nonviolent resistance, dissenters organize forms of power including economic power, labor power, and the power of public opinion in order to undermine consent and force authorities to change policies.

The use of these theories and techniques remains important in stable, democratic societies as a way of resolving conflict, generating social change, and challenging power structures, especially on behalf of the powerless, whose rights are often ignored. Without the legal sanctions which permit such protest, the only recourse becomes open societal violence and conflict, even to the point of civil war. — *Charles L. Kammer*

See also Civil disobedience; Civil Rights movement; Conscription; Gandhi, Mahatma; King, Martin Luther, Jr.; Montgomery bus boycott.

BIBLIOGRAPHY
Broad views of the topic are presented in Peter Ackerman and Christopher Kruegler, *Strategic Nonviolent Conflict: The Dynamics of People Power in the Twentieth Century* (Westport, Conn.: Praeger, 1994); David P. Barash, *Introduction to Peace Studies* (Belmont, Calif.: Wadsworth, 1991); Robert Conney and Helen Michalowski, eds., *The Power of the People: Active Nonviolence in the United States* (Philadelphia: New Society, 1987); and Gene Sharp, *The Politics of Nonviolent Action* (3 vols. Boston: Porter Sargent, 1973). A more personal view is contained in Martin Luther King, Jr., *A Testament of Hope: The Essential Writings and Speeches of Martin Luther King, Jr.*, edited by James M. Washington (San Francisco: Harper, 1991).

Nuclear radiation testing with human subjects

DATE: 1950's and 1960's
SIGNIFICANCE: The radiation testing on humans that was performed by the U.S. government raises critical questions about informed consent and government ethics

For a quarter century after the end of World War II, the United States government conducted a number of tests that involved subjecting humans to nuclear radiation. These tests were designed to study various phenomena: the effect of nuclear fallout on soldiers in the battlefield, the ability of radiation to sterilize men, the salubrious and deleterious effects of radiation on persons with cancer, the movement in nuclear particles in the atmosphere, and the potential effects of radiation exposure on astronauts, among others. The tests were conducted on soldiers, prison inmates, the terminally ill, retarded children, and apparently healthy paid volunteers. In some cases the subjects were informed of the purpose of the experiments and the likely dangers. In other cases the subjects were not informed or were even misled.

The experiments were terminated in the early 1970's, as knowledge of the health dangers associated with even low levels of radiation improved, as changing medical and ethical standards opposed the tests, and as increased public awareness confronted the government. The government apparently tried to minimize public knowledge of the experiments. Nevertheless, revelations about the scope and extent of the tests continued into the 1990's, bringing calls for reparations and official apologies.

The U.S. government's nuclear testing raises a number of justice issues. The first concerns informed consent. In those cases where consent was not sought, or where it was obtained under false representation of the test, clearly an injustice was done. Even in those cases where consent was obtained, extenuating circumstances may cloud the ethical basis and even the legality of the testing. For example, there is some question as to whether conscripted soldiers are in a position to withhold consent freely. Certainly the "informed" quality of consent is problematic with retarded children.

Another justice issue concerns how justice can best be served *ex post facto*, many years after an event has occurred. Possibilities range from, on the one hand, giving financial compensation to the families of persons who died from the testing to, on the other, viewing the testing as something that, although it seems inexcusable today, seemed necessary and justifiable at a time when little was known about radiation and when learning how to survive a nuclear war seemed to be a pressing issue. In 1995, President Bill Clinton addressed the issue. He officially apologized on behalf of the government and announced that reparations would be made in a number of the most egregious cases.

See also Environmental law; Moral relativism; Natural law and natural rights; Nuclear weapons.

Nuclear weapons

DEFINITION: Powerful explosive devices which operate on the principles of nuclear fission or fusion, thus releasing large, lethal doses of radioactivity
SIGNIFICANCE: Nuclear bombs are considered the "ultimate" weapon by virtue of their enormous destructive potential and lingering radioactive effects, which themselves raise unique moral questions

Thousands of military personnel were exposed to radiation during tests and military exercises in the years following World War II. (AP/Wide World Photos)

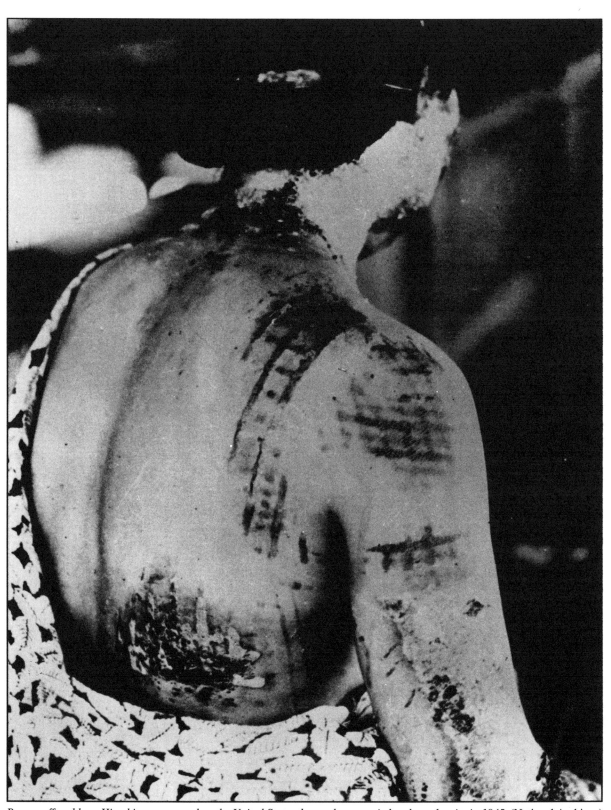

Burns suffered by a Hiroshima woman when the United States dropped an atomic bomb on the city in 1945. (National Archives)

The "nuclear era" began with the ending of World War II, when the United States dropped two atomic fission bombs on Japan. The destructive force of those bombs was unprecedented. Yet it was the devastating environmental and biological effects of the radiation they unleashed which raised the most difficult questions of morality and justice. Partly because of that controversy, nuclear weapons have not been used in war since 1945.

Nevertheless, continuing technological advances steadily increased the destructive power and targeting accuracy of nuclear weapons. Over the years the United States amassed thousands of nuclear warheads, ready for delivery by missiles, bombers, and submarines. The United States has not been alone in these efforts; fifty years after the atomic bombing of Japan there were about a dozen countries with nuclear weapons. In short, nuclear weapons have increased in destructive potential, accuracy, number, and accessibility.

Recognizing the increasing dangers posed by nuclear weapons, countries have devised various treaties to provide some safeguards. The Nuclear Non-Proliferation Treaty of 1968 prohibits nuclear countries from providing nuclear weapons technology or material to non-nuclear countries and prohibits non-nuclear countries from seeking to develop the same. There also have been a number of treaties restricting nuclear tests and limiting the number of deployed nuclear weapons.

One of the most important treaties for discouraging the use of nuclear weapons has been the Antiballistic Missile (ABM) Treaty of 1972. This treaty restricted the United States and the Soviet Union to a small number of ABMs for protection from nuclear attack. In effect, both countries agreed to leave themselves vulnerable to a nuclear strike. In this way, the ABM Treaty institutionalized the situation of "mutual assured destruction" (MAD), whereby a country launching a nuclear strike against the other would have no effective defense against a retaliatory nuclear attack. Both sides would be destroyed in any nuclear war. This was seen by Soviet and American leaders to be the only way of ensuring that neither country would have an incentive to use nuclear weapons.

A basic controversy concerns the use of nuclear weapons against a non-nuclear country. The only actual occurrence of this was the American attack on Japan in 1945, and that decision continues to be questioned. There are those who believe that nuclear weapons are qualitatively and morally different from other weapons. They argue that the use of nuclear weapons is patently unjust in that their destructive and lethal effects spread well beyond the battlefield to include thousands, or millions, of civilians. They claim that no military victory could be worth the sickness and deformity that nuclear weapons inflict not only on their immediate victims but also on successive generations.

See also International law; Morality and foreign policy; Nuclear radiation testing with human subjects.

Nuisance

DEFINITION: An activity that infringes on the rights of others to enjoy their own property or that adversely affects a community's general welfare

SIGNIFICANCE: Private and public nuisance laws have in many cases been supplanted by regulations such as antipollution legislation and zoning restrictions

Nuisance law, a broad area of tort law, is divided into public and private nuisance causes of action, which are often unrelated. A private nuisance is usually viewed as the unreasonable interference with the use and enjoyment of one's land. In other words, a private nuisance exists when the actions of one party interfere with the ability of another party or parties to enjoy their home or to function effectively in their place of business. The interference may involve a direct, trespassory invasion, such as smoke, dirt, dust, or flooding. It may also be an indirect invasion, such as noise, odors, vibration, light, poor aesthetics, or causing fear. Oftentimes the location of an activity is the critical factor in determining whether the activity constitutes a nuisance. Supreme Court Justice George Sutherland once wrote, "A nuisance may be merely a right thing in the wrong place, like a pig in the parlor instead of the barnyard." Private nuisances usually affect only a few persons and are redressible in the courts through damages and injunctive relief.

Public nuisances tend to affect the general community and to threaten the public health, safety, morals, or welfare. Thus, activities as diverse as prostitution and water pollution may constitute public nuisances. One significant limitation in public nuisance law is that, traditionally, only an attorney general, district attorney, or similar official could enforce public nuisance law. To a large extent, public nuisance law has been supplanted by criminal statutes and regulatory schemes (as is the case with pollution). Similarly, many issues that were once dealt with through nuisance litigation are now resolved through zoning decisions.

See also Commercialized vice; Environmental law; Tort; Zoning.

O'Brien, United States v.

COURT: U.S. Supreme Court

DATE: Decided May 27, 1968

SIGNIFICANCE: Upholding a criminal conviction for burning a draft card, the Court devised a four-part test for determining the kinds of symbolic speech that are protected by the First Amendment

In front of the Boston courthouse in 1966, David Paul O'Brien and two companions burned their Selective Service registration cards as a symbolic expression of protest against the Vietnam War and the draft. Agents of the Federal Bureau of Investigation protected O'Brien from an angry crowd and then arrested him for disobeying a 1965 federal law that made it illegal to mutilate or destroy a draft card knowingly. After a trial and conviction, the young man was sentenced to the custodial supervision of the attorney general for a maximum of six years. A court of appeals found that the 1965 law was unconstitutional insofar as it allowed punishment for the symbolic expression of ideas protected by the First Amendment,

In United States v. O'Brien*, the Supreme Court held that burning a draft card was not constitutionally protected "symbolic speech."* (AP/Wide World Photos)

but this court also ruled that O'Brien could be prosecuted for nonpossession of a draft card. The government petitioned for review by the U.S. Supreme Court, arguing that the court of appeals had erred in holding the statute unconstitutional.

Granting the petition, the Court voted 7 to 1 to reverse the ruling of the court of appeals and to uphold O'Brien's conviction. Writing for the majority, Chief Justice Earl Warren referred to several precedents in holding that when "speech" and "nonspeech" are combined in a single conduct, the government might place incidental limitations on First Amendment freedoms according to a four-part test. First, the governmental regulation must be based on a power that is constitutional; second, the regulation must advance "an important or substantial governmental interest"; third, the governmental objective must be unrelated to the suppression of free expression; and finally, the incidental limitations on free expression must be no greater than essential to further the governmental objective. Based on the importance of draft cards within the selective service system, Warren concluded that a sufficient governmental interest existed to justify the 1965 statute.

The *O'Brien* decision was important because of its four-part test, which provided a useful instrument for deciding when the government may punish illegal actions that are designed as symbolic expression of ideas. The test would later be used by the Court in cases dealing with matters such as nude dancing and the desecration of the flag.

See also *Barnes v. Glen Theatre, Inc.*; Speech and press, freedom of; *Texas v. Johnson*; *Tinker v. Des Moines Independent Community School District*.

Obstruction of justice

DEFINITION: Interference with the operation of a court or its officials

SIGNIFICANCE: Obstructing justice may deny a party the right to due process or justice

Obstruction of justice is an attempt to impede justice by any means. Obstruction includes physical disruption of a trial court in session, an attempt to interfere with a judge or court officials, including jurors, or an attempt to bribe or create doubt regarding the integrity of those involved in a court proceeding. Concealing or falsifying evidence obstructs justice, as does resisting a court-appointed process server.

Because police are officers of the court, intentional interference with their duties may be considered an obstruction of justice. In federal practice, obstruction extends to agencies, departments, and committees conducting their work. A witness concealing evidence from an investigation by a congressional committee is as guilty of obstruction as a person concealing evidence in a trial court.

See also Bribery; Contempt of court; Evidence, rules of; Lying to Congress; Subpoena power.

Occupational Safety and Health Administration (OSHA)

DATE: Created by law December 29, 1970

SIGNIFICANCE: Although Congress had previously legislated safety or health standards for specific industries, the Occupational Safety and Health Administration was the first federal agency given jurisdiction over safety and health in the workplace across the breadth of American industry

The idea of national legislation to ensure safety and health in the workplace for all Americans originated in the Democratic administration of President Lyndon B. Johnson but did not become law until the Republican administration of President Richard M. Nixon.

Partisan Conflict. In 1969, a majority of Congress supported an occupational safety and health bill, but there was considerable disagreement over what the content should be. Most of the legislative battles took place largely out of public view in congressional committees, with voting occurring along party lines. The final compromise version of the bill was closer to what the Democrats wanted, since the Democrats were the majority party in each house of Congress. The bill easily passed in each house because even Republicans who had opposed parts of the bill in committee did not want to appear to be opposed to the health and safety of American workers; thus, most voted for the bill.

President Nixon found himself in much the same situation as Republican members of Congress. He had supported a bill to provide a safe and healthy workplace for Americans as a part of his strategy for drawing blue-collar workers away from the Democratic Party. In the bill that he supported, the workplace would have been regulated by an independent regulatory commission. The Occupational Safety and Health (OSH) Act, however, placed the Occupational Safety and Health Administration (OSHA) in the Department of Labor, headed by an assistant secretary of labor. Nixon signed the bill into law on December 29, 1970, even though it was not what he had wanted. He feared that Labor Department bureaucrats might be biased against business.

The Functions of OSHA. OSHA sets safety and health standards for the workplace and enforces those standards. When the agency sets standards, it does so by adopting regula-

Established in 1970, OSHA sets safety and health standards for the workplace. (Jim West)

tions through the administrative rule-making process. A proposed new regulation is published in the *Federal Register*, and interested parties, such as those who would be affected by the rule, have an opportunity to submit written comments. There can be an oral hearing presided over by an administrative law judge if an interested party requests one. Thirty days after receiving comments, OSHA may promulgate the new regulation or decide that it is unnecessary. If adopted, the new regulation is as binding as if it had been enacted by Congress.

OSHA's enforcement responsibility is primarily carried out by its ten regional offices. Enforcement involves inspections of businesses to determine whether they are complying with safety and health standards. The constitutional prohibition on unreasonable searches and seizures prevents inspectors from entering nonpublic areas of a business without the consent of the management unless they have a warrant. They may obtain an administrative warrant, which is more easily obtained than warrants used in the criminal process. More than forty-six hundred rules issued during OSHA's first two years, as well as the agency's inspections and fines for safety violations, some of them minor, made OSHA exceedingly unpopular with American business during its early years.

Benzene and Cotton Dust Cases. In the late 1970's, OSHA began placing greater emphasis on the regulation of health hazards. Such agency activity was sometimes challenged in court. When the secretary of labor attempted to lower the permissible level of exposure to benzene, a substance used in the petroleum industry and known to cause cancer, the Supreme Court decided on July 22, 1980, in *Industrial Union Department, AFL-CIO v. American Petroleum Institute*, that the secretary had exceeded his authority under the OSH Act. He had acted without evidence that the previous standard for exposure to benzene constituted a significant health hazard, and he did not have any evidence that the lower level of exposure would significantly decrease the risk of cancer. The language of the OSH Act, however, required that the secretary act on the basis of the best available evidence. This decision recognized that OSHA regulations impose significant costs on business and that they are justified only when supported by evidence that they will significantly improve health in the workplace.

When the textile industry challenged an OSHA regulation lowering the permissible level of cotton dust in the air breathed by workers, there was an attempt to get the Supreme Court to read into the OSH Act a requirement that OSHA use cost-benefit analysis prior to imposing new regulations on industry and show that the value of the health benefits resulting from the regulations would exceed the costs to industry. This would have been extremely difficult to do and would have brought OSHA regulation of the workplace to a virtual halt. On June 17, 1981, in *American Textile Manufacturers Institute v. Donovan*, the Supreme Court refused to read cost-benefit analysis into the OSH Act. The agency did, however, become quite cautious in the issuance of new regulations as a result of the Supreme Court's decision in the benzene case and the policy of deregulation pursued by President Ronald Reagan. — *Patricia A. Behlar*

See also Administrative law; Environmental law; Labor law; Welfare state; Workers' compensation.

BIBLIOGRAPHY

Several works on regulation include chapters on OSHA, including Gary C. Bryner, *Bureaucratic Discretion: Law and Policy in Federal Regulatory Agencies* (New York: Pergamon, 1987); Joseph A. Page and Mary-Win O'Brien, *Bitter Wages* (New York: Grossman, 1973); Jeremy Rabkin, *Judicial Compulsions: How Public Law Distorts Public Policy* (New York: Basic Books, 1989); Susan J. Tolchin and Martin Tolchin, *Dismantling America: The Rush to Deregulate* (Boston: Houghton Mifflin, 1983); and James Q. Wilson, ed., *The Politics of Regulation* (New York: Basic Books, 1980).

Ogden v. Saunders

COURT: U.S. Supreme Court

DATE: Decided February 19, 1827

SIGNIFICANCE: The Supreme Court took a first important step in restricting the operation of the contract clause of the U.S. Constitution

A New York State law, passed in 1801, gave relief to people who could not pay their debts. The Constitution forbids the states to "pass any . . . Law impairing the Obligation of Contracts." Therefore the New York law could not constitutionally be applied to contracts made prior to the passage of the law. *Ogden v. Saunders* tested whether the New York law could be applied to contracts made after the law's passage. It was argued that all contracts carry with them the state laws which prescribe the rules for the enforcement of contracts—including debtor relief provisions.

After elaborate and protracted argument in 1824, in which Daniel Webster and Henry Clay participated, the Supreme Court decided 4 to 3 that a state bankruptcy law such as the New York law does not impair the obligation of contracts which are entered into after passage of the law. The decision was accompanied by six separate extensive opinions by the justices, which revealed deep disagreements within the Court. Chief Justice John Marshall was in the minority in this case for the only time in his judicial career. Marshall's conservative view was that the constitutional grant of power to Congress to establish uniform bankruptcy rules necessarily excluded the operation of all state bankruptcy laws.

A second issue settled by *Ogden v. Saunders* was whether a debtor discharged under the New York State law could claim that discharge for a contract or debt owed to a citizen of another state. On this issue the Court split differently. Chief Justice Marshall and the other conservatives on the Court held that the debt was still collectible in a federal court. To hold otherwise would produce "a conflict of sovereign power and a collision with the judicial powers."

In sum, then, the Court decided that state bankruptcy and debtor relief laws are unconstitutional when applied to contracts entered into before passage of the law and constitutional with respect to contracts made after passage of the law. Second, such laws are unconstitutional if they attempt to invalidate a debt owed to a citizen of another state.

This decision began the restoration of state powers which had been restricted by the contract clause as the Court had previously interpreted it. *Ogden v. Saunders* presaged a broader view of the state's police powers which soon became dominant and has prevailed in the United States ever since.

See also Bankruptcy; Clay, Henry; Contract law; Marshall, John; *Sturges v. Crowninshield.*

Olmstead v. United States

COURT: U.S. Supreme Court
DATE: Decided June 4, 1928
SIGNIFICANCE: Although a majority of justices rejected the argument that government wiretaps on telephones constituted illegal searches and compelled self-incrimination, Justice Louis D. Brandeis' famous dissenting opinion laid the groundwork for the later development of a constitutional right to privacy

During the Prohibition era, Roy Olmstead was convicted of being the general manager of a significant illegal smuggling operation that brought liquor to the United States from Canada in violation of federal law. Olmstead's illegal business had fifty employees and reportedly earned more than two million dollars each year. The evidence that produced the convictions of Olmstead and his associates was gathered through the use of wiretaps. Law enforcement officials had attached wires to the telephone lines leading from Olmstead's residence and office. Officials had listened to and had stenographers take notes on the conversations secretly overheard through the telephone lines.

Olmstead and his codefendants challenged the use of such investigative techniques and evidence. They claimed that the wiretaps constituted an illegal search and seizure in violation of the Fourth Amendment and that the use of private conversations as evidence violated the Fifth Amendment's prohibition on compelled self-incrimination.

In an opinion by Chief Justice William Howard Taft, the Supreme Court rejected Olmstead's arguments. Taft concluded that the Fourth Amendment protected only against unreasonable searches of material things and that telephone lines running between two people's property could not be considered protected against intrusion by government. Taft also declared that the defendants' conversations were voluntary and therefore could not be regarded as compelled self-incrimination.

In a famous dissenting opinion, Justice Louis D. Brandeis made an eloquent plea for the recognition of a constitutional right to privacy. According to Brandeis, the authors of the Constitution "sought to protect Americans in their beliefs, their thoughts, their emotions, and their sensations. They conferred, as against the government, the right to be let alone—the most comprehensive of rights and the right most valued by civilized men."

Brandeis was not the lone dissenter in the case; Justices Oliver Wendell Holmes, Jr., Pierce Butler, and Harlan F. Stone also found fault with Taft's conclusions. Brandeis, however, was the lone justice to place great emphasis on a general right of privacy. The other justices were also concerned about the definition of a search under the Fourth Amendment or the legality of police methods.

Brandeis could not manage to gain majority support for his ideas during his lifetime. Instead, his eloquent defense of a right to privacy stood for more than thirty years as the primary argument against government intrusions into citizens' private lives. Beginning in the 1960's, when the Supreme Court's composition had changed significantly, Brandeis' words were used by a generation of justices who followed his ideals and established the existence of a constitutional right to privacy in *Griswold v. Connecticut* (1965).

See also Brandeis, Louis D.; Electronic surveillance; Evidence, rules of; Privacy, right of; Taft, William Howard.

Omnibus Crime Control and Safe Streets Act of 1968

DEFINITION: Legislation designed to help states and cities to control crime
SIGNIFICANCE: The Crime Control and Safe Streets Act of 1968 marked the beginning of major efforts by the federal government to help states and cities in the control of crime

In his 1967 State of the Union Address, President Lyndon B. Johnson first suggested the adoption of legislation that would become the Omnibus Crime Control and Safe Streets Act of 1968. Increasing crime rates and the riots in U.S. inner cities in the mid-1960's had generated widespread public concern over crime. In its original form, the proposed act reflected many suggestions of the Katzenbach Commission, which Johnson had appointed in July, 1965. The proposed bill provided for categorical grants to state and local governments. These grants would provide funds for police training, for innovative criminal rehabilitation programs, and for increased restrictions on guns and on electronic surveillance.

Legislation. The bill that finally emerged for Johnson's signature was considerably different from that originally proposed, sufficiently different that Johnson delayed signing the bill for several days and considered a veto. Legislative support for the bill (which was approved by margins of 72 to 4 in the Senate and 368 to 7 in the House), combined with the upcoming Democratic National Convention, served to pressure the president into signing the bill. The revised legislation provided for block grants to states and eliminated any direct aid to cities; it also banned wiretaps and electronic surveillance by private individuals. Nevertheless, the bill sanctioned the issuance of warrants for electronic surveillance by cities, states, and the national government, and it eased restrictions on gun licensing.

Administration. Congress took the administration of the program out of the hands of the Justice Department and placed it in the hands of the Law Enforcement Assistance Administration (LEAA), a new agency designed with a three-person leadership. In an attempt to avoid partisanship, no two members of the leadership could be members of the same political party; moreover, all three top administrators had to form a consensus before taking any action. This design slowed the implementation of the program, however, and the leadership structure was revised.

Operation. Over a period of twelve years, the LEAA provided more than $8 billion to state and local governments. States and cities used these funds for modernizing equipment, communication improvement, criminal-identification facilities, and laboratories. Funding was also available for police patrols in high-crime areas, for training and recruitment of police, for criminal-rehabilitation efforts, and for crime-prevention programs. For several reasons, the largest portion of the funding usually went to equipment rather than personnel. A provision of the initial act limited funding for personnel to one-third of the total. States and cities were also often wary about using federal funds for personnel, because if a cutback in federal funds occurred, reductions in personnel would be more difficult than reductions in equipment expenditures. By the end of the Jimmy Carter Administration, budget requests exceeded $400 million a year, and Congress essentially stopped the funding. In the early part of President Ronald Reagan's first term, Attorney General Edwin Meese presided over the final days of the LEAA.

See also Arms, right to keep and bear; Electronic surveillance; Law Enforcement Assistance Administration (LEAA); President's Commission on Law Enforcement and Administration of Justice.

Opium Exclusion Act

DATE: Enacted February 9, 1909
DEFINITION: The Opium Exclusion Act prohibited the use and importation of the drug for other than medicinal purposes
SIGNIFICANCE: The sponsors of the 1909 Opium Exclusion Act intended to suppress illicit uses of the drug and to send a signal urging countries involved in the production and trade of opium to do the same

Senator Henry Cabot Lodge of Massachusetts introduced the opium exclusion bill on January 4, 1909. Drafted by Elihu Root, chairman of the American Opium Commission, the bill was part of the commission's attempt to root out the Chinese opium trade through international cooperation. A bill regulating the importation of opium into the United States was needed as a signal to other countries.

Enemies of the bill opposed it on the grounds that the act, by placing the Department of Agriculture in charge of executing it, would give the federal government police powers constitutionally reserved for the states. To accommodate the critics, the authors of the bill changed it to transfer responsibility for implementing the law from the Agriculture Department to the Treasury Department, thereby declaring it a revenue bill.

See also Comprehensive Drug Abuse Prevention and Control Act of 1970; Drug legalization debate; Drug use and sale, illegal; Harrison Narcotic Drug Act; Marijuana Tax Act.

Organized crime

DEFINITION: A group of enterprises dedicated to providing illicit and illegal goods and services, sometimes with the use or threat of violence

SIGNIFICANCE: Organized crime groups, or syndicates, operate in almost every major city in the United States; it is estimated that organized crime syndicates earn more than $50 billion annually

Modern organized crime grew out of nineteenth century gangs operating primarily in New York and New Orleans. Groups were formed by German, Irish, Italian, Jewish, and Polish immigrants desperate to make a living in their new homeland. When they were not competing among themselves for control of various areas of the city, they engaged in operations such as gambling, prostitution, and extortion.

The key to the rise of American organized crime, however, was Prohibition. The demand for alcohol, made illegal by the Eighteenth Amendment, provided criminal elements across the United States with the opportunity to organize and profit. Indeed, bootlegging—the producing, supplying, or shipping of illegal alcoholic beverages—was the motivation for Johnny Torrio, the mastermind behind the first organized criminal syndicate in the United States. To avoid conflict and even warfare over bootlegging territories and gang jurisdictions, Torrio called for the division of Chicago into several zones, each under the sole jurisdiction of one gang. In return, each gang provided Torrio with a portion of its profits.

As new gangs moved into Chicago, however, warfare once again erupted despite Torrio's efforts to prevent it. When Torrio retired, he turned control of his criminal empire, then earning some $50 million annually, over to Alphonse "Scarface Al" Capone. Under Capone's leadership, the outfit soon grew to a national level, and profits grew at unprecedented rates. The new national syndicate was created, and the Mafia was born.

The Power of Criminal Syndicates. The power of the Mafia can easily be demonstrated through an examination of the power and influence of Capone's gang during Prohibition. In only a few short years, Capone and his gang rose from common hoods to the criminal elite, earning millions of dollars annually and controlling the political affairs of an entire city. By working with both legitimate businesses and illegal operations, Capone was able to gain powerful allies and rise to the undisputed leadership of Chicago's criminal underworld.

Perhaps the best example of the power and influence of organized criminal syndicates, however, is provided by Murder, Incorporated. Murder, Inc., created in the 1930's as part of a nationwide syndicate, operated from a twenty-four-hour candy store in Brooklyn. Under the direct leadership of Albert Anastasia and the guidance of some of the most famous gangsters of the time, including Charles "Lucky" Luciano, Meyer Lansky, and Louis "Lepke" Buchalter, Murder, Inc. received "contracts" (orders) to "hit" or "pop" (kill) people. The purpose of the organization was to ensure the loyalty of members of the syndicate. Bosses, associates, and family members who did not follow the decrees of the ruling council could be executed by the organization. During its brief life, it is estimated that Murder, Inc. killed between four and five hundred victims.

In 1940, however, Murder, Inc. was all but destroyed by multiple arrests of lower-level associates for killings commit-

Legendary organized crime boss Al Capone (left). (AP/Wide World Photos)

ted under the direction of the organization. After one upper-level associate gave authorities details on over two hundred murders, the national syndicate quickly changed its methods and distanced itself from Murder, Inc. Instead of one nationwide organization, each family provided several hit men. If a "hit" was contracted in New York, a family in Chicago or San Francisco would provide the hit man. This system proved extremely effective, as it prevented direct association with the victim and thereby hindered efforts to prosecute the murderer, and it is the system still used by the syndicate.

The Structure of Organized Crime. With the repeal of Prohibition, bootlegging quickly gave way to the provision of other illegal goods and services, but the structure of the organization remained. The usual structure centers on a "boss" who presides over a "family." The boss is the ultimate authority within each family and has power over the life and death of each member. The boss is served by an underboss and a *consiglieri*, or counselor. Together, these three form the centralized leadership of each family. Several *capo*, or captains, report to the leaders of the family, and each *capo* in turn controls several soldiers and associates responsible for the day-to-day operations of the family, including its legal and illegal enterprises.

Between families, a strict code of conduct is maintained, designed primarily to prevent conflict. This code, enacted by Capone, still exists among professional criminals today. Central to the code is the belief that one's loyalties begin and end with the syndicate. According to the code, the organization must be more important than an individual's wife, children, religion and country; orders must be followed without question; an individual must never provide information to any law enforcement officials or any other outsiders; and an individual will respect all members despite personal feelings, pay all debts owed to other members, and never harm or steal from any other members, unless directed to do so by a family boss.

Organized Crime Today. Many organized criminal groups operate within the United States. These range from the Japanese Yakuza to the Society of Thieves-in-Law, from Chinese street gangs to Colombian drug cartels. Most engage in the same criminal activities and have similar structures. Although formed primarily within particular ethnic communities, there is a significant degree of cooperation between organized crime groups. An example of this cooperation is a gasoline "racket" (scam) that was conducted by the Russian Mafia and La Cosa Nostra (LCN). In exchange for the protection that LCN offered the Russian Mafia, the Mafia provided LCN with a portion of the revenue generated by shorting customers a few cents' worth of gasoline on every sale in the northeastern United States.

Syndicates usually hire and promote individuals, at least partially, on the basis of their national heritage. The resulting criminal groups are therefore quite homogeneous in their composition. Major criminal organizations include Italian, Colombian, Chinese, and Russian descendants.

The primary syndicate operating today, however, is referred to as "La Cosa Nostra" (Italian for "this thing of ours"). LCN grew out of Capone's efforts to organize gangs in Chicago. LCN is

ruled by the Commission, a group composed of the five New York families, as well as families from Philadelphia, Chicago, and Detroit. The Commission coordinates operations and mediates disputes between the various families. The organization and structure guaranteed by the strict leadership of the Commission is the primary reason the LCN has grown to be the most influential organized criminal gang in the United States.

The Federal Bureau of Investigation (FBI) has identified twenty-five LCN families across the United States. In addition to the eight families that compose the Commission, families operate in Buffalo, Cleveland, Denver, Kansas City, Los Angeles, Milwaukee, New England, Newark, New Orleans, Pittston (New York), Pittsburgh, Rochester, St. Louis, San Francisco, San Jose, Tampa, and Tucson. Atlantic City, Las Vegas, and Miami have been declared "open cities" in which all families can operate. Although LCN families do not strictly enforce their territorial jurisdictions, operations in a family's territory can be conducted only with its permission.

Although the terms "La Cosa Nostra" and "Mafia" are frequently used to denote the entire spectrum of criminal syndicates, the terms technically apply to only one small portion of organized crime composed primarily of those groups of Italian descent. Many other major criminal organizations operate within the United States. Some, such as the Chinese Triads and the Russian Mafia, work closely with LCN families in various operations. Others, such as Toa Yuai Jingya Kumiai (TYJK), operate relatively independently. Other than the LCN, however, most organized crime groups operate on a local or regional level. Nevertheless, their influence within their own jurisdiction is significant.

Criminal organizations are involved in many activities. Although gambling and narcotics provide the majority of income, criminal syndicates are also involved in prostitution, labor racketeering, extortion, loan-sharking, and even hijacking cargoes. To launder (disguise) illegally earned funds, syndicate operations frequently employ legal enterprises—from cleaning companies to vending machines, from construction firms to waste disposal businesses.

The Internationalization of Organized Crime. The trend of organized crime has been toward international cooperation between criminal syndicates operating within different countries. Motivated by the potential for greater profits, criminal groups in the United States have allied with similar organizations in countries such as Colombia and Russia. Through complex relationships, foreign contracts provide American syndicates with drugs, primarily heroin and cocaine, in exchange for huge sums of money.

Although domestic crime groups are moving toward international cooperation, an even greater threat to law enforcement efforts is posed by groups such as the Chinese Triads and Colombian cartels—groups that are truly international in scope. With ties to terrorist organizations across the globe, international organized crime has the ability to threaten international stability and American interests worldwide. In 1988, the FBI estimated that the LCN had two thousand members in twenty-five U.S. cities. In 1989, the U.S. Senate estimated that the Colombian drug cartels had one hundred thousand members, earning some $20 billion annually. If for no other reason, the ability of international criminal groups to escape domestic prosecution while earning unprecedented profits will allow the internationalization of organized crime to continue.

Combating Organized Crime. Attempts to combat organized crime are hampered on several fronts. A report compiled in the 1980's under the direction of President Ronald Reagan identified three characteristics of organized crime which have limited the effectiveness of law enforcement officials' efforts. First, the decentralized structure and limited central membership of the syndicate make it difficult for law enforcement officials to convict Mafia leadership for acts committed by other family members under their direction. Furthermore, if one family is caught, the remaining families can continue their operations unhindered. Second, the ability of syndicates to bribe and corrupt government officials, police, lawyers, and businesspeople has provided organized crime with many allies in various fields. Finally, the social prestige afforded by membership in an elite criminal group provides both allies for and incentives not to prosecute family members. Together, these factors have acted to limit the impact of law enforcement operations against organized criminal groups.

Perhaps the most important law in the prosecution of organized crime is the Racketeer Influenced and Corrupt Organizations Act (RICO), adopted by Congress in 1970. Under RICO, law enforcement officials could prosecute an entire criminal family for operations conducted by one of its members under its direction. RICO has resulted in increasing success in law enforcement efforts, most notably in the prosecution of Joey Gambino, head of the New York Gambino family.

Other methods of combating organized crime have also been suggested. Most center on increasing surveillance of syndicate members and sharing resources and information between the various branches of law enforcement. Despite increasing efforts, however, organized crime groups have continued to prosper as the undisputed elite of the criminal underworld.

— *Noah Zerbe*

See also Anti-Racketeering Act; Capone, Alphonse (Al); Commercialized vice; Money laundering; Organized Crime Control Act; Prohibition; Racketeer Influenced and Corrupt Organizations Act (RICO).

BIBLIOGRAPHY

An excellent introduction to the structure of organized crime is provided in *An Introduction to Organized Crime in the United States* (Washington, D.C.: U.S. Department of Justice, 1993). The historical evolution of syndicates, primarily the Mafia, is traced in Gus Tyler, *Organized Crime in America* (Ann Arbor: University of Michigan Press, 1962). For a slightly more detailed analysis of criminal groups, including legal frameworks and organized crime, see Nikos Passas, *Organized Crime* (Brookfield, Vt.: Dartmouth Publishing, 1995). A thorough analysis of operations and businesses of criminal groups, as well as a general overview of related concepts, is provided by Howard Abadinsky, *Organized Crime* (Boston: Allyn and

Bacon, 1981). Interesting interviews with and descriptions of the lifestyles of Mafia leaders and members can be found in Howard Abadinsky, *The Criminal Elite* (Westport, Conn.: Greenwood Press, 1983). Information on the internationalization of criminal groups can be found in Roy Godson and William J. Olson, "International Organized Crime," *Society* 32 (January/February, 1995), and Louise I. Shelley, "Transnational Organized Crime: An Imminent Threat to the Nation-State?" *Journal of International Affairs* 48 (Winter, 1995). Finally, significant reference works on organized crime include Jay Robert Nash, *World Encyclopedia of Organized Crime* (New York: Da Capo Press, 1993), and Cal Sifakis, *The Mafia Encyclopedia* (New York: Facts on File, 1987).

Organized Crime Control Act

DATE: Became law October 15, 1970

DEFINITION: A set of amendments to existing law and authorizations of new law enforcement entities to combat organized crime

SIGNIFICANCE: The Organized Crime Control Act was a key element of the Nixon Administration's "war on crime"

The 1960's were seen by many at the time as an era of increasing crime, disrespect for authority, and corruption. Richard M. Nixon's election as president in 1968 marked the beginning of a series of conservative policies designed to address those problems under the rubric of a "war on crime." The Organized Crime Control Act was a key element of that program.

In general, the act strengthened the ability of law enforcement authorities to gather evidence against organized crime, provided for the protection of government witnesses, revised explosives regulations, and increased penalties for "dangerous special offenders." The act also established a commission to investigate criminal involvement in gambling. Title IX of the act, known as the Racketeer Influenced and Corrupt Organizations Act (RICO), identified various illegal activities and specified penalties.

The legislation encountered some resistance from those who argued that it provided the government with unconstitutional powers, violating individual rights. The final version of the act included a provision establishing a commission to review federal laws and practices for potential infringements of individual rights.

See also Anti-Racketeering Act; Gambling law; Organized crime; Racketeer Influenced and Corrupt Organizations Act (RICO).

Osborne v. Ohio

COURT: U.S. Supreme Court

DATE: Ruling issued April 18, 1990

SIGNIFICANCE: In this case, the Supreme Court upheld the states' rights to prohibit the possession and viewing of child pornography

Clyde Osborne was convicted of possessing child pornography after police found sexually explicit photographs of a nude minor male in his home. Ohio law prohibited any person from possessing or viewing materials that include a nude minor who is not their child unless they have a "bona fide purpose" or written consent from the minor's parents for such materials. Sentenced to six months in prison, Osborne appealed on the contention that the First Amendment protected his right to possess and view the photographs. In 1990, the Supreme Court ruled 6 to 3 to uphold Ohio's law, although Osborne's conviction was reversed and a new trial ordered. Essentially, the case contained three elements: whether Ohio's law was constitutional; whether Ohio's law was overbroad; and whether Osborne was denied due process.

In appealing the constitutionality of Ohio's child pornography law, Osborne relied on the Supreme Court's 1969 ruling in *Stanley v. Georgia* in which the court struck down the state's right to prohibit obscene materials. Justice Byron White, however, writing for the majority, pointed to the different underlying motivations for the Georgia and Ohio laws. In the case of *Georgia*, the state wished to prevent the "poisoning of the viewer's mind," while in Ohio's law, the motivation was to protect the victims of child pornography and to destroy the market for such materials. The Court ruled that the state's interest in this case was sufficiently compelling and deemed the law constitutional.

Osborne's second contention, that the Ohio law was overbroad, was also struck down by the Court. The Ohio statute prohibited only "lewd exhibition" or "graphic focus of the genitals" of a child who was not the child of the person charged. The court ruled that this interpretation was specific in its intentions and therefore denied Osborne's overbroad arguments. Osborne's due process arguments were noted, however, and the Court ruled that he should receive a new trial.

Justice William Brennan wrote the dissenting opinion, with Justices Thurgood Marshall and John Paul Stevens concurring. Brennan saw the Ohio law as overbroad, especially concerning its definition of "nudity." While the photographs were "distasteful," Brennan contended that Osborne had the right to possess the photographs under the protection of the First Amendment. The dissenting opinion also suggested that the state's interest was better served through other laws prohibiting the "creation, sale and distribution of child pornography."

Although somewhat weak in its ruling, the *Osborne* case is significant in its upholding of the states' rights to prohibit the possession of child pornography. As the dissenting opinion reveals, however, to stand up to further Supreme Court scrutiny, such laws need to be carefully worded to avoid overbroad interpretation.

See also Child molestation; *New York v. Ferber*; Pedophilia; Privacy, right of; Rape and sex offenses; Statutory rape.

Palko v. Connecticut

COURT: U.S. Supreme Court

DATE: Ruling issued December 6, 1937

SIGNIFICANCE: In this case, while refusing to apply the Fifth Amendment right against double jeopardy to the states, the Supreme Court established an influential test for determining which fundamental rights contained within the Bill of Rights are incorporated into the Fourteenth Amendment's due process clause

On the night of September 29, 1935, Bridgeport, Connecticut, police officers Wilfred Walker and Thomas J. Kearney were shot and killed. Frank Palko was charged with first-degree murder, a charge which carried a death sentence. On January 24, 1936, a trial jury found Palko guilty of only second-degree murder because the killings were not sufficiently premeditated. Palko received a sentence of life imprisonment. On July 30, 1936, the Supreme Court of Errors of Connecticut ordered a new trial by finding that the trial judge gave improper instructions to the jury. On October 15, 1936, a second jury found Palko guilty of first-degree murder, and he was sentenced to death. Palko's case came to the U.S. Supreme Court with the claim that the second trial violated his Fifth Amendment right to not "be subject for the same offense to be twice put in jeopardy of life or limb." At the time, however, the Supreme Court had applied the Fifth Amendment right against double jeopardy only to criminal cases in federal, rather than state, courts.

For most of American history, the provisions of the Bill of Rights protected individuals only against actions by the federal government. The ratification of the Fourteenth Amendment in 1868 applied constitutional rights to protection against the states, but those rights were vaguely worded protections involving "due process" and "equal protection." People repeatedly brought cases to the Supreme Court asserting that the provisions of the Bill of Rights should apply against state as well as federal government officials. Beginning in 1925, the Supreme Court gradually incorporated a few rights—speech, press, and religion—into the Fourteenth Amendment's due process clause and thereby made those rights applicable to the states.

Unfortunately for Palko, the Court was unwilling to incorporate the Fifth Amendment's protection against double jeopardy in 1937. Thus Palko's conviction was affirmed, and he was subsequently executed for the murders. Justice Benjamin Cardozo's majority opinion, however, established a test for determining which rights to incorporate by declaring that only rights which are "fundamental" and "essential" to liberty are contained in the right to due process in the Fourteenth Amendment. In analyzing Palko's case, Cardozo decided that many criminal justice rights contained in the Bill of Rights, such as trial by jury and protection against double jeopardy and self-incrimination, are not fundamental and essential because it is possible to have fair trials without them.

The importance of *Palko v. Connecticut* is that Cardozo's test established an influential standard for determining which provisions of the Bill of Rights apply against the states. Although justices in later decades disagreed with Cardozo's specific conclusions and subsequently incorporated double jeopardy and other rights for criminal defendants, most justices continued to use Cardozo's basic approach of evaluating whether each specific right was fundamental and essential to liberty.

See also Bill of Rights, U.S.; Cardozo, Benjamin Nathan; Civil War Amendments; Double jeopardy; Incorporation doctrine; Supreme Court of the United States.

Palmer raids and the "red scare"

DATE: January 2-5, 1920

PLACE: United States

SIGNIFICANCE: The Palmer raids represented one of numerous aspects of post-World War I hysteria which resulted in the infringement of rights of citizens

A strong desire to eliminate political dissent arose during World War I. It was intensified by the Communist overthrow of the Russian government in 1917 and the perceived Communist threat to American institutions, and it continued in the post-World War I era. In 1918, Congress enacted a law allowing the secretary of labor to deport any alien belonging to a revolutionary organization.

It was the belief of Attorney General Alexander Mitchell Palmer that the law was not being applied to the extent necessary. Without the knowledge of Secretary of Labor William Wilson, Palmer obtained arrest warrants from a subordinate in Wilson's department, the aim being an application of the deportation law. Beginning the night of January 2, 1920, a series of raids were carried out which resulted in the arrest of more than three thousand "radicals" in thirty-three cities. The "Palmer raids" continued on January 5. Arrested were any persons even remotely connected with revolutionary organizations, including family members visiting the jail.

Secretary Wilson, outraged by Palmer's abuse of power, took charge of the deportation hearings. Eventually, 556 aliens were deported; the remainder of those arrested were released. Though the "red menace" was always more perceived than real, in the years following World War II another "threat" would result in the rise of Joseph McCarthy.

See also Communist Party, American; House Committee on Un-American Activities (HUAC); McCarthyism; Presumption of innocence; Smith Act.

Pandering

DEFINITION: Catering to the gratification of another's desire for sexual or other illicit pleasures

SIGNIFICANCE: Solicitation, enticing, or purveying of particular types of illicit services is widely viewed as undermining community morals, whether barred by law or not

Even though many localities have laws against this type of intermediation, which exploits commercialized vice, these laws are infrequently enforced, as is the case for many so-called victimless crimes. There are several reasons for such inconsistency. The demand for the services of panderers, procurers, and pimps is high. Contemporary mores tend not to regard gratification of various desires as immoral or harmful. Law enforcement personnel are occupied with more serious crimes.

Failing specific statutes or sufficient evidence, the government frequently has to use tax evasion or other laws to curtail actions it considers antisocial or immoral. Because customers rarely sign complaints, the police often have to use questionable entrapment procedures in seeking convictions of panderers. Organized crime is often involved in prostitution and pornography, and pandering and related activities tend to generate secondary criminality. Public prosecutors and police vice squads therefore continue their intermittent countermeasures.

See also Commercialized vice; Disorderly conduct; Moral turpitude; Public order offenses; Solicitation to commit a crime; Vagrancy laws; Victimless crimes.

Pardoning power

DEFINITION: The power granted to the president of the United States and to state governors to forgive an offense or crime

SIGNIFICANCE: A pardon removes any punishment or penalty attached to an offense or crime, and it legally restores the pardoned person to a state of innocence regarding the crime

A pardon is an "act of grace" to mitigate the punishment the law demands for a crime and to restore the rights and privileges forfeited because of the offense. The executive authority can either commute or pardon the convicted criminal. To commute is to reduce the penalty, such as the length of time in prison. To pardon is to excuse the person from any penalty under the law. In *Ex parte Garland* (1867), the Supreme Court stated, "When the pardon is full, it releases the punishment and blots out of existence the guilt, so that in the eyes of the law the offender is as innocent as if he had never committed the offense."

An amnesty is a group pardon of several or many people. "Pardon" applies to one individual. A pardon totally restores the individual, whereas a "parole" simply releases the person early, subject to the supervision of the public authority. A person violating the conditions of parole may be returned to imprisonment. This is usually not the case with a pardon, but there can be a "conditional pardon" that requires the pardoned person to meet some condition such as leaving the state or refraining from certain actions. A violation of the condition could lead to the revocation of the pardon.

President Gerald Ford speaking to the nation announcing his pardoning of former president Richard Nixon. (Courtesy Gerald R. Ford Library)

CLEMENCY APPLICATIONS FOR FEDERAL OFFENSES					
Fiscal year	Received	Granted		Denied	Pending
		Pardons	Commutations		
1979	710	143	10	448	617
1980	523	155	11	500	474
1981	548	76	7	260	679
1982	462	83	3	547	508
1983	447	91	2	306	556
1984	447	37	5	326	635
1985	407	32	3	279	728
1986	362	55	0	290	745
1987	410	23	0	311	821
1988	384	38	0	497	673
1989	373	41	1	392	612
1990	354	0	0	116	681
1991	318	29	0	588	289
1992	379	0	0	192	476
1993	868	36	2	251	928

Source: U.S. Department of Justice, Bureau of Justice Statistics, *Sourcebook of Criminal Justice Statistics—1993.* Washington, D.C.: U.S. Government Printing Office, 1994.

Note: Numbers reflect executive clemency applications received, disposed of, and pending in the Office of the U.S. Pardon Attorney. The pardon attorney reviews, investigates, and recommends action regarding all petitions for executive clemency.

There can also be a partial pardon, which remits only a part of the punishment or only the part for a specific portion of the legal consequences of a crime. Most pardons, though, are absolute or unconditional. No further legal actions can be taken against a recipient of a complete pardon. This legally applies to collateral as well as direct consequences of an incident. Governors and the president have a systematic procedure to consider applications for pardons. The official in the Department of Justice who considers these applications and makes recommendations to the president is known as the pardon attorney.

The most famous, and probably most controversial, pardon in American history was granted to former President Richard Nixon by President Gerald Ford in 1974. Before Nixon could be impeached by Congress for his role in the Watergate cover-up, Ford granted him a "full, free, and absolute pardon."

See also Appellate process; Ford, Gerald R.; Impeachment; Nixon, Richard M.; Sentencing.

Parole

DEFINITION: The practice of releasing inmates to serve the last portion of their sentence in the community, under supervision of the criminal justice system

SIGNIFICANCE: Rates of arrest for offenders free on parole have caused some to question whether parole is an effective strategy for monitoring recently released offenders

Parole serves several different purposes in the United States. It allows for a period of transition following release from a prison, theoretically allowing an individual the opportunity to find employment while still under the supervision of the criminal justice system. In addition, keeping offenders under supervision following release from prison helps them remain crime-free until they are able to take care of themselves. Finally, parole helps to alleviate overcrowding in prisons through the early release of persons who have not committed any new crimes while incarcerated.

When inmates are released from prison, they are released either unconditionally or conditionally. Unconditional release occurs when the inmate has served all the time sentenced except for any time subtracted for good behavior. Some inmates eventually become eligible for mandatory release. This occurs when they have served the amount of time to which they were sentenced (less any good time credit). These individuals are not literally parolees; they have served their time, and supervision is not usually required. In some cases the sentence can be commuted, or changed.

When inmates are released conditionally, they are expected to behave according to certain criteria; otherwise they will be returned to prison. Conditional release can include parole, probation, mandatory release, or some other method of supervision. Parole is far and away the most common method of conditionally releasing inmates in the United States. In 1991, approximately 47 percent of inmates conditionally released were released on parole.

History of Parole. The idea of parole is believed to have started in England in the late sixteenth century. Inmates were sometimes released from incarceration to serve as cheap labor for landowners in the new North American colonies. Later, this system became more formalized when inmates who worked while incarcerated were rewarded with early release. This idea of "good behavior" during incarceration endures in the modern correctional system. Inmates who stay out of trouble while incarcerated are eligible for early release (sometimes referred to as "good time").

During the early nineteenth century, prisons were built in the United States with the expectation that prisoners would work as laborers. During this time, an indeterminate sentenc-

ing system was used in the criminal justice system. Prisoners' behavior and earned "good time" determined when they would be released from incarceration. Eventually, prison labor came to be an important part of the economy for the area serving the prison. With the Industrial Revolution and a dramatic increase in business, however, prison labor came to be seen as a threat to individual businesses. In addition, state and local government began to purchase goods from private business, whose products were of higher quality. As part of a crusade against prison labor, the Progressive movement in the early twentieth

A parole officer meeting with a parolee under his supervision; keeping regular appointments with a parole officer is frequently a condition of parole. (Ben Klaffke)

CONDITIONAL RELEASES FROM STATE PRISONS, 1991

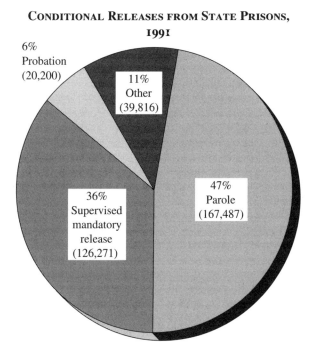

6%
Probation
(20,200)

11%
Other
(39,816)

36%
Supervised
mandatory
release
(126,271)

47%
Parole
(167,487)

Source: U.S. Department of Justice, Bureau of Justice Statistics, *Sourcebook of Criminal Justice Statistics—1993.* Washington, D.C.: U.S. Government Printing Office, 1994.

century focused on the benefit of using the community to help rehabilitate incarcerated offenders. These reformers believed that prisoners could be released from their sentence and allowed to live in their community during a time of transition from prison to life outside prison.

The U.S. parole system had been formally implemented a few decades earlier, in the late nineteenth century. Before it began, the only way an inmate could leave prison early was to win a pardon or clemency from the governor of the state. As the use of clemency began to increase, politicians found it too time-consuming to pardon every prisoner who was worthy of early release. This, in conjunction with the reforms of the Progressive era, made parole a very attractive solution to several of the concerns of citizens.

Conditions of Parole. While jurisdictions have many different conditions for their parolees, all parolees have one thing in common. They are all regularly monitored by the criminal justice system. Infractions of conditions may result in the inmate's being returned to prison. Conditions may include keeping regular appointments with a parole officer, abstaining from drug and alcohol use, undergoing urine tests (for the presence of drugs), attending school, or keeping a full-time job.

When parolees violate the conditions set by the criminal justice system, they are usually returned to prison to complete their sentence. In some cases, extra time is added to the sentence if a crime was committed during parole.

Making Parole Decisions. Decisions about which inmates will or will not be released are typically made by a parole board. In most states in the United States, the parole board is under the supervision of the state department of corrections. A typical parole board includes members of the local community as well as some criminal justice practitioners. Parole boards are also responsible for continued monitoring of released offenders.

When inmates become eligible for parole, they are called in by the parole board to a parole hearing. In this hearing, inmates are interviewed about their desire to leave prison and how they plan to support themselves following release. Occasionally, crime victims will appear at parole hearings to protest the release of an inmate on parole. — *Christina Polsenberg*

See also Good time; House arrest; Prison and jail systems; Probation; Punishment.

BIBLIOGRAPHY

A history of parole in the United States is contained in Jonathan Simon, *Poor Discipline* (Chicago: University of Chicago Press, 1993), while an overview of the modern parole system is contained in Howard Abadinsky, *Probation and Parole: Theory and Practice* (Englewood Cliffs, N.J.: Prentice-Hall, 1977). Statistical information on parolees can be found in Bureau of Justice Statistics, *Sourcebook of Criminal Justice Statistics* (Washington, D.C.: U.S. Government Printing Office), published annually.

Pasadena City Board of Education v. Spangler

COURT: U.S. Supreme Court

DATE: Decided June 28, 1976

SIGNIFICANCE: In this school desegregation case, the Supreme Court held that a federal district court exceeded its authority in ordering annual reassignments of students to facilitate changes in the racial makeup of schools caused by demographic shifts

In 1968, several students and their parents filed suit against the Pasadena Unified School District in California, alleging that the district's schools were segregated as a result of official action on the part of the district. In 1970, the federal district court found for these plaintiffs, concluding that the district had engaged in segregation and ordering the district to adopt a plan to cure the racial imbalances in its schools. The federal court's order provided that no school was to have a majority of minority students. The district thereafter presented the court with a plan to eliminate segregation in the Pasadena schools; the court approved the plan, and the district subsequently implemented it.

Approximately four years later, the Pasadena Unified School District asked the district court to modify its original order and eliminate the requirement that no school have a majority of minority students. The district contended that though it had abandoned its racially segregative practices, changing racial demographics had created new racial imbalances in the district's schools. The federal district court refused to modify its original order, however, and the Ninth Circuit Court of Appeals upheld the district court's ruling.

Reviewing this decision, Justice William H. Rehnquist, joined by five other justices, concluded that the district court had abused its authority in refusing to remove the requirement that no district school have a majority of minority students. According to the Court, there had been no showing that changes in the racial mix of the Pasadena schools had been caused by the school district's policies. Since the school district had implemented a racially neutral attendance policy, the federal district court was not entitled to require a continual reshuffling of attendance zones to maintain an optimal racial mix. Justices Thurgood Marshall and William J. Brennan dissented from this holding, emphasizing the breadth of discretion normally allotted to federal district courts to remedy school segregation once a constitutional violation had been shown.

The majority's decision signaled that the broad discretion with which the Court previously had seemed to have invested federal district courts was not without limits. It had been widely thought that once officially sanctioned or *de jure* segregation had been shown, a federal court had great latitude in eliminating not only such *de jure* segregation but also *de facto* segregation—that is, segregation not necessarily tied to official conduct. The majority's decision in this case, however, signified otherwise.

See also Racial and ethnic discrimination; Segregation, *de facto* and *de jure*; *Swann v. Charlotte-Mecklenburg Board of Education*.

Patent law. *See* Copyrights, patents, and trademarks

Payne v. Tennessee

COURT: U.S. Supreme Court
DATE: Decided June 27, 1991
SIGNIFICANCE: In a dramatic departure from *stare decisis* (the practice of basing decisions on precedents of previous cases) the Supreme Court overruled two cases it had decided within the past four years and held that victim impact evidence would be permitted in capital sentencing hearings

In 1987, the Supreme Court in *Booth v. Maryland* had held that prosecutors in capital cases would not be permitted to use victim impact evidence to persuade the jury that the defendant deserved to be executed. The five members of the *Booth* majority held that evidence about the personal characteristics of the murdered person and evidence about the impact of the crime on surviving family members was irrelevant to the jury's decision whether the character of the defendant and the circumstances of the crime called for the death penalty or for some lesser punishment. Because victim impact evidence focused the jury's attention on the victim and surviving family members, it diverted the jury's attention from the defendant. Most important, it created a risk that a death sentence might be based on arbitrary and capricious reasons, such as the willingness and ability of surviving family members to articulate their grief, or the relative worth of the murder victim to the community.

Four justices had sharply dissented. In their view, victim impact evidence was relevant to the defendant's moral blameworthiness because it gave the jury important information about the extent of the harm caused by the defendant.

The *Booth* decision was reaffirmed two years later in *South Carolina v. Gathers*, when another bare majority of the Court held that prosecutors could not present victim impact evidence to the jury during closing arguments in death penalty cases. By 1991, however, two members of the *Booth* majority had retired from the Court and had been replaced by more conservative justices. That same year, the Court agreed to reconsider its recent decisions and granted *certiorari* in *Payne v. Tennessee*.

Pervis Tyrone Payne had stabbed to death twenty-eight-year-old Charisse Christopher and her two-year-old daughter, Lacie. Payne also stabbed and left for dead Charisse's three-year-old son, Nicholas. Nicholas survived his stab wounds, several of which passed completely through his body. During Payne's trial, Nicholas' grandmother testified emotionally as to the effect of the murders on Nicholas. In addition, during closing arguments to the jury, the prosecutor strongly implied that returning a death sentence would somehow help Nicholas. The jury sentenced Payne to die.

In the Supreme Court, Payne argued that the grandmother's testimony and the prosecutor's argument to the jury constituted victim impact evidence and thereby violated *Booth* and *Gathers*. In a radical departure from past practice, the Supreme Court discarded those recent decisions and announced a new rule: Victim impact evidence would be permitted in capital sentencing proceedings. According to the majority, victim impact evidence gave the jury important information about the extent of the harm caused by the defendant.

Justice Thurgood Marshall, who voted with the majority in *Booth* and *Gathers*, was enraged and disheartened. Breaking tradition, Justice Marshall read his dissent from the bench on the last day of the Court's 1991 term. He said: "Neither the law nor the facts supporting *Booth* and *Gathers* underwent any change in the last four years. Only the personnel of this Court did." Within two hours of reading his dissent, Justice Marshall announced his resignation from the Court.

See also *Booth v. Maryland*; Marshall, Thurgood; Sentencing; *Stare decisis*.

Pedophilia

DEFINITION: Attraction to children as objects of sexual desire
SIGNIFICANCE: While being sexually attracted to children is not, in and of itself, a crime, most pedophiles feel compelled to act on their feelings, leading to various crimes related to sexual assault of a minor

"Paraphilia" is the term used to refer to any unusual and compulsive sexual desire. While having a paraphilia is not illegal, acting upon a paraphilia may be, as in the case of voyeurism (being a "peeping Tom") or exhibitionism (being a "flasher"). Of all the paraphilias that may lead to crime, the one which is regarded as the most heinous, and perhaps the one that causes the most harm to society, is pedophilia—sexual attraction to children. Because pedophilia is one of the most powerful of the sexual compulsions, individual pedophiles may victimize hundreds of children before being arrested. Once identified, they are also among the most difficult of all paraphiliacs to treat or rehabilitate.

Pedophilia is, essentially, a condition of males: More than 90 percent of pedophiles are heterosexual males, with the remainder consisting primarily of homosexual males. Thus, the majority of victims are young girls. Some pedophiles, on the other hand, consider themselves heterosexual in terms of their adult sexual orientation and choice of partners but find themselves attracted to prepubescent children of both sexes. The typical pedophile is married, is religiously and politically conservative, and has a dominant or even domineering relationship over his wife and family. Sometimes the pedophile acts on his compulsion within his own family, engaging in incest. Other forms of abuse may also be occurring within the family, but this is not necessarily the case. Most pedophiles do not commit incest, but instead seek potential victims where children congregate, such as at schools, church, and summer camps.

To the best of psychologists' knowledge, pedophilia is acquired during early childhood and adolescence based on the principles of associative learning, especially classical conditioning. Some pedophiles were sexually abused when they were children; others may have feelings of fear or inadequacy relating to adult relationships.

Since what is learned can theoretically be "unlearned," treatment of pedophiles generally consists of a variety of behavior modification techniques that have proven to be very successful for the unlearning (or reconditioning) of other attitudes and behaviors (such as smoking, phobias, and other nonsexual compulsions). Perhaps because sexual pleasure is such a powerful reward, however, pedophiles are very resistant to treatment, and behavior modification programs to date have not been very successful. Other therapies focus on social skills training, trying to make appropriate adult sexual interactions more appealing, and thus lessening the relative attractiveness of children as sexual objects. Drug treatment ("chemical castration") is the most successful but also the most controversial of treatments.

Although pedophilia is listed in the American Psychiatric Association's *Diagnostic and Statistical Manual of Mental Disorders*, it is not among the disorders that can invoke the insanity defense; pedophiles generally have no psychologically distinguishing attributes other than their sexual compulsion.

See also Child molestation; Incest; Moral turpitude; Rape and sex offenses; Statutory rape.

Pendleton Act

DATE: Became law January 16, 1883
DEFINITION: Reformed the federal civil service by ending the spoils system and created the Civil Service Commission
SIGNIFICANCE: This act instituted the first merit system of appointment to the civil service; at first its provisions were limited to about 10 percent of federal employees, but a merit system now covers more than 90 percent

Early in American history the selection of government workers was based on the applicant's "fitness of character." George Washington used such criteria as family background, education, social status, and loyalty to appoint individuals to government positions. As political parties developed, partisan appointments to government offices became increasingly common. By the time Andrew Jackson became president in 1828, the attitude toward government appointments was, "to the victor belong the spoils." Even Abraham Lincoln skillfully used patronage to win reelection in 1864.

As the "spoils system" spread to state and local governments, a reform movement emerged to combat the practice, which too often led to corruption and incompetence in government. The effort to reform the civil service was led by many different groups. The first reform association was formed in New York in 1877. The National Civil Service Reform League was created in 1881 to make changes nationwide. Business leaders and professionals wanted more efficiency and participation in government, while the public was becoming outraged at the abuses of the spoils systems. The decisive event in the reform movement came in 1881 when Charles Guiteau shot and killed President James A. Garfield after he was refused a government job.

In the end, politics sealed the fate of patronage. The Republicans suffered heavy losses in the 1882 congressional elections and feared defeat in the 1884 presidential elections. They reluctantly joined the reform movement to prevent a new president from making wholesale changes in government positions. In 1881, Dorman B. Eaton, a member of the Reform League, went to England to discuss reform with leading reformers, including John Stuart Mill. Upon his return, Eaton met with Democrat George H. Pendleton of Ohio, who introduced legislation to end the spoils systems.

The Pendleton Act—also known as the Civil Service Act of 1883—dramatically changed government employment and instituted "merit principles" into the federal government. The act called for open, competitive entrance examinations to test applicant abilities. It disallowed the removal of employees for political reasons and prohibited coercing any person's political activity. The objective of the new merit system was a politically neutral government bureaucracy.

The initial impact of the Pendleton Act was modest. Only 13,924 positions (11 percent) were affected by its provisions. By the beginning of the twentieth century, 95,000 jobs were covered by the act, while 110,000 positions were outside its guidelines. Franklin D. Roosevelt was able to appoint 60 percent of the federal workforce (400,000 jobs) according to political criteria. Eventually Congress saw the danger of a president being able to appoint large numbers of politically loyal bureaucrats and brought almost all federal workers under merit protection.

Currently, more than 99 percent of the more than three million federal workers are covered by a merit system. The president can appoint about 5,000 positions when a new administration takes office.

The Pendleton Act has remained relatively unchanged since 1883. The next important civil service law passed by Congress was the Civil Service Reform Act of 1978. This law provided for changes in the administration of the merit system, improved management flexibility, created a Senior Executive Service, and gave managers the capacity to reward or discipline employees.

See also Civil service system; Machine politics; Political corruption; Spoils system and patronage.

Perjury

DEFINITION: A crime in which a person deliberately lies or bears false witness while under oath, either in court or in such extrajudicial testimony as sworn affidavits and depositions

SIGNIFICANCE: Because it can confound justice, perjury is considered an extremely serious crime; undetected, it can result in the conviction of the innocent or the acquittal of the guilty

Although the Ninth Commandment, in the Old Testament book of Exodus, proscribed bearing false witness, laws against perjury are of relatively recent derivation. In England until the fourteenth century, coerced confessions or trials by ordeal or combat, rather than eyewitness testimony, were normally used to determine guilt. Even as English common law and the jury system developed, witnesses were first limited to a suspect's accusers. They were not even required to appear at trials; if they did appear, they were treated as jurors. Verdicts, but not testimony, could be found false through "the writ of attaint," under which juries could be punished and their verdicts nullified.

In England, testimony of Crown witnesses given under oath was first allowed in the sixteenth century, but it was not until 1702 that sworn testimony of witnesses for the defense was permitted. By that time, juries no longer had a testimonial function. Witnesses had become the only means of bringing evidence before criminal courts, and perjury was a punishable offense under common law.

One important concept that shaped early laws against perjury involved the "material" nature of sworn testimony. That is, for a person to be convicted of perjury, his or her perjured testimony had to be significant enough to influence the outcome of the trial. Most modern state statutes defining perjury retain the "material" qualifier, though a few state laws no longer make it a mandatory requirement. Even in those states where materiality is required, it has served not so much as an impediment to conviction as a factor in determining the severity or grade of the crime.

While convictions for perjury have at times hinged on some subtle distinctions, the basis of perjury remains the same: A witness must deliberately lie while presenting testimony under oath. In many states, perjury is not limited to lying while under oath in court. It has been extended to include lying or "false swearing" before governmental agencies empowered to subpoena witnesses and take sworn testimony. Further, a witness may commit perjury even giving true testimony if the witness believes that the testimony is actually false. Perjury thus depends not only on the truth or falsity of a sworn statement but also on the intent to deceive. Inconsistent or contradictory testimony does not constitute perjury if no such intent is involved.

Perjury, a felony, carries major penalties, including both heavy fines and imprisonment. It is, however, difficult to prove. In most cases, perjury convictions must meet the "two-witness rule" requiring some corroboration of testimony that contradicts the allegedly perjured testimony. For this reason the charge of perjury is more often threatened than invoked.

See also Evidence, rules of; Judicial system, U.S.; Jury system; Lying to Congress; Model Penal Code; Obstruction of justice.

Pierce v. Society of Sisters

COURT: U.S. Supreme Court
DATE: Decided June 1, 1925
SIGNIFICANCE: This case, which struck down state legislation requiring parents to send their children to public rather than private schools on grounds that such legislation violated the liberty clause of the Fourteenth Amendment, has provided important authority in Supreme Court cases in the areas of contraceptive, abortion, and homosexual rights

In 1922, the state of Oregon adopted the Compulsory Education Act, which compelled general attendance at public schools by normal children between the ages of eight and sixteen. The Society of the Sisters of the Holy Names of Jesus and Mary, a private parochial school, challenged this legislation on the grounds that it conflicted with the right and liberty of parents to send their children to schools of their own choosing and violated the right of private schools and teachers therein to engage in a useful business and profession.

In a unanimous decision, the U.S. Supreme Court held that "the Act of 1922 unreasonably interferes with the liberty of the parents and guardians to direct the upbringing and education of children under their control." Justice James C. McReynolds, writing for the Court, explained that "rights guaranteed by the Constitution may not be abridged by legislation which has no reasonable relation to some purpose within the competency of the state."

This decision has since become a focal point for vigorous judicial debate over the application of the Ninth Amendment as authority for the invalidation of state legislation in such areas as contraceptive, abortion, and homosexual rights. That amendment states: "The enumeration in the Constitution, of certain rights, shall not be construed to deny or disparage others retained by the people." One judicial view, espoused by Justices Arthur Goldberg and William Brennan, is that the Ninth Amendment clearly implies that there are other rights, not specifically set forth in the Bill of Rights, which are protected from government infringement and that the Court may therefore strike down state legislation deemed to infringe upon such other rights as might be subsumed under the liberty clause.

An opposing view expresses alarm that the Ninth Amendment, adopted by the states as a means of ensuring that the federal government did not exceed its limited and enumerated powers, might be used in a way to expand federal veto power over state legislation. As Justice Potter Stewart stated in his dissenting opinion in *Griswold v. Connecticut* (1965), "The Ninth Amendment was passed, not to broaden the powers of this Court . . . but . . . to limit the federal government."

The former view has prevailed in cases such as *Roe v. Wade* (1973), in which the Court, upholding a woman's right to an abortion, cited *Pierce v. Society of Sisters* for the proposition that personal rights that can be deemed "implicit in the concept of ordered liberty" are guaranteed by the Constitution. In *Bowers v. Hardwick* (1986), however, the Court narrowly declined to find the freedom to engage in homosexual conduct as a right subsumed under the Fourteenth Amendment.

See also Civil liberties; Civil War Amendments; *Griswold v. Connecticut*; Ninth Amendment; *Roe v. Wade*; School law; *Wisconsin v. Mitchell*.

Pinkerton, Allan (Aug. 25, 1819, Glasgow, Scotland— July 1, 1884, Chicago, Ill.)

IDENTIFICATION: American private detective

SIGNIFICANCE: Allan Pinkerton's private detective agency was the first to collect and circulate photographs and detailed physical descriptions of criminals, anticipating the later work of the Federal Bureau of Investigation and Interpol

A radical political agitator in Scotland, Pinkerton immigrated to the United States in 1843, working as a cooper until counterfeiting cases drew him into law enforcement. In 1849, he became Chicago's first detective and was later a special agent for the post office. About 1850, he formed the North-Western Police Agency, later the Pinkerton Agency; its early motto, "The Eye That Never Sleeps," gave the term "private eye" to the language.

The agency's strength was its ability to cross local and state lines to protect banks and stagecoach and train shipments against bandits on the lawless frontier. Pinkerton opened offices in New York and Philadelphia in 1866 and 1867. Shortly after, he established his Rogues' Gallery, a collection of photographs and descriptions that formed the earliest clearinghouse for this information. Pinkerton's exploits became so popular that, by 1876, he had employed seven writers to produce what became eighteen volumes about his activities. (He sketched outlines and generally ensured the authenticity of investigative techniques.) One former operative, William J. Burns, was asked to establish a coast-to-coast crime-fighting force that became the federal government's Bureau of Investigation, later renamed the Federal Bureau of Investigation (FBI).

See also Bank robbery; Frontier, the; Police and guards, private.

Planned Parenthood of Central Missouri v. Danforth

COURT: U.S. Supreme Court
DATE: Decided July 1, 1976
SIGNIFICANCE: The Court ruled that states cannot require a spouse's consent for an abortion and upheld the right of minors to receive abortions without parental consent

In June of 1974, the Missouri Abortion Act was passed. It required a woman to sign a consent form prior to abortion, spousal consent for abortions, and parental consent for abortions for minors. It also required that physicians make every effort to preserve the life of viable fetuses and prohibited the use of saline amniocentesis as a method of abortion. Planned Parenthood of Central Missouri filed a suit on behalf of itself, women seeking abortions, and physicians who perform abortions. The defendant was John Danforth, attorney general of Missouri. The U.S. District Court, Eastern Missouri, upheld most of the provisions of the law, leading to the case's appeal to the Supreme Court.

The Supreme Court, in a 5-4 decision, overturned the law's central provisions. It ruled that the law did not provide adequate definition of viability and further that the restrictions on physicians placed improper legal constraints in an area that was a matter of medical judgment. Drawing on its *Roe v. Wade* (1973) decision, the Court struck down the prohibition of saline amniocentesis as a method of abortion, for its earlier ruling permitted restriction on abortion methods during the second trimester only on the grounds of health risks to the mother. It found no serious health threats to maternal life from this procedure. The court also ruled that requiring parental consent for minors was improper, since such consent was not legally required for other medical procedures. Significantly, it argued that rights do not emerge at a certain age but that competent minors already have a "right to privacy" that assures them access to abortion. Its most far-reaching decision involved the denial of a right of spousal consent for abortion. The Court ruled that the woman's right to privacy takes precedence over any claims that others may have.

The minority opinion objected that the state's interest in developing fetal life, as articulated in *Roe v. Wade*, permitted states to require physicians to attempt to save viable fetal life. It also argued that the *Roe* decision did not establish an absolute right to abortion. Consequently, they supported provisions for spousal consent in cases where the spouse was willing to assume the burden of care for the child. Similarly, they indicated that parental consent for minors would be acceptable if there was provision for court intervention in the case of conflict or for court permission in lieu of parental consent in potentially abusive family situations. This last provision has been enacted in a number of subsequent state laws and upheld by the Court.

See also Abortion; *Akron v. Akron Center for Reproductive Health*; *Doe v. Bolton*; *Harris v. McRae*; *Maher v. Roe*; *Planned Parenthood v. Casey*; *Roe v. Wade*; *Thornburgh v. American College of Obstetricians and Gynecologists*.

Planned Parenthood v. Casey

COURT: U.S. Supreme Court
DATE: Decided June 29, 1992
SIGNIFICANCE: The Supreme Court reaffirmed its holding in *Roe v. Wade* (1973) that the constitutional right of privacy protects a woman's right to choose to have an abortion

before the fetus she is carrying becomes viable; a controlling plurality of the Court also determined that regulations making it more difficult for a woman to obtain an abortion will be upheld as long as they do not unduly burden the woman's decision to terminate her pregnancy

Five medical clinics and one physician challenged the constitutionality of certain provisions of the Pennsylvania Abortion Control Act, which restricted access to abortion services. The Supreme Court, however, could not reach a consensus on the appropriate standard of review to apply to these regulations. Three justices wrote a joint opinion upholding all but one of the challenged provisions on the grounds that they did not unduly burden the right to have an abortion. Four other justices, arguing that the Constitution does not recognize a right to have an abortion, concurred in that result. Thus, seven justices voted to uphold the following abortion regulations. Prior to obtaining her informed consent to surgery, physicians must provide a woman seeking to have an abortion with specific information about the nature of an abortion, the risks associated with this medical procedure, and the gestational age of the fetus. A woman must wait twenty-four hours after receiving this information before she can obtain an abortion. A woman under the age of eighteen may not obtain an abortion without either the informed consent of one of her parents or the determination by a court that the woman is mature enough to make this decision for herself or that having an abortion is in her best interests.

The three-justice plurality struck down as unduly burdensome a regulation prohibiting a married woman from obtaining an abortion unless she first notifies her spouse of her decision to terminate her pregnancy. Two other justices, who argued that all abortion regulations should be strictly scrutinized, concurred in declaring this provision unconstitutional.

The Court's decision in Casey, particularly the plurality opinion of Justices David Souter, Anthony Kennedy, and Sandra Day O'Connor, appeared to reflect a constitutional compromise on the abortion issue. On the one hand, the right to have an abortion was explicitly affirmed by a majority of the Court out of respect for stare decisis, the obligation of judges to respect past precedent, if for no other reason. Under the authority of Casey, any law attempting to criminalize abortion, as many state laws did prior to the Court's decision in Roe v. Wade in 1973, would be declared unconstitutional on its face.

On the other hand, the "undue burden" standard applied by the plurality to determine the constitutionality of abortion regulations in Casey represented a significant retreat from the trimester framework and rigorous review the Court had applied during the twenty-year period after Roe was decided. Unlike the old approach, under which virtually any regulation of abortion during the first two trimesters of the gestation period would be struck down, regulations that increased the cost of having an abortion after Casey would be upheld unless plaintiffs challenging their constitutionality could demonstrate the severity of the resulting burden on a woman's right to choose to terminate her pregnancy.

Not only was this new standard of review more lenient than its predecessor, but also it seemed more ambiguous in its meaning and less predictable in its application. The plurality opinion in Casey defined an undue burden as "shorthand for the conclusion that a state regulation has the purpose or effect of placing a substantial obstacle in the path of a woman seeking an abortion of a nonviable fetus." Exactly what constituted a substantial enough burden to justify a court invalidating an abortion regulation remained unclear. The plurality's language left unanswered many important questions that could only be resolved by further litigation and additional judicial decisions.

Notwithstanding this criticism, the Court's decision in Casey did resolve one important constitutional question in unambiguous terms. The core holding of Roe v. Wade was not overruled. As the plurality stated emphatically, "a State may not prohibit any woman from making the ultimate decision to terminate her pregnancy before viability."

See also Abortion; *Akron v. Akron Center for Reproductive Health*; *Doe v. Bolton*; *Harris v. McRae*; *Maher v. Roe*; *Planned Parenthood of Central Missouri v. Danforth*; *Roe v. Wade*; *Thornburgh v. American College of Obstetricians and Gynecologists*.

Plea bargaining

DEFINITION: The negotiation process in which defendants agree to plead guilty in exchange for the expectation of fewer or lesser charges or more lenient punishments

SIGNIFICANCE: In the American justice system, more than 90 percent of all criminal convictions are obtained through guilty pleas produced after negotiations between the prosecution and the defense

In the minds of the public, decisions about the guilt or innocence of criminal defendants are supposed to be made after lawyers battle one another in the courtroom under the watchful eyes of a judge and jury. The central role of trials in the American justice process is emphasized in a variety of information sources, ranging from textbooks to television dramas. In reality, however, more than 90 percent of all criminal convictions are obtained through negotiations between the prosecution and the defense. The negotiation process through which the prosecution attempts to reach an agreement with the defendant is called "plea bargaining." The defendant voluntarily admits responsibility for the crime by entering a guilty plea, and, in turn, the prosecution agrees to reduce the number or severity of criminal charges pursued against the defendant or, alternatively, recommends that the judge impose a less-than-maximum sentence. Although the American public had little recognition of the existence of plea bargaining prior to the 1960's, historical studies show that such activities have taken place in American courts since the nineteenth century.

Plea Bargaining and the Law. Although the Sixth Amendment to the U.S. Constitution guarantees that people charged with serious crimes have a "right to a speedy and public trial by an impartial jury," there is no requirement that cases actually go to trial. The U.S. Supreme Court permits people to waive their constitutional rights as long as such waivers are undertaken knowingly and voluntarily. When criminal defendants enter guilty pleas, they are, in effect, waiving their right to a jury trial.

In several judicial decisions, the Supreme Court has endorsed and provided rules for plea bargaining. In particular, the Court has insisted that guilty pleas be entered voluntarily and that both prosecutors and defendants fulfill promises made during the bargaining process. Defendants, for example, will often gain a lighter sentence by pleading guilty and promising to testify against other individuals. If they do not testify, their plea agreement can be nullified. Prosecutors often promise to recommend a specific sentence, and they must keep their promises if those promises were a primary inducement to gain the guilty plea. The Supreme Court also permits prosecutors to pressure defendants during the plea negotiations by threatening severe charges or punishments if a guilty plea is not forthcoming.

The Plea-Bargaining Process. Plea bargaining may begin at any time after a defendant is arrested and may continue throughout the justice process. In fact, some plea agreements are even reached after the prosecution and defense have begun to present evidence in front of a jury. Some plea bargains involve actual negotiated exchanges between the prosecution and defense. For example, the prosecutor may agree to drop serious charges if the defendant will agree to plead guilty to one lesser charge. Alternatively, some plea bargaining involves the prosecutor and defense attorney in merely settling the facts of the case. Both lawyers may know, for example, that a certain judge always imposes specific sentences for first-degree burglary and "breaking and entering." Thus the plea-bargaining discussions involve reaching agreement on the provable facts in the case, to determine which crime the prosecutor is likely to be able to prove. The defendant will then plead guilty to whatever crime both sides agree can be proved. In this way the defendant gains certain knowledge about what the sentence will be and avoids uncertainty about which punishment is likely to be imposed after a trial.

Plea bargaining exists because it serves the interests of all parties involved in criminal cases. Prosecutors gain certain convictions without expending the resources required for trials. Defendants gain fewer charges as well as punishments that are less than the maximum possible. Defense attorneys have cases resolved so that they can move ahead to work on other cases. Judges gain efficiency in the quick processing of criminal cases that might otherwise absorb weeks of court time in trials.

Critics of plea bargaining claim that it is an illegitimate process that permits criminals to escape the harsh punishments that they deserve. Defenders of plea bargaining assert that such negotiations tend to give offenders precisely what they deserve by focusing on a determination of provable facts and also save significant time and money by keeping cases from going to trial. Some prosecutors and legislatures have attempted to abolish plea bargaining for specific charges, but most studies indicate that plea bargaining never disappears. Because the process serves the interests of all involved, it will

continue to occur informally whenever prosecutors and defense attorneys talk to one another at various stages of the justice process. Although many members of the public believe that the prevalence of plea bargaining is one of the worst flaws in the American justice system, most professionals who work in the courts view plea bargaining as a desirable and necessary process that permits the courts to conclude cases quickly and impose punishment efficiently.   — *Christopher E. Smith*

See also Arraignment; Counsel, right to; Criminal procedure; Defense attorney; Prosecutor, public; Public defender; *Santobello v. New York*; Sentencing.

BIBLIOGRAPHY

The ways in which lawyers and judges learn about plea bargaining are discussed in Milton Heumann, *Plea Bargaining* (Chicago: University of Chicago Press, 1978). Plea-bargaining strategies are examined in Douglas Maynard, *Inside Plea Bargaining* (New York: Plenum Press, 1984), and Lynn Mather, *Plea Bargaining or Trial?* (Lexington, Mass.: Lexington Books, 1979). Studies of plea bargaining in specific court contexts can be found in Peter F. Nardulli, James Eisenstein, and Roy B. Flemming, *The Tenor of Justice: Criminal Courts and the Guilty Plea Process* (Urbana: University of Illinois Press, 1988). Efforts to reform plea bargaining are discussed in Candace McCoy, *Politics and Plea Bargaining* (Philadelphia: University of Pennsylvania Press, 1993).

Plessy v. Ferguson

COURT: U.S. Supreme Court
DATE: Decided May 18, 1896
SIGNIFICANCE: In this case, the U.S. Supreme Court ruled that Louisiana's requirement of segregation on railroad passenger cars was constitutional; this ruling set the stage for the creation of the "separate but equal" policies that shaped U.S. race relations until the mid-1950's

Ultraconservative white Democrats in the Louisiana legislature approved the Separate Car Act in 1890, which required that railroads provide segregated seating accommodations for Caucasian and African American passengers. The railroads could provide either separate cars or separate sections of a car. Homer Plessy, an African American, deliberately violated the law in 1892 in order to test its constitutionality. Critics maintained that the measure violated the "equal protection of the law" guarantee of the Fourteenth Amendment to the United States Constitution.

The Supreme Court ruled in its hearing of Plessy's appeal that the Separate Car Act was a constitutional exercise of the state's power to promote the common good, peace, and order. The Court held that the Fourteenth Amendment "could not have been intended to abolish distinctions based upon color, or to enforce social . . . equality." The majority opinion approving Louisiana's required segregation formed the constitutional basis for the "separate but equal" doctrine that permeated American race relations for nearly sixty years: As long as accommodations for people of the two races were equal, then it was constitutional for them to be separate. Even though the ruling technically applied only to railroad passenger cars, the "separate but equal" doctrine allowed many states to impose "Jim Crow" laws upon their black citizens, segregating almost all aspects of public intermingling. The resulting segregated facilities were most often unequal, with those provided for the majority clearly superior to those provided for the minority.

Only Justice John M. Harlan dissented from the opinion of the other eight justices in the Plessy decision. His dissent established an interpretation of constitutional equality that would wait nearly sixty years before it became the guiding principle for American race relations: "[I]n view of the Constitution . . . there is in this country no superior, dominant, ruling class of citizens. . . . Our constitution is color-blind and neither knows nor tolerates classes among its citizens."

As this 1930's photograph of a school for black children shows, the separate facilities allowed for blacks and whites by Plessy v. Ferguson were rarely equal. (Library of Congress)

The Supreme Court began signaling during the late 1930's that it might be reconsidering the constitutionality of the "separate but equal" doctrine. Beginning with *Gaines v. Canada* in 1938 and including *Morgan v. Virginia* in 1946 and *Shelley v. Kraemer* in 1948, the court chipped away at the doctrine. It finally overturned "separate but equal" in the *Brown v. Board of Education* case in 1954. "Separate educational facilities are inherently unequal," the justices ruled unanimously. "Therefore, we hold that the plaintiffs . . . are, by reason of the segregation complained of, deprived of the equal protection of the law guaranteed by the Fourteenth Amendment." The influence of the *Plessy v. Ferguson* decision had ended at last.

See also *Brown v. Board of Education*; Jim Crow laws; Racial and ethnic discrimination; Segregation, *de facto* and *de jure*; *Shelley v. Kraemer*; *Sweatt v. Painter*.

Plyler v. Doe

COURT: U.S. Supreme Court
DATE: Decided June 15, 1982
SIGNIFICANCE: This case, which held that Texas' refusal to provide free public education to illegal aliens was unconstitutional, provided a basis for injunctions against implementation of laws seeking to deny certain public benefits to illegal aliens

In May of 1973, the Texas legislature amended its education laws to require that persons who were illegally in the United States and in the state of Texas pay a modest tuition charge for attending the public schools. In passing the amendments, the Texas legislature noted that the federal government denied the benefits of at least eight federal programs, including the food stamp program and Supplemental Security Income (SSI), to illegal aliens. According to the state, the purpose of the amendment was to "prevent undue depletion of its limited revenues available for education, and to preserve the fiscal integrity of the State's school-financing system against an ever-increasing flood of illegal aliens." It further claimed that it did not have the same responsibility to provide free benefits at taxpayer expense to those people illegally within the state as to its own citizens.

A bare majority of five Supreme Court Justices disagreed, on the grounds that a policy of charging illegal aliens a modest tuition fee was not a rational means of furthering the state's legitimate fiscal ends.

The majority conceded both that public education is not a fundamental right granted by the Constitution and that illegal aliens cannot be treated as a suspect class since they are in violation of federal law. The Court declined, however, to accept any suggestion that "illegal immigrants impose any significant burden" on the economy and therefore concluded that the policy, which provided free tuition to lawful citizens but declined free benefits to unlawful ones, failed to further a substantial state interest and therefore violated the equal protection clause of the Constitution.

The minority view, expressed by Chief Justice Warren Burger, argued that the legislative policy was clearly related to the legitimate state purposes of preserving the fiscal integrity of the state

school system and not placing the burden of educating foreign nationals illegally in the state on its own taxpaying citizens: "It is simply not 'irrational,' " Burger concluded, for a state to determine that "it does not have the same responsibility to provide benefits for persons whose very presence . . . is illegal as it does to provide for persons lawfully present." Noting that Congress itself had denied certain benefits to illegals, the dissent was of the view that "by definition, illegal aliens have no right whatever to be here, and the state may reasonably, and constitutionally, elect not to provide them with governmental service at the expense of those who are lawfully within the state."

This case was cited in an injunction against the implementation of Proposition 187, passed by the California electorate in 1994, which sought to deny certain benefits to illegal aliens in California. *Plyler v. Doe* has been a focal point in the debate over immigration policy and the problems in providing services to illegal immigrants. It should be noted that the Court in this case found only that Texas had failed to put forward sufficient evidence of the state's legitimate purpose in enacting the statute. This left open the possibility that future litigation on this issue may turn on the ability of a state to provide more complete evidence in the record of the state's objective and interest in such policies.

See also Illegal aliens; Immigration, legal and illegal; School law.

Police

DEFINITION: A modern law enforcement agency generally associated with urban areas
SIGNIFICANCE: The police force is the principal law enforcement agency in cities and towns around the world

The word "police" has its origin in the ancient Greek word *polis*, which the Greeks used for their form of city-state government. *Polis*, broadly associated with government, has a distinctly urban connotation; other words derived from the same root are "polity," "politics," and "policy." The concept of the police force has evolved substantially through the years but is still associated with the law enforcement agency that governs concentrations of people in villages, towns, and—particularly—large metropolitan areas. Nearly every municipality refers to its law enforcement agency as the police, whereas many counties refer to their law enforcement agency as the sheriff or sheriff's department.

The first law enforcement in the United States was provided by the "night watch" system, prevalent in the East until the early nineteenth century. The night watch usually was overseen by local businessmen, who took turns maintaining nightly guard duty at their stores. These "solid citizen" law enforcement figures gave a parochial cast to law enforcement that has survived until today. As villages grew into towns, the night watch was supplemented with a day patrol. Constables were added in some areas. In the South and West, the local law enforcement officer was usually the sheriff. Eventually, however, the need for round-the-clock law enforcement agencies became clear.

Modern patrol officers frequently patrol their assigned areas in automobiles equipped with a variety of communication and computer devices. (James L. Shaffer)

Modern police departments originated in Europe in the nineteenth century as people moved to the cities during the Industrial Revolution. Using the London police department as its model, New York City established a police department with eight hundred officers in 1844. It in turn became a model for other large American departments. Local police forces had become fairly common by the late nineteenth century; they were locally funded. Local tax revenues are still the biggest single source of support for municipal police departments. By the early twentieth century, police departments were an accepted part of most communities. Slowly the problems of the early years, such as corruption, incompetence, and lack of training, were being recognized and addressed. Today, municipal police maintain a broad role in the enforcement of federal, state, and local laws and the apprehension of all types of criminals.

In the years immediately after World War II, police training and roles expanded noticeably. In the 1950's, police became increasingly involved in enforcing traffic laws. Also, as cities and their suburbs expanded, foot patrolmen were replaced by police officers in patrol cars. Police could thus patrol larger areas, but the fact that they were in automobiles isolated them from the people they were protecting. This trend began to be reexamined in the 1980's, and many communities attempted to return to what has become known as "community-oriented policing," emphasizing foot and bicycle patrols.

Functions of Police Departments. The traditional jobs that Americans want their police departments to perform include preventing crime, preserving order or peace, protecting people and property, and protecting personal liberties. Patrolling designated areas (whether on foot or in automobiles), educating the public through crime-prevention programs, and working with others in the criminal justice system (such as the district attorney) have been the main approaches to achieving the first goal. Preserving public order involves activities ranging from crowd control to traffic control to responding to domestic violence complaints. Both the general public and most police officials view the police's most important task as protecting the well-being and property of law-abiding citizens. In order to accomplish this goal, the police enforce laws, apprehend violators, recover stolen property, investigate suspected criminal activities, and assist in the prosecution and conviction of violators.

A newer and in some ways simpler model has also been proposed for police departments. The new model holds that police should fill three basic roles: responding to citizens' complaints, providing services to the community, and arresting suspected criminals. Proponents of this model note that a significant number of calls to police involve not crimes per se but immediate needs for help in a wide variety of areas, as when a person's automobile is disabled or when parents discover drugs in the possession of their children.

Organization. The typical large American municipal police organization is quasi-military in nature. Officers are promoted to ranks such as sergeant, lieutenant, and captain; a rigid hierarchy is involved. On the plus side, this allows a tight organization and a clearly delineated chain of command; on the minus side, it does not allow much adaptability or flexibility. The chief of police is at the top of the chain of command, and below him are one or more deputy chiefs. Below them are commanders and precinct captains; below them are lieutenants, sergeants, and patrol officers. Each person in this struc-

ture should have no more than one supervisor. This policy is complicated by the fact that police departments operate twenty-four hours a day, so personnel frequently have different supervisors on different days and at different times. Organizational charts, rules, and manuals define the divisions of authority within the department.

The patrol officer, although low in the hierarchy, is in many ways the central figure in the police department's law enforcement efforts. Investigations are most often initiated by patrol officers. The duties of patrol officers comprise a wide range of activities, including patrolling assigned areas, responding to emergencies, investigating suspicious situations, issuing traffic citations, administering first aid to injured people, searching for stolen or lost property and missing persons, providing public information, and maintaining effective relationships with other law enforcement agencies and personnel.

A TYPICAL LARGE MUNICIPAL POLICE DEPARTMENT

Source: Adapted from Foster, Charles A., ed., *Introduction to the Administration of Justice.* New York: John Wiley & Sons, 1979.

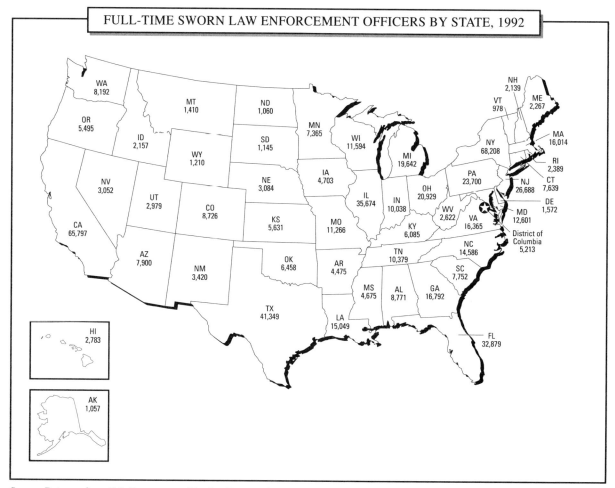

FULL-TIME SWORN LAW ENFORCEMENT OFFICERS BY STATE, 1992

Source: Data are from U.S. Department of Justice, Bureau of Justice Statistics, *Census of State and Local Law Enforcement Agencies, 1992* (bulletin NCJ-142972). Washington, D.C.: U.S. Government Printing Office, 1993.

Large police departments also have specialized officers to handle such matters as juvenile delinquency, vice and narcotics, traffic control, and plainclothes (detective) investigations. There are also support personnel who maintain records (which are crucial when criminal cases go to court) and maintain the department's communication system as well as its communications with other parts of the criminal justice system.

The Evolution of Modern Police Techniques. Before the development of identification techniques such as fingerprinting, police had to rely on eyewitness testimony or the help of informants. One method was to arrest petty criminals and give them partial immunity for their crimes if they would help law enforcement officials to locate other wrongdoers. These informants would provide information that would lead to the arrest of more serious criminals. The use of informants continues to this day. The identification of criminals took a great stride with the invention of fingerprinting, using a system developed by Francis Gaulton in Great Britain. Fingerprinting, now one of the most widespread methods of identifying crimi-

nals, has been supplemented by the analysis and classification of footprints, tire marks, bloodstains and other body tissues and fluids, and by the use of deoxyribonucleic acid (DNA) tests to identify the perpetrator of a crime.

Modern communication via radio, television, computer networks, and a whole range of satellite facilities has materially increased the ability of police agencies to communicate with one another and to receive reports of crime. For the apprehension of criminals and recovery of stolen property, modern techniques include the use of computers to track license plates, vehicle identification numbers (VINs), and serial numbers on stolen property, particularly firearms. The comparatively recent development of the 911 emergency calling system, which provides quick access to firefighting and emergency medical services, is said to be a deterrent to crime.

Training of Police. As the number and range of crimes grew along with U.S. cities, specialized training for police officers became increasingly imperative. Any large city today maintains its own academy for the training of police officers.

The Federal Bureau of Investigation (FBI) also plays an important support role for state and local police by providing national crime laboratories, extensive legal services, and specialized training. No longer can police forces maintain a simple "watchman" function or limit themselves to the apprehension of criminals. The role of the police in mediating domestic disputes, for example, has grown dramatically in the late twentieth century. Thus, police find themselves extending their training beyond mere law enforcement into the family-service area. The complexity of the legal and cultural environment in which police officers operate, and the resultant need for psychological and sociological training, has made sophisticated training of police mandatory.

Police Brutality and Corruption. Despite the growth of professionalism and the increased availability of training, major concerns remain about two related issues that erode professionalism: police brutality and corruption. Both these problems are related to the parochial origin of police in the United States. Police forces are generally funded by local taxpayers, who use the purse strings to maintain local control over the police. Local police, in turn, nearly always favor residents over outsiders, majority ethnic groups members over minorities, and the well-to-do over the poor. Outsiders, minorities, and poor people are the most likely targets for police brutality. Police corruption nearly always involves the differential application of law enforcement. Again, local well-to-do citizens are most likely to benefit from corruption by obtaining favorable treatment from the police. Local control of both city and county law enforcement continues to make these problems endemic. Attempts to combat corruption and brutality nearly always require the intervention of state or federal agencies.

—*Richard L. Wilson*

See also Arrest; Chief of police; Community-oriented policing; Criminal justice system; Deadly force, police use of; Discretion; Federal Bureau of Investigation (FBI); Forensic science and medicine; Police and guards, private; Police brutality; Police corruption and misconduct; Sheriff; State police.

BIBLIOGRAPHY

Robert M. Fogelson, *Big City Police* (Cambridge, Mass.: Harvard University Press, 1977), is a history of police reform in the United States. David R. Johnson, *American Law Enforcement: A History* (St. Louis: Forum Press, 1981), is an overview that includes discussion of the federal government's role in fighting crime. Roger G. Dunham and Geoffrey P. Alpert, eds., *Critical Issues in Policing: Contemporary Readings* (Prospect Heights, N.J.: Waveland, 1992), is a comprehensive collection of essays by a variety of specialists. A solid account of basic organization among various law enforcement agencies can be found in Robert H. Langworthy, *The Structure of Police Organizations* (New York: Praeger, 1986). The link between police behavior and public policy is made by Stuart A. Scheingold in *The Politics of Law and Order: Street Crime and Public Policy* (New York: Longman, 1984). A classic book on police behavior is James Q. Wilson's *Varieties of Police Behavior* (Cambridge, Mass.: Harvard University Press, 1968).

Police and guards, private

DEFINITION: Persons employed by individuals and organizations to provide protective services and to enforce organizational rules

SIGNIFICANCE: The high crime rate since the 1960's has helped spur the growth of the private security industry; measured by the amount of money spent on it, it is the United States' primary protective resource

Private security began as an eighteenth century practice whereby victims of street crime could recover their stolen property through the dubious offices of a "thief-taker." In the twentieth century it has grown into a vast industry that includes uniformed private security companies, loss prevention officers, private investigators, and protective services. The private security industry is estimated to employ 1.5 million people and to generate some $52 billion a year, 73 percent more than is spent on public law enforcement.

As demand for protection has grown, the private security industry has expanded to meet the needs left unfilled by civil police. Private security is provided either by direct hiring, known as "proprietary security," or by hiring specific services or equipment, known as "contract security." A typical security guard working for an established private security company such as Wells Fargo might engage in watch-clock tours (patrolling a building or area by making "rounds"), traffic control, fire prevention, access control, and property protection. Major transit centers, such as airports, also employ numerous security personnel who screen passengers and visitors for weapons, explosives, and other banned materials.

Private security services go far beyond uniformed guards and patrols, alarm services, and armored escorts; they include private investigations, security analysis, employee drug and honesty testing, evacuation planning, forensic analysis, crowd control management, loss prevention, risk management, and computer security planning. Private police and guards also investigate crimes against business, including white-collar crimes, copyright and trademark infringements, industrial espionage, fraud, and embezzlement.

Some large private security companies, as well as large corporations with established in-house security, provide extensive training for their personnel; others do not. There is no national regulation of the industry, but thirty-five states license private security firms, and thirty-seven license private detectives. In fifteen states, private security is regulated by the state police.

Many states authorize private security officers to make felony arrests when there is "reasonable cause" to believe that a crime has been committed; in such cases there is no obligation to inform arrestees of their rights. Private security personnel are generally prohibited from detaining suspects, however, or from searching persons or property without consent. There are exceptions to these latter rules in situations where security personnel are policing a specified area, such as a company plant, department store, or college campus. Roughly 80 percent of public police departments allow their officers to moonlight as private police, and about 20 percent of acting officers are estimated to do so. Retired police officers are a rich source of trained personnel for private security agencies.

On the other hand, the ambivalent relationship between crime and protection established by Britain's notorious eighteenth century "thief-taker general" Jonathan Wild—who employed thieves to steal the property he later recovered for a reward—continues to taint some of today's private security companies. Some companies employ personnel with questionable backgrounds, pay very low wages, and provide little training. The public image of the private security industry has not been helped by employers who use private police to spy on employees or break strikes. The latter practice was established in the nineteenth century by Allan Pinkerton, who could be called the United States' first private security officer.

See also Neighborhood watch programs; Pinkerton, Allan; Police; Vigilantism.

Police brutality

DEFINITION: The excessive use of force by those whose duty it is to use force if necessary to maintain law and order
SIGNIFICANCE: From the early 1960's into the early 1990's, the issue of police brutality repeatedly inflamed relations between the police and racial minorities

Police brutality includes the excessive use of force to compel a citizen to obey police orders or to arrest someone, the excessive use of force to compel an assembly of people to disperse, the physical maltreatment of someone who has already been taken into police custody (often for purposes of extracting a confession), and the use of deadly force against a fleeing suspect unless it is necessary to save the officer's own life or the lives of others.

Because of the stresses inherent in their work, some tendency toward brutality has probably always existed among police officers since the first police forces were established in the United States in the 1840's and 1850's. In the second half of the twentieth century, however, the changing racial makeup of large cities has made the American public (and that of some other countries) more sensitive to the problem than ever before. Although urban riots triggered by allegations of police brutality made headlines in the 1960's, 1980's, and early 1990's, a less-publicized peaceful struggle against police brutality has proceeded throughout the United States along several fronts: the push for civilian complaint review boards, civil suits and criminal prosecutions, Supreme Court decisions, and reforms within the police departments themselves.

Police Subculture and Police Brutality. To do their job, police officers must be able to use physical force as a last resort to compel obedience, and they inevitably must be granted a certain amount of leeway, or discretion, as to when such force is to be used. The decision to use force, although it can easily be second-guessed at leisure, often must be made with great speed, and it is often difficult to know exactly how much force is "excessive" in any particular instance. The main protection that police officers believe they possess is the respect and fear that others have of them; if they encounter signs of defiance or disrespect on the part of a citizen, they may feel

compelled to arrest the person—and to use force if the person resists. The possibility of death and maiming at the hands of criminals is a hazard of the job. The trust that police officers must place in one another in order to survive often produces an "us versus them" attitude of distrust of citizens. When the public at large demands that police crack down on crime at all costs, police officers are tempted to violate individual rights in order to get results. Moreover, police officers' need to make split-second decisions tempts them to stereotype citizens by age, sex, and race; hence, decisions regarding whom to stop and frisk and when to use force may seem to be made (and in fact sometimes are made) in a discriminatory manner.

Urban Racial Change and Police Brutality. From 1940 to 1990, the major cities of the northern and western United States, once overwhelmingly white, witnessed dramatic increases in their African American and Hispanic populations. Until the 1970's, however, the ranks of police officers consisted overwhelmingly of non-Hispanic whites. The tendency of big-city police officers, as time went on, to live in predominantly white suburbs further alienated them from many of those they policed, as did the replacement of foot patrols by two-person patrol cars. High unemployment among young urban blacks promoted petty crime and disorderly conduct, thereby making police-citizen confrontations more likely. The high physical identifiability of most African Americans, and the tendency of white Americans to stereotype them as potential criminals, made police brutality an issue with resonance for middle-class as well as poor blacks. In New York City, Chicago, Denver, and Los Angeles, complaints about police brutality frequently arose among Hispanics as well as blacks.

Although many controversial incidents of police use of force have elicited only peaceful protests, minority group anger over alleged police brutality has sometimes exploded into violence. Riots erupted in New York City in July, 1964 (after a police officer killed a black youth); in Los Angeles in 1965; in cities throughout the United States in 1967; in Miami in May, 1980 (after the police officers who had beaten to death a black motorcyclist were acquitted); in Miami again in January, 1989 (after a black motorcyclist was shot to death by a police officer); and in Los Angeles on April 29-May 1, 1992 (after the acquittal of police officers involved in the videotaped beating of black motorist Rodney King).

Police Brutality and Public Assembly. Excessive use of force against people demonstrating publicly for particular causes was a common complaint in the 1960's, a decade of unusual political ferment in the United States; even after that era ended, such incidents sometimes occurred. Examples include the use of police dogs against blacks demanding desegregation in southern cities in the early 1960's, the clubbing of youthful (and mostly white) demonstrators against the Vietnam War in Chicago in August, 1968, and the use, in 1989, of nunchakus (particularly painful restraint devices) against predominantly white antiabortion demonstrators in Los Angeles.

Civilian Police Review Boards. Handling citizen complaints about police brutality was the exclusive concern of

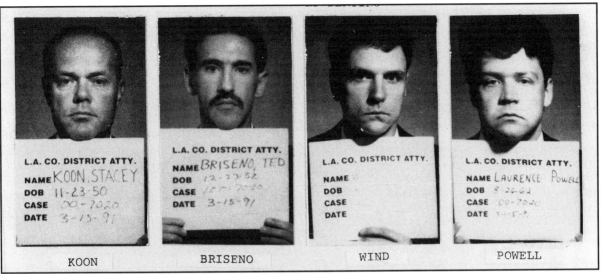

L.A. CO. DISTRICT ATTY.
NAME KOON, STACEY
DOB 11-23-50
CASE 00-7020
DATE 3-15-91

KOON

L.A. CO. DISTRICT ATTY.
NAME BRISENO, TED
DOB 12-23-52
CASE 00-7020
DATE 3-15-91

BRISENO

L.A. CO. DISTRICT ATTY.
NAME
DOB
CASE
DATE

WIND

L.A. CO. DISTRICT ATTY.
NAME LAURENCE POWELL
DOB 8-26-62
CASE 00-7020
DATE 3-15-9

POWELL

The four Los Angeles police officers indicted for brutality in the 1991 police beating of Rodney King. (AP/Wide World Photos)

police department internal affairs units until the late 1950's and early 1960's, when the American Civil Liberties Union joined minority civil rights activists in demanding the establishment of civilian review boards (bodies with at least half their members from outside the police department) to hear such complaints. A civilian review board was instituted in New York City in 1966 but was abolished after a referendum; it was not re-established until 1993. By 1990, about half of the fifty largest American cities had some form of civilian oversight over the police.

Police officers who opposed civilian review boards feared that such bodies would be dominated by militant antipolice activists; on the other hand, it was also argued that civilian arbiters would accept excuses for brutality that would never pass muster with professional police officers. By the early 1990's, scholarly advocates of civilian review boards, while conceding their imperfections, viewed them as a necessary (although inefficient) way to assure citizens that complaints of brutality would be treated fairly.

Fighting Police Brutality Through the Courts. Even though the beating of Rodney King by members of the Los Angeles Police Department on March 3, 1991, was recorded on videotape, the four officers who had beaten him were acquitted in their first jury trial, before a state court, on April 29, 1992. For a number of reasons, many police officers suspected of acts of brutality are never brought to trial at all. District attorneys, who need willing police cooperation to try cases, are usually reluctant to prosecute police; police officers are usually unwilling to testify against other officers; it is widely understood that jurors often sympathize with police officers; and victims of police brutality are not always entirely blameless individuals. One of the few cases in which a police officer was both prosecuted and convicted of brutality in a state criminal trial was that of New York City patrolman Thomas Ryan, sentenced in 1977 to four years in prison by a Bronx jury for beating Israel Rodriguez to death in 1975.

Another was the sentencing of two white Detroit police officers to stiff prison terms in 1993 for the 1992 death of a black man, Malice Green.

Police officers can also be tried on federal criminal charges of having violated the brutality victim's civil rights: In April, 1993, two of the four officers who had beaten Rodney King were convicted of such charges. In *Monroe v. Pape* (1961), the Supreme Court laid the basis for such legal action by holding that the Civil Rights Acts of 1871 (originally passed to protect African Americans in the South) applied to abuses of power by local police officers anywhere in the country. As of the early 1990's, however, federal trials of local police officers were rare. The Department of Justice lacked the personnel to check up on police abuses throughout the country.

Two milestones made civil suits a more effective means of obtaining redress: the Supreme Court decision (unconnected with police brutality) in *Monell v. New York City Department of Social Services* (1978), holding local governments financially liable for the transgressions of their employees, and a 1976 act of Congress permitting judges to award attorneys' fees to a plaintiff if the plaintiff wins the case. In April, 1994, Rodney King was awarded $3.8 million in damages from the city of Los Angeles; other American cities have also paid out considerable sums. Brutality lawsuits have the best chance of success when the victim has suffered obvious physical harm.

The Supreme Court and Police Brutality. In the decisions *Brown v. Mississippi* (1936) and *Rochin v. California* (1952), the Supreme Court voided criminal convictions based on confessions extracted by torture. Under Chief Justice Earl Warren (whose term lasted from 1953 to 1968), the Supreme Court increasingly imposed on state and local police forces the restrictions of the Bill of Rights, which had been formerly imposed only on federal authorities. In *Mapp v. Ohio* (1961), the Court ordered local police to obey the Fourth Amendment's ban on searches without warrant; in *Miranda v. Arizona*

(1966), it ordered the police to inform those in custody of their rights to remain silent and to have legal counsel. The Court provided no guidelines for disciplining erring officers; it only stated that evidence obtained through torture or illegal searches could not be used in a trial.

After Warren's retirement, the Supreme Court no longer led the way in the fight against police brutality. In *Rizzo v. Goode* (1976), the justices, in a 5-4 decision, declined to interfere in the operations of the Philadelphia police department, which had been accused of systematic brutality toward minorities. In *Lyons v. Los Angeles* (1982), the Court refused to outlaw the use of chokeholds by the Los Angeles Police Department. In two cases decided in 1984, the Court allowed certain exceptions to the rules established in *Mapp* and *Miranda*. In 1985, in *Tennessee v. Garner*, the justices decreed that the police should no longer automatically have the right to shoot at a fleeing felony suspect, but this doctrine had already been adopted by many local police departments before the Supreme Court ratified it.

Police Chiefs' Efforts at Reform. In the 1960's, critics of the police accused police chiefs of automatically defending any officer accused of brutality. During the 1970's and 1980's, however, chiefs of police in many American cities took measures to discipline officers guilty of brutality and to reduce the number of incidents in the future. Black and Hispanic police chiefs, becoming more common by the 1980's, made special efforts in this regard. In 1972, New York City police commissioner Patrick V. Murphy instituted strict new rules governing the use of deadly force; in 1985, New York City police commissioner Benjamin Ward punished officers who had used the stun gun against suspects in their custody. In 1990, Kansas City police chief Steven Bishop summarily dismissed officers who had severely beaten a suspect involved in a high-speed car chase. Police departments in Oakland, California, and Miami, Florida, aided by social scientists, instituted programs to teach officers how to defuse potentially violent police-citizen confrontations. Some departments brought back foot patrols to enable officers to get to know people in minority neighborhoods better. Even in Los Angeles, where real reform began only after the 1992 riot and the subsequent retirement of Chief Daryl Gates, widespread public outcry in the early 1980's ended the use of chokeholds.

Minority Recruitment and Police Brutality. Affirmative action has increased the percentage of minority officers in police departments and reduced somewhat the level of prejudice-motivated brutality, but it has not worked miracles. Minority police officers are sometimes guilty of brutality themselves. In 1994, in Detroit, Michigan, and Compton, California, black police officers were accused by Hispanic activists of brutality against Hispanics. The Miami police officer who shot to death a black motorcyclist in 1989 was Hispanic.

Progress in Controlling Brutality. Although considerable progress in decreasing police brutality was made in the 1980's, the Rodney King beating brought home the fact that brutality was still a problem in the 1990's. Three examples of events that engendered protests from 1994 and 1995 illustrate the continued existence of the problem. Protests arose in New York City in April, 1994, after a black man died in police custody; in Paterson, New Jersey, in February, 1995, after police shot a black teenager; and in Cincinnati, Ohio, in April, 1995, after a white police officer was videotaped beating an eighteen-year-old black youth.

In spite of such examples, however, many scholars see a general trend toward stricter regulation of the police use of force. They view the actions and attitudes (and what was described by an investigative commission as the "siege mentality") of the pre-1992 Los Angeles Police Department, for example, as an exception rather than the rule. Although in 1990 civil libertarians in Chicago accused the police of torturing alleged police-killer Andrew Wilson while he was in custody, torture of suspects by the police was almost certainly much less common by the mid-1990's than it had been in 1931, when the federally appointed Wickersham Commission found such "third-degree" tactics to be widespread. Between 1970 and 1984, shooting deaths of fleeing suspects, although not completely eliminated, decreased in number, and the once yawning gap in police shooting deaths between blacks and whites had appreciably narrowed. —*Paul D. Mageli*

See also Civilian review boards; Deadly force, police use of; King, Rodney, case and aftermath; *Mapp v. Ohio*; Miami riots; Race riots, twentieth century; Reasonable force; *Tennessee v. Garner*; Wickersham Commission.

BIBLIOGRAPHY

Jerry Bornstein's concise *Police Brutality: A National Debate* (Hillside, N.J.: Enslow, 1993), which relies heavily on newspaper and magazine sources, is suitable for the high-school-age reader; it contains synopses of a wide range of brutality incidents of the 1980's and early 1990's. Chapters 8, 9, and 11 of Samuel Walker's *The Police in America: An Introduction* (2d ed. New York: McGraw-Hill, 1992), which is suitable for college students, connects the brutality problem to the broader issues of police discretion, accountability, and police-minority group relations. The chapter endnotes include many sources for further study.

For the general reader, *Above the Law: Police and the Excessive Use of Force* (New York: Free Press, 1993), by Jerome H. Skolnick and James J. Fyfe, ably combines grand theory with down-to-earth examples and offers both historical and comparative perspectives (including insights from the British experience). The authors, a sociologist turned law professor and a police officer turned criminology professor, sharply criticize the pre-1992 Los Angeles Police Department, whose harsh policing style is thoroughly documented; they provide much less information on alleged instances of brutality in other cities. The book is particularly informative on brutality against antiwar and antiabortion activists. *The New Blue Line: Police Innovation in Six American Cities* (New York: Free Press, 1986), by Jerome H. Skolnick and David H. Bayley, is enlightening on efforts to curb police brutality in Houston, Texas, and Oakland, California. In the chapter on police discretion in *Taming the System: The Control of Discretion in Criminal Justice, 1950-*

1990 (New York: Oxford University Press, 1993), Samuel Walker provides a brief summary of two decades of effort to regulate the police use of deadly force.

Works written by onetime police chiefs can be as revealing about the dilemmas of police use of force as books written by scholars. Defensive and self-justifying, *Chief: My Life in the LAPD* (New York: Bantam, 1992), by Daryl Gates, exemplifies the "us versus them" mentality to which police officers are susceptible. Another retired police chief, Anthony V. Bouza, offers a more liberal viewpoint in *The Police Mystique: An Insider's Look at Cops, Crime, and the Criminal Justice System* (New York: Plenum Press, 1990).

Police corruption and misconduct

DEFINITION: Police corruption involves violation of department procedure or of civil or criminal law by members of a police force

SIGNIFICANCE: Police corruption endangers the society the police are entrusted to protect; it can hinder the apprehension and investigation of criminals, thus crippling the entire justice system's ability to function

Corruption undermines a police force's ability to perform its duties—namely, to protect its citizenry by enforcing and upholding civil and criminal law. The term "misconduct" is often applied to actions that violate the requirements of police behavior; misconduct ranges from the disregarding of department policy to the commission of criminal acts.

The International Association of Chiefs of Police defines police misconduct in terms of a continuum that is divided into three levels. The first level includes violation of police procedure as defined by the department's official policy, procedure, and review, including personal and professional conduct and procedural violations. The second level involves violations of criminal law. While actions designated as second-level infractions may overlap with the procedural policy violations covered by level one, level two extends to include activities that are prosecutable both inside and outside an officer's department. Examples include stealing at the scene of a crime, bribery, and other criminal activities. The third level is the illegal use of force. Improper use of force, such as police brutality, runs parallel to the other two categories but is listed separately because of the unique nature of the police department's legal monopoly on force. Illegal use of deadly force may render an officer liable to criminal homicide charges in addition to departmental discipline.

These definitional levels represent police misconduct in terms of the violation of formally written regulations, informal operating procedures, and guidelines that pertain to police and other public-service agencies and of criminal and civil laws. However, controversy surrounds the issue of defining and punishing misconduct. Such controversy results from differing views on the cause of misconduct; some see corrupt officers as atypical, while others suggest that corruption stems from the structure of law enforcement itself and that it is spread by succeeding generations of officers via group socialization.

Historical Trends. Police misconduct has been recorded by reports, commissions, committees, and the media throughout the history of American policing. The severity of wrongdoings has varied greatly from period to period. The trend of reform waves suggests that corruption rises to an intolerable level and then is combated by agents both inside and outside the police force. Tensions between reformers and those defending the status quo often result in a change in the upper-management level of police administration, the inception of well-publicized departmental reorganizations, or the removal of an entire administration from office.

Reform Movements. Reform movements increase public awareness of corruption within police forces and call for improvement in the organization of police forces and in the implementation of policing. The first reform wave in American policing came in the late nineteenth century. Organized crime was a powerful force in large cities. Several reports of police involvement in criminal activities caught the attention of the public and incited movements to restructure the police system.

In 1894, the Lexow Committee held hearings on charges of corruption in the New York City Police Department. The investigation revealed that patrolmen had intimidated and framed prospective witnesses, that commissioners had suspended a captain for speaking out against department wrongdoings, and that agents of Tammany Hall, an organization of New York City politicians, had bribed and removed certain witnesses who were under subpoena to testify in court. In the late 1890's, further indications of big-city police corruption became apparent. A Los Angeles police chief went into business with a prominent pimp to monopolize the city's prostitution business, and in New York City, a gunman was hired by a police lieutenant to assassinate a noted gambler.

The struggle between reformers and those in power centered on several issues. Political machines dominated big-city politics and provided services to their constituents. The police were used by these organizations to collect payoffs and perform other duties for political "bosses." In return, police officers were rewarded with career opportunities inside and outside their departments. The officers themselves were also generally cynical about everyday crimes. Many held the assumption that gambling, prostitution, and drinking were irrepressible instincts. Thus, they were leery of reformers who believed that these common ills could be eradicated.

In order to sever the connection between police and political machines, reformers worked to replace machine-employed police administrations with independently elected officers. Another reform objective was the centralization of big-city police, affording a system to establish corruption controls and a central administration powerful enough to enforce those controls. This centralization was achieved by delegating responsibilities to chiefs, commissioners, superintendents, and public-safety directors and by providing these officials with large staffs equipped to meet their assigned responsibilities. In addition, reformers pushed to lengthen the tenure of office for police chiefs in order to grant more stability and power to that office. Lastly, reformers moved to restructure departments; specialized squads were trained to control vice and deal with other issues previously delegated to ordinary patrol officers. Efforts were also made to build morale from within by upgrading the status of police personnel and by narrowing police jurisdiction, granting health, welfare, and other nonpolice functions to other public agencies.

Court precedents that sought to control police practices include the suggestion by a federal court in *Boyd v. United States* (1896) that evidence obtained by means that violated the Fourth Amendment should be judged inadmissible. This concept has been upheld by the U.S. Supreme Court. The Court applied it to federal cases in *Weeks v. United States* (1914) and to state proceedings in *Wolf v. Colorado* (1949).

Postwar Reform. Shortly after World War II, reports of scandals in police departments in major American cities prompted a second reform wave. The aims of this reform were similar to those of the previous movement: enhancing the power of police chiefs, employing specialized squads to deal with specific criminal actions, centralizing police agencies, and reorganizing departments along functional, rather than territorial, lines. In addition, reformers moved to streamline the administrative sector of the police force by minimizing the number of high-level officials who reported directly to police chiefs, worked to raise the standards of police officers by revising disciplinary standards and procedures, lobbied to create external review mechanisms, and began to use civilians to fulfill many of the departments' clerical duties.

Judges gained more control over police conduct in 1961 with the Supreme Court's ruling in *Mapp v. Ohio*. The ruling created the "exclusionary rule," which prohibited the use in court of evidence that was gained by illegal means. While previous court rulings had restricted the use of such evidence in court proceedings, the *Mapp* ruling established a means of enforcing such a dictum by declaring such actions to be in violation of a defendant's constitutional rights.

The late 1960's and early 1970's saw a third reform wave. Tensions between urban racial minorities and a primarily white police force erupted into open confrontations during this period. Other groups that saw law enforcement as symbolic of governmental repression also sought open conflict with police. The police themselves were frustrated with what they saw as a system that did not protect their interests, and many officers began to assert themselves more aggressively. This assertion often took the form of alliances and police unions that took a firmer stance toward elements of society that were perceived as hostile to the police.

Reports of corruption surfaced, fueling the tensions between the police and the citizenry. In 1970, New York police officers Frank Serpico and David Durk informed their department and the city's administration of widespread corruption, but the charges went unnoticed. The officers took their story to *The New York Times*, where it was verified and published. Public awareness prompted the appointment of a mayoral

committee to investigate the matter. At the committee's recommendation, the mayor created the Commission to Investigate Allegations of Police Corruption and the City's Anti-corruption Procedures, known as the Knapp Commission. As a result of the commission's uncovering of widespread corruption, New York police commissioner Howard Leary resigned. Governor Nelson Rockefeller then created the office of special prosecutor, designed to investigate and prosecute any present or former public servant who committed a corrupt act or dealt illegally with narcotics.

Civilian review mechanisms also became more common during this period. These organizations provided resources for communities of racial minorities who believed that they needed countervailing forces to balance police. Police unions and some political forces typically opposed these review organizations; as a result, many of these groups lasted only a short time. Other groups, however, did survive and proved themselves instrumental in reviewing police misconduct inquiries.

Handling Police Corruption. Disciplinary policy and procedures differ among police forces. Some departments handle all questions of police misconduct from within, except in the case of criminal prosecutions. Others use an independent review board created specifically to deal with issues of corruption. The Police Executive Research Forum's Model Policy Statement lists a variety of options for handling misconduct. The penalties suggested include verbal reprimands, letters of reprimand, imposition of additional duty, monetary fines, loss of vacation, transfer, suspension without pay, loss of promotion opportunity, orders to seek counseling, demotion, discharge, and criminal prosecution. The statement makes a distinction between violations of department rules and actions that violate civil and criminal laws.

Contemporary Corruption Issues. The rise of aggressive criminality among police officers poses a major threat to the criminal justice system. Foremost among such criminal activities is the sale of crack cocaine. While few in number, police officers involved in drug trafficking actively collaborate with—or compete against—the dealers that they have been hired to pursue. Los Angeles, New York, Washington, D.C., New Orleans, and Miami have particularly severe problems with criminal drug activity among their police forces. Studies of cases such as New York's "Dirty Thirty," Miami's "Miami River" case, and Washington, D.C.'s "Dirty Dozen" indicate that officers generally become corrupt in groups. These investigations suggest that policing widespread violence often requires that officers go beyond the law to do their jobs but that they risk harsh discipline for doing so. They must also bear the responsibility of life-or-death decisions. Analysts suggest that such stress creates the tendency for officers to be clannish and secretive and to maintain an antagonistic mentality. The temptation of cocaine money and the inefficiency of the legal system further frays the integrity of the officers who daily combat violent drug criminals.

Law enforcement agencies hope that community policing, which brings an officer in direct and daily contact with a single neighborhood, will create a sense of trust and accountability in local citizens while granting officers personal insight into the specific concerns of a given community. This approach has received bipartisan political support and has been endorsed by both police departments and the communities they serve. Community policing, however, depends upon the integrity of police forces to instill the necessary trust and respect among community members. Corruption involving drugs and the violent crimes associated with them can easily damage the effectiveness of such programs.   —H. C. Aubrey

See also Bribery; Civilian review boards; Commercialized vice; International Association of Chiefs of Police; Knapp Commission; Machine politics; Organized crime; Police.

BIBLIOGRAPHY

Discussions of police corruption and disciplinary tactics include Gilda Brancato and Elliot Polebaun's *The Rights of Police Officers* (New York: Avon Books, 1981); *Complaints Against the Police: The Trend to External Review*, edited by Andrew J. Goldsmith (Oxford, England: Oxford University Press, 1991); Herman Goldstein's *Police Corruption: A Perspective on Its Nature and Control* (Washington, D.C.: Police Foundation, 1975); V. A. Leonard and Harry W. More's *Police Organization and Management* (7th ed. Mineola, N.Y.: Foundation Press, 1987); James Mills's *The Underground Empire: Where Crime and Governments Embrace* (Garden City, N.Y.: Doubleday, Inc., 1986); Samuel Walker, *A Critical History of Police Reform: The Emergence of Professionalism* (Lexington, Mass.: Lexington Books, 1977); and Robert M. Fogelson's *Big-City Police* (Cambridge, Mass.: Harvard University Press, 1977). Insights on contemporary corruption and its effects on society are presented in "Why Good Cops Go Bad," by Tom Morganthau et al. (*Newsweek*, December 19, 1994).

Political campaign law

DEFINITION: A collection of laws that regulate the conduct of individuals seeking elected office

SIGNIFICANCE: The manner in which elections are conducted and regulated is an essential component of a country's commitment or antagonism to the principles of representation and universal suffrage

The very term "campaign" evokes images of pitched military battles in which various factions vie for the spoils of war. To some, the conduct of a modern political campaign in the United States is similar to a large military operation, with leaders developing strategies to vanquish political opponents on the field of battle.

In its formative years, the United States lacked cohesive political organizations to assist in large-scale campaigning for elected offices. It was not until after the Civil War that political campaigns became larger with the infusion of money from business interests. As money became more and more integral to seeking office, observers began to call for electoral reform. A central component of the move for reforming campaign practices in the United States was the fear that a small segment of the society would corrupt the system and breach certain central tenets of the American political system, that all persons are created equal and that the power of the government is derived from the consent of the governed.

Moves Toward Regulation. The first law to regulate political campaign was the 1883 Civil Service Act, which prohibited federal employees from being solicited for campaign contributions. The first attempts to force disclosure of campaign funding came during the reformist era of the early 1900's. In response to the Teapot Dome scandal of the Harding Administration, Congress passed the Federal Corrupt Practices Act of 1925, which established limits on general election spending and directed candidates to report spending made with their "knowledge and consent." The law's vague wording was an invitation for lawmakers to sidestep its enforcement provisions. Although successive presidents spoke of the need for strengthening campaign laws, it was not until the 1960's that lawmakers seriously began to consider revising and strengthening campaign laws.

Reforming the System. In a 1966 letter, President Lyndon Johnson described existing campaign laws as "more loophole than law." Following initiatives begun in the Kennedy Administration, Johnson proposed several campaign finance laws. Like many of his predecessors' bills, Johnson's legislation lingered and died in congressional committees. It was not until 1971 that significant reform proposals were seriously considered by both houses of Congress.

Landmark legislation in the area of political campaign law came in two pieces of legislation passed by Congress in 1971, the Federal Election Campaign Act (FECA) and the Revenue Act. Replacing the 1925 law, the FECA mandated full disclosure of campaign contributions and set monetary limits on campaign spending. The Revenue Act permitted taxpayers to contribute to a general election fund by checking a box on federal income-tax forms. The Revenue Act created the Presidential Election Campaign Fund to provide federal subsidies to candidates who meet specific campaign contribution levels from private donors. At the time, lawmakers saw a need to provide government funding of campaigns, since the FECA placed strict limits on a candidate's ability to raise money from donors or use his or her own funds to conduct campaigns.

Investigations of Richard Nixon's 1972 reelection campaign in the wake of the Watergate scandal brought renewed enthusiasm to establish laws to monitor campaign contributions. In 1974, Congress passed a reform proposal that placed a ceiling on campaign spending and created an independent Federal Election Commission to monitor candidates. Under intense public pressure, President Gerald R. Ford signed the Federal Election Campaign Act Amendments of 1974, after expressing reservations about the public financing of presidential elections. "The times demand this legislation," Ford said. To many observers, the most significant aspect of the 1974 law was the one-thousand-dollar limit placed on individual contributions for each primary, runoff, or general election. It also placed a cap of twenty-five thousand dollars per year on an individual's contribution to federal candidates.

While this did not directly affect the average voter, it did prohibit wealthy individuals from contributing large sums to federal candidates.

Immediately after the law took effect, its constitutionality was challenged by Senator James Buckley and others on the grounds that its spending limits placed restrictions on First Amendment free speech guarantees. In *Buckley v. Valeo* (1976), the U.S. Supreme Court held that provisions to limit individual contributions to candidates, public financing of presidential campaigns, and disclosure laws did not violate the Constitution. The Court concluded, however, that spending caps that limited the candidates' own funds did violate free speech guarantees, because "virtually every means of communicating ideas in today's society requires the expenditure of money."

In response, Congress passed the Federal Election Campaign Act Amendments of 1976 to integrate the *Buckley* decision into the existing law. The 1976 amendments provided the option for candidates to refuse public funding, thereby avoiding campaign limits. If candidates do accept public money, they must limit the use of their own money in the conduct of the campaign.

Contemporary Campaign Law. As federal elections rely increasingly on electronic communication to reach voters, observers point out that media access, along with money, has become a powerful force in elections. Since the 1970's, resources devoted to television advertising have grown rapidly. Critics of television's influence on campaigns have proposed regulating content of advertising, mandating free time for candidates, and limiting exposure for individual candidates. So-called equal time proposals have failed, however, in part because of the possible violations of free speech rights that were examined in the *Buckley* decision.

Congress has modified the laws passed in the 1970's to accommodate inflation as well as to limit the influence of political action committees (PACs). Individuals are now able to contribute two thousand dollars per election cycle, one thousand in the primary and one thousand in the general election. In addition, individuals may give up to five thousand dollars to PACs and twenty-five thousand dollars to national party committees. No individual may exceed twenty-five thousand dollars in total contributions in one calendar year. Candidates are required to disclose all contributions they receive to the Federal Election Commission. The candidate is required to disclose the names and the amounts of contributions of all individuals or groups that contribute to federal campaigns.

—*Lawrence Clark III*

See also *Buckley v. Valeo*; Civil service system; Political corruption.

BIBLIOGRAPHY:
Valuable sources detailing the quickly changing regulations of congressional and presidential campaigns are Suzanne M. Coil, *Campaign Financing: Politics and the Power of Money* (Brookfield, Conn.: Millbrook Press, 1994); Congressional Quarterly, *Congressional Campaign Finances: History, Facts, and Controversy* (Washington, D.C.: Congressional Quarterly Press, 1992); Herbert Alexander, *Financing Politics: Money,* *Elections, and Political Reform* (4th ed. Washington, D.C.: Congressional Quarterly Press, 1992); David B. Magleby and Candice J. Nelson, *The Money Chase: Congressional Campaign Finance Reform* (Washington, D.C.: Brookings Institution Press, 1990); Anthony Corrado, *Creative Campaigning: PACs and the Presidential Selection Process* (Boulder, Colo.: Westview Press, 1992).

Political corruption

DEFINITION: A general term for the abuse of office by public officials who exploit the public trust for private gain; the term is difficult to define precisely because of differences in the interpretation of ethical practices of public officials across time, cultures, and nations

SIGNIFICANCE: Ethical violations by elected and nonelected representatives erode the public's overall trust in public institutions and the political process

Political corruption is a worldwide phenomenon that has afflicted political systems since the earliest forms of government. As Lord Acton observed in 1887, "Power tends to corrupt and absolute power corrupts absolutely." Like their modern descendants, ancient systems of government in all parts of the world were afflicted with such problems as bribery, vote buying, influence peddling, illegal gift giving, and a host of other practices deemed unethical by twentieth century standards. Many observers have directly correlated the level of a nation's development with the level of political corruption. As political systems expand and gain authority over their citizens, the powers of elected representatives and bureaucracies generally expand, increasing the opportunities for individuals to use their offices to gain personal advantage.

America's European roots were extremely influential in colonial attitudes toward political corruption. The early colonists had seen first-hand the electoral corruption that plagued European monarchies since the Middle Ages. The poor and minority groups seeking independence from imperial control had long been denied a voice in government. The founders, drawing from the liberal traditions of writers such as English philosopher John Locke, set out to establish a government that would establish a contract between the people and its elected government. In theory, the people would possess certain inalienable rights, and the government would be established with the sole purpose of protecting these rights.

The colonists believed that political power was by its very nature likely to be used to restrict rather than to protect liberty. The unrestricted and undemocratic power of European monarchies had established a legacy of patronage that benefited large landowners and supporters of monarchical rule. According to the founders of the U.S. government, the roots of corruption lie in centralized nonrepresentative political entities composed of self-serving individuals. As the United States developed as an economic power during the nineteenth century, however, so did the size and influence of government. Rapid development after the Civil War, in particular, brought with it a rise in the level of political corruption.

The Grant Administration. The administration of Ulysses Grant is an example of how corruption in the United States had grown by 1869, when the Civil War hero was elected president. Grant's administration was by no means unique; since the nation's founding there have been numerous examples of wrongdoing in all branches and levels of U.S. government. In the atmosphere of the post-Civil War era it was possible for entrepreneurs such as Jay Gould and Jim Fisk to make millions simply by maneuvering financial markets in various ways. Sometimes their "luck" had more to do with political connections than with prognostication. Some commentators have labeled this period the age of "robber barons," a time when large financial interests used and abused democratic institutions and financial markets to make money.

While a number of political scandals tarnished Grant's administration, one episode stands out because of its impact on the public's perception of the political process and American justice. The scandal involved a group of midwestern distillers of whiskey who had been in collusion to cheat the U.S. government out of millions of dollars in taxes on whiskey and other liquors. The "whiskey ring" put millions into the pockets of the distillers and corrupt politicians who turned a blind eye to the practices in exchange for a portion of the stolen tax money. When the news first broke, Grant declared, "Let no man escape," and he pledged a full-scale investigation into the

The administration of President Ulysses S. Grant is often used as an example of political corruption at the highest level of government. (Library of Congress)

crimes. When he discovered that many federal officials, including his private secretary, were involved, however, he actively obstructed justice to salvage the reputations and careers of many of his political supporters and friends. The public was outraged. Yet in the end the only men to be prosecuted were low-level conspirators in the tax-fraud operation. A large segment of the public came to believe that the rich and powerful had escaped prosecution with the help of the highest official in the federal government, President Ulysses S. Grant.

Civil Service and Attempts at Reform. American politics in the nineteenth century was dominated by a system of political patronage dubbed the spoils system during the administration of Andrew Jackson. In practice the spoils system distributed government jobs and political favors on the basis of political affiliation rather than merit. For people elected to public office, the spoils of office were a powerful tool to generate and retain political support. The power of state and local political "machines" of the period flowed directly from the spoils system of government.

The most famous example of political machines of the period was controlled by William M. "Boss" Tweed, the leader of New York City's Democratic organization, Tammany Hall. Along with the mayor, comptroller, and city chamberlain, Tweed consolidated his power with the electorate not by proposing solutions to the growing problems of poverty and education but by distributing patronage jobs and city projects. As his ability to control the levers of the city government grew, his ability to profit personally through bribes and kickbacks grew as well. Tweed and Tammany Hall fell in 1871 after Tweed and many of his associates were implicated in the misappropriation of city funds. Tweed was indicted and eventually convicted.

The American public grew tired of the scandals associated with political machines in the late 1800's. The assassination of President James Garfield in 1881 by a frustrated job seeker highlighted the disadvantages of the allocation of government jobs to nonelected civil servants. The assassin, Charles Guiteau, had been turned down for a job in the Garfield Administration after his offer to work as a volunteer in Garfield's New York presidential campaign had been ignored. In response to the assassination and the abuses of the spoils system across the country, a reform-minded Congress enacted the Pendleton Civil Service Act of 1883 to reduce political patronage in the federal government. The law established the Civil Service Commission to conduct examinations for job seekers, forbade the practice of requiring political contributions from federal employees, and reduced direct political influence on civil servants in many areas of the federal government.

While patronage remained in state and municipal governments, successive administrations expanded the scope of the law to include most federal workers. As civil servants became more isolated from political influence, presidents began to complain that the distance between the bureaucracy and elected political leaders made the civil servants much less responsive to the needs of elected politicians and the public. Despite these criticisms, efforts to reform the civil service structure were not reversed. In a number of decisions the Supreme Court ruled against patronage practices in the hiring and firing of public employees except when political affiliation can be proven to be an essential requirement for the position. The 1978 Civil Service Reform Act expanded protection for civil service jobs and replaced the Civil Service Commission with the Office of Personnel Management.

In the 1940's, lawmakers further isolated civil servants from political influence when they passed legislation to prohibit federal employees from overtly engaging in partisan politics. The 1939 Hatch Act, sponsored by New Mexico Senator Carl Hatch, prohibited executive branch employees from using their "official authority and influence" to interfere in the results of elections and from taking "an active part in political management or in political campaigns." An amendment enacted in 1940 expanded the law to prohibit campaign contributions from federal employees and extended the act to cover state and city employees in departments receiving federal funds. An attempt to weaken the Hatch Act was successfully vetoed by President Gerald Ford in 1976.

Problems of Enforcement. As the electorate began to scrutinize the ethics of public officials more closely in response to the corruption of the late 1800's, unethical practices became increasingly covert. The Teapot Dome scandal involving President Warren G. Harding's secretary of the interior further eroded the public's confidence in elected politicians. The secretary of the interior, Albert B. Fall, was convicted in 1929 of receiving $385,000 in bribes from oil companies in exchange for leases of government oil fields and became the first cabinet official in U.S. history to receive a prison term for ethical improprieties in office. So-called muckraking newspaper and magazine stories further detailed unethical politicians and aided reformers in gaining support for additional legislation to curb corruption.

As the public began to be less tolerant of open attempts to profit from public office, some observers began to notice a subtle change in the nature of political corruption. With less leverage over civil service jobs, politicians came increasingly to count on campaign funds rather than patronage jobs to draw support from the electorate. Politicians were becoming less dependent on political machines and more reliant upon the corporate and private supporters who possessed resources needed to run effective political campaigns. Reformers began to lobby for a new law that would directly address campaign funding of federal officials.

The 1925 Federal Corrupt Practices Act required presidential and congressional candidates to provide details of campaign spending and contributions. The language of the act was so general, however, that presidential and congressional candidates had little trouble finding loopholes to exceed the contribution limits outlined in the law. In a system of government that rewards individualism and material success, it proved difficult to devise enforcement bodies to curb corruption effectively without violating the rights of individuals to engage in the political process.

Watergate. The most important political corruption scandal of the modern era began as a plot by members of the Richard M. Nixon Administration to influence the 1972 presidential election through illegal means. In the end the Watergate affair became a constitutional crisis that removed a president from office and forced the nation to face unethical conduct in the highest office in the land. The scandal eventually included the administration's involvement in political espionage, campaign violations, illegal break-ins of the offices of political opponents, improper use of the Internal Revenue Service and the Central Intelligence Agency, and a conspiracy to obstruct justice. Many Americans were astounded at the extent of the involvement of high-level officials who abused the highest offices in the federal government to advance their political fortunes.

The Watergate scandal began on the night of June 17, 1972, when five men with surveillance equipment were arrested inside the Democratic Party's national headquarters. The men were eventually connected with two officials associated with the Republican Committee to Re-elect the President ("CREEP"). Even after the five burglars and the two officials were convicted in January of 1973, administration officials denied any White House connection with the affair. Soon after, one of the burglars alleged that former attorney general John Mitchell was involved in the conspiracy to break into the Democratic headquarters. The growing scandal forced the resignation of Nixon's chief of staff H. R. Haldeman, chief presidential adviser John D. Ehrlichman, and White House counsel John Dean, who began cooperating with government investigators.

The White House also denied allegations of unethical campaign practices during the 1972 presidential campaign. Allegations included wiretapping of political opponents' offices, circulating false information, harassing speakers, and using prostitutes to discredit delegates to the Democratic national convention. In May of 1973, the Senate began televised hearings into these allegations. John Dean testified that high-level White House officials knew of the plans for the break-in and that Nixon himself had participated in a conspiracy to obstruct the investigation of ethical violations. Special Prosecutor Archibald Cox, appointed by Attorney General Elliot Richardson, uncovered further damaging evidence as well as the existence of a secret taping system inside the White House. When Cox attempted to obtain the tapes, Nixon cited executive privilege and ignored a subpoena to turn them over. When Cox sought further legal means to obtain the tapes, Nixon fired him in October of 1973. Attorney General Richardson resigned in protest. Nixon's political problems were exacerbated when his vice president, Spiro Agnew, was forced to resign in October after being indicted on charges of income tax evasion (he later pleaded no contest to the charges).

After the firing of Cox, the president appointed a new special prosecutor and released edited versions of the tapes. An increasingly cynical public and press put little faith in Nixon's denials and began to talk openly of the need to impeach the president. The House of Representatives Judiciary Committee conducted dramatic hearings in July, 1974. In the end, the committee voted for three articles of impeachment against Nixon for obstruction of justice, abuse of power, and defiance of congressional subpoenas. With pressure building from Republican leaders, Richard Nixon announced on August 8, 1974, that he would resign from the presidency. Nixon was succeeded by Gerald R. Ford, who granted him an unconditional pardon for all federal crimes he "may have committed or taken part in."

Post-Watergate Reforms and Altered Perspectives. In a response to the loss of public confidence in government over its conduct of the Vietnam War, the Congress enacted legislation in 1972 to require candidates and political committees to provide financial information and close loopholes that existed in the 1925 Federal Corrupt Practices Act. By requiring more detailed disclosure and enforcement mechanisms, the Federal Election Campaign Act of 1972 sought to bring campaign financing under the scrutiny of federal officials and the public at large. In the early 1970's, widespread support for public financing of presidential campaigns forced Congress to address that issue. The Revenue Act of 1971 provided tax credits for political contributions and gave taxpayers the opportunity to provide one dollar from their tax returns to finance presidential campaigns. In the post-Watergate period Congress also moved to place limits on campaign spending and limited personal contributions to campaigns. In 1976, however, the Supreme Court ruled that certain rules limiting the amount of money a candidate could spend on a campaign violated free speech rights and struck down the provisions.

In the post-Watergate era, any scent of impropriety by elected officials was actively investigated by journalists. A cynical public came to expect their elected officials to meet strict ethical standards, both in their work and in their private lives. Distinguishing "scandal" (damage to a person's reputation) from political corruption became more difficult in the aftermath of Watergate. While some commentators conclude that corruption and scandal proliferate in government as never before, others point out that stricter regulation and the general public's fascination with media-driven scandals magnify corruption that in the past would have been considered typical behavior if it was even reported at all.

The accusation of corruption has become a frequently used tool in the battle for political power. Many politicians do not hesitate to level charges of ethical indiscretions at their opponents. The willingness of the two major political parties to charge each other with corrupt practices invites the minority party to defeat opponents not by offering alternatives to failed policies but rather by uncovering misdeeds. While some charges later prove to contain merit, the personal attacks tend to fuel public cynicism about elected politicians and government as a whole. —*Lawrence Clark III*

See also Color of law; Long, Huey; Machine politics; Police corruption and misconduct; Political campaign law; Spoils system and patronage; Teapot Dome scandal; Watergate scandal.

BIBLIOGRAPHY

For a survey of political scandals, see Barbara S. Feinberg's *American Political Scandals: Past and Present* (New York:

Franklin Watts, 1992) and Nathan Miller's *Stealing from America: A History of Corruption from Jamestown to Reagan* (New York: Paragon House, 1992). A detailed examination of popular scandal and political corruption can be found in George C. Kohn's *Encyclopedia of American Scandal* (New York: Facts on File, 1989). For an overview of political corruption and how past scandals have influenced American political culture, see Suzanne Garment's *Scandal: The Crisis of Mistrust in American Politics* (New York: New York Times Books, 1991). For a study of the efforts of individuals to expose ethical violations in the government and the private sector, see Myron P. Glazer and Penina M. Glazer's *The Whistleblowers: Exposing Corruption in Government and Industry* (New York: Basic Books, 1989). For a unique view of corruption and organized crime, see William J. Chambliss' *On the Take: From Petty Crooks to Presidents* (2d ed. Bloomington: Indiana University Press, 1988). For an overview of the Watergate scandal, see United States, Watergate Special Prosecution Force, *Watergate Special Prosecution Force Report* (Washington, D.C.: U.S. Government Printing Office, 1975). An excellent examination of the role of "soft money" on national politics can be found in Brooks Jackson's *Honest Graft: Big Money and the American Political Process* (New York: Alfred A. Knopf, 1988). For the decline in the public's confidence in public officials as well as the connection of lobbyists and pressure groups with political corruption, see Kevin Phillips' *Arrogant Capital: Washington, Wall Street, and the Frustration of American Politics* (Boston: Little, Brown, 1994).

Poll tax

DEFINITION: A tax which must be paid as a qualification for voting

SIGNIFICANCE: Poll taxes were used by southern states to restrict the voting rights of blacks as well as many poor white southerners

Poll taxes originated after the American Revolution in order to expand, not restrict, the electorate. Since only white, male, property holders could vote in the post-revolutionary period, the poll tax payment became a substitute for property requirements. It was not until after the Civil War that southern states used the poll tax to restrict the electorate. Florida was the first state to adopt a poll tax, in 1889, and other southern states quickly followed.

Most states imposed a tax of between one and two dollars, and the tax was cumulative. A person had to pay the tax every year, not only the year the person wanted to vote. In Alabama the tax could accumulate for twenty-four years. Many states gave exemptions for the aged and disabled and for veterans. The veterans' exemption angered many women, once women gained the vote, as women were prohibited by law from serving in the military and therefore had to pay the tax. As a result, many women led the opposition to the poll tax.

Another unique feature of the poll tax was that the tax frequently had to be paid six months to a year before the election. If one forgot to pay, one could not vote. Most states also required people to keep poll tax receipts. Those blacks and poor whites who could pay the tax had to retain receipts for several years to prove they had paid it.

Poll taxes successfully eliminated most black voters and many whites as well. The taxes also led to political corruption, as candidates, political organizations, and interest groups would pay the taxes of their supporters even though this was illegal. The corrupting influence of the poll tax led a number of states to seek its repeal.

Many national organizations, including the National Association for the Advancement of Colored People (NAACP) and the National Committee to Abolish the Poll Tax, sought to eliminate the tax. One approach was the attempt to get Congress to ban poll taxes in federal elections. On five occasions the House of Representatives passed legislation to repeal the poll tax, and each time it was killed by southern-led filibusters in the Senate.

Another approach to banning the poll tax was by constitutional amendment. In 1964, the Twenty-fourth Amendment was adopted, which banned poll taxes in federal elections. Poll taxes were still permitted in state and local elections until 1966, when the U.S. Supreme Court ruled that poll taxes violated the equal protection clause of the Fourteenth Amendment in *Harper v. Virginia Board of Elections*.

See also *Harper v. Virginia Board of Elections*; Racial and ethnic discrimination; Taxation and justice; Vote, right to.

Polygamy

DEFINITION: The marriage of a person to more than one spouse
SIGNIFICANCE: In the United States, polygamy has been a legal, religious, social, and moral issue

Polygamy is a very broad term and will be narrowed here for ease of discussion. Polygamy can be divided into two distinct categories: a man having more than one spouse, and a woman having more than one spouse. The first case, a much more common practice, is called polygyny; the second is called polyandry. In general discourse the term polygamy is used interchangeably with polygyny. Historically, where polygyny has been allowed, the vast majority of men were monogamous, having only one wife, either because of the shortage of marriageable women or because only the well-off man could afford to provide for more than one wife.

In the United States, the issue of polygamy is primarily linked with the history of the Church of Jesus Christ of Latter-Day Saints (the Mormon church). The practice of polygamy, integral to the early Mormon church, caused considerable animosity and even violence to be directed at the church in the nineteenth century. The first antibigamy act in the United States was passed in 1862. In 1879, the constitutionality of bigamy laws was challenged under the First Amendment in *Reynolds v. United States*, a test case brought by Mormons in Utah (then a territory). In this case the Supreme Court limited the free exercise of religion, at least where multiple spouses are concerned. The Court held that, although freedom of religious thought is constitutionally protected, religious practices (such as church-sanctioned polygamy) are not necessarily protected if they go against the public interest.

The Edmunds Act of 1882 formalized tough penalties for polygamy. Eight years later (as upheld in *Church of Jesus Christ of Latter-Day Saints v. United States*), the corporate charter of Utah was revoked over the issue of polygamy; its property was ruled to be forfeit to the U.S. government. The Court declared that polygamy was "contrary to the spirit of Christianity." That same year Mormon prophet Wilford Woodruff published the 1890 Manifesto, which ended the church-sanctioned disobedience. On January 4, 1893, President Benjamin Harrison granted amnesty to all Mormons who moved into compliance with the law after the Manifesto was published. Polygamy and its attendant controversy persisted into the twentieth century, however; in 1946, in *Cleveland v. United States*, the Supreme Court called on the Mann Act in upholding a conviction of Mormons who were living in a polygamous marriage of transporting women across state lines for purposes of "debauchery."

See also Adultery; Mann Act; Religion, free exercise of; *Reynolds v. United States*.

Polygraph

DEFINITION: Literally, "multiple graphs"; a "physiograph" that monitors physiological changes
SIGNIFICANCE: Law enforcement agents and attorneys sometimes use physiographs as "lie detectors"

For the purpose of "lie detection," physiographs are generally set up to measure four things: blood flow, breathing, heart rate, and skin conductance (a measure of sweating). All these functions are controlled by a person's autonomic nervous system and are generally not under conscious control. Part of the autonomic nervous system is activated during times of emotion. Thus, during a lie detection test, a person is put into what is assumed to be a nonemotional setting and asked questions related to a crime; it is assumed that a person who has "guilty knowledge" and knows the correct answers but lies will experience fluctuations in nervous system activity which can be read on the chart.

Polygraphs do work better than chance; however, there are three major problems with their use. First, they implicate innocent people as guilty ("false positives") much more often than they indicate that guilty people are innocent ("false negatives"), because innocent people often feel anxious and frightened during the test. Second, people who are pathological liars do not experience guilt or anxiety during the test, and therefore the worst criminals are the ones who are most likely to "beat the system." Third, it takes substantial training to administer the test properly and interpret the results; very often, zealous interrogators do not follow the proper protocols.

See also Evidence, rules of; Forensic science and medicine; Perjury.

Poor People's March on Washington

DATE: May-June, 1968
PLACE: Washington, D.C.
SIGNIFICANCE: Martin Luther King, Jr.'s Poor People's Campaign, carried out after King's death, was a major mass-

Polygraph testing involves a number of problems, including the occasional implication of innocent people who feel nervous or frightened while taking the test. (James L. Shaffer)

Resurrection City being constructed on the Mall in Washington, D.C. (Library of Congress)

participation event designed to dramatize to the nation and the government the plight of the poor

By 1967, Martin Luther King, Jr., had come to see the Vietnam War and the War on Poverty as inseparable issues: The war overseas was taking needed money and government attention away from the more important goal of ending poverty in the United States. The Poor People's Campaign was designed to demonstrate the problem of poverty vividly and graphically by bringing thousands of poor Americans to Washington, D.C., to camp and lobby.

Organizing for this massive march on Washington was interrupted while King went to Memphis in support of a sanitation workers' strike. While there, he was assassinated, the event stunning the movement and the nation. The Southern Christian Leadership Conference (SCLC), now led by Ralph Abernathy, decided to carry out King's Poor People's March in his honor and memory. From all parts of the nation, thousands of poor people of all races set out for Washington, arriving five weeks after King's death. They built Resurrection City, a campground-city, on the Washington Mall.

In the few weeks of its existence, Resurrection City provided "freedom schools" and free food and medical care for its poor residents. Demands were made on the government through such actions as marching to the Department of Agriculture and demanding an end to American hunger in a land of such plenty. Jesse Jackson, a long-time member of the SCLC and King associate, came into prominence, leading marches and giving speeches. Running a city sapped all the energy from the SCLC, however; the group had no time to plan other actions and no clear agenda. Then it began to rain. The rain and mud made life in Resurrection City miserable, and the protesters soon had to abandon the project.

A few government actions can be attributed to the Poor People's Campaign—provision of food to some of the country's neediest counties, some funding for low-income housing, and additional funds for the Office of Economic Opportunity—but, in general, the campaign had only very limited success.

See also Civil Rights movement; Jackson, Jesse; King, Martin Luther, Jr.; Southern Christian Leadership Conference (SCLC); Student Nonviolent Coordinating Committee (SNCC).

Populism

DEFINITION: A third-party movement of the 1890's, consisting of farmers, miners, and small businessmen, that urged economic reform

SIGNIFICANCE: Although the Populist movement faded quickly after William Jennings Bryan's defeat in 1896, the legacy of Populism is said by some to include the direct election of Senators and the Federal Reserve system

The Populist movement evolved from the Grange and the National Farmers' Alliance groups (which all had variations of the name National Farmers' Alliance) that originated in 1877 in New York, although some historians argue that an earlier association from Kansas was the true forerunner of the Populists. By the 1880's, various farm organizations had organized in several midwestern states for the purpose of addressing the perceived monopoly powers of the railroads, grain elevators, and other businesses. In the early 1890's, those numerous organizations coalesced into the People's Party. That party held organizational meetings throughout 1891 and planned to run candidates in 1892. In the elections of 1892, most of the other bodies started to abandon their own names for the People's Party or, after October, 1892, the Populist Party.

In its mature form, Populism focused on two major issues: government control of the railroads and "cheap money," especially the famous "free silver" movement. Farmers who made up the first wave of Populists were more concerned about railroad rates and grain elevator charges, while the miners who joined the movement later emphasized inflation as a social remedy to falling prices that hurt workingmen.

Farmers had settled the West, and the farm areas depended on railroads to get their crops to market. In some cases, the farmers had to store their grain in silos, or elevators, near the train route, until a train arrived. In many cases only one railroad served a geographic area, and most farmers resented these monopolies. Freight rate increases in the 1880's combined with generally falling agricultural prices to cause greater anxiety. Wheat prices, for example, dropped steadily from the late 1870's to the mid-1890's. Farm mortgages, on the other hand, generally had long, fixed terms that left farmers vulnerable to falling prices. By the late 1800's, the Populists argued that the farmers' position had declined so much that market forces no longer would protect them; they demanded that government directly intervene to protect farmers and agricultural prices.

Falling prices constituted the other major concern of the Populists. A deflationary wave hit the United States in the late 1870's, and although the U.S. Treasury had attempted to contract the money supply to return to gold redemption for greenbacks, it is likely that world forces fed the deflation. Nevertheless, farmers and common laborers chafed at the "tight money" policies, and sought ways to get easier credit and "loose money." Several plans were offered, including a program to reissue greenbacks. The most popular from the 1870's on was to convert the United States to a bimetallic (gold and silver) standard.

Populist concepts of social justice played into the silver and the railroad issues. "Big business" supported a tight money standard, which favored creditors. That same big business owned the railroads that charged—in the minds of the Populists—usurious rates. Thus, the movement became infused with a paranoia of eastern business, specifically New York bankers. Ultimately, the election of 1896, which pitted William Jennings Bryan of Nebraska (a Democrat who was supported by the Populists for his free silver position) against Republican William McKinley, who favored a gold standard, resulted in Bryan's defeat and, in essence, that of the Populists as well. The party faded away not long after. Some writers, such as John Hicks, have attributed political reforms such as direct election of senators to the Populist influence. On other

issues, such as the "loose money" policy, some have viewed the creation of the Federal Reserve system in 1913 as a legacy of Populism.

See also Bryan, William Jennings.

Positive law

DEFINITION: The command, or law, of a recognized political authority

SIGNIFICANCE: Those who stress the concept of positive law, as differentiated from such ideas as natural law and higher law, argue that law should be enforced and obeyed, irrespective of whether it is just

One feature common to all types of law is that laws are enacted by a recognized political authority, whether it be a legislature, a court, or an administrative agency. This common feature is known as legal positivism, or positive law. Legal positivists generally define law as the command of a political authority. The seventeenth century British political philosopher, Thomas Hobbes, said, "Law properly, is the word of him, that by right hath command over others."

Law is basically a command. This fact has bearing on the relationship between law and morality. The commands made by recognized political authorities may be good, bad, or indifferent. To legal positivists, such commands are valid law, irrespective of their goodness or badness. In other words, legal validity and moral validity are different questions. Sometimes this view is expressed: "Law is law, just or not." For this reason, some positivists say that every validly enacted positive law should be enforced and obeyed, whether it is just or not. Some positivists adopt a more general definition of law by defining it as the command of society's ultimate political authority, or sovereign. In this view, different kinds of positive law are valid because the sovereign has delegated some of its ultimate lawmaking power to various subordinates, such as the courts.

Both these definitions dovetail with the general positivist position that law and morality are separate and distinct things. Yet the positivist may insist that the validity of law is distinct from the question of its moral rightness even while adhering to some system of moral values. The positivist does not suggest that the law is not subject to moral condemnations if it deserves to be condemned, but the positivist does say that positive law is concerned with what the law is and not with what the law ought to be. Positive law also does not deny that rational arguments may be applied to moral evaluation of the law. In examining such arguments it prefers to concentrate on the study of values that are inherent in a particular civilization and on exploring how these may best be realized in present conditions rather than to postulate absolute and unprovable values. The positivist believes that a clearer understanding of human social problems can be attained by keeping questions of legal validity and moral worth separate and distinct.

The concept of positive law may be contrasted with the concept of natural law, which holds that certain rules or commands are universally true because they come from nature. Historically, positive law was a reaction against this older tradition, and it rooted law in the command of the sovereign, not in an understanding of what is right or just by nature.

See also Civil disobedience; Jurisprudence; Justice; Law; Natural law and natural rights.

Posse comitatus

DEFINITION: A group of people pressed into service to aid civilian officials in enforcing the law

SIGNIFICANCE: The *posse comitatus* concept requires able-bodied adults to assist civilian law enforcement when requested to do so; the Posse Comitatus Act restricts military involvement in the posse

Posse comitatus means "the entire power of the county" from which the sheriff can draw able-bodied adults to help quell civil disturbances. The name derives from ancient Roman times, when traveling government officials were accompanied by their retainers, a practice known as *comitatus*. The *posse comitatus* can be traced to the *jurata ad arma* of the feudal kings of England, whereby all freemen over fifteen years of age were required to own weapons and to be available for the king's defense. Eventually this civilian force became known as the *posse comitatus*, or simply posse.

The issue of who should be allowed to be in a posse has long been scrutinized. Except in extreme circumstances, the *posse comitatus* is composed of civilians under a civilian authority. In English tradition, this separation of civil from military law enforcement can be traced to the signing of the Magna Carta (1215). In the United States, the Posse Comitatus Act (1878) stated that military personnel were not to be included in posses.

Passed in response to the defeated Confederacy's complaint that federal troops were being used to enforce civilian laws, the Posse Comitatus Act instituted the separation between civilian forces under a civil control from martial forces under military control and proscribed the use of the military to quell civilian disturbances. Although the Navy and Marines are not specifically governed by the act, those branches of the military adhere to the act's prohibitions as a matter of policy. The air force was included in later amendments.

The 1981 amendments to the act eroded its stand against the involvement of the military in law enforcement. These amendments, enacted in response to the increased power of drug smugglers, whose organizations and equipment rivaled those of some countries' military forces, delineated the military's role in civil law enforcement. In theory, the separation between civil and military law enforcement is still intact, but the 1981 amendments allow the military to supply civilian law enforcement authorities with equipment, information, and facilities. They do not allow direct involvement of military personnel in civilian law enforcement.

The familiar posse of the American frontier was used to apprehend felons. Members of the community were deputized by the sheriff or marshal to chase rustlers and others who had violated a breach of the peace. Sometimes the formation of the posse led to abuses and vigilantism under the color of law, including abuses by groups such as the Ku Klux Klan.

In more recent times, the name Posse Comitatus was taken by an antitax vigilante group. This Posse Comitatus, a militant, armed survivalist group founded in the 1960's, believes in a reading of the United States Constitution to exclude any amendments beyond the first ten.

See also Color of law; Constitutional law; Frontier, the; National Guard; Sheriff; Vigilantism.

Pound, Roscoe (Oct. 27, 1870, Lincoln, Nebr.—July 1, 1964, Cambridge, Mass.)

IDENTIFICATION: American jurist and educator

SIGNIFICANCE: A distinguished legal philosopher and a prolific writer, Pound's major contribution was his development and advocacy of "sociological jurisprudence"

After studying law at Harvard University, Roscoe Pound practiced law in Nebraska and taught at the state university while directing the state botanical survey. After serving as commissioner on uniform state law for Nebraska (1904-1907), he taught at several law schools, joining the Harvard faculty in 1910 and serving as dean of the law school from 1916 to 1936. After World War II he helped organize the judicial system of Taiwan. His influential legal perspective, "sociological jurisprudence," emphasized that law should recognize the "social interests" of humanity and should attempt to deal with contemporary social issues. Thus, his theories of jurisprudence suggested an activist, instrumental approach, and he criticized a "mechanical jurisprudence," contrasting "the law in the books and the law in action." Pound's many books include *The Spirit of the Common Law* (1921) and *Social Control Through Law* (1942).

See also Jurisprudence; Legal ethics; Legal realism; Progressivism.

Powell v. Alabama

COURT: U.S. Supreme Court

DATE: Decided November 7, 1932

SIGNIFICANCE: The Court ruled that the concept of due process requires states to provide effective counsel in capital cases when indigent defendants are unable to represent themselves

In 1931, Ozie Powell and eight other black youths whose ages ranged from twelve to nineteen, known as the "Scottsboro boys," were tried and convicted before an all-white jury in Scottsboro, Alabama, charged with having raped two white women while traveling on a freight train. Although the Alabama constitution required the appointment of counsel for indigents accused of capital crimes, no lawyer was definitely appointed to represent the defendants until the day of their trial. An atmosphere of racial hostility influenced the proceedings, and after a trial lasting one day, seven of the youths were sentenced to death, while the two youngest were transferred to the juvenile authorities. The trial attracted considerable attention, so that procommunist lawyers of the International Labor Defense volunteered to represent the young men on appeal. After the majority of the Alabama Supreme Court affirmed the convictions, the U.S. Supreme Court granted review.

The Court voted 7 to 2 to reverse the conviction and to remand the case to Alabama for a new trial. Writing for the majority, Justice George Sutherland did not speak of the Sixth Amendment, which had not yet been made applicable to the states, but rather he asked whether the defendants had been denied the right of counsel, contrary to the due process clause of the Fourteenth Amendment. Sutherland noted that from the time of arraignment to the time of the trial, the defendants had not had "the aid of counsel in any real sense." The right to be heard implied the right to be heard with the assistance of counsel, for even most educated and intelligent persons would not have the training or experience to represent themselves in a criminal trial. Sutherland was impressed with "the ignorance and illiteracy of the defendants" and with the "circumstances of public hostility." In this particular case, therefore, the failure of the trial court to make "an effective appointment of counsel" was a denial of due process within the meaning of the Fourteenth Amendment.

The "Scottsboro boys case" represented transitional steps in three important directions. First, the decision came very close to incorporating the right to counsel into the meaning of the Fourteenth Amendment, so that this portion of the Sixth Amendment would apply to the states. Second, it recognized that at least in capital cases, the state must provide counsel for indigents unable to defend themselves. Third, it included the provocative suggestion that the state had the obligation to provide "effective" assistance of counsel. These three issues would become increasingly important in subsequent cases.

See also *Argersinger v. Hamlin*; *Barron v. Baltimore*; Counsel, right to; Due process of law; *Gideon v. Wainwright*; Incorporation doctrine; Scottsboro cases.

President of the United States

DEFINITION: The nation's chief elected executive officer, armed by the Constitution, laws, and custom with extensive powers to influence the way justice is or is not achieved

SIGNIFICANCE: Though limited by the other branches of government, the president remains an important and controversial figure able to affect how the nation's justice system is organized and how it acts

The United States Constitution created the presidency as one of the three branches of the federal government. Although an electoral college exists, today the president is elected for all practical purposes by the vote of the people for a term of four years and can be reelected once. The Constitution directly states a number of the president's duties and powers, such as serving as commander in chief of the armed forces, seeing that the laws of the country are properly enforced, advising Congress, vetoing legislation, negotiating treaties, and making appointments to both executive and judicial positions. At the same time, the Constitution contains checks on the unlimited exercise of these and other powers by the president. For example, the president's veto can be overridden by a two-thirds vote of both houses of Congress, presidential appointments and treaties must be ratified by the Senate, and the president can be

Since George Washington's two terms as the first U.S. president, the powers—and the burdens—of the office have expanded significantly. (Library of Congress)

impeached for "high crimes and misdemeanors" and, if convicted, removed from office.

Presidential Powers. Since 1787 the presidency has expanded and taken on additional powers as well as unanticipated burdens. From Thomas Jefferson's nearly single-handed acquisition of the huge territory of the Louisiana Purchase through Abraham Lincoln's freeing of Confederate slaves in the Emancipation Proclamation to the expansion of the office's powers by activists such as Theodore Roosevelt and Franklin D. Roosevelt, many presidents have interpreted their responsibilities broadly as requiring the addition of powers beyond the process of governing—this despite the absence of a clear basis in the original Constitution. Although occasionally they have had to relinquish such powers (as when, in 1950, the Supreme Court nullified President Harry S Truman's seizure of steel mills on strike during the Korean War), most of the actions of presidents which have been justified as inherent or implied in the nature of the executive office have survived challenges in the courts and have generally been accepted by the public. In the twentieth century the ability of presidents to make news and to stay in the spotlight has made it possible for them to forge links directly with the people and to appeal to public opinion over the heads of their opponents. Nevertheless, the powers of the office are not without limits, especially if one or both branches of the Congress are controlled by a rival political party, or if the president remains unpopular or cannot effectively assert military power or diplomacy abroad.

Justice Issues. The president has several roles to play in the justice arena. As chief executive, the president assumes ultimate responsibility for policies involving law-and-order questions. With senatorial approval, the president appoints the attorney general to head the Department of Justice and usually also appoints the director of the Federal Bureau of Investigation (FBI). Members of the federal judiciary, most notably

Generalized Organization of the Executive Office

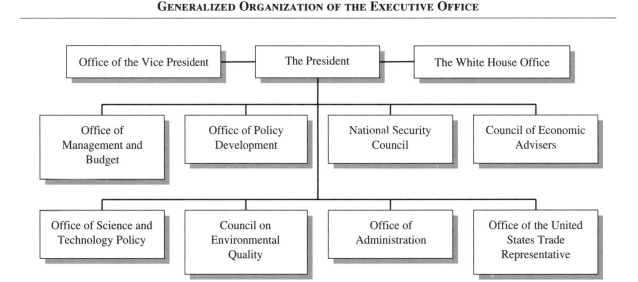

Source: Adapted from Jay M. Shafritz, *The Dorsey Dictionary of American Government and Politics.* Chicago: Dorsey Press, 1988.

those who sit on the U.S. Supreme Court, are presidential appointments. As these judges serve for life, their impact on the character of justice in the country is likely to extend well beyond the term of the person who appointed them. The president is also able to pardon persons convicted of federal crimes, a power that has been used sparingly. In 1974 President Gerald R. Ford used it to forestall the impeachment of former President Richard M. Nixon for the Watergate cover-up.

The president has the power to order national authorities to take actions to ensure that the country's laws are properly executed, with or without the consent of Congress. President Truman used his power as commander in chief to order the racial desegregation of the armed forces in 1947. President Dwight D. Eisenhower sent federal marshals into Little Rock, Arkansas, in 1957 to integrate its high schools after local authorities refused to do so. Using the argument that he was enforcing a court order against a felon who had violated U.S. laws, President George Bush sent troops into an independent country, Panama, to seize its leader, Manuel Noriega, and return him to Florida for criminal trial. President Bill Clinton ordered federal marshalls to protect abortion clinics after a series of bombings aimed at them.

Presidents often respond to the mood of the times regarding the way criminal activity should be defined, prevented, and punished. In the 1980's and 1990's, candidates for the presidency of both major parties campaigned heavily on law-and-order themes, promising to stiffen penalties for miscreants and accusing their opponents of being soft on crime. President Ronald Reagan used his visibility to launch a "war against drugs." Regardless of whether they have wanted the responsibility, more and more presidents are expected to assume the mantle of chief law enforcer.   —*James B. Christoph*

See also Attorney general of the United States; Constitution, U.S.; Constitutional law; Justice, U.S. Department of; Lincoln, Abraham; Roosevelt, Franklin D.; Solicitor general of the United States; Supreme Court of the United States.

Bibliography

Good basic treatments of the modern presidency are Thomas Cronin, ed., *Inventing the Presidency* (Lawrence: University of Kansas Press, 1989), and Richard E. Neustadt, *Presidential Power* (New York: John Wiley & Sons, 1980). James David Barber's *The Presidential Character: Predicting Performance in the White House* (4th ed. Englewood Cliffs, N.J.: Prentice Hall, 1992) explores the relationship between presidents' personalities and their conduct in office. Useful biographies include James MacGregor Burns, *Roosevelt: The Lion and the Fox* (New York: Harcourt, Brace, 1956); David McCullough, *Truman* (New York: Simon & Schuster, 1992); Arthur M. Schlesinger, *A Thousand Days: John F. Kennedy in the White House* (Boston: Houghton Mifflin, 1965); Doris Kearns Goodwin, *Lyndon Johnson and the American Dream* (New York: Harper & Row, 1976); and Stephen E. Ambrose, *Nixon* (3 vols. New York: Simon & Schuster, 1987-1991).

President's Commission on Law Enforcement and Administration of Justice

Date: Established July, 1965

Significance: Also known as the Katzenbach Commission, its 1967 report, *The Challenge of Crime in a Free Society*, investigated the perpetrators and victims of crime as well as the agencies responsible for diminishing its effect on American society

In the 1964 presidential campaign, Republican Barry Goldwater campaigned on a platform that emphasized "law and order" and decried "crime in the streets." After defeating Goldwater, President Lyndon B. Johnson appointed his attorney general, Nicholas Katzenbach, as chair of the President's Commission on Law Enforcement and Administration of Justice. The commission's purpose was to examine how widespread crime had become and how crime and delinquency had influenced American society.

The commission was made up of 19 commissioners, 63 staff members, 175 consultants, and hundreds of advisers. In the fall of 1965, the commission created working groups to examine four areas: police, courts, corrections, and the extent of the crime problem.

The research on which the commission's report was based is still considered one of the most extensive analyses of crime ever completed in the United States. The commission's final report included two hundred recommendations to combat the influence of crime. It concluded that contrary to popular opinion, crime is not the vice of a small number of people. Research showed that perpetrators and victims of crime exist in all segments of society. The commission found that much crime generally went unreported and that the fear of crime had "eroded the basic quality of life of many Americans."

In response to the conclusions of the commission, Congress passed the Omnibus Crime Control and Safe Streets Act of 1968, creating the Law Enforcement Assistance Administration. Despite the fact that the effect of crime on society has grown in the decades following, many experts cite the commission's report as one of the first efforts by the government to understand the roots of the crime problem.

—Lawrence Clark

See also Comprehensive Crime Control Act of 1984; Crime; Criminal; Criminal justice system; Law Enforcement Assistance Administration (LEAA); Omnibus Crime Control and Safe Streets Act of 1968.

Presumption of innocence

DEFINITION: The idea that a person accused of a crime does not need to prove innocence; rather, the prosecution must prove the person guilty

SIGNIFICANCE: The presumption that an accused person is innocent until proven guilty is an essential element of the American criminal justice system

The presumption of innocence traces its roots to Roman law. Its role in the early common law of England is obscure, but it was clearly established by 1802. In England and the United States it is viewed as the source of the "proof beyond a reasonable doubt" requirement in criminal trials.

The presumption of innocence is not explicitly provided for in the Constitution. It is inferred from the due process clauses of the Fifth and Fourteenth Amendments (as held in the Supreme Court cases *Coffin v. United States*, 1895, and *Taylor v. Kentucky*, 1978, respectively). The presumption of innocence describes the right of a defendant to offer no proof of innocence in a criminal case. It also describes the duty of the prosecution to offer evidence that the defendant committed the crime charged and to convince the jury beyond a reasonable doubt that, in the light of the offered evidence, the defendant is guilty of the crime charged. The fact that a jury is instructed to presume that a defendant is innocent until proven guilty assists the jury in understanding the limited circumstances under which it should vote to convict a defendant. It also cautions a jury to not convict based on the fact the defendant was arrested and is being tried or on mere suspicion that the defendant committed the crime charged. In this sense the presumption of innocence aids the jury in understanding the requirement that the prosecution prove its case beyond a reasonable doubt, a concept which can be difficult for a jury to understand.

A defendant charged with a federal crime is entitled to receive a presumption of innocence jury instruction if he or she requests it, as established in *Coffin v. United States*. This is not the rule in state crime trials. Despite the long history of its importance and function, the Supreme Court has held that a presumption of innocence instruction need not be given to every jury in state criminal trials. The Supreme Court has interpreted the due process clause of the Fourteenth Amendment as requiring it only when the failure to give such an instruction in the case would deprive a defendant of a fair trial in the light of the totality of the circumstances. Many states, however, have held that the presumption of innocence charge to a jury is required by their state constitutions or statutes.

If a defendant is presumed innocent, then what is the justification for holding a criminal defendant in jail pending trial? Holding the defendant in jail prior to trial certainly seems to be imposing punishment before the defendant has been found guilty, which would appear to be logically inconsistent with the ideal of the presumption of innocence. In *Bell v. Wolfish* (1979), the Supreme Court explained why the presumption of innocence does not apply to pretrial proceedings. The Court held that the role of the presumption of innocence is limited to the guilt-determining process at the defendant's trial. Before trial, the defendant's right to freedom is defined by the Fourth, Fifth, and Eighth Amendments. The government may need to hold a defendant in jail prior to trial to ensure that he or she appears for the trial or to protect the community from possible criminal conduct by the defendant prior to trial. In many, but not all, circumstances, the Eighth Amendment provides that a defendant has a right to bail before trial.

See also Bail system; Burden of proof; Criminal justice system; Criminal procedure; Due process of law; House Committee on Un-American Activities (HUAC); McCarthyism; Reasonable doubt; Standards of proof.

Preventive detention

DEFINITION: Confinement of a criminal defendant before final conviction and sentencing

SIGNIFICANCE: Federal and state statutes permit preconviction detention upon finding that the accused is likely to flee or is a threat to the safety of the community

Under the English system at the time of the American Revolution, some criminal defendants were released on bail while those accused of the most serious felony offenses, especially crimes subject to capital punishment, were detained pending trial. Although some legal writers suggest that this pretrial detention was to protect the community from the dangerous propensities of the accused, case law indicates that detention was to make sure the defendant was present at trial. Current American practice, which evolved from English law, allows defendants to remain free on bail or on personal recognizance except in capital offenses with abundant evidence of guilt, when the defendant is likely to flee, or when the accused poses a danger to the community or to witnesses.

Preventive detention statutes call into question three important principles of American law: the presumption of innocence, the right to due process, and the prohibition against excessive bail. Indispensable to the American criminal justice system is the proposition that one who is accused of a crime is presumed innocent until proven guilty. Opponents of preventive detention contend that an accused person has no less of a right to freedom than any other member of society and that the only proper basis for preconviction confinement is the risk of flight. Nevertheless, other grounds for detention are recognized by federal and state law. The Fifth Amendment prohibits the deprivation "of life, liberty, or property, without due process of law." However, due process is satisfied by a hearing before a judicial officer in which the person to be detained has the right to be present and to contest the evidence favoring detention. The mandate of the Eighth Amendment, that "[e]xcessive bail shall not be required," is also frequently cited by those who condemn preventive detention. They argue that this implies a right to be released on bail in all cases, except perhaps capital cases for which bail was not available under English common law. The courts, however, have consistently held that this amendment only limits the discretion of judges to set high bail in cases for which Congress or a state legislative body has authorized that bail be granted. The right to bail is fundamental but not absolute. It is not a constitutional violation to provide bail in some cases and deny it in others. The requirement is only that courts must act reasonably and conform to the Constitution and statutes.

The Bail Reform Act gives judicial officers the discretion to detain defendants in federal criminal cases upon finding that no condition or combination of conditions will reasonably assure the appearance of the accused to stand trial or protect the safety of others in the community. Preventive detention may be ordered for those accused of crimes of violence, of offenses which may be punishable by life imprisonment or death, or of certain drug-related offenses. It also may be ordered for defendants with two or more previous felony convictions, for those who pose a serious risk of flight, and for those who the court finds will obstruct justice or intimidate witnesses or jurors.

State courts also have the power to deny bail in order to assure the presence of the accused at trial and to protect the community unless such powers are limited by the Constitution or by statute. Typical statutes permit criminal defendants to be released on bail except in capital cases where the facts are evident or the presumption of guilt is great. Some statutes also allow preventive detention for felony offenses involving acts of violence in which guilt is obvious or when the defendant would be likely to harm another if released.

See also Arrest; Bail system; Criminal justice system; Criminal procedure; Discretion; Due process of law; Presumption of innocence; Prison and jail systems.

Price fixing

DEFINITION: A crime involving an agreement to eliminate competition with respect to price

SIGNIFICANCE: This violation of the antitrust laws is often considered the most serious interference with consumer welfare and the free market

Price fixing is most often an agreement among direct competitors, but it may appear in other forms. Because price fixing eliminates competition, it is thought to be a fundamental attack on the free market; thus making it illegal is considered to be in the public interest. This has been done through various state and federal antitrust laws. At the federal level, the Sherman Antitrust Act of 1890 provides criminal and civil penalties for contracts, combinations, and conspiracies in restraint of trade. Various state laws penalize many of the same activities. The Clayton Antitrust Act of 1914 and the Federal Trade Commission Act of 1914 expanded the scope of federal antitrust law, but they provide only civil remedies.

The antitrust laws were originally enacted in response to the predatory actions of large corporations in the nineteenth century. Unfettered competition, especially in regard to price, is in the best interests of consumers, because competition will lead to the best product at the lowest possible price. Some businesses have distorted this price mechanism by making agreements among themselves to eliminate competition.

A criminal conviction can be obtained only when it can be shown that various persons conspired or agreed to fix prices in a manner that shows an intention to interfere with the price mechanism. It is enough to show that the parties agreed or conspired, even if they never succeeded in actually fixing prices.

Price fixing can be accomplished in various ways. The classic case is an agreement to set a single price for a commodity, but there are other forms of agreement whose effect is also price fixing. Collusive bidding is illegal because it prevents the free operation of the price mechanism. An agreement to set a maximum or a minimum price is similarly illegal. An agreement between producers to limit production is price fixing, because prices will tend to rise as supplies fall. Resale price maintenance is a form of price fixing in which a distributor attempts to fix the price at which the commodity can be resold: A wholesaler may sell to a retailer only on the condition that the retailer charge its customers a particular price.

Those charged with price fixing cannot defend themselves by arguing that the price charged is reasonable or that the industry was facing ruinous competition before the price-fixing conspiracy. The public policy of the antitrust laws is that any supposed benefits gained by price fixing will never outweigh the detriment to consumer welfare. In the language of antitrust law, price fixing is per se illegal.

Price fixing is a felony under the Sherman Antitrust Act, but prison sentences have been rare, and the fines imposed are never large. This may be because the criminals are often respected businesspersons, or it may result from uncertainty regarding what conduct is illegal, given the vague language of some of the statutes.

See also Antitrust law; Capitalism; Consumer fraud; Regulatory crime; Sherman Antitrust Act.

Prison and jail systems

DEFINITION: Prisons are institutions operated by states and the federal government to incarcerate individuals convicted of serious crimes; local jails hold offenders sentenced for lesser crimes and detain persons awaiting trial, sentencing, or transportation to a prison

SIGNIFICANCE: American prisons and jails are responsible for securing offenders sentenced by federal, state, and local courts to some period of incarceration as punishment for their crimes

In the United States a person found guilty of committing a criminal offense is punished through a sentence imposed by a court. Incarceration in either jail or prison is generally reserved for the most serious offenders and is used as a sanction in fewer than half of the sentences handed down by courts. Imprisonment at the state or federal level usually involves a sentence of more than one year, while jails receive criminals facing less time.

The last quarter of the twentieth century witnessed a dramatic increase in the number of persons incarcerated in American prisons and jails. Excluding jails, the number of inmates in state and federal prisons reached the one million mark by the mid-1990's, giving the United States one of the highest incarceration rates (the number of persons incarcerated per 100,000 population) in the world.

Local Jails. The oldest American institution for incarcerating people is the local jail, dating back to the colonial period. By the 1990's, slightly more than three thousand jails and detention centers could be found in forty-four states. Six states (Alaska, Connecticut, Delaware, Hawaii, Rhode Island, and Vermont) have adopted combined jail-prison systems which are administered by state government. Jails in the other states continue to be a local responsibility, with approximately 80 percent of the facilities falling under the jurisdiction of county governments and the remainder operated by municipalities. This does

Most county jails—pictured is Iowa's Grant County jail—are administered by a local agency such as a sheriff's department. (James L. Shaffer)

not include approximately thirteen thousand temporary "lock-ups" which secure persons for relatively brief periods.

Jails serve a number of functions. First, jails detain persons awaiting trial for whom bond was denied or could not be posted. This includes individuals accused of violating state laws and, through contracts with the national government, about two-thirds of the persons accused of breaking federal laws. Second, jails incarcerate persons convicted of lesser crimes, serving short sentences for misdemeanor and some felony offenses. A little under half of the persons held by jails are convicted offenders, typically guilty of committing some type of property crime. Third, jails detain convicted offenders awaiting sentencing by the court. Fourth, jails hold sentenced offenders for transportation to state and federal prison facilities. By 1991, this included approximately eighteen thousand prisoners held in local jails because of state prison crowding.

Accurate and reliable counts of jail inmate populations and their characteristics are difficult to secure. In 1992, the U.S. Department of Justice reported an average daily jail population of almost 450,000 inmates, roughly double the daily population enumerated ten years earlier. When one considers that most jail inmates are incarcerated for relatively brief periods, this translates into one to five million people passing through the jail system per year. Based on various surveys of jail facilities, the typical jail inmate is male, lacks a high school degree, and is in his mid- to late twenties. In 1989, three-fourths of the jail population was found to be between the ages of eighteen and thirty-four. African Americans and whites are incarcerated in similar numbers and together account for 80 percent of all inmates.

Most county jails are administered by a law enforcement agency, usually the county sheriff's office. In many counties the sheriff is elected rather than appointed. City-operated jails also tend to be administered by law enforcement agencies, though some larger cities have created separate departments for jail management. Approximately 50 percent of all jails were designed to contain twenty-five or fewer inmates, with the smallest jails distributed primarily in the midwestern and western states. The designed capacity of some larger jails reaches into the thousands, with many being located in California. The nation's one hundred largest jails account for roughly 40 percent of all jail inmates on any given day. Smaller jails, which are generally older and have smaller cells, are gradually disappearing through replacement and other institutional arrangements, such as the creation of regional facilities.

State Prisons. Offenders convicted of violating state laws and incarcerated for more than one year are usually sentenced to serve time in state prisons rather than jail. In 1990, there were almost one thousand confinement facilities administered by state governments, almost all of which hold general adult populations. Ninety percent of these prisoners were serving sentences longer than one year for felony convictions. In addition, many states operate juvenile detention centers and community based facilities which permit inmates to work or go to school without supervision.

Between the end of World War II and the early 1970's, the prison population of states remained remarkably stable at around 200,000 inmates per year. This was followed by a rapid increase in the number of sentenced prisoners over the next two decades, as the inmate population of state prisons more than quadrupled. More than 50 percent of the prisons in operation in the late 1980's were less than twenty-five years old. In 1991, almost half of state prisoners were serving time for violent offenses, followed by property offenders at 25 percent. One of every five state prisoners was convicted of a drug violation. Most state prison inmates have been incarcerated previously or are "recidivist," with only one-fifth having no prior sentence upon entry.

Type of offense committed and recidivism status are but two factors considered by prison personnel in the evaluation and classification of a newly sentenced inmate. States operate multiple prisons to handle different classifications of inmates, with the most common assignments being to minimum (low), medium, and maximum (high) security facilities. Classification also serves to identify rehabilitative programs for which an inmate may qualify, such as drug treatment.

State prisoners are predominantly male, with two-thirds between the ages of eighteen and thirty-four. More than half of

An inmate walks through a cell block in California's Folsom Prison. (Ben Klaffke)

SENTENCED PRISONERS IN STATE AND FEDERAL INSTITUTIONS

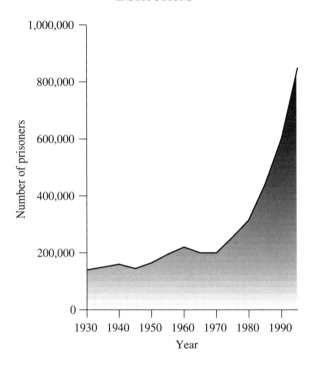

Source: U.S. Department of Justice, Bureau of Justice Statistics, *Sourcebook of Criminal Justice Statistics—1993.* Washington, D.C.: U.S. Government Printing Office, 1994.

the inmates in 1991 were high school graduates, and many had attended college for some duration. The largest proportion of inmates are African Americans, followed closely by non-Hispanic whites. Together these two groupings account for approximately 80 percent of all inmates.

The operation and administration of prisons are primarily an executive branch responsibility, though state legislatures play a critical role in the provision of general policy guidance and the allocation of financial resources. In most states, prison management is organizationally situated within a department of corrections. Many departments deal with juvenile institutions as well, and may also have the authority to oversee probation and parole programs. Depending on the state, the corrections department may report directly to the governor or indirectly as a subunit within a larger "superagency" dealing with a broader array of functional concerns. Independent corrections departments are administered by a director or secretary appointed by the governor, sometimes with senate confirmation.

Individual prisons are administered by superintendents or wardens. Wardens are responsible for institutional security and daily operations. Wardens usually serve at the pleasure of the governor or corrections secretary. Assisting the warden are two or more deputy wardens, each responsible for some spe-

cialized component of institutional operations such as inmate programs, custody, and general management. Custody is of primary importance, as it is fundamental to institutional security. The provision of custodial services is labor intensive, involving around 60 percent of a prison's workforce.

Federal Prison System. In comparison with state prisons and local jails, the federal prison system is much simpler. Prior to the twentieth century, persons awaiting trial or convicted of violating federal laws were held in either state prisons or local jails through contractual agreements. This practice still continues, especially in the detention of accused persons. In response to a growing prison population, however, the federal government began holding sentenced offenders at a former military prison in 1895. Shortly thereafter, Congress appropriated funds to begin developing additional facilities. One hundred years later there were roughly eighty federal confinement facilities in operation to maintain an inmate population approaching 100,000. In 1991, 80 percent of federal inmates were serving sentences exceeding one year. Branches of the armed forces also operate prisons, with the Army providing the only long-term facility, the U.S. Disciplinary Barracks.

Since 1930, federal prisons have been under the authority of the Bureau of Prisons, an administrative subdivision of the U.S. Justice Department. The bureau is a centralizing agent in the federal prison system, providing policy guidance and institutional coordination at the top of a structured, hierarchical organization. The bureau is divided into regional areas for management purposes. Wardens are accountable to the regional offices from whom they receive policy directives. In 1934, it was the Bureau of Prisons that developed the first classification system for assigning new inmates to appropriate facilities. The classification system still exists, with prisoners and facilities associated with one of six security levels, with six being maximum security. In 1993, almost 40 percent of all federal prisoners were confined to at least a medium security facility.

Federal prisoners are slightly older than state inmates, with the average age of new admissions in the early thirties and only half of the population between eighteen and thirty-five. More than 90 percent of federal prisoners are male, and slightly less than two-thirds are white, far outnumbering members of minority groups. In the mid-1990's, six of every ten federal inmates were incarcerated for drug offenses.

Purpose of Incarceration. Underlying the use of imprisonment for convicted felons and misdemeanants are fundamental questions about the use of incarceration. Four perspectives on the role of imprisonment are that (1) it serves as a deterrent to committing crimes; (2) it is a means of realizing retribution against those found guilty of committing crimes; (3) it incapacitates those responsible for crime; and (4) it offers an opportunity to rehabilitate criminals for a return to society. The relative dominance of these perspectives has varied throughout history, and to some extent elements of all four are reflected in contemporary state and federal imprisonment practices.

Coinciding with the increased use of incarceration in the latter part of the twentieth century was a movement away from

ENROLLMENT IN ACADEMIC, WORK, AND COUNSELING PROGRAMS IN STATE CORRECTIONAL FACILITIES

	Percent of All Inmates/Residents Enrolled in Programs					
	Total		Confinement Facilities		Community-Based Facilities	
Type of Program	1984	1990	1984	1990	1984	1990
Academic programs						
Adult basic education	8.2%	8.7%	8.3%	8.8%	4.6%	4.3%
Secondary[a]	7.5	5.9	7.6	5.9	5.7	5.4
Special[b]	1.5	1.3	1.5	1.3	0.7	0.6
College	5.4	4.8	5.5	4.9	2.2	0.7
Work programs						
Prison industries	11.0	6.9	11.5	7.1	(c)	0.2
Facility support services[d]	30.7	40.5	31.7	41.3	(c)	10.7
Farming/agriculture/ranching	5.1	4.0	5.3	4.1	(c)	0.3
Vocational training	8.4	8.5	8.7	8.7	(c)	0.4
Work release[e]	3.5	2.8	0.9	0.8	76.5	76.9
Counseling programs						
Psychological/psychiatric[f]	14.2	30.8	14.0	30.3	20.7	49.7
Employment	4.0	5.5	2.9	5.0	37.7	24.4
Life skills/community adjustment	8.7	5.0	7.7	4.4	34.5	25.0
Parenting	0.4	0.9	0.4	0.8	2.1	1.8

Source: U.S. Department of Justice, Bureau of Justice Statistics, *Sourcebook of Criminal Justice Statistics—1993.* Washington, D.C.: U.S. Government Printing Office, 1994.

Notes:
[a] Includes General Education Development (GED) programs.
[b] For example, programs for inmates with learning disabilities.
[c] Not included in the 1984 Census of State Adult Correctional Facilities.
[d] Includes office work, administration, food services, laundry, building maintenance, repair, construction, and similar programs.
[e] Inmates work in the community and return to the facility at night.
[f] Including drug and alcohol programs.

the goal of rehabilitating or treating offenders. Laws enacted by state legislatures and the U.S. Congress during this period rejected uncertainty (discretion) in sentencing, a cornerstone of the rehabilitation model, in favor of practices giving courts less or no discretion in how convicted offenders are to be punished. Some states adopted determinate sentencing, which mandates a certain prison sentence for a given crime and is consistent with the retribution model of punishment. Most states and the federal government also enacted mandatory sentencing laws designed to deter the commission of certain crimes, such as using a handgun in committing a crime.

Regulating Inmate Populations. The "in-flow" of sentenced offenders is not under the immediate control of the officials responsible for operating prisons and jails. Sentencing practices are reflected in the laws promulgated by legislatures and in the behavior of individual judges in sentencing convicted offenders. Correctional facilities must react to the flow or stream of prisoners channeled to them by the legal system. Prisons and jails must respond to the number of persons involved and to the length of the sentences imposed. More prisoners facing longer sentences places greater pressure on the ability of these institutions to care for persons under their charge.

One way to address the pressure of greater in-flow is through the regulation of "out-flow"—inmates leaving prison and jail by release. Some of this occurs naturally as prisoners fulfill the sentences imposed by courts. The granting of parole is a mechanism for releasing prisoners early, as parole time is counted as part of an inmate's prison time in indeterminate sentencing states. Many states and the federal government have parole boards which enjoy broad discretion in granting parole. In some states, however, the discretion afforded parole boards is more limited, or parole has been eliminated altogether with the adoption of determinate sentencing. A third method for releasing inmates is through good-time credits which inmates earn and then apply toward reducing their sentences. In many states, credits are earned for good behavior and program participation. Credit is also usually granted for time spent in jail awaiting trial or sentencing. As a result of these different practices, most prisoners do not serve their full sentences but rather some proportion of them. Studies of felony offenders suggest that persons committing more serious crimes generally serve a smaller proportion of their sentences in comparison with individuals committing lesser crimes.

In 1980, Minnesota adopted sentencing guidelines for judges to follow in sentencing offenders to prison. The guidelines require judges to consider various factors in reaching a given sentence, including the availability of prison space. Following adoption, Minnesota experienced slower growth in its inmate population. In other states, prison officials are empowered to release prisoners nearing the end of their sentences in order to accommodate new admissions.

Prisoners' Rights. Historically, federal courts took a "hands-off" position when it came to the administration of state prisons and local jails. Institutional corrections was considered to fall within the domain of state powers, and federal courts refused to become entangled in how these governments elected to operate confinement facilities. Lawsuits brought by inmates challenging the conditions of their incarceration were ignored as federal judges deferred to the authority of state governments.

In the 1960's, lower federal courts began abandoning the hands-off doctrine. Initially, courts issued orders dealing with the rules and practices of state prisons in selected, narrow areas, such as the religious freedoms afforded inmates. This piecemeal approach lasted until 1969, when a federal district court judge declared that the entire Arkansas prison system violated the U.S. Constitution's Eighth Amendment prohibiting cruel and unusual punishment. The court focused on the totality of conditions of the state prison system and found the cumulative impact of individual deficiencies was sufficient to establish a constitutional violation. The court delineated problems ranging from security and custodial treatment to living conditions and sanitation.

In the twenty years following the Arkansas case, nearly every state and countless local governments became the subject of this newer, more comprehensive attempt to reform prisons and jails. During this period, eight states' prison systems were declared unconstitutional, and more than thirty states had one or more facilities operating under judicial supervision. Courts have identified numerous problems in how facilities are administered; the most common problems are overcrowding and the association of overcrowding with other conditions. In response, many state and local governments have attempted to construct more or bigger institutions to accommodate expanding inmate populations. Population caps have been employed by other governments to limit the number of inmates assigned to a given facility. If a facility is operating at capacity, releases are required before new inmates can be accepted. Courts have ordered caps in many situations, while some have been self-imposed by state and local governments.

Costs of Confinement. Prisons and jails represent a significant financial undertaking for governments. First, there is the ever-increasing cost of constructing facilities. At the close of the late 1980's, the per-inmate cost of building a facility ranged between $25,000 and $80,000. Once built, there is the cost of operation. In 1990, approximately 22 billion dollars was spent on institutional corrections by all governments, representing about one-third of all criminal justice expenditures. State governments accounted for slightly less than two-thirds of this amount, with local governments contributing another 30 percent. Corrections was the fastest growing finan-

cial obligation of state governments during the 1980's and into the 1990's. Between 1979 and 1990, direct expenditures for corrections increased more than 300 percent.

These expenditures translate into high annual operating costs per inmate. In 1990, the federal government spent more than $14,000 per inmate, while the state average was $1,000 higher. States with the lowest expenditures per inmate are generally found in the South. States in other regions spend considerably more, with some having per-inmate expenditures almost double the average. Prisons and jails are labor-intensive organizations, and most of their costs are in terms of personnel. Almost half a million people were employed in institutional settings in 1990, with more than 50 percent working for state governments. This translated into roughly one correctional officer for every four to five inmates.

In the light of these growing costs, governments have been exploring various options designed to reduce public spending. One set of options involves efforts to develop alternatives to imprisonment which have lower price tags. Community-based facilities and electronic supervision are two options employed by many governments. Alternatively, state and local governments have turned to the private sector for assistance. Private companies are building and operating facilities on the promise of being able to hold costs down. The true cost savings of these measures continue to be evaluated and debated.

—*William A. Taggart*

See also Attica prison riot; Auburn system; Boot camps; Criminal justice system; Good time; Just deserts; New Mexico State Penitentiary riot; Parole; Prisons, Bureau of; Punishment; Rehabilitation; Walnut Street Jail.

BIBLIOGRAPHY
The single best source of annual statistical information about prisons and jails is the U.S. Department of Justice, Bureau of Justice Statistics, *Sourcebook of Criminal Justice Statistics* (Washington, D.C.: U.S. Government Printing Office). The Bureau of Justice Statistics is responsible for a number of other publications, including the *Bulletin* and *Special Reports* (Washington, D.C.: U.S. Department of Justice). Both appear on a semiregular basis (six to ten times a year), and many issues deal with institutional corrections. Two comprehensive introductory textbooks on corrections are Harry E. Allen and Clifford E. Simonsen, *Corrections in America: An Introduction* (6th ed. New York: Macmillan, 1992), and Todd R. Clear and George F. Cole, *American Corrections* (3d ed. Belmont, Calif.: Wadsworth, 1993). A more advanced treatment of corrections is offered by Neal Shover and Werner J. Einstadter, *Analyzing American Corrections* (Belmont, Calif.: Wadsworth, 1988). Jails have not received much attention in comparison with prisons. One readable exception is a book edited by Joel A. Thompson and G. Larry Mays, *American Jails: Public Policy Issues* (Chicago: Nelson-Hall, 1991). A useful edited volume on the development of the federal prison system is John Roberts' *Escaping Prison Myths: Selected Topics in the History of Federal Corrections* (Lanham, Md.: American University Press, 1994). John Irwin, an ex-convict

turned professor, has written a number of books from an "insider's" perspective, including *Prisons in Turmoil* (Boston: Little, Brown, 1980).

Prisons, Bureau of

Date: Created 1930

Significance: The creation of the U.S. Bureau of Prisons to oversee the confining of criminals convicted in federal courts reflected the general expansion of federal criminal law and the growing role of federal law enforcement agencies

The first two federal prisons were opened in Leavenworth, Kansas, and Atlanta, Georgia, in 1905. Before that time, persons convicted of federal crimes were confined either in a facility on a military reservation or in a state or local corrections facility. Prohibition and the expansion of federal powers to combat organized crime in the 1920's and 1930's increased federal responsibilities for law enforcement and created a need for a separate federal prison system. In 1930, the Bureau of Prisons was created to administer the expanding federal corrections programs and a growing network of prison facilities. High-profile federal law enforcement agencies, particularly the Federal Bureau of Investigation under J. Edgar Hoover's leadership, focused attention on violent crime, and new pris-

ons were built. Alcatraz, perhaps the best known of the maximum-security facilities, was opened in 1934 and held some of the United States' most notorious criminals until its closing in 1963.

The Bureau of Prisons, a unit of the U.S. Department of Justice, is divided into six geographic regions that have a significant amount of autonomy. The directors of the regions also serve on the executive staff of the bureau and provide national coordination of the agency's programs. The organization of the bureau includes the executive office of the director, with a general counsel and an internal affairs section. There are also divisions for administration, correctional programs (with responsibility for managing the facilities), health services, human resource management, program review, community corrections and detention, and information, policy, and public affairs. The Bureau of Prisons is also responsible for UNICOR, a public corporation and the successor to Federal Prisons Industries, founded in 1934, which provides employment and training for inmates. It produces goods and services ranging from furniture to electronics to data entry. The Bureau of Prisons also operates the National Institute of Corrections, which supports state and local corrections agencies and operates the National Academy of Corrections, an information

The federal penitentiary at Marion, Illinois, is overseen by the U.S. Bureau of Prisons. (James L. Shaffer)

center, and the National Jail Center. The institute has a budget separate from that of the Bureau of Prisons.

The Bureau of Prisons began to experience problems in the 1980's and 1990's because of the age of its facilities, the need for increased capacity, and the increasing costs of corrections programs. In particular, prison overcrowding, the need to accommodate a wide variety of inmate populations, and increasing costs of treating drug abuse problems and addressing health problems related to acquired immune deficiency syndrome (AIDS) have taxed the agency. The lack of strong political constituencies in the corrections profession and the increasing unwillingness of Congress to expand funding for federal programs are making it difficult to address the growing problems, even though the need for additional resources and new programs has been noted in numerous U.S. General Accounting Office reports. The Bureau of Prisons is also facing challenges in the form of recommendations for privatization of its facilities, and it has been targeted periodically by Congress for elimination.

See also Auburn system; Boot camps; Model Penal Code; Parole; Prison and jail systems; Rehabilitation.

Privacy, right of

DEFINITION: The right of individuals to be free from unwarranted publicity or uninvited intrusions into their personal affairs

SIGNIFICANCE: Although the U.S. Constitution does not use the word "privacy," the Bill of Rights secures specific kinds of privacy interests, and the Supreme Court has interpreted the Constitution to protect a general right to privacy which includes personal autonomy and intimate relationships

Many of the provisions of the U.S. Constitution protect values which people commonly include under the multifaceted label "privacy." The First Amendment means that people should be allowed privacy in their beliefs and expressions of beliefs. The Third Amendment permits individuals to refuse to take soldiers into their homes in peacetime. The Fourth Amendment protects against unreasonable searches of persons, homes, and property. The Ninth Amendment recognizes that rights exist that are not enumerated in the Constitution. Both the Fifth and Fourteenth Amendments appear to give some substantive rights to liberty and property, concepts at the core of an individual's private interests.

Publicity and Invasions of Privacy. The modern notion of a legal, expansive right to general privacy really began in 1890, when lawyers Louis Brandeis and Charles Warren published a famous article in the *Harvard Law Review* entitled "The Right to Privacy," arguing that "the right to be let alone" was "the most comprehensive of rights and the right most valued by civilized man." Brandeis and Warren advocated the use of tort law to deter invasions of privacy by the press and others. Beginning with New York in 1903, most states gradually allowed civil suits for the unauthorized use of one's name, the public disclosure of private affairs, and publicity presenting one in a false light.

Any legal restraint on publicity eventually comes in conflict with the First Amendment guarantee of a free press. For this reason, in *Time, Inc. v. Hill* (1967), the Supreme Court applied its standards for libel of public persons to unwanted publicity about private individuals if the publicity relates to a "newsworthy" story. Thus, a private individual described in a story of public interest is able to collect damages only if the writer or publisher resorts to "deliberate falsity or a reckless disregard for the truth."

The Court extended this test in *Cox Broadcasting Corporation v. Cohn* (1975), in which it overturned a civil award arising under a Georgia privacy statute that made it illegal to publicize the name of a rape victim. The Court declared it unconstitutional to punish the news media for providing "truthful information available in the public record." If the state wished to protect the privacy of victims, it could delete the relevant information from public court documents. In a subsequent case, *Florida Star v. B.J.F.* (1989), the Court again emphasized press freedom over privacy when it overturned a civil award against a newspaper for illegally reporting the full name of a rape victim, the name coming from police records. A minority of three justices argued that more weight should be given to the privacy of innocent victims.

Privacy and the Fourth Amendment. Because of the British colonial experience, the framers of the Fourth Amendment wanted to deny the government the power to conduct general searches of buildings with writs of assistance. In the famous Massachusetts trial of 1761, *Paxton's Case*, James Otis had argued against the use of general writs, declaring that an individual in his house should be "as secure as a prince in his castle."

The Supreme Court only gradually tried to prevent the police from violating the Fourth Amendment. In one of the first important cases, *Boyd v. United States* (1886), Justice Joseph Bradley insisted that the courts had the duty to uphold the spirit of the amendment, writing that it applied "to all invasions on the part of the government and its employees of the sanctity of a man's home and the privacies of life." In *Weeks v. United States* (1914), the Court began a rigorous assault on unreasonable searches by mandating the "exclusionary rule," which disallows any use of illegally obtained evidence in criminal trials.

In his famous dissent in *Olmstead v. United States* (1928), Justice Brandeis interpreted the Fourth Amendment broadly to prohibit "every unjustifiable intrusion on the privacy of the individual." Most of Brandeis' ideas were accepted in *Katz v. United States* (1967), a case in which the Court interpreted the amendment to require a valid search warrant whenever the police enter into a zone in which a person has a "reasonable expectation of privacy." The Court has reaffirmed the *Katz* principle on numerous occasions. In *Terry v. Ohio* (1968), for example, the Court allowed the police to stop and frisk based on reasonable suspicion but insisted that whenever individuals harbor a reasonable expectation of privacy they are "entitled to be free from unreasonable governmental intrusion."

One controversial question is whether mandatory drug testing is contrary to Fourth Amendment rights, especially when there is no basis for individualized suspicion. When the U.S. Customs Service began to require drug tests of employees entering sensitive positions in the service, the Court in *National Treasury Employees Union v. Van Raab* (1989) voted 5 to 4 that the government's compelling interest in law enforcement outweighs the "privacy interests" of the employees. The Court, however, insisted that only the special demands of the positions justified this "diminished expectation of privacy."

Privacy of Association. The Constitution does not explicitly mention a freedom of association, but First Amendment rights for free expression and peaceful assembly logically imply the privilege to meet with others to establish organizations for the advancement of ideas and opinions. The Supreme Court recognized this expansive view in *National Association for the Advancement of Colored People v. Alabama* (1958), with Justice John Harlan speaking of constitutional protection for "privacy in group association."

In general, private associations may decide to include or exclude people for any reason, even prejudices based on race or gender. In *Rotary International v. Rotary Club of Duarte* (1987), however, the Court upheld a California statute that required large business clubs to include women. Insisting that the club was not a small, intimate organization and that its mission would not be changed by admitting women, the Court was careful to acknowledge that "the freedom to enter into and to carry on certain intimate or private relationships is a fundamental element of liberty protected by the Bill of Rights."

Substantive Due Process and Privacy. The period from 1897 to 1937 is often called the "Lochner age." During these years the Supreme Court insisted that the due process clauses of the Fifth and Fourteenth Amendments protected substantive rights to liberty and property. This approach meant that any restraint on these substantive rights would be judged unconstitutional unless justified by a legitimate objective of law enforcement. The conservative Court emphasized the right of persons to make private contracts without governmental interference; this "liberty of contract" almost invariably supported laissez-faire economic policies, as in *Lochner v. New York* (1905).

During the Lochner age, however, there were at least two substantive due process decisions recognizing liberties which would later be incorporated into a generic right to privacy. In the first case, *Meyer v. Nebraska* (1923), the Court struck down a state law making it illegal to teach non-English languages in all schools. The rationale was a broad conception of liberty which included family relationships, education, and the "orderly pursuits of happiness by free men." Second, the Court in *Pierce v. Society of Sisters* (1925) overturned a state law which prohibited parents from sending their children to private schools. The ruling affirmed "the liberty of parents and guardians to direct the upbringing and education of children under their control." Although the Court in 1937 stopped striking down economic regulations based on the application of substantive due process, it never overturned the *Meyer* and *Pierce*

precedents, and years later these cases would often be quoted to defend the libertarian notion that government may not intrude into a zone of private family life and personal autonomy.

Privacy and Reproductive Freedom. In gradually developing an explicit right of general privacy, the Supreme Court dealt with issues of sexuality and reproduction. In the watershed case *Skinner v. Oklahoma* (1942), the Court unanimously overturned Oklahoma's Habitual Criminal Sterilization Act, which allowed the sterilization of "habitual criminals." Justice William O. Douglas, a partisan of Brandeis' views on privacy, utilized the argument that the individual's right to procreate was "a basic liberty." Later, in *Loving v. Virginia* (1967), the Court declared that a state miscegenation law was unconstitutional because it violated the right of individuals to choose their own marriage partners.

The most influential case that specifically proclaimed reproductive privacy rights was *Griswold v. Connecticut* (1965). Overturning a state statute that prohibited the use of contraceptives, Justice Douglas argued for the majority that there were penumbras (partial shadows) to the Bill of Rights that created "zones of privacy" not specifically mentioned in the Constitution and that one such zone was the right of a married couple to practice family planning. Marriage and procreation, he wrote, were associated with "a right to privacy older than the Bill of Rights—older than our political parties, older than our school system." While six other justices agreed with the outcome in *Griswold*, at least one justice wanted to find the right of privacy in the Ninth Amendment, and others wanted to find it in a substantive due process reading of the due process clause.

A few years later, the Court in *Eisenstadt v. Baird* (1972) expanded the right of privacy somewhat by overturning a Massachusetts law which prohibited the distribution of contraceptives to unmarried people. The *Eisenstadt* decision recognized that the right of privacy inhered in the individual rather than the marital relationship, and it explicitly declared that the right included freedom from governmental intrusion into one's personal choice about whether to give birth to a child.

Privacy and Abortion Rights. The Court's decisions proclaiming the right to use birth control were in the background to *Roe v. Wade* (1973), the controversial case in which the Court ruled that laws outlawing abortion violated a woman's right to privacy. Justice Harry Blackmun, writing for the majority, found the right of privacy primarily in the "concept of personal liberty" guaranteed by the Fourteenth Amendment. He declared that this right "is broad enough to encompass a woman's decision whether or not to terminate her pregnancy." Whatever the rights of a fetus, he argued, they are secondary to the woman's right of privacy, at least until the fetus becomes viable.

During the subsequent two decades, the Court approved of many restrictions on a woman's right to have an abortion, but it continued to guarantee the basic right. In these later cases, the Court increasingly emphasized that the underlying right to privacy was an aspect of liberty based on a substantive due process reading of the Fourteenth Amendment. Thus the term "liberty interest" tended to replace the term "right to privacy."

Privacy and Personal Autonomy. One problem with building privacy rights on the concept of substantive due process is that subjective judgments inevitably determine which rights are protected and which are not. Thus, in *Kelly v. Johnson* (1976), the Court upheld a regulation which limited the length of policemen's hair, but in *Moore v. East Cleveland* (1977) the Court overturned a city ordinance limiting the occupancy of any dwelling to a narrow definition of a family, prohibiting a grandmother from living with her grandchildren. In *Moore*, Justice Lewis Powell referred to the string of privacy cases and concluded that "freedom of personal choice in matters of marriage and family life is one of the liberties protected by the Due Process Clause." The most controversial aspect of Powell's opinion was his suggestion that protections of substantive due process should be limited to institutions and practices "deeply rooted in this Nation's history and tradition."

In the controversial case *Bowers v. Hardwick* (1986), the Court considered the nation's history and tradition when it concluded that the right of privacy gave no protection for the right to engage in homosexual practices, even in a private bedroom. Writing for the majority, Justice Byron White accepted that the due process clause protected many substantive liberties, but he insisted that the Court should show "great resistance to expand the substantive reach of those Clauses." In *Cruzan v. Director, Missouri Department of Health* (1990), on the other hand, the Court found enough history and tradition to conclude that competent adults possess the constitutional right to refuse unwanted medical intervention, even when death is the result of such a refusal.

Informational Privacy. In contrast to the Court's recognition of claims for personal autonomy in regard to one's body and relationships in the traditional family, it has found little occasion to expand protection for "informational privacy." In its major decision dealing with the issue, *Whalen v. Roe* (1977), the Court upheld a state law which required the keeping of computer files on all patients obtaining dangerous but legal drugs. While acknowledging an individual's interest in maintaining autonomy over some personal information, the Court considered that the law did not "pose a sufficiently grievous threat" to establish a constitutional violation. As *Whalen* illustrates, courts have generally allowed legislative bodies to decide on appropriate means to safeguard interests in informational privacy. Congress has recognized the public's concern for the issue, as seen in the Privacy Act of 1947, which allows individuals to have access to personal information in files of federal agencies, except for law enforcement and national security files. —*Thomas T. Lewis*

See also Abortion; Birth control, right to; *Bowers v. Hardwick*; Due process of law; Electronic surveillance; *Griswold v. Connecticut*; *Katz v. United States*; *Lochner v. New York*; Ninth Amendment; Search and seizure.

BIBLIOGRAPHY

Any good text in American constitutional law includes material on the right of privacy. Two helpful treatments are in chapter fifteen of Laurence Tribe, *American Constitutional Law* (2d ed. Mineola, N.Y.: Foundation Press, 1988), and chapter seven of Lee Epstein and Thomas Walker, *Constitutional Law for a Changing America* (2d ed. Washington, D.C.: Congressional Quarterly, 1995). A concise historical account is in Darien McWhirter and Jon Bible, *Privacy as a Constitutional Right* (New York: Quorum Books, 1992). John Shattuck's *Rights of Privacy* (Skokie, Ill.: National Textbook, 1977) is a well-organized handbook for the ACLU. For useful documents, see P. Allan Dionisopoulos and Craig Ducat, *The Right to Privacy: Essays and Cases* (St. Paul, Minn.: West, 1976). Peter Irons' *The Courage of Their Convictions* (New York: Free Press, 1988) presents fascinating accounts of several privacy cases. Henry Glick's *The Right to Die: Policy Innovation and Its Consequences* (New York: Columbia University Press, 1992) presents an interesting account of an important issue. Many stimulating essays are included in Ferdinand Schoeman, ed., *Philosophical Dimensions of Privacy: An Anthology* (New York: Cambridge University Press, 1984). Robert Bork's *The Tempting of America* (New York: Free Press, 1990) criticizes the substantive due process approach to privacy.

Privileged communications

DEFINITION: Those statements made by individuals within a protected relationship such as attorney-client, husband-wife, physician-patient, cleric-penitent, and journalist-source, which the law of some states protects from compelled disclosure at trial or deposition

SIGNIFICANCE: Privileged communication laws encourage full and free disclosure between certain classes of individuals when the speaker needs to be able to make confidential statements, including statements about the person's own misdeeds, with the assurance that the recipient of this information cannot be compelled to reveal it at a later date

Legal scholars, such as John Wigmore, have observed that there are four fundamental conditions necessary to the establishment of a privilege against the disclosure of communications. First, the communications must originate in a confidence that they will not be disclosed. Second, the element of confidentiality must be essential to the maintenance of the relation between the parties. Third, the relationship must be one which, in the opinion of the community, ought to be diligently fostered. Finally, any injury which would occur to the relationship by disclosure of the communication must be greater than the benefit which would be gained by requiring it to be revealed.

The concept of privileged communications goes against the fundamental judicial principal that the courts have a right to require anyone who may have relevant information to testify. Therefore, the courts strictly construe such privileges and accept them "only to the very limited extent that permitting a refusal to testify or excluding relevant evidence has a public good transcending the normally predominant principal of utilizing all rational means for ascertaining the truth" (*Elkins v. United States*, 1960).

Attorney and Client. Clients have a privilege to refuse to disclose, and to prevent their attorneys from disclosing, confidential communications made for the purpose of facilitating the rendition of professional legal services to them. The attorney-client privilege has been justified by the theory that disputes which could result in litigation can be handled most expeditiously by attorneys who have been candidly and completely informed of the facts by their clients. Such full disclosure will best be promoted if clients know that their disclosures cannot, over their objections, be repeated by their attorneys in court. In the criminal context, the attorney-client privilege is necessary to protect the accused's Fifth and Sixth Amendment rights to the effective assistance of counsel.

Privileged attorney-client communications can be waived only by the client. Further, if the client is called to testify during trial, the client can assert the privilege when asked by the opposing counsel what he told his own attorney. In most states, the death of the client will not relieve the attorney from the privilege that existed while the client was alive.

The privilege is not recognized if the client's purpose is the furtherance of an intended future crime or fraud. The privileged communications may be a shield of defense as to crimes already committed, but it cannot be used as a sword or weapon of offense to enable persons to carry out contemplated crimes against society (*Gebhart v. United Railways Co.*, 1920).

Husband and Wife. This privilege is considered necessary for the encouragement of marital confidences, which promote harmony between husband and wife. It is most commonly asserted in criminal proceedings, in which accused persons can prevent their spouses from testifying against them. Either spouse may assent the privilege.

In some states, the privilege extends past the death of one of the spouses. Communications between the husband and wife before marriage or after divorce are not privileged, however, and the privilege does not extend to proceedings in which one spouse is charged with a crime against the person or property of the other or against a child of either.

Physician and Patient. The American physician-patient privilege originated in a New York testimonial provision of 1828 which reads:

> No person authorized to practice physic or surgery shall be allowed to disclose any information which he may have acquired in attending any patient, in any professional character, and which information was necessary to enable him to prescribe for such patient as a physician, or to do any act for him as a surgeon.

This statute set forth the general scope and purpose of the privilege. In some states it has been extended to communications between a patient and nurse, psychologist, psychotherapist, or social worker. The policy behind the privilege is that the physician must know all that a patient can articulate in order to identify and treat disease; barriers to full disclosure would impair diagnosis and treatment.

For the privilege to apply, the patient must have consulted the physician for treatment or diagnosis. Only that information which is necessary to enable the doctor to prescribe or act for the patient is privileged. The privilege is not recognized where the patient sees the physician at the request of another, such as a public officer. It does not apply in an examination by a court-appointed doctor or prosecutor or in an examination requested by the patient's own attorney for personal injury litigation purposes. The privilege is not recognized if the patient has an unlawful purpose in the consultation, such as to secure an illegal abortion, to obtain narcotics in violation of the law, or to have his or her appearance disguised by plastic surgery when a fugitive from justice.

In most jurisdictions, an implicit waiver of the privilege occurs when a plaintiff files a civil suit for personal injury damages. Plaintiffs are not permitted to sue for personal injuries while preventing their doctors, pursuant to the physician-client privilege, from disclosing pertinent treatment information. The privilege is also often statutorily waived in actions for workers' compensation, prosecutions for homicide, assault with a deadly weapon, commitment proceedings, and will contests.

Cleric and Penitent. The cleric-penitent privilege recognizes the need to disclose confidentially to a spiritual or religious counselor what are believed to be flawed acts or thoughts and to receive guidance in return. This privilege also recognizes that members of the clergy often assume roles as counselors, doing much work that overlaps with psychiatrists and psychologists, both of whom have the benefit of privileged physician-patient communications in most states. —*David R. Sobel*

See also Attorney; Defense attorney; News media; News sources, protection of; Public defender.

BIBLIOGRAPHY

A number of general works include good discussions of privileged communications, among them Charles Tilford McCormick, *McCormick on Evidence* (4th ed. St. Paul, Minn.: West, 1992); *American Jurisprudence* (2d ed. Rochester, N.Y.: Lawyers' Co-operative, 1979); Eric D. Green, *Problems, Cases, and Materials on Evidence* (Boston: Little, Brown, 1993); and John Henry Wigmore, *Evidence in Trials at Common Law* (2d. ed. Boston: Little, Brown, 1961). More specific discussions include Alan B. Vickery, "Breach of Confidence: An Emerging Tort," in *Columbia Law Review* 82 (November, 1982), and "Communication to Clergyman as Privileged," in *American Law Reports* (3d ed. Rochester, N.Y.: Lawyers' Co-operative, 1975).

Probable cause

DEFINITION: The likelihood that a search or seizure warrant is justified; the Fourth Amendment states that no search or arrest warrants "shall issue, but upon probable cause"

SIGNIFICANCE: The probable cause requirement, an important concept in search and seizure law, protects individuals against government abuse of its power to seize evidence and arrest people suspected of a crime

In Great Britain a series of statutes beginning in the fourteenth century authorized government officials and, in some cases, private individuals to search for and seize certain items. The power to search and seize was not effectively limited, and many abuses occurred in terms of indiscriminate searches and seizures. For example, the Licensing Act of 1662 authorized almost unlimited searches and seizures by the king's secretaries of state in their efforts to seek out any seditious or unlicensed publication of books and pamphlets. General warrants and writs of assistance, some of the most obnoxious forms of unlimited search and seizure power, were used extensively by England to enforce its mercantile taxation policies and to investigate illegal smuggling activities in the American colonies.

The Fourth Amendment to the U.S. Constitution was designed to prevent the federal government from using the much-hated general warrants and writs of assistance. The requirement of probable cause ensured that warrants for searches and seizures would not be issued based on only vague claims that they were necessary for the protection of the state or its citizens.

The Fourth Amendment's probable cause requirement was never intended to prevent or frustrate law enforcement. The Supreme Court has consistently emphasized that the determination of probable cause is pragmatic inquiry, the outcome of which is dependent on the specific facts in each case. In each case, probable cause should be determined using a practical, nontechnical approach in examining the facts. Whether probable cause exists in a case involving a warrant turns on the question of whether, based on the totality of the circumstances disclosed in the warrant application, a magistrate using common sense could conclude that there was a fair probability that evidence sought would be found in the place to be searched or that the person sought committed the alleged crime. According to the U.S. Supreme Court in *Illinois v. Gates* (1983), when a warrant is used, an appellate court should give great deference to the magistrate's determination of probable cause so long as it has a substantial basis in facts disclosed in the affidavits supporting the request for a warrant.

In some cases probable cause is also the standard used by judges in determining whether action taken by the police without a warrant was an unreasonable search or seizure. In a warrantless circumstance, the determination of probable cause turns on the question of whether trustworthy facts and circumstances within a police officer's knowledge at the time he or she acted would lead a person of reasonable caution to conclude that a crime was being or had been committed or that the evidence sought may be found in the place searched (*Draper v. United States*, 1959). In *Terry v. Ohio* (1968), the Supreme Court authorized brief warrantless detention and, in some circumstances, a limited search of individuals based on reasonable suspicion. Subsequently, the Supreme Court has reemphasized that in most cases when a finding of probable cause is required, the facts must establish the presence of more than a reasonable suspicion.

See also Arrest; Presumption of innocence; Reasonable doubt; Search and seizure; *Terry v. Ohio*.

Probation

DEFINITION: A judicial act that permits convicted criminals to remain free in society under conditions set by, and under the supervision of, officers appointed by the court

SIGNIFICANCE: Probation reduces the cost of maintaining people convicted of crimes and protects nonviolent offenders from corruption by the hardened criminals they would encounter in prison

Probation, parole, and pardon are three elements of the justice system that are somewhat akin to one another but serve significantly different purposes. Probation is a court-ordered action that permits convicted criminals, particularly those without previous criminal records, to continue to function in society under the close supervision of a probation officer for whatever period of time the court has mandated. Parole, on the other hand, is an executive action that releases prisoners, who have served part of their sentences, from confinement under the close supervision of a parole officer. Both probation and parole can be revoked if probationers or parolees fail to meet the conditions of their releases. Pardon, like parole, is an executive action, but it exempts a person from punishment for a crime, even when evidence or implication of guilt exists.

Probation in the United States. The concept of probation was introduced into the United States in 1841 by John Augustus, a respected Boston businessman, who convinced a judge to release to his custody a man convicted of public drunkenness. Augustus took the convict home, cleaned him up, outfitted him with new apparel, and helped him to find a job. When this totally changed and rehabilitated person appeared in court weeks later, the judge, impressed by his transformation, fined him one cent and released him.

In the eighteen years before Augustus' death in 1859, this civic-minded man had nearly two thousand convicted criminals released into his custody, which marked the beginning of the probation system in the United States. Initially, Augustus rescued only those convicted of drunkenness, but in time he also supervised the release of people convicted of graver crimes. The success record of those released to Augustus' supervision and care is impressive. Fewer than twelve ran away, and few were convicted of future crimes.

Soon the practice of probation, which is now a vital and necessary part of the judicial system, spread to venues throughout the United States. Pioneers who followed Augustus in helping to promote this form of social control were Rufus W. Cook and William J. Mullen.

Advantages of Probation. For many convicted criminals, particularly first offenders convicted of nonviolent crimes, probation is a more effective punishment than imprisonment and the removal from society that accompanies it. Probationers are viewed as being clearly guilty of the crimes of which they are accused, but they are given the opportunity to put their convictions behind them and to build a future for themselves. Many probation programs offer probationers extensive counseling. The word "probation" is derived from the Latin word that means to prove, and proving themselves is precisely what probationers are charged with doing. It is estimated that rehabilitation occurs in more than 70 percent of all probation cases.

The economic advantages of probation are sufficiently great that, as state budgets come under increasing strain, probation

AVERAGE MONTHS OF PROBATION SENTENCES IMPOSED BY STATE COURTS, 1990					
	Probation Sentence in Case of				
			Split Sentence of Probation with:		
Most Serious Conviction Offense	*Total*	*Straight Probation*	*Total*	*Prison*	*Jail*
All offenses	42	42	42	48	40
Violent offenses	48	46	49	58	45
Murder	64	67	63	69	49
Rape	64	61	65	68	63
Robbery	50	50	49	59	44
Aggravated assault	43	43	43	53	40
Other violent	47	45	49	46	50
Property offenses	43	44	42	49	39
Burglary	49	48	47	60	41
Larceny	40	41	37	40	37
Fraud	42	43	41	43	40
Drug offenses	41	42	41	47	38
Possession	38	39	37	38	37
Trafficking	43	44	43	50	40
Weapons offenses	35	34	36	39	35
Other offenses	39	40	39	39	40

Source: U.S. Department of Justice, Bureau of Justice Statistics, *Sourcebook of Criminal Justice Statistics—1993.* Washington, D.C.: U.S. Government Printing Office, 1994.

becomes a much more appealing solution to crime control than imprisonment. The cost of maintaining a probationer is one-tenth the cost of confining a prisoner. Further, probationers can work to support themselves and their dependents, whereas the families of imprisoned criminals often become wards of the state. From a purely humanitarian perspective, it is generally thought beneficial to society for the families of convicted criminals to be disrupted as little as possible. With skillful guidance from probation officers, probationers often learn to adapt to a society in which they have previously found it impossible to function productively. At its best, probation can turn criminals around by alerting them to opportunities of which they had never before been aware.

Probation is an obvious and ready solution to prison over-crowding, which has become a major problem in the United States. The country's prison population grew from just over two hundred thousand in 1980 to 1.1 million in 1990. The cost of maintaining one prisoner in confinement for a year is close to twenty thousand dollars nationally, whereas less than two thousand is spent annually on the average probationer.

Reservations About Probation. The courts have found that prisoners assured of being given probation are more likely to plead guilty to the crimes of which they are accused than they would be if they faced time in prison. This is advantageous to courts, whose calendars are clogged, but it may be distinctly disadvantageous to those accused of crimes of which they are not actually guilty.

Fear of being convicted and sent to prison if their cases go to trial has encouraged some accused people to plead guilty to felonies they did not commit. This is especially true among the impoverished and those against whom a circumstantial case is strong. Some jurists question the ethics of courts that promise probation in return for guilty pleas while implying that a trial will be likely to result in incarceration.   *—R. Baird Shuman*

See also Criminal procedure; Good time; House arrest; Pardoning power; Parole; Punishment.

BIBLIOGRAPHY

Helpful sources on probation are Howard Abadinsky, *Probation and Parole: Theory and Practice* (3d ed. Englewood Cliffs, N.J.: Prentice-Hall, 1987); Robert Carter and Leslie T. Wilkins, eds., *Probation and Parole: Selected Readings* (New York: John Wiley & Sons, 1970); Dean J. Champion, *Criminal Justice in the United States* (Columbus, Ohio: Merrill, 1990); Dean J. Champion, *Felony Probation: Problems and Prospects* (Westport, Conn.: Praeger, 1988); Dean J. Champion, *Probation and Parole in the United States* (Columbus, Ohio: Merrill, 1990); Reed K. Clegg, *Probation and Parole: Principles and Practices* (Springfield, Ill.: Charles C Thomas, 1974); Barbara A. Kay and Clyde B. Vedder, *Probation and Parole* (Springfield, Ill.: Charles C Thomas, 1974).

Products liability

DEFINITION: The area of law that governs under what circumstances a manufacturer, seller, or other party may be held liable for injury or damage resulting from the use of a product

SIGNIFICANCE: Products liability law reflects the idea that consumers need greater protection against the manufacture and sale of unsafe products than warrantee protection offers

The term "products liability" refers to the liability of a manufacturer or seller of a product when personal injury or damage to property is caused by a defect in the product. Generally, a defect is defined as a condition that makes the product unreasonably dangerous to the user or consumer. Products liability typically does not encompass a dissatisfied purchaser's claim for breach of a contract because of a bad bargain in cases where there is a demand for a refund of the purchase price or cost of obtaining a replacement in the absence of any personal injury, property damage, or commercial loss.

Origin of the Doctrine. The law of products liability has its origin in both tort and contract law. The public policy giving rise to the doctrine of products liability dictated that consumers needed more protection against dangerous products than is afforded by the law of warranty. As the complexity of products has increased, so has the opportunity for mishap in design, manufacturing, marketing, or use. This fact has resulted in significant increases in the incidence of—and the severity of damage caused by—defective products. The law of products liability led to the burden of loss being shared between product purchasers and users (who primarily bore the burden in the past) and manufacturers and vendors. The responsibility of manufacturers and vendors was increased in recognition of their ability most effectively and least expensively to prevent damage caused by their own products, while being in a superior position to absorb and distribute loss as an expense of production and sale.

Generally, a product is viewed as any object possessing intrinsic value, whether capable of delivery either as an assembled whole or as a component part, which is produced for introduction into trade or commerce. Most states have enacted statutes expressly excluding human tissue, organs, blood, blood components, and approved animal tissue from the law of products liability.

What Constitutes a Defective Condition. To be defective, a product must be either unreasonably dangerous in normal use per se or dangerous in normal use because of its construction or composition, the manufacturer's failure to warn, or its design. The "normal use" of a product includes foreseeable misuse, and a manufacturer is obligated to take into account such misuse in designing its product.

A product is unreasonably dangerous per se if a reasonable person would conclude that the danger-in-fact of the product or risks inherent in it, whether foreseeable or not, outweigh the product's utility or benefit. A product is unreasonably dangerous in construction or composition if at the time it leaves the control of its manufacturer it contains an unintended abnormality or condition that makes the product more dangerous than it was designed to be.

A product is unreasonably dangerous if the manufacturer fails to warn adequately about a danger related to the way the product was designed. A manufacturer is required to provide an adequate warning of any danger inherent in the normal use of its product which is not within the knowledge of, or obvious to, the ordinary user. A product is unreasonably dangerous in design if, while not unreasonably dangerous per se, alternative products were available to serve the same needs or desires with less risk of harm or there was a feasible way to design the product with less harmful consequences.

Theories for Recovery of Damages. The manufacturer is not an absolute ensurer that its product's design will not produce injury. There are three basic legal theories for liability that can be used in most jurisdictions as bases on which a plaintiff can sue a manufacturer in a products liability action: strict liability, which focuses on the quality of the product; negligence, which focuses on the conduct of the defendant; and expressed warranty and implied warranty, which focuses on the performance of the product against the explicit or implicit representations made on its behalf by the manufacturer or seller.

Strict liability in tort is the doctrine most commonly associated with products liability. It had its origin in 1963, when the California Supreme Court held in *Greenman v. Yuba Power Products, Inc.* that "a manufacturer is strictly liable in tort when an article he places on the market, knowing that it is to be used without inspection for defect, proves to have a defect that causes injury to a human being." The liability is "strict" in the sense that the plaintiff need not prove the defendant's negligence. It is said to be "in tort" because it applies to situations in which defendants cannot avail themselves of the usual contract or warranty defenses which may be available in an action for breach of warranty.

Under the strict liability doctrine, the conduct of the defendant is often irrelevant. Further, it is unnecessary for the plaintiff to be the purchaser of the product. Most often, a plaintiff need only prove that the defendant placed the product on the market; that at the time the product left the defendant's possession, it was defective; that this defect made the product unreasonably dangerous for its intended (or a reasonably foreseeable) use; and that this defect was a proximate cause of some damage to the plaintiff. The plaintiff must also prove the nature and extent of the damage.

Negligence exists where there has been a failure to do something that a person of ordinary prudence would have done in the same or similar circumstances. Products liability on the ground of negligence can be found against the manufacturer, the seller, or even a corporation engaged in testing products and affixing a label thereon indicating its work on such products. Typically, the requirement of showing that the defendant failed to exercise due care makes it more burdensome for a plaintiff to prevail in a products liability action based on negligence, as opposed to an action in strict tort liability or on breach of an express or implied sales warranty.

In a products liability setting, a warranty is a contractual representation, whether implicit or express, that a product is appropriate for certain specified purposes or usages. It has also been considered an agreement by the manufacturer to be responsible for all foreseeable damages that arise from defects in its product. In most jurisdictions a warranty claim is the preferred legal theory for establishing liability for a product-caused injury, because proof of negligence is not required. In some jurisdictions a warranty has the disadvantage of being available only to the product's purchaser. The plaintiff must only prove his or her injury and damages, that the existence of the product's defect or condition breached the warranty, and that the breach of warranty was the proximate cause of the injury or loss. *David R. Sobel*

See also Civil law; Civil procedure; Class action; Consumer fraud; Consumer rights movement; Contract law; Tort; Tort reform.

BIBLIOGRAPHY

Good sources include Robert D. Hursh and Henry J. Bailey, *American Law of Products Liability* (Rochester, N.Y.: Lawyers Co-operative, 1994); Noel W. Dix and Jerry J. Phillips, *Products Liability Cases and Materials* (St. Paul, Minn.: West, 1976); William Lloyd Prosser, *Handbook of the Law of Torts* (4th ed. St. Paul, Minn.: West, 1971); Charles O. Smith, *Products Liability: Are You Vulnerable?* (Englewood Cliffs, N.J.: Prentice-Hall, 1981); and Alvin S. Weinstein, *Products Liability and the Reasonably Safe Product: A Guide for Management, Design, and Marketing* (New York: John Wiley & Sons, 1978).

Progressivism

DATE: 1890's-1917
DEFINITION: A movement involving a broad coalition of reformers and reform groups with the goal of creating a more just social and economic order; it resulted in an era of sweeping reforms in the United States
SIGNIFICANCE: The Progressive era is generally considered one of the most reform-oriented periods in American history, foreshadowing in some aspects the New Deal reforms of the 1930's

Historians have long debated the character and nature of Progressivism and the Progressive era. It is as difficult to date the beginning of Progressivism as it is problematic to pinpoint its exact origins. The changes which resulted from the social and economic transformation of American society in the late nineteenth century affected people of diverse backgrounds, and this diversity is reflected in the make-up of progressive reformers. They included labor and women's rights' activists, doctors, environmentalists, politicians, consumer advocates, professionals, and Americans from virtually all walks of life.

Despite their diversity, some common criteria were shared by all Progressives. Broadly inspired by evangelical Protestantism and scientific expertise, Progressives shared a faith in the ability of humanity to improve the conditions of its existence and to create a more just social and economic order through political means. They set out to ameliorate the conditions of the United States' urban industrial order, not to dismantle it. Most Progressives were outraged over the worst consequences of industrialization and abuses of business but also by signs of social disintegration. Because Progressives shared a strong concern with social disintegration, they also believed in control. Ideas of social justice and social control were closely intertwined in the Progressive mind.

Progressives gave different emphasis to the elements of justice and control. Arthur Link and Richard McCormick have divided the Progressives into three groups: social Progressives, reforming professionals, and coercive Progressives. Among the social Progressives, the element of control appeared in a rather benign form, such as the control of the conditions surrounding people to guarantee decent lives for all Americans. Reforming professionals, such as social hygiene experts, educators, city planners, and social workers, expected unquestioning conformity with their methods and expertise; however, reforming professionals frequently had to give in to the demands of business elites, represented by the philanthropic foundations which funded many of their projects. Coercive Progressives, on the other hand, tended to emphasize control over justice. Particularly in the American South, Progressivism for whites went hand-in-hand with segregation and disfranchisement of African Americans. Coercive attitudes were not limited to southern Progressives. Some northern Progressives publicly extolled the benefits of immigration restriction, Americanization of immigrants, and Prohibition. The combined notions of social justice and social control were an intrinsic part of Progressive reform, and in some cases justice was sacrificed in favor of control.

See also Addams, Jane; Brandeis, Louis D.; *Hammer v. Dagenhart*; Holmes, Oliver Wendell, Jr.; Hughes, Charles Evans; *Muller v. Oregon*; Sanger, Margaret; Sinclair, Upton; Steffens, Lincoln.

Prohibition

DATE: Eighteenth Amendment ratified January 16, 1919; effective January 17, 1920; repealed December 5, 1933
SIGNIFICANCE: Called a "noble experiment" by President Herbert Hoover, Prohibition (the national banning of the production, sale, and distribution of alcoholic beverages) was the most prominent attempt to legislate morality in the twentieth century; its failure brought an end to a major reform effort

The prohibitionist movement existed as early as the colonial period, but most historians date the modern form to the 1850's. The movement met with local and state successes in the late nineteenth century. By 1900 a quarter of the U.S. population was living in "dry" areas (areas where the sale of alcohol was illegal); by 1917, twenty-nine states were dry.

The Eighteenth Amendment. Congress first enacted a temporary prohibition of the sale of alcohol in 1917 as a war measure. Then, in December, 1917, a proposed amendment to the U.S. Constitution stating that the "manufacture, sale, or transportation of intoxicating liquors within, the importation thereof into, or the exportation thereof from the United States and all territory subject to the jurisdiction thereof for beverage purposes is hereby prohibited" was introduced into Congress. It speeded its way through the Senate and the House of Representatives and was sent to the states for ratification. Mississippi was the first state to ratify (on January 8, 1918), and a little more than a year later, Nebraska became the thirty-sixth, the last required. Passage of the Volstead Act, a measure designed both to continue the wartime prohibition and to provide enforcement of Prohibition as mandated by the Eighteenth Amendment, followed on October 28, 1919. The Volstead Act defined alcoholic beverages as those containing at least 0.5 percent alcohol.

The Prohibition Era. Almost from the first, Prohibition appeared to be largely unenforceable. Those who wanted to drink had little trouble locating bootleggers, and speakeasies (clubs that served alcohol illegally) abounded. The Prohibition Bureau's budget was small, and all the presidents of the period—Warren G. Harding, Calvin Coolidge, and Herbert Hoover—expressed doubts about its viability.

One of the side effects of Prohibition was the rise of organized crime. Until the 1920's gangs had been local, but that soon changed. Although there were bootleggers and illicit distillers and brewers in all parts of the country, "Scarface Al" Capone, who operated out of Chicago, became the symbol of them all. By 1927 the Capone gang was grossing an estimated $60 million a year on beer alone, and by 1929 the figure approximated $100 million. Capone's beer earnings were said to be larger than the profits of Standard Oil of Indiana, Ford, or General Electric. Without Prohibition, this situation would have been impossible. That Prohibition was considered the most divisive American political question of the 1920's is generally conceded by historians who study the period. The matter was addressed directly in the 1928 presidential election, when the country was presented with a choice between Republican Herbert Hoover, who supported Prohibition, and Democrat Al Smith, who opposed it. The election resulted in a Hoover landslide, although it was attributable more to the fact that the nation was basking in prosperity than to other issues. Despite his support of Prohibition, Hoover indicated his conviction that the Volstead Act was unenforceable. On May 29, 1929, he appointed a group to study Prohibition and make recommendations. The National Commission on Law Observation and Enforcement, headed by former attorney general George Wickersham, released its findings in 1931. The Wickersham Report concluded that a more serious attempt at enforcement would be required if Washington expected the public to take the Volstead Act seriously.

Prohibition was a major issue in the 1932 presidential race. The Republicans renominated Hoover and at his insistence adopted a conciliatory position on Prohibition, calling for the Eighteenth Amendment to be resubmitted to the states for ratification. The Democrats, led by Franklin D. Roosevelt, supported outright repeal.

Repeal of Prohibition. Roosevelt's election spelled the end of Prohibition. On December 7, 1932, the House Ways and Means Committee held hearings on the matter of modifying the Volstead Act. Shortly thereafter, Representative James Collier introduced a measure to legalize beer with a 2.75 percent alcohol content. It won approval in the House and was sent on to the Senate. There it became the Collier-Blaine Bill, which in its new form upped the alcoholic content to 3.05 percent—another sign that Prohibition was a fading crusade.

On February 20, 1933, Congress passed what would become the Twenty-first Amendment, repealing the Eighteenth. It was sent to the states for ratification. Roosevelt did not have to wait until ratification to ask for changes in the Volstead Act, however; legislation based on the Collier-Blaine Bill, now known as the Cullen-Harrison Bill, which legalized 3.2 percent beer, was passed by Congress. On March 22, in the midst of his famous "hundred days," in which a rush of legislation was passed to fight the Great Depression, Roosevelt signed into law the Beer and Wine Revenue Act—the title was significant—which legalized beer and wine with an alcohol content of 3.2 percent, effective April 7, 1933, in those states and areas without local laws to the contrary.

At the same time, the proposed amendment made its way through the states. Utah ratified it on December 5, whereupon it became part of the Constitution. Prohibition at the federal level died.

Most historians agree that Prohibition marked a major step in the development of a federal presence in law enforcement. The modern Federal Bureau of Investigation had its origins in the enforcement of Prohibition statutes. Prohibition also made possible the growth of organized crime. Defenders of the "war against drugs" observe that liquor consumption fell in the 1920's; opponents point to the experience of Prohibition as an indication that criminalization of such behavior does not work. Both sides agree, however, that the way in which the laws were enforced (or not enforced) prompted a disrespect for law in general. —*Robert Sobel*

See also Capone, Alphonse (Al); Commercialized vice; Organized crime; Temperance movement; Victimless crimes.

BIBLIOGRAPHY

The history of Prohibition has been studied carefully by many historians and legal scholars. For background, there is Donald Barr Chidsey, *On and Off the Wagon: A Sober Analysis of the Temperance Movement from the Pilgrims Through Prohibition* (New York: Cowles, 1969), and John Krout, *The Origins of Prohibition* (New York: Alfred A. Knopf, 1925). Passage of the legislation may be found in K. Austin Kerr, *Organized for Prohibition* (New Haven, Conn.: Yale University Press, 1985). For the Prohibition experience, see Charles Merz, *The Dry Decade* (Garden City, N.Y.: Doubleday, Doran, 1931); Andrew Sinclair, *Era of Excess: A Social History of the Prohibition Movement* (New York: Harper & Row, 1964); Herbert Asbury, *The Great Illusion: An Informal History of Prohibition* (New York: Alfred A. Knopf, 1950); and J. C. Furnas, *The Life and Times of the Late Demon Rum* (London: W. H. Allen, 1965). Repeal is covered in Fletcher Dobyns, *The Amazing Story of Repeal* (Chicago: Willett, Clark, 1940), and Arthur M. Schlesinger, *The Age of Roosevelt: The Crisis of the Old Order, 1919-1933* (Boston: Houghton Mifflin, 1957).

Property rights

DEFINITION: The right to possess, use, and dispose of something

SIGNIFICANCE: The combination of control, reward, and responsibility provides a strong incentive for owners of property to use it productively, but the distribution of rewards may appear unfair

The surveying and registration of land are essential for maintaining rights to land, as are police forces and the courts.
(James L. Shaffer)

Property rights underlie all transactions involving buying and selling and are a fundamental requirement for effective functioning of a market economy. Exactly what constitutes property, and what rights go with it, must be determined by law. Usually the property owner has the right to use it, sell it, rent it out, or give it to someone else.

Three fundamental elements of property rights are control, reward, and responsibility. To own property is to have authority to determine how it is used and who may use it. The owner benefits from the property, perhaps through enjoyments, perhaps from revenue generated by the property (in such forms as rent, interest, and profits) and the proceeds from selling the property. The owner of property is responsible for paying taxes on the property and for any harm the property might cause. Legal liability may arise when one's property hurts others.

Complex issues associated with property rights arise from the institution of the "corporation." A corporation can be a legal entity entitled to own property, make contracts, buy and sell, borrow and lend, and sue and be sued. The corporation is owned by its stockholders. Their influence in corporate decision making may be relatively weak, however, and their rewards may be subordinated to management and employees.

Property rights can be judged by their influence on the behavior and character of persons involved. Owners of property have a strong incentive to use it in ways that generate high incomes and raise the market value of the property. A tract of land will yield the highest rent or capital gain if it is used in the manner which best serves the desires of consumers. Capital is most productive when invested in products which are in demand and processes which are efficient. Ownership of property also protects the freedom and independence of owners, but it raises important questions of social justice.

Rights and Government. Most fundamentally, property rights are limitations on the power of government. Such limitations were written into the U.S. Constitution, particularly in the Fifth Amendment, which states that no person shall "be deprived of life, liberty, or property, without due process of law; nor shall private property be taken for public use without just compensation." The Thirteenth Amendment abolished slavery—the ownership of one person by another.

Many government policies limit private property rights. Taxes take away some of the rewards of ownership. Zoning laws restrict uses of real estate. Owners of rental housing find their rewards and authority limited by rent controls and legislation regarding eviction procedures. Licensing, franchising, and chartering policies may restrict the ability of individuals to use their property in certain types of production. Civil-asset forfeitures permit law enforcement officers to seize property even without a conviction for any crime, as with persons accused of drug offenses. The manner in which business firms use their property is affected by many types of labor legislation, particularly regulation of health and safety conditions. Federal agricultural policies adopted in the 1930's restricted farmers' opportunities to use their land as they wished. In the 1970's and 1980's, policies aimed at protecting the environ-ment conflicted with traditional property rights, especially concerning so-called wetlands and land areas where endangered species were to be found.

Property rights require much support from government. Land property, for example, is protected through the surveying of land and recording of ownership and, more generally, through a system of police and courts of law. Criminal law protects property owners against theft and trespass, while much private law concerns relationships between property owners and other people. Inheritance, marriage, and divorce law all involve property.

Social Justice Issues. While seventeenth century philosopher John Locke defended the right to property as the right to the fruits of one's own labor, nineteenth century socialists argued that property often gave the owners an unfair privilege to enjoy the fruits of other people's labor. Karl Marx claimed that private ownership of the means of production led to widespread poverty and inequality. Indeed, property ownership is usually quite unequal, and wealthy persons often acquire their property through gift or inheritance rather than through work. On the other hand, when Communist revolutions in Russia and China abolished private ownership of production and replaced it with systems of state ownership and control, oppression and grossly inefficient economic systems resulted.   —*Paul B. Trescott*

See also Capitalism; Eminent domain; Marxism; *Nollan v. California Coastal Commission*; Real estate law; Takings clause; Wills, trusts, and estate planning; Zoning.

BIBLIOGRAPHY

A wide range of viewpoints, historical and modern, on property rights can be found in James Bovard, *Lost Rights: The Destruction of American Liberty* (New York: St. Martin's Press, 1994); Richard T. Ely, *Property and Contract in Their Relations to the Distribution of Wealth* (New York: Macmillan, 1914); Werner Hirsch, *Law and Economics: An Introductory Analysis* (2d ed. Boston: Academic Press, 1988); Richard Posner, *Economic Analysis of Law* (2d ed. Boston: Little, Brown, 1977); and Richard H. Tawney, *The Acquisitive Society* (New York: Harcourt, Brace and Howe, 1920). *Property Rights and the Limits of Democracy*, edited by Charles K. Rowley (Brookfield, Vt.: Edward Elgar, 1993), includes an essay by Nobel Prize winner James Buchanan.

Prosecutor, public

DEFINITION: The attorney serving as the public official responsible for overseeing the prosecution of criminal cases by setting charges, conducting plea negotiations, and presenting evidence in court on behalf of the government

SIGNIFICANCE: The prosecutor is one of the most powerful actors in the justice system because of the office's broad discretionary powers to determine which cases will be pursued and which defendants will be permitted to plead guilty to lesser charges

The prosecutor is the public official who acts as the attorney representing the government and the public in pursuing criminal convictions. The prosecutor possesses broad powers to determine which defendants to prosecute, what charges to pursue, and which cases to terminate through plea bargains. The prosecutor must oppose the defense attorney during trials and present sufficient and appropriate evidence to persuade a judge or jury to render a verdict of guilty.

The Prosecutorial System. The concept of the American prosecutor was drawn from English legal tradition, in which a representative of the king sought to persuade jurors that a particular individual should be charged and convicted of a crime. In the United States, prosecutorial responsibilities are divided among the various levels of government. Federal prosecutors are known as U.S. attorneys. They are appointed to office by the president and are each responsible for prosecuting federal crimes in one of the ninety-four federal district courts throughout the United States. Within each courthouse, they are assisted with their tasks by teams of assistant prosecutors. Their work is often coordinated by the attorney general of the United States and the U.S. Department of Justice.

At the state level, each state has an elected attorney general who, in most states, possesses the power to initiate prosecutions for violations of state laws. In three states—Alaska, Delaware, and Rhode Island—the attorney general oversees all local prosecutors. In most states, however, the focus of prosecutorial power is the local prosecutor. These local prosecutors are sometimes known as district attorneys or states' attorneys. In all states except Connecticut and New Jersey, local prosecutors are elected officials who have primary responsibility for investigating and prosecuting violations of state criminal laws within their counties. In Connecticut and New Jersey, local prosecutors are appointed and supervised by state officials. By contrast, local prosecutors in other states are accountable to the voters within their counties. They are usually visible political figures who seek to please and impress the voters with their efforts to combat crime.

Many attorneys use the office of county prosecutor as a stepping-stone to higher offices as judges, state legislators, or members of Congress. The prosecutor's office serves this purpose especially well because of its high visibility in the local community and because the prosecutor can show tangible success in battling crime—an issue of widespread concern to voters. Moreover, prosecutors do not have to become involved in controversial issues that divide the community such as welfare spending or education. They can devote their time to publicizing their success in the battle against crime, which enjoys unified public support.

Because of the visibility and power of the local prosecutor's office, political parties frequently devote significant energy and resources to battling each other during election campaigns for the prosecutor's office. As a result, political leaders often select prosecutorial candidates based on their ability to raise campaign funds and their attractiveness to the voters rather than on their prior experience as attorneys. Attorneys who have never handled criminal cases before in their lives sometimes win elections as prosecutors. If their offices are anywhere but in rural areas, however, they usually have experienced assistant prosecutors who handle the steady flow of cases and teach them about criminal law. In small towns and rural counties, the local prosecutor may not have many assistant prosecutors, if any.

Because of prosecutors' involvement in politics, political considerations sometimes affect their decisions. They may use their offices to provide jobs (as assistant prosecutors and investigators) for loyal members of their political party. They may prosecute vigorously any questionable activity by political opponents while turning a blind eye to wrongdoing by influential citizens or by their political supporters. Because no official supervises or commands the local prosecutors in most states, it is up to the local voters to ensure that prosecutors perform according to professional standards. Voters are the only ones who possess the power to remove most prosecutors from office.

Prosecutors' Decision Making. Prosecutors possess broad powers. They can use their discretion to determine which defendants are charged, what charges are pursued, which plea bargains to approve, and what strategies to employ during trials. Prosecutors even possess the power to drop charges against defendants without providing any reasons. This power to drop charges cannot be stopped or reversed by any other official, not even a judge or the governor. The primary pressure that keeps prosecutors from having unchecked power is the risk that the public will be unhappy with the prosecutor's decisions and vote him or her out of office at the next election.

Prosecutors are responsible for many key decisions in the criminal process. They must evaluate the evidence brought to them by the police in order to determine which charges, if any, to file against each defendant. Prosecutors make recommendations about whether defendants should be released on bail. Studies show that judges are usually very deferential to prosecutors' recommendations about whether bail is to be granted, the bail amount, and the conditions of release. Prosecutors also control the grand jury process by presenting evidence against the suspects that they have chosen without any defense attorneys in the courtroom to argue against the issuance of indictments. In states that do not use grand juries, prosecutors initiate charges against a defendant by filing an information describing the charges to be pursued based on the evidence thus far available. Prosecutors handle plea negotiations on behalf of the government and recommend sentences when defendants plead guilty. Prosecutors also develop trial strategies and determine how evidence will be presented to the jury for those few cases that are not terminated through plea bargains.

Prosecutors' decision making is influenced by their need to please several constituencies. Because prosecutors' jobs depend on public support, prosecutors typically try to develop good relations with the news media. They want news reports to show them as making tough, intelligent decisions in identifying and prosecuting criminal suspects. Prosecutors must also have good relationships with the police, because they must rely on the police to do a good job in making arrests and gathering appropriate evidence. Prosecutors do not want to displease police officers by dropping charges or agreeing to light sentences during plea bargaining, because the police then may be less enthusiastic and cooperative in investigating subsequent cases. Prosecutors also rely on good relationships with the local county commission, city council, or state legislature that provides the annual budget for the prosecutor's office. If the prosecutors cannot please these elected officials, then they may receive inadequate resources in the following year's

Under the direction of District Attorney Gil Garcetti, Marcia Clark led the prosecution team that unsuccessfully attempted to convict celebrity athlete O. J. Simpson of murder in 1995. (AP/Wide World Photos)

budget. Although prosecutors have broad discretionary power, their relationships with political constituencies influence their decisions and actions.

Prosecutors' decisions are also influenced by their need to process a steady flow of cases with their office's limited resources. For most prosecutors, this situation helps to encourage their participation in plea bargaining. Most offices do not have the time, money, or personnel to bring every case to trial. Moreover, prosecutors gain definite convictions when they can negotiate a guilty plea. If cases go to trial, there is always a risk that unpredictable juries might not render guilty verdicts. Through plea bargaining, prosecutors gain quick convictions with a minimal expenditure of resources.

Prosecutors usually hold the upper hand in plea bargaining because they can initially charge defendants with multiple offenses, even if they are not sure that they can prove all the charges. This gives the prosecutor the ability to apply pressure to the defendant by scaring the defendant with the prospect of multiple convictions and punishments if a guilty plea is not forthcoming. The U.S. Supreme Court has decided that prosecutors can threaten defendants with additional charges during plea negotiations. Although the judge officially controls sentencing, most judges will routinely approve whatever sentence the prosecutor recommends as part of a plea agreement. Because more than 90 percent of cases terminate through plea bargains, the prosecutor effectively influences the sentences imposed on offenders in most cases.

The plea-bargaining process in many courthouses becomes streamlined through cooperative relationships that develop among prosecutors, public defenders, and judges. Frequently, the same assistant prosecutor, public defender, and judge are in the same courtroom day after day discussing plea bargains in one case after another. Before long, they come to understand one another's assessments of the seriousness of specific kinds of crimes and of the appropriate severity of punishment for each crime. Once they develop common understandings about the sentences to be imposed for specific offenses or repeat offenders, they can quickly develop consistent plea agreements in each new case that arrives before them.

PROSECUTION AND LEGAL SERVICES EMPLOYEES, 1990			
	Employment		
Level of Government	Total	Full-Time	Full-Time Equivalent
Federal	24,947	24,947	24,947
State	30,199	27,871	29,046
County	42,018	38,484	40,049
Municipal	20,562	17,615	18,365
Total	117,726	108,917	112,407

Source: U.S. Department of Justice, Bureau of Justice Statistics, *Sourcebook of Criminal Justice Statistics—1993.* Washington, D.C.: U.S. Government Printing Office, 1994.

Prosecutors and the Adversary System. Because the American justice process employs an adversary system that pits prosecutors against defense attorneys, many critics fear that prosecutors are encouraged to seek convictions at all costs rather than examine each case carefully to determine whether someone arrested by the police is, in fact, guilty. In an adversary system, attorneys can become too focused on simply defeating the opponent rather than ensuring that justice is accomplished through the conviction of guilty defendants. There is a risk that attorneys, including prosecutors, will attempt to hide information from their opponents, even when that evidence might cast doubt on the guilt of a defendant and thereby increase the probability that an innocent person receives unjustified punishment.

In other countries (in Germany, for example), prosecutors are appointed government officials who are under the supervision of a national office. They have secure positions, and their decisions are less susceptible to political pressures. They are obligated to reveal any evidence that questions the defendant's guilt, and their ultimate objective as professionals is to see that correct decisions are made. By contrast, as elected officials in an adversary system, American prosecutors are under pressure from the community to solve crimes. They may be blamed by the public and subsequently lose office if highly publicized crimes remain unsolved. This pressure may create incentives for prosecutors to pursue cases aggressively against defendants, even in instances in which the available evidence may be less than compelling. If prosecutors are unethical, their lack of the job security possessed by government-employee prosecutors in other countries may lead them to manufacture evidence against selected individuals simply to avoid public blame for unsolved crimes. Such problems are not widespread, but they have occurred with sufficient frequency over American history to raise questions about whether elected prosecutors in an adversarial system can make sufficiently objective decisions to avoid misuse of prosecutors' broad powers.

—*Christopher E. Smith*

See also Attorney, United States; Attorney general, state; Attorney general of the United States; Criminal justice system; Defense attorney; District attorney; Grand jury; Indictment; Plea bargaining; Public defender.

BIBLIOGRAPHY

A basic interpretation of the prosecutor's role in the various stages of the criminal justice process is contained in George F. Cole, *The American System of Criminal Justice* (7th ed. Belmont, Calif.: Wadsworth, 1995). A history and overview of American prosecutors and their roles is presented in Joan E. Jacoby, *The American Prosecutor: A Search for Identity* (Lexington, Mass.: Lexington Books, 1980). A collection of scholarly essays about prosecutors' work is presented in William F. McDonald, ed., *The Prosecutor* (Beverly Hills, Calif.: Sage, 1979). First-person accounts of prosecutors' work are contained in David Heilbroner, *Rough Justice: Days and Nights of a Young D. A.* (New York: Pantheon Books, 1990), and Judith Rowland, *The Ultimate Violation* (Garden City, N.Y.: Doubleday, 1985).

Psychopath and sociopath

DEFINITION: Psychopathy is a psychological phenomenon: Psychopaths have an egocentric, impulsive personality and lack the "social emotions"; sociopathy is a sociological phenomenon: Sociopaths exhibit recurrent criminal antisocial behavior

SIGNIFICANCE: The great majority of crimes are committed by a small proportion of individuals (sociopaths) who are "career criminals"; some sociopaths have psychopathic personalities and may commit particularly brutal and heartless crimes, and these individuals are the hardest to rehabilitate

The terms "psychopath" and "sociopath" are typically used very loosely, often interchangeably. While there is substantial overlap between these categories, there are also meaningful distinctions; not every member of one category is automatically a member of the other. It is important, in terms of prevention and rehabilitation, to clarify the differences.

Psychopaths. Psychopathy is a personality type exhibited mostly by men; about 4 percent of males and 1 percent of females are psychopaths. The typical psychopath is superficially amiable and extroverted but cannot maintain deep interpersonal ties; he is socially irresponsible, exhibits marked impulsivity, and is exceedingly egocentric and manipulative. Because of his superficial sociability and charm, a psychopath is often able to deceive and manipulate others through use of elaborate scams and ruses, such as fraud, bigamy, and embezzlement.

Psychopaths are not, in any standard sense, intellectually handicapped; in terms of intelligence, they are average or above average. Thus, they are well aware of the concepts of right and wrong. Despite this knowledge, however, psychopaths do not internalize moral values. They can verbally state what behaviors are considered moral and ethical, but they feel no compunctions about acting the opposite way. Because they are characterized by an inability to experience the "social emotions" of love, shame, guilt, empathy, and remorse, nineteenth century philosophers referred to psychopaths as being "morally insane." The psychopathic personality type seems to be a result of having a nervous system that is chronically understimulated. Because of this, psychopaths are constantly experimenting, seeking thrills, and pushing boundaries to their limits. This behavior is often destructive, but in a sense the psychopath is only trying to get enough mental and physical stimulation to feel "normal."

The first signs of psychopathy appear at a very early age (approximately four years). Children who inherit this physiology and personality are very hard to control (because of their impulsiveness) and very hard to socialize (because of their lack of fear and guilt). In fact, psychopaths do not experience emotional or even physical pain in the same way that others do; this inability makes it hard for them to empathize with others and makes it difficult for them to learn from punishment—two processes that are important for normal moral development. While it is not completely clear how psychopathy develops, it is clear that it has a large genetic component. Studies of adopted children in a variety of cultures have shown that psychopathy is transmitted from biological, not adoptive, parents. It is also

Serial killers, such as David Berkowitz, the "Son of Sam" killer who murdered six in New York City in the 1970's, are often classic psychopaths. (AP/Wide World Photos)

clear that hormones are somehow involved, in that males are much more likely to be psychopathic than females.

Because of its biological nature, psychopathy is difficult to prevent or change, and rehabilitation of psychopaths is notoriously difficult. Because they are not intellectually handicapped, psychopaths often use their intelligence to mimic feelings of remorse and elicit sympathy from others. When criminal psychopaths are released from prison, their recidivism rates are much higher than those of other released offenders. It seems that the only ways to prevent criminal psychopaths from repeating their behavior are either to offer them opportunities for a noncriminal life with prestige and excitement (which society is generally unwilling to do, but which occasionally happens—as when a psychopath becomes famous by writing a book of his or her exploits) or to keep them imprisoned for the greater part of their life until hormone levels drop enough to reduce their impulsivity and need for sensation. There are indications that this occurs at approximately age fifty.

Finally, while it is the case that many psychopaths seek excitement and challenge through crime, not all become criminals. Thrill-seeking and risk-taking individuals have attributes that can make them good scientists or entrepreneurs; they are also particularly well-suited for occupations that require a kind of detached, fearless approach, such as being soldiers, pilots, or firefighters.

Sociopaths. Unlike psychopathy, sociopathy is a behavior, not a personality type. As such, it is much more flexible; a person may be sociopathic only during certain times in his or her life, or only under certain circumstances.

Sociopathic behavior is directly related to what has been called the "criminogenic environment." That is, criminal antisocial behavior occurs in the greatest frequencies in poor, crowded neighborhoods by individuals who have few resources, poor education, few job opportunities, and few positive social skills. Many have been victims of parental neglect or abuse. Some individuals living in such stark and hopeless circumstances perceive that they have nothing to lose and everything to gain by engaging in criminal behavior. Thus, the proportion of sociopaths in a population fluctuates directly with environmental circumstances.

Members of urban gangs are a good example of the sociopathy that results from the criminogenic environment. Some people have referred to gang territories as "war zones," and the behavior of gangs is in some ways much like that of soldiers in wartime situations: constant paranoia, hair-trigger responses to any environmental disturbance, and sometimes the cold, detached harming of innocent people.

Because it seems to have its roots in social, not biological, conditions, sociopathy is more easily preventable and more easily reversed than psychopathy. Sociopaths do not lack social emotions, and so can learn to empathize with their victims and to feel true pain and remorse for their actions. As a result, compared with psychopaths, sociopaths are more likely to profit from therapy and/or social and occupational skills training programs. They are also more likely to desist from further criminal activity after rehabilitation. —*Linda Mealey*

See also Competency to stand trial; Criminal; Insanity defense; Moral turpitude; Murders, mass and serial; Pedophilia; Rehabilitation.

BIBLIOGRAPHY

Robert D. Hare, *Without Conscience: The Disturbing World of the Psychopaths Among Us* (New York: Pocket Books, 1993), is the most readable book describing adult psychopaths. The best book on child and adolescent psychopaths is *High Risk: Children Without Conscience*, by Ken Magid and Carole A. McKelvey (New York: Bantam Books, 1987). For more historical background and a more diverse set of perspectives, see *Personality Theory, Moral Development, and Criminal Behavior*, edited by William S. Laufer and James M. Day (Lexington, Mass.: Lexington Books, 1983). *Crime and Human Nature*, by James Q. Wilson and Richard J. Herrnstein (New York: Simon & Schuster, 1985), is an excellent general book on the causes of crime and sociopathy. For more specific reading on the biological and social causes of antisocial behavior, see, respectively, Adrian Raine and Jennifer Dunkin's 1990 article "The Genetic and Psychophysiological Basis of Antisocial Behavior: Implications for Counseling and Therapy," in the *Journal of Counseling and Development* 68 (July-August, 1990), and G. R. Patterson, Barbara DeBarsyshe, and Elizabeth Ramsey's 1989 article "A Developmental Perspective on Antisocial Behavior," in *The American Psychologist* 44 (February 1, 1989).

Public defender

DEFINITION: An attorney compensated by the government to provide legal representation to criminal defendants who are too poor to hire their own lawyers

SIGNIFICANCE: The public defender is a key actor in the American adversarial system of criminal justice because this attorney is responsible for ensuring that each defendant's rights are protected and each defendant's case is presented in a forceful, professional manner

The public defender represents criminal defendants who cannot afford to hire their own attorneys. Although the public defender is paid by the government, this attorney bears the professional responsibility of vigorously defending accused persons, even those against whom there is clear-cut evidence of guilt. The public defender must make sure that each indigent defendant's constitutional rights are protected and that the prosecution proves its case before any poor person is convicted of a crime and receives a sentence of incarceration or death. The public defender must play this role through the processing of criminal cases, from the initial police interrogations of suspects through jury trials and initial appeals. American history has demonstrated that when there are no lawyers assigned to represent poor defendants, there are grave risks that innocent people will be convicted of crimes or that police officers and prosecutors will violate constitutional rights in the course of seeking criminal convictions.

The Constitution and Adversarial Justice. The colonists who established the United States and wrote the U.S. Constitution brought with them from England a profound distrust of governmental power. From English legal traditions they borrowed institutions and practices that they hoped would diminish the risk that police and prosecutors could arrest, convict, and imprison people unfairly. In the Bill of Rights, they established people's rights to fair trials, trial by jury, freedom from compelled self-incrimination, and other mechanisms designed to reduce the risk that prosecutors would wield excessive power. In drawing from these English traditions, the American founders established an adversarial system of justice in which the defendant would have the right to present arguments and evidence in opposition to the prosecution before a decision was rendered by a neutral group of citizens making up the jury. A key element of this adversarial system established by the Sixth Amendment was Americans' right to counsel during criminal proceedings.

During the nineteenth century, the Sixth Amendment right to counsel was interpreted in a limited fashion. The provision was considered to apply only in federal cases, and it was regarded as barring any governmental effort to prevent defendants from hiring their own attorneys. As a result, poor defendants' access to adversarial justice was limited to whatever ability they possessed to represent themselves in making arguments and presenting evidence. Illiterate, uneducated, and inarticulate defendants were inevitably overwhelmed by the prosecution, regardless of their actual guilt or innocence. Eventually, the Supreme Court interpreted the Sixth Amendment to require that the government supply attorneys to represent poor defendants in federal cases, so that all defendants would have genuine access to the adversarial process (*Johnson v. Zerbst*, 1938).

During the twentieth century, many states acted on their own to supply attorneys for indigent criminal defendants in state court cases. By the early 1960's, fewer than a dozen states still refused to supply attorneys for poor defendants. The Supreme Court remedied this problem by reinterpreting the Sixth Amendment to require that attorneys be provided free of charge to represent indigent defendants facing felony charges in state courts (*Gideon v. Wainwright*, 1963). This interpretation was expanded to require representation in initial appeals after conviction (*Douglas v. California*, 1963) and, subsequently, in any case in which a defendant faced the possibility of incarceration (*Argersinger v. Hamlin*, 1972). As a result of these judicial decisions, state and county governments were required to develop methods for hiring, compensating, and assigning attorneys to represent indigent criminal defendants.

Methods of Providing Representation. Three primary means have developed for providing attorneys for indigent criminal defendants. In most urban areas, states and counties have established public defender offices, employing salaried attorneys full time to provide representation for indigent defendants. These attorneys become specialists in criminal law and frequently bring great zeal to their representation of defendants, having made a conscious career choice to become public defenders. Although these attorneys benefit from specialized training and expertise, they are often hampered by relatively low salaries and high caseloads. If there is a surge in criminal cases, each attorney in the office will have to assume a greater burden, because limited government budgets frequently preclude the possibility of hiring additional attorneys. Many attorneys suffer from "burnout," and the high turnover rate in the office means that many public defenders are young, inexperienced attorneys who may not stay with their initial career choice long enough to develop the expertise necessary for skilled advocacy. In addition, these attorneys often find that their clients are uncooperative. Because the defendants know that their attorneys are on the government's payroll, they sometimes erroneously believe that the public defenders are actually working for the prosecution. When the defendants do not cooperate in supplying information necessary for mounting a vigorous defense, public defenders' jobs are made much more difficult.

Many states and counties, especially those outside urban areas, provide representation through an appointed counsel system. Attorneys in private practice ask to be placed on the local court's list of lawyers willing to accept appointments to represent indigent defendants. As the need arises, an individual lawyer will be asked to represent a specific poor defendant. The government pays the lawyer a modest hourly rate for

PUBLIC DEFENSE EMPLOYEES, 1990			
	Employment		
Level of Government	Total	Full-Time	Full-Time Equivalent
Federal	589	589	589
State	7,377	7,055	7,255
County	7,348	6,615	7,038
Municipal	437	306	325
Total	15,751	14,565	15,207

Source: U.S. Department of Justice, Bureau of Justice Statistics, *Sourcebook of Criminal Justice Statistics—1993*. Washington, D.C.: U.S. Government Printing Office, 1994.

handling each case. In some counties, the court clerk simply assigns the next available attorney from the list when a defendant cannot afford to hire a lawyer. In other places, judges choose attorneys for each assignment. When the list is not followed in order, there are risks that judges will steer cases to their political supporters and allies.

Attorneys who participate as appointed counsel do not always possess interest or expertise in criminal law. Frequently, inexperienced attorneys fresh out of law school take criminal case appointments as a means to pay their bills while they work toward establishing a law practice for tax cases, corporate matters, or other legal issues that interest them. As a result, there may be questions about the enthusiasm and skill employed by these attorneys on behalf of indigent defendants. Many defendants believe that their appointed attorneys were too quick to engage in plea bargaining simply because they were not interested in mounting a vigorous defense. Moreover, the relatively low hourly pay scale can encourage appointed attorneys to seek quick plea bargains rather than risk assuming uncompensated costs in preparing for expensive, time-consuming trials. Some private attorneys earn all of their income from handling a high volume of quick plea bargains in order to accumulate fee payments for many cases. As a result, there are serious questions about the quality of representation provided for indigent defendants by appointed counsel.

The third method of providing representation is used in only 10 percent of counties nationwide. In the contract counsel system, each year attorneys bid for the opportunity to represent all the indigent defendants in a county. One attorney or law firm will be awarded the contract to handle all cases for a specified hourly rate or predetermined annual fee. The quality of representation will vary according to the skill and dedication of the attorney or attorneys who win the annual contract.

The American mechanisms for providing public defenders do not exhaust all possible solutions. Denmark seeks to ensure that defendants receive skilled representation by limiting appointments to experienced attorneys who are certified to represent criminal defendants. In Ontario, Canada, defendants are given vouchers that they can use to select their own attorneys, who will be compensated by the government by taking the case. In a few countries, and occasionally in American counties that exhaust their annual budget for public defense before the end of the year, judges require attorneys to represent indigent defendants without any compensation. In such situations, however, the attorneys have little incentive to prepare and present an extensive defense on behalf of the defendant.

The Process of Indigent Representation. The U.S. Supreme Court issued several decisions identifying which stages in the justice process require the opportunity to be represented by counsel. Fairness in an adversarial system of justice requires professional representation early in the criminal process in order to monitor and counteract the actions taken by the prosecution and police in gathering evidence. Yet public defenders often have fewer resources than prosecutors. While the police serve as investigators who gather evidence for the prosecution, public defenders are often completely on their own in gathering evidence and preparing a case.

Indigent people arrested for crimes are entitled to be represented by a public defender during any questioning by police or prosecutors. The public defender is responsible for ensuring that the suspect's constitutional right against compelled self-incrimination is not violated through improper or coercive questioning techniques. The presence of the defense lawyer also guards against the risk that the police or prosecutor may testify untruthfully about what the suspect said during questioning. Although defendants have a right to have a public defender present, many poor defendants waive their right to have a lawyer present during questioning, either because they do not understand the importance of professional representation or because they believe that they gain leniency by immediately cooperating with the police.

Poor defendants also have a right to a public defender during other preliminary stages. Bail hearings are a particular important stage for these defendants because they are unlikely to be able to secure release if a judge requires them to post cash in order to be released from jail pending trial. The public defender must attempt to persuade the judge that the indigent defendant can be released on his or her own recognizance without posing a risk of flight or danger to the community.

In most cases, public defenders seek favorable plea bargains in which the indigent defendant will enter a guilty plea to a reduced charge. Such plea bargains terminate more than 90 percent of cases that are not dismissed for lack of evidence early in the proceedings. Plea agreements may be discussed with the prosecution during each stage of the criminal process until an agreement is reached. Many indigent defendants do not realize that all defense attorneys, including those representing affluent clients, discuss possible plea bargains with the prosecution. Poor defendants may automatically assume that their public defender is "selling them out" because they are too poor to hire their own attorney. There may be some truth to this assumption if the public defender is not aggressively advancing the client's interests during the negotiations. Such perceptions can contribute to friction and a lack of cooperation between indigent defendants and public defenders.

Public defenders play an important role in the adversarial justice process. Yet because they are frequently hampered by low pay, limited resources, high caseloads, and uncooperative clients, there are continuing questions about whether poor criminal defendants receive adequate representation and protection of their constitutional rights.   —*Christopher E. Smith*

See also *Argersinger v. Hamlin*; Assigned counsel system; Counsel, right to; Criminal procedure; Defense attorney; *Escobedo v. Illinois*; *Gideon v. Wainwright*; *Miranda v. Arizona*; *Powell v. Alabama*; Prosecutor, public; Scottsboro cases.

BIBLIOGRAPHY
Studies of public defenders in trial courts are presented in Lisa McIntyre, *The Public Defender: The Practice of Law in the Shadows of Repute* (Chicago: University of Chicago Press, 1987); Lynn Mather, *Plea Bargaining or Trial? The Process of Criminal-Case Disposition* (Lexington, Mass.: Lexington Books, 1979); and Robert Hermann, Eric Single, and John Boston, *Counsel for the Poor: Criminal Defense in Urban America* (Lexington, Mass.: Lexington Books, 1977). One study of public defenders' appellate work is David T. Wasserman, *A Sword for the Convicted* (New York: Greenwood Press, 1990). One of the most famous articles discussing public defenders is Jonathan Casper's "Did You Have a Lawyer When You Went to Court? No, I Had a Public Defender," *Yale Review of Law and Social Change* 1 (Spring, 1971).

Public order offenses

DEFINITION: Minor offenses, including vagrancy and disorderly conduct, that are considered disruptions of order or tranquillity

SIGNIFICANCE: Statutes involving public order are used to protect the general public from harassment or annoyance in public places

Public order offenses, or public tranquillity offenses, comprise a variety of behaviors that fall into the overlapping categories of vagrancy, disorderly conduct, and breach of the peace (or disturbing the peace). Behaviors ranging from loitering to panhandling to playing loud music may be prohibited by state or local public order ordinances, which have as their goal the regulation of public behavior in order to keep a community orderly and pleasant. The illegalization of behaviors such as vagrancy and public drunkenness has a long history and is based in English common law. Although public order offenses are considered minor and are handled by the lower ("inferior") courts, they are important because they are widely used by police in maintaining order; they account for much of the caseload of the lower courts. Public order laws have often been treated as "catch-all" categories for handling a wide range of social problems—including people deemed undesirable but not truly criminal—and, through police discretion, have sometimes been applied unfairly. A number of vagrancy laws have been held by the courts to be unconstitutionally vague, and many laws dealing with public order have been either abolished or redrawn to be more precise.

See also Breach of the peace; Discretion; Disorderly conduct; Misdemeanor; Vagrancy laws.

AMERICAN JUSTICE

LIST OF ENTRIES BY CATEGORY

AREAS OF LAW

Administrative law
Admiralty law
Antitrust law
Banking law
Civil law
Commercial law
Constitutional law
Contract law
Copyrights, patents, and
  trademarks
Criminal law
Environmental law
Family law
Gambling law
Immigration laws
Insurance law
International law
Labor law
Medical and health law
Real estate law
School law
Sports law
Telecommunications law
Transportation law

CIVIL AND CRIMINAL JUSTICE

Adultery
Appellate process
Arraignment
Arrest
Attorney
Bail system
Bailiff
Bankruptcy
Bar examinations and
  licensing of lawyers
Bar, the
Battered child and battered
  wife syndromes
Burden of proof
Capital punishment
Case law
Chief of police
Civil disobedience
Civil procedure
Civilian review boards
Commercialized vice
Common law
Community-oriented policing
Conscientious objection
Coroner
Corporal punishment
Counsel, right to
Crime
Crime Index
Criminal
Criminal intent
Criminal justice system
Criminal procedure
Criminology
Deadly force, police use of
Defamation
Detectives, police
Deterrence
Discretion
District attorney
Domestic violence
Drug legalization debate
Drug use and sale, illegal
Equitable remedies
Equity
Espionage
Evidence, rules of
Felony
Fiduciary trust
Forensic science and medicine
Gangs, youth
Hate crimes
Illegal aliens
Immigration, legal and illegal
Immunity of public officials
Incapacitation
Indictment
Judicial system, U.S.
Jurisprudence
Jury system
Justice
Juvenile delinquency
Juvenile justice system
Labor unions
Law
Law schools
Legal ethics
Legal realism
Lynching
Machine politics
Malfeasance, misfeasance,
  and nonfeasance
Malice
Mandatory sentencing laws
Medical examiner
Medical malpractice
Military justice
Miscarriage of justice
Miscegenation laws
Misdemeanor
Mistrial
Moral relativism
National debt
Negligence
News media
News sources, protection of
Nonviolent resistance
Nuisance
Organized crime
Pardoning power
Pedophilia
Plea bargaining
Police
Police and guards, private
Police brutality
Police corruption and
  misconduct
Political corruption
Positive law
Presumption of innocence
Prison and jail systems
Privileged communications
Products liability
Property rights
Prosecutor, public
Psychopath and sociopath
Public defender
Punishment
Reasonable doubt
Reasonable force
Rehabilitation
Reparations
Restrictive covenant
School prayer
Seditious libel
Self-defense
Sentencing
Sexual harassment
Sheriff
Special weapons and tactics
  (SWAT) teams
Spoils system and patronage
State police
Sterilization and American
  law
Suicide and euthanasia
Ten most wanted criminals
Terrorism
Tort
Tort reform
Vigilantism
Wills, trusts, and estate
  planning
Zoning

CONSTITUTIONAL LAW AND ISSUES

Abortion
Affirmative action
Arms, right to keep and bear
Assembly and association,
  freedom of
Bill of Rights, U.S.
Birth control, right to
Busing
Censorship
Civil liberties
Civil rights
Civil War Amendments
Clear and present danger test
Commerce clause
Constitution, U.S.
Constitutional interpretation
Contract, freedom of
Counsel, right to
Cruel and unusual
  punishment
Double jeopardy
Due process of law
Equal protection of the law
Establishment of religion
Federalism
Incorporation doctrine
Judicial review
Ninth Amendment
Privacy, right of
Religion, free exercise of
Retroactivity of Supreme
  Court decisions
Search and seizure
Self-incrimination, privilege
  against
Speech and press, freedom of
Speedy trial, right to
States' rights
Supremacy clause
Supreme Court of the United
  States
Takings clause

COURT CASES

Wards Cove Packing Co. v. Atonio
Washington v. Davis
Webster v. Reproductive Health Services
Weeks v. United States
Wesberry v. Sanders
West Coast Hotel Co. v. Parrish
West Virginia State Board of Education v. Barnette
Wickard v. Filburn
Wisconsin v. Mitchell
Wisconsin v. Yoder
Witherspoon v. Illinois
Wolf v. Colorado
Yates v. United States

CRIMES

Accessory, accomplice, and aiding and abetting
Arson
Assault
Attempt to commit a crime
Bank robbery
Battery
Blackmail and extortion
Breach of the peace
Burglary
Bribery
Carjacking
Child abuse
Child molestation
Computer crime
Conspiracy
Consumer fraud
Contributing to the delinquency of a minor
Counterfeiting and forgery
Crime
Crime Index
Criminal
Disorderly conduct
Drive-by shootings
Driving under the influence
Dueling
Embezzlement
Fraud
Hate crimes
Incest
Indecent exposure
Insider trading
Kidnapping
Lying to Congress
Mail fraud
Manslaughter
Money laundering
Moral turpitude
Motor vehicle theft
Murder and homicide
Murders, mass and serial
Obstruction of justice
Organized crime
Pandering
Perjury
Polygamy
Price fixing
Public order offenses
Rape and sex offenses
Regulatory crime
Robbery
Skyjacking
Solicitation to commit a crime
Status offense
Statutory rape
Tax evasion
Theft
Treason
Vagrancy laws
Vandalism
Victimless crimes
War crimes
White-collar crime

GOVERNMENT AGENCIES, OFFICERS, AND COMMISSIONS

Alcohol, Tobacco, and Firearms (ATF), Bureau of
Attorney, United States
Attorney general, state
Attorney general of the United States
Campus Unrest, President's Commission on
Coast Guard, U.S.
COINTELPRO
Commission on Civil Rights
Drug Enforcement Administration (DEA)
Equal Employment Opportunity Commission (EEOC)
Federal Bureau of Investigation (FBI)
Federal Trade Commission (FTC)
Food and Drug Administration (FDA)
Immigration and Naturalization Service (INS)
Internal Revenue Service (IRS)
Interstate Commerce Commission (ICC)
Justice, U.S. Department of
Justice Statistics, Bureau of
Juvenile Justice and Delinquency Prevention, Office of
Knapp Commission
Law Enforcement Assistance Administration (LEAA)
Legal Services Corporation
Marshals Service, U.S.
National Advisory Commission on Civil Disorders
National Commission on the Causes and Prevention of Violence
National Crime Information Center
National Guard
National Institute of Justice
Occupational Safety and Health Administration (OSHA)
President of the United States
President's Commission on Law Enforcement and Administration of Justice
Prisons, Bureau of
Secret Service
Securities and Exchange Commission (SEC)
Solicitor general of the United States
Supreme Court of the United States
Treasury, U.S. Department of the
United States Parole Commission
United States Sentencing Commission
Warren Commission
Wickersham Commission

HISTORICAL EVENTS, MOVEMENTS, AND TRENDS

Abolitionist movement
American Revolution
Animal rights movement
Attica prison riot
Auburn system
Black codes
Black Power movement
Boston police strike
Branch Davidians, federal raid on
Chicago seven trial
Civil Rights movement
Civil War
Consumer rights movement
Court-packing plan of Franklin D. Roosevelt
Emancipation Proclamation
Fries Rebellion
Frontier, the
Iran-Contra scandal
Jacksonian democracy
Japanese American internment
Jeffersonian democracy
Jim Crow laws
Kefauver investigation
Kent State student killings
King, Rodney, case and aftermath
Lincoln-Douglas debates
Little Rock school integration crisis
McCarthyism
Magna Carta
Manhattan Bail Project
Miami riots
Montgomery bus boycott
MOVE, Philadelphia police bombing of
My Lai massacre
Neighborhood watch programs
New Mexico State Penitentiary riot
Nuclear radiation testing with human subjects
Palmer raids and the "red scare"
Poor People's March on Washington
Populism
Progressivism
Prohibition
Pullman strike
Race riots, twentieth century
Reconstruction

Rosenberg trial and
  executions
Sacco and Vanzetti trial
  and executions
Saint Valentine's Day
  massacre
Salem witchcraft trials
Scopes "monkey" trial
Scottsboro cases
Selma-to-Montgomery civil
  rights march

Seneca Falls Convention
Simpson, O. J., trial
Slavery
Tax revolt movement
Teapot Dome scandal
Temperance movement
Triangle Shirtwaist Factory
  fire
Vietnam War
Walnut Street Jail
Watergate scandal

LEGAL TERMS AND PROCEDURES

Advisory opinion
Amicus curiae brief
Appellate process
Arbitration and mediation
Arraignment
Arrest
Assigned counsel system
Autopsy
Bench warrant
Bill of attainder
Bill of particulars
Blue laws
Boot camps
Cease and desist order
Certiorari, writ of
Change of venue
Citizen's arrest
Civil remedies
Class action
Color of law
Community service as
  punishment for crime
Compensatory damages
Competency to stand trial
Consent decree
Contempt of court
Declaratory judgment
Deposition
Dictum
Diversion
DNA testing
Electronic surveillance
Eminent domain
Entrapment
Ex post facto law
Expert witness
Extradition
Fingerprint identification
Forfeiture, civil and criminal
Good time
Grand jury
Habeas corpus

Harmless error
Hearsay rule
House arrest
Immunity from prosecution
Impeachment
In forma pauperis petition
In loco parentis
Indictment
Information
Injunction
Insanity defense
Jury nullification
Just deserts
Litigation
Majority, age of
Mala in se and *mala
  prohibita*
Mandamus, writ of
Mandatory sentencing laws
Mens rea
Mitigating circumstances
Parole
Plea bargaining
Polygraph
Posse comitatus
Preventive detention
Probable cause
Probation
Punitive damages
Restitution
Restraining order
Reversible error
Small-claims court
Standards of proof
Standing
Stare decisis
Statute of limitations
Sting operation
Strict liability
Subpoena power
Suit
Voir dire

LEGISLATION AND GOVERNMENT

Age Discrimination in
  Employment Act
Aid to Families with
  Dependent Children
  (AFDC)
Alien and Sedition Acts
Americans with Disabilities
  Act (ADA)
Anti-Racketeering Act
Chinese Exclusion Act
Civil Rights Act of 1957
Civil Rights Act of 1960
Civil Rights Act of 1964
Civil Rights Act of 1968
Civil Rights Act of 1991
Civil Rights Acts of
  1866-1875
Civil service system
Clayton Antitrust Act
Comprehensive Crime
  Control Act of 1984
Comprehensive Drug Abuse
  Prevention and Control
  Act of 1970
Comstock Law
Conscription
Copyrights, patents, and
  trademarks
Employee Retirement
  Income Security Act
  (ERISA)
Employment Act of 1946
Enforcement Acts
Equal Employment
  Opportunity Act
Equal Pay Act
Equal Rights Amendment
  (ERA)
Espionage Act
Ethics in Government Act
Family Medical Leave Act
Federal Crimes Act
Federal Tort Claims Act
Food stamps
Freedom of Information Act
Fugitive Slave Laws
GI Bill of Rights
Great Society
Harrison Narcotic Drug Act
Hatch Act
Hobbs Act
Immigration Reform and
  Control Act
Insanity Defense Reform Act

Judiciary Acts
Juvenile Justice and
  Delinquency Prevention
  Act
Kansas-Nebraska Act
Labor-Management Relations
  Act
Landrum-Griffin Act
Lindbergh law
Louisiana Civil Code
Mann Act
Marijuana Tax Act
Martial law
Missouri Compromise of 1820
Model Penal Code
Motor Vehicle Theft Act
Motor Vehicle Theft Law
  Enforcement Act
National Crime Victimization
  Survey
National Firearms Act and
  Federal Firearms Act
National Labor Relations Act
  (NLRA)
National Narcotics Act
New Deal
Omnibus Crime Control and
  Safe Streets Act of 1968
Opium Exclusion Act
Organized Crime Control Act
Pendleton Act
Political campaign law
Pure Food and Drug Act
Racketeer Influenced and
  Corrupt Organizations Act
  (RICO)
Sentencing guidelines, U.S.
Sherman Antitrust Act
Smith Act
Social Security system
Tariff
Tax Reform Act of 1986
Truth in Lending Act
Uniform Crime Reports
  (UCR)
United States Code
Victim assistance programs
Victims of Crime Act
Violent Crime Control and
  Law Enforcement Act of
  1994
Voting Rights Act of 1965
War on Poverty
Workers' compensation

ORGANIZATIONS

American Bar Association (ABA)
American Civil Liberties Union (ACLU)
American Federation of Labor-Congress of Industrial Organizations (AFL-CIO)
American Indian Movement (AIM)
Anti-Defamation League (ADL)
Black Panther Party
Communist Party, American
Congress of Racial Equality (CORE)
Democratic Party
Federalist Party
Free Soil Party
House Committee on Un-American Activities (HUAC)
International Association of Chiefs of Police
International Brotherhood of Police Officers
Interpol
Jeffersonian Republican Party
John Birch Society
Ku Klux Klan (KKK)
Mexican American Legal Defense and Education Fund (MALDEF)

Mothers Against Drunk Driving (MADD)
Nation of Islam
National Association for the Advancement of Colored People (NAACP)
National Association for the Advancement of Colored People Legal Defense and Educational Fund
National District Attorneys Association
National Organization for Victim Assistance (NOVA)
National Organization for Women (NOW)
National Rifle Association (NRA)
National Urban League
Republican Party
Socialist Party, American
Southern Christian Leadership Conference (SCLC)
States' Rights Party
Student Nonviolent Coordinating Committee (SNCC)
Students for a Democratic Society (SDS)
United Farm Workers (UFW)
Weather Underground
Whig Party
World Court

PERSONS

Addams, Jane
Anthony, Susan B.
Bentham, Jeremy
Black, Hugo L.
Blackstone, William
Brandeis, Louis D.
Brown, John
Bryan, William Jennings
Burger, Warren
Bush, George
Calhoun, John C.
Capone, Alphonse (Al)
Cardozo, Benjamin Nathan
Carter, Jimmy

Chase, Samuel
Chávez, César
Clay, Henry
Cooley, Thomas
Daugherty, Harry M.
Debs, Eugene V.
Dix, Dorothea Lynde
Douglas, Stephen A.
Douglas, William O.
Douglass, Frederick
Du Bois, W. E. B.
Eisenhower, Dwight D.
Ellsworth, Oliver
Field, Stephen J.

Ford, Gerald R.
Frankfurter, Felix
Fuller, Melvin Weston
Gandhi, Mahatma
Garrison, William Lloyd
Garvey, Marcus
Gompers, Samuel
Greeley, Horace
Hand, Learned
Holmes, Oliver Wendell, Jr.
Hoover, J. Edgar
Hughes, Charles Evans
Jackson, Jesse
Jay, John
Johnson, Lyndon B.
Kennedy, John F.
Kennedy, Robert F.
Kent, James
King, Martin Luther, Jr.
Lewis, John L.
Lincoln, Abraham
Livingston, Edward
Long, Huey
Mack, Julian William
Malcolm X
Marshall, John
Marshall, Thurgood
Muhammad, Elijah

Nader, Ralph
Nixon, Richard M.
Pinkerton, Allan
Pound, Roscoe
Randolph, A. Philip
Reagan, Ronald
Rehnquist, William
Roosevelt, Eleanor
Roosevelt, Franklin D.
Rush, Benjamin
Sanger, Margaret
Sinclair, Upton
Stanton, Elizabeth Cady
Steffens, Lincoln
Stone, Harlan Fiske
Story, Joseph
Stowe, Harriet Beecher
Taft, William Howard
Taney, Roger Brooke
Truman, Harry S
Vinson, Fred M.
Waite, Morrison Remick
Warren, Earl
Washington, Booker T.
White, Edward Douglass
Wilson, James
Wilson, Woodrow

SOCIAL JUSTICE AND POLITICAL RIGHTS

Acquired immune deficiency syndrome (AIDS)
Age discrimination
American Indians
Capitalism
Citizenship
Civil rights
Civil Rights movement
Comparable worth
Conservatism, modern American
Declaration of Independence
Democracy
Equality of opportunity
Feminism
Gay rights
Homelessness
Japanese American internment
Liberalism, modern American
McCarthyism
Marxism

Morality and foreign policy
Natural law and natural rights
Nuclear weapons
Poll tax
Racial and ethnic discrimination
Religious sects and cults
Representation: gerrymandering, malapportionment, and reapportionment
Segregation, *de facto* and *de jure*
Sex discrimination
Socialism
Taxation and justice
Veterans' rights
Vietnam War
Vote, right to
War on Poverty
Welfare state
Woman suffrage